Exploring Corporate Strategy

Text and Cases

THIRD EDITION

Exploring Corpo...
Strategy

Text and Cases

THIRD EDITION

Gerry Johnson
Cranfield School of Management

Kevan Scholes
Sheffield Business School

PRENTICE HALL
NEW YORK   LONDON   TORONTO   SYDNEY   TOKYO   SINGAPORE

First published 1989
This edition published 1993 by
Prentice Hall International (UK) Ltd
Campus 400, Maylands Avenue
Hemel Hempstead
Hertfordshire, HP2 7EZ
A division of
Simon & Schuster International Group

© Prentice Hall International (UK) Ltd, 1993

Typeset in 10/12pt ITC Century Book by Goodfellow & Egan Ltd,
Cambridge

Printed and bound at the University Press, Cambridge

Library of Congress Cataloging-in-Publication Data

Johnson, Gerry.
    Exploring corporate strategy Text and Cases / Gerry Johnson,
Kevan Scholes. – 3rd ed.
        p. cm.
    Includes bibliographical references and index.
    ISBN 0–13–297441–X
    1. Corporate planning.   2. Strategic planning.   I. Scholes,
Kevan.   II. Title.
HD30.28.J648 1993
658.4'012–dc20   92–25521
                                                            CIP

British Library Cataloguing in Publication Data

A catalogue record for this book is available from the British Library

ISBN 0–13–297441–X

---

5 97 96 95 94

Contents

List of illustrations *xiii*
List of figures *xv*
Preface *xix*

PART I   INTRODUCTION

Chapter 1   Corporate strategy: an introduction 3

1.1   The nature of corporate strategy *4*
    1.1.1   The characteristics of strategic decisions *5*
    1.1.2   Levels of strategy *10*
    1.1.3   The vocabulary of strategy *12*
1.2   Strategic management *14*
    1.2.1   Strategic analysis *17*
    1.2.2   Strategic choice *20*
    1.2.3   Strategy implementation *21*
    1.2.4   A summary of the strategic management process *22*
1.3   Strategic management in different contexts *23*
    1.3.1   The small business context *26*
    1.3.2   The multinational corporation *26*
    1.3.3   Manufacturing and service organisations *27*
    1.3.4   Strategy in the public sector *27*
    1.3.5   The voluntary and not-for-profit sectors *29*
    1.3.6   Professional organisations *29*
1.4   Summary: the challenge of strategic management *30*
    References *32*
    Recommended key readings *33*
    Work assignments *33*

Chapter 2   Strategic management in practice 34

2.1   Introduction *34*

2.2   Patterns of strategy development *35*
  2.2.1   Incremental strategy development *35*
  2.2.2   Intended and realised strategies *38*
  2.2.3   Emergent, opportunistic and imposed strategies *38*
2.3   Explaining strategy development *39*
  2.3.1   The 'natural selection' view *40*
  2.3.2   The planning view *40*
  2.3.3   The logical incremental view *43*
  2.3.4   The cultural view *46*
  2.3.5   The political view *51*
  2.3.6   The visionary view *52*
  2.3.7   Integrating views of strategy development *54*
2.4   Strategic decision-making processes in action *56*
  2.4.1   Elements of strategic decision-making processes *58*
  2.4.2   The cultural web *60*
  2.4.3   The risk of strategic drift *63*
2.5   Summary and implications for the study of strategy *65*
       References *69*
       Recommended key readings *71*
       Work assignments *71*

PART II   STRATEGIC ANALYSIS

Chapter 3   Analysing the environment *75*

3.1   Introduction *75*
3.2   Understanding the nature of the environment *77*
3.3   Auditing environmental influences *79*
  3.3.1   PEST analysis *82*
  3.3.2   The use of scenarios *85*
3.4   Structural analysis of the competitive environment *87*
  3.4.1   The threat of entry *88*
  3.4.2   The power of buyers and suppliers *90*
  3.4.3   The threat of substitutes *93*
  3.4.4   Competitive rivalry *93*
  3.4.5   Key questions arising from structural analysis *94*
3.5   Identifying the organisation's competitive position *96*
  3.5.1   Competitive analysis *97*
  3.5.2   Strategic group analysis *98*
  3.5.3   Market segments and market power *101*
  3.5.4   Market share and market growth *103*
  3.5.5   Market attractiveness and business strength *106*
3.6   Summary *107*
       References *111*

Recommended key readings *112*
Work assignments *113*

Chapter 4   Analysing resources and strategic capability *115*

4.1   Introduction *115*
4.2   Resource audit *119*
4.3   Value chain analysis *120*
    4.3.1   Resource utilisation *123*
    4.3.2   Analysing cost efficiency *128*
    4.3.3   Analysing effectiveness *132*
    4.3.4   Control of resources *133*
    4.3.5   Financial analyses *135*
4.4   Comparative analysis *138*
    4.4.1   Historical analysis *138*
    4.4.2   Comparison with industry norms *139*
    4.4.3   Best practice analysis *140*
4.5   Assessing the balance of resources *143*
    4.5.1   Portfolio analyses *144*
    4.5.2   Balance of skills/personalities *146*
    4.5.3   Flexibility analysis *148*
4.6   Identification of key issues *148*
    4.6.1   SWOT analysis *148*
    4.6.2   Core competences *151*
4.7   Summary *152*
    References *153*
    Recommended key readings *154*
    Work assignments *154*

Chapter 5   Culture and stakeholder expectations *156*

5.1   Introduction *156*
5.2   The cultural context of strategy *158*
    5.2.1   External influences *158*
    5.2.2   Internal influences *162*
5.3   Stakeholder analysis *171*
    5.3.1   Conflicts of expectations *172*
    5.3.2   Identifying stakeholders *173*
    5.3.3   Stakeholder mapping *175*
5.4   Power *178*
    5.4.1   Sources of power within organisations *178*
    5.4.2   Sources of power for external stakeholders *182*
    5.4.3   Methods of assessing power *183*
5.5   Organisational purposes *186*
    5.5.1   Mission *186*

        5.5.2   Corporate objectives *188*
        5.5.3   Unit objectives *190*
        5.5.4   The precision of objectives *190*
    5.6   Business ethics *191*
        5.6.1   The role of business in society *192*
        5.6.2   Corporate social responsibility *194*
        5.6.3   The role of individuals/managers *195*
    5.7   Summary *198*
        References *198*
        Recommended key readings *199*
        Work assignments *200*

PART III   STRATEGIC CHOICE

Chapter 6   Strategic options *203*

    6.1   Introduction *203*
    6.2   Generic strategies *204*
        6.2.1   Porter's generic strategies *204*
        6.2.2   Some problems with generic strategy concepts *205*
    6.3   Market-based generic strategies: the 'strategy clock' *209*
        6.3.1   Price-based strategies (routes 1, 2) *210*
        6.3.2   Value added, or differentiation strategies (route 4) *212*
        6.3.3   The hybrid strategy (route 3) *213*
        6.3.4   Focused differentiation (route 5) *213*
        6.3.5   Failure strategies (routes 6, 7, 8) *216*
    6.4   Sustaining and operationalising generic strategies *216*
        6.4.1   Cost and the value chain *217*
        6.4.2   Differentiation and linkages within the value chain *217*
        6.4.3   Differentiation through linkages across value chains *218*
        6.4.4   The management challenge of generic strategies *219*
    6.5   Alternative directions for strategy development *221*
        6.5.1   Withdrawal *222*
        6.5.2   Consolidation *223*
        6.5.3   Market penetration *225*
        6.5.4   Product development *226*
        6.5.5   Market development *227*
        6.5.6   Diversification *227*
    6.6   Alternative methods of strategy development *231*
        6.6.1   Internal development *231*
        6.6.2   Mergers and acquisitions *233*
        6.6.3   Joint development and strategic alliances *235*
    6.7   Summary *239*
        References *240*

Recommended key readings *242*
Work assignments *243*

Chapter 7   Strategy evaluation 1: Assessing the suitability of strategies *244*

7.1   Introduction *244*
7.2   Evaluation criteria *244*
    7.2.1   Suitability *244*
    7.2.2   Feasibility *245*
    7.2.3   Acceptability *246*
7.3   A framework for evaluating strategies *246*
7.4   Strategic logic *248*
    7.4.1   Portfolio analyses *249*
    7.4.2   Life cycle analyses *250*
    7.4.3   Value chain analyses *254*
7.5   Cultural fit *259*
    7.5.1   Embryonic stage *259*
    7.5.2   Growth *260*
    7.5.3   Maturity *261*
    7.5.4   Decline *261*
7.6   Research evidence *263*
    7.6.1   The importance of market share *264*
    7.6.2   Consolidation strategies *264*
    7.6.3   Related developments *266*
    7.6.4   Diversification and performance *268*
    7.6.5   Public-sector strategies *270*
7.7   Screening options *271*
    7.7.1   Bases for comparison *272*
    7.7.2   Ranking *273*
    7.7.3   Decision trees *274*
    7.7.4   Scenarios *275*
7.8   Summary *277*
    References *278*
    Recommended key readings *279*
    Work assignments *279*

Chapter 8   Strategy evaluation 2: Making choices *281*

8.1   Introduction *281*
8.2   Analysing return *281*
    8.2.1   Profitability analyses *282*
    8.2.2   Cost/benefit analysis *285*
    8.2.3   Shareholder value analysis *288*
8.3   Analysing risk *289*

8.3.1   Financial ratio projections *289*
8.3.2   Sensitivity analysis *291*
8.3.3   Decision matrices *292*
8.3.4   Simulation modelling *296*
8.3.5   Heuristic models *297*
8.4   Analysing stakeholder reactions *297*
8.5   Analysing feasibility *300*
8.5.1   Funds flow analysis *300*
8.5.2   Break-even analysis *301*
8.5.3   Resource deployment analysis *302*
8.6   Selection of strategies *304*
8.6.1   Selection against objectives *304*
8.6.2   Referral to a higher authority *305*
8.6.3   Partial implementation *305*
8.6.4   Outside agencies *306*
8.7   Summary *307*
References *308*
Recommended key readings *308*
Work assignments *309*

PART IV   STRATEGY IMPLEMENTATION

Chapter 9   Planning and allocating resources *313*

9.1   Introduction *313*
9.2   Resource planning at the corporate level *314*
9.2.1   Few resource changes *315*
9.2.2   Allocations during growth *316*
9.2.3   Allocating resources in static or declining situations *317*
9.2.4   Allocating shared resources *317*
9.3   Resource planning at the business level *320*
9.3.1   Resource identification *321*
9.3.2   Fit with existing resources *325*
9.3.3   Fit between required resources *326*
9.4   Preparing resource plans *326*
9.4.1   Critical success factors and key tasks *328*
9.4.2   Planning priorities *329*
9.4.3   Testing key assumptions *332*
9.4.4   Financial planning and budgeting *333*
9.4.5   Manpower planning *334*
9.4.6   Network analysis *337*
9.5   Summary *339*
References *341*
Recommended key readings *342*
Work assignments *342*

Chapter 10   Organisation structure and design *344*

10.1   Introduction *344*
10.2   Structural types *345*
    10.2.1   The simple structure *345*
    10.2.2   The functional structure *345*
    10.2.3   The multidivisional structure *346*
    10.2.4   The holding company structure *347*
    10.2.5   The matrix structure *349*
    10.2.6   Intermediate structures and structural variations *353*
    10.2.7   Structural types in multinational companies *353*
10.3   The elements of organisational design *356*
10.4   Centralisation vs devolution *358*
    10.4.1   Strategic planning *358*
    10.4.2   Financial control *361*
    10.4.3   Strategic control *362*
10.5   Organisational configurations *364*
    10.5.1   Choosing a configuration *367*
10.6   Management systems and control *370*
    10.6.1   Control through information and measurement *370*
    10.6.2   Control through reward systems *373*
10.7   Influences on organisational design *376*
    10.7.1   Type of strategy *377*
    10.7.2   Operational processes and technology *378*
    10.7.3   Organisational type *379*
    10.7.4   The environment *380*
10.8   Summary *381*
    References *383*
    Recommended key readings *384*
    Work assignments *385*

Chapter 11   Managing strategic change *386*

11.1   Introduction *386*
11.2   Understanding processes of strategic change *387*
    11.2.1   A systems view of incremental change *388*
    11.2.2   Unfreezing and the management of strategic change *389*
11.3   Diagnosing strategic change needs *390*
    11.3.1   Detecting strategic drift *391*
    11.3.2   Identifying barriers to strategic change *393*
11.4   Managing the strategic change process *394*
    11.4.1   Styles of managing strategic change *395*
    11.4.2   Changes in organisational routines *398*
    11.4.3   Symbolic activity in managing change *401*
    11.4.4   Political processes *405*

11.5   Leadership and change agency *411*
11.6   Conclusions *414*
    11.6.1   Environmental assessment *414*
    11.6.2   Leading change *414*
    11.6.3   Linking strategic and operational change *415*
    11.6.4   Strategic human resource management *416*
    11.6.5   Coherence in managing change *416*
    11.6.6   Pulling it all together *417*
    References *417*
    Recommended key readings *421*
    Work assignments *422*

CASE STUDIES

A guide to using the case studies *427*
British Steel *431*
Planning in Shell *435*
The European brewing industry 1992 *444*
Courage Ltd *475*
Brasseries Kronenbourg *482*
Laura Ashley Holdings plc *495*
The Crucible Theatre *526*
A note on the world automobile industry *558*
Peugeot SA Group *571*
The Rover/Honda alliance *591*
Vitalograph *603*
The News Corporation *623*
Electrolux: the acquisition and integration of Zanussi *651*
A strategy for change at KPMG *676*
The Burton Group (A) *686*
The Burton Group (B) *697*
The Burton Group (C) *710*

Index of companies and organisations *725*
General index *727*

Illustrations

1.1 IKEA's ideal *4*
1.2 British Airways and the vocabulary of strategy *14*
1.3 Strategic issues in different contexts *24*
2.1 Incremental strategy development in Ford of Europe *37*
2.2 A logical incrementalist view of strategic management *45*
2.3 Beliefs and assumptions in UK retail banking *48*
2.4 The politics of change: championing HIV/AIDS *52*
2.5 Different perceptions of how strategies develop *56*
2.6 The cultural web of a UK bank in the 1980s *62*
2.7 The Icarus Paradox *66*
3.1 Examples of environmental influences *80*
3.2 Shell's global scenarios for the energy industry *86*
3.3 A five-forces analysis of the oil industry in Ireland *90*
3.4 Increasing competition in the European chemical industry *95*
3.5 Strategic groups and strategic space *100*
3.6 Segments and power in the 'grumpits' market *104*
3.7 NFC's directional policy exercise *108*
4.1 Competitive advantage through resources *116*
4.2 Opportunity 2000: women into management *122*
4.3 Companiex *126*
4.4 Amstrad and the single European market for telecommunications/ computing equipment *129*
4.5 The Patient's Charter *140*
4.6 R & D scoreboard *142*
4.7 SWOT analysis *150*
5.1 Culture clash at CMB Packaging *161*
5.2 Cultural web of a regional newspaper *164*
5.3 Peace at the Savoy – at last *170*
5.4 Shifts in stakeholder positioning in UK local government *179*
5.5 Organisational purposes *188*
5.6 Business ethics: the Anglo-Saxon and the French view – the case of private TV channels *196*
6.1 The generic strategy of Sainsbury *208*
6.2 Breadth or focus in European businesses *214*

6.3   The search for efficiency and value added in the UK National Health Service *218*

6.4   Information systems provide linkages within and between value chains *220*

6.5   VNU withdraws from printing *224*

6.6   Directions of growth *232*

6.7   Why we're merging: Nationale Nederland and NMB Postbank *236*

6.8   A loose network aids the textile industry in Denmark *240*

7.1   State-owned railways: assessment of options *247*

7.2   Making vertical integration work at Linfield *255*

7.3   Synergy as a reason for mergers in the new Europe *257*

7.4   Nurses show the way to total quality *262*

7.5   Privatisation *272*

7.6   Ranking options: Churchill Pottery *276*

8.1   Sewerage construction project *286*

8.2   Strategy evaluation at BP and Rolls-Royce *290*

8.3   Sensitivity analysis *294*

8.4   Power struggle in the UK telecommunications industry *299*

8.5   Using break-even analysis to examine strategic options *303*

9.1   Changing approaches to resource allocation in UK higher education *318*

9.2   Resource identification: adjusting to crisis *324*

9.3   United Stationers turn distribution into a fine art *330*

9.4   Base budget reviews at Cheshire County Council *335*

9.5   Shortening the development cycle: the Land Rover Discovery *340*

10.1   Matrix structure at Shell *352*

10.2   ICI's structure for Europe *357*

10.3   Centralisation and devolution in Sheffield City Council *366*

10.4   State/company relationship changes in China *371*

10.5   Changes in reward systems at ICL *375*

10.6   Coping with 'Big Bang' in the investment banking industry *382*

11.1   Managing change at Kindercare *390*

11.2   Blockages to change in Zolotoy Kolos *394*

11.3   Styles of managing change *399*

11.4   Symbolic activity and strategic change *404*

11.5   Machiavelli on political processes *409*

11.6   Longman *418*

Figures

1.1   The vocabulary of strategy *13*
1.2   Strategic management and operational management *16*
1.3   A basic model of the strategic management process *17*
1.4   Aspects of strategic analysis *18*
1.5   A summary model of the elements of strategic management *23*
1.6   Some characteristics of strategic management in
        not-for-profit organisations *30*
2.1   Patterns of strategic change *35*
2.2   Strategy evolution and consolidation *36*
2.3   Strategy development routes *38*
2.4   Decision flow in product/market strategy formulation *41*
2.5   Notional incremental change *46*
2.6   Frames of reference of managers *47*
2.7   The role of the paradigm in strategy formulation *50*
2.8   Profiles of strategy development *55*
2.9   Phases of strategic decision making *58*
2.10 The cultural web of an organisation *61*
2.11 The dynamics of paradigm change *64*
2.12 The risk of strategic drift *65*
3.1   Steps in environmental analysis *76*
3.2   Growing uncertainty according to the nature of the environment *78*
3.3   A PEST analysis of environmental influences *82*
3.4   Impact analysis *84*
3.5   A model for structural analysis *88*
3.6   Some characteristics for identifying strategic groups *99*
3.7   Some criteria for market segmentation *102*
3.8   The growth/share matrix *105*
3.9   Indicators of SBU strength and market attractiveness *107*
3.10 Market attractiveness/SBU strength matrix *110*
4.1   Analysing strategic capability *118*
4.2   The value chain *121*
4.3   The value system *123*
4.4   Resource utilisation and competitive advantage *124*
4.5   Sources of cost efficiency *130*

4.6   Assessing effectiveness *132*
4.7   Aspects of resource control *134*
4.8   The relationship between various financial ratios
        – The Dupont model *137*
4.9   Product portfolio matrices *145*
4.10   Personality types for the effective team *147*
4.11   Flexibility analysis: an example *149*
5.1   Culture, stakeholder expectations and organisational purposes *157*
5.2   National culture and organisational strategies *160*
5.3   Analysing the cultural web: some useful questions *163*
5.4   Different types of organisational culture and their influences on
        strategic decision making *171*
5.5   Some common conflicts of expectations *172*
5.6   The attitudes of stakeholders towards possible future changes *174*
5.7   Stakeholder mapping: power/dynamism matrix *176*
5.8   Stakeholder mapping: power/interest matrix *177*
5.9   Sources of power *180*
5.10   Assessing the relative power of stakeholders *185*
5.11   Stakeholder mapping: an example *186*
5.12   Organisational purposes *187*
5.13   Business ethics: ten roles of organisations *193*
5.14   Some questions of corporate social responsibility *195*
6.1   Development strategies *204*
6.2   Three generic strategies *206*
6.3   The strategy clock: competitive strategy options *211*
6.4   Alternative directions for development *222*
6.5   Alternatives open to a manufacturer to develop by related
        diversification *229*
6.6   Some reasons for related diversification *230*
6.7   Some reasons for unrelated diversification *231*
6.8   Types of and motives for strategic alliances *238*
7.1   A framework for evaluating strategies *248*
7.2   The life cycle portfolio matrix *251*
7.3   The assessment of synergy for a grocery retailer *256*
7.4   Conditions for synergy *258*
7.5   Culture, the life cycle and strategic choices *260*
7.6   Basis for assessing strategic potential *263*
7.7   Market share drives profitability *265*
7.8   On average, market position has an important, positive
        influence on profits *265*
7.9   The PIMS findings relating to various types of consolidation strategy *267*
7.10   The PIMS findings relating to other related strategies *269*
7.11   Gap analysis *274*
7.12   A simplified strategic decision tree for a sweet manufacturer *275*
8.1   Some useful measures of profitability for strategic evaluation *283*

8.2   Decision matrices: an example *293*
8.3   A funds flow forecast for strategy X (1988–1990), (£000) *301*
8.4   Resource deployment analysis *304*
8.5   'Rolling-out' strategies in a multinational *307*
9.1   Resource allocation at the corporate level *314*
9.2   Matching operational resource plans to strategies *321*
9.3   Some resource implications of strategic change *322*
9.4   Key skills and resources to support different strategies *323*
9.5   Resource integration in a product launch *327*
9.6   Elements of a resource plan *328*
9.7   Critical success factors and key tasks: an example – office
        systems supplier *329*
9.8   Methods of training and development for managing strategic change *337*
9.9   Network analysis for a customer survey project *338*
10.1   A basic functional structure *346*
10.2   A multidivisional structure *347*
10.3   Levels of divisions *348*
10.4   A holding company structure *349*
10.5   Two examples of matrix structures *350*
10.6   Structural types in multinational companies *354*
10.7   Role of subsidiaries in transnational corporations *356*
10.8   Centre–division relationships *359*
10.9   Strategic planning *360*
10.10   Financial control *361*
10.11   Strategic control *363*
10.12   Some benefits of centralisation and devolution *365*
10.13   The six basic parts of an organisation *368*
10.14   Mintzberg's six organisational configurations, plus network
        organisations *369*
10.15   Different types of responsibility centre *373*
10.16   Individual or group incentives *376*
10.17   Characteristics of mechanistic and organic systems in organisations *377*
10.18   Environmental influences on organisational structure *381*
11.1   A framework for managing strategic change *387*
11.2   'Unfreezing' and the management of change *392*
11.3   Mechanisms and processes for managing strategic change *396*
11.4   Styles of managing strategic change *397*
11.5   Types of rite (ritual) and their roles in culture change *402*
11.6   Political mechanisms in organisations *406*
11.7   Political manoeuvres and change *410*
11.8   Fifteen key competences of change agents *412*
11.9   Managing change for competitive success: the five central factors *415*

Preface

It is now five years since our second edition was published and nine since the first edition. There have been many interesting and important developments in the subject of corporate strategy during that time. Equally important has been the vastly increased recognition of the importance of the subject to practising managers in both the public and private sectors. This has been reflected in the widespread inclusion of corporate strategy in educational programmes at under-graduate, postgraduate and professional levels, as well as its adoption in short courses and consultancy assignments. It is now widely accepted that an under-standing of the principles and practice of strategic issues are not just the con-cern of top managers but are essential for most levels of management – although clearly the detailed requirements will vary. Since we have consistently argued the importance of this wider 'uptake', these are changes which we welcome.

The combined sales of our first and second editions exceeded 100,000. In revising the book for this third edition we have therefore tried to ensure that we reflect the changing views, attitudes and approaches to corporate strategy but that we do this within the framework and style of the previous editions, which many of you have kindly complimented us on. We hope we have achieved this and that you continue to find *Exploring Corporate Strategy* a useful and stimu-lating text. Some of its content has changed – and this is explained more fully below – but the purpose of the book remains the same: to develop a greater capability for strategic thinking among managers and potential managers.

We began the first edition by quoting the group corporate planner of one of the UK's biggest companies explaining that the main problem he faced was to get managers to understand that it was their responsibility to formulate strategy:

> This is my biggest difficulty. First, because they seem to think it's someone else's responsibility and, second, because they think there is some set of techniques which is going to create strategy for the company. I try to get them to understand that if the managers of the business aren't responsible for strategy, then no one is: and that they already have – or can easily get – any techniques that are necessary. The problem is the inability of managers to think strategically.

Nine years on we would still regard this as the core issue which this book aims to address through providing readers with an understanding of:

- What corporate strategy is.
- Why strategic decisions are important.
- Approaches to formulating and implementing strategy.

It is not a book of corporate planning techniques but rather builds on the practice of good strategic management, as researchers and practitioners in the area understand it. It is a book primarily intended for students of strategy on undergraduate, diploma and masters courses in universities and colleges; students on courses with titles such as Corporate Strategy, Business Policy, Strategic Management, Organisational Policy, Corporate Policy and so on. However, we know that many such students are already managers anyway who are undertaking part-time study: so this book is written with the manager and the potential manager in mind.

Traditionally, the study of corporate strategy in organisations had been taught using intensive case study programmes. There remain teachers who argue that there can be no substitute for such an intensive case programme. At the other extreme there is a growing school of thought which argues that the only reason cases were used was that there was an insufficient research base to the problems of strategy, resulting in a lack of theoretical underpinning. They argue that since the 1960s the strides made in research and the development of theory make such intensive case programmes redundant. It seems to us that this is a fruitless division of opinion probably rooted in the academic traditions of those involved, rather than a considered view of the needs of students.

The position taken here is that case work, or appropriate experiential learning, is of great benefit in the study of strategy for it allows students both to apply concepts and theories and – just as important – to build their own. However, it is also the case that the growing body of research and theory can be of great help in stimulating a deeper understanding of strategic problems and strategic management. Our approach builds in substantial parts of such research and theory, and encourages readers to refer to more; but we also assume that readers will have the opportunity to deal with strategic problems through such means as case study work or projects or, if they are practising managers, through their involvement in their own organisations. Our view in this respect is exactly the same as the writers of a medical or engineering text, and we encourage readers to take the same view: it is that good theory helps good practice, but that an understanding of the theory without an understanding of the practice is very dangerous – particularly if you are dealing with a patient, a bridge or, as with this book, organisations.

For this reason the book is again available in two versions – text only or text and cases. The seventeen case studies consist of twelve entirely new cases and five which have been completely updated and rewritten from the last edition. We have also included a new feature in both versions of the book. Each chapter is concluded with a set of work assignments. These take the main issues from each chapter and suggest ways in which readers can consolidate their understanding by applying these concepts to appropriate case studies, illustrations and/or organisations of their own choice. These assignments are provided at three levels of difficulty, in order to give maximum flexibility in their use:

- Level 1 (normal script) are straightforward applications of concepts or techniques to specific situations.
- **Level 2 (bold script) require the comparison of concepts and/or of different situations.**
- *Level 3 (italic script) require a comprehensive analysis usually linking two or more concepts and/or situations and requiring 'reading round' the issues.*

Strategic management is a responsibility of *all managers* and, what is more, a responsibility that is becoming more and more important. It is not sufficient for managers to think of management in some operational or functional context, simply to know their piece of the jigsaw well and trust that others know theirs equally as well. Modern organisations exist in a complex environment with an increasing demand for fast and effective strategic responses. The very least that managers require is to understand how their piece of the jigsaw fits into the rest in the context of the strategic problems and direction of the organisation. If they do not, the effectiveness of strategic management, and particularly the implementation of strategy, can be severely impaired.

In preparing this third edition, we have tried to bear in mind the needs of the manager in understanding strategic problems in many different organisations. In so doing, we have developed further some of the themes running through the previous editions.

The text more explicitly develops the theme that strategy and the management of strategy can be thought of in at least two rather different ways. First, it can be seen as a matter of essentially *economic analysis and planning*. And second, it can be seen as a matter of *organisational decision making* within a *social, political and cultural context*. Both these aspects of strategic management are relevant to the study of strategy, and the text incorporates both. For example, one of the themes running through the book is the importance of a clear analysis of the strategic situation facing the organisation and a rational assessment of the future options available to it. In considering such issues, the book includes, for example, discussion of the value of environmental audits, structural and strategic group analysis of competitive environments, the relevance of experience curve concepts, value chain analysis, life cycle models of strategic analysis and choice, and the findings of those researchers who have tried to understand the relationship between strategic positioning of organisations and financial performance. In short, one of the themes is that the employment of rational models of analysis and choice in organisations is important to strategic management.

There is also a growing expectation that managers will be able to take decisions about change and implement change with a great deal more assurance and skill than hitherto. Yet the evidence is that managers are not good at handling change, particularly of the magnitude involved with strategic change. Strategic management cannot be developed by providing 'a bag of management techniques'; it is also to do with developing in managers a sensitivity to an increasingly turbulent environment, together with an understanding of the culture of the organisation in which they work and the means whereby they can manage change within that culture. Herein lies one of the fundamental problems of strategic management. The environment that organisations face is increasingly turbulent, so the need for management sensitivity to change is growing. Yet the values, expectations and assumptions of members of an organisation working within a particular culture can be a very constraining and conservative influence on the understanding of strategic problems and the development of solutions.

This third edition develops this theme much further. It draws on the growing amount of research and literature on decision-making processes within a political and cultural context, and considers explicitly how such influences can be analysed and what mechanisms exist for managing strategic change within such systems. In particular, readers familiar with previous editions will note the important changes made to the content of Chapters 2, 5 and 11. There is, therefore, an expectation that readers will seek to reconcile 'scientific management' about the complex issues of strategy with an understanding of the human and social side of management. While this is a demanding task, it is the key to the effective management of strategy and a fundamental task of managers in today's organisations.

As in the previous editions, the book also recognises that strategic management is as relevant to the public sector and to not-for-profit organisations as it is to the private sector of industry and commerce. Indeed, the period since the second edition was published has seen unprecedented changes in the recognition of strategic management in the public sector against the background of significant changes in their role and method of operation. This 'new era' is reflected in discussions and examples throughout the book. We also have a good many references, examples and illustrations of the application of strategic management concepts to the public sector.

Another issue of major importance to many more organisations over the past five years has been the need to think of corporate strategy and an organisation's performance much more in an *international context*. In Europe this has clearly been pushed along by the impetus to the single European market – indeed, this book is published on the very first day of the market 'for proper'. But this issue of internationalisation has spread much wider than those narrowly and immediately effected by the single market. It is now expected in many industries and public services that an aspiration to perform well – by *international standards* – is important. The rapidly growing communications of all types is making managers – and those who judge their performance – much more familiar with what *best international practice* means in their context. The third edition of this book has made major changes in recognising the importance of this international dimension through additional concepts and analytical methods – but more importantly through the tone of the discussion, and particularly the choice of illustrations and (in the text and cases edition) a much wider international choice of case studies.

The book, while using up-to-date theory and research, is not primarily an academic treatise, but a book for managers and those who intend to be managers: so a few words about its style are in order. The reader will find that throughout the book there are 'illustrations' which enlarge upon or give case material related to a point in the text. These illustrations are all taken from actual incidents reported in the press or in journals, from case studies, or from the authors' personal experience, and wherever possible the organisation or individuals involved are named.

As far as terminology is concerned, we have tried to avoid some of the pitfalls of jargon that management writers often fall into; if we have failed to do so on occasions, it is not for the want of trying. The word 'organisation' has been used most frequently, but there are times when 'company', 'enterprise' or 'firm' is used: these tend to be where commercial operations are being discussed, but it does not mean that the discussion relates only to the private sector. We have also chosen not to make dogmatic distinctions between descriptions of the subject such as 'corporate strategy', 'business policy', 'strategic management' and so on.

The structure of the book is explained in some detail in Chapter 1. However, it might be useful to explain the basic structure of the book here and some of the changes from the second edition. The book is in four parts. Part I comprises an introduction to corporate strategy, first in terms of its characteristics, and the elements of strategic management (Chapter 1), and then in terms of how strategic decisions actually come about in organisations (Chapter 2), and also examines the relationship between organisational strategy and culture.

Part II of the book is concerned with strategic analysis. The chapter structure remains the same, but a number of key themes have been expanded. For example, Chapter 3 has much more on the analysis of an organisation's competitive position. Chapter 4 devotes more time to the analysis of the factors underpinning strategic capability – particularly cost and value creation. Chapter 5 now has a much fuller and more integrated treatment of the two major issues underlying the expectations and purposes of organisations. The *cultural* context is explored – both externally and internally – and the *political* context includes a more systematic treatment of stakeholder analysis.

Part III is concerned with strategic choice, and the division of material between the chapters has been changed a little in the new edition. Chapter 6 focuses on the identification of strategic options and updates the discussion of generic strategies in the light of the debate which has occurred since 1988 on the acceptability of Porter's generic strategies. Chapter 7 now focuses on assessing the suitability of strategies, using the three approaches of strategic logic, research evidence and cultural fit. It includes a discussion of the screening of options together with an assessment of acceptability and feasibility. Chapter 8 is now entitled 'making choices' and two important additions are a discussion of 'shareholder value' and a sharper critique of the use of financial analysis techniques.

The final section of the book – Part IV – is about strategy implementation. Again we have moved some material around between chapters. Chapter 9 remains devoted to resource planning; an important addition is a fuller discussion of *critical success factors*. Chapter 10 has been refocused a little to bring together all of the aspects of organisational design: namely, structure, centre/division relationships, configuration and control/regulatory systems. We feel that this makes for a clearer discussion. This now leaves Chapter 11 to give an expanded treatment of managing change and to underpin the links with the theme of strategy and culture in Chapters 2 and 5.

Many people have helped us with the development of this new edition. First and foremost have been the adopters of the current edition – a number of whom we have had the pleasure of meeting at our annual seminars. Many of you have provided us with constructive criticism and thoughts for the new edition – we hope you are happy with the results! Also our students and clients at Sheffield and Cranfield are a constant source of ideas and challenge. It would be impossible to write a book of this type without this direct feedback. The Strategic Planning Institute has been helpful in commenting on Chapter 7, as have Tony Grundy and David Pitt-Watson on Chapters 4 and 8. In addition many others have contributed illustrations and we would like to thank them too. They include: John Darwin, Glyn Owen, Bernard Jones, Peter Jones and Graham Worsdale, all from Sheffield Business School; David Cowley, Roger Lazenby, Julie Verity and Elaine Burton, all from Cranfield School of Management; Christine Bennett and Ewan Fairlie from Warwick University Business School; Kent Nielsen, University of Aarhus; Michel Bougon, Bryant College, USA; Richard Whipp, Cardiff Business School; Eleanora Cattaneo, International Institute of St Petersburg, Bocconi University; Harry Sminia, University of Groningen; M. Salgado, Groupe ESC Lyon and Glyn Roberts, Cheshire County Council. Our thanks are also due to those who have had a part in preparing the manuscript for the book: Jenny Scholes, Claire Larkin and Jayne Barker at Sheffield, and Elaine Burton and Julia Newton at Cranfield. Finally, we would like to thank all those who have contributed to the book directly through case studies.

Gerry Johnson
Kevan Scholes
January 1993

PART I
Introduction

CHAPTER 1

Corporate strategy: an introduction

By 1991 Ingvar Kamprad had seen IKEA transformed from the mail-order furniture business he set up in Sweden in 1949 to a £2 billion retail furnishing empire with 96 stores in 24 countries. Retail commentators and business analysts saw the firm as a major success story: its success based on its customer focus, its clear long-term strategy and its skill in implementing that strategy. The issue that faced Ingvar Kamprad and Anders Moberg, the chief executive of IKEA, was whether the strategy pursued so successfully in the past could be maintained in the 1990s. Illustration 1.1 gives an overview of the developments of IKEA and its strategic plans.

The approach IKEA had taken to meeting customer needs and developing its business had followed a consistent pattern over many years. However, the changes that had taken place, albeit in an evolutionary way, had substantially changed the direction of the business in that time: they were changes which were long-term in nature and had far-ranging implications for organisational structure and control, and the logistics of the operation. They also raised major challenges for the future. In short, they were major *strategic* developments.

All organisations are faced with the need to manage strategies: some developing from a position of strength, like IKEA; some needing to overcome significant problems. This book deals with why reviews of strategic direction take place in organisations, why they are important, how such decisions are taken and some of the tools and techniques that managers can use to take such decisions. This chapter is an introduction and explanation of this theme, and of the structure of the book as a whole. It also draws on the IKEA illustration for the purposes of discussion; and as the book progresses, other such illustrations are used to help develop discussion.

This first chapter deals with the questions of what is meant by 'corporate strategy' and 'strategic management', why they are so important and what distinguishes them from other organisational tasks and decisions. In discussing these it will become clearer how the book deals with the subject area.

One other point should be made before proceeding. The term 'corporate strategy' is used here for two main reasons: first, because the book is concerned with strategy and strategic decisions in all types of organisation – small and large commercial enterprises as well as public services – and the word 'corporate' embraces them all; and second, because, as the term is used in this book (discussed more fully in section 1.1.2), 'corporate strategy' denotes the most general level of strategy in an organisation and in this sense embraces other levels of strategy. Readers will undoubtedly come across other terms, such as 'strategic management', 'business policy', 'management policy' and 'organisational strategy', all of which deal with the same general area.

1.1 The nature of corporate strategy

Why are the issues facing IKEA described as 'strategic'? What sorts of decision are strategic decisions, and what distinguishes these from other decisions that were no doubt being taken in the company?

ILLUSTRATION 1.1
IKEA's ideal

We shall offer a wide range of furnishing items of good design and function, at prices so low that the majority of people can afford to buy them.
                                                              Ingvar Kamprad

Aged nineteen, Ingvar Kamprad produced his first mail-order furniture catalogue in 1949; it featured locally produced furniture. Within four years his first store opened in Almhult, Sweden. By August 1991 the IKEA Group's annual sales, to over 100 million customers, exceeded £2 billion through 96 stores in 24 countries.

Growth had been impressive but incremental. During the 1960s growth was limited to six stores in Scandinavia. The first test of the retail concept outside Scandinavia was near Zurich in 1973. This small market was chosen as a 'failure would not be too damaging'. Success led to expansion in Switzerland and then entry into other countries. The 1970s saw 24 stores open and entry into eight new countries. The 1980s were the boom years with 53 stores opened and nine new countries entered. The growth was fuelled by changing customer attitudes from status and designer labels to functionality, encouraged by an economic recession. However, in countries with significant perceived risk, IKEA worked through franchise operations.

A key feature of IKEA's retailing concept was universal customer appeal that crossed national boundaries. The products and the shopping experience were both designed to support this appeal. IKEA aimed to get to know its customer needs and then remove any cost or activity from its offer that did not meet them. Customers came from many lifestyles, from

1.1.1 The characteristics of strategic decisions

The characteristics usually associated with the words 'strategy' and 'strategic decisions' are these:

1. Strategic decisions are likely to be concerned with the *scope of an organisation's activities*: does (and should) the organisation concentrate on one area of activity, or does it have many? For example, IKEA had clearly defined the *boundaries* of its business in terms of the type of product – 'furnishing items of good design and function' – and mode of service – large retail outlets and mail order. While not owning its manufacturing, it also had an in-house design capability which specified and controlled what manufacturers supplied to the company. Perhaps most significantly, it had

---

new homeowners to business executives needing more office capacity. They all expected well-styled, high-quality home furnishings, reasonably priced and readily available. IKEA believed that customers need time and information to make their purchase decisions. The information was provided in a 200-page glossy catalogue, which was the primary selling vehicle. Sales staff participated only if asked: this reduced the number of staff required and ensured customer participation in the process. Furnishing items were displayed in 100 model rooms for customers to try. Supervised children's activity areas were provided, as were cafés where customers could get a taste of Swedish culture as well as Swedish food.

Large sales volumes reduced purchase prices to IKEA but cost reduction was taken even further. IKEA employed twenty designers to design for low cost and ease of manufacture. Low-cost modern materials (plastics and chipboard) were used wherever possible, but traditional materials (pine and linen) were used in the visible parts to emphasise Scandinavian style. The most economical suppliers were chosen over traditional suppliers: for examples, a shirt manufacturer produced seat covers. All items were flat packed, even pillows, as this made distribution less costly and enabled customers to collect goods and assemble them at home.

The end result was that IKEA was able to offer a core range of 12,000 items, both large and small, from 1,800 suppliers in 45 countries at prices 20 to 40 per cent lower than for comparable quality goods elsewhere. It was a one-stop shop for all the home's needs.

A pattern of development emerged, illustrated by IKEA's entry into the USA. Small trial stores were opened to test the concept and allow local adaptation. Then larger stores, the largest by 1992 being between 200,000 and 250,000 square feet, were built and increased in numbers

(Continued on p.6)

steadily. A local support office was set up to help store management train market and set up stock. Stores were usually based on greenfield sites outside, but within easy access of, population centres. The stores had a quality feel with parquet flooring and human-scale dimensions inside, despite being the size and style of aircraft hangers. The Swedish national colours were strongly in evidence along with other cultural elements such as low-key dress, relaxed interpersonal style, and traditional food and drink. This seemed a recipe for success as figures showed that yield per square foot was three times the industry average.

The IKEA Group located in Denmark to escape Swedish taxation. Anders Moberg became the chief executive, Ingvar Kamprad having retired to Switzerland as a tax exile. The company shares were held in trust by a Dutch charitable foundation and not traded. IKEA's expansion plans envisaged internal funding with 15 per cent of turnover reinvested, and a liquidity target of 12 per cent of turnover. IKEA was organised around four functions: product range, purchasing, distribution services and retailing. Anders Moberg headed the wholesale activities that included product range, purchasing and distribution service. By 1991 the retailing function was developing a regional structure to manage the global expansion.

While Ingvar Kamprad was no longer in control of IKEA, his influence could still be found. His sayings were still quoted: 'There is no more effective method than setting a good example.' 'The fear of making a mistake is the root of bureaucracy and the enemy of evolution.' 'The feeling of having finished is an effective sleeping pill.' Indeed, echoes of

also decided to widen its geographic scope substantially.

The issue of scope of activity is fundamental to strategic decisions because it concerns the way in which those responsible for managing the organisation conceive its boundaries. It is to do with what they want the organisation to be like and to be about.

2. Strategy is to do with the *matching of the activities of an organisation to the environment* in which it operates. While the market for furnishings was mature with little prospect of overall growth, the management of IKEA had seen that the retail provision of furnishing in most countries did not meet the expectations of customers. Customers frequently had to wait for delivery for items which were highly priced. The market had one other advantage. It appeared that customer tastes seemed relatively common except in specialised segments of the market: buyers wanted everyday furniture which was well designed and looked good, but was reasonably priced.

IKEA had also realised in the first two decades of its trading that it was less susceptible to economic downturn than many of its competitors. This may have

his philosophy and style could be seen in Anders Moberg. He would arrive at the office in the company Nissan Primera, dressed in informal clothes, and clock in just as other employees did. When abroad he travelled on economy-class air tickets and stayed in modest hotels. He expected his executives to do likewise.

IKEA did not always get it right first time; rather the company tried to improve continuously. Its most serious problem was being 'out of stock'. When stores initially set up in a new country, customers made long journeys to get to them. Non-availability was therefore bad news. This could be compounded by lack of information available over the telephone, caused by low staff levels and an increasingly world-wide sourcing network that did not allow rapid replenishment. On the other hand, IKEA adopted the attitude that, as customers became involved in the process, the process itself evolved better to meet their needs. It believed a partnership between customers and employees would grow.

So what of the future? IKEA believed that the changes in eastern Europe and the one-time Soviet republics represented great potential. Specific issues for IKEA in these regions included how to support and modernise local suppliers and the usefulness of local currency. Globally, IKEA's challenge centred on the tension between 'universal appeal' and 'unwillingness to adapt to local markets'. As a securities analyst said: 'If you go into other stores you'll see different furniture for each region. At IKEA it's pretty much the same thing in all their stores.'

Prepared by David Cowley, Cranfield School of Management.

been because its prices were often lower: but it was also because when someone took a purchasing decision at IKEA, they walked away with the goods. In other stores, since delivery was often delayed, purchase decisions were also often delayed.

However, IKEA also knew that it faced significant differences in its markets. By 1991 the number of countries in which IKEA was represented was a great deal larger than in the company's early days. This meant that IKEA had to understand buying habits and preferences from a much wider base, from markets close to its Swedish home, to the USA, and even to the Far East and eastern Europe. IKEA could no longer assume that its knowledge of earlier markets would necessarily apply: for example, it had found that shopping habits in the USA differed substantially from those in Europe, and this had required a change in the way it serviced the market. Therefore, while the core principles of IKEA's business idea were adhered to around the world to produce consistent product quality and shopping experience, store management had been given a greater degree of freedom to adapt to local market needs.

IKEA's management had, however, decided that there were some markets, attractive though they were, where it did not make sense to try to control IKEA's operations directly. In the Far East and Australia, IKEA stores operated under a franchise arrangement. Here the company recognised that local knowledge in fine tuning the business to local needs was vital; or the problems of long-distance control too great to manage the operation effectively on this basis.

There were wider environmental issues with which IKEA had to be concerned, and which affected its strategic development: for example, the economic conditions in the countries in which it operated; and the growth in car ownership, particularly in less highly developed countries, a factor directly linked to the percentage of the population which could shop at a store. Other organisations might find their environment a good deal more hostile than IKEA, with perhaps much higher degrees of competition, reduction in demand for goods, technological obsolescence, or rapid change in buyer requirements.

3. Strategy is also to do with the *matching of the organisation's activities to its resource capability*. It is not just about countering environmental threats and taking advantage of environmental opportunities; it is also about matching organisational resources to these threats and opportunities. There would be little point in trying to take advantage of some new opportunity if the resources needed were not available or could not be made available, or if the strategy was rooted in an inadequate resource base. IKEA had found that the strengths it could draw on, not only in terms of experience but also in terms of resources, had allowed it to develop the business to take advantage of the opportunities existing in the market. The product range IKEA had designed and developed was not only low cost but unique in its style and its flat-pack design: this design had deliberately emphasised the Scandinavian image of the product, and therefore distinguished it from other ranges of furnishings. Moreover, IKEA benefited from years of design experience dedicated to its operation and markets. Product range was further enhanced by the design of the stores, even down to the food served in them. The logistics of the operation, from sourcing of product to control of stock, had been learned over many years and provided not only a quite distinct way of operating, but a service greatly appreciated by customers. The policy to finance development internally had also led to a concentration on strong and secure financing, and careful evaluation of projects to ensure adequate cash flow. In short, both the physical aspects of resources and the experience built up over the years had been consciously developed to service the opportunity afforded in the marketplace.

4. Strategic decisions therefore often have *major resource implications* for an organisation. For example, the decision that IKEA took to develop its operations internationally had significant implications in terms of its need to obtain properties for development and access to funds by which to do this,

sometimes for projects which might be seen as high risk – for example, entering new markets in times of recession. The size of the operation in terms of numbers of people working in it, managerial levels and sheer physical stock held had to rise significantly. The need to control a multinational enterprise, as opposed to a national operation, had also began to require skills and control systems of a different sort. It was a problem which many retailers had found difficulty coping with. In the 1980s a number of UK retail firms had attempted to develop overseas with little success; and one of the major reasons was that they had underestimated the extent to which their resource commitments would rise and how the need to control them would take on quite different proportions. Strategies, then, need to be considered not only in terms of the extent to which the existing resource capability of the organisation is suited to the environmental opportunities; but also in terms of the extent to which resources can be obtained and controlled to develop a strategy for the future.

5. Strategic decisions are therefore likely to *affect operational decisions*, to 'set off waves of lesser decisions'.[1] The changes that have taken place in IKEA required a whole series of decisions at operational level. Management and control structures to deal with the international spread of the firm had to change. The methods of developing and distributing stock required revision to deal with the extended distribution logistics. Marketing and advertising policies needed to be reviewed by country to ensure their suitability to different customer behaviours and tastes. Personnel policies and practices, originated in the Swedish firm, also had to be reviewed. Store operations needed to change too, as geographical scope increased. For example, in the USA, IKEA saw the need to add to the core product range from local suppliers, install serviced loading bays, and erect bollards to stop the shopping trolleys being taken to all parts of the car parks, which like almost everything else were bigger in the USA.

6. The strategy of an organisation will be affected not only by environmental forces and resource availability, but also by the *values and expectations* of those who have *power* in and around the organisation. In some respects, strategy can be thought of as a reflection of the attitudes and beliefs of those who have most influence on the organisation. Whether a company is expansionist or more concerned with consolidation, and where the boundaries are drawn for a company's activities, may say much about the values and attitudes of those who influence strategy – the *stakeholders* of the organisation.

    In IKEA the insistence on internal financing, or Anders Moberg's emphasis on frugality and simplicity, were likely to influence the long-term development and direction of the company and the way it operated. Certainly, in IKEA the powerful influences of the founder and the chief executive were pronounced. Indeed, Anders Moberg took direct executive responsibility for core activities of the company. It would be difficult to imagine IKEA following a strategy which involved quite different sorts of retailers, operating in different sorts of ways throughout the world within a loose federation of businesses. It had a way of doing things – a culture – which provided a rationale for its business.

There are, of course, other stakeholders who have influence: in other companies, shareholders or financial institutions; certainly management and the workforce, buyers and perhaps suppliers; and the local community. The beliefs and values these stakeholders have will have a more or less direct influence on the strategy development of an organisation.

7.   Strategic decisions are likely to affect the *long-term direction* of an organisation. IKEA set out along a path which was difficult to reverse. In the 1950s and 1960s the company could have been defined, essentially, as a Scandinavian furnishing retailer. The whole thrust of its strategy now moved to being a multinational retailer; and as explained above, the resource and managerial commitments of this were such that it was difficult to envisage how they could return to their previous state.

Overall, if a *definition* of a strategy is required, these characteristics can provide a basis for one. **Strategy is the *direction* and *scope* of an organisation over the *long term*: ideally, which matches its *resources* to its changing *environment*, and in particular its *markets*, *customers* or *clients* so as to meet *stakeholder* expectations.**

Strategic decisions are, then, often *complex in nature*:[2] it can be argued that what distinguishes strategic management from other aspects of management in an organisation is just this complexity. The complexity arises for at least three reasons. First, strategic decisions usually involve a *high degree of uncertainty*: they may involve taking decisions on the basis of views about the future which it is impossible for managers to be sure about. Second, strategic decisions are likely to demand an *integrated* approach to managing the organisation. Unlike functional problems, there is no one area of expertise, or one perspective that can define or resolve the problems. Managers, therefore, have to cross functional and operational boundaries to deal with strategic problems and come to agreements with other managers who, inevitably, have different interests and perhaps different priorities. This problem of integration exists in all management tasks but is particularly problematic for strategic decisions. Third, as has been noted above, strategic decisions are likely to involve *major change* in organisations. Not only is it problematic to decide upon and plan those changes, it is even more problematic actually to implement them. Strategic management is therefore distinguished by a higher order of complexity than operational tasks.

1.1.2 Levels of strategy

Strategies will exist at a number of levels in an organisation. Individuals may say they have a strategy – to do with their career, for example. This may be relevant when considering influences on strategies adopted by organisations, but it is not what is meant by corporate strategy. Taking IKEA as an example, it is possible to distinguish at least three different levels of strategy. First, there is the *corporate* level: for IKEA as for many corporate headquarters, the main issues seem to be about overall scope of the organisation; how it is to be run in structural and financial terms; and how resources are to be allocated to the different IKEA operations across the world. As has been seen, all of these are likely to be influenced by the overall mission of the organisation. This was so in IKEA: the mission was to provide good-value home furnishings around the world at such a price that the majority of people were able to afford them. This is based on ideas of egalitarianism and Swedish social values as much as on good business through the creation of a large market. IKEA truly believed it had something of value to offer the world. These are factors common in other large organisations, although they might also be expressly concerned at the corporate level with financial markets and issues of diversification and acquisition.

The second level can be thought of in terms of *competitive or business strategy*. Here strategy is about how to compete in a market: the concerns are therefore about which products or services should be developed and offered to which markets; and the extent to which these meet customer needs in such a way as to achieve the objectives of the organisation – perhaps long-term profitability, market growth or measures of efficiency. So, whereas corporate strategy involves decisions about the organisation as a whole, business strategy is more likely to be related to a unit within the whole.

For IKEA, issues of business strategy will, then, be concerned with the sorts of store, product and service they should offer within the particular markets in which they compete. This is a good illustration of the way in which corporate-level strategy interacts with business-level strategy. At the business level, IKEA strategy needs to take account of the markets within which it is operating. However, at the corporate level IKEA wishes to ensure that its image, ranges and style of operation are consistent throughout the world. This matching of competitive-level strategy with corporate-level strategy is an issue which exists for most multinational corporations. For IKEA, it is resolved by the overall corporate mission and strategy guiding the choice of markets in which it operates, and the sorts of product and service it provides. Other organisations might choose to compete differently in different markets, in which case the corporate influence may be much less.

The third level of strategy is at the operating end of the organisation. Here there are *operational strategies* which are concerned with how the different functions of the enterprise – marketing, finance, manufacturing and so on – contribute to the other levels of strategy. Such contributions will certainly be important in terms of how an organisation seeks to be competitive. For example, in IKEA it was of crucial importance that design, store operations and sourcing operations dovetailed into higher-level decisions about product range and market entry. Indeed, in most businesses, successful business strategies depend to a large extent on decisions which are taken, or activities which occur, at the operational level. The integration of operations and strategy is therefore of great importance.

The ideas discussed in this book are of relevance to all three levels of strategy but are most specifically concerned with the areas of corporate and business strategy – what businesses (or areas of operation) should an organisation be in, and how should it compete in each of these?

1.1.3 The vocabulary of strategy

At the end of section 1.1.1 a definition of strategy was given. It can be dangerous to offer a definition, because lengthy semantic discussions can follow about whether or not it is precise enough, and whether everyone would agree with it. In fact, it is clear enough in the literature on strategy that many authors would have different definitions.[3] The concern in this book is not to provide a categoric definition, but rather to summarise the characteristics of strategic decisions that readers need to understand. However, there are indeed many terms used when discussing the notion of strategies in organisations. It is therefore worthwhile devoting a little space to clarifying some of these. There is another reason for doing this: as has already been explained, strategic issues shade into more general expectations of stakeholders and the operational detail of running organisations. This shading can give rise to confusion of terminology. Perhaps reviewing the terms here might lead to greater clarity.

Figure 1.1 and Illustration 1.2 employ some of the terms that readers will come across in this and other books on strategy. Figure 1.1 explains these in relation to a personal strategy we may have followed ourselves – dieting. Illustration 1.2 shows how these relate to an organisation – in this case, British Airways.

Not all these terms are always used in organisations, or in strategy books: indeed, in this book the word 'goal' is rarely used. Moreover, it may or may not be that mission, goals, objectives, strategies and so on are written down precisely. In some organisations this is done very formally. In others it is not: as will be shown in Chapter 2, a mission or strategy especially might sometimes more sensibly be conceived as that which can be deduced about an organisation from what it is doing. However, as a general guideline the following terms are often used.

A *mission* is a general expression of the overriding premise of the organisation, which, ideally, would be in line with the values and expectations of major stakeholders. It is likely to be concerned with the overall purpose of the organisation, its scope and its boundaries. It is sometimes referred to in terms of the apparently simple, but actually quite challenging question: *'What business are we in?'*.

If the word *goal* is used, it usually means a general statement of direction in line with the mission. It may well be qualitative in nature. On the other hand, an *objective* is more likely to be quantified, or at least to be a more precise state-

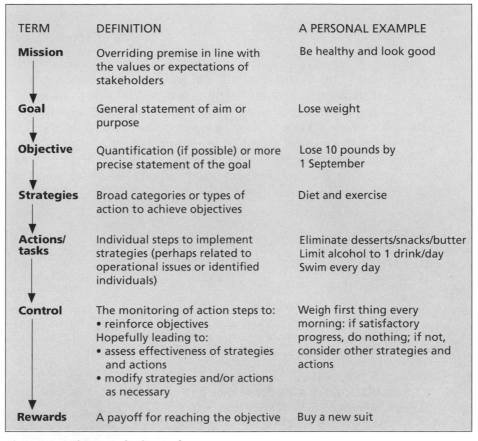

TERM	DEFINITION	A PERSONAL EXAMPLE
Mission	Overriding premise in line with the values or expectations of stakeholders	Be healthy and look good
Goal	General statement of aim or purpose	Lose weight
Objective	Quantification (if possible) or more precise statement of the goal	Lose 10 pounds by 1 September
Strategies	Broad categories or types of action to achieve objectives	Diet and exercise
Actions/ tasks	Individual steps to implement strategies (perhaps related to operational issues or identified individuals)	Eliminate desserts/snacks/butter Limit alcohol to 1 drink/day Swim every day
Control	The monitoring of action steps to: • reinforce objectives Hopefully leading to: • assess effectiveness of strategies and actions • modify strategies and/or actions as necessary	Weigh first thing every morning: if satisfactory progress, do nothing; if not, consider other strategies and actions
Rewards	A payoff for reaching the objective	Buy a new suit

Figure 1.1 The vocabulary of strategy

ment in line with the goal. (However, in this book the word 'objective' is used whether or not there is quantification.)

Strategies, when stated, are likely to be fairly broad statements of intent which show the types of action required to achieve the objectives.

To be effective, strategies need to translate into *actions* and *tasks* which link broad direction to specific operational issues and individuals.

It is then important to exercise some degree of *control* so as to monitor the extent to which the action is achieving the objectives and goals.

Another term used in this book is *SBU*, or *strategic business unit*, a term often used in relation to business strategy. SBU means a unit within the overall corporate entity for which there is an external market for its goods and services which is distinct from that of another SBU. (In public-sector organisations a corresponding definition of an SBU might be a part of the organisation or service for which there is a distinct client group.) An SBU may not therefore be defined in terms of organisational structure. For example, a company might have a number

ILLUSTRATION 1.2
British Airways and the vocabulary of strategy

The annual reports and public statements of companies will often contain elements of the vocabulary of strategy used in this book.

The mission and goals of British Airways are boldly proclaimed in the annual accounts. Several goals are associated with the mission and two have been repeated here. They relate to global leadership and service and value. The mission and goals are supported and amplified by comments from the company's executives in their reports in the annual accounts. Examples of these comments can be seen under objectives, strategies, actions and rewards.

Mission

'To be the best and most successful company in the airline industry'

Goals

'GLOBAL LEADER'
'To secure a leading share of air travel business world-wide with a significant presence in all major geographical markets'

'SERVICE AND VALUE'
'To provide overall superior service and good value for money in every market segment in which we compete'

Objectives

'Our objective is to maintain the growth of British Airways' business and to take advantage of the expected overall global expansion of the industry ...'

'... we seek to excel in anticipating and responding quickly to customer needs and competitor activity ...'

of divisions, but these could serve a number of markets. It might be more useful to consider business – or competitive strategy – at the level of the distinct market, and this is where the notion of an SBU is helpful.[4]

1.2 Strategic management

What, then, is 'strategic management'? It is not enough to say that it is the man-

During the preparation of British Airways for public ownership in 1986 the then chief financial officer Jim Harris also publicly stated a quantified objective: '. . . the airline must achieve profits of over £200m a year after all charges in order to meet the demands that are placed on it.'

Strategies

'. . . competition will increase in many of our markets and success will depend on our ability to keep costs firmly under control.'

'Our strategy is to expand our core business globally by creating marketing alliances where beneficial or, if there is a sufficient return on capital, by investing in other airlines.'

'. . . maintaining a pace of quality, innovation and service delivery which keeps us ahead of the competition . . .'

Actions

'. . . we agreed a marketing partnership with United Airlines in 1987.'

'. . . we reached agreement for a partnership with Air New Zealand . . . Our two airlines services connect at Singapore, Hong Kong, Kuala Lumpur and Los Angeles.'

'. . . we are investing £35 million to acquire a 70% stake in a restructured Sabena World Airlines.'

Reward

'We operate a profit sharing scheme, which allows eligible staff to acquire shares in the Company, and a savings-related share scheme.'

Sources: *British Airways Plc Annual Report and Accounts 1989–1990*; *British Airways Plc Annual Report and Accounts 1990–1991*; *Financial Times*, 2 June 1986, p. 10.

Prepared by David Cowley, Cranfield School of Management.

agement of the process of strategic decision making. This fails to take into account a number of points important both in the management of an organisation and in the area of study with which this book is concerned.

First, it should be pointed out that the nature of strategic management is different from other aspects of management. Figure 1.2 summarises some of these differences. An individual manager is most often required to deal with problems of operational control, such as the efficient production of goods, the management of a salesforce, the monitoring of financial performance or the design of

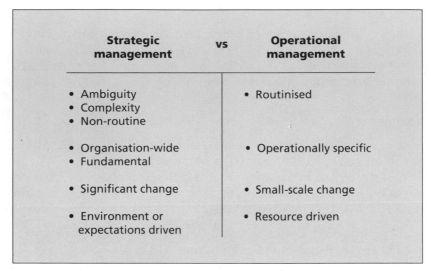

Strategic management	vs	**Operational management**
• Ambiguity • Complexity • Non-routine		• Routinised
• Organisation-wide • Fundamental		• Operationally specific
• Significant change		• Small-scale change
• Environment or expectations driven		• Resource driven

Figure 1.2 Strategic management and operational management

some new system that will improve the efficiency of the operation. These are all very important tasks, but they are essentially concerned with effectively managing a limited part of the organisation within the context and guidance of a more overarching strategy. Operational control is what managers are involved in for most of their time. It is vital to the effective implementation of strategy, but it is not the same as strategic management.

Nor is strategic management concerned only with taking decisions about major issues facing the organisation. It is also concerned with ensuring that the strategy is put into effect. It can be thought of as having three main elements within it, and it is these that provide the framework for the book. There is *strategic analysis*, in which the strategist seeks to understand the strategic position of the organisation. There is *strategic choice*, which is to do with the formulation of possible courses of action, their evaluation and the choice between them. And there is *strategy implementation*, which is concerned with planning how the choice of strategy can be put into effect, and managing the changes required.

Before discussing these elements in detail it is important to make clear how they relate to each other and, therefore, why Figure 1.3 is shown in the form it is. The figure could have been shown in a linear form – strategic analysis preceding strategic choice, which in turn precedes strategy implementation. Indeed, this would seem quite logical, and many texts on the subject do just this. However, in practice, the stages do not take this linear form. It is very likely that the elements are interlinked: it is quite possible that one way of evaluating a strategy would be to begin to implement it, so strategic choice and strategy implementation may overlap. It is also likely that strategic analysis will be an on-going activity and so will overlap with the implementation of strategy. The process is examined more fully in the light of research on the subject in Chapter 2, so as to provide readers

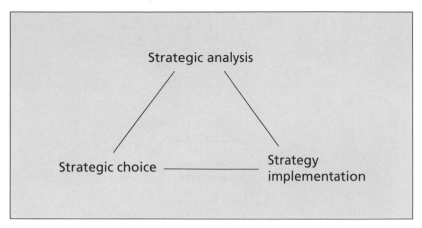

Figure 1.3 A basic model of the strategic management process

with a better 'feel' for the realities of strategic management. It is for structural convenience only that the process has been divided into sections in this book.

1.2.1   Strategic analysis

Strategic analysis is concerned with understanding the strategic position of the organisation. What changes are going on in the environment, and how will they affect the organisation and its activities? What is the resource strength of the organisation in the context of these changes? What is it that those people and groups associated with the organisation – managers, shareholders or owners, unions and so on – aspire to, and how do these affect the present position and what could happen in the future?

The history of IKEA suggests that a great deal of care was taken by those planning the development of the business in analysing different strategic moves. The decision to enter a new geographic market required careful consideration about the economy in that country, current and future demand in the market for furnishings, the historical and likely future activities of competitors, the most attractive locations in terms of demographic profiles of potential customers, and so on. It also required managers in IKEA to match opportunities to resource capability and availability in terms of finances, manpower and skills. All these considerations had to be considered in the light of the expectations and values of the corporate centre, and quite probably those of IKEA's founder, Ingvar Kamprad.

The aim of *strategic analysis* is, then, to form a view of the key influences on the present and future well-being of the organisation and therefore on the choice of strategy. These influences are summarised in Figure 1.4 and discussed briefly below. Understanding these influences is an important part of the wider aspects of strategic management which this section also goes on to discuss.

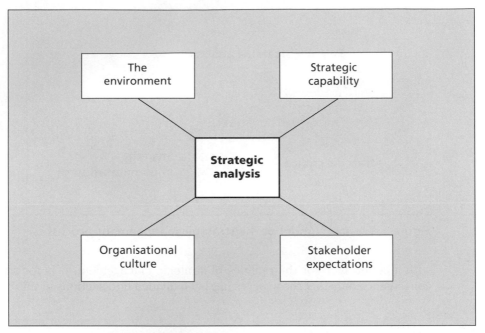

Figure 1.4 Aspects of strategic analysis

1. The *environment*. The organisation exists in the context of a complex commercial, economic, political, technological, cultural and social world. This environment changes and is more complex for some organisations than for others. Since strategy is concerned with the position a business takes in relation to its environment, an understanding of the environment's effects on a business is of central importance to strategic analysis. The historical and environmental effects on the business must be considered, as well as the present effects and the expected changes in environmental variables. This is a major task because the range of environmental variables is so great. Many of those variables will give rise to *opportunities* of some sort, and many will exert *threats* upon the firm. The two main problems that have to be faced are, first, to distil out of this complexity a view of the main or overall environmental impacts for the purpose of strategic choice; and second, the fact that the range of variables is likely to be so great that it may not be possible or realistic to identify and analyse each one. Chapter 3 examines how it might be possible to tackle these problems.

2. The *resources* of the organisation. Just as there are outside influences on the firm and its choice of strategies, so there are internal influences. One way of thinking about the *strategic capability* of an organisation is to consider its *strengths* and *weaknesses* (what it is good or not so good at doing, or where it is at a competitive advantage or disadvantage, for example). These strengths and weaknesses may be identified by considering the resource

areas of a business such as its physical plant, its management, its financial structure and its products. Again, the aim is to form a view of the internal influences – and constraints – on strategic choice. Chapter 4 examines resource analysis in detail.

3.   The *expectations* of different *stakeholders* are important because they will affect what will be seen as acceptable in terms of the strategies advanced by management. However, the beliefs and assumptions that make up the *culture* of an organisation, though less explicit, will also have an important influence. The environmental and resource influences on an organisation will be interpreted through these beliefs and assumptions; so two groups of managers, perhaps working in different divisions of an organisation, may come to different conclusions about strategy, although they are faced with similar environmental and resource implications. Which influence prevails is likely to depend on which group has the greatest *power*, and understanding this can be of great importance in recognising why an organisation follows or is likely to follow, the strategy it does. Chapter 2 discusses the important influences of beliefs and organisational culture on the formulation of strategy, and this is followed through in Chapter 5 with a discussion of how the culture, expectations and power structures in an organisation can be analysed and the ways in which such beliefs and expectations are likely to affect organisational objectives.

Together, a consideration of the *environment*, the *resources*, the *expectations* and the *objectives* within the *cultural* and *political* framework of the organisation provides the basis of the strategic analysis of an organisation. However, to understand the strategic position an organisation is in, it is also necessary to examine the extent to which the direction and implications of the current strategy and objectives being followed by the organisation are in line with and can cope with the implications of the strategic analysis. In this sense, such analysis must take place with the future in mind. Is the current strategy capable of dealing with the changes taking place in the organisation's environment or not? If so, in what respects and, if not, why not?

It is unlikely that there will be a complete match between current strategy and the picture which emerges from the strategic analysis. The extent to which there is a mismatch here is the extent of the strategic problem facing the strategist. It may be that the adjustment that is required is marginal, or it may be that there is a need for a fundamental realignment of strategy. For example, it is likely that when IKEA examines market potential for the development of new stores in new countries, opportunities suggest themselves which are not necessarily compatible with the resource base, or the expectations of the corporate centre. Indeed, some analysts believe that IKEA have underestimated the problems in the USA of customer resistance to a 'do it yourself' approach to home furnishing. There may also be opportunities in a market which could be taken advantage of only by trading in some other way than that which IKEA wishes to pursue. Profits may be capable of being made, but not in ways which IKEA wishes to follow. Or it may be that the analysis shows that different resources or different skills are required to develop such a market: this may be one of the reasons why IKEA has developed its franchising operations in the 1980s.

1.2.2 Strategic choice

Strategic analysis provides a basis for strategic choice. This aspect of strategic management can be conceived of as having three parts.

1. *Generation of strategic options.* There may be several possible courses of action. In the 1970s and 1980s, IKEA had faced a decision about the extent to which it was to become a truly multinational firm. By 1991 the international scope of their operations posed them other choices: which areas of the world were now most important to concentrate on; was it possible to maintain a common basis of trading across all the different countries? or was it necessary to introduce variations by market focus? These were critical questions because the fundamental or *generic strategy* of the organisation was based on a world-wide basis of retailing which was quite unique – or differentiated. Within these choices, what *strategic directions* were necessary in terms of product development and product range? Should the company attempt to follow these strategies by internal development, or was increasing joint venture activity through franchising more sensible: in other words, what *methods* of strategic direction were most appropriate?

   All of these considerations are important and needed careful consideration: indeed, in developing strategies, a potential danger is that managers do not consider any but the most obvious course of action – and the most obvious is not necessarily the best. A helpful step in *strategic choice* can be to generate *strategic options*.

2. *Evaluation of strategic options.* Strategic options can be examined in the context of the strategic analysis to assess their relative merits. In deciding any of the options that they faced, IKEA management might have asked a series of questions. First, which of these options built upon strengths, overcame weaknesses and took advantage of opportunities, while minimising or circumventing the threats the business faced? This is called the search for strategic fit or *suitability* of the strategy. However, a second set of questions is important. To what extent could a chosen strategy be put into effect? Could required finance be raised, sufficient stock be made available at the right time and in the right place, staff be recruited and trained to reflect the sort of image IKEA was trying to project? These are questions of *feasibility*. Even if these criteria could be met, would the

choice be *acceptable* to the stakeholders? For example, suppose in reviewing strategic options, IKEA management could see a logic in substantial variation by country in product range and store design. Would this be acceptable to the corporate centre, and perhaps ultimately to the heritage established by Ingvar Kamprad?

3. *Selection of strategy.* This is the process of selecting those options which the organisation will pursue. There could be just one strategy chosen or several. There is unlikely to be a clear-cut 'right' or 'wrong' choice because any strategy must inevitably have some dangers or disadvantages. So in the end, choice is likely to be a matter of management judgement. It is important to understand that the selection process cannot always be viewed or understood as a purely objective, logical act. It is strongly influenced by the values of managers and other groups with interest in the organisation, and ultimately may very much reflect the power structure in the organisation.

Strategic choice is dealt with in Part III of the book. In Chapter 6 there is a discussion of the various strategic options that organisations most typically consider. Chapter 7 discusses the criteria of evaluation in more detail and discusses several approaches to assessing the suitability of different types of strategy. Chapter 8 goes on to consider some techniques for evaluating specific options and the ways in which strategy selection might occur.

1.2.3 Strategy implementation

Strategy implementation is concerned with the translation of strategy into action. Implementation can be thought of as having several parts. It is likely to involve *resource planning,* including the logistics of implementation. What are the key tasks needing to be carried out? What changes need to be made in the resource mix of the organisation? By when? And who is to be responsible for the change? It is also likely that changes in *organisational structure* will be needed to carry through the strategy. There is also likely to be a need to adapt the *systems* used to manage the organisation. What will different departments be held responsible for? What sorts of information system are needed to monitor the progress of the strategy? Is there a need for retraining of the workforce? When IKEA decided to expand its international operations in the 1980s it was faced with an extension to its operations that required a restructuring of the organisation, which it decided could most appropriately be done by geographical area; and the revision of the means by which it controlled the different geographical operations, as well as more detailed logistics of the business, such as distribution and stock control. In addition there was a major problem of training. It was one thing to maintain the carefully preserved Swedish image of the organisation when it was trading in Scandinavia, and perhaps northern Europe. But how was this to be done for stores as far apart as Australia, Singapore and Los Angeles?

The implementation of strategy also requires the managing of *strategic change*; and this requires action on the part of managers in terms of the way they manage change processes, and the mechanisms they use for it. These mechanisms are likely to be concerned not only with organisational redesign, but with changing day-to-day routines and cultural aspects of the organisation, and overcoming political blockages to change.

Part IV of the book deals with strategy implementation. The planning of resource allocation is discussed in Chapter 9, the issues of organisational structure and systems of control are dealt with in Chapter 10, and the issues of managing strategic change are discussed in Chapter 11.

1.2.4 A summary of the strategic management process

The influences on, and elements of, strategic management discussed above are summarised in Figure 1.5. The figure is intended not as a prescription of what strategic management should be, but as a framework which readers can use to think through strategic problems. It also forms the structure of the remainder of the book.

It was stated earlier that there is a danger of thinking of the process of strategic management as an orderly sequence of steps; the danger is that readers might not find the elements described here existing in practice, and might therefore argue that strategic management in their organisation does not take place. It is important to stress that the model used in this book, and summarised in this chapter, is a useful device for the structuring of the book and a means by which managers and students of strategy can *think through* complex strategic problems. It is not, however, an attempt to describe how the processes of strategic management necessarily take place in the political and cultural arenas of an organisation. The traditional view of strategic management, common in books of the 1960s and 1970s, was that strategy was, or should be, managed through planning processes, in the form of a neat sequence of steps building on objective setting and analysis, through the evaluation of different options, and ending with the careful *planning* of the strategy implementation.[5] Many organisations do have such systems, and find that they contribute usefully to the development of the strategy of their organisation. However, not all organisations have them, and even when they do, it would be a mistake to assume that the strategies of organisations necessarily come about through them.

The management of the strategy of an organisation can also be thought of as a process of *crafting*.[6] Here strategic management is seen not so much as a formal planning process, but rather as a process by which strategies develop in organisations on the basis of managers' experience, their sensitivity to changes in their environments and what they learn from operating in their markets. This does not mean that managers are not thinking about the strategic position of their organisation, or the choices it faces; but this may not be taking place in a highly formalised way.

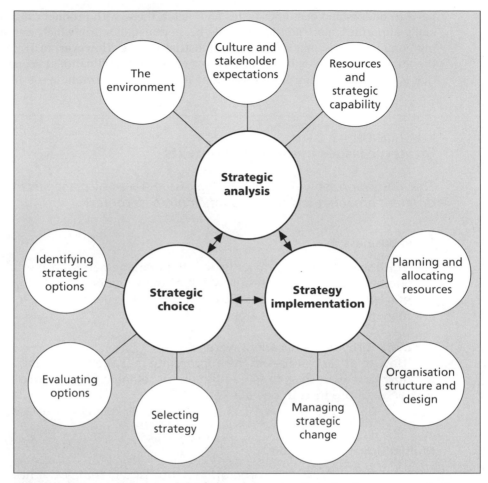

Figure 1.5 A summary model of the elements of strategic management

These and other views about the management of strategy and how strategies develop in organisations are discussed in Chapter 2.

1.3 Strategic management in different contexts

The multinational retail development of IKEA has been used in this chapter to illustrate different aspects of strategic management. To a greater or lesser extent all these aspects are relevant for most organisations. However, it is likely that different aspects will be more important in some contexts, and some organisations, than in others. For example, IKEA is a retail business, and in retailing the need to understand customer tastes and match these with product range is crucially important, more so than it would be, perhaps, in a firm which was supplying commodity raw materials in an industrial setting. However, in IKEA itself, the strategic emphases have changed over time. Its multinational scope meant that structural and control issues became much more important in the 1980s and

---

ILLUSTRATION 1.3
Strategic issues in different contexts

This illustration shows how the strategic issues faced by managers in different organisations depend on their business context.

Small Business

'For a small business a major issue is the management of growth. Successful small businesses grow out of the founder's entrepreneurial vision, but growth means the founder can no longer manage all the activities alone.'

For Mark Kirby the implications were:
'How to attract and select the appropriate management talent; and how to market so as to spread the risk of selling a single or small range of products to one market sector'.

Mark Kirby, managing director of Medic Aid.

Multinational Corporation

'Any big multinational corporation is intrinsically complex. It has multiple layers of managers and, in most cases, multiple businesses – it develops products, manufactures and sells them, and services them in multiple countries ... A choice (of strategy) in principle ... has to be embedded in a complex industrial and managerial structure so that the myriad choices made daily within the organisation fall in line with the chosen strategic orientation.'

Y. Doz, introduction to *Strategic Management in Multinational Companies*,
Pergamon, 1986, pp. 6–7.

Professional Partnership

'In recent years, "Professional Partnerships" like accountants have become huge organisations with sales in excess of $5 billion. Yet they still tend to be organised to serve national or regional markets, with partners being responsible for all aspects of service delivery to clients,

1990s than they had been when it was more geographically limited in the 1960s. It would, then, be wrong to assume that all aspects of strategic management are equally important in all circumstances: this section briefly reviews some of the ways in which aspects differ in different contexts. Differences are also shown in Illustration 1.3.

---

with which they may personally identify. You also need to remember that partnerships are not hierarchies: you can't easily tell partners what to do. However clients are beginning to require international service delivery. This cuts across the traditional structure and culture of partnerships; for example in the way it requires team working across national boundaries, and therefore planned integration of resources. It is not always easy to get partners to go along with this. As one of my colleagues said: A great deal of management of a professional service organisation has to do with "keeping the fleas in the bucket".'

David Pitt-Watson, director of Braxton Associates

Charity Sector

'Many charitable organisations comprise groups with diverse values and beliefs. An example might be the voluntary workers who are committed to the ideals of the organisation and those people employed to provide a professional service to the organisation. These different groups need to be co-ordinated so that the ideals are changed into works.'

John Naylor, National Secretary, YMCA

Public Sector

'In public-sector organisations, where the government is the major stakeholder, and not the market, the motivation to meet customer needs is reduced. Staff adopt the attitude that if a particular service is considered essential then, if not economic, it will be supported by the government. The consequences for the organisation and the individual of failure to provide an appropriate level of service are reduced. Being dependent on government policy also means that objectives may change rapidly as policy changes ... And this political dimension also reduces the scope of management options and increases the time for decisions to be taken.'

Stephen Colloff, formerly director of personnel development, British Railways

Prepared by David Cowley, Cranfield School of Management.

1.3.1 The small business context

Small businesses are likely to be operating in a single market, or a limited range of markets, probably with a limited range of products or services. The scope of the operation is therefore likely to be less of a strategic issue than in larger corporations. It is also likely that, unless the firm is specialising in some particular market segment, it will be subject to significant competitive pressures: so issues of competitive strategy are likely to be especially important for the small firm. Decisions on competitive strategies are likely to be strongly influenced by the experience of those running the business. It is unlikely that they will have central service departments to undertake complex analysis and market research; rather, it may be senior managers themselves, perhaps even the founder of the firm, who has direct contact with the marketplace and whose experience is therefore very influential. Indeed, in small firms the values and expectations of senior executives who may be in an ownership position are likely to be very important. Even when current management are not owners, it may be that the values and expectations of the founders still linger on.

Small firms are also likely to be private companies. This significantly affects their ability to raise capital. Combined with the legacy of the founder's influence on choice of product and market, this may mean that choices of strategy are significantly limited. The firm may see its role as consolidating its position within a particular market. If it does not, and is seeking growth, then the raising of finance for the development of strategy may become a key strategic issue; and in many such firms, relationships with funding bodies such as banks become a major resource issue.

1.3.2 The multinational corporation[7]

The key strategic issues facing multinationals are substantially different from those facing the small business. Here the firm is likely to be very diverse in terms of both products and geographic markets. It may be that the firm is in a range of different types of business in the form of subsidiary companies within a holding company structure, or divisions within a multidivisional structure. Therefore issues of structure and control at the corporate level, and relationships between businesses and the corporate centre, are usually a major strategic issue for multinational firms. At the business unit level, many of the competitive strategic issues will, perhaps, be similar to those faced by smaller firms – though the strength of the multinational within a given geographical area may be greater than for any small firm. However, for the multinational parent company a significant issue will be how corporate business units should be allocated resources given their different, and often competing, demands for them; and how this is to be co-ordinated. Indeed the co-ordination of operational logistics across different business units and different countries may become especially important. For example, a multinational manufacturing company such as Ford or General Motors has to decide upon the most sensible configuration of plants for the manufacture of cars. Most have moved from manufacturing a particular car at a particular location, and now manufacture different parts of cars in different locations, bringing together such components for the assembly of a given car in a given location. The logistics problems of co-ordinating such operations are immense, requiring sophisticated control systems and management skills far removed from those in the smaller firm. An important choice that a major multinational has to make is the extent to which it controls such logistics centrally, or devolves autonomy to operating units. It is, again, an issue of structure and control, the subject of Chapter 10 of this book.

1.3.3 Manufacturing and service organisations[8]

Important differences exist between organisations providing services and those providing products, particularly with regard to competitive strategy. Competitive strategy for a manufacturing firm is likely to be concerned with the product itself to a greater extent than in the case of service organisations. Ford's ability to compete effectively with Japanese manufacturers critically depends on the extent to which it has a physical product which gives it advantages over Japanese producers, at a price which is also competitive. These factors are likely to be linked back into the production process to a considerable extent. In contrast, in a firm which competes on the basis of the services it provides – for example, insurance, management consultancy, professional services and so on – there is no physical product. Here competitive advantage is likely to be much more related to the extent to which customers value less tangible aspects of the firm. This could be, for example, the soundness of advice given, the attitude of staff, the ambience of offices, the swiftness of service and so on.

Senior management in manufacturing organisations can therefore usually exercise more direct control over competitive strategy than can be exercised in a service firm. In the service firm, the factors which determine competitive advantage are much more likely to be controlled by people at the point of delivery; and this may be well removed from the control of central management. In short, the direct control of senior executives on competitive strategy in the service firm is likely to be less strong than in the product-based firm.

1.3.4 Strategy in the public sector[9]

The development of concepts and techniques of corporate strategy has, in the past, occurred mainly in commercial enterprises. However, many of the concepts are just as important in the public sector. There are, of course, differences; and what matters is that managers in the public sector can identify what these differences are, and therefore what the focus of attention should be in considering strategic developments in their organisations. Some examples are as follows:

- *Nationalised companies* are similar in many respects to commercial organisations; the differences are associated with the nature of ownership and control. A commercial enterprise that is state controlled may well have differences in planning horizons and in bases of financing, and may require that top management control their organisation more centrally for reporting purposes – for example, to government ministers.
- A *government agency* is also similar in some respects to a commercial enterprise – it has a labour market, and a money market of sorts; it also has suppliers and users or customers. The fundamental difference is that at its heart lies a 'political market which approves budgets, and provides subsidies'.[10] It is the explicit nature of this political dimension which managers – or officers – have to cope with which particularly distinguishes government bodies, be they national or local, from commercial enterprises. This may in turn change the horizons of decisions, since they may be heavily influenced by political considerations, and may mean that analysis of strategies requires the norms of political dogma to be considered explicitly. However, although the magnitude of the political dimension is greater, the model of strategic management discussed here still holds. What is different is that certain aspects of strategic analysis and choice, notably those to do with political influences, are more important.
- Many public-sector organisations are in monopoly or *quasi-monopoly situations*, and they may be in these situations because they provide services which are required by the public but are difficult to provide through market mechanisms. For example, health services and many of the amenities run by local government may not be attractive commercial propositions. Their role in providing *public services* is problematic from a strategic point of view because they may not be able to specialise, and may not be able to generate surpluses from their services to invest in development. As is frequently pointed out by government, the press and users alike, this combination of lack of market focus, lack of involvement and a very broad role can lead to a mediocrity of service.
- In the public sector the notion of competition is often different. It is usually competition for *resource inputs*; therefore the need to demonstrate *value for money* in outputs becomes particularly important. Indeed, many of the developments in management practices in the public sector, such as changes to internal markets, performance indicators, competitive tendering and so on, are attempts to introduce elements of competition in order to encourage improvements in value for money.
- Overall, the role of ideology in the development of strategy in the public sector is probably greater than that in commercial organisations. Putting it in the terminology of this book, the criterion of *acceptability* in strategic

choice is probably of greater importance in the public sector than in the commercial sector.

1.3.5   The voluntary and not-for-profit sectors[11]

In the voluntary sector it is likely that underlying values and ideology will be of central strategic significance. It has already been noted that the values and expectations of different stakeholder groups in organisations play an important part in the development of strategy. This is particularly the case where the *raison d'être* of the organisation is rooted in such values. This tends to be the case, most obviously, in organisations providing services traditionally not for profit, such as charities.

In not-for-profit organisations such as charities, churches, private schools, foundations and so on, the sources of revenue are different from most businesses: funding bodies may be diverse and are quite likely not to be direct beneficiaries of the services offered. Moreover, they may provide funds in advance of the services being offered – in the form of grants, for example. The implications are several. Influence from funding bodies may be high in terms of the formulation of organisational strategies. Moreover, since such organisations are so dependent on funds which emanate not from clients but from sponsors, there is a danger that they become more concerned with resource efficiency than service effectiveness. The multiple sources of funding likely to exist, linked to the different objectives and expectations of the funding bodies, might also lead to a high incidence of political lobbying, difficulties in clear strategic planning, and a requirement to hold decision making and responsibility at the centre, where it is answerable to external influences, rather than delegate it within the organisation. The characteristics and difficulties of strategic management in not-for-profit organisations are summarised in Figure 1.6.

1.3.6   Professional organisations

Traditionally based values are often of particular importance in professional service organisations where professional advice has historically been seen as more important than revenue-earning capability. To a large extent this remains the case in medicine, accountancy, law and other professions.

Private-sector professional firms may also have a partnership structure. Partners may be owners and perhaps bear legal responsibility for advice and opinion offered by the firm; they may therefore carry considerable power. And there may be many of them – each of the top four accountancy firms in the UK has over 400 partners. However, although interacting with clients and exercising actual or potential control over resources, they may not regard themselves as managers at all. As a partner in a major accountancy firm put it: 'We see ourselves as the largest network of sole traders in the world.' The problems of

CHARACTERISTICS	LIKELY EFFECTS
Objectives and expectations • May be multiple service objectives and expectations • May be multiple influences on policy • Expectations of funding bodies very influential	• Complicates strategic planning • High incidence of political lobbying • Difficulties in delegating/ decentralising responsibilities and decision making
Market and users • Beneficiaries of service not necessarily contributors of revenue/resources	• Service satisfaction not measured readily in financial terms
Resources • High proportion from government, or sponsors • Received in advance of services • May be multiple sources of funding	• Influence from funding bodies may be high • May be emphasis on financial or resource efficiency rather than service effectiveness • Strategies may be addressed to sponsors as much as clients

Figure 1.6 Some characteristics of strategic management in not-for-profit organisations

developing and implementing strategy within such a context are, therefore, heavily linked to the management of internal political influences and the ability to take account of, and where necessary to change, organisational culture.

Another factor is the pressure those in the professions find themselves under to be more 'commercial' in their approach. Such pressure may come from government, as in the case of doctors; or it may be a function of size, as has been found in the growing accountancy firms. This has meant that such organisations have had to ask many of the questions of strategy that profit-making organisations have to ask, particularly those concerned with competitive strategy. Accounting or law firms may in future find themselves competing for customers more directly than hitherto.

1.4 Summary: the challenge of strategic management

This chapter has set out to explain the focus, concept and scope of the study of corporate strategy, and to propose a framework with which to approach the subject. The aim is that by this stage readers will have some idea about the types of issue with which strategic management is concerned. The rest of the book expands on these issues, but it is worthwhile emphasising four key implications for the effective strategic manager at this stage.

1. It should be clear that the scope of strategic management is much greater than that of any one area of functional management. This was seen in Figure 1.2. To a much greater extent, strategic management is concerned with complexity arising out of ambiguous and non-routine situations with organisation-wide rather than functional specific implications. This is a major challenge for managers who are used to managing the resources they control on a day-to-day basis.

    This can be a particular problem because of the background of managers who may have been trained, perhaps over many years, to undertake operational tasks and to take operational responsibility. Accountants find that they still tend to see problems in financial terms, marketing managers in marketing terms and so on. Each aspect in itself is important, of course, but none is adequate alone. The manager who aspires to manage, or influence, strategy needs to develop a capability to take an overview, to conceive of the whole rather than just the parts of the situation facing an organisation.

2. To develop an ability as a strategist therefore requires that the manager is able to conceptualise key strategic issues. Most aspects of management involve:

    *   *Analysis and planning* required to gather and organize *information* about the situation or issue faced.
    *   *Action* to undertake tasks: this may vary from action in the form of arranging for analysis to take place, to action in terms of ensuring change takes place.
    *   *Conceptualisation* of problems and choices: this is not simply a matter of analysis but is to do with *making sense* of the situation.

    Because strategic management is characterised by its complexity, it is necessary to make decisions and judgements based on the conceptualisation of difficult issues. Yet the early training of managers is often about taking action, or about detailed planning or analysis. This book discusses analytical approaches to strategy, and it is also concerned with action related to the management of strategy; but the emphasis is on developing concepts of relevance to the complexity of strategy which informs this analysis and action.

3. A major challenge for the strategic manager is to build an organisation that, simultaneously, is able to match stakeholder expectations and resource

capability and efficiency with a responsiveness to changes in the environment. This cannot be done by the intellectual understanding or the sheer energy of the strategist alone. The need is to build organisational capability in strategic response and action. This book should be regarded less as a guide for the individual manager than as a guide for building this organisation-wide capability.

4. Managing strategic change is a particular problem for managers. To cope with the vast variety and range of environmental outputs in the strategic decision process, managers have to operate within some simplified model of that environment. Essentially, managers reduce the 'infinite' to a personally manageable frame of reference. More precisely, there is evidence to show that to some extent these frames of reference are inherited by the manager in terms of managerial experience which relates to key factors for business success in a particular business environment. However, this experience can be a significant restraint on change. For example, it would probably not be easy for senior executives with long experiences in IKEA to envisage, or implement, a significant shift in the type of retail business they operate. For IKEA in 1991 this was not a problem, but for many organisations it was. The ability to understand strategic issues outside such constraining frames of reference is of particular importance, and this is discussed more fully in Chapter 2.

References

1. From D. J. Hickson, R. J. Butler, D. Cray, G. R. Mallory and D. C. Wilson, *Top Decisions: Strategic decision making in organisations*, Basil Blackwell, 1986, p. 28.
2. These reasons for the complexity of strategic management are based on the explanations given by Gerry Johnson in *Strategic Change and the Management Process*, Basil Blackwell, 1987, pp. 5–6.
3. For a discussion of alternative definitions, see C. W. Hofer and D. Schendel, *Strategy Formulation: Analytical concepts*, West, 1978, pp. 16–20.
4. The term 'SBU' can be traced back to the development of corporate-level strategic planning in General Electric in the USA in the early 1970s. For an early account of its uses, see W. K. Hall 'SBUs: hot, new topic in the management of diversification', *Business Horizons*, vol. 21, no. 1, (1978), pp. 17–25.
5. There are many books on 'strategic planning', particularly from the 1970s. For example, see J. Argenti, *Practical Corporate Planning*, George

Allen and Unwin, 1980. Other references are given in Chapter 2.
6. See H. Mintzberg, 'Crafting strategy', *Harvard Business Review*, vol. 65, no. 4, (1987), pp. 66–75.
7. The importance of issues of organisation and control in multinational corporations is reflected in the books and papers written on multinationals. For example, see C. A. Bartlett, Y. Doz and G. Hedlund, *Managing the Global Firm*, Routledge, 1990.
8. See R. Normann, *Service Management: Strategy and leadership in service businesses*, Wiley, 1984.
9. J. Rabu, G. J. Miller and W. B. Hildreth (eds), *Handbook of Strategic Management*, Marcel Dekker, 1989, is one of the few books on strategy which sets out to provide a public-sector bias to its coverage.
10. An interesting discussion of strategy in government departments can be found in H. Tendam, 'Strategic management in government agency', *Long Range Planning*, vol. 19, no. 4, (1986), pp. 78–86.

11. This discussion of strategy in not-for-profit organisations is based on chapter 11 of T. L. Wheelan and J. D. Hunger, *Strategic Management* (2nd edn), Addison-Wesley, 1987.

Recommended key readings

It is useful to read different explanations of the concepts of strategy. For example some of the papers in *The Strategy Process*, edited by Henry Mintzberg and James Brian Quinn (Prentice Hall, 1991) are helpful, see:

In chapter 1, 'Strategies for change' by J. B. Quinn which discusses some of the military derivations of strategy, and the chapter by Mintzberg, 'Five P's for strategy' which provides different perspectives on the strategy concept.

In chapter 3 'The concept of corporate strategy' by Kenneth Andrews is a good example of a traditional 'business policy' approach to the subject.

Work assignments

1.1 Using the characteristics discussed in section 1.1.1, write out a statement of strategy for IKEA, British Steel* or an organisation with which you are familiar.

1.2 Using Figure 1.1 and Illustration 1.2 as a guide, identify, note down and explain examples of the vocabulary of strategy used in the annual report of a company.

1.3 Using annual reports and press articles, write a brief case study (similar to the IKEA illustration or the British Steel case) which shows the strategic development and current strategic position of an organisation.*

1.4 Using Figure 1.5 as a guide, identify the influences on strategy for British Steel* or an organisation of your choice.

1.5 Using Figure 1.5 as a guide, show how the different elements of strategic management differ in:
   (a) a multinational business (e.g. Electrolux* or Peugeot*)
   (b) a professional services firm (e.g. KPMG*)
   (c) a public-sector organisation (or The Crucible Theatre*).

* This refers to a case study in the Text and Cases version of this book.

CHAPTER 2

Strategic management in practice

2.1 Introduction

In Chapter 1 the idea of corporate strategy was introduced, as were the elements of strategic management – strategic analysis, strategic choice and strategy implementation. It needs to be emphasised that these elements make up a model, the purpose of which is to help readers think about strategic problems and formulate strategy. It is also important, however, to understand that the model does not necessarily describe how strategies followed by organisations *actually* come about. There now exists a good deal of evidence about how this does occur, so before going on to examine the elements of the model in more detail in Parts II, III and IV, it is useful to have a clearer understanding of how strategies come about in practice. This chapter provides a basis for that understanding.

The first part of the chapter is concerned with *patterns of strategic change*, i.e. the ways in which strategies are observed to develop over time in organisations. The conclusion reached is that strategic changes may take different forms but that, usually, they occur not as major, one-off changes in direction but as more gradual, incremental developments, with only occasional more 'transformational' change.

The second part of the chapter explains how *strategic decisions* are made. Here different explanations of *processes of decision making* are given; and it is argued that different types of organisation are likely to exhibit different processes. However, what does emerge is the strong influence of the social, political and cultural processes at work in organisations. The different perspectives are therefore brought together within a framework which links strategy to these social and cultural aspects of organisations.

In the *summary* at the end of the chapter, lessons are drawn from the practice of strategic decision making in terms of *implications for the study of strategy* and the content of this book. It is, however, important to sound something of a warning: just because managers behave in particular ways does not mean these are the right ways or the most sensible ways. The approach taken in this book is that readers will be able to assess a good deal better for themselves which of the techniques and concepts in the rest of the book are most useful if they have an understanding of strategic decision making as it happens: and that is the role of this chapter.

2.2 Patterns of strategy development

Since strategy is about the long-term direction of an organisation, it is typically thought of in terms of major decisions about the future. However, it would be a mistake to conceive of organisational strategy as necessarily developing through one-off major changes. The strategic development of organisations is better described and understood in terms of continuity. There is a tendency towards 'momentum' of strategy:[1] once an organisation has adopted a particular strategy then it tends to develop from and within that strategy, rather than fundamentally changing direction.

2.2.1 Incremental strategy development

Henry Mintzberg's historical studies of organisations[2] over many decades showed that 'global' or *transformational* change did take place but was infrequent. More typically, organisations changed *incrementally*, during which times strategies formed gradually; or through *piecemeal* change, during which times some strategies changed and others remained constant; there were periods of *continuity*, in which established strategy remained unchanged; and also periods of *flux*, in which strategies did change but in no very clear direction. Figure 2.1 illustrates these patterns.

One strategic move – an acquisition, product launch, or significant investment decision perhaps – may well grow out of the existing mainstream strategy,

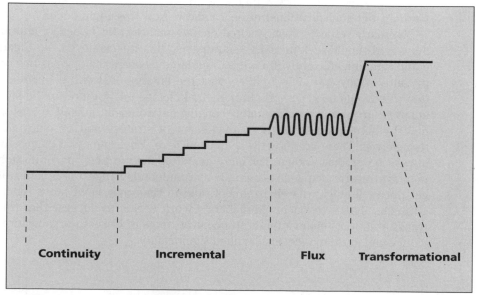

Figure 2.1 Patterns of strategic change

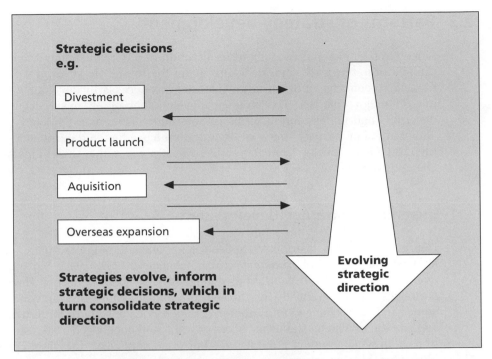

Strategic decisions e.g.

Divestment

Product launch

Aquisition

Overseas expansion

Strategies evolve, inform strategic decisions, which in turn consolidate strategic direction

Evolving strategic direction

Figure 2.2 Strategic evolution and consolidation

which in itself gradually changes. Such moves may over time form an overall strategic approach of the firm, so that as time goes on each decision taken is informed by this *emerging* strategy and, in turn, reinforces it. Figure 2.2 shows this. Over time, this process could, of course, lead to a quite significant shift in strategy, but gradually. Illustration 2.1 shows how this might occur.

In many respects such gradual change makes a lot of sense, and arguably managers should seek to manage strategy so that it is achieved. No organisation could function efficiently if it were to undergo frequent major revisions of strategy; and, in any case, it is unlikely that the environment will change so rapidly that this would be necessary. Incremental change might therefore be seen as an adaptive process in a continually changing environment; indeed, this is the view held by some writers on the management of strategy and by many managers themselves. There are, however, dangers here. Environmental change may not always be gradual enough for incremental change to keep pace: if such incremental strategic change lags behind environmental change, the organisation may get out of line with its environment, and in time may need more fundamental strategic change to occur. Mintzberg's work seems to suggest that this is so: transformational change tends to occur at times of crisis in organisations, typically when performance has declined significantly.

ILLUSTRATION 2.1
Incremental strategy development in Ford of Europe

Ford's strategy was to move from an international to a global business. However, this move was being achieved through incremental strategy development.

Under Henry Ford II's chairmanship in the late 1960s, Ford divided its world into four areas – Europe, North America, Latin America and Asia-Pacific. Prior to this move the two manufacturing companies in Europe – based in Britain and Germany – had independent product development and engineering teams, and developed different and competing ranges of vehicles. The setting up of Ford of Europe changed this.

Lindsey Halstead, chairman of Ford of Europe explained: 'Instead of competing, our two product development and engineering teams in Britain and Germany began co-operating on the single range of European products we have today.' However, in the early 1970s Ford products in European and North American markets were still very different. Lindsey Halstead explains how this changed: 'America's automobiles, under the pressure of oil prices, began a transformation. As they became smaller, the possibility of building components – particularly high cost-for-volume items like engines and gearboxes – suitable for the products of both continents, became a reality.'

Ford reaped the benefits in terms of economies of scale and also the releasing of engineering resources to develop a wider range of products to meet the demands of an increasingly sophisticated marketplace. This led them to the next stage: 'We are now embarked upon the next step of putting into practice on a global basis the sort of changes we made when we set up Ford of Europe and the other regional entities . . . With the experience we have gained, most particularly I think in Europe, in eliminating duplication in product development, supply and manufacturing in what were once a diversified series of operations, we are now aiming to concentrate product development in global "centres of responsibility" . . . It took over a decade for the changes we made in Europe in the late '60s and early '70s to bear full fruit. The plans we have to turn Ford's different regions into global "centres of responsibility" will take at least as long.'

As these developments have progressed, so too have others which have gradually enabled Ford to develop regional and national variations. These include co-operation with Mazda in Japan, and Australia and for the North American version of the Escort, with Volkswagen in Brazil and Argentina, and with Kia in Korea, which builds Ford's smallest American car. 'At Ford, everyone's horizon has already been moved many times. The way they did things yesterday is frequently out-of-date by tomorrow.'

Source: 'Close encounters of the Ford kind', *Business Strategy International*, vol. 1, no, 1.

Prepared by Roger Lazenby, Cranfield School of Management.

2.2.2 Intended and realised strategies

Conceiving of organisations' strategies in terms of such patterns of change means it is important to be careful about just what is meant by 'strategy'. Typically, strategy is written about as though it is developed by managers in an *intended*, planned fashion. Strategy is conceived of as being formulated, perhaps through some planning process, resulting in a clear expression of strategic direction, the implementation of which is also planned in terms of resource allocation, structure and so on. The strategy then comes about, or is *realised* in actuality. In this way, strategy is conceived of as a deliberate, systematic process of development and implementation (route 1 in Figure 2.3).[3] As explained in Chapter 1, this is broadly the framework adopted in this book because it is a convenient way of thinking through the issues relating to strategy. However, it does not necessarily explain how strategies are actually realised. It has to be said that such evidence as exists about the effectiveness of planning systems suggests that in many organisations that have them, and which attempt to formulate strategies in such systematic ways, the intended strategies do not become realised; or only part of what is intended comes about. In effect, much of what is intended follows route 2 in Figure 2.3 and becomes *unrealised*: that is, statements of strategy which do not come about in practice. There may be all sorts of reasons for this, and the rest of the chapter helps explain some of these.

2.2.3 Emergent, opportunistic and imposed strategies

The fact that a planned, intended strategy does not come about, does not necessarily mean that the organisation has no strategy at all. If strategy is regarded as

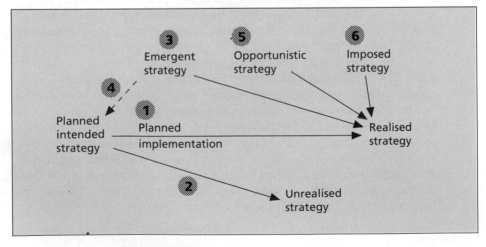

Figure 2.3 Strategy development routes

the direction of the organisation, which develops over time, then it can also be conceived of as an *emergent* process (route 3 in Figure 2.3). How this happens will also be explained later in the chapter. It should also be pointed out that, despite the existence of a stated, intended strategy which appears to have come about through a planning mechanism, strategy development may still be of an emergent nature. For example, the planning process may perform the role of monitoring the progress or efficiency of an emergent strategy. On the other hand, it may do little more than pull together the views and 'wisdom' of management or industry experts which have been built up over time. Indeed, it is a frequent complaint of chief executives that their planning systems seem to have degenerated into little more than rather routinised elaborations of where the organisation has come from, and the received wisdom which has been built up in it. This is, in effect, route 4 in Figure 2.3. It can be dangerous because the firm appears to be taking a proactive, systematic approach to strategy development, and this may mask a somewhat complacent view of the situation the organisation is in.

Strategies may also come about in *opportunistic* ways (route 5 in Figure 2.3). For example, as changes occur in the environment, or new skills are recognised, these may be taken advantage of in an opportunistic manner. Indeed, a firm may be set up in the first place because an entrepreneur sees an opportunity in the market; and the likelihood is that, if the initial strategic approach of that firm is successful, that strategy will persist for some time. On the other hand, a long-established firm may enter a new market sector because of an opportunistic acquisition, for example. This is not to suggest that such opportunistic developments are always wise, but they do occur, and can lead to changes in the realised strategy of an organisation.

Finally strategy may be *imposed* (route 6 in Figure 2.3). A strategy of retrenchment, with divestments and the cutting of costs, may be forced by recession or a threatened take-over. Developments of new products may be forced by the obsolescence of existing products. Government action may have a direct impact on organisational strategy: for example, in the public sector; or by privatisation of public utilities or state-owned enterprises, as has happened most dramatically in recent years in eastern Europe. Again such pressure may be dealt with through planning mechanisms within the organisation; or it may be handled through some other mechanism, such as individual decision making by senior executives. In any event, such imposed strategy development can result in significant long-term changes for an organisation.

2.3 Explaining strategy development

This section reviews in more detail the different explanations of how strategies develop. However, it is important to stress that it is most unlikely that any one of the explanations will account entirely for the processes at work in an organisation: strategy formulation needs to be understood in terms of a mix of processes.

2.3.1 The 'natural selection' view[4]

Some writers on management argue that the strategic choice available to an organisation is severely limited: that the environment is such a dominant influence that most organisations, save the very large, are unable to influence their operating environments; they merely buffer from, or respond to, changes in that environment. Such strategy development as exists occurs through a process similar to natural selection. Variations occur within organisational processes, structures and systems which may or may not be deliberate. These variations are more or less relevant to the environmental pressures the organisation faces, and therefore result in one organisation performing better, or worse, than another. Those organisations that perform better may then be able to retain, duplicate or reproduce such positive variations, and so improve their standing in relation to other organisations.

Certainly in some organisations, managers themselves see their scope for strategic choice as severely limited. For example, in the oil industry, many senior executives argue that they have to manage strategy for a commodity in a market dominated by raw material prices and availability, and that all they can do is keep costs down, learn to be as good as possible at forecasting changes in that environment and respond as rapidly as possible to such changes.

The view taken in this book is that for some organisations the impact of the environment is, indeed, very large, and that degrees of managerial latitude are severely reduced. However, this is not so in all environments, and even where those pressures are severe, it is the job of managers to develop the skills and strategies to cope with the situation.

2.3.2 The planning view[5]

Strategic planning is perhaps the most traditional view of how strategic decisions are made in organisations; and it has already been touched upon in Chapter 1.

In the 1960s and 1970s books were written about strategy which took the view not only that strategy could, but that it *should*, come about through highly systematised forms of planning. They advocated the setting up of corporate planning departments and prescribed tools and techniques. For example, Figure 2.4 shows a planning framework from Ansoff's highly influential book on corporate strategy.[6] It is characterised by being highly systematised, but it contains within it the same sorts of elements of strategic decision making already discussed in Chapter 1. These include the setting of objectives or goals; the analysis of the environment and the resources of the organisation, so as to match environmental opportunities and threats with resource-based strengths and weaknesses; the

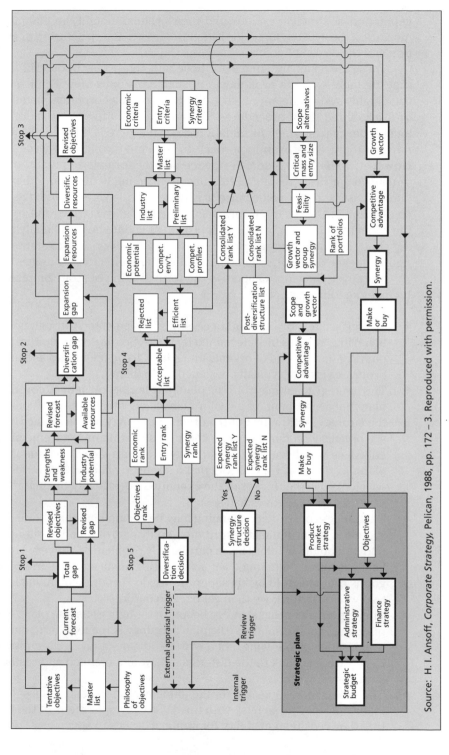

Figure 2.4 Decision flow in product/market strategy formulation

Source: H. I. Ansoff, *Corporate Strategy*, Pelican, 1988, pp. 172 – 3. Reproduced with permission.

generation of strategic options and their evaluation; and the planning of implementation through resource allocation processes, the structuring of the organisation and the design of control systems.

These elements are similar to those adopted in this book. The difference is that the more extreme proponents of such a planning view emphasise the need for a highly systematic approach, perhaps through a corporate planning function, or a structured set of procedures. Their view is that this is *the* rational approach and sequence to strategy formulation. The view here is that the elements of planning do represent a useful approach to thinking through the issues of strategy. However, while there is some evidence that the formalised pursuit of such a systematised approach results in that firm performing better than others,[7] such evidence must be tentative because it is difficult to isolate planning as a dominant or determining factor in performance. It is probably more useful to conceive of the elements within the planning approach as useful means of analysis and thinking about complex strategic problems; their formalisation into some sort of planning sequence does not, in itself, guarantee more effective strategies.

Moreover, there are dangers in the formalisation of strategic planning. These include the following:

- Strategies are more or less successfully implemented through people. Their behaviour will not be determined by plans. So the social, cultural and political dimensions of organisations have to be taken into account. Planning processes are not typically designed to do this.
- The strategy resulting from the plan may not be 'owned'. A corporate planning department, or a senior management team, may be convinced of the strategy, but the rest of the organisation may not be. Indeed, the rest of the organisation may not even know what it is. In one extreme instance, a colleague was discussing the strategy of a pharmaceutical company with its planning director. He was told that a strategic plan existed, but found that it was locked in the drawer of the executive's desk. Only the planner and a few other senior executives had seen it!
- The process of strategic planning may be so cumbersome that individuals or groups in the firm might contribute to only part of it and might never understand the whole. This is particularly problematic in very large firms. One executive, on taking over as marketing manager in a large consumer goods firm, was told by his superior: 'we do corporate planning in the first two weeks of April; we then get back to our jobs'.
- There is a danger that strategy becomes thought of as 'the plan'. Strategy is, of course, not the same as 'the plan': strategy is the long-term direction the organisation is following, not a written document on an executive's shelf. Here we come back to the difference between intended and realised strategies.
- The managers responsible for the implementation of strategies, usually line managers, may be so busy with the day-to-day operations of the business that they cede responsibility for strategic issues to specialists. However, the

specialists do not have power in the organisation to make changes. The result can be that strategic planning becomes an intellectual exercise removed from the reality of operation. As General William Sherman said in 1869, in the context of the American Civil War: 'I know there exist many good men who honestly believe that one may, by the aid of modern science, sit in comfort and ease in his office chair, and, with figures and algebraic symbols, master the great game of war. I think this is an insidious and most dangerous mistake.'[8]

- Strategic planning can become too detailed in its approach, concentrating on extensive analysis which, while sound in itself, may miss the major strategic issues facing the organisation. For example, it is not unusual to find companies with huge amounts of information on their markets, gathered with little clarity about the strategic importance of that information. The result can be 'information overload'.

- Planning can become obsessed with historical analysis, or the search for absolute determinants of performance – perhaps a set of economic indicators, for example. Particularly in dynamic environments, the danger is that this orientation reduces managers' readiness to cope with the uncertainty of the future.

- The planning process itself may become little more than the financial extrapolation of previous years' allocation of resources rather than being used for the long-term development of the firm.

However, the discipline and components of planning approaches can be useful because they may provide a framework for strategic thinking; and if managers also address the problems of managing strategy within the social, cultural and political world of organisations, then such thinking can be very helpful.

2.3.3 The logical incremental view

In the late 1950s Lindblom[9] suggested that managing strategies through logical, sequential planning mechanisms was unrealistic. He argued that, given the complexity of organisations and the environments in which they operate, managers cannot consider all possible strategic options in terms of all possible futures and evaluate these against preset, unambiguous objectives. This is particularly so in an organisational context in which there are likely to be conflicting views, values and power bases. Rather, strategic choice takes place by comparing options against each other and considering which would give the best outcome and would be possible to implement. Lindblom called this strategy building through 'successive limited comparisons', but argued that it took place in the everyday world of managing, not through planning systems.

It is a position in many respects similar to that argued by Quinn.[10] His study of nine major multinational businesses concluded that the management process could best be described as *logical incrementalism*. By this he meant that managers have a view of where they want the organisation to be in years to come, but try to move towards this position in an evolutionary way. They do this not only by attempting to ensure the success and development of a strong, secure but flexible core business, but also by continually experimenting with 'side bet' ventures. There is also a recognition that such experiments cannot be expected to be the sole responsibility of top management – that they should be encouraged to emerge from lower levels, or 'subsystems' in the organisation. Effective managers accept the uncertainty of their environment because they realise that they cannot do away with this uncertainty by trying to 'know' factually about how the environment will change; rather they seek to become highly sensitive to environmental signals through constant environmental scanning and by testing changes in strategy in small-scale steps. Commitment to the strategic option may therefore be tentative in the early stages of its development. There is also a reluctance to specify precise objectives too early as this might stifle ideas and prevent the sort of experimentation which is desired. Objectives are therefore likely to be fairly general in nature.

Such a process is seen by managers to have benefits. Continual testing and gradual strategy implementation provide improved quality of information for decision making and enable the better sequencing of the elements of major decisions. There is also a stimulation of managerial flexibility and creativity, and, since change will be gradual, the possibility of creating and developing a commitment to change throughout the organisation is increased. Such processes also take account of the political nature of organisational life, since smaller changes are less likely to face the same resistance as major changes. It is also possible to accommodate the variety of resource demands and political ambitions of different groupings – or coalitions – in the organisation (see Chapter 5).

The logical incrementalist view does not, then, view strategic management in terms of a neat sequential model. The idea that the implementation of strategy somehow follows a choice, which in turn has followed analysis, does not hold. Rather strategy is seen to be worked through in action.

This view of strategy making is sometimes called 'adaptive' by other writers,[11] and bears similarity to the descriptions managers themselves often give of how strategies come about in their organisations. Illustration 2.2 provides some examples of managers explaining the strategic decision-making process in their organisation. They see their job as 'strategists' involving continually, proactively, pursuing a strategic goal, countering competitive moves, adapting to their environment, while not 'rocking the boat' too much, so as to maintain efficiency and performance. Quinn himself argues that 'properly managed, it is a conscious, purposeful, pro-active, executive practice'.[12]

Quinn also suggests that different decisions should not be seen as entirely separate. Because the different parts, or 'subsystems', of the organisation are in a continual state of interplay, the managers of each know what the others are doing and can interpret each other's actions and requirements. They are, in effect, learning from each other about the feasibility of a course of action in terms of resource management and its internal political acceptability. Moreover,

ILLUSTRATION 2.2
A logical incrementalist view of strategic management

Managers often see their jobs as managing adaptively: continually changing strategy to keep in line with the environment, while maintaining efficiency and keeping stakeholders happy. Some quotes from managers illustrate this.

1. 'I begin wide-ranging discussions with people inside and outside the corporation. From these a pattern eventually emerges. It's like fitting together a jigsaw puzzle. At first the vague outline of an approach appears like the sail of a ship in a puzzle. Then suddenly the rest of the puzzle becomes quite clear. You wonder why you didn't see it all along.'

2. 'The real strength of the company is to be able to follow these peripheral excursions into whatever … one has to keep thrusting in these directions; they are little tentacles going out, testing the water.'

3. 'We haven't stood still in the past and I can't see with our present set up that we shall stand still in the future; but what I really mean is that it is a path of evolution rather than revolution. Some companies get a successful formula and stick to that rigidly because that is what they know – for example, [Company X] did not really adapt to change, so they had to take what was a revolution. We hopefully have changed gradually and that's what I think we should do. We are always looking for fresh openings without going off at a tangent.'

4. 'The analogy of a chess game is quite useful in this context. The objective of chess is clear: to gain victory by capturing your opponent's king. The resources to do this are the various pieces available. Most players will begin with a strategic move, that assumes a countermove by the opponent. If the countermove materialises, then the next move follows automatically, based on a previous winning strategy, and the game will proceed to its logical (and victorious) conclusion. However, the beauty of chess is the unpredictability of one's opponent's moves, and as with any precipitating event, a strategy must be reappraised in the light of the unusual. To attempt to predict the outcome of chess is impossible, and therefore players limit themselves to working on possibilities and probabilities of moves that are not too far ahead.'

Sources: Extract 1 from J. B. Quinn, *Strategies for Change*, Irwin, 1980; extracts 2 and 3 from G. Johnson, *Strategic Change and the Management Process*, Basil Blackwell, 1987; extract 4 from a manager on an MBA course.

the formulation of strategy in this way means that the implications of the strategy are continually being tested out. This continual readjustment does, of course, make a lot of sense if the environment is considered as a continually changing influence on the organisation. It is a process through which the organisation keeps itself in line with such change, as shown notionally in Figure 2.5.

2.3.4 The cultural view[13]

Traditionally, strategy has been viewed as the response of an organisation to its environment. However, faced with similar environments, organisations respond differently; these differences are accounted for by the influence of managerial decision making on strategy. However, management cannot be conceived of simply in terms of the manipulation of techniques or tools of analysis. Management is also about the application of managerial experience gained over many years, and often within the same organisation or industry. Nor do managers typically work in isolation; they interact with others. Their experience is not only rooted in individual experience, but based on group and organisational experience built up over time. It is therefore important to recognise the significance of cultural aspects of management.

By 'organisational culture' is meant the 'deeper level of basic *assumptions and beliefs* that are shared by members of an organisation, that operate unconsciously and define in a basic "taken for granted" fashion an organisation's view of its self and its environment'.[14] A cultural perspective suggests that managerial experience is likely to be based on 'taken-for-granted' frames of reference which

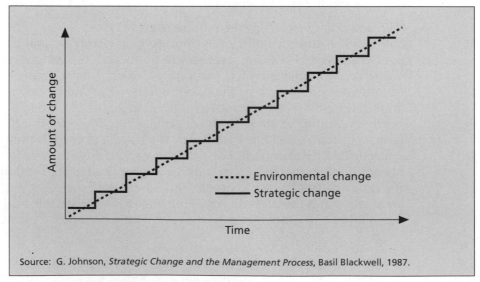

Source: G. Johnson, *Strategic Change and the Management Process*, Basil Blackwell, 1987.

Figure 2.5 Notional incremental change

are brought to bear by a manager – or group of managers – and which will affect how a given situation is perceived and how it is responded to. This taken-for-grantedness is likely to be handed on over time within a group. That group might be, for example, a managerial function such as marketing or finance; a professional grouping, such as accountants; an organisation as a whole; or more widely an industry sector, or even a national culture.

There are, then, many cultural frames of reference which influence managers. Figure 2.6 shows this graphically. However, among these frames of reference two are especially important for the strategic management of most organisations. These are:

- The industry frame of reference, which here is termed an 'industry *recipe*'.[15]
- The organisational frame of reference, which here is termed the 'organisational *paradigm*'.[16]

The recipe and the paradigm are likely to be most readily surfaced in discussion with managers. It is less likely that they will be surfaced by structured planning systems, for example. The reason for this is that many of the constructs within these frames of reference are deep rooted. A paradigm, for example, may contain within it the beliefs which managers talk about in their day-to-day lives, but it will also contain assumptions which are rarely talked about, which are not

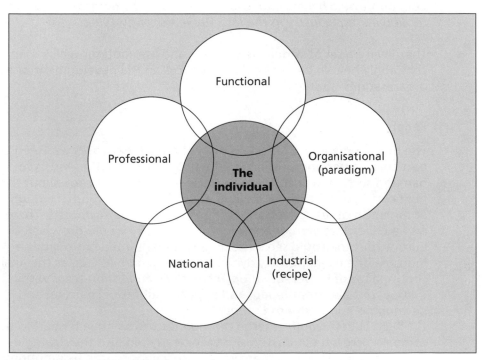

Figure 2.6 Frames of reference of managers

considered problematic, and about which managers are unlikely to be consciously explicit.

These deep-rooted assumptions can often play an important part in strategy development. For example, in retail banking in the UK the deep-seated assumptions of the importance of secure lending and the permanence of the banking institutions have strongly influenced the development of strategy by the banks; and have also influenced the strategic direction of firms to which banks lend. Illustration 2.3 gives examples of the beliefs and ·assumptions in the UK retail banking industry in the late 1980s. In retail banking many of the beliefs and assumptions were shared across organisations – in this sense the influence of the recipe is marked. In other industries there are more differences between organisations; the influence of the paradigm is more marked.

An organisation's paradigm can be traced to different influences, and the strength of these will depend on a number of factors. For example, an organisation with a relatively stable management and a long-term momentum of strategy is likely to have a more homogeneous paradigm than one in which there has

---

ILLUSTRATION 2.3
Beliefs and assumptions in UK retail banking

Commonly held beliefs and assumptions could be detected across the UK retail banking industry in the late 1980s and early 1990s.

There were a set of widely held beliefs and assumptions which managers commonly held to be important influences on the development of their organisations' strategies.

Beliefs

The development and rationalisation of *branch networks* was seen as of particular importance, reflecting the heavy investment in assets for most banks in such networks. There was also a common concern about the high *cost base* of retail banks, and equally the opportunity through *automation* of reducing staff costs and so reducing such costs. There was also a belief that *merger and acquisition* activity would grow across Europe, but this could see a rise in government intervention in the industry. The main industry dynamics were generally seen as the likely continuance of EC *deregulation*; *increased competition* from within Europe, but also from Japan; and opportunities for expansion and development in *southern Europe*.

Such beliefs would emerge through discussion; they tended to be common across the industry; and they clearly fed into the strategies of organisations. However, there were also deeper-rooted assumptions

been rapid turnover of management and significant change forced upon it. An organisation with a dominant professional influence, perhaps an accountancy firm, is likely to demonstrate a homogeneous paradigm. Industry influences may be particularly strong if the transfer of staff between firms is limited to that industry, as it often is in engineering or banking, for example.

For an organisation to operate efficiently it must, to some extent, have a generally accepted set of beliefs and assumptions. It may not be a static set of beliefs – although it is likely that it will evolve gradually rather than change suddenly. What it does represent, however, is collective experience without which managers would have to 'reinvent their world' afresh for all circumstances they face. The paradigm allows the experience gathered over years to be applied to a given situation so that managers can decide upon relevant information by which to assess the need for change, a likely course of action, and the likelihood of success of that course of action.

The relationship and distinction between the paradigm and organisational strategies needs to be made clear. Figure 2.7 helps to do this. Environmental

which could be discerned. Indeed, one of the major problems UK banks faced in the 1980s and early 1990s was the difficulty of effecting strategic change faced with the deep-seated assumptions about the nature of banking.

Assumptions

Executives tended to be *conservative*; this often took the verbal form of not wanting to 'rock the boat'. This itself was rooted in a *risk aversion* about bank operations which took several forms. At lower levels in the organisation, it might be as simple as the view that 'mistakes equal death', and that rules and procedures needed to be followed to the letter. More generally, the need for *secure lending* was paramount. This could be traced to an internal point of reference for managers: the bank was primarily about its own long-term security, and customers were essentially a means of achieving this. The effect, in the UK at least, was a reliance on established procedures to avoid risk, and a short-termism in financial transactions. All this was within the context of the assumption that the bank, perhaps established for 200 years, would *always be in existence*.

At the individual level, managers saw themselves as *professionals*, providing a fair and reasonable service to the retail and corporate community; and they also believed that, like other professionals, they had a *'job for life'* – an assumption that was to be challenged harshly in the late 1980s and early 1990s.

Source: Authors

forces and organisational capabilities do not in themselves create organisational strategy; people create strategy. The forces at work in the environment, and the organisation's capabilities in coping with these, are made sense of through the assumptions and beliefs here called the paradigm. However, environmental forces and organisational capabilities, while having this indirect influence on strategy formulation, nonetheless impact on organisational performance more directly. For example, an engineering firm making electrical switchboards and switchgear had built its reputation on the manufacture of the switchgear. By the 1980s overseas manufacturers had developed substitute, cheaper and smaller products. The company took for granted, however, that its own switchgear products were superior from an engineering point of view, and continued to build them into its manufactured switchboards. Customers, however, preferred the cheaper, smaller overseas products, and in consequence sales and profits of the firm declined. It took many years before managers in the company recognised the need to change strategy fundamentally, during which time loss of revenue and profits had substantially reduced its ability to reinvest in product development and new plant. The potential difference between the actual influences and managerial perceptions of the influences on the organisation can give rise to significant problems – and is an issue to which we shall return later.

The paradigm or recipe may, then, be very conservative influences on strategy. This is the more so since, at the organisational level at least, it is likely to be linked to other aspects of organisational culture. For example,[17] in organisations which tend to be conservative, where low-risk strategies, secure markets and well-tried potential solutions are valued, organisational stories are typically concerned with historical stability and consensus, routines and control systems

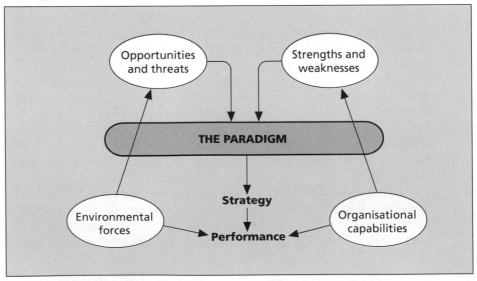

Figure 2.7 The role of the paradigm in strategy formulation

more formalised, and personal relationships also more formal. In contrast, in organisations in which innovation and breaking new ground are valued, growth strategies, and perhaps higher-risk strategies, are more likely; and the stories here are likely to be concerned with growth and change, and routines of decision making and control less rigid and less formal.

Chapter 5 considers further how cultural aspects of organisations can be analysed and the links to other aspects of strategic management.

2.3.5 The political view[18]

Strategy development can also be explained in political terms. Organisations are political entities and powerful internal and external interest groups influence the inputs into their decisions. Different interest groups (or stakeholders) may be in conflict there may, for example, be differences between groups of managers, between managers and shareholders, or between powerful individuals. These differences are likely to be resolved through processes of bargaining, negotiation or perhaps edict, but they will certainly affect the objectives of the organisation. Powerful individuals or groups may also influence the sort of information that is seen as being important. Information is not politically neutral, but rather is a source of power for those who control that information which is seen to be important. The withholding of information, or the power of one manager over another because that manager controls sources of information, can therefore be important. Powerful individuals and groups may also strongly influence the identification of key issues and even the strategies eventually selected. It would be wrong to assume that these emerge in a politically neutral environment. Differing views will be fought for not only on the basis of the extent to which they reflect environmental or competitive pressures, but also because they have implications for the status or influence of different stakeholders.

A political perspective on decision making would therefore suggest that strategies emerge through processes of bargaining, negotiation and the trading-off of political interests. Illustration 2.4 shows how political processes played an important part in the strategic response to the growth of AIDS in the UK.[19] Understanding the influence of such political processes is important; Chapter 5 returns to this in more detail.

The links between the power structure in the organisation and the paradigm may also be strong. The paradigm is, in some respects, the 'formula for success' which is taken for granted and likely to have grown up over years; the most powerful groupings within the organisation are likely to be closely associated with this set of beliefs.[20] For example, accountancy firms in the UK may now offer a whole range of services, but typically the most powerful individuals or groups have been qualified accountants with a set of assumptions about the business and its market rooted in the audit practice. Similarly, in many retail businesses the powerful individuals and groups are those with years of experience in 'the retail trade', in which the skill of operating on a day-to-day basis, especially in the field of merchandising, is often regarded as of prime importance. One implication of this is that it is likely that a purely analytical questioning of the paradigm may be taken as evidence of a lack of understanding of the problems of the business, even as a political threat, since it will be perceived as an attack on those most associated with those core beliefs, and an attempt to 'rock the boat'. Even if managers 'intellectually' accept such analysis, they may be influenced by the paradigm and its cultural underpinnings in formulating, persisting with or adjusting strategy.

2.3.6 The visionary view

Illustration 2.4 also shows that the development of strategies can be seen as the outcome of the influence of visionary leaders too. This might be especially so if the organisation is dominated by a charismatic leader; and such leaders may exist, particularly, in organisations which they have founded, or in situations

---

ILLUSTRATION 2.4
The politics of change: championing HIV/AIDS

The vision and political activity of individuals galvanised the early response to AIDS/HIV in the UK.

AIDS was identified in 1981. Ten years later over 400,000 cases worldwide had been reported, with millions estimated to have HIV, the causative virus. In the UK, national strategic action was initiated by the Department of Health in 1985, but some health authorities started to respond to HIV/AIDS from 1982. Research in six such districts suggested that, though predisposing conditions were important, a strategic service response was triggered only when particular individuals recognised the issue's importance and took an early lead.

These 'product champions', became key agents of change, attracting resources, stimulating organisational learning and influencing the development of policy and practice both locally and at national level. They were not a homogeneous group, coming from a wide range of specialities (which influenced the nature of the services that evolved), and differing in individual character and style. They did, however, share a missionary enthusiasm and perspectives beyond the narrow confines of their own specialities (initially, colleagues often saw the issue as a 'hobby-horse'). They were the 'doers', often overcoming opposition by ignoring it, and developing services with minimal resources.

Crucial to the success of the early champions was their personal positions. Many were medical consultants; all were respected members of professional groups with considerable status and autonomy. They used

where an organisation has reached a point of crisis. Less commonly, perhaps, vision could be associated with a small group of individuals rather than one individual.

There are those[21] who argue that strategic management has so consistently emphasised the importance of analysis (as in the planning view) or experimentation and doing (as in the logical incremental view) that the role of intuition and vision has been lost. They argue that the history of business would suggest that new businesses, new ventures, turnaround and new strategies are the products of just such creative management rather than detailed planning.

What then is visionary strategic management? One explanation is that it is associated with executives who have especially high intuitive capacities – excutives who relate more naturally to the identification of new possibilities, new patterns and ideas, rather than the detailed search for cause and effect, or the day-to-day detail of management. They are likely to see what other managers do not see, to espouse new ways of working and perhaps sometimes to disregard practical implications.

this power to promote their objectives, though in different ways according to their personal styles. All saw coalition building as important, recruiting key figures from other occupational groups to support their cause. However, diplomatic skills and ease of access to the great and good varied, making some coalitions more influential than others. Personal clout could sometimes be used to railroad people into co-operating: 'People know me by now, that if I say I'm going to do something, and I've got the money to do it, then they're not going to stop me . . . they can decide to be on my side or not, and it's probably better for them if they're on my side.'

Lack of hard information about the epidemic gave champions opportunity to use, and sometimes manipulate, statistical predictions to create a mobilising perception of crisis. Some became adept at exerting pressure through the media: 'I recognised early on that the only way we'd get [funders] to move was to embarrass them, and . . . we got onto the newspapers and the box and turned the temperature up and got them to respond.'

Such activities were fundamental to raising the profile of HIV/AIDS and driving early service development. However, emergent strategies formed through political processes may not always address long-term requirements. By the time special government funding began in the mid-1980s, champions had been accorded 'expert' status and the new resources tended to flow into service infrastructures around their specialities institutionalising particular patterns of service delivery and decreasing flexibility – a potential problem given the nature of the epidemic and changing patient needs.

Source: Prepared by Chris Bennett and Ewan Ferlie, Centre for Corporate Strategy and Change, University of Warwick.

Visionary management might also be seen as the capacity of managers more generally to envisage, rather than plan, the future of their organisation. It can be argued that some market environments are so turbulent that trying to forecast, predict or plan what they will be like is futile.[22] On the other hand, experienced managers have a 'feel' for what makes sense in those markets – again there are links here with the notion of the paradigm – and can make decisions about the future on this basis. Here, then, the notion of visionary capacity is not limited to the leadership role of the organisation, but is seen as a more general aspect of management.

A third explanation is more mundane. It is that new visions in organisations come about because a new executive applies his or her existing frame of reference from another context to the new organisation to which they have been appointed. For example, some of the new chief executives appointed to UK privatised industries in the 1980s came from private-sector companies. They brought with them frames of reference from competitive environments in which profit motivation was taken as given. What was normal and obvious to them, was often seen as new and visionary in the organisations they moved into. In terms of the definition of vision and its influence in organisations, this approach links into the cultural and political views.

A difficulty is that visionary strategies may be short lived. They may be very influential at a particular time, and may overwhelm objective analysis of the organisation's position. The history of organisations may suggest that visionary capacity is an important influence on strategy development. However, there are examples of organisations in which visionary leaders have been effective in turning the organisation around, perhaps, but whose influences then continued at times when a cooler examination of the business situation might have suggested that the vision was becoming inappropriate.

2.3.7 Integrating views of strategy development

These different views about how strategies develop are not mutually exclusive. Indeed, in most organisations managers see strategies developing through a mix of such processes. The series of diagrams in Figure 2.8 show different patterns that exist in organisations.[23]

Figure 2.8(a) shows a large retailer in which vision is deemed to be particularly important, but planning too is seen to play a significant role. The organisation represented in Figure 2.8(b) is a public-sector organisation in which the forces of the environment are such that there is relatively little choice, and the natural selection view predominates within a political context. And in Figure 2.8(c) a common pattern is shown: here the logical incremental, cultural and political views are pronounced. This is typical in organisations in which adaptive or incremental strategy development predominates.

Of course, very real problems can emerge if different parts of an organisation see markedly different influences on the development of strategy. Illustration 2.5 shows two such examples.

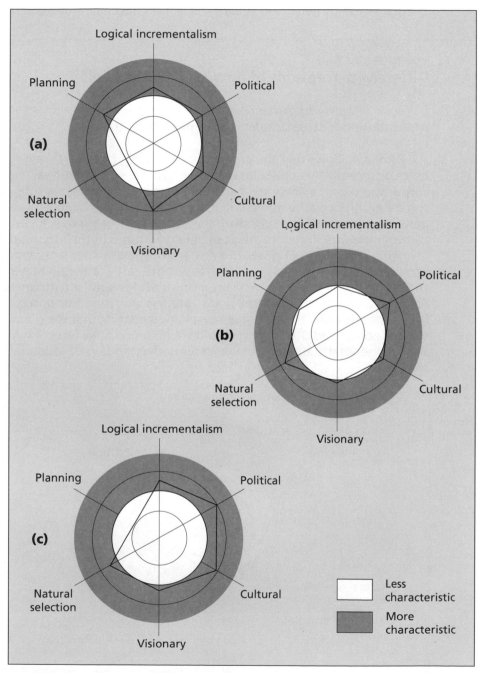

Figure 2.8 Profiles of strategy development

2.4 Strategic decision-making processes in action

There now exist a number of studies which have traced how decisions are made

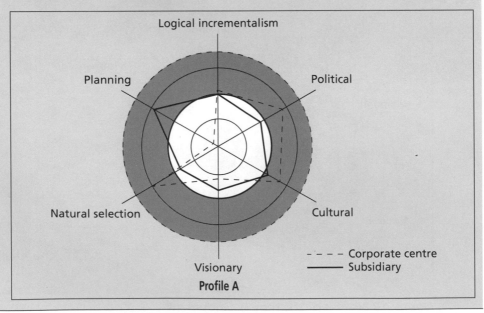

in organisations. They also show that, to a greater or lesser extent, each of the views described above can be seen in different decisions that are examined. However, some general patterns do emerge and these are now summarised.

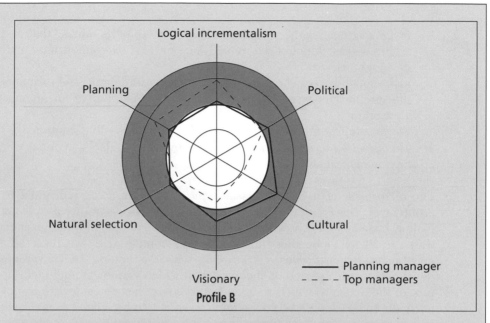

Profile B

Profile B illustrates disagreement between a corporate planner and fellow senior figures within a financial services organisation. Most managers saw strategy formulation within the organisation driven by the culture, history and shared beliefs of the organisation, its political processes and a 'vision' inherited from the founders of the firm. The corporate planner, however, viewed the process differently. He saw strategy as the product of logical planning and experimenting, with careful adaptation to the needs of the market. Perhaps not surprisingly, the managers were not persuaded that the planning processes were much value; and the planner believed that the managers really did not take strategic planning seriously enough.

Prepared by Andy Bailey, Cranfield School of Management.

☐ Less characteristic

■ More characteristic

2.4.1 Elements of strategic decision-making processes

There are four stages which can be discerned in decision processes.[24] These are represented in Figure 2.9.

1. *Issue awareness*: the recognition that 'something is amiss', that a state of affairs exists which need remedying, or that an opportunity exists for development.
2. *Issue formulation*: the collection of information about, and examination of the circumstances of, the issue and the formulation of an organisational view about it.
3. *The development of solutions*: the generation of possible solutions.
4. *The selection of a solution*: the means by which a decision about what is to be done is reached.

The *awareness* of a strategic issue typically occurs at an individual or small group level. This is not likely to be an analytical process; rather people get a 'gut feeling' based on their previous experience. These people may not be managers – they are likely to be those in most direct contact with whatever stimulates awareness, perhaps sales staff dealing with customers. This awareness will develop through a period of 'incubation' in which various stimuli build up a picture of the extent to which an organisation's circumstances deviate from what is normally to be expected. These stimuli are likely to be related to internal performance measures such as turnover or profit performance; customer reaction to the quality and price of service or products; and changes in the environment, in terms of competitive action, technological change and economic conditions.

The importance of the individual's role in problem recognition needs to be emphasised. There is evidence to suggest that successful business performance is associated with management's capability in sensing its environment. This does not necessarily mean that the company has complex or sophisticated means of

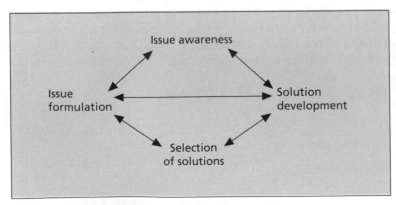

Figure 2.9 Phases of strategic decision making

achieving this, but rather that people in the organisation – not only managers – respond to or take into account a wide range of influences.[25]

This accumulation of stimuli eventually reaches a point where the presence of a problem cannot be ignored and requires an organisational response. Typically, this *triggering point* is reached when the formal information systems of the organisation begin to highlight the problem; perhaps a variance against budget becomes undeniable or a number of sales areas consistently report dropping sales. At this stage, however, issues may still be ill-defined.

Issue formulation involves a number of processes. Information gathering is likely to take place, but not necessarily in a highly structured, objective manner. Information is sought and gathered on a verbal and informal basis, particularly among more senior management. This may, of course, be supplemented through more formal analysis. However, the rationalisation of information so as to clarify the situation is a process which draws heavily on existing managerial experience. Indeed, the role of information generated from more formalised environmental analysis in this process is often to post-rationalise or legitimise managers' emerging views of the situation.

The resolution (or definition) of what constitutes the nature of the issue may prove difficult. Overall, formal analysis appears to play much less of a role than is suggested in some management texts. Through debate and discussion, there will probably be an attempt to reach an organisational view or consensus on the problem to be tackled. The emerging view will therefore take shape in terms of both individual and collective experience, and different views will be resolved through social and political processes. It may also be that these processes of issue formulation could trigger a different problem, so the process tends to be iterative.

In *developing solutions*,[26] managers search for ready-made solutions through *memory search*, in which the manager seeks for known, existing or tried solutions; or *passive search*, which means waiting for possible solutions to be thrown up. It is likely that there will be a number of these searches in which managers draw on what they have experienced and tried in the past before there is an attempt to *design* a solution; that is, to custom-build a strategy to handle the problem at hand. In either search or design the process of choice tends to be iterative. Managers begin with a rather vague idea of a possible solution and gradually refine it by recycling it through selection routines (see below) back into problem identification or through further search routines. The process is developmental, based on debate and discussion within the organisation and, again, on the collective management wisdom and experience in the organisation. Indeed, the logical incrementalist view of strategy development suggests that successful managers actively use bargaining processes in order to challenge prevailing strategic inclinations and generate information from other parts of the organisation to help in making decisions.

As has been seen, the process of *developing solutions* may overlap with the processes of *selecting solutions*. They are somewhat arbitrary categorisations for the purpose of description and might be regarded as part of the same process, in which a limited number of potential solutions gradually get reduced until one or more emerges. This may occur through 'screening', in which managers eliminate that which they consider not to be feasible. However, the predominant criterion for assessing feasibility is not formal analysis but managerial judgement followed by political bargaining. Formal analysis is the least observed of these three approaches, and needs again to be seen in the context of social and political processes.

It should also be remembered that the process might well be taking place below the most senior levels of management, so it may be necessary to refer possible solutions to some higher level, and seeking this *authorisation* is another way of selecting between possibilities. Typically, though not always, authorisation is sought for a completed solution after screening has taken place. This raises the question of whether it is sensible to view this referral as a sort of checking of an incrementally generated strategic solution against some overall strategy.

2.4.2 The cultural web[27]

It is clear in examining decision processes that experience carries an important influence. Managers draw heavily on frames of reference which are built up over time and which are especially important at a collective organisational level. The beliefs and assumptions which comprise this paradigm are, however, also likely to be hedged about and protected by different aspects of organisational culture.

- The *routine* ways that members of the organisation behave towards each other, and that link different parts of the organisation, comprise 'the way we do things around here', which at their best lubricate the working of the organisation and may provide a distinctive and beneficial organisational competency.[28] However, they can also represent a take-for-grantedness about how things should happen which is extremely difficult to change and highly protective of core assumptions in the paradigm.
- The *rituals* of organisational life, such as training programmes, promotion and assessment, point to what is important in the organisation, reinforce 'the way we do things around here' and signal what is especially valued.
- The *stories* told by members of the organisation to each other, to outsiders, to new recruits and so on, embed the present in its organisational history and flag up important events and personalities, as well as mavericks who 'deviate from the norm'.
- The more *symbolic aspects* of organisations, such as logos, offices, cars and titles, or the type of language and terminology commonly used, become a short-hand representation of the nature of the organisation.
- The *control systems*, measurements and reward systems emphasise what is important in the organisation, and focus attention and activity.
- *Power structures* are also likely to be associated with the key constructs of the paradigm. The most powerful managerial groupings in the organisation

are likely to be the ones most associated with core assumptions and beliefs about what is important.

● The formal *organisational structure*, or the more informal ways in which the organisations work, are likely to reflect power structures and, again, to delineate important relationships and emphasise what is important in the organisation.

It would therefore be a mistake to conceive of the paradigm as merely a set of beliefs or assumptions removed from organisational action. They lie within a cultural web which bonds them to the day-to-day action of organisational life. This notion of the paradigm within a cultural web is shown in Figure 2.10, and an organisational example of it is given as Illustration 2.6.

This illustration builds on Illustration 2.3. It shows the cultural web for a major UK clearing bank in the mid-1980s. At that time the UK banking system was beginning to feel the effects of the deregulation of the banking industry – known as 'Big Bang'. Most of the banks were reviewing their strategies, attempting to become more market and customer focused, diversifying their services and trying to introduce a business-oriented culture rather than a traditional banking culture. This bank, together with most of the others, was finding difficulty in implementing an intended strategy very much along these lines.

The difficulties encountered by the bank can be explained both in terms of

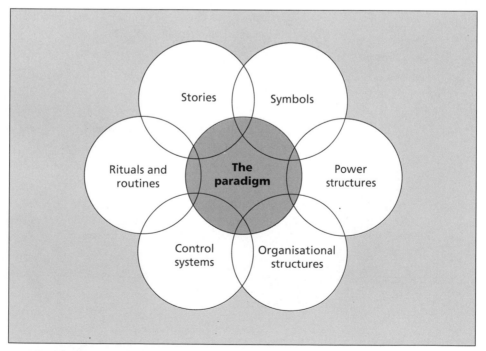

Figure 2.10 The cultural web of an organisation

ILLUSTRATION 2.6
The cultural web of a UK bank in the 1980s

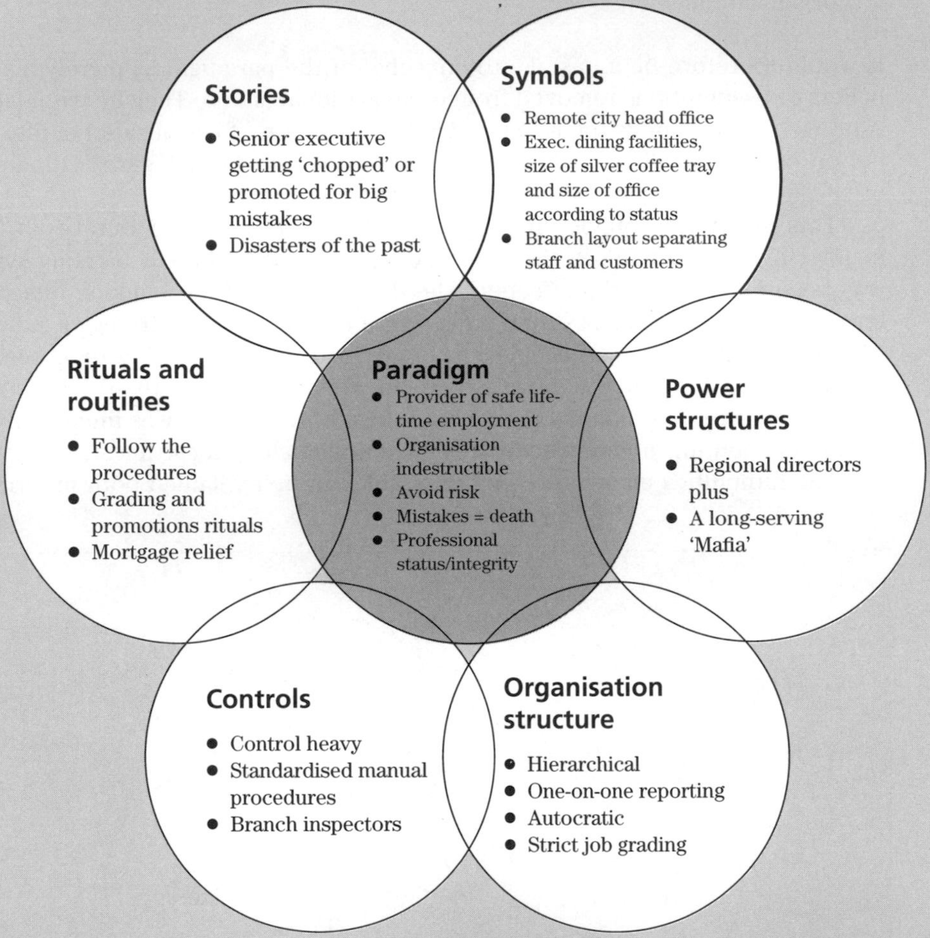

Stories
- Senior executive getting 'chopped' or promoted for big mistakes
- Disasters of the past

Symbols
- Remote city head office
- Exec. dining facilities, size of silver coffee tray and size of office according to status
- Branch layout separating staff and customers

Rituals and routines
- Follow the procedures
- Grading and promotions rituals
- Mortgage relief

Paradigm
- Provider of safe life-time employment
- Organisation indestructible
- Avoid risk
- Mistakes = death
- Professional status/integrity

Power structures
- Regional directors plus
- A long-serving 'Mafia'

Controls
- Control heavy
- Standardised manual procedures
- Branch inspectors

Organisation structure
- Hierarchical
- One-on-one reporting
- Autocratic
- Strict job grading

Source: Authors

the paradigm itself, in which security, risk aversion and the paramount importance of professionalism were significant, and also in terms of the different aspects of the cultural web. The power structure lay not only in the hands of the main board, but was devolved through powerful regional directors. These directors had considerable influence on many of the rituals and routines of the organisation, including appointments, promotions and grading systems. The organisation was hierarchical in nature, a feature bolstered by status symbols and the ritualised promotions and grading systems. The control systems, particularly at branch level, were manual, time consuming and standardised, and had to be carried out without exception. Moreover, there was a branch inspectorate system which checked this was being done; and a prevalent view that what really mattered was the efficiency in following such procedures, rather than looking after customers. The risk aversion was, itself, magnified by many stories about senior executives who had suffered because of taking risky decisions, and the giving of mortgage relief to very many of the bank's employees. It was a cultural system which had evolved around security, safety, hierarchy and bureaucracy, and it was proving difficult to change.

The cultural web is, then, a useful conceptual tool for understanding the way in which beliefs and assumptions, linked to political, symbolic and structural aspects of the organisation, guide and constrain the development of strategy. It will be used in Chapter 5 as a basis for considering the cultural audit of organisations, and again in Chapter 11 in discussing processes of strategic change.

2.4.3 The risk of strategic drift[29]

The conservative influence of the paradigm and 'the way we do things around here' is likely to have important implications for the development of strategy in organisations.

Faced with pressures for change, managers will be likely to deal with the situation in ways which protect the paradigm from challenge. This raises difficulties when managing strategic change, for it may be that the action required is outside the scope of the paradigm and the constraints of the cultural web, and that members of the organisation would therefore be required to change substantially their core beliefs or routines. Desirable as this may be, the evidence is that it does not occur easily.[30] Managers are much more likely to attempt to deal with the situation by searching for what they can understand and cope with in terms of the existing paradigm, and this seems to be especially so in organisations in which there is a particularly high degree of homogeneity in the beliefs and assumptions which comprise it. Managers will, then, typically attempt to minimise the extent to which they are faced with ambiguity and uncertainty by looking for that which is familiar.

Figure 2.11 illustrates how this might occur. Faced with a stimulus for action, in this case declining performance, managers first seek for means of improving the implementation of existing strategy: this could be through the tightening of controls. In effect, they will tighten up their accepted way of operating. If this is not effective, a change of strategy may occur, but still a change which is in line with the existing paradigm. For example, managers may seek to extend the market for their business, but may assume that it will be similar to their existing market, and therefore set about managing the new venture in much the same way as they have been used to. There has been no change to the paradigm and there is not likely to be until this attempt to reconstruct strategy in the image of the existing paradigm also fails. What is occurring is the predominant application of the familiar and the attempt to avoid or reduce uncertainty or ambiguity.

This is, of course, an alternative explanation of incremental or adaptive strategy development. Indeed, it may be that changing the strategy within the paradigm makes sense: after all, it does encapsulate the experience of those in the organisation, and permits change to take place within what is familiar and understood. However, the outcome of processes of decision making of this kind may not be the adaptive strategy making which keeps in line with environmental change, as was shown in Figure 2.4. Rather it may be an adaptation in line with the experience enshrined in the paradigm. Nonetheless the forces in the environment will have an effect on performance. Over time this may well give rise to the sort of strategic drift shown in Figure 2.12 (phase 1), in which the organisation's strategy gradually, if imperceptibly, moves away from the forces at work in its

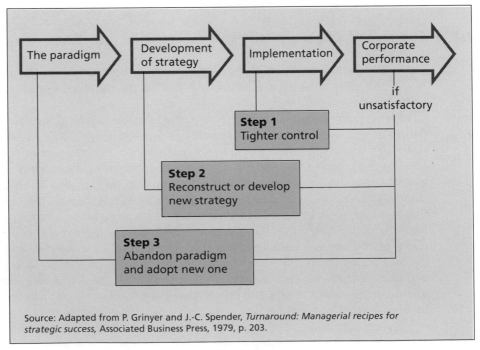

Source: Adapted from P. Grinyer and J.-C. Spender, *Turnaround: Managerial recipes for strategic success,* Associated Business Press, 1979, p. 203.

Figure 2.11 The dynamics of paradigm change

environment. Illustration 2.7 shows how even the most successful companies may drift in this way. Indeed, they may become a victim of the very success of their past.[31]

This pattern of drift is made more difficult to detect and reverse because although changes are being made in strategy – albeit within the parameters of the paradigm – such changes are the application of the familiar and may achieve some short-term improvement in performance, thus tending to legitimise the action taken.

However, in time either the drift becomes apparent or environmental change increases, and performance is affected (phase 2 in Figure 2.12). Strategy development is, then, likely to go into a state of flux, with no clear direction (phase 3), further damaging performance. Eventually more transformational change is required, if the demise of the organisation is to be avoided (phase 4).

The paradigm is, then, an inevitable feature of organisational life which can be thought of either as encapsulating the distinctive competences of the organisation or, more dangerously, as a conservative influence likely to prevent change and result in a momentum of strategy which can lead to strategic drift.

2.5 Summary and implications for the study of strategy

This chapter has dealt with the processes of strategic management as they are to be found in organisations: it is therefore descriptive not prescriptive. There is no

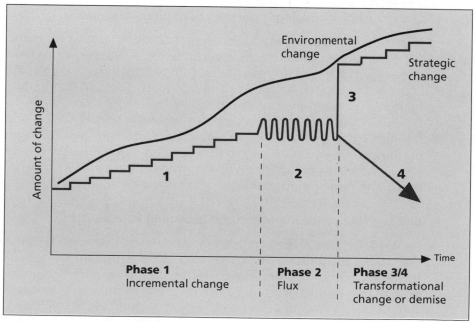

Figure 2.12 The risk of strategic drift

suggestion here that, because such processes exist, this is how strategy *should* be managed. However, it is important to understand the reality of strategy making in organisations not least because those who seek to influence the strategy of organisations must do so within that reality. There is little point in formulating strategies which may be analytically elegant without having an understanding of the processes which are actually at work. Moreover, it is this book's intention that the subject should be approached in such a way that it builds upon this understanding of reality and, wherever possible, relates an essentially analytical approach to the real world of managers.

ILLUSTRATION 2.7
The Icarus Paradox

In The Icarus Paradox, Danny Miller draws a parallel between Icarus, who persisted in flying towards the sun and melted his wings, and exceptional companies which persist in pursuing previously successful strategies until they too become unstuck.

Miller identifies four 'trajectories' by which outstanding companies amplify their strengths to the point where 'one goal, one strategic vision, one department, and one skill overwhelms all others': excesses and deficiencies very much related to their once successful strategies.

Craftsmen (the focusing trajectory) becoming Tinkerers.

Founder Ken Olsen of Digital Equipment Corporation and his team of design engineers invented the minicomputer, a cheaper, more flexible alternative to its mainframe cousins. Digital honed their minis until they could not be beaten for quality and durability. Their VAX series proved highly reliable and the profits poured in.

But Digital turned into an engineering monoculture. Technological fine tuning became such an obsession that customers' needs for smaller machines, more economical products and more user-friendly systems were ignored. By focusing too closely on product refinement, customer needs and new markets were forgotten.

Builders (the venturing trajectory) becoming Imperialists

Harold S. Geneen, an entrepreneurial accountant, examined ITT's diverse operations and through divestment and consolidation forged a cohesive corporate entity. He installed state-of-the-art management information systems and built a head office corps of young executives to help him control his growing empire and identify opportunities for creative diversification.

In this concluding section, some of the lessons of this chapter are summarized and related to what follows in the rest of the book.

- It is important to distinguish between the *intended* strategy of managers – that which they say the organisation will follow – and the *realised* strategy of an organisation – that which it is actually following. This is particularly important when considering how relevant current strategy is to a changing environment: it may be more useful to consider the relevance of realised strategy than intended strategy.

Unfortunately, ITT's success at diversification and controlled decentralisation led to managers' overconfidence, resulting in 'too much of the same'. Consequently, diversification went from a selective tactic, to an engrained strategy, to a fanatical religion. ITT expanded and diversified too aggressively and indiscriminately.

Pioneers (the inventing trajectory) becoming Escapists

Rolls-Royce was a most progressive, state-of-the-art aircraft engine manufacturer, with an impressive history of innovation – the first aircooled turbine blades, turbo-fan engines and vertical take-off engine.
However, Rolls' unequalled history of design innovation was to be its downfall. Its senior executives were virtually all engineers concerned with engineering excellence; and when competing for the engine contract for Lockheed's Tristar, the design proved far too costly to develop and impossible to implement. Time delays, manufacturing problems and costs far exceeding budgets all plagued the project. The downfall was caused by dedicated engineers getting carried away by invention.

Salesmen (the decoupling trajectory) becoming Drifters

In his five years as CEO, Lynn Townsend doubled Chrysler's US market share and tripled its international share – a success due to aggressive marketing, involving forceful selling and promotion, and to sporty styling of the cars.
However, the company's concern with style and image led to a proliferation of product lines, the 'triumph of packaging over content' and a consequent lack of focus, which raised costs, reduced quality, confused the customer and heightened political tension in the organisation.

Source: Danny Miller, *The Icarus Paradox,* Harper Business, 1990.

Prepared by Roger Lazenby, Cranfield School of Management.

- Strategy usually evolves *incrementally*. Strategic change tends to occur as a continual process of relatively small adjustments to existing strategy through activity within the subsystems of an organisation. However, there is likely to be an overall strategic direction, a strategic *momentum*, which is persistent over time.

- The incremental change in organisations is likely to occur through *cultural, social and political processes*, or by managers experimenting and 'learning by doing' – the notion of *logical incrementalism*.

- Formal *planning* (e.g. corporate planning systems) may be important as an aid to analysing strategic positions and thinking through options, but it is not necessarily the vehicle by which strategies are formulated.

- Over time the organisation may become out of line with a changing environment (*strategic drift*), eventually reaching a point of crisis. At this time, more fundamental or transformational change may occur.

- The way in which managers assess the need for strategic change is through an essentially *qualitative assessment of signals* which accumulate from inside and outside the organisation.

- The definition of strategic problems and choice of strategies by managers rely not so much on dispassionate analysis of data as on (a) perceptions of what powerful individuals in the organisation see as the problem, and (b) the manager's reconciliation of the circumstances of the situation with past experience and the received wisdom encapsulated in the core assumptions and beliefs of the organisation, termed here the *paradigm*.

- The *cultural web* of an organisation – its political structures, routines, rituals and symbols – is likely to exert a preserving and legitimising influence on the core beliefs and assumptions that comprise the paradigm, hence making strategic change more difficult to achieve.

The approach taken in this book has been influenced by this understanding of how strategies develop in organisations. First, as has been said in Chapter 1, the idea of a purely sequential model of strategic management has been rejected. The headings of strategic analysis, choice and implementation are a useful structure for the book, and for thinking about the problems of strategy, but readers are urged to regard these aspects of strategic management as interdependent and an influence on one another.

This chapter has highlighted the substantial influence of the beliefs and assumptions of the managers within a cultural setting. If the strategist is to have an influence on the formulation of strategy and is to consider sensibly the ability of the organisation to implement that strategy, it is important that these cultural aspects of the organisation are explicitly understood. For this reason, emphasis is placed in this book on the importance of understanding the nature of the beliefs and assumptions of managers, and the cultural, social and political context in which they exist. In Chapter 5 there are sections on how an analysis of such systems may be undertaken. This is also regarded as a factor to be considered in strategy evaluation and is therefore considered again in Chapter 7 when the notion of 'cultural fit' is discussed. In Chapter 11 it is recognised that such aspects of the organisation may well provide the major stumbling blocks to the implementation of strategic change. The chapter therefore returns to the processes of strategic management with a view to examining how strategy and strategic change can be implemented within the cultural and political context of the organisation.

While the reality of judgement and the prevalence of bargaining processes in organisations are accepted, the book also contains examples of, and references to, many techniques of quantitative and qualitative analysis. The value of such analytical approaches is not to be underestimated. Not only do they provide an essential tool for managers to think through strategic problems and analyse possible solutions, they also provide means whereby the taken-for-granted wisdom of the organisation and assumed courses of action can be challenged.

The overall aim is, then, to provide a framework for strategy and strategic management which usefully combines the rigour of analysis with the reality of the processes of management.

References

1. The idea of strategy 'momentum' is discussed fully in D. Miller and P. Friesen, 'Momentum and revolution in organisational adaptation', *Academy of Management Journal*, vol. 23, no. 4, (1980), pp. 591–614.
2. These generalised patterns of strategy development are based on those discussed by Henry Mintzberg in 'Patterns of strategy formation', *Management Science*, vol. 24, no. 9, (1978), pp. 934–48, although his own categorisation is a good deal more complex than the one used in this book.
3. The framework used here is, in part, derived from the discussion by H. Mintzberg and J. A. Waters, 'Of strategies, deliberate and emergent', *Strategic Management Journal*, vol. 6, no. 3, (1985), pp. 257–72.
4. See H. E. Aldrich, *Organisations and Environments*, Prentice Hall, 1979; and B. McKelvey and H. E. Aldrich, 'Populations, natural selection and applied organisational science', *Administrative Science Quarterly*, vol. 28, no. 1, (1983), pp. 101–28.
5. For an avowedly planning approach to strategy, see the books by J. Argenti, e.g. *Practical Corporate Planning*, George Allen and Unwin, 1980; see also G. A. Steiner, *Strategic Planning: What Every Manager Must Know*, The Free Press, 1979. For a text based on a similar approach, see A. J. Rowe, K. E. Dickel, R. O. Mason and N. H. Snyder, *Strategic Management:*

A methodological approach, Addison-Wesley, 1989.
6. This figure is taken from H. Igor Ansoff's summary to chapter 9 (on 'Choice of strategy') in *Corporate Strategy*, Pelican, 1988.
7. The research of J. A. Pearce, K. Robbins and R. B. Robinson ('The impact of grand strategy and planning formality in financial performance', *Strategic Management Journal*, vol. 8, no. 2, (1987), pp. 125–34) does suggest a positive link between formalised planning and performance, as does that of L. C. Rhyne ('The relationship of strategic planning to financial performance', *Strategic Management Journal*, vol. 7, no. 5, (1986), pp. 423–36. However, the Rhyne paper also shows that, while most research on the subject does show some benefits from financial planning, some of the studies on the subject give contrary or non-conclusive findings.
8. Sherman's quote is taken from Barrie G. James, *Business Wargames*, Penguin, 1985, p. 190.
9. Lindblom's paper 'The science of muddling through' (*Public Administration Review*, vol. 19, (1959), pp. 79–88) is one of the earliest which criticises an overrational view of strategy formation and argues for an incremental perspective within a social and political context.
10. J. B. Quinn's research involved the examination of strategic change in companies and has been published in *Strategies for Change*, Irwin, 1980.
11. 'Adaptive' is a word used, for example, in a useful

paper by E. E. Chaffee as one of her 'three models of strategy': see the *Academy of Management Review*, vol. 10, no. 1, (1985), pp. 89–98.

12. See Quinn, *Strategies for Change*, reference 10, p. 58.

13. The 'cultural view' resembles Chaffee's 'Interpretative' view of strategy (see reference 10).

14. Edgar Schein, *Organisational Culture and Leadership*, Jossey Bass, 1985, p. 6.

15. The term 'industry recipes' is used by J.-C. Spender in *Industry Recipes: The nature and sources of management judgement*, Basil Blackwell, 1989.

16. 'Paradigm' is a term used by a number of writers. See, for example, A. Sheldon, 'Organisational paradigms: a theory of organisational change', *Organisational Dynamics*, vol. 8, no. 3, (1980), pp. 61–71; G. Johnson, *Strategic Change and the Management Process*, Basil Blackwell, 1987.

17. This section is based on the work of R. Miles and C. Snow, which can be found in *Organisational Strategy, Structure and Process*, McGraw-Hill, 1978.

18. There has been relatively little published which has examined strategic management from a political perspective, but for a general book on the subject of power and organisations, see H. Mintzberg, *Power In and Around Organisations*, Prentice Hall, 1983.

19. For a fuller account of the managerial processes surrounding the response to AIDS, see E. Ferlie and C. Bennett, 'Patterns of strategic change in health care: district health authorities respond to AIDS', *British Journal of Management*, vol. 3, no. 1, (1992), pp. 21–38.

20. A number of writers and researchers have pointed to the links between the locus of power in organisations and the perceived ability of such powerful individuals or groups to 'reduce uncertainty'. See D. J. Hickson *et al.*, 'A strategic contingencies theory of intra-organisational power', *Administrative Science Quarterly*, vol. 16, no. 2, (1971), pp. 216–29; D. C. Hambrick, 'Environment, strategy and power within top management teams', *Administrative Science Quarterly*, vol. 26, no. 2, (1981), pp. 253–76. Since the paradigm is, in effect, the 'perceived wisdom' of how to operate successfully in the organisation, it is likely that those most associated with it will be the most powerful in the organisation.

21. For a discussion of the intuitive role of strategic management, see D. K. Hurst, J. C. Rush and R. E. White, 'Top management teams and organisational renewal', *Strategic Management Journal*, vol. 10, Special issue, (1989), pp. 87–105.

22. See R. Stacey, *The Chaos Frontier*, Butterworth Heinemann, 1991 and *Managing Chaos*, Kogan Page, 1992.

23. The figures here are based on research being undertaken at Cranfield School of Management: see A. Bailey and G. Johnson, 'How strategies develop in organisations', in D. Faulkner and G. Johnson (eds), *The Challenge of Strategic Management*, published in 1992 by Kogan Page.

24. This section brings together the work of a number of researchers. For a thorough discussion of the problem of awareness and diagnosis stages of the decision-making process, see M. A. Lyles, 'Formulating strategic problems: empirical analysis and model development', *Strategic Management Journal*, vol. 2, no. 1, (1981), pp. 61–75; H. Mintzberg, O. Raisinghani and A. Theoret, 'The structure of unstructured decision processes', *Administrative Science Quarterly*, vol. 21, no. 2, (1976), pp. 246–75; and L. M. Fahey, 'On strategic management decision processes', *Strategic Management Journal*, vol. 2, no. 1, (1981), pp. 43–60.

25. This proposition is supported by the research of P. Grinyer and D. Norburn, 'Director without direction', *Journal of General Management*, vol. 1, no. 2, (1973/4), pp. 37–48; Quinn, (reference 10), D. Miller and P. Friesen, 'Archetypes of strategy formulation', *Management Science*, vol. 24, no. 9, (1978), pp. 922–33; and A. Pettigrew and R. Whipp, *Managing Change for Competitive Success*, Basil Blackwell, 1991.

26. This is borne out in much of the research into strategic decision making and corporate planning. For example, see Mintzberg, Raisinghani and Theoret, (see ref. 24)

27. A fuller explanation of the cultural web can be found in G. Johnson, 'Managing strategic change: strategy, culture and action', *Long Range Planning*, vol. 25, no. 1, (1992), pp. 28–36.

28. The organisational benefits of routines are discussed by economists such as R. R. Nelson and S. G. Winter, *An Evolutionary Theory of Economic Change*, Harvard University Press, 1982; and by management researchers such as J.-C. Spender, (see op. cit. reference 15)

29. For a fuller discussion of strategic drift, see G. Johnson, 'Rethinking incrementalism', *Strategic Management Journal*, vol. 9, no. 1, (1988), pp. 75–91.

30. Chris Argyris vividly illustrates the extent to which 'theories-in-use', as a code of behaviour, are very resistant to change and challenge. See *Organisational Learning: A theory of action perspective*, Addison-Wesley, 1978.

31. See D. Miller, *The Icarus Paradox*, Harper Business, 1990.

Recommended key readings

For a review of different explanations of the strategic management process, see Gerry Johnson, *Strategic Change and the Management Process*, Basil Blackwell, 1987, chapter 2; and C. R. Schwenk, *The Essence of Strategic Decision Making*, Lexington Books, 1988.

On incremental strategic change, see J. B. Quinn, *Strategies for Change: Logical incrementalism*; Irwin, 1980; and compare this with Gerry Johnson,

'Rethinking incrementalism', *Strategic Management Journal*, vol. 9, no. 1, (1988), pp. 75–91; and Danny Miller, *The Icarus Paradox*, Harper Business, 1990.

On the effects of cultural and political processes on strategy development and strategic change, see Gerry Johnson, 'Managing strategic change: strategy, culture and action', *Long Range Planning*, vol. 25, no. 1, (1992), pp. 28–36.

Work assignments

2.1 For an organisation with which you are familiar (or for the three Burton* cases) characterise how strategies have developed in terms of each of the explanations given in section 2.3, and explain your categorisation.

2.2 Based on Illustrations 2.3 and 2.6, and your own research and experience, what were the characteristics of banks' *realised* strategies in the early 1990s? How does this differ from what the banks' *espoused* strategies were?

2.3 Identify the advantages and any potential dangers or disadvantages of planning systems in an organisation (e.g. in Shell*). What steps might you take to avoid or overcome the dangers?

2.4 In Ford of Europe (see Illustration 2.1), the National Health Service (see Illustrations 2.4 and 6.3) and many banks (see Illustrations 2.3 and 2.6) planning systems exist. What role should planning play given the nature of strategy development in these organisations?

2.5 What is the difference between 'logical incrementalism', 'muddling through' and 'intuitive management'? (References 9, 10, 13 and 21 will be helpful here.)

2.6 *Incremental patterns of strategy development are common in organisations, and managers see advantages in this. However, there is also the risk of strategic drift. How might such drift be avoided, while retaining the benefits of incremental strategy development? (Reference to the recommended readings by Quinn (1980) and Miller (1990) and familiarity with the chapters which follow in this book will be useful here.)*

2.7 Explain the difference between a 'paradigm' and a 'strategy'.

2.8 What are the beliefs and assumptions concerning organisational strategy (the paradigm) prevalent in (a) the organisation in which you work; or (b) your university or college department; or (c) Burton A* compared with Burton B.*

2.9 For further exercises relating to the cultural web, see assignments 5.2 and 5.5 at the end of Chapter 5.

* This refers to a case study in the Text and Cases version of this book.

PART II
Strategic analysis

The first part of this book has shown that any organisation needs to adjust strategy as circumstances within and around it change. To effect these changes successfully, managers need to form a view of the key influences on their choice of strategy. Strategic analysis is concerned with providing an understanding of the strategic situation which an organisation faces. Such an understanding provides the background against which sensible future choices may be made and also insights into the difficulties of implementing a strategy. Readers should remember, however, that this relationship between analysis, choice and implementation is not a simple one in practice, and therefore strategic analysis should not be viewed as a one-off exercise which precedes choice and implementation. Strategic analysis is about becoming more aware and better informed about an organisation's situation, and in some circumstances this can be done only by implementing changes (perhaps on a limited scale). Indeed, the process of strategic choice and strategic implementation described in Parts III and IV will constantly challenge the validity of the analysis as well as building upon it.

Analysing an organisation's situation can be a complex task, and for convenience it is helpful to divide the analysis into the different types of influence on strategy as described in Chapter 1.

- Chapter 3 is concerned with the influences of the environment on an organisation. The challenge is to make sense of this complexity so as to understand the key variables affecting the performance of the organisation and how well the organisation is positioned in terms of such influences.
- Chapter 4 looks at the resources which an organisation possesses in an attempt to understand the organisation's strategic capability. These resources might include plant, people and their skills, finance and systems. The need is to understand how the configuration of such resources (the organisation's value chain) influences its strategic capability.
- Chapter 5 shows how the culture of an organisation might be understood as an influence on strategy. It also examines how individuals and groups can influence the development of strategy in terms of their own interests or expectations. The importance of assessing the bases and configurations of power is also discussed. The objectives of organisations are seen as an

outcome of these cultural and political processes rather than as preordained targets.

Although this part of the book is divided into three chapters, it should be remembered that there are strong links between these various influences on strategy. For example, environmental pressures for change may be constrained by the resources available to make changes, or by an organisational culture which may lead to resistance to change. The relative importance of the various influences will change over time and will show marked differences from one organisation to another.

CHAPTER 3

Analysing the environment

3.1 Introduction

Managers, faced with the need to understand the effects of the environment, are dealing with a difficult problem. The formulation of strategy is concerned with matching the capabilities of an organisation to its environment. But there are two major problems. First, the notion of the environment encapsulates very many different influences; the difficulty is understanding this diversity in a way which can contribute to strategic decision making. The danger is a 'listing' approach to this problem – setting down all conceivable environmental influences in an attempt to see what the organisation has going for it and against it. Long lists can be generated for most organisations, but no useful, overall picture emerges of the really important influences on the organisation. What is more, there is the danger that attempts will be made to deal with environmental influences in a piecemeal way, rather than identifying more fundamental strategic responses. A second difficulty is that of uncertainty. Understanding the history of external influences on an organisation is problematic; understanding likely future influences is much more so.

In these circumstances, managers typically cope with making sense of environmental influences by evolving, over time, accepted wisdom about their industry, its environment and what are sensible responses to different situations. This was discussed in Chapter 2. However, there are models which permit a more integrated and analytical understanding of the environment. This chapter uses some of these models to facilitate an assessment of the impact of the environment on the organisation. This is done in a series of steps briefly introduced here and summarised in Figure 3.1.

1. It is useful to take an initial view of the *nature of the organisation's environment* in terms of how uncertain it is. Is it relatively static or does it show signs of change, and in what ways; and is it simple or complex to comprehend? This helps in deciding what focus the rest of the analysis is to take. Given a fairly simple/static environment, detailed, systematic, historical analysis may be very helpful. If the environment is in a dynamic state or shows signs of becoming so, a more future-oriented perspective is more sensible.

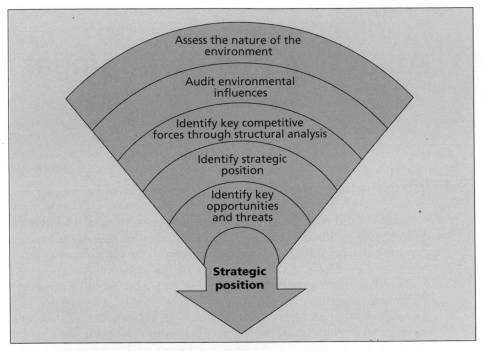

Figure 3.1 Steps in environmental analysis

2. A second step might involve an *auditing of environmental influences*. Here the aim is to identify which of the many different environmental influences have affected the organisation's development or performance in the past. It may also be helpful to construct pictures – or scenarios – of possible futures, to consider the extent to which strategies might need to change.

3. The third step moves the focus more towards an explicit consideration of individual environmental influences. The general understanding already begun can be enhanced by a *structural analysis* which aims to identify the key forces at work in the immediate or competitive environment and why they are significant.

From these three steps should emerge a view of the really important developments taking place around the organisation. It may be that there are relatively few of outstanding significance; or it could be that there are many interconnected developments. What matters is that there should be an attempt to understand why these are of strategic significance.

4. The fourth step is to analyse the organisation's *strategic position*: that is, how it stands in relation to those other organisations competing for the same resources, or customers, as itself. This may be done in a number of ways, but this chapter concentrates on: (a) *competitor analysis*; (b)

strategic group analysis, which maps firms in terms of similarities and dissimilarities of the strategies they follow; (c) the *analysis of market segments and market power*, which seeks to establish the segments in which the organisation is most likely to be effective; (d) building on this, *growth/share analysis*, which maps the organisation's market power in relation to market growth; and (e) *attractiveness analysis*, which maps the organisation's competitive position in relation to the attractiveness of the market(s) in which it operates.

The aim of such analysis is to develop an understanding of *opportunities* which can be built upon and *threats* which have to be overcome or circumvented: an understanding which needs to be considered in terms of the resource base of the organisation (Chapter 4) and which will contribute to strategy choice (Part III).

3.2 Understanding the nature of the environment

Since one of the main problems of strategic management is coping with uncertainty, it is useful to begin an analysis of the environment by asking: (a) How uncertain is the environment? (b) What are the reasons for that uncertainty? (c) How should the uncertainty be dealt with?

As Figure 3.2 suggests, environmental uncertainty increases the more environmental conditions are dynamic or the more they are complex.[1] Dynamism is to do with the rate and frequency of change. The idea of complexity perhaps needs a little more explanation because it may exist for a number of different reasons, including the following.

● The *diversity* of environmental influences faced by an organisation. For a multinational company operating in many different countries, the sheer . number of influences it has to cope with increases uncertainty.
● The amount of *knowledge* required to handle environmental influences. An extreme example of this would be a space agency like NASA.
● Different environmental influences being *interconnected*. If influences such as raw material supplies, exchange rates, political changes and consumer spending are not independent of each other but are related, it is more difficult to understand influence patterns.

In *simple/static* conditions an organisation faces an environment which is relatively straightforward to understand and is not undergoing significant change. Raw material suppliers and some mass manufacturing companies are, perhaps, examples: technical processes may be fairly simple, competition and markets are fixed over time and there may be few of them. Another example historically were many public services in 'monopoly' positions, protected from competitive influences and in the business of 'rationing' scarce resources. In such circumstances,

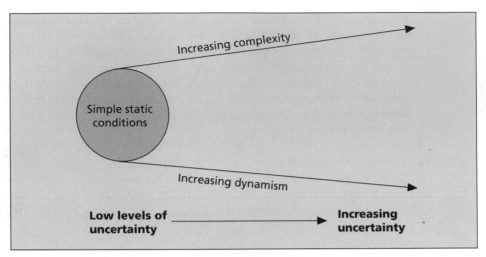

Figure 3.2 Growing uncertainty according to the nature of the environment

if change does occur it is likely to be predictable, so it makes sense to analyse the environment on a historical basis.

In situations of relatively low complexity, it may also be possible to identify some predictors of environmental influences. For example, in public services, demographic data such as birth rates might be used as lead indicators to determine the required provision of schooling, health care or social services.

In *dynamic* conditions, managers sensibly address themselves to considering the environment of the future, not just of the past. They may do this by intuitive means, or may employ more structured ways of making sense of the future, such as scenario planning. This involves identifying possible future changes significant to the organisation and building logically consistent alternative views of the future based on these. Scenario planning is discussed later in the chapter (see section 3.3.2).

Organisations in *complex* situations face environmental influences difficult in themselves to comprehend. They may, of course, face dynamic conditions too. With the growth and application of more and more sophisticated technology there is an increasing move to this condition of greatest uncertainty. The computer industry, airlines and the electronics industry are all in, or moving into, this dynamic/complex situation. A multinational may, as a corporate body, also be in a complex condition because of its diversity, while different operating companies within it face varying degrees of complexity and dynamism. There are both organisational and information-processing approaches to deal with such complexity.

Complexity as a result of diversity might be dealt with by ensuring that different parts of the organisation responsible for different aspects of diversity are separate and given the resources and authority to handle their own part of the environment. This is discussed in Chapter 10.

An information-processing approach to dealing with complexity might entail an attempt to model the complexity so as to simulate the effects on the finances of an organisation of different environmental conditions (see also section 8.3.4). In its extreme form there may be an attempt to model the environment itself: for example, in the 1980s the UK Treasury Office drew on a model of the UK economy. However, for most organisations facing complexity, organisational responses are probably more useful than extensive model building. Indeed it can be argued[2] that since the environment in which organisations operate cannot be predicted other than for the short term, what really matters is that managers are, themselves, sensitive to signals in their environment and flexible and intuitive in their responses to such signals; and that they build organisations capable of such responses. Strategic management is, then, seen as much more to do with the skills and characteristics of managers than with tools of analysis and planning. Analysis is here much more concerned with helping sensitize managers to their environment than arriving at precise explanations or bases of prediction.

The purpose of taking an initial view of the nature of the environment is to consider the most useful ways of understanding and dealing with its influences. In practice, an auditing of past and current influences, discussed in the section which follows, is likely to be important. What needs to be considered is the extent to which these influences can be expected to persist, and how complexity – if it exists – can be handled.

3.3 Auditing environmental influences

Illustration 3.1 shows some of the environmental influences important to organisations. It is not intended to provide an exhaustive list, but it does give examples of ways in which strategies of organisations are affected by such influences and also indicates some of the ways in which organisations seek to handle aspects of their environment.[3]

Over time different environmental forces will be more, or less, important to an organisation. For example, the economies of most western countries moved from recession in the late 1970s and early 1980s, into recovery in the mid-1980s, and back into recession by 1990. It is also the case that the key environmental

ILLUSTRATION 3.1

ILLUSTRATION 3.1

The following are examples of ways in which

Economic factors and restructuring

In the united Germany a domestic boom that sheltered the economy from the world recession slowed in 1992. German industry faced low-cost competition from Japan and some west European countries. A short working week, high wages and high environmental standards affected productivity. In the face of reduced demand, Degussa had to restructure. Plans were created to cut labour costs by 10 per cent; reduce foreign investment; float a pharmaceutical subsidiary to raise cash; and form joint venture partnerships to spread product development costs.

Capital markets

In 1991 Vickers reported losses for the first time in its post-war history. Losses of £60m at Rolls-Royce Motor Cars were blamed. The losses were attributed to the recession halving sales and to restructuring costs of £30m. Substantial development costs were also anticipated to develop a new model. Vickers' total dividend in 1991 was 6 pence, down from 9.9 pence in 1990. Vickers came under pressure from the City to stem losses, improve dividends and reduce capital requirements – perhaps by finding a buyer for Rolls.

Demographics

During the 1980s America's ageing population faced the highest medical costs in the world and falling real incomes. Traditional hedges against inflation such as certificates of deposit and real estate began to look less attractive. As a result, some stockbroking firms developed new business around equity-based savings products. Not only did these products produce new revenue, but they also helped to support share prices on the markets.

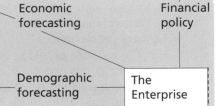

Economic forecasting

Financial policy

Demographic forecasting

The Enterprise

Environmental sensing R & D policy

Socio-cultural

- During the 1980s in Britain, people became more concerned with the quality of their lives and their health. The demand declined for foods perceived as unhealthy, such as sugar, butter and fried foods. The demand rose for fresh foods and foods perceived as being healthy, such as rice, pasta and fish.
- Increasingly, Europeans became more mobile, working and visiting countries other than their own. Manufacturers therefore found it more difficult to sell similar products with different propositions or prices in different countries.

Technology

Technological change reduces the length of the product life cycle and therefore the time to recoup investment. Investment costs can also be increased as the number of technologies in a product is increased. To reduce these costs to a minimum and to stay in the product development race, many electronics groups formed strategic alliances. For example, Philips joined with Motorola to design and develop semiconductor chips for Compact Disk Interactive, a new CD-based multi-media product combining graphics, data, CD video and CD audio.

Prepared by David Cowley, Cranfield School of Management.

Examples of environmental influences

organisations interact with aspects of the environment.

Labour market

By the 1990s UK accountancy firms began to face client demands for reduced fees and better service. The firms responded in two ways. First, the use of information technology was increased for routine services, to reduce the need for large numbers of junior staff, and to reduce costs. Second, firms began to recruit more experienced staff backed with appropriate qualifications to meet specific client needs. Both of these moves led to a reduction in graduate recruitment by the firms.

Competition

- In the 1990s the UK government introduced a competitive element into the National Health Service. For example, providers of services (e.g. hospitals) were required to price their services, and health authorities were obliged to choose between the services offered by different providers based on value for money and services offered.
- With a strong position at home, National Australia bank decided to enter the UK market and bought the Clydesdale and Northern banks from Midland, becoming the first large foreign competitor to enter the UK retail banking market.

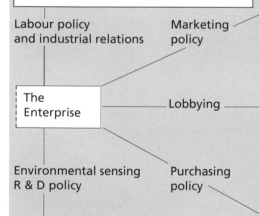

Labour policy
and industrial relations

Marketing
policy

The
Enterprise

Lobbying

Environmental sensing
R & D policy

Purchasing
policy

Government

- Given improving East–West relations, western governments announced cuts in defence expenditure that accelerated the restructuring of defence industries and caused thousands of job losses.
- In the 1980s the British government controlled the economy through interest rates, which also affected exchange rates. Joining the ERM limited the use of interest rates.
- Among measures to stimulate the UK car market the government announced in the 1992 budget that the special car tax would be halved to 5 per cent.

Ecology

The collapse of the communist regimes in eastern Europe brought evidence of enormous ecological devastation: food contaminated by heavy metals; up to 60 per cent of some forests damaged by acid rain; and up to 80 per cent of rivers in some countries polluted to the extent that they could not support life. However, this yielded opportunities for companies such as Deutsche Babcock and Metallgesellschaft, which were able to respond by providing environmental monitoring and decontamination technologies for soil water and waste treatment.

Supplies

In March 1992 zinc supply was disrupted and price structures were in confusion. Zinc smelters in the USA and Mexico suffered strikes, and in Peru a drought induced a power shortage. These factors kept prices on an upward trend despite rising stock levels caused by reduced demand from recession-hit companies and increases in supply from Russia. Demand was anticipated to increase in the latter half of 1992 as the recession receded. For purchasers such as manufacturers of batteries, the dilemma was to buy now or later – a decision which could affect their competitive price position.

issues for one organisation may not be the same as for another. A multinational corporation might be primarily concerned with government relations, since it may be operating plants or subsidiaries within many different countries with different systems of government and policies. Exchange rates will be particularly important for an export-led firm; a retailer, on the other hand, may be primarily concerned with customer tastes and behaviour. A computer manufacturer is likely to be concerned with the technical environment which leads to innovation and perhaps obsolescence of equipment. Public-sector managers and civil servants are likely to be especially concerned with public policy issues, public funding levels and perhaps demographic changes. The point is that there is unlikely to be any definitive set of environmental issues which are especially important for all organisations, and they will shift over time.

3.3.1 PEST analysis

It is useful to consider as a starting point what environmental influences have been particularly important in the past and the extent to which there are changes occurring which may make any of these more or less significant in the future for the organisation and its competitors. Figure 3.3 can help with such an audit by providing a summary of some of the questions to ask about likely key forces at

---

1. **What environmental factors are affecting the organisation?**
2. **Which of these are the most important at the present time? In the next few years?**

Political/legal
Monopolies legislation •
Environmental protection laws •
Taxation policy • Foreign trade
regulations • Employment law •
Government stability

Socio-cultural
Population demographics •
Income distribution • Social
mobility • Lifestyle changes •
Attitudes to work and leisure •
Consumerism • Levels of
education

Economic
Business cycles • GNP trends • Interest
rates • Money supply • Inflation •
Unemployment • Disposable income
• Energy availability and cost

Technological
Government spending on research •
Government and industry focus of
technological effort • New
discoveries/development • Speed of
technology transfer • Rates of
obsolescence

Figure 3.3 A PEST analysis of environmental influences

Paramount Publishing International

(PRENTICE HALL/HARVESTER WHEATSHEAF/ELLIS HORWOOD/ALLYN &
BACON/WOODHEAD FAULKNER/APPLETON & LANGE)
Campus 400, Maylands Ave, Hemel Hempstead, Herts., HP2 7EZ, England
Tel: Hemel Hempstead (0442) 881900 Fax:(0442 257115) Telex: 82445
Registration: London 714516   VAT Registration No. GB 490 5885 08

REFERENCE
IU165070

Date and
Tax Point

INSPECTION COPY   23/10/94

MR D FITZSIMMONS
SCHOOL OF MANAGEMENT
UNIVERSITY CENTRAL LANCS
PRESTON
LANCS PR1 2HE

W/H Order No. P271585

SBN	TITLE	AUTHOR	PRICE
013297441X	EXPLORING CORPORATE STRATEGY:	JOHNSON/SCHOLES	£ 19.95

This book is sent to you for 60 days examination following: YOUR REQUEST BY TELEPHONE

When you have had the opportunity to examine the book and its suitability to your reading requirements and considered the
options outlined below, please complete the details below and return this form.

☐ This book will be recommended for purchase as a main course text on the following course: ------------

Beginning on:----------   Student Numbers: --------------   I am therefore retaining the book as a desk copy.

NB   Books may only be retained, without purchase, if they are the main recommended or dual recommended text.
If you wish to retain the book as a supplementary recommended text or for your own interest, please refer to the new
boxed section below.
Which book shop will you inform of your students' requirements? -----------------

Comments on the book (Academic quality, course applicability, etc):-------------------
----

We would be grateful for the names of colleagues whom you think may be interested in this book:

Book(s) currently recommended as main text: -------------------

☐ I return the book herewith.

☐ I am retaining the book and enclose a cheque for £/$ ------------- made payable to **INTERNATIONAL BOOK
DISTRIBUTORS LTD**

☐ I am retaining the book and wish you to debit my credit card account with the amount of £------
My Access/American Express/Diners Club No. is: ☐☐☐☐

Name: ---------

work in the wider environment. It is sometimes known as a PEST analysis, indicating the importance of political, economic, social and technological influences on organisations. There are four main ways in which this can contribute to strategic analysis:

1. The headings in Figure 3.3 can be used as a *checklist* when considering and analysing the different influences. However, although a great deal of information can be generated in this way, it will be of limited strategic value if it remains a listing of influences. It is, therefore, important that the sort of models discussed in the rest of the chapter are used to inform and guide analysis.

2. It may, however, be possible to identify a smaller number of *key environmental influences*. For example, the hospital services in western industrialised countries face short-term pressures in terms of patient care, but their ability to provide such care in the long term is critically dependent on how management reconcile themselves to the convergence of at least three crucial factors. The first is demographic, and concerns in particular the ageing population and therefore increasing demands on health care; the second is the rapid development of technology, at one and the same time prolonging life, improving the prospects of care and yet demanding huge amounts of funding; and the third is the uncertain economic conditions within which they operate when linked to government policy on public funding. The point is that the strategy for an organisation must address these key influences. The danger is that managers, faced with pressing day-to-day problems – as in the health service – fail to address them; and strategy becomes short-term response rather than long-term development.

3. PEST analysis may also be helpful in identifying long-term *drivers of change*. For example, given the increasing globalisation of some markets, it is important to identify the forces leading to this development. These include rapid change in technology, leading to shorter life spans of such technology, and therefore to the need for greater scale economies in its use. The world-wide convergence of consumer tastes in markets such as radios, television and entertainment leads to the possibility of major economies being gained through global marketing and manufacturing. The growth of multinational customers and competitors has also increased the shift towards global markets, as has the overall pressure on business for cost reduction and therefore the search for scale economies. A further force for global development is the world-wide search for raw materials, energy and often skills to service global business networks.[4]

4. PEST analysis may also help to examine the *differential impact* of external influences on organisations either historically or in terms of likely future impact. This approach builds on the identification of key trends or influences, and asks to what extent such external influences will affect

different organisations – perhaps competitors – differently. Figure 3.4 shows a simplified example of such an analysis, which builds on the trends towards globalisation of markets discussed above. Here, the shorter life span of technology, the convergence of customer requirements and the need to access supplies of skills internationally are the three key forces identified. The three competitors, A, B and C have been assessed in terms of their differential ability to cope with these three key forces. The analysis shows that firm A is best placed to deal with technological change, given its track record and investment in R & D and its high market share, allowing the cost of R & D to be readily offset. Like C, it is also well placed, given its centralised product planning, to cope with the development of more convergent customer requirements. However, both A and C, are not as well placed as B when it come to accessing supplies, and particularly technical skills world-wide, because A and particularly C, are much more centralised in procurement; and C, in particular, has a tradition of recruiting and promoting from within its own national boundaries.

This is a simplified example of what might be a much more complex analysis, but it does show how the identification of key trends or influences can be taken further to examine differential impact on organisations.

KEY EXTERNAL INFLUENCES	COMPETITORS		
	A	**B**	**C**
Shorter technological life span	+ + Track record in R & D and high volume share	– – Lowest investment in R & D and lowest market share	+ Track record in R & D and substantial share
Convergence of customer requirements	+ + Central product planning	– – Diverse products from many SBUs	+ + Central product planning
Access to supplies and skills internationally	– Centralised procurement policies	+ Widest networks of operating units	– – Centralised procurement policies. Staffing traditionally from one national SBU

Figure 3.4 Impact analysis

3.3.2 The use of scenarios[5]

The identification of major trends can also usefully be built into the construction of scenarios as a way of analysing environmental influences. Scenario planning is especially useful in circumstances where it is important to take a long-term view of strategy – probably a minimum of five years – and where there are a limited number of key factors influencing the success of that strategy. For example, in the oil industry there is a need for views of the business environment of up to 25 years; and while a whole host of environmental issues are of relevance, a number, such as raw material availability, price and economic conditions, are of crucial importance. Obviously, it is not possible to forecast precisely economic conditions, or the price of oil, over 25-year time horizons. However, it is helpful to have a coherent view of the future against which strategies can be considered and developed.

Scenario building is an attempt to construct views of possible future situations. These are not just based on hunch, but try to build consistent views of possible developments around identified key factors. The aim is to draw up a limited number of logically consistent, but different scenarios such as those shown in Illustration 3.2. There are two main benefits to such an exercise. The first is that managers can examine strategic options against the scenarios and ask: 'what should we do if ...', or 'what would be the effect of ...'? In effect, the scenarios can be used for sensitivity testing of possible strategies. The second benefit is that managers can examine the implications of scenarios so as to challenge the taken-for-granted assumptions about the environment in which they operate. This may be particularly important where there are long time horizons because operating managers may be so concerned with the short term that they neglect to consider long-term changes.

The main steps in drawing up scenarios are as follows:

● First, it is necessary to identify the key assumptions, or forces, that are to be worked on. This may build on the sort of PEST analysis described above. It is best to restrict these assumptions to environmental forces, rather than including the strategic action of the organisation or of competitors. It is also important that the number of assumptions is kept relatively low, since the complexity in drawing up scenarios will rise dramatically with the number of assumptions included.

● It is important to understand historically the trend with regard to assumptions being considered, their impact on market conditions and organisational strategies, and what these assumptions themselves depend upon. For example, if oil prices are being considered, what affects oil prices? However, this analysis is for the purposes of gaining an understanding of the assumptions to be used, rather than for forecasting. Scenario building is not about quantitative forecasting.

- Scenarios are built by considering logically consistent, possible futures, usually on the basis of an optimistic future, a pessimistic future and a 'dominant theme', or mainline, future. Most experts agree that two to four scenarios are appropriate to aim for.
- These future scenarios may be built in one of two ways:
  (a) The first way is to build up scenarios from the assumptions. This is a sensible approach if the number of assumptions is very low, perhaps if there are three or five key assumptions. Different, consistent configurations of these factors might be systematically examined to build towards three, or perhaps four, scenarios.
  (b) If the number of factors being considered is larger, then it may not be feasible to undertake this 'building-up' process. Instead the 'tone' of scenarios is set – for example, according to optimistic and pessimistic extremes, or in terms of perhaps three dominant themes. Then from the

ILLUSTRATION 3.2
Shell's global scenarios for the energy industry

In 1990 Shell produced two scenarios for use in their planning process: 'global mercentilism' and 'sustainable world'.

Every two or three years the Central Planning Group of Shell revises its thinking about the future on behalf of the Shell Group. The process results in two scenarios, the purpose of which is to sensitise decision-makers in the group to recognise signals of possible changes in the world. The proposition is that a more rapid and appropriate business response can then be effected compared with that likely to occur if such changes came as a surprise.

In 1990 Shell's Central Planning Group produced two scenarios entitled 'global mercantilism' and 'sustainable world'. The world at this time was seen in terms of three areas of potentially far-reaching change: geopolitics, international economics and the natural environment. These form a common starting point from which two different logic-flows branch towards the distinct scenarios. The branching point for these two stories is a (hypothetical) coincident economic downturn in several major countries.

Global mercantilism is the outturn of a weak international order as a result of the end of the cold war. There is instability in the world's economic and political systems which leads to a focus on building a new, more managed, regional system. The emphasis is on regional pacts and bilateral agreements rather than a global system. It encourages internal, protectionist thinking within countries or blocs, but it also recognises that companies need to be competitive. The route to competitiveness is seen to lie in the free-market approach, so that deregulation and

array of factors available, those consistent with these themes are chosen. In either case, in using the factors to build scenarios the allocation of probabilities to factors should be avoided: it endows the scenarios with spurious accuracy, which can be unhelpful given the purpose of the scenarios.

3.4 Structural analysis of the competitive environment

So far the concern has been with broad aspects of the environment. However, for most organisations, there is a set of external influences which are more immediate, and which they are likely to be able to affect directly by their own actions. This is the immediate or competitive environment, and the concern here

privatisation are the prescription. Environmental concerns are not high on the political agenda in this picture: although local/regional actions may be taken, international environmental issues prove too difficult to resolve.

Here the energy industry faces changing rules and the continuous reconfiguration of markets. Regional self-sufficiency is the emphasis and non-OPEC production is continued. Oil marketers and producers develop tight bonds and reciprocal arrangements, while volatile economic growth makes it hard to control oil prices, which are liable to large fluctuations, largely outside the influence of OPEC.

In contrast, *sustainable world* puts the environment at the top of the list. Political and economic thinking converge in a world where the importance of international trade agreements is recognised and pursued. Large economic powers in particular recognise that there are limits to the burden that can be placed on the environment, so there is a shift to tighter environmental regulation and taxation. This world has a global, caring outlook, with concern for the developing countries and aid given to try and help achieve environmental improvements in these resource-scarce regions.

Here implications for the energy industry are centred on increasing governmental pressure to reduce environmental impact. Pressure is exerted as regulation for lower emissions into the atmosphere and incentives to gain greater energy efficiency. The technology exists to meet the challenge, and economic conditions are made favourable so that, with time, the environmental payback is reaped.

Source: *Challenges and Opportunities for the Petroleum Industry*, Shell, October 1991; *Global Scenarios for the Energy Industry: Challenge and response*, Shell, January 1991.

Prepared by Julie Verity, Shell International Fellow, Cranfield School of Management.

is with the factors which directly influence the capability of an organisation to position itself more or less effectively against its rivals.

This section draws on the 'five-forces' approach proposed by Porter,[6] and is summarised in Figure 3.5. It is a structured means of examining the competitive environment of an organisation so as to provide an understanding of the forces at work. Although designed primarily with commercial organisations in mind, it is of value to most organisations. Illustration 3.3 shows how the analysis of the five forces might help an organisation to understand a changing industry environment.

3.4.1 The threat of entry

Threat of entry will depend on the extent to which there are *barriers to entry*. Most typically, these are as follows:

● *Economies of scale.* In some industries, economies of scale are extremely important: for example, in the car or airline industry. However, the importance of scale economies differs by industry: for example, in the

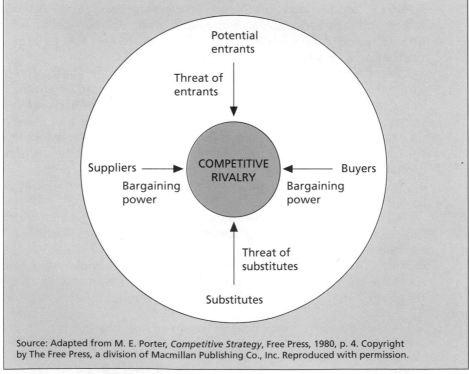

Source: Adapted from M. E. Porter, *Competitive Strategy*, Free Press, 1980, p. 4. Copyright by The Free Press, a division of Macmillan Publishing Co., Inc. Reproduced with permission.

Figure 3.5 A model for structural analysis

machine tool industry the optimum scale of production is theoretically very high, but the cost of producing at half that level is relatively low.

- *The capital requirement of entry.* The capital cost of entering a market will vary according to technology and scale. The cost of setting up a retail clothing business with leased premises and stock from wholesalers is minimal when compared to the cost of, for example, entering capital-intensive industries such as chemicals and heavy machinery.

- *Access to distribution channels.* For decades the UK brewing companies, like many of their German and French counterparts, invested in the ownership or financing of pubs, which guaranteed the distribution of their products and excluded competitive products. This made it difficult for competitors to break into the market. However, in the late 1980s the Monopolies and Mergers Commission in the UK demanded that the larger brewing companies do away with this 'tied house' system, with the aim of allowing a freer entry of competitor products.

- *Cost advantages independent of size.* To a large extent these are to do with early entries into the market and the experience so gained. It is difficult for a competitor to break into a market if there is an established operator who knows that market well, has good relationships with the key buyers and suppliers, and knows how to overcome, market and operating problems. This phenomenon relates to the 'experience curve' and is dealt with in more detail in section 4.3.2.

- *Expected retaliation.* If a competitor considering entering a market believes that the retaliation of an existing firm will be so great as to prevent entry, or will mean that entry would be too costly, then this is also a barrier. Entering the breakfast cereal market to compete with Kelloggs, or the motorcycle market to compete with Honda, would be unwise unless careful attention was paid to a strategy to avoid retaliation.

- *Legislation or government action.* The most obvious example of the way in which government action can influence competitive activity was in the command economies of eastern Europe. The move towards demand-driven economies means that managers in hitherto protected environments face the pressures of competition for the first time. To a lesser extent the situation is similar in many public services such as the postal system, health service or rail system in western countries, traditionally operated as monopolies, but increasingly facing deregulation and privatisation.

- *Differentiation.* By differentiation is meant the provision of a product or service regarded by the user as meaningfully different from the competition; its importance will be discussed more fully in Chapter 6. However, here it is important to point out that organisations able to achieve differentiation provide for themselves real barriers to competitive entry. For example, Marks and Spencer is perceived by its customers as a unique retailer with an image for reliability and quality which it seeks to ensure through a co-ordinated mix of staff training, product and quality specification and control at supplier level, and strong corporate values supportive of the quality

ILLUSTRATION 3.3
A five-forces analysis of the oil industry in Ireland

Structural analysis can provide a basis for understanding the forces at work in a competitive environment, and the effects of changes in these forces.

Over the past twenty years the global trend has been towards free-market economies, away from controlled ones. Liberalisation has occurred through acts of privatisation and deregulation by governments. This trend started in the USA in the 1970s, was followed enthusiastically in the UK during the 1980s, and is one of the fundamental principles of the EC post-1992.

The five-forces tool provides a useful way of understanding the nature of industries and how these might change. The oil industry provides a good example of an industry which has traditionally been regulated to some extent by national governments. What happened in Ireland in the 1980s was typical of the sorts of change occurring more widely. Four major companies dominated the oil industry in Ireland, and government regulation existed in order to secure supply of an important product for which Ireland had no indigenous substitute. The fuel-oil sector (which supplied oil for electricity generation and for heating) had fewer restrictions of operations than did the retail sector (selling gasoline to the car-owning public) and was a natural entry point for new competition to penetrate the industry, which had grown profitable in an environment of weak competitive forces:

image. Nor is the idea of differentiation peculiar to the private sector. For example, museums, art galleries and exhibition centres have sought to differentiate themselves from competitors through the services they offer, the architecture of buildings or featured special exhibitions; and symphony orchestras through their repertoire and style of performance.

These barriers to entry differ by industry, so it is impossible to generalise about which are more important than others. But it is important to establish: (a) which barriers, if any, exist; (b) to what extent they are likely to prevent entry in the particular environment concerned; and (c) the organisation's position in all this – is it trying to prevent entrants, or is it attempting to gain entry, and if so, how?

3.4.2 The power of buyers and suppliers

The next two forces can be considered together because they are linked – all

- *Threat of entry* had been low due to lack of knowledge outside the industry about how to trade in oil products. But by the early 1980s the threat was increasing as spot-market trading developed, enabling entrepreneurs to enter.
- *Threat of substitution* was very low. Until the late 1970s oil had met over 70 per cent of the country's primary energy requirements. At the end of the decade, however, natural gas had been discovered off the south coast and a gas distribution system was being built by the government. By 1984 fuel oil had lost more than 20 per cent of its market share to natural gas.
- *Power of buyers* was low. A maximum price was set by the regulator which was based on the oil companies' costs, plus an allowable margin. All four majors priced at the regulated price since market demand was high and rising.
- *Rivalry* was low. Price was set to meet company costs and provide a margin to traders. Demand was high, but due to the introduction of natural gas was falling.

The result was a market with low competitive rivalry and high margins. However, entrepreneurs saw an opportunity to capitalise on the margins they could earn from entering the fuel-oil sector with lower operating costs than the established players. The effect was to undermine the government's set price and remove effective regulation at a time when market forces were changing. The final result was a significant increase in the competitiveness of the sector.

Prepared by Julie Verity, Shell International Fellow, Cranfield School of Management.

organisations have to obtain resources and provide goods or services. Moreover, buyers and sellers can have similar effects in constraining the strategic freedom of an organisation and in influencing the margins of that organisation. However, it is also important to remember that different types of suppliers and buyers will be important for different organisations in different ways. For example, consider the relationship between buyer and seller in the provision of goods in grocery manufacturing and retailing in the UK. The power of multiple retailers has grown enormously since the 1970s. At that time grocery manufacturers could expect to exert strong marketing power over retail channels. By the early 1990s, however, around 55 per cent of grocery sales were accounted for by just five retail chains. Any one supplier was relatively unimportant to these major companies. In the largest of the retailers – Sainsbury – most sales were accounted for by own-label or own-packed products: here Sainsbury itself exercised control over product quality and, to a large extent, specification of prices. For the grocery supplier, the balance of power had changed entirely within a period of less than fifteen years.

So when is supplier power, and buyer power, likely to be important? Supplier power is likely to be high when:

- There is a concentration of suppliers rather than a fragmented source of supply.
- The 'switching costs' from one supplier to another in the industry are high, perhaps because a manufacturer's processes are dependent on the specialist products of a supplier, or a product is clearly differentiated.
- The brand of the supplier is powerful. This links to 'switching costs' because, as might be the case for consumer goods, a retailer might not be able to do without a particular brand.
- There is the possibility of the supplier integrating forward if it does not obtain the prices, and hence the margins, it seeks.
- The supplier's customers are of little importance to the supplier, in which case the supplier is not likely to regard the long-term future of the customers as particularly important.

Buyer power is likely to be high when:

- There is a concentration of buyers, particularly if the volume purchases of the buyers are high.
- There are alternative sources of supply, perhaps because the product required is undifferentiated between suppliers or, as for many public-sector operations in the 1980s, the deregulation of markets spawns new competitors.
- The component or material cost is a high percentage of the total cost. Buyers will then be likely to 'shop around' to get the best price and therefore 'squeeze' the suppliers.
- There is a threat of backward integration by the buyer if satisfactory prices or suppliers cannot be obtained.

Some organisations may rely on supplies other than tangible goods. For example, the provision of finance may be crucial to an organisation, and therefore the power of the supplier of finance may be vital. For example, the British Rail system had, by the 1980s, become in critical need of reinvestment in its infrastructure. Yet the public-sector finance controls of the Conservative government in the 1980s, and the legislation that prevented British Rail raising capital from financial markets, meant that British Rail's freedom to act in this regard was severely limited; and this damaged its ability to compete with road transport.

People, too, can be a critical area of supply. For professional services, such as management consultancy, corporate tax advice, medicine or teaching, the availability of skilled staff is crucial. However, while this may be a significant constraint, it may not give the suppliers power, since they may not be organised to exert it. In other cases, most obviously if trade union power is strong, labour supply may not only be important, but may exercise power.

The problem of constructing strategies to achieve strategic aims is therefore likely to depend on the extent to which power can be enhanced, or mutual interest accommodated, in the supplier–buyer channel. For example, local government authorities in the UK, having realised that their historically fragmented mode of buying reduced buying power, sought to increase this by forming buying groups in the 1980s. And Ford, faced with competitive demands for higher productivity at lower cost, reduced suppliers of components from 2,500 in 1985 to 900 by 1990. The suppliers which remained gained in volume orders, but they had to prove themselves against strict criteria of quality and delivery. The converse is also the case, of course: it might be possible for a supplier to seek out market segments with less powerful buyers, or to differentiate products so that buyers become more dependent on that product. It might also be possible to build mutually advantageous links with suppliers and buyers: a point discussed more fully when considering the strategic capability of organisations in section 4.2.

3.4.3 The threat of substitutes

The threat of substitution may take many forms. There could be actual or possible substitution of one product for another – the fax for the telephone, for example. A new process may render a product superfluous: for example, if more precise casting means that engine blocks are cast to a finer specification, it may reduce demand for cutting tools. Substitutes may also be thought of as those competing for discretionary expenditure: for example, furniture manufacturers or retailers need to understand that they compete for available household expenditure with suppliers of televisions, videos, cookers, cars and holidays. 'Doing without' can also be thought of as a substitute; certainly for the tobacco industry this is so.

It is the strategic impact of actual or potential substitutes that needs careful consideration. The availability of substitutes can place a ceiling on prices for a company's products, or make inroads into the market and so reduce its attractiveness. The key questions that need to be addressed are: (a) whether a substitute poses the threat of obsolescence of a firm's product or service, or provides a higher perceived benefit or value; (b) the ease with which buyers can switch to substitutes, usually determined by the one-time costs facing the buyer making such a change; and (c) to what extent the risk of substitution can be reduced by building in switching costs, perhaps through added product or service benefits meeting buyer needs.

3.4.4 Competitive rivalry

Organisations will also be concerned with the extent of rivalry between themselves and competitors. What is it based upon? Is it likely to increase or decrease in intensity? How can it be influenced? The most competitive markets will be those in which *entry* is likely, *substitutes* threaten, or *buyers* or *suppliers* exercise control; so the previously discussed forces are relevant here. However, there are likely to be other forces which affect competitive rivalry:

- The extent to which competitors in the industry are *in balance*. Whatever their number, where competitors are of roughly equal size there is the danger of intense competition as one competitor attempts to gain dominance over another. Conversely, the most stable markets tend to be those with dominant organisations within them.
- A market undergoing *slow growth* may increase rivalry if it is entering maturity and competitors are keen to establish themselves as market leaders.
- *High fixed costs* in an industry, perhaps through high capital intensity or high costs of storage, are likely to result in competitors cutting prices to obtain the turnover required. This can result in price wars and very low-margin operations.
- If the addition of *extra capacity is in large increments*, the competitor making such an addition is likely to create at least short-term overcapacity and increased competition.
- Again *differentiation* is important. In a commodity market, where products or services are not differentiated, there is little to stop customers switching between competitors.
- If the *acquisition of weaker companies* by stronger companies results in the provision of funds to improve the competitive standing of such firms, their ability to compete more effectively may be enhanced.
- Where there are *high exit barriers* to an industry, there is again likely to be the persistence of excess capacity and consequently increased competition. Exit barriers might be high for a variety of reasons: they might vary from a high investment in non-transferable fixed assets such as specialist plant, to the cost of redundancy, to the reliance on one product in order to be credible within a market sector even if the product itself makes losses.

Illustration 3.4 shows how the European chemical industry became increasingly competitive in the early 1990s.

3.4.5 Key questions arising from structural analysis

The 'five forces' framework can be employed simply as a checklist to describe what is going on in the market. However, this is not its only purpose. The analyst should be seeking to gain insights into the forces which need the particular attention of the organisation. The following questions help focus the analysis:

- What are the *key forces* at work in the competitive environment? These will differ by industry. For example, for grocery manufacturers the power of retail

ILLUSTRATION 3.4
Increasing competition in the European chemical industry

Increasing competition in the European chemical industry in the early 1990s resulted from a combination of declining demand, overcapacity, rising costs, lack of differentiation and overseas competitors.

The European chemical industry comprises many subsectors including basic organic and inorganic chemicals, agrochemicals, plastics, pharmaceuticals and speciality chemicals. It experienced boom conditions in 1988. In 1991 growth turnover and profits started to decline, and the view in the industry was that this more competitive environment would continue until 1994 because:

- World-wide recession had *reduced demand*. An example from the plastics industry showed that polyethylene plants were operating at *85 per cent capacity* compared to 100 per cent in 1988.
- Awareness of the environmental impact of certain chemicals – polystyrene, chlorofluorohydrocarbons and 1,1,1-trichloroethane – caused whole *market segments to disappear*. Developing substitutes wherever possible, incurred costs.
- The economics of production required large capital expenditure on process-specific, large-scale plant. Moreover, *capacity increases* planned during 1988 came on stream in 1991. The industry continued to invest in plant after the market had peaked: for example, ethylene capacity was expected to grow at 6 per cent per annum until 1996. Demand was expected to be between 2.5 and 5 per cent.
- Further *capital investment* and *higher operating costs* were due to improvements in environmental monitoring and control required in law by government policy. The industry also faced *higher raw material costs* for petroleum-based feedstocks due to the Gulf crisis.
- Heavy investment in the Far East (for example, South Korea invested $7 billion in petrochemical plant between 1987 and 1991) reduced European export business and increased competition as these countries become net exporters, gaining *entry to the European market*.
- *Exit barriers* were high due to the highly capital-intensive nature of the industry and its process-specific assets.
- Many basic-grade chemicals are *commodity items*, presenting the market with little differentiation or basis for creating switching costs.

Source: FT Surveys, *Chemistry in Britain*.

Prepared by David Cowley, Cranfield School of Management.

buyers is of extreme importance; whereas for computer manufacturers the growing power of chip manufacturers and the growth in competitive intensity might be regarded as most crucial; and for a deregulated public service new entrants with more commercial experience might be the central problem.

- Are there *underlying forces* – perhaps identified from the PEST analysis – which are driving the competitive forces? For example, government constraints on expenditure may affect the availability of sufficiently educated staff, or finance for investment in the public sector.
- Is it likely that the forces will *change*, and if so how? For example, a company with a strong market position within a given country may have built its strategy on that market strength. However, if forces for globalisation in the industry are occurring, strength in the national market might become much less important. For example, historically Bass built its strength on its UK base in brewing. However, the brewing industry shows signs of globalisation and, while Bass has retained interests in the brewing industry, its strategic development in the 1980s has concentrated much more on its hotel businesses.
- How do particular competitors stand in relation to these competitive forces? What are their strengths and weaknesses in relation to the key forces at work? The issues of *competitive standing* and *competitive positioning* are therefore important and are dealt with next.
- What can be done to *influence* the competitive forces affecting the organisation? Can the organisation build barriers to entry, increase its power over suppliers or buyers, or find ways of diminishing competitive rivalry? These are the fundamental questions relating to *competitive strategy* and will be a major concern of Chapter 6.
- Are some industries more attractive than others? It can be argued that some industries are intrinsically more profitable than others because, for example, entry is more difficult, or buyers and suppliers less powerful. In theory, then, the corporate strategist might use industry analysis as a means of identifying which industries are more or less attractive than others (see section 3.5.5). While this may be helpful, it is dangerous to assume that the forces identified in such an analysis are deterministic of business success. For example, given the situation in the chemical industry described in Illustration 3.4, why would the Koreans wish to enter what appears to be a highly unattractive market? The answer may be that they believe that they can achieve some competitive advantage which others cannot achieve: that success depends more on competitive strategy than on the characteristics of the industry.

3.5 Identifying the organisation's competitive position

All organisations – public or private – are in a competitive position in relation to each other, in so far as they are competing either for customers or, perhaps in the case of public services, for resources. It is therefore important that they understand the nature of their relative positioning and its implications in strategic terms. The auditing of environmental influences outlined in section 3.3 and the structural analysis in section 3.4 provide indications of key factors which will affect positioning, but there are some useful ways of pulling these factors together to help analysis. This section reviews different ways of doing this: first generally in terms of competitor analysis; then by employing a number of analytical frameworks, in particular strategic group analysis, market segmentation, and different ways in which an organisation's competitive position can be related to market attractiveness.

3.5.1 Competitor analysis[7]

A first step in understanding the position of an organisation is to examine it against competitors or rivals it faces. These may be competitors in market situations or, as in the public sector, competitors for resources. In either case the first step in such analysis requires the identification of key environmental influences (see section 3.3), and the identification of key competitive forces, which have been discussed above. The main competitors can then be assessed in terms of the extent to which they are well positioned in terms of these forces. This can be done through the sort of *impact analysis* discussed in section 3.3.1 and shown in Figure 3.4. However, to do this, it is necessary to understand the strategic direction of other organisations, which requires an analysis of the elements of strategy for those organisations, similar to that outlined in this book. For example, in order to understand how a given competitor is attempting to cope with the environment it faces, the following questions could usefully be asked:

- What are the *objectives* of the organisation: is it seeking growth, for example; and if so, is it mainly concerned with profit growth, revenue growth or market share?
- What *resource strengths* do competitors have, and what are their weaknesses? The review of resources in Chapter 4 can help here.
- What is the *record of performance* of each competitor? Financial analysis of performance trends (see section 4.3.5) can be helpful here.
- What is the *current strategy* of competitors? Is there evidence of a consistent approach to strategy development: for example, by long-term

concentration on cost reduction, or differentiation; or by market or product development? At the corporate level, has it been an acquisitive firm, or does it prefer to develop new ventures internally? On all these questions Chapter 6 can provide useful guidelines.

- What are the *assumptions* underlying competitors' approach to their strategy development? Chapter 2 argued that organisational paradigms are important. Is it possible to detect what the core beliefs and assumptions are for each competitor? For example, it is quite clear that the subsidiaries in the UK-based GEC hold to the core assumption that financial measures are the main indicators of performance, rather than, for example, market-based measures. For a company like Marks and Spencer, it is clear that quality is of essential importance. In universities in many parts of the world, research is regarded as of paramount importance rather than teaching.

Uncovering these strategic aspects of organisations can help understand how competitors have in the past dealt with the forces identified as important in the competitive and wider environment, and how they are likely to deal with them in the future.

3.5.2 Strategic group analysis

Strategic group analysis can help build on competitor analysis so as to gain an understanding of the *positioning* of an organisation in relation to the strategies of other organisations. It poses the question: who are the most direct competitors, and on what basis is competition likely to take place?

One problem in analysing competition is that the idea of the 'industry' is not always helpful because its boundaries can be unclear and they are not likely to provide a sufficiently precise delineation of competition. For example, Guinness and Albani of Denmark are presumably in the same industry – brewing – but are they competitors? The former is a publicly quoted multinational drinks business; the latter is owned by a foundation and concentrates on a local market in Denmark. And what of Bass or Kronenbourg, both in brewing, but within much more diverse corporate groups? In a given industry there may be many companies, each of which has different interests and competes on a different basis. In analysing the relative positions of organisations there is a need for some intermediate level of understanding between that of the individual firm and that of the industry. One such level is the market segment, and this is taken up in section 3.5.3 below; another is the strategic group.

With strategic group analysis the aim is to identify finely defined groupings so that each represents organisations with similar strategic characteristics, following similar strategies or competing on similar bases. Porter argues that such groups can usually be identified using two, or perhaps three, sets of key characteristics. The sort of characteristics which distinguish between organisations and help to identify strategic groupings are summarised in Figure 3.6.[8] Which of these characteristics are particularly relevant in terms of a given organisation or industry needs to be understood in terms of the history and development of that industry, and identification of the forces at work in the environment, the competitive activities of the firms being studied and so on. The analyst is seeking to establish which characteristics most differentiate firms or groupings of firms from one another.

For example, in Illustration 3.5, diagram (a) shows a strategic group map of the European food manufacturing industry[9] in the 1980s. Here the key characteristics of geographic coverage of Europe and marketing intensity are used, showing clear distinctions between four groupings. A1 are multinational companies operating across the world with strong brands. A3 are national companies with major brands and high levels of marketing support, though for a more limited range than A1 companies. B2 companies operate nationally but are typically not market leaders. C3 are companies specialising in own-label supplies and focusing on low-cost production.

This sort of analysis is useful in three ways:

1. It helps to gain a better understanding of the bases of rivalry within strategic groups; and also how this is different from that within other groups. For

It is useful to consider the extent to which organisations *differ* in terms of **characteristics** such as:

- Extent of **product (or service) diversity**
- Extent of **geographic coverage**
- Number of **market segments served**
- **Distribution channels** used
- Extent (number) of **branding**
- **Marketing effort** (e.g. advertising spread, size of salesforce, etc.)
- Extent of **vertical integration**
- Product of service **quality**
- **Technological leadership** (a leader or follower)
- **R & D capability** (extent of innovation in product or process)
- **Cost position** (e.g. extent of investment in cost reduction)
- **Utilisation of capacity**
- **Pricing policy**
- Level of **gearing**
- **Ownership structure** (separate company or relationship with parent)
- Relationship to **influence groups** (e.g. government, the City)
- **Size** of organisation

Source: Adapted from M. E. Porter, *Competitive Strategy*, Free Press, 1980; and J. McGee and H. Thomas, 'Strategic groups: theory, research and taxonomy', *Strategic Management Journal*, vol. 7, no. 2 (1986), pp. 141–60.

Figure 3.6 Some characteristics for identifying strategic groups

ILLUSTRATION 3.5
Strategic groups and strategic space

Mapping of strategic groups in the food industry can provide insights into the competitive structures of industries, and the opportunities and constraints for development.

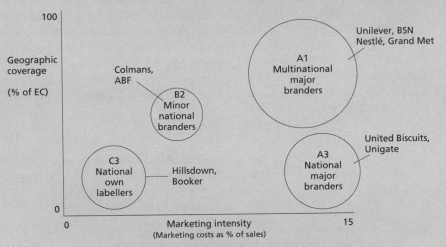

(a) Strategic groups: food industry 1980s

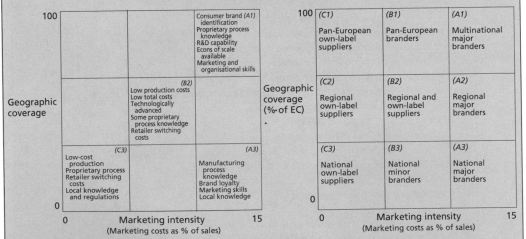

(b) Summary of mobility barriers

(c) Strategic space analysis

Source: Adapted from J. McGee and S. Segal-Horn, 'Strategic space and industry dynamics', *Journal of Marketing Management*, vol. 6, no. 3 (1990).

example, the multinationals compete in terms of marketing (and especially branding), and the control of manufacturing resources across countries. The own-label suppliers are especially concerned with keeping down costs.

2. It raises the question as to how likely or possible it is for an organisation to move from one strategic group to another. Mobility between groups is a matter of considering the extent to which there are barriers to entry between one group and another. In Illustration 3.5, diagram (b) shows the sort of mobility barriers for the groupings identified in the industry. These may to be substantial, particularly for the multinational group, but probably also for the own-label producers; the minor national branders are, perhaps, less secure in their position, being susceptible to both major-brand and low-price competition.

3. Strategic group mapping might also be used to predict market changes or identify strategic opportunities. For example, in illustration 3.5, diagram (c) suggests there are vacant 'spaces' in the European food industry which could provide opportunities for new strategies and new strategic groups. Of course, it is important to ask to what extent any of these spaces provide viable strategic opportunities; but B1 (pan-European branders) could be attractive, for example, since it would permit economies of scale across a market which is developing its logistics network, harmonising legislation and showing signs of converging consumer tastes in some product areas. Indeed, by the 1990s it was becoming clear that Unilever, Nestlé and Mars were beginning to focus on just such a strategy.

3.5.3 Market segments and market power

Strategic groups are defined primarily in terms of the characteristics of organisa-tions. However, strategy is necessarily concerned with an organisation's position with regard to its customers or users, so assessing the *market position* (or *demand position* in the public sector) in relation to other organisations is impor-tant. In doing this, an important issue is the definition of the market.

A rudimentary understanding of marketing tells us that not all users are the same: they have different characteristics and needs, behave differently and so on. Markets are therefore most usefully thought of in terms of market segments; and identifying which organisations are competing in which market segments is, in itself, a valuable exercise.[10]

In undertaking a market segmentation analysis the following should be con-sidered:

1. There are many bases of market segmentation: Figure 3.7 summarises some of these. It is important to consider which bases of segmentation are most important. For example, in industrial markets segmentation is often thought

Type of factor	Consumer markets	Industrial/organisational markets
Characteristics of people/organisations	Age, sex, race Income Family size Life-cycle stage Location Lifestyle	Industry Location Size Technology Profitability Management
Purchase/use situation	Size of purchase Brand loyalty Purpose of use Purchasing behaviour Importance of purchase Choice criteria	Application Importance of purchase Volume Frequency of purchase Purchasing procedure Choice criteria Distribution channel
Users' needs and preferences for product characteristics	Product similarity Price preferences Brand preferences Desired features Quality	Performance requirements Assistance from suppliers Brand preferences Desired features Quality Service requirements

Figure 3.7 Some criteria for market segmentation

of in terms of industrial classification of buyers – 'we sell to the car industry', for example. However, it may be that this is not the most useful basis of segmentation when thinking of strategic development. For example, segmentation according to buyer behaviour or purchase value might be more appropriate in some markets. Indeed, it is often useful to consider different bases of segmentation in the same market to help explain the dynamics of that market and suggest strategic opportunities for development.

2.   It is also important to assess the attractiveness of different market segments. This can be done by applying the principles of structural analysis described in section 3.4 to the market segments being examined. However, because it is the segments that are being examined, it is necessary to conceive of entry and substitution from other market segments. For example, in the late 1980s a software developer was attempting to build market share in the provision of financial control systems to hospitals. The company found that the major competitor in that segment was not another software house, but an IT consultant who had previously concentrated on consultancy services rather

than software development in another market segment. It had become involved in the development of software in that segment and was finding a ready market for its skills and software products in hospitals.

3. When linked to the notion of market power, the value of market segmentation increases further. Relative market share (i.e. a firm's share in relation to its competitors) is a measure of market power. It has been shown[11] that there is an important relationship between market power and performance in commercial organisations. This is not just because of benefits of scale but also because of 'experience curve' effects which are discussed more fully in the next chapter (see section 4.3.2). Given the importance of market power, it is helpful to break down a market according to its segments and to examine market shares within those segments. This may be done in a quantitative way by establishing the size of market segments and competitor shares by segment; or a more qualitative approach may be sensible. In either case, what is needed is a breakdown of the market into the segments which are important from a strategic point of view: for example, because certain segments are more competitive than others; or because some segments are growing and others are not; or because some segments are much bigger than others. Illustration 3.6 shows how an examination of market power by segment might provide insights into strategic positioning.

4. To what extent is it beneficial to concentrate on a narrower, more specialist focus in one or more segments, or to take a broad approach to a market? This issue of *focus* is a key issue relating to strategic choice and forms an important part of the discussion in Chapter 6.

3.5.4 Market share and market growth

One of the most widely used ways of considering the position of a strategic business unit (SBU) in relation to others and in relation to the nature of the market, or the market segment in which it operates, is the *growth/share matrix*.[12] The matrix is centrally concerned with examining SBUs in relation to (a) market (segment) share, and in this sense relative market power; and (b) the growth rate of that market. Market growth rate is important for an SBU seeking to dominate a market because it must normally gain dominance when the market is in the growth stage. In a state of maturity, a market is likely to be stable with customer loyalties fairly fixed; it is therefore more difficult to gain share. But if all competitors in the growth stage are trying to gain market share, competition will be very fierce and only those prepared to invest in order to gain share will achieve dominance. This is likely to mean that an SBU following these principles will need to price low and/or spend high amounts on advertising and selling. Such a strategy is one of high risk unless this low-margin activity is financed by

ILLUSTRATION 3.6
Segments and power in the 'grumpits' market

An analysis of market power by market segment can provide important strategic insights.

The market for grumpits is worth £100 million, and all the companies involved are manufacturing much the same sort of product. If company C thinks of its market in overall terms, then it considers itself to be weak. But suppose the segments shown in the table below are based on different customer types: then company C is strong in one part of the market – segment IV – and this could open strategic possibilities depending on the opportunities and threats in that segment.

Other implications about the competitive environment emerge. Segments I and II are the largest, where the competitive battle is at its most fierce. Companies A and B are concentrating on these segments with company D running behind. Company C specialises in segment IV, which it dominates. But what of segments III and V, which are growing? They account for £25 million and no one is really concentrating on them. Company D with, say, a 25 per cent share of I (£10 million), a 10 per cent share of II (£2.5 million) and a 10 per cent share of III (£1.5 million) has a turnover of £14 million and is probably having to operate at low margins to try to compete in I and II. Is there an opportunity to concentrate on dominating III and V, achieving perhaps a 40 per cent share of each and sales of £10 million at higher margins? Companies A and B, of course, are probably more concerned with retaining their dominance of I and II respectively.

Competitor analysis by market segment

Segment	Size (£m)	Competitor positions			
		A	B	C	D
I	40	Dominant	Weak		No. 2
II	25	No. 2	Dominant		Weak
III	15	Weak		Weak	Weak
IV	10			Dominant specialist	
V	10 (growing)	No one specialising (all weak)			
Total market	100				

higher-profit-earning products. This leads to the idea of a balanced mix of SBUs. The resulting portfolio is shown as Figure 3.8.

● A *star* is an SBU which has a high market share in a growing market. As such, the firm may be spending heavily to gain that share, but experience curve benefits (see section 4.3.2) should mean that costs are reducing over time and hopefully at a faster rate than those of the competition.
● The *question mark* (or problem child) is also in a growing market but does not have a high market share. A company may be spending heavily to increase market share, but it is then unlikely to be achieving sufficient cost reduction benefits to offset such investments.
● The *cash cow* has a high market share in a mature market. Because growth is low and market conditions more stable, the need for heavy marketing investment is less. But high relative market share means that the SBU should be able to maintain unit cost levels below those of competitors. The cash cow should then be a cash provider.
● *Dogs* have low share in static or declining markets and are thus the worst of all combinations. They may be a cash drain and use up a disproportionate amount of company time and resources.

The growth/share matrix is useful in providing a visual display of the strengths of a portfolio, particularly in identifying the balance between SBUs and links to potential cash generators and cash users. In this respect it can also be helpful in guiding the strategic direction of each business (see 7.4.1). However, there are problems in the use and interpretation of the matrix. It is difficult to be

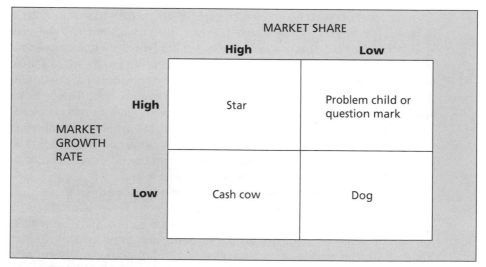

Figure 3.8 The growth/share matrix

exact in the positioning of SBUs: for example, precisely what are high or low market growth rates; or indeed dominant, or less dominant, market shares? Given lack of precise measures, a danger is that managers will position their SBUs in line with internalised and rather wishful thinking. A second danger is that the positioning of the business units will then be taken over – literally, in terms of the implications for strategic action. For example, a 'dog' could be written off without regard for the competitive consequences of pulling out of a market, and therefore handing a more dominant competitor even more market power and the chance of strengthening its own portfolio.

A different problem often arises for managers in public-sector organisations. They may find it difficult to develop 'stars' – that is, services with real growth potential – or to generate surpluses to be reinvested, because this may not be their brief from government. They may be expected to manage the very sorts of service which cannot make money but which are public necessities. Further, if they seek to develop services which can grow and make money, these may be privatised or put out to private tender. For example, it may be seen as legitimate for a local government leisure department to manage public parks and recreation grounds, but the development of squash, indoor tennis and swimming pools with profit potential may be seen as an inappropriate activity. The definition of the appropriate portfolio of activities therefore requires a clarity of strategy in relation to political influence groups and stakeholders (see Chapter 5) as well as an evaluation and careful planning of funding bases (see Chapters 8 and 9).

3.5.5 Market attractiveness and business strength (or directional policy matrix)

Another form of portfolio analysis maps SBUs according to (a) how attractive the industry (or market) is in which they are operating; and (b) the competitive strength of the SBU: this is sometimes called the *Directional policy matrix*.[13] Each business unit is positioned within the matrix according to a series of indicators of attractiveness and strength. The factors typically considered are set out in Figure 3.9. However, these should not be thought of as preordained. The factors included should be those most relevant to the organisation and its market: for example, those identified by the PEST or five forces analysis. Although positioning on this matrix is essentially judgemental, some organisations do use 'scoring' methods to construct the portfolio. Illustration 3.7 shows how the international transport company NFC used this approach in its strategy review in the late 1980s.

The resulting matrix positions the different SBUs of the organisation according to both attractiveness and strength. Some analysts also choose to show graphically how large the market is for a given business unit's activity, and even the market share of that SBU. So the resulting output might look something like Figure 3.10. This matrix provides a useful way of directing managers' attention to key forces in the environment and raises questions about appropriate strategies

Indicators of SBU strength	Indicators of market attractiveness
• Market share • Sales force • Marketing • Customer service • R & D • Manufacturing • Distribution • Financial resources • Image • Breadth of product line • Quality/reliability • Managerial competence	• Market size • Market growth rate • Cyclicality • Competitive structure • Barriers to entry • Industry profitability • Technology • Inflation • Regulation • Workforce availability • Social issues • Environmental issues • Political issues • Legal issues

Figure 3.9 Indicators of SBU strength and market attractiveness

for different business units and the portfolio as a whole (see section 7.4.1). However, it should be borne in mind that its value does depend on information of a comparative nature between competitors being available; and obtaining the depth of information required is not always straightforward. Moreover, it should not necessarily be assumed that markets that appear 'unattractive' are necessarily unprofitable. This will strongly depend on the competitive strength of the firm.

There are other portfolio approaches. These are not reviewed here, but since they can be helpful for other purposes, they are referred to later. Section 4.4.1 refers to such portfolios in considering the balance of an organisation's activities; and in section 7.4.2 the life cycle mapping approach is used as a basis for strategy evaluation.

3.6 Summary

The ability to sense changes in the environment is important because perceived changes in environmental influences signal the possible need for changes in strategy: they throw up opportunities and warn of threats. The evidence is that organisations which are better at sensing the environment perform better than those which are poor at it.[14]

ILLUSTRATION 3.7
NFC's directional policy exercise

NFC, the multinational transport company, used a 'scoring' mechanism to build the directional policy matrix for its different businesses in the late 1980s. The following are extracts from the company's briefing document.

The aim of the Directional Policy Matrix is to assess the overall health and prospects of a corporation's portfolio and to determine the relative position of each product group within that portfolio. The two axes of the matrix are:

 (i) the attractiveness of the industry or *sector prospects* and
(ii) the strength or *competitive position* of the business unit or product.

Sector Prospects

There are four criteria in assessing the prospects for market sectors. Each can be scored, on a scale of 1–5:

i)   *Sector Growth Rate per year*   ii) *Sector Profitability*   Growth Rate

	Growth Rate
12% and over	5
9% to 11%	4
6% to 8%	3
3% to 5%	2
0% to 2%	1

...

iii) *Market Structure*: high scores if answers to these questions are 'yes'.

1) *Power of Suppliers*: is the market supplied by relatively few suppliers?
2) *Power of Buyers*: is the market free from domination by a small group of powerful customers?
3) *Substitute Services*: is the service free from the risk of substitution by alternative services?
4) *Threat of Entry – Barriers to Entry*: is the entry to the sector made more difficult by: (i) the need for particular expertise? (ii) the need for special licences? (iii) a high capital requirement?
5) *Intensity of Rivalry Among Existing Competitors*: is the market 'orderly' without fierce competition between the players?

iv) *Quality Considerations*: high scores if answers to these questions are 'yes'.

1) Does the service have characteristics which make it more difficult for a customer to change supplier?

2) Is the service normally sold on a contractual basis?
3) Is the sector stable and not subject to wide fluctuations in (i) demand and (ii) margins?

Competitive Position

In this section, the aim is to assess the company's own competitive position in the sector; by reference to three main elements:

i) *Market Position*: in terms of relative market share, and the degree to which this share is secured.

5 Leader. A company with 25% of the market in a field of 10 competitors may be so placed. A company with 50% in a field of 2 competitors will not be.
4 Major Producer. No one 'leader', but several competitors so placed.
3 A strong viable stake in the market but below the top league.
2 Minor market share.
1 Current position negligible.

ii) *Resources and Structure*: the capability of the business to supply the services required by the market.

(a) Quality of resources. Has the business the necessary resources to meet the market's requirements in terms of: a) staff resources and quality; b) management resources and quality; c) location, suitability and availability of physical resources; d) IT capability?
(b) Flexibility of response. The speed with which the business is able to respond to market pressures to invest, disinvest or change the service offered.
(c) Synergistic considerations. A market or cost advantage to the business in offering a service alongside another activity so that one may benefit from the existence of the other.

Higher than average ratings apply where the business has used its resources and skills to create a continuing competitive advantage in the market.

iii) *Performance*

The assessment of performance should consider: a) business growth relative to market trends; b) profit record; c) service levels *vis-à-vis* market; d) image in the market place.'

Source: Used with the permission of NFC plc.

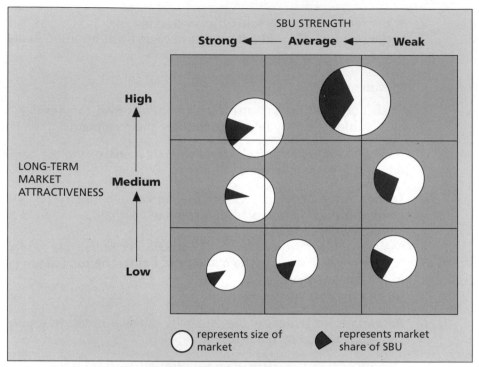

Figure 3.10 Market attractiveness/SBU strength matrix

A major problem is the difficulties managers have in perceiving and internalising external influences – an important theme of Chapter 2 – and their effect on strategy. This chapter has discussed some analytical ways in which this can be done. It began by warning against the analysis degenerating into a trivial listing of the ways in which different forces affect an organisation. The approach here is a structured way of avoiding this, so as to move towards an interpretation, or synthesis, of such forces. The proposed sequence of analysis is as follows:

- Clarifying the nature of the environment in terms of its level of *uncertainty* in order to take an initial view on appropriate ways of undertaking analysis.
- Carrying out an initial *audit* of environmental influences to gain an overall view of the variety of forces at work, but also to identify key forces and significant changes.
- Focusing more specifically on the forces which determine the nature of the competitive environment through *structural analysis*.
- Considering the *positioning* of the organisation in relation to others with which it competes for customers or resources, in order to establish its relative strengths in its market.

All this should help in at least three ways:

- First, it moves the focus of attention from the operational detail of running the organisation to the wider world in which the organisation exists. It should also help sensitize managers to the environment which influences the organisation.
- Second, it should help identify the threats and opportunities the organisation faces, and its relative strengths in facing them. However, a more detailed consideration of resource capabilities is required to do this; and therefore the points in this chapter need to be considered in conjunction with those in Chapter 4 concerned with the analysis of resources. Indeed, at the end of Chapter 4 environmental and resource analysis are brought together in an explanation of SWOT analysis (see section 4.6.1).
- Third, it begins to provide bases for thinking through strategic options. For example, analysis of the forces in the competitive environment, or the positioning of the organisation relative to competition, raises constraints and signals opportunities that feed into a consideration of options discussed in Part III of the book.

However, it is important to stress that techniques of analysis, or the presence of individuals or departments to undertake such analysis, are in themselves no guarantee that organisations will be able to respond to change. The extent to which an organisation will be successful in adapting to changes in its environment will depend on the sensitivity and flexibility of the people in that organisation, and their ability to effect change. This will, of course, be affected by the quality of its management, its organisational culture and its structure, the subject of later chapters in the book.

References

1. R. Duncan's research, on which this classification is based, can be found in 'Characteristics of organisational environments and perceived environmental uncertainty', *Administrative Science Quarterly*, vol. 7, no. 3, (1972), pp. 313–27.
2. See, for example, the discussion of the implications of chaos theory on management by Ralph Stacey in *The Chaos Frontier*, Butterworth Heinemann, 1991 and *Managing Chaos*, Kogan Page, 1992.
3. There are books which do review environmental influences on organisations: for example, M. Glew, M. Watts and R. Wells, *The Business Organisation and Its Environment* (books 1 and 2), Heinemann Educational, 1979; and L. Fahey and V. K. Narayanan, *Macroenvironmental Analyses for Strategic Management*, West Publishing, 1986.
4. The forces for globalisation here are based on C. K. Prahalad and W. L. Doz, *The Multi-National Mission: Balancing Local Demands and Global Vision*, Free Press, 1987; and C. A. Bartlett and S. Ghoshal, *Managing Across Borders*, Hutchinson Business Books, 1990.
5. See S. P. Schnaars, 'How to develop and use scenarios', in R. G. Dyson (ed.), *Strategic Planning: Models and analytical tech-*

niques, Wiley, 1990. Also the Shell approach to scenario planning has been well written up: for example, in Pierre Wack, 'Scenarios: shooting the rapids', *Harvard Business Review*, vol. 63, no. 6, (1985), pp. 139–50.

6. See M. E. Porter, *Competitive Strategy: Techniques for analysing industries and competitors*, Free Press, 1980.

7. Porter (see reference 6) discusses competitor analysis in chapter 3 of *Competitive Strategy*.

8. The characteristics listed in Figure 3.6 are based on those discussed by Porter, (reference 6) and by J. McGee and H. Thomas, 'Strategic groups: theory, research and taxonomy', *Strategic Management Journal*, vol. 7, no. 2, (1986), pp. 141–60. This paper also provides a useful background to strategic group analyses.

9. This discussion on strategic group mapping and strategic space is based on the paper by J. McGee and S. Segal-Horn, 'Strategic space and industry dynamics', *Journal of Marketing Management*, vol. 6, no. 3, (1990), pp. 175–94.

10. A useful discussion of segmentation in relation to competitive strategy is provided by Michael Porter in chapter 7 of *Competitive Advantage*, Free Press, 1985. See also the discussion on market segmentation in P. Kotler, *Marketing Management* (6th edn), Prentice Hall, 1988.

11. A useful discussion of the relationship between market share and business performance is to be found in R. D. Buzzell and B. T. Gale, *The PIMS Principles: Linking strategy to performance*, Free Press, 1987, especially chapter 5.

12. For further information on the growth/share matrix, see B. Hedley, 'Strategy and the business portfolio', *Long Range Planning*, vol. 10, no. 1, (1977), pp. 9–15, and A. Hax and N. Majluf, 'The use of the growth–share matrix in strategic planning', in R. G. Dyson (ed.), *Strategic Planning: Models and analytical techniques*, Wiley, 1990.

13. See A. Hax and N. Majluf, 'The use of the industry attractiveness–business strength matrix in strategic planning', in R. G. Dyson (ed.), *Strategic Planning: Models and analytical techniques*, Wiley, 1990.

14. D. Norburn's work supports this and is summarised in 'Directors without direction', *Journal of General Management*, vol. 1, no. 2, (1974), pp. 37–48. See also D. Miller and P. Friesen, 'Strategy making in context: ten empirical archetypes', *Journal of Management Studies*, vol. 14, no. 3, (1977), pp. 253–80, and A. Pettigrew and R. Whipp, *Managing Change for Competitive Success*, Basil Blackwell, 1991.

Recommended key readings

L. Fahey and V. K. Narayanan, *Macro-environmental Analyses for Strategic Management*, West Publishing, 1986, is a sound and structured approach to analysing the strategic effects of environmental influences on organisations.

M. E. Porter, *Competitive Strategy: Techniques for analysing industries and competitors*, Free Press, 1980, is essential reading for those who are faced with the structural analysis of an organisational environment.

The book of readings edited by R. Dyson, *Strategic Planning: Models and analytical techniques*, Wiley, 1990, contains useful readings on scenario planning and different forms of portfolio analysis.

As an antidote to analytical approaches to understanding the environment see R. Stacey, *Managing Chaos*, Kogan Page, 1992.

Work assignments

In the assignments which follow the analysis of an industry is normally required. This could be the European Brewing Industry,* the World Automobile Industry,* an industry of your choice, or a section in public services.

3.1   Using Illustration 3.1 or Figure 3.3 as a guide, undertake an audit of an industry environment. What are the key environmental influences on firms in that industry? What are the main drivers of change?

3.2   Drawing on section 3.4, carry out a structural analysis of an industry. What are the key competitive forces at work in that industry? Are there any changes that might occur which would significantly affect bases of competition in the industry?

3.3   **Compare two industries in terms of the key environmental influences and competitive forces in them. Assess and compare the entry barriers, and competitive rivalry in the two industries.**

3.4   **Building on assignments 1 and 2, identify the main changes likely in an industry. Following the guidelines in section 3.3.2 and Illustration 3.2, construct scenarios for the industry for an appropriate time period.**

3.5   **Within an industry undertake a competitor analysis, identifying the important differences in the strategic characteristics of organisations. Also assess the extent to which the environmental influences and competitive forces identified in assignments 1 and 2 will have a differential impact on these organisations (see Figure 3.4).**

3.6   **Building on section 3.5.2 and Illustration 3.5:**
      (a) Identify the strategic characteristics which most distinguish organisations in an industry. Construct one or more strategic group maps on these bases.
      (b) Assess the extent to which mobility between strategic groups is possible. (If you have constructed more than one map for the industry, do the mobility barriers you identify differ between them? What does this signify?)
      (c) Identify any vacant strategic spaces in the maps. Do any represent viable strategic positions? What would be the characteristics of an organisation competing in such a space?

3.7   **Using both the growth/share matrix and the directional policy matrix, undertake an analysis of the relative competitive position of the SBUs within a firm. Assess the value of the two matrices.**

3.8   *Using the tools of analysis in this chapter, write a report for an organisation (e.g. Peugeot,* Kronenbourg* or Courage*) which assesses their industry environment and their competitive position within it.*

3.9 *Discuss, and show with examples, the extent to which techniques in this chapter are relevant to analyses of the environment of public-sector organisations.*

3.10 *In a highly complex, dynamic environment, which analytic approaches might be more or less useful? What other aspects of strategic management described in other chapters would be especially important?*

* This refers to a case study in the Text and Cases version of this book.

CHAPTER 4

Analysing resources and strategic capability

4.1 Introduction

The previous chapter has emphasised the importance of matching the organisation's strategies to the environment within which the organisation is operating. However, any organisation must pursue strategies which it is capable of sustaining. This chapter is concerned with understanding an organisation's *strategic capability*, and ways in which resource analysis can contribute to this understanding.

Some authors[1] have suggested that traditional methods of strategic analysis have overemphasised the environment as the lead-edge of strategy formulation. They have argued that in many circumstances *resource-based* strategies would provide a better focus for strategy formulation. This requires a good understanding of the strategic capability of the organisation. This chapter discusses how resource analysis can contribute to understanding an organisation's strategic capability. This will require an assessment of the *core competences* which have been built up through the delivery of the organisation's old strategies. It is likely that managers will favour new strategies which exploit these core competences in preference to strategies which a market-led analysis might suggest. There is, of course, a danger of *strategic drift* in this approach (as discussed in Chapter 2). The *resource management systems* and the *resource heritage* of the organisation will reinforce this tendency, since they are geared to the management of resources for their current purpose: for example, its plants are located in particular places, its communication systems have been set up in certain ways, etc. So strategy formulation is not occurring in a greenfield site situation. The danger is that these resource considerations are allowed to overshadow factors in the environment or the expectations of stakeholders. Good strategic management should pay proper attention to each of these 'pressures'.

In order to understand strategic capability it will be necessary to consider organisations at various levels of detail. There are broad issues of capability which are relevant to the organisation as a whole. These are largely concerned with the *overall balance* of resources and mix of activities. There are also assessments to be made of the quantity and quality of each *key resource area*, such as buildings, machines and people. However, a major theme of this chapter is that the capability of any organisation is fundamentally determined by the separate

ILLUSTRATION 4.1
Competitive advantage through resources

British Airways and Guinness have built competitive advantage by exploiting a key resource.

British Airways and information technology

In 1991 British Airways was spending the equivalent of two jumbo jets per annum – £150m – on information technology. Although the core business activity of British Airways was flying passengers around the world, doing this profitably and maintaining excellence of service was highly dependent on the management of information. To help sell seats BA used one of the largest computers outside the defence industry. The system could extract data from anywhere in the BA network in two seconds. The airline could link seat availability to the currency a passenger used – limiting availability for those paying in weaker currencies. Indeed, maximising the profit from each seat – yield management – became a critical task. This included sophisticated management of overbooking to ensure that the majority of passengers would not be upset – or that those who were would be handsomely compensated. The chairman of the company regarded IT as an inseparable part of the business operations and a key strategic tool for competitive – and profitable – performance.

activities which it undertakes in designing, producing, marketing, delivering and supporting its products or services. It is an understanding of these various *value activities* and the *linkages* between them which is crucial when assessing strategic capability. This will normally be assessed *relative* to competitors or other providers.

The concern about an organisation's resource profile is not confined to strategic analysis. It should be a key determinant during strategic choice, helping to identify directions which best match the organisation's strategic capabilities. Detailed resource planning and deployment are also important ingredients in the successful implementation of strategies. These two further aspects of resources will be discussed in Chapters 8 and 9 respectively. Illustration 4.1 shows the importance of various resources in company performance.

An organisation's resources are not confined to those which it 'owns'. Strategic capability is strongly influenced by resources outside the organisation which are an integral part of the chain of activities between the product or service design, through production and marketing to the use of the product or service by consumers. Section 4.3 will introduce this important concept of the *value system* and the way in which it relates resources to strategic capability and the competitive performance of an organisation.

Guinness and international brands

When Anthony Tennant took over as chairman of Guinness in 1987 he inherited a range of spirits (Johnnie Walker, Dewars, Gordon's, Pimms and others) which had been undermarketed, underpriced and overproduced. They had been viewed by the previous owners – Distillers – as volume products.

Tennant set about redefining the company's strategy around the exploitation of the brand names which were internationally famous. This required some critical changes in how the value chain activities were planned to gain a clearer positioning of each brand in the various segments of the spirits market. First, the company reorganised its international distribution – concentrating on Guinness-owned distributors to ensure control and consistency of marketing. They also reduced the number of brands available in each market and concentrated efforts on building up brand image and awareness. This allowed brand extensions to be introduced in certain markets – such as Johnnie Walker Premier in the Far East, where expensive European brands were important – particularly to Japanese businessmen. The success of the international strategy showed in the Distillers profits, which grew by 87 per cent between 1987 and 1990 and even held up through the Gulf War and recession of early 1991.

Sources: *Financial Times*, 8 January 1991; *Sunday Times Business World*, 1991.

Before reviewing methods which can be used to analyse an organisation's resource position, it is necessary to understand how the various analyses will contribute to the overall assessment of strategic capability. Figure 4.1 provides a systematic way to move from a simple audit of resources to a deeper understanding of strategic capability.

- *The resource audit.* This identifies the resources 'available' to an organisation in supporting its strategies. It will be seen that some of these resources will reside outside the organisation. Both the quantity and quality of resources needs to be audited.
- *Value chain analysis.* This is a useful method of relating resources to the strategic purposes for which these resources are to be used. It is the key to understanding strategic capability, since it requires an analysis which goes beyond a resource *audit* and looks in detail at how resources are being *utilised, controlled and linked together.* Usually the reasons for good or poor performance are found here rather than in the resources *per se.*
- *Comparison.* Strategic capability is often difficult to assess in absolute terms. Indeed, if the concern is with competitive advantage or value for money, these are likely to be assessed in relative terms. The two most

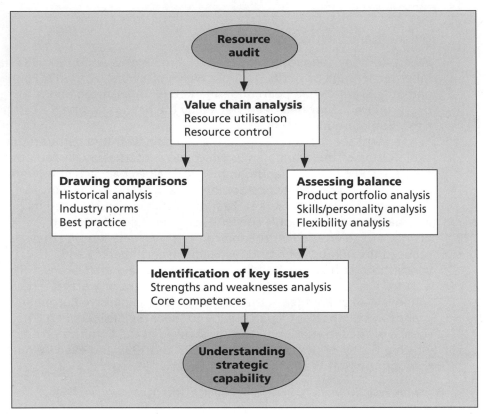

Figure 4.1 Analysing strategic capability

frequently used comparisons are *historical* – improvement or decline over time – or *industry norms* – comparison with the performance of similar organisations. A third basis of comparison is now in common use: namely, comparison with *best practice*, including comparisons beyond the industry.

● *Balance.* Very often an organisation's strategic capability is impaired, not because of problems with individual activities or resources but because the balance of these resources is inappropriate. For example, there may be too many new products, resulting in cash flow problems, or a board of directors all with experience which is too similar.

● *Identification of key issues.* Resource analysis can often prove difficult or fruitless if attempts are made to list the key issues (such as *strengths and weaknesses*) before some of these other analyses have been undertaken. This identification of key issues is critical and is best undertaken as a means of summarising the key strategic insights which have emerged from the other analyses.

4.2 Resource audit[2]

The resource audit can be a useful starting point in understanding strategic capability. It attempts to assess the inherent strength of the resource base – the quantity of resources available and the nature of those resources. Typically, these can be grouped under the following four headings:

- *Physical resources.* An assessment of a company's physical resources should stretch beyond a mere listing of the number of machines or the production capacity, and should ask questions about the nature of these resources such as the age, condition, capability and location of each resource.
- *Human resources.* The analysis of human resources should examine a number of questions. An assessment of the number and types of different skills within an organisation is clearly important, but other factors such as the adaptability of human resources must not be overlooked.
- *Financial resources.* This should include the sources and uses of money, such as obtaining capital, managing cash, the control of debtors and creditors, and the management of relationships with suppliers of money (shareholders, bankers, etc.).
- *Intangibles.*[3] One mistake which can be made in a resource analysis is to overlook the importance of intangible resources. There should be no doubt that these intangibles have a value, since when businesses are sold part of their value is 'goodwill'. In some service-based businesses in particular, such as professional services, retail shops or the catering industry, goodwill could represent the major asset of the company and may result from brand names, good contacts, company image or many other sources.

If the resource audit is to be useful as a basis for further analyses, two important points need to be borne in mind:

- The audit should include all resources which the organisation can *access* to support its strategies, and should not be narrowly confined to the resources which it owns in a legal sense. Many strategically important resources are outside the organisation's ownership, such as its network of contacts or customers.
- Although later analyses will be needed to establish the links between resources and strategic capability, some initial considerations can be made while drawing up the resource audit. The audit needs to be comprehensive, but it is helpful to identify the resources which are critical in underpinning the organisation's distinctive capabilities – in contrast to those which are necessary, but which are not the basis of the organisation's distinctiveness. Illustration 4.1 shows the importance of this link to competitive advantage in the cases of Guinness and British Airways.

4.3 Value chain analysis[4]

The first step in moving from a resource audit to an understanding of strategic capability is to find a way of relating an organisation's resource profile to its strategic performance: that is, to identify how the *activities* of the organisation underpin its competitive advantage. *Value chain analysis* has been widely adopted as a method of achieving such an understanding. Value analysis[5] was originally introduced as an accounting analysis to shed light on the 'profitability' of separate steps in complex manufacturing processes, in order to determine where cost improvements could be made and/or value creation improved. These two basic step, identifying *building blocks* and assessing the *value added* from each, were linked to an analysis of an organisation's competitive advantage by Michael Porter. He argued that an understanding of strategic capability must start with an identification of these separate *value activities*.

Figure 4.2 is a schematic representation of the value chain. The *primary activities* of the organisation are grouped into five main areas: inbound logistics, operations, outbound logistics, marketing and sales, and service.

- *Inbound logistics* are the activities concerned with receiving, storing and distributing the inputs to the product/service. These include materials handling, stock control, transport, etc.
- *Operations* transform these various inputs into the final product or service: for example, machining, packaging, assembly, testing, etc.
- *Outbound logistics* collect, store and distribute the product to customers. For tangible products this would involve warehousing, materials handling, transport, etc.; in the case of services it may be more concerned with arrangements for bringing customers to the service if it is in a fixed location (e.g. sports events).
- *Marketing and sales* provide the means whereby consumers/users are made aware of the product/service and are able to purchase it. This would include sales administration, advertising, selling, etc. In public services, communication networks which help users access a particular service are often important. For example, this became one key role for Passenger Transport Executive bodies following the deregulation of buses in the UK in 1986.
- *Service* covers all those activities which enhance or maintain the value of a product/service, such as installation, repair, training, spares, etc.

Each of these groups of primary activities is linked to support activities. These can be divided into four areas:

- *Procurement.* This refers to the process for acquiring the various resource inputs to the primary activities (not to the resources themselves). As such, it occurs in many parts of the organisation.

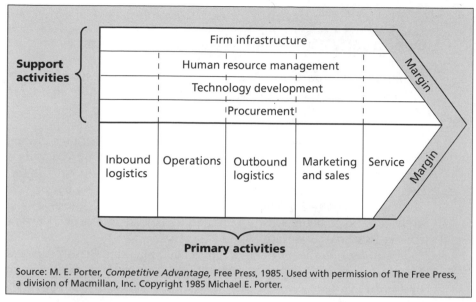

Figure 4.2 The value chain

- *Technology development.* All value activities have a 'technology', even if it is simply 'know-how'. The key technologies may be concerned directly with the product (e.g. R & D product design) or with processes (e.g. process development) or with a particular resource (e.g. raw materials improvements).
- *Human resource management.* This is a particularly important area which transcends all primary activities. It is concerned with those activities involved in recruiting, training, developing and rewarding people within the organisation. Illustration 4.2 shows that many organisations are looking at this issue more strategically in relation to women in management.
- *Infrastructure.* The systems of planning, finance, quality control, etc. are crucially important to an organisation's strategic capability in all primary activities. Infrastructure also consists of the structures and routines of the organisation which sustain its culture.

One of the key features of most industries is that very rarely does a single organisation undertake all of the value activities from the product design through to distribution to the final consumer. There is usually specialisation of role and any one organisation is part of the wider *value system* which creates a product or service (see Figure 4.3). In understanding how value is created it is not sufficient to look at the organisation's internal position alone. Much of the value creation will occur in the supply and distribution chains, and this *whole process* needs to be analysed and understood. For example, the quality of a motor car when it reaches the final purchaser is not only influenced by the activi-

ILLUSTRATION 4.2
Opportunity 2000: women into management

Sometimes an organisation's performance may improve only if attention is paid to one of the critical support activities in the value chain: for example, human resource development.

In a blaze of publicity in late 1991 a cross-section of Britain's influential employers publicly declared a commitment to improve the quality and increase the quantity of jobs for women in their workforce. They set themselves specific targets and pledged to achieve them by the year 2000. *Opportunity 2000* declared the pressing need to improve skills at all levels and to avoid wasting the abilities of women especially at the top levels of management.

Founder members of Opportunity 2000 included British Airways, ICI, Sainsbury, Midland Bank and the BBC. Apart from the social injustice of neglecting women's interests, organisations supporting the movement were aware that business and other organisations cannot be making best use of existing talent, let alone anticipating future trends, unless they are able to attract, and retain, more female employees. Peter Davies, the chairman of Reed International, commented: 'In business we ignore at our peril the potential women have to offer. It is a matter of common sense that we should not throw away the investment we have made in their development.'

The idea was not to impose positive discrimination from on high, but to share ideas on goals and practical plans for action. It was also hoped to foster a spirit of competition among participating companies – but precisely how their aims were to be achieved was left to them. Some, like the BBC, set quantitative targets of 40 per cent middle management and 30 per cent senior posts to be women by 1996. Others, such as Sainsbury, already had a majority of female employees but pledged to spur talented women to climb the management ladder. British Airways' goals included that women managers in the airline's UK workforce reflect the proportion of women currently in full-time employment (20 per cent in 1991, forecast to be 27 per cent by the year 2000). Finally, it was recognised that, if significant changes were to be achieved in this important area of human resource development, implementation had to be accompanied by the key ingredients needed for any significant cultural change: namely, commitment at board level, widespread training and education, substantial resources and prompt feedback on results achieved.

Source: British Airways, *Business Life*, February 1992.

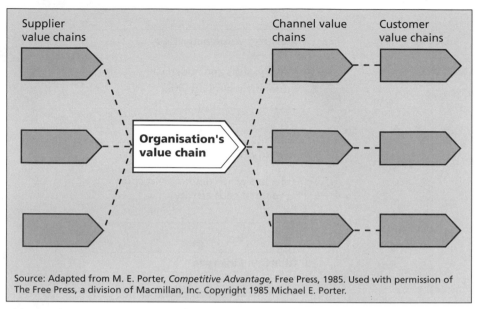

Source: Adapted from M. E. Porter, *Competitive Advantage*, Free Press, 1985. Used with permission of The Free Press, a division of Macmillan, Inc. Copyright 1985 Michael E. Porter.

Figure 4.3 The value system

ties which are undertaken within the manufacturing company itself. It is also determined by the quality of the components and the performance of the distributors.

4.3.1 Resource utilisation

One of the key aspects of value chain analysis is the recognition that organisations are much more than a random collection of machines, money and people. These resources are of no value unless organised into routines and systems which ensure that products or services are produced which are valued by the final consumer/user. In other words, it is value activities and linkages between them which are the source of competitive advantage for organisations. A resource analysis must therefore proceed beyond an audit of resources to an assessment of how those resources have been *utilised*.

Figure 4.4 shows how an analysis of resource utilisation can be undertaken and linked to competitive advantage:

- The organisation can be disaggregated into the various *value activities* which underpin the production and delivery of its products or services. These should include the value activities in the supply and distribution chains (Figure 4.3).
- Although all of these activities are necessary to the organisation's successful

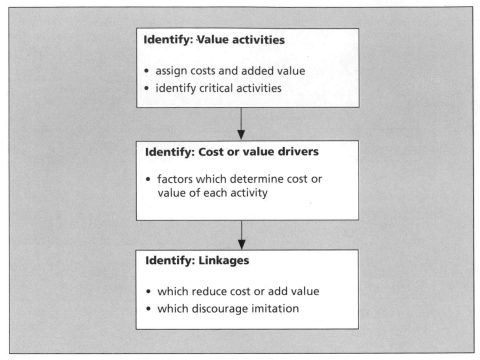

Figure 4.4 Resource utilisation and competitive advantage

operation, it is important to identify those value activities which critically underpin the organisation's competitive position. So, for one organisation the low price of its products to the final consumer may be underpinned by the low-cost supply of components and the low mark-up in the distributor organisations. Illustration 4.3 shows how an understanding of the resource issues underpinning competitive advantage can be crucial. It is strengthening and building on the key value activities which is likely to achieve success. For example, much of Black and Decker's success is built around the manufacturing of electric motors and consumer franchising. Brother, who originally manufactured sewing machines, built on the key activities of electrical and electronic assembly to create a leading position in the computer printer market. It will be seen in Chapter 9 (Figure 9.7) that in planning implementation of strategies a detailed resource analysis related to this issue of *critical success factors* can also be helpful.

● The concept of value must be assessed from the viewpoint of the final consumer or user of the product of service. This is often not done by organisations for several reasons. First, many manufacturers may be distanced from the final users by several intermediaries – other manufacturers and distributors. Although it is important to recognise the role of intermediaries, there is a danger that an understanding of value is therefore filtered through or interpreted by these other parties rather than assessed directly from the final consumer. In other words, many manufacturers are out of touch with the realities of their markets. Second, in service organisations value is often conceived of by the professional employees and not tested out with customers or clients. This is an important criticism of many public-service organisations. Third, consumers' concept of value changes over time – either because they become more experienced (through repeat purchase) or because competitive offerings become available which offer better value for money. So value is a relative rather than an absolute measure.

- The next step is to identify those factors which *sustain* the competitive position through each of these critical factors. These are called the *cost-drivers* or *value-driver*s. For example, the low-cost supply situation might be related to the physical proximity of the suppliers and could therefore disappear with any geographical expansion.

- Competitive advantage is likely to be sustained by the linkages which have been made between value activities and also within the wider value system of suppliers, channels or customers. It is the planning of these linkages which can either provide distinctive cost advantages or become the basis on which the organisation's product/services are differentiated from other offerings. Whereas competitors can often imitate the separate activities of an organisation, it is more difficult to copy linkages within and between value chains, as will be discussed in Chapter 6. In understanding the strategic capability of an organisation, the strategic importance of the following types of linkage should be analysed in order to assess how they contribute to cost reduction or value added.

- There may be important links between the *primary activities*. In particular, choices will have been made about these relationships and how they influence value creation and strategic capability. For example, a decision to hold high levels of finished stock might ease production scheduling problems and provide for a faster response time to the customer. However, it will probably add to the overall cost of operations. An assessment needs to be made as to whether the added value of stocking is greater than the added cost. *Specialisation* of role tends to occur in most organisations – often around the primary activities identified in Figure 4.2. This specialisation can militate against the creation of value if the primary activities are not well linked and working towards a common end. It is easy to miss this point in an analysis if, for example, the marketing activities and operations are assessed separately. The operations may look good because they are geared to high-volume, low-variety, low-unit-cost production. However, at the same time the marketing team may be selling speed, flexibility and variety to the customers. These two potential strengths when put together are a weakness as they are not in harmony, which is what a value chain requires.

- The link between a *primary activity* and a *support activity* may be the

ILLUSTRATION 4.3
Companiex

An important starting point in strategic analysis can be an understanding of a company's resources relative to those of its competition. It is a company's relative position in all the activities in which it competes, not just its market or product position, which will determine its success.

In 1990 Companiex manufactured small domestic appliances: hand-held mixers, electric knives and electric pencil sharpeners. The market for hand-held mixers was mature and the company had a strong market position. Traditional strategic analysis would suggest that such a business should be harvested for cash. In electric slicing knives, the market was also mature, but no company's market position was weak. Traditional strategic analysis would suggest that such a business should be de-emphasised ... or even liquidated. In electric pencil sharpeners, the company's market position was strong and the market growth was high; it should be invested in to hold share and to consolidate the strong market position. Such an analysis seemed intuitively appealing, and had gained considerable influence in the company's strategic thinking.

However, the position looked different if the activities which were involved in producing and selling these products were analysed. Many of the products shared similar *activities*, as seen in the diagram opposite. Mixers and slicing knives shared components, housing, motors, assembly and distribution. Pencil sharpeners shared motors and assembly, but little else.

Comparing the company's *activity* position with its market position is useful. The company was very strong at assembly, at manufacturing electric motors, and in metal housings. This suggested that it had correctly identified its position in mixers, because in each of the activities which added cost and value to this product the company was very strong. However, it was entirely wrong to characterise the slicing knives market as one which should be de-emphasised. On the basis of its activity strengths, this product should have generated high profits and should have been expanded. Finally, it was not true that the company would have a strong position in pencil sharpeners. In fact, its weakness in plastic housing was likely to prove to be an Achilles' heel – the company's relative weakness in the activity was likely to increase because the use of plastic housings was growing faster than the market for pencil sharpeners. As a result, the company would lose share on an activity basis.

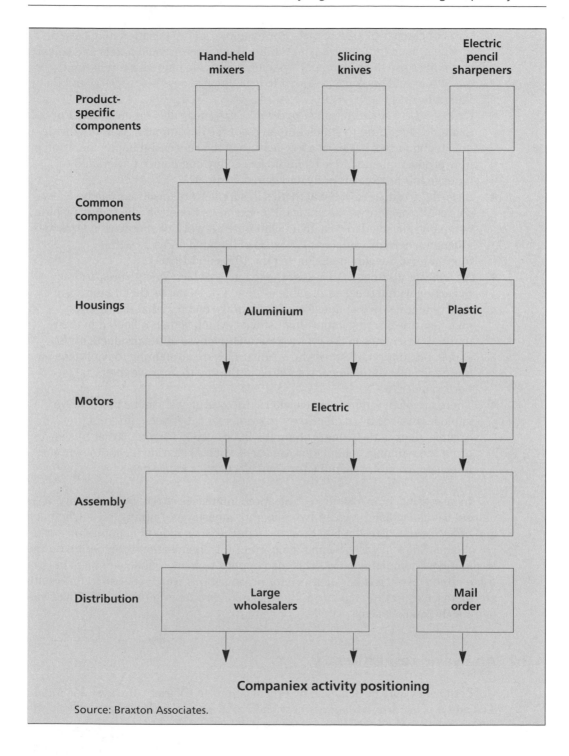

Product-specific components

Hand-held mixers

Slicing knives

Electric pencil sharpeners

Common components

Housings
Aluminium

Plastic

Motors
Electric

Assembly

Distribution
Large wholesalers

Mail order

Companiex activity positioning

Source: Braxton Associates.

basis of competitive advantage. For example, an organisation may have a unique system for procuring materials. Many international hotels and travel companies use their computer systems to provide immediate 'real-time' quotations and bookings worldwide from local access points (as seen in Illustration 4.1).

● Linkages between different *support activities* may also create value. For example, the extent to which human resource development is in tune with new technologies has been a key feature in the successful implementation of new production and office technologies. Many companies have failed to manage this linkage properly and gain advantage.

● *External linkages* to value activities in supplier organisations can be a key source of competitive advantage. For example, Benetton, the Italian fashion company, managed to sustain an elaborate network of suppliers, agents and independent retail outlets as the basis of its rapid and successful international developments during the 1970s and 1980s.

● An analysis also needs to assess the extent to which *suboptimisation* is occurring within the overall value system. For example, the organisation may reduce its own in-house costs of storage and find that distribution channels are carrying unduly high stocks, which is then reflected in their mark-up and hence in the relative competitiveness of the products in the shops. Illustration 4.4 shows how Amstrad were attempting to capitalise on harmonisation of technical standards in Europe to improve their performance.

● There are often circumstances where the overall cost can be reduced (or value increased) by *collaborative arrangements* between different organisations in the value system. It will be seen in Chapter 6 that this is often the rationale behind joint ventures, such as sharing technology in the international motor manufacture and electronics industries.

In assessing how resource utilisation influences strategic capability it is helpful to distinguish between two separate measures of utilisation – *efficiency* and *effectiveness*. These relate directly to discussions in later chapters on strategic choice. Efficiency is especially important for organisations competing on the basis of cost competitiveness. This also applies to many public services. In contrast, effectiveness is a key measure for organisations which choose to differentiate themselves from competitors by sustaining products/services which are valued for their uniqueness.

4.3.2 Analysing cost efficiency

Cost efficiency may be achieved by organisations in a variety of ways (see Figure 4.5) and it is important to assess how each of these potential sources of cost efficiency relate to the *cost-drivers* discussed above.

ILLUSTRATION 4.4
Amstrad and the single European market for telecommunications/computing equipment

The acceptance of common technical and product standards often requires companies to reconfigure the management of their value chain.

Historically, computer companies wishing to market in Europe had to produce country-specific products. What was acceptable to the French could not be sold in Germany and so on. The result was that companies like Amstrad – the UK-based consumer electronics company – were denied the flexibility which they required to become a genuinely European operator. An economic slowdown in Italy, for instance, meant that a product delivered in Milan had to be shipped back to the UK and reworked to meet the technical requirements of the German market. However, with growing acceptance of European standards Amstrad was changing its approach. From a central warehouse in Rotterdam it could ship a standard computer system in one box, a monitor in another and the only country-specific items – the keyboard and foreign language manual – in a third box. Each subsidiary could draw from this central stock as and when required for its local market.

This allowed the company considerable advantages in reducing the risk of unwanted stock in its various local warehouses, and hence in controlling costs. However, by 1991 the advances which had been made in the computing field had not been matched in the facsimile (fax) market. Amstrad had gained a substantial share of the UK market, but attempts to gain penetration of other European markets had met a barrage of technical objections – many of which were not even related to published national standards. So the removal of these barriers was seen as critical to creating genuine competition within Europe – on a truly `level playing field' – and to enabling Amstrad to exploit its skills in marketing.

Source: *Single Market News*, DTI, Summer 1991.

1. *Economies of scale* are traditionally an important source of cost advantage in manufacturing organisations, since the high capital costs of plant need to be recovered over a high volume of output. In other industries, similar economies are sought in distribution or marketing costs.

2. *Supply costs* clearly influence an organisation's overall cost position and are of most importance to organisations which act as intermediaries, where the added value through their own activities is low and so the need to identify and manage input costs is critically important to success. Trading

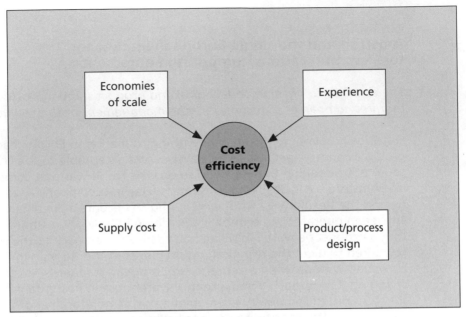

Figure 4.5 Sources of cost efficiency

organisations sustain their competitive advantage in this way. The way in which supplier relationships are controlled is of major importance in sustaining this position and will be discussed in section 4.3.4 below.

3. *Product process design* also influences the cost position. Assessments of efficiency in production processes has been undertaken by many organisations over a number of years through the monitoring of *capacity fill, labour productivity, yield* (from materials) or *working capital* utilisation. The important issue is to analyse which of these are the cost-drivers underpinning the competitive advantage of the organisation.

   In contrast there has been much less attention paid to how product design may contribute to the overall cost competitiveness of the company. Where it has been undertaken it has tended to be limited to the production processes, e.g. ease of manufacture. However, product design will also influence costs in other parts of the value system – for example, in distribution or after-sales service.

4. *Experience*[6] is a key source of cost advantage. The work of the Boston Consulting Group (BCG) established important relationships between the cumulative experience gained by an organisation and its unit costs – this is described as the *experience curve*. The premise of the BCG findings is that, in any market segment of an industry, price levels tend to be very similar for similar products. Therefore what makes one company more profitable than

the next must be the level of its costs. The *experience curve* suggests that an organisation undertaking any tasks learns to do them better over time. Therefore, cost is also a function of market share. Hence the importance of gaining and holding market share, referred to as *market power* in Chapter 3.

It is the *relative market share* in definable market segments which matters. In highly fragmented industries it is quite possible to operate profitably without dominating a segment. The objective is to have more experience than anyone else in that segment, as will be seen in Chapter 6.

There are two important implications of the experience curve work which should influence organisations' thinking about their strategic position:

- Growth is not optional in many markets. If an organisation chooses to grow more slowly than the competition, it should expect the competitors to gain cost advantage in the longer term – through experience. The Japan car manufacturers are an example of this phenomenon occurring on an international scale from the 1970s onwards.
- Organisations should *expect* their real unit costs to decline year on year. In high-growth industries this will happen quickly, but even in mature industries this decline in costs should occur. Organisations which fail to recognise and respond to this are likely to suffer fierce competition. One of the criticisms of public services is that their quasi-monopoly status has tended to shield them from the pressures to push down unit costs and provide better value for money.

When analysing the strategic importance of experience the following factors must be borne in mind:

- There is often some collective learning/experience *across* firms in the same industry (say, when a new production technology is introduced). This blurs the simple model of BCG.
- Learning from experience is not the only determinant of cost. Other factors such as technology and relative labour and energy costs also affect cost. Indeed, if experience were the only driver of cost then the most experienced company would be able to sustain a competitive advantage through cost indefinitely. This does not happen.
- The analysis of experience should be applied to *parts* of the value chain. This explains how inexperienced operators can gain a better cost position than the market leader through changes in the way the product is designed, produced or distributed. The analysis of experience should be applied to *value activities* and not products. For example, a retail organisation may gain cost advantage in terms of its stocking and purchasing costs through the introduction of electronic point of sale (EPOS) systems. They may not be more experienced overall than their main competitive rivals, but they gain advantage through the rapid learning and experience related to these particular value activities.

4.3.3 Analysing effectiveness

The assessment of effectiveness is essentially related to how well the organisation is matching its products/services to the identified needs of its chosen client groups, and the factors which underpin this effectiveness. Unlike cost analysis, the potential sources of value added or effectiveness are likely to be many and varied. Therefore this section will concentrate on how the critical factors for effectiveness can be established in any particular situation. Figure 4.6 summarises the key issues, and the value chain can be used as a framework to assess the following:

● How well matched are the product or service features to the requirements of clients? More importantly, is the added cost of providing unique features more than recovered through the value which clients place on this uniqueness (through better prices or improved budget allocation)?
● Are the services which support the product matched with client expectations, and, again, do these represent perceived value? This would apply to delivery, technical back-up, credit, etc.
● Are the systems for communicating with clients before, during and after purchase adding value to the relationship? This would apply to issues such as brand name, corporate image, marketing literature and technical information.

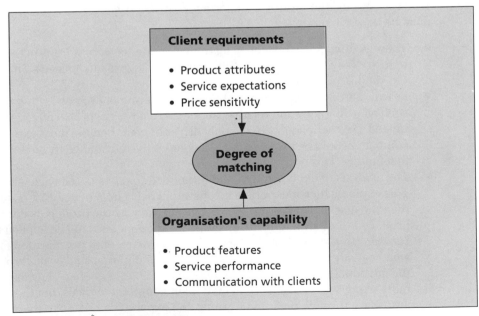

Figure 4.6 Assessing effectiveness

Readers are reminded that this effectiveness evaluation is most important to apply to the activities which critically underpin competitive strategy, and should be a means of clearly establishing the *value-drivers* for each of these activities. For example, if product durability is the major source of competitive advantage, this could be underpinned by sourcing of components, product design and maintenance regimes in use. In turn the value-drivers for each of these activities might be supplier *accreditation procedures*, use of *freelance designers* and in-house *after-sales service* teams.

4.3.4 Control of resources

Another criterion against which a company's strategic capability needs to be assessed is the extent to which the resources have been properly controlled. Figure 4.7 identifies some controls which might be investigated. There could be situations where good-quality resources have been deployed in the right way and used efficiently, but performance is still poor as the resources are poorly controlled. There are a number of questions to ask in assessing whether the resource control arrangements add to or detract from the strategic capability of the organisation:

- Are *performance measures* related to the basis on which the organisation is competing or providing value for money? For example, a high level of stock may be disastrous for a company needing to cut costs, but critically important to customer service.
- Do managers differentiate between the *important* and the trivial in the way they exercise control? For example, do they know what the four or five most important resource measures, or performance indicators should be?
- Are managers informed by the control system *in time* to affect their judgements and decisions? This is often a criticism of many costing systems – they provide information after the event.

Since critically important value activities may be undertaken outside the organisation's direct control, a resource analysis should assess the extent to which the organisation is able to evaluate and influence the creation of value throughout the value system. There are many different ways in which organisations could attempt to achieve this control:

- *Vertical integration* attempts to achieve control through ownership of more parts of the value system. Many organisations are now disillusioned with this as a solution, since the practical difficulties and costs of co-ordinating a wide range of activities often outweigh the theoretical benefits.
- Within manufacturing industry the concept of closely *specifying* requirements and controlling the performance of suppliers has been used for many years.

Resource area	Typical controls to investigate
Physical resources	
Buildings	Security, maintenance
Plant, machinery	Production control Maintenance system
Financial	Costing system Budgets Investment appraisal
Materials	Supplier control (quantity, quality and cost) Control of stock
Products	Stock control Quality control Losses (e.g. theft)
Human resources	Control of key personnel Leadership Working agreements Control of outlets (e.g. distributors)
Intangibles	Control of image (e.g. public relations) Industrial relations climate Control of vital information

Figure 4.7 Aspects of resource control

- A more recent philosophy has been *total quality management*,[7] which seeks to control value creation through closer working relationships between the various specialists within the value system. So, for example, many manufacturers will now involve their suppliers and distributors at the design stage of a product or project.
- The *merchandising* activities of many manufacturers are now much improved and are an important means of improving their control over distributor performance through training, incentives, joint promotions, etc.

Public-sector organisations in many countries have been questioning whether the traditional *administered monopoly* really does deliver value for money. This has led to some very significant changes in how the value system for public services is managed and controlled. The philosophy underlying most of the changes has been to exert control by separating and specialising roles within the value system in a way that tends to exist in the private sector. So, for example, the creation of *internal markets* in the health service and other public services separates the role of the client (the health authority) from the provider of services (e.g. hospitals). Hitherto, these activities were controlled directly by the same body.

Competitive tendering[8] takes the process one stage further and introduces market pressure as a key controlling mechanism. Perhaps the most common response has simply been the adoption of more devolved management structures, which often bring into sharper focus the performance of internal suppliers – particularly if there is the opportunity to 'source' or 'sell' services from and to third parties. This issue is discussed more fully in Chapter 10.

Many of the items discussed above relate to how an organisation is able to manage and control *linkages* in its value system to strategic advantage. This is crucial since linkages provide an advantage which is robust and difficult to imitate. This will be discussed more fully in section 6.4. There are often points in the history of an organisation's development where the need to extend these linkages while maintaining adequate control becomes a key issue. For example, *internationalisation* requires organisations to reassess their links and relationships with suppliers and channels and to reshape them to service a much wider geographical area.

4.3.5   Financial analyses[9]

Understanding the strategic capability of an organisation will inevitably return to the issue of financial capability and performance. There is a plethora of financial information within organisations which can help in an assessment of the strengths and weaknesses of that organisation. The danger is that financial ratio analysis is undertaken without a strategic perspective. This section is concerned with providing such a perspective.

The first important issue to recognise is that there will not be a single agreed view on how to assess the financial standing of a company, since different groups (*stakeholders*) will have different expectations of the company. This concept of stakeholder expectations is covered more fully in Chapter 5, but for the current purpose it is important to distinguish between four different types of financial expectation:

- *Shareholders* are essentially concerned with assessing the quality of their *investment* and the payoffs they can expect both in dividends and in capital growth (reflected in share price). Therefore they will be mainly concerned with measures such as earnings per share, P/E ratio, dividend yield, etc. Comparisons across companies are a key measure of investment attractiveness. Shareholder value analysis is discussed in more detail in section 8.2.3.
- *Bankers* and other providers of interest-bearing loans are concerned about the *risk* attached to their loans. This might be assessed through looking at

the capital structure of the company – particularly the gearing ratio (of debt to equity), which indicates how sensitive the solvency of the company is to changes in its profit position. Interest cover is a similar measure which relates interest payments to profit.

- *Suppliers* and *employees* are likely to be concerned with the *liquidity* of the company, which is a measure of its ability to meet short-term commitments to creditors and wages. Bankers will share this concern because a deteriorating liquidity position may require correction through loans and an increased risk profile as discussed above.
- *Managers* within the company should be using financial analyses to help them assess the *performance* of the company, which is a prerequisite to achieving the aspirations of the other stakeholders over a period of time. This is the use of financial analysis which traditionally has received the most attention. Which of these financial measures are of particular importance depends upon which stakeholders are being considered and over what timescale.

Figure 4.8 shows some of the most commonly used ratios. When using financial analyses as part of a resource analysis, the following issues need to be borne in mind:

- Financial ratios[10] (such as stock-turn, sales margin, etc.) are of no importance in themselves. It is the implications of these ratios which are critical. This may not emerge until some sensible basis of comparison is established (see below). Even then a word of warning is necessary. It may be that an organisation is successfully differentiating itself from its competitors by extra spending in selected areas (e.g. advertising). Provided this results in added value (possibly through price or market share), this may well be a defensible spending pattern.
- Only some value activities will be of critical importance to an organisation. The financial analyses which relate to those activities will be particularly useful. For example, rate of stock turnover may be important to a high street store, unit profit margins to a market stallholder, or sales volume to a capital-intensive manufacturer. It is important to be selective in the use of ratios. Indeed, some of the most successful uses of ratio analysis have been in the identification of this relationship between market characteristics, the key value activities which are critical to success, and establishing *benchmarks* of best practice, say, in stock turnover, etc.
- The key value activities may change over time, and so should the key financial measures to monitor. For example, during the introduction of a new product the key factor may be *sales volume*; once established, *profit/unit* might be most important, while during decline *cash flow* may be essential to support the introduction of the next generation of products.

In addition to published financial data, management would normally have access

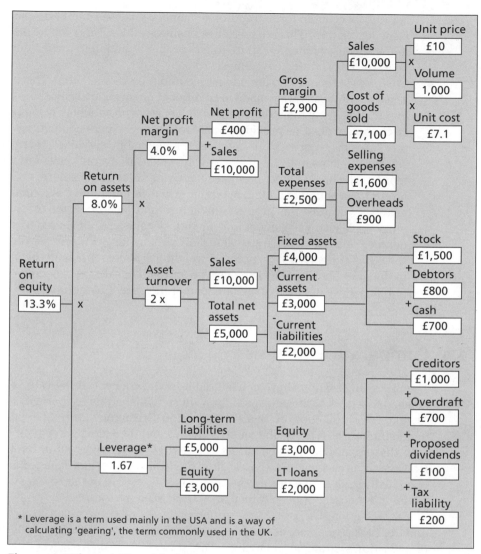

Figure 4.8 The relationship between various financial ratios –
The Dupont model; an example ('000 units)

to additional financial information (such as cost data) which would help provide
a fairly comprehensive analysis of many of the resource utilisation and control
issues raised above.

A major concern about traditional financial analysis from a strategic perspective is that it has tended to exclude two key stakeholder groups:

● *The community*, which is concerned with the *social cost* of an
organisation's activities in terms of pollution, marketing activities, etc. This

is rarely accounted for in traditional financial analyses, but is an issue of growing concern. This is a matter of business ethics,[11] and will be discussed more fully in Chapter 5. Failure to pay proper attention to these issues could be a source of strategic weakness.

● *Customers/clients*, who are concerned about *perceived value*. This assessment too is rarely made in traditional financial analysis, the implication being that companies which survive profitably in a competitive environment must be providing value for money. Where competitive pressures have not existed – such as in many public services – there are now serious attempts to develop performance measures more related to value for money. The fundamental premise underlying value chain analysis is built around this notion of adding maximum value at minimum cost. Financial analysis can assist this process only if information is collected for that purpose. Many management information systems are not geared to such a detailed analysis of separate value activities, making this process difficult. In the UK of the early 1990s, political weight has been put behind this process in the development of a *citizen's charter* defining what is expected of each public service in terms of client expectations (see Illustration 4.5).

4.4 Comparative analysis

The preceding sections have considered how the concept of the value chain can be used to assess strategic capability. Value chain analysis encourages managers to take a critical look at their organisation's resources with the purpose of understanding how particular value activities and the linkages between activities help the organisation to sustain its competitive advantage within its 'industry'. However, it is also useful to assess how the value system has changed and developed historically, since this gives insights into how (and perhaps why) the organisation has chosen, or been forced, to shift its resource base.

This section discusses these different bases of comparison, the *historical* and the *industry norm*, as valuable means of improving the understanding of an organisation's strategic capability. The section will also suggest that further insights can be developed by comparing *best practice* beyond the industry within which the organisation currently operates. Again the value chain concept will be useful in analysing this best practice.

4.4.1 Historical analysis

A historical analysis looks at the deployment of the resources of an organisation by comparison with previous years in order to identify any significant changes. Typically, financial ratios like sales/capital and sales/employees will be used, as well as any significant variations in the proportions of resources devoted to different activities. This can reveal trends which might not otherwise be apparent. For example, a retailing company which owns its own property may find that a comparison with the deployment of resources five years previously reveals that there has been a drift from retailing to property management as the focal point of the company's activities. In some cases it has prompted companies to reassess where the major thrust of their business should be in the future. In the public sector, historical analyses have been used extensively and are also the subject of heated political debate as different measures are chosen according to the various shades of political opinion.

4.4.2 Comparison with industry norms

A historical analysis can normally be improved significantly by an additional comparison with similar factors analysed for the industry as a whole or for similar public-service providers. It helps to put the company's resources and performance into perspective, and reflects the fact that it is the *relative* position of a company which matters in assessing its capability. This needs to be assessed in relation to the value activities and not just the product or market position, as was seen in Illustration 4.3.

One danger of industry-norm analysis is that the company may overlook the fact that the whole industry is performing badly, and is losing out competitively to other countries with better resources or even other industries which can satisfy customers' needs in different ways. Therefore if an industry comparison is performed, it is wise to make some assessment of how the company's resources compare with those in other countries and industries. This can often be done by looking at a few of the more important measures of resource utilisation, such as stock turnover, yield from raw materials, etc. Illustration 4.6 shows an example of comparisons of R & D expenditure.

However, readers are reminded of the preceding discussion concerning the importance of establishing and maintaining a distinctive value chain for an organisation. A comparison of similar value activities between organisations can be useful if the strategic context is not forgotten. For example, a straight comparison of resource deployment between two competitive companies (say, in terms of an analysis of cost structures) may reveal quite different situations in the labour cost as percentage of total cost. The conclusions drawn from this, however, depend upon circumstances. If the firms are competing head on, largely on the basis of price, then differentials in labour costs could be of crucial importance. In contrast, the additional use of staff by one organisation may be an essential support for the special services provided which differentiate that organisation from its competitors.

ILLUSTRATION 4.5
The Patient's Charter

A commitment to address the needs of customers/clients requires the development of appropriate targets and standards of performance.

In the early 1990s many public services, in the UK and elsewhere, were keen to redress the balance of attention they were paying to their various stakeholders. In particular, the voice of the client was encouraged through various means including, in the UK, what became known as the *citizen's charter*. This was promoted by the government, and major public services adopted their own charter.

In the case of the National Health Service this was known as the *Patient's Charter* and was launched in 1992. The charter contained three main elements: a reaffirmation of seven existing rights of patients; the introduction of three new rights; and the publication of performance standards (both national and local). Standards were not rights, but helped clarify the expectations which government had of management in the health service in terms of quality of service.

Seven existing rights

- Health care on the basis of clinical need not ability to pay.
- Registration with a family doctor (GP).
- Emergency care at any time.
- Referral to a hospital consultant (through GP).
- Clarification of proposed treatment, including risks and alternatives.

4.4.3 Best practice analysis

The shortcomings of industry-norm analysis have encouraged many organisations to develop different approaches to intra-industry comparisons. Rather than attempting to establish the 'norm', there is a search for *best practice* and the establishment of *benchmarks of performance* related to that best practice. Some specific examples of this approach are as follows:

- *Competitor profiles*[12] where detailed dossiers/analyses are built up on the performance of key competitors. These are particularly valuable where data are available to disaggregate the overall performance measures (such as return on capital) to specific measures which relate to the critical value activities as mentioned above.
- *Benchmarking* establishes key performance targets to be met in the

- Access to health records.
- Freedom of whether to take part in medical research/training.

Three new rights

- Detailed information on local health services, including quality standards and maximum waiting time.
- Guaranteed admission for treatment by a specific date no longer than two years after being placed on a waiting list.
- Any complaints to be fully and promptly investigated and a written reply sent by the chief executive or general manager.

Nine national standards

- Respect for privacy, dignity, and religious and cultural beliefs.
- All people – including those with special needs – to be able to use services.
- Information to relatives and friends.
- Waiting time for ambulance (14 minutes maximum in urban areas).
- Waiting time for assessment in emergency (immediate assessment).
- Waiting time in outpatients (within 30 minutes of appointment time).
- Cancellation of operations (no cancellations on the day).
- A *named* nurse – or other professional – responsible for each patient.
- Discharge arrangements (follow-up needs).

In addition, local health authorities were required to develop a series of more detailed local standards for the guidance of patients.

Source: *Patient's Charter*, Department of Health, 1991.

execution of these key value activities if a sustainable competitive position is to be established. This analysis can also contribute significantly to the discussion of positioning and strategic groups (Chapter 3), since it sharpens up considerably the resource profile and performance measures which are necessary for long-term survival in each strategic group. Over the past ten years the most valuable use of this type of analysis has been where international competitiveness has been of critical importance – which has applied to many manufacturing companies world-wide.[13]

Benchmarking is best analysed for separate value activities. In this way, best practice may be found in other industries. For example, many aspects of hospital and patient care are compared against the hotel and catering industry standards of performance.

- *Base budget reviews*[14] (see also Illustration 9.4) are a similar process used by

ILLUSTRATION 4.6
R & D scoreboard

Comparative analysis can also be usefully applied to any value activity which underpins the competitive strategy of an organisation, an industry or a nation. R & D is one such activity for many sectors of industry.

In 1991 the *Independent* newspaper published the first ever detailed analysis of the R & D spend of UK companies – in the form of an 'R & D scoreboard'. Comparisons were made with previous years, between industry sectors and – perhaps most critically – with international competitors. Some examples of the data are as follow:

(a) Change on previous year

	% increase in spend
All industry	12%
Aerospace	27%
Chemicals	7%
Food	2%
Leisure	46%
Service industries	5%

(b) Inter-industry comparisons

	R & D per employee (£000s)	R & D/sales (%)
Aerospace	2.32	3.33
Chemicals	2.72	3.29
Food	1.01	1.22
Leisure	0.22	0.37
Service industries	2.59	2.65

many public-sector organisations where historically the idea of external benchmarking has been ignored or even resisted. Such reviews are most effective where they are applied to specific services and where four fundamental questions are asked: first, *why* is this service provided at all?; second, why is it provided *in that particular way*?; third, what are the examples of *best practice* elsewhere?; and fourth, how should the service be *reshaped* in the light of these comparisons? Although this process is at least partially subjective, there are many examples of its successful application.

(c) International comparisons (top 100)

	UK	USA	Germany	Japan
1. R & D per employee (£000s)				
All industries	1.53	3.73	4.32	n/a
Aerospace	2.34	2.42	17.48	n/a
Chemicals	3.02	4.96	5.57	n/a
Leisure	0.21	4.85	n/a	n/a
Service industries	5.82	n/a	1.89	n/a
2. R & D/sales (%)				
All industries	1.69	3.80	5.09	3.71
Aerospace	3.34	4.20	23.78	n/a
Chemicals	3.56	4.50	5.79	3.88
Leisure	0.36	6.80	n/a	3.62
Service industries	4.51	n/a	2.75	n/a

In a foreword to the publication Peter Lilley, the secretary of state for trade and industry, said: 'In part this scoreboard is encouraging with an overall increase in spend of 12% – and much greater in some industries such as Aerospace and electrical and electronics. However, this must be put into perspective by international comparisons. The evidence is that UK firms are still not doing enough to match the efforts of their main competitors in other countries ... I believe that the R & D Scoreboard should now stimulate investors to question companies who appear to be under investing in R & D.'

4.5 Assessing the balance of resources

The previous sections have been concerned with analysing the strategic capability of an organisation through a detailed look at the value activities which are undertaken, and also the way that linkages are managed between these separate activities and within the wider value system. Such an analysis should provide a useful analysis of the capability which an organisation derives from its separate products, services or business units. However, in many organisations there is an additional resource issue which is of equal, and complementary, importance: namely, the extent to which the organisation's resources are balanced as a whole. Three important aspects of such an analysis are as follows:

- The extent to which the various activities and resources of the organisation complement each other. Portfolio analysis is particularly useful in analysing this issue.
- The degree of balance of the people within the organisation in terms of both individual skills and personality types.
- Whether the degree of flexibility in the organisation's resources is appropriate for the level of uncertainty in the environment and the degree of risk the company is prepared to take.

4.5.1 Portfolio analyses[15]

Very few organisations are pursuing single-product/single-market strategies. So an important part of a strategic capability analysis is to assess the extent to which the activities that make up the company's portfolio are complementary (as against competitive or simply unrelated). It is a key responsibility of strategic managers to ensure that the portfolio is strong.

An acceptance that this mix is important requires some experience in deciding how to describe and assess the current range of activities – as a basis for adapting the mix in the future. The Boston Consulting Group (BCG) proposed one of the first ways of classifying business units – in relation to market growth and company relative market share. This was introduced in Chapter 3 (section 3.5.4 and Figure 3.8) as a means of assessing the positioning of an organisation's activities *vis-à-vis* competitors or other providers. Figure 4.9 shows a number of other matrices.

Portfolio analysis can be very valuable in assessing how the balance of activities contributes to the strategic capability of the organisation. However, some caution needs to be exercised in their use:

- The analysis should be applied to *strategic business units*, i.e. units dealing with particular market segments not whole markets.
- Corporate management must develop the capability to review the role of each strategic business unit in the overall mix of company activities, and devote time to it.
- Proper use of portfolio planning will result in different targets and expectations for different parts of the organisation. This can be a major cultural change for many managers. However, it is critical and should extend to the resource allocation processes (both capital and revenue budgets). All too often this critical stage is avoided and everything is levelled down to the weakest part of the business.

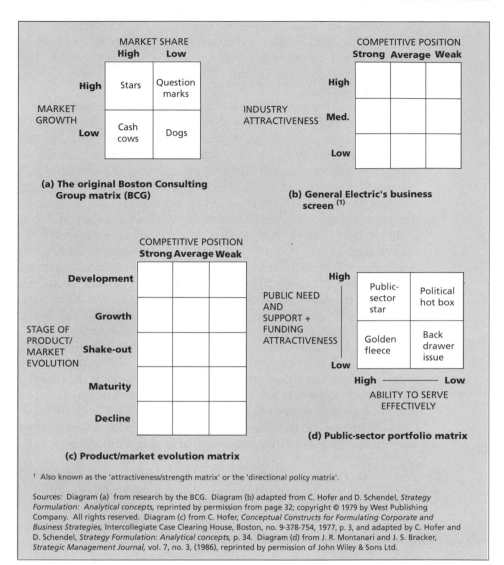

Figure 4.9 Product portfolio matrices

- The original BCG analysis concentrated on the needs of a business to plan its cash flow requirements across its portfolio. So *cash cows* will be used to fund the development of *question marks* and *stars*. However, little is said about the behavioural implications of such a strategy. How do central management motive the *cash cows*, who see all their hard-gained surpluses being invested in other businesses? Indeed, perhaps the single factor which makes the creation and management of a balanced portfolio difficult in practice is the jealousy which can arise between the various strategic business units. This often has to be reflected in the organisation structure –

placing some distance between the potential friction points.

- In many organisations the critical resource to be planned and balanced will not be cash but the time and creative energy of the organisation's managers, designers, engineers, etc. *Question marks* and *stars* are very demanding on these types of resource.
- Some authors[16] are somewhat sceptical as to whether the corporate headquarters really do add value to the company through this constant process of buying, selling, developing or running down individual units to keep the portfolio balanced. They suggest that the free market may well allocate resources more effectively if the activities are separated and the corporate centre closed down. This issue will be discussed more fully in Chapter 10.
- The portfolio approach has also been used in the public sector,[17] as seen in Figure 4.9 (d). Here the key judgements are concerned with the organisation's ability to provide perceived value for money within the resources which are likely to be available, and the political requirement to offer services. This latter point is often forgotten by public-sector managers when reviewing their portfolio of activities for the future. A provider of public services will often need to keep a wider portfolio of services in order to satisfy the political objectives within which they operate.
- The position of *dogs* is often misunderstood. Certainly there may be some products which need immediate deletion – but even then there may be political difficulties if they are the brainchild of people with power in the organisation. However, other *dogs* may have a useful place in the portfolio. They may be necessary to complete the product range and provide a credible presence in the market. They may be held for defensive reasons – to keep competitors out. They may be capable of revitalisation.

Despite these concerns, however, portfolio analysis remains an important method of assessing the balance of resources within an organisation.

4.5.2   Balance of skills/personalities

Organisations must possess the balance of skills needed to run a business successfully. They need the capability to manage their production and marketing systems as well as controlling the financial and personnel aspects properly. Indeed, the way in which these different skills are *linked* together in the value chain is likely to be a source of competitive advantage, and they have been referred to as the *non-tradable assets* of the organisation. This is particlarly important for professional service organisations, where a variety of different skills have to be blended together in circumstances where each professional group can be fiercely independent.

Belbin[18] has looked at another aspect of the balance of human resources: namely, the extent to which management teams contain an adequate balance of personality types to operate effectively. Some of the more common personality types needed within an effective team are identified in Figure 4.10. For example, it is often argued that one of the strengths of the British government services is the complementary nature of the team within departments – particularly the relationship which ministers, as the political leaders, share with the senior civil servants, and, in turn, the latter's relationship with the analysts within their department. An analysis of the effect of skills and personalities on an organisation's strategies is essentially concerned with the role of *people*. This will be discussed in detail in Chapter 5.

Chairman/team leader
Stable, dominant, extrovert
Concentrates on objectives
Does not originate ideas
Focuses people on what they do best

Plant
Dominant, high IQ, introvert
A 'scatterer of seeds', originates ideas
Misses out on detail
Thrustful but easily offended

Resource investigator
Stable, dominant, extrovert
Sociable
Contacts with outside world
Salesperson/diplomat/liaison officer
Not original thinker

Shaper
Anxious, dominant, extrovert
Emotional, impulsive
Quick to challenge and respond to challenge
Unites ideas, objectives and possibilities
Competitive
Intolerant of woolliness and vagueness

Company worker
Stable, controlled
Practical organiser
Can be inflexible but likely to adapt to established systems
Not an innovator

Monitor evaluator
High IQ, stable, introvert
Measured analyses not innovation
Unambitious and lacking enthusiasm
Solid, dependable

Team worker
Stable, extrovert, low dominance
Concerned with individual's needs
Builds on others' ideas
Cools things down

Finisher
Anxious, introvert
Worries over what will go wrong
Permanent sense of urgency
Preoccupied with order
Concerned with 'following through'

Sources: R. M. Belbin, *Management Teams: Why they succeed or fail*, Heinemann, 1981; and R. M. Belbin *et al.*, 'Building effective management teams', *Journal of General Management*, vol. 3, no. 3.

Figure 4.10 Personality types for the effective team

4.5.3 Flexibility analysis

Another issue which needs to be assessed is the extent to which an organisation's resources are flexible and adaptable. It is important to assess how far flexibility is balanced with the uncertainty faced by the organisation; flexibility has no strategic significance without an understanding of this uncertainty. A manufacturing company facing a highly volatile raw materials market may choose to spread its sources of supply despite the fact that this could prove more costly. In contrast, it may be happy to have a highly inflexible, high-volume production system if it is trading in a stable market, and this system of production ensures a highly competitive cost structure.

A flexibility analysis need be no more sophisticated than a simple listing of the major areas of uncertainty and the extent to which the company's resources are geared to cope with each of these. Figure 4.11 sets out such an analysis, which seeks to compare the major areas of uncertainty faced by a company with the degree of flexibility in the related resource areas. These range from areas where uncertainties can be fairly easily accommodated (e.g. using overtime to flex capacity), to ones which currently represent a constraint on strategic development (e.g. design skills).

4.6 Identification of key issues

The last major aspect of resource analysis is the identification of the key issues arising from previous analyses. It is only at this stage of the analysis that a sensible assessment can be made of the major strengths and weaknesses of an organisation and the strategic importance of these (see Illustration 4.6). The resource analysis then starts to be useful as a basis against which to judge future courses of action. There are several assessments which can be made.

4.6.1 SWOT analysis[19]

SWOT analysis can be a very useful way of summarising many of the previous analyses and combining them with the key issues from environmental analysis, thus bringing together the key issues from Chapters 3 and 4. The aim is to identify the extent to which the current strategy of an organisation and its more specific strengths and weaknesses are relevant to, and capable of dealing with, the changes taking place in the business environment. SWOT stands for strengths, weaknesses, opportunities and threats, but rather than just listing these in terms of managers' perceptions, the idea is to undertake a more structured analysis so as to yield findings which can contribute to the formulation of strategy. Although what follows is somewhat crude as an analytical device, it has proved in practi-

| Major areas of uncertainty | Flexibility | | Comments |
	Required	Actual (at present)	
Demand for product A	Capacity (possibility + 20%) or Stocks	Overtime could cover

Low | Probably OK |
Price of raw materials from present supplier	New suppliers New materials	None known at present Production system cannot cope	Problem area Seek information on new suppliers
Major customer may go bankrupt	Replacement customer	No leads	Sound out potential customers
Long-term loan may not be renewed next year	Other sources of capital	Good image on stock market	New share issue looks favourable
Chief design engineer may retire	Design capability for products presently in development	Deputy not suitable Chief may agree to part-time 'consultancy' arrangement	Training and/or recruitment needs urgent attention

Figure 4.11 Flexibility analysis – an example

cal application to be a helpful means of achieving these aims. The procedure can be undertaken in a number of steps:

- Identify the current or prevailing strategy or strategies that the organisation is following. This is not necessarily the strategy as advocated or published, but the realised strategy (see Chapter 2) of the organisation. This in itself might be problematic, since managers do not always agree on the strategy they are following – so this debate is often very important.
- Identify the key changes in the organisation's environment following the procedures outlined in Chapter 3. While there is no fixed number which should be agreed upon, it is helpful if the list does not exceed seven or eight key points.
- The same process should then be undertaken in terms of the resource profile of the organisation, following the procedures outlined in this chapter to identify the key capabilities (strengths) and key limitations (weaknesses) of the organisation. It is useful to keep the total list to no more than eight points. It is important to avoid overgeneralising this analysis and to keep to quite specific points: a statement such as 'poor management' means very little, for example and could be interpreted in any number of ways. If it means that senior managers have, historically, not been good at motivating change in the organisation, then that is a more specific and more useful point.

Illustration 4.7 gives an example of the types of list drawn up by a regional police force in the UK when undertaking this exercise.

The statements need to be examined one against another. This can be done by taking each statement in the left-hand column in turn, examining it in terms of the key environmental issues and *scoring* either a + (or a weighted + +) or a – (or a – –), as follows:

1.   Mark + if there would be a benefit to the organisation: that is, if:

ILLUSTRATION 4.7
SWOT analysis

A SWOT analysis can be a useful way to summarise the relationship between key environmental influences, the strategic capability of the organisation and hence the agenda for developing new strategies.

The results below are from a SWOT analysis undertaken by a regional police force within the UK.

Key issues in environment	Politics/legislation	New technologies	Changing roles in justice system/Europe	Public expectations (citizen's charter)	Increase in major crime	Social trends (demography)	+	–
Main strengths								
Committed employees	0	+	+	+	0	0	3	0
Good community links	+	–	+	+	–	+	4	2
New 'top team'	+	+	+	+	+	0	5	0
New equipment (transport)	0	+	0	+	+	0	3	0
Operational planning	+	+	–	–	+	0	3	2
Main weaknesses								
Undercapacity	–	0	0	–	–	–	0	4
Reactive approach	–	–	–	+	+	0	2	3
IT systems	–	–	0	–	–	0	0	4
Financial planning systems	–	–	0	–	0	0	0	3
+	3	4	3	5	4	1		
–	4	4	2	4	3	1		

Source: Authors.

- A strength would enable the organisation to take advantage of or counteract a problem arising from an environmental change.
- A weakness would be offset by the environmental change.

2. Mark – if there would be an adverse effect on the organisation: that is, if:

- A strength would be reduced by the environmental change.
- A weakness would prevent the organisation from overcoming the problems associated with an environmental change, or would be accentuated by that change.

When this procedure is completed the analysis will look something like the completed Illustration 4.7. What this yields is a much clearer view of the extent to which the environmental changes and influences provide opportunities or threats, given current strategies and organisation capabilities. For example, Illustration 4.7 shows that a major opportunity for the organisation lies in the availability of new technologies (communications, etc.) It also reveals that it was reasonably well placed to deal with the growing expectations of the public around quality of service. However, other environmental issues seem to be rather limited in opportunity, and there are significant threats in terms of new legislation and the increase in major crime. Some issues could be either opportunities or threats, depending on the extent to which the organisation can utilise and develop the strengths of good community relations and new equipment.

It is important when undertaking the analysis not just to relate it to the historical situation. Some strengths of the organisation may not be so relevant in terms of the way the organisation's environment is developing. Similarly, an analysis of perceived weaknesses should recognise that their importance varies depending on the types of strategy the organisation is likely to pursue. So the reactive approach is only a weakness in relation to strategies requiring a comprehensive and planned approach – such as crime prevention. It remains a strength in relation to the readiness to deal with emergencies.

A SWOT analysis, therefore, provides a mechanism for systematically thinking through the extent to which the organisation can cope with its environment. However, this analysis requires an understanding of both the environment and the resource capabilities of that organisation.

4.6.2 Core competences

A strengths and weaknesses analysis can be particularly powerful if it incorporates a comparison with competitors. This can be done using the concept of *core competences*. Core competences are concerned with identifying those particular strengths which give the company an edge over its competitors, and those areas of particular weakness which are to be avoided. This may require a parallel analysis of competitors' resources as previously mentioned. A supermarket's core competence might be found in its layout, display and control systems, which allow for high-volume trading at minimal cost. Its particular weakness would be its inability to provide advice to customers. This analysis would help in assessing how viable a move into new product areas might be, such as DIY or furniture.

A tangible way in which core competence is recognised in the public services is through the establishment of *centres of excellence* which receive special funding (e.g. in health care). The main reason why there has been so much emphasis on value chain analysis in this chapter is because it is a useful way of understanding the core competence of an organisation, particularly where a comparison is made with the value chains of major competitors.

The strategic importance of the core competences of an organisation can be tested during resource analysis by asking four questions.[20]

- Who *owns* the core competences? For example, in professional service organisations the knowledge and skills of the professional employees are essentially owned by the individuals and not the firms, and can be taken to a competitor firm.
- How *durable* are the competences? Where technology is changing rapidly or where product life cycles are short, the key source of competitive advantage may be short lived. This is one way in which rapid technological change can help small firms compete with larger companies in their industry. Although they are at a disadvantage in their ability to afford new technologies, the speed of change brings new opportunities to organisations that are flexible and opportunistic. This is often the core competence of the small firm.
- How *transferable* are the competencies? The extent to which competitors are able to acquire a similar competence base will vary. Some resources, such as raw materials, may be very transferable; others, such as brand name or reputation, may not be so easily transferred.
- How *replicable* are the competences? This requires an assessment of whether competitors could develop (rather than purchase) a similar resource base: that is, the threat of imitation.

Together these factors determine how robust is a particular core competence.

4.7 Summary

Resource analysis is an important means of assessing an organisation's strategic capability, which is necessary if sensible choices of future strategy are to be made. Traditionally, much of the discussion of resource analysis has centred around the idea of strengths and weaknesses.

The concept of the value chain is particularly useful in understanding an organisation's strategic capability, since it concentrates on value activities and the linkages between activities rather than simply resources *per se*. This underlines the fact that capability is strongly related to the way in which resources are utilised and controlled. It has also been emphasised that a resource analysis must not be confined to those resources which an organisation owns. Often it is the linkages with the value chains of suppliers, channels and customers which are the cornerstones of an organisation's capability, and which prevent imitation by competitors.

The idea of linkages is a reminder that it is the *configuration* of resources which provides strategic capability. Another aspect of configuration is the balance (or mix) of resources which the organisation possesses. Lack of balance can be a key weakness even if the detailed appraisal of separate resources looks strong.

Perhaps the most crucial issue has been the contention that strategic capability is best understood in relation to other (competitive) organisations. It is the core competences of the organisation *vis-à-vis* competitors or other providers which are so important to unearth in a resource analysis.

Finally, it should be remembered that resource capability is only one piece of the jigsaw. The strategic importance of the environment has been discussed in Chapter 3. The next chapter considers the third ingredient: namely, the extent to which an organisation's culture and power structure can influence strategy.

References

1. The concept of resource-based strategies is discussed by B. Wernerfelt in 'A resource-based view of the firm' *Strategic Management Journal*, vol. 5, no. 2, (1984), pp. 171–8, and an example is given by D. J. Collis, 'A resource-based analysis of global competition', *Strategic Management Journal* vol. 12, summer, 1991, pp. 49–68.

2. There are a number of papers and standard texts which include traditional resource audits. See, for example, G. A. Steiner, *Strategic Planning*, Free Press, 1979, Chapter 8; R. M. Grant, *Contemporary Strategy Analysis*, Blackwell, 1991, p. 99; and R. B. Buchele, 'How to evaluate a firm', *California Management Review*, Fall 1962, pp. 5–16. The latter provides extensive checklists under functional areas. Readers who are unfamiliar with resource analysis in any functional area may wish to consult one of the following standard texts: P. Kotler, *Marketing Management: Analysis, planning, implementation and control* (7th edition), Prentice Hall, 1991; R. Wild, *Production and Operations Management* (3rd ed), Nelson, 1984; M. W. E. Glautier and B. Underdown, *Accounting Theory and Practice* (4th ed), Pitman, 1991; D. Torrington and L.

Hall, *Personnel Management: A new approach*, Prentice Hall, 1986; C. Fombrun, N. Tichy and M. Devanna, *Strategic Human Resource Management*, Wiley, 1990.

3. Intangible resources have become increasingly recognised to be of strategic importance, as discussed in R. Hall, 'The strategic analysis of intangible resources', *Strategic Management Journal*, vol. 13, (1992), pp. 135–44.

4. An extensive discussion of the value chain concept and its application can be found in M. E. Porter, *Competitive Advantage*, Free Press, 1985. The concept is introduced in Chapter 2.

5. Value analysis was developed in the immediate post-war period by Lawrence Miles. See, for example, L. D. Miles, *Techniques for Value Analysis and Engineering*, McGraw-Hill, 1961.

6. P. Conley, *Experience Curves as a Planning Tool*, available as a pamphlet from the Boston Consulting Group. Also A. C. Hax and N. S. Majluf in R. G. Dyson (ed.), *Strategic Planning: Models and analytical techniques*, Wiley, 1990, Chapter 3.

7. Useful reference books on total quality management are J. M. Juran, *Juran on Planning for Quality*, Free Press, 1988; and J. S. Oakland, *Total Quality Management*. Heinemann, 1989.

8. The details of compulsory competitive tendering can be found in D. Parker, 'The 1988 Local Government Act and compulsory competitive tendering', *Urban Studies*, vol. 27, no. 5, (1990), pp. 653–68.

9. M. W. E. Glautier and B. Underdown, *Accounting Theory and Practice*, (4th edition), Pitman, 1991.

10. Glautier and Underdown, (reference 9) deal with financial ratio analysis in detail.

11. Business ethics are discussed more fully in section 5.6. For an overview see J. Mahoney, 'An international look at business ethics: Britain', *Journal of Business Ethics*, vol. 9, no. 7, (1990), pp. 545–50.

12. Competitor profiles are discussed in M. E. Porter, *Competitive Strategy*, Free Press, 1980, p. 49.

13. A practical example of benchmarking can be found in the 'competitiveness achievement plans' used by Lucas and reported in *Management Today*, June 1986. Also R. C. Basil Camp, *Benchmarking: The search for industry best practices that lead to superior performance*, Quality Press, 1989. Many articles on competitor analysis include references to benchmarking for example; S. Ghoshal and D. E. Westney, 'Organisational competitor analysis systems', *Strategic Management Journal*, vol. 12, no. 1, (1991), pp. 17–31, and R. Walker.

'Rank Xerox: Management revolution', *Long Range Planning*, vol. 25, no.1, (1992), pp. 9–21.

14. Base budget reviews have been used by a number of public-sector organisation in an attempt to take on board the philosophy of zero-based budgets (see D. Wise, *Management Today*, July 1986) in a way that could be worked in practice.

15. The use of growth/share matrices is discussed by A. C. Hax and N. S. Majluf in R. G. Dyson, *Strategic Planning: Models and analytical techniques*, Wiley, 1990, Chapter 4. Some authors have warned of the need to use portfolio matrices with care. See for example, S. P. Slatter, 'Common pitfalls in using the BCG portfolio matrix', *London Business School Journal*, Winter 1980, pp. 18–22.

16. See, for example, a discussion of the diversified context in H. Mintzberg and J. B. Quinn, *The Strategy Process*, (2nd edn), Prentice Hall, 1991, p. 672.

17. J. R. Montanari and J. S. Bracker, 'The strategic management process at the public planning unit level', *Strategic Management Journal*, vol. 7, no. 3, (1986), pp. 251–65.

18. R. M. Belbin, *Management Teams: Why they succeed or fail*, Heinemann, 1981.

19. The idea of SWOT as a commonsense checklist has been used for many years. See, for example, S. Tilles, 'Making strategy explicit', in I. Ansoff (ed.), *Business Strategy*, Penguin, 1968.

Recommended key readings

An extensive discussion of the value chain concept and its application can be found in M. E. Porter, *Competitive Advantage*, Free Press, 1985.

M. W. E. Glautier and B. Underdown, *Accounting Theory and Practice* (4th edn), Pitman, 1991, is a good reference text for the financial analyses which underpin resource analysis.

The use of growth/share matrices is discussed by A. C. Hax and N. S. Majluf in R. G. Dyson (ed.), *Strategic Planning: Models and analytical techniques*, Wiley, 1990, chapter 4.

The importance of balanced management teams to the success of strategy is discussed by R. M. Belbin, *Management Teams: Why they succeed or fail*, Heinemann, 1981.

Work assignments

4.1 Use Figures 4.2 and 4.3 to map out the key value activities for Laura Ashley* (or an organisation of your choice) – both within the company and in the wider value system in which it operates.

4.2 **By referring to Figure 4.4, explain how the organisation you have analysed in assignment 1 does or does not gain competitive advantage from:**
(a) The separate value activities.
(b) Linkages within the value chain.

4.3 Use Figures 4.5 and 4.6 to explain how the management and control of relationships within the value chain could be changed to improve the efficiency and/or effectiveness of an organisation. Illustrate your answer by reference to and an organisation of your choice, Laura Ashley,* Companiex (Illustration 4.3) or Amstrad (Illustration 4.4), and by comparison between two or more of these.

4.4 **Choose two organisations in the same industry and compare the configurations of their value chain. Explain how these relate to the organisations' competitive positioning.**

4.5 To what extent are changes like the Patient's Charter (Illustration 4.5) effective in influencing the way in which resources are utilised and controlled in public services? Would similar initiatives be valuable in the private sector?

4.6 Choose an organisation for which you have access to financial data and calculate as many of the ratios shown in Figure 4.8 as possible. What do these ratios tell you about the strategic capability of the organisation? What are the shortcomings of such an analysis in understanding strategic capability?

4.7 How would you use the data in Illustration 4.6 to assess the R & D strategy of an organisation? Are there other comparisons you would wish to make before changing the strategy of the organisation?

4.8 **Identify the strategic business units in an organisation of your choice. Use one of the portfolio matrices shown in Figure 4.9 to assess the extent to which this represents a well-balanced portfolio. How would you strengthen this portfolio?**

4.9 Prepare a SWOT analysis for an organisation of your choice (see Illustration 4.7). Explain carefully why you have chosen each of the key items on your shortlists.

---

*This refers to a case study in the Text and Cases version of this book.

CHAPTER 5

Culture and stakeholder expectations

5.1 Introduction

There is a temptation to look for a neat and tidy way of formulating strategy. Such a method might, apparently, be obtained through the analysis of the organisation's environment (Chapter 3) and the extent to which the company's resources, or strategic capability (Chapter 4), are matched with the environment. However, this strategic logic can fail to recognise the complex role which people play in the evolution of strategy as introduced in Chapter 2. This chapter looks at how the *cultural* and *political* situation of an organisation can be analysed and understood as part of a strategic analysis. Strategy formulation is also a product of the taken-for-granted assumptions about the *purposes* of the organisation and what people want the organisation to be like. There has been a growing awareness of the central importance of these issues in understanding strategy formulation and implementation since the early 1980s.

A strategic analysis can help provide an understanding of the factors and processes which drive the strategy of an organisation. This can be done in two broad ways. First, by analysing the way in which *culture* drives organisational strategies – building on the discussions in Chapter 2. This is discussed in section 5.2. Second, by systematically analysing the *political* processes which shape strategy (sections 5.3 and 5.4). The final parts of the chapter discuss how these various influences determine the *purposes* and the *ethical* stance of an organisation. Figure 5.1 provides a framework for such an analysis.

- The *cultural context* of the organisation needs to be analysed as mentioned above. Externally, this will require an understanding of the dominant *values of society* and the influence of *organised groups*. Internally, the cultural context can be understood through analysing the *cultural web*, which was introduced in Chapter 2. This cultural context reflects the taken-for-granted beliefs of people both inside and around the organisation.
- An analysis of the *political* context requires an assessment of how the *expectations* of individuals and groups influence the *purposes* of the organisation. *Stakeholder* analysis can be useful in understanding this process. Stakeholders are groups or individuals who have a stake in, or an expectation of, the organisation's performance, and include employees,

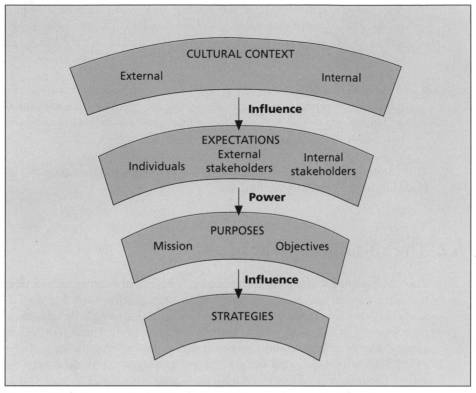

Figure 5.1 Culture, stakeholder expectations and organisational purposes

managers, shareholders, suppliers, customers and the community at large. Stakeholders may be identified within the formal structure of the organisation because they undertake a common task (e.g. functional departments). However, stakeholders also arise as a result of specific events and can transcend the formal structure. *Power* is the mechanism through which stakeholders influence an organisation's strategies. Power can be derived from a number of sources which will be discussed in section 5.4.

● The *purposes* of an organisation are often expressed through *mission* statements or more specific *objectives*. Organisational objectives have traditionally been afforded a central/dominant role in influencing strategy: that is, strategy is seen as the means of achieving preordained and unchangeable objectives. This is not the view taken in this book. Whereas organisations do have objectives which are often important in strategy formulation, they should not be regarded as unchangeable. They should be viewed as an important part of the strategic equation, and open to amendment and change as strategies develop. Objectives tend to emerge as the wishes of the most dominant stakeholder – usually the managers in the organisation, although there are notable exceptions. However, in pursuing these objectives the members of the dominant group are very strongly influenced by their reading of the political situation and are likely to set aside some of their expectations in order to improve the chance of achieving others.

- Whereas most of this chapter is concerned with how these various issues influence an organisation's strategies, the final section on **business ethics** will consider the reverse question: namely, how organisations influence the behaviour of individuals and the values of society.

This chapter is concerned with providing some approaches to analysing these issues as part of a strategic analysis.

5.2 The cultural context of strategy

There are a wide variety of factors which influence the expectations that individuals and groups are likely to have of an organisation (see Figure 5.1). When analysing the significance of these factors in the strategic development of any organisation, it is useful to ask three questions: first, which factors inside and outside the organisation have most influence on the expectations of groups and individuals within the organisation?; second, to what extent do current strategies reflect the influence of any one factor or a combination of factors?; third, how far would these factors help or hinder the changes which would be needed to pursue new strategies? Readers are encouraged to bear these questions in mind while reading this section.

5.2.1 External influences

The expectations of individuals are influenced by a number of factors which are *external* to the organisation: in particular, the *values of society* and *organised groups*.

Values of society

Attitudes to work, authority, equality and a number of other important issues are constantly shaped and changed by society. From the point of view of corporate strategy, it is important to understand this process for two reasons. First, values of society change and adjust over time, and, therefore policies which were acceptable twenty years ago may not be so today. There has been an increasing trend within many countries for the activities of companies to be constrained by legislation, public opinion and the media. Second, companies which operate *internationally* have the added problem of coping with the very different standards and expectations of the various countries in which they operate.

There have been a number of research studies[1] into how national culture influences employee motivation, management styles and organisational structures. The conclusions are that individual countries are markedly different from each other. For example, British culture appears to be far more tolerant of uncertainty than many other societies – notable European examples being France, Spain and Germany.

This research is as a reminder that the way in which organisations analyse and respond to their environment is strongly tied up with national culture, which is a key *frame of reference* for managers (see Chapter 2). It is not surprising against this background that there have been markedly different reactions among member countries to the European moves towards a single market. It has been suggested, for example, that Latin European managers – such as the French – are more risk averse than others. They react to uncertainty by referring it to higher authority and expecting government action to provide a buffer from adverse environmental influences.

Figure 5.2 is a checklist against which the influence of national culture on strategic management process can be assessed. This is clearly of major importance to multinational organisations in determining how the strategic management process might best be undertaken in the various divisions or companies which make up the organisation, and can be particularly important following mergers across more than one country, as shown in Illustration 5.1.

Although it is difficult and perhaps dangerous to stereotype nations against the checklist, two extreme stereotypes can be identified:

- A culture where uncertainty is managed by attempting to reduce it; when organisations are seen as having control and being proactive; and where the hierarchy, the individual and the work tasks are stressed. Here strategies are likely to be *planned*. US culture comes close to this stereotype.
- In contrast, the *adaptive* model of strategic management is more likely to be found in cultures where uncertainty is accepted as given; where the organisation has less control and is reactive; and where the orientation is towards the group and social concerns. Japanese culture is close to this stereotype.

Organised groups

Individuals often have allegiances to organised groups which are very influential on their beliefs, values and assumptions and are a key *frame of reference*, as mentioned above. These allegiances may be highly institutionalised and directly related to their working situation (such as membership of trade unions), or they may be more informal and unrelated (such as membership of churches or political groups). Within an industry the concept of an industry *recipe* (see Chapter 2)

STRATEGIC ISSUES	APPROACH TO MANAGING ISSUES
(a) Relationships with environment	In that culture do managers generally:
• Coping with uncertainty	avoid *or* tolerate? reduce *or* accept?
• Influencing the environment	manage *or* adapt? behave proactively *or* reactively? prefer action *or* fatalism?
• Assessing truth/reality	analyse facts *or* theoretical logic? assess inductively *or* deductively?
• Attitude to time/change	relate to past *or* future? prefer continuous *or* step change?
(b) Internal relationships	
• Power and status	use hierarchy *or* networks?
• Individualism	respect individuals *or* groups?
• Social orientation	emphasise tasks *or* social needs?

Source: Adapted from S. Schneider, 'Strategy formulation: the impact of national culture', *Organisation Studies,* vol. 10, no. 2, (1989).

Figure 5.2 National culture and organisational strategies

is a reminder of the importance of common values and expectations in shaping the dominant strategies of the industry (or strategic groups within the industry). The membership of professional bodies or institutions can be particularly important in organisations with a high proportion of professional staff. Engineering companies, R & D departments, accountancy sections and many public-service departments are all dominated by people who very often have a strong 'professional' view of their role, which may not be in accord with the managerial view of how these people can best be used as a resource.

At the corporate level, the whole organisational ethos of the company may be influenced by its membership of a trade association or similar body. These bodies may exert influence informally, but often seek to impose norms of behaviour on member companies through the development of 'codes of conduct'. These relate to issues like quality of service, dealing with disputes, employment practices, etc. There are many examples in UK industries, such as the Association of British Travel Agents (ABTA), the National House Builders Registration Council (NHBRC) and the British Insurance Brokers Association

ILLUSTRATION 5.1
Culture clash at CMB Packaging

Although the strategic logic for cross-country mergers in Europe may be strong, making them work successfully is not easy.

CMB Packaging was formed in 1989 as an Anglo-French merger of the old Metal Box company and Carnaud. On the surface there were good reasons to be optimistic about the merger, which was worth about £800m. The packaging industry was fragmented and facing increased concentration in its major buyer industries of consumer goods and food. Mergers had already occurred in packaging and appeared to be relatively successful. The two companies' activities seemed fairly complementary. Carnaud was strong in France, Germany, Italy and Spain, while Metal Box was the leader of the UK market with some Italian activities.

In the event the real world interfered with the vision and highlighted differences in management philosophy. Although this is a common problem even with mergers in the same country, many of the problems could be traced back to cross-country differences. At the top level the president, Jean-Marie Descarpentries, was described as 'flamboyant, a showman, an archetypal Frenchman full of French management school ideas, like the inverted pyramid with customers at the top and management at the bottom'. By contrast, the old Metal Box group operated with a typical British, top-down, centralised management approach. This clash of cultures at the top led to indecision about the company's strategy and organisation. This in turn led to declining performance.

The conclusion drawn by many people was that perhaps this friendly type of merger is the most dangerous form of cross-European co-operation – particularly if there are significant differences in management style. Unfortunately, management styles are different throughout Europe and present a challenge to European corporate integration. They vary from the authoritarian Italian *padrone*, to the German consensus approach. If cultures clash, perhaps the best way forward is either through outright takeover – where one culture triumphs over another – or, if this is impractical, through a loose and simple form of co-operation. Maybe CMB Packaging had fallen between these two stools?

Source: *The Times*, 12 September 1991.

(BIBA). This process also occurs on an international scale, a well-known example being the Organisation of Petroleum Exporting Countries (OPEC).

5.2.2 Internal influences

Chapter 2 introduced the concept of the *cultural web* as a means of explaining the various factors within an organisation which preserve and sustain the commonly held core beliefs and assumptions – the *paradigm* (Figure 2.10). This section suggests how the elements of the cultural web might be analysed as a means of understanding the cultural context within which new strategies may be developed. This is an important background against which an assessment of future choices can be made (Chapter 7), both in relation to options which might be possible within the current paradigm and for those which require more significant change. Where change is likely to be required, the analysis provides a background against which to assess how change might be achieved (Chapter 11). Each of these various facets of the cultural web will be discussed separately in the sections which follow. However, readers are reminded that it is often the interrelationships between these various issues which is of most importance.

The paradigm

It was explained in section 2.4.2 that the core of an organisation's culture is encapsulated in the *paradigm* of the organisation. Whereas it is easy to talk about culture in vague and generalised terms, the need is to *analyse* and understand culture in much more precise terms. It is therefore useful to conceive of the paradigm as consisting of three layers[2]:

- *Values* may be easy to identify in an organisation, and are often written down as statements about the organisation's mission, objectives or strategies. However, these tend to be vague – such as 'service to the community' or 'equal employment opportunities'.
- *Beliefs* are more specific, but again they are issues which people in the organisation can surface and talk about: for example, a belief that the company should not trade with South Africa, or that professional staff should not have their professional actions appraised by managers.
- *Assumptions* are the real core of an organisation's culture. They are the aspects of organisational life which are *taken for granted* and which people find difficult to identify and explain. For example, Illustration 5.2 shows that in a regional newspaper the culture was based on the assumption that people were prepared to pay for local news and that the newspaper was a key part of the local community. Advertising revenue, which accounted for a large part of the newspaper's income, was seen as necessary but not as the core of the business.

(a) Stories

1. What core beliefs do stories reflect?
2. How pervasive are these beliefs (through levels)?
3. Do stories relate to:
   - strengths or weaknesses?
   - successes or failures?
   - conformity or mavericks?
4. Who are the heroes and villains?
5. What norms do the mavericks deviate from?

(b) Routines and rituals

1. Which routines are emphasised?
2. Which would look odd if changed?
3. What behaviour do routines encourage?
4. What are the key rituals?
5. What core beliefs do they reflect?
6. What do training programmes emphasise?
7. How easy are rituals/routines to change?

(c) Symbols

1. What language and jargon is used?
2. How internal or accessible is it?
3. What aspects of strategy are highlighted in publicity?
4. What status symbols are there?
5. Are there particular symbols which denote the organisation?

(d) Organisational structure

1. How mechanistic/organic are the structures?
2. How flat/hierarchical are the structures?
3. How formal/informal are the structures?
4. Do structures encourage collaboration or competition?
5. What type of power structures do they support?

(e) Control systems

1. What is most closely monitored/controlled?
2. Is emphasis on reward or punishment?
3. Are controls related to history or current strategies?
4. Are there many/few controls?

(f) Power structures

1. What are the core beliefs of the leadership?
2. How strongly held are these beliefs (idealists or pragmatists)?
3. How is power distributed in the organisation (see section 5.4)?
4. Where are the main blockages to change?

(g) Overall

1. What is the dominant culture (defender, prospector, analyser)?
2. How easy is this to change?
3. Are there any linking threads through the separate elements of the web?

Figure 5.3 Analysing the cultural web: some useful questions

ILLUSTRATION 5.2
Cultural web of a regional newspaper

The cultural web is a useful conceptual tool for understanding the way in which beliefs and assumptions – linked to political, symbolic and structural aspects of the organisation – both guide and constrain the development of strategy.

The newspaper business illustrated was based in the north of England, operating in a market in which it had enjoyed long-standing dominance with its local evening newspaper. By the early 1990s it faced increasing competitive pressure from free newspapers and entry by competitors historically based elsewhere. Moreover, a changing local population meant less traditional loyalty to the newspaper, and longer-term developments of media alternatives raised both strategic opportunities and possible threats.

The need was for a substantial short-term rethink of competitive strategy and a longer-term rethink of the direction of the business. Yet it became clear that the managers took for granted that their paid-for daily newspapers 'would always be around' and that the local community somehow needed them. Moreover, the technology, structure and routines of the business did little to promote strategic thinking: the business was necessarily run on short-term deadlines – hours, not days; and the 'macho' self-image of those running the business, and the vertical, hierarchical ways of managing the business, prevented a free flow of ideas across management boundaries.

Suggestions by some younger managers that the prime purpose of the business was to create an effective advertising medium (the main source of revenue) were set aside, given the dominant belief that 'we are a *news*paper' – a view reinforced by the symbolic significance of the presses, the associated technical jargon, the street distribution system and the stories linked to news gathering and coverage.

This taken-for-grantedness can be very difficult to surface. Nonetheless, unless these beliefs and assumptions are surfaced and challenged, very little will change in the organisation. The assumptions are likely to override the logical, explicit statements of the organisation's preferred strategies.

Insights into the paradigm can be gained by analysing the elements of the cultural web (see Figure 5.3). The *process* by which this analysis might be undertaken can vary, from listening to people talk about their organisation to asking managers to undertake the analysis themselves using the cultural web as a checklist. It can also be done by observing the organisation's day-to-day operation and building a 'picture' of the web in that way. Figure 5.3 provides a check-

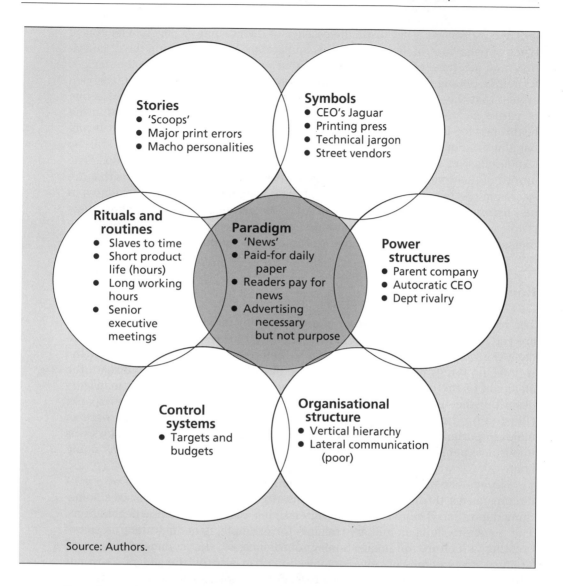

Source: Authors.

list of questions which can be used to guide an analysis using the cultural web (by any of these processes).

Stories

The stories[3] in organisations provide valuable insights into the core beliefs and assumptions of the organisation. Stories arise and develop over time through the experiences of individuals and groups undertaking the day-to-day tasks of the organisation, and typically deal with the *heroes and villains, successes, disas-*

ters and *mavericks*. They distill the essence of the company's past and legitimise types of behaviour of those individuals and groups currently within the organisation, and attitudes of outsiders towards that organisation. They are the devices for telling people what is important in the organisation. For example, it has been argued that the dominant culture of the health service in many countries is one of curing sickness rather than promoting health. Most of the stories within the health service concern spectacular developments in curing – particularly terminal illnesses. In contrast, community medicine and preventative care are still the 'Cinderellas' of the health service and receive little attention and kudos. The heroes of the organisation are in curing not caring. Illustration 5.2 shows that the stories in the regional newspaper are about spectacular successes or failures in news stories and the macho personalities of the organisation. Stories about mavericks can be useful since, by pointing up what is regarded as unacceptable or unusual, they emphasise what are the normal expectations.

Routines and rituals

The *routines* of an organisation represent the way in which the value activities are carried out in delivering the organisation's strategies. Routines are the mundane aspects of organisational life which often become taken for granted as 'the way we do things round here'. Indeed, the outsider might be able to discern the elements of the organisation's paradigm by listening to the way that managers describe the routines of their organisation. In the regional newspaper (Illustration 5.2) the routines for meeting tight publication deadlines were of major importance. They were part of a culture where up-to-the-minute news was important, people were slaves to time and short-term performance was dominant.

Rituals are of a higher order than routines. They are the special events or circumstances through which the organisation highlights or emphasises something important. Examples of rituals are training, meetings or union negotiations. The 'square-bashing' in military training, for example, is an important means of creating a culture of unquestioning obedience to the command structure. Training programmes of other organisations can also be thought of as rituals which give useful pointers to core beliefs. For example, some organisations have training only in the technical skills of the job, whereas others place more emphasis on the development of general skills and attitudes. By the 1990s many of the major international accountancy firms had extended their services beyond auditing and taxation into management consultancy. This required a major shift of emphasis in their training programmes towards business skills and awareness, which had beneficial effects on their core business too. International expansion also led to the use of training events to build a new international culture within the organisation – with some considerable difficulty. Other examples of rituals in organisations are given in Figure 11.5.

Symbols

The importance of symbols[4] and symbolic behaviour is often underplayed both in understanding organisational culture and also in assisting strategic change. They can be an important means of understanding the types of behaviour which are expected and rewarded in the organisation. For example, the symbols of hierarchy such as office size, carpets and car-parking spaces are useful clues to the extent to which the organisation is rooted to its established way of doing things.

The type of *language* used in an organisation can also be helpful in understanding the organisational paradigm. For example, when the the hovercraft service started Channel crossings in the late 1960s, the companies deliberately mimicked airlines rather than ships, and this was sustained throughout by rituals and symbols – they had a 'pilot', dressed their 'cabin staff' as did airlines, had 'flights' not sailings, etc. In the newspaper example (Illustration 5.2) the technical *jargon* was inaccessible to outsiders, indicating the clannish and somewhat exclusive nature of the enterprise as perceived by the managers and, arguably, a somewhat inward looking culture.

Although symbols are shown separately in the cultural web, it should be remembered that many elements of the web are symbolic in the sense that they convey messages beyond their functional purpose. Routines, control and reward systems, and structures are symbolic in so far as they signal the type of behaviour which is valued in the organisation.

Public statements, such as in the company annual report, are a visible symbol of which stakeholder groups the organisation is most concerned with serving.

Organisational structure

Chapter 10 will discuss how the organisational structure and design is crucial to the successful implementation of strategy. However, organisational structures also preserve the core beliefs of the organisation and are legitimised by its power structure. It is therefore important to understand how the structure relates to the paradigm of the organisation, and how easy or difficult it will be to change in support of new strategies.

The way in which responsibility and authority are distributed within the organisational structure is also an important part of the culture. For example, an organisation which is structured and managed as a series of separate and competitive units is likely to have a cohesive culture at the level of these subunits which makes collaborative ventures (between units) difficult. Indeed, in many such organisations the systems of control and reward are also likely to have developed in a way which encourages and supports competitive (rather than collaborative) behaviour. It is not surprising, therefore, that individuals and groups are likely to favour strategies which can be pursued in a devolved rather than an integrated way. As devolution sweeps through the large organisations in the

1990s, there is a considerable danger that one casualty will be the ability to co-ordinate joint ventures between businesses, divisions or service departments as the culture at subunit level strengthens at the expense of a cohesive corporate culture.

Control systems

Understanding of an organisation's paradigm can be assisted by observing the types of control system in the organisation, and the issues which are most close-ly monitored or promoted. For example, many public-service organisations have been obsessed with stewardship of funds rather than quality of service. This can be clearly seen in their bureaucratic procedures, which were almost entirely con-cerned with accounting for spending and had little regard for outputs. The move to develop output-related *performance indicators* is of major concern to many public- and private-sector service organisations in the 1990s as the paradigms of the organisations shift towards service and client care.

Reward systems are important indicators of what behaviours are encour-aged within the organisation, and can prove to be a major barrier to the success of new strategies. For example, an organisation which has individually based bonus schemes related to volume of throughput will find this a difficult culture within which to promote strategies requiring teamwork and an emphasis on quality not volume. In a more general sense, it is useful to observe whether con-trol systems are geared to reward or punishment, since this will influence the dominant attitudes to risk taking. In the newspaper example (Illustration 5.2) the control systems were geared to short-term targets and budgeting – again reflect-ing the centrality of *news* as the core business, as distinct from long-term plan-ning or development.

Power structures

Power is a key force which shapes organisation culture, and also a means where-by some expectations influence strategy more strongly than others. Power will be discussed more fully in section 5.4 below. It will be seen that power often accrues to those perceived most able to reduce the uncertainty in the organisa-tion.[5] Since the paradigm is the set of assumptions by which people reduce their personal uncertainty, change may require an attack on the power structures which protect and legitimise the paradigm. Therefore an important issue to assess is the strength of belief among the most powerful individuals and groups: in other words, whether they are *idealists* or *pragmatists*.

Overall

The cultural web has so far been used to analyse culture through the separate elements of the web. However, it is important to be able to describe the dominant culture of the organisation *as a whole* – as manifested in these separate elements. This can be done in several ways:

- One means of achieving an overall view of culture is through observing the way in which strategies have developed *historically*. History is a powerful influence on an organisation's culture and, in turn, affects the choices of strategies. Stinchcombe[6] found that the way that companies were organised and managed bore a strong relationship to the era in which their particular industry had its foundations. For example, the pre-industrial revolution industries, such as farming or construction, still retain many of the features associated with craft industries despite modern methods of operation.
- History and tradition can often be forces which prevent organisations from recognising the need to respond to key changes in the environment, such as new technologies. The extent to which this is a potential problem for an organisation needs to be assessed, particularly if it is likely to cause *strategic drift* (as discussed in Chapter 2). Illustration 5.3 shows how important history and tradition can be in mergers.
- Miles and Snow,[7] whose findings were discussed in Chapter 2, categorise organisations into three basic types in terms of how they behave strategically (Figure 5.4). When undertaking a strategic analysis this categorisation provides a means of assessing the dominant culture of the organisation. By reviewing the historical choices of strategy, the analyst can distinguish between a *defender* and a *prospector* organisation, and hence judge the extent to which new strategies might fit the current paradigm.
- The extent to which a *cohesive culture* is a strength or a weakness for the organisation needs to be assessed. A cohesive culture almost demands, and often produces, a situation where more and more like-minded individuals are selected into key leadership roles or become socialised into the organisation's dominant beliefs and approaches. The symptoms are usually clear: established routines are not deviated from; powerful symbols and stories exist which encourage a commitment to the strategies which the organisation has pursued *historically*; there is little tolerance of questioning and challenge; and so on. These are the circumstances where strategic drift is likely to occur. However, managers may be unable to detect this drift themselves. It is often the case that it is not until performance has significantly dropped that the stimulus for change occurs. Perhaps a more healthy situation is one of constructive friction – where a strong corporate culture is maintained, but where the core beliefs and assumptions are continuously subjected to critique.
- The dominant culture also tends to vary from one industry to another, making the transition of managers between sectors quite difficult. A number

ILLUSTRATION 5.3
Peace at the Savoy – at last

History is a powerful force in shaping the values and expectations within a company, and these are not easy to change – even for a major new shareholder.

In November 1989 four of the most distinguished hoteliers in the world met to shake hands on a deal to end a corporate feud which had lasted almost nine years. Lord Charles Forte and his son Rocco – the dynasty at the helm of Trusthouse Forte (THF) – eventually agreed to shelve their long-cherished dream to take over the Savoy Hotel Company, owner of Claridges, the Connaught, the Berkeley, Simpsons and the Savoy itself. It had been a classic octogenarian battle between the blue-blooded Savoy – personified in its 81-year-old former chairman Sir Hugh Wontner, and the upstart Charles Forte, who started with one milkbar after the Second World War and built up a £3bn catering and hotel empire.

Although THF had held 69 per cent of the Savoy's shares since 1981, it only had 42 per cent voting rights. After failing to gain representation on the board, THF had resorted to legal action. The deal in 1989 eventually gave it two seats on the board for Rocco Forte and the THF finance director, Donald Main. In return they agreed not to acquire any more Savoy shares and to drop all litigation. Giles Shephard, the managing director of the Savoy, remained as determined as Sir Hugh Wontner to preserve the special identity of the Savoy hotels. He believed that hotels of that type were best run by small companies. Nevertheless he acknowledged that the THF directors could bring knowledge and experience of another type of business to the board. But any decisions on changes and developments would clearly need the approval of the full board where Rocco Forte and Donald Main would have to act as Savoy directors and not competitors.

Source: *Sunday Times*, 3 December 1989.

of private-sector managers were encouraged to join public services during the 1980s in an attempt to inject new cultures/outlooks into the public sector. Many were surprised at the difficulties they experienced in adjusting their management style to the different traditions and expectations of their new organisation.

Organisation type	Characteristics of strategic decision making		
	Dominant objectives	Preferred strategies	Planning and control systems
1. Defenders	Desire for a secure and stable niche in market.	Specialisation; cost-efficient production; marketing emphasises price and service to defend current business; tendency to vertical integration.	Centralised, detailed control; emphasis on cost efficiency; extensive use of formal planning.
2. Prospectors	Location and exploitation of new product and market opportunities	Growth through product and market development (often in spurts); constant monitoring of environmental change; multiple technologies.	Emphasis on flexibility, decentralised control, use of *ad hoc* measurements.
3. Analysers	Desire to match new ventures to present shape of business.	Steady growth through market penetration; exploitation of applied research; followers in the market.	Very complicated; co-ordinating roles between functions (e.g. product managers); intensive planning.

Source: Adapted from R. E. Miles and C. C. Snow, *Organizational Strategy, Structure and Process*, McGraw-Hill, 1978.

Figure 5.4 Different types of organisational culture and their influences on strategic decision making

5.3 Stakeholder analysis[8]

The attitudes of individuals – both inside and around an organisation – will be strongly influenced by the cultural context described above. Few individuals have sufficient power to determine unilaterally the strategy of their organisation. Influence is likely to occur only because individuals share expectations with others by being a part of a stakeholder group. Individuals will need to identify themselves with the aims and ideals of these stakeholder groups, and this may occur within departments, at different geographical locations, at different levels in the hierarchy, etc. Most individuals will belong to more than one stakeholder group. It will be seen below that stakeholder groups are not necessarily ever present and enshrined within the organisation's structure – they tend to arise as a result of events.

Equally important are the external stakeholders of the organisation, and these would typically include bankers, customers, suppliers, shareholders or unions. Often they may seek to influence company strategy through their links with internal stakeholders. For example, customers may pressurise sales managers to represent their interests within the company. Even if external stakeholders are passive, they may represent real constraints on the development of new strategies. Understanding stakeholders and how they are likely to influence the organisation's strategy is a very important part of any strategic analysis and forms the core of an assessment of the cultural/political dimension of strategy.

5.3.1 Conflicts of expectations

Since the expectations of stakeholder groups are likely to differ, it is quite normal for conflict to exist within organisations regarding the importance and/or desirability of many aspects of strategy. This section considers some of the typical expectations that exist and how they might conflict (see Figure 5.5). In most situations a compromise will need to be reached between expectations which cannot all be achieved simultaneously – between, for example, growth and profitability; growth and control/independence; cost efficiency and jobs; volume/mass provision and quality/specialisation – and the problems of suboptimisation will have to be tackled where the development of one part of an organisation may be at the expense of another.

What emerges is the need to understand the expectations of different stakeholder groups, and to weigh these in terms of the power that they exercise. For example, banks may not have a shareholding in a company, but may well have a direct interest through the funds they loan. Their main expectation is to achieve

---

1. In order to grow, short-term profitability, cash flow and pay levels may need to be sacrificed.

2. When family businesses grow, the owners may lose control if they need to appoint professional managers.

3. New developments may require additional funding through share issue or loans. In either case financial independence may be sacrificed.

4. Public ownership of shares will require more openness and accountability from the management.

5. Cost efficiency through capital investment can mean job losses.

6. Extending into mass markets may require a decline in quality standards.

7. In public services, a common conflict is between mass provision and specialist services (e.g. preventative dentistry or heart transplants).

8. In public services, savings in one area (e.g. social security benefits) may result in increases elsewhere (e.g. school meals, medical care).

Figure 5.5 Some common conflicts of expectations

a secure return on their investment in terms of interest, and a company with high borrowings may well discover that meeting the bank's expectation becomes a dominant requirement.

Government (both central and local) is an example of how a variety of stakeholder groups with different expectations attempt to influence the formulation of strategy. The electorate is able to influence the situation by allocating power to political parties. They in turn are subject to their own internal pressures from groupings with differing expectations, and must reconcile their policies with the views of opposition parties and the administrators in the government departments.

Mapping out the various expectations within an organisation and where they conflict contributes significantly to an understanding of the core beliefs in the organisation and its strategic position. Together with an assessment of the power structure of the organisation (see below) this is necessary in order to assess future strategies in relation to their *cultural fit* and how easy or difficult change is likely to be.

5.3.2 Identifying stakeholders

When analysing stakeholders there is a danger of concentrating too heavily on the formal structure of an organisation as a basis for identification, since this can be the easiest place to look for the divisions in expectations mentioned previously. It is, however, necessary to unearth the 'informal' stakeholder groups and assess their importance.

Other problems in analysis are that individuals tend to belong to more than one group, and stakeholders will also line up in different groupings depending on the issue in hand. For example, marketing and production departments could well be united in the face of proposals to drop certain product lines, while being in fierce opposition regarding plans to buy in new items to the product range. It is often *specific events* which trigger off the formation of stakeholder groups. For this reason it is helpful to speculate on the degree of unity or diversity between the various groups if faced with a number of possible future events. In this respect what we are considering here is also a tool of strategic evaluation. Nevertheless this process can be very helpful during strategic analysis in uncovering potential alliances or rifts which may be significant when thinking about future strategic choices.

Figure 5.6 shows a typical analysis in the case of a company which operated on two sites in the UK (Nottingham and Lincoln). The various internal and external stakeholders are identified and the table is used to map out their expected reactions to a variety of possible changes. Several useful points emerge from this analysis:

●   There will always be some events about which the majority of stakeholders can unite. Such solidarity tends to occur during the early stages of

Possible changes	A Whole company	B Internal stakeholders						C External stakeholders			
		1 Market. dept	2 Prod. dept	3 Notts plant	4 Lincoln plant	5 Gradu-ates	6 Clerical staff	1 Suppl. A	2 Cust. X	3 Shr.hdr M	4 Local comm.
1. Sell out to competitor	−	−	−	−	−	−	−	0	−	0	−
2. Introduce computerised systems	+	+	?	+	0	+	−	0	+	+	0
3. Close Lincoln plant	?	+	−	+	−	0	0	0	+	0	−
4. Develop new EC markets	?	?	−	+	−	0	0	+	−	+	0
5. Subcontract production	?	+	−	−	−	0	0	−	0	−	−

+ = support   0 = neutral   − = oppose   ? = divided opinion

Figure 5.6 The attitudes of stakeholders towards possible future changes

development of new companies, or when survival is threatened by such events as a possible takeover by a major competitor.

- New groups may become important in certain of the situations envisaged. For example, the proposal to close the Lincoln plant would meet resistance not only from the employees there, but also from the local support which they would be able to muster. Equally, computerisation would be resisted by clerical staff, who had hitherto never been viewed as a cohesive group.

- In some cases there would be divided views within one of the stakeholder groups. For example, the export section of the marketing department might be delighted by plans to expand sales in the EC, but not so their UK counterparts. Thus these would need to be viewed as separate stakeholders in such circumstances.

- At this stage it is important to identify potential alliances between stakeholders regarding any of these future options. In this example, a particularly significant observation is that the possibility of closing the Lincoln plant could well see an alliance between the Nottingham plant and the marketing department with strong support from the major customer X. In any such move the Lincoln plant could only rely on production staff and local community action; others seem to be broadly indifferent.

5.3.3 Stakeholder mapping[9]

Assessing the importance of stakeholder expectations is an important part of any strategic analysis. It consists of making judgements on three issues:

- How likely each stakeholder group is to impress its expectations on the company.
- Whether they have the means to do so. This is concerned with the power of stakeholder groups (see section 5.4).
- The likely impact of stakeholder expectations on future strategies.

Two methods of mapping stakeholders will be considered: the power/dynamism matrix; and the power/interest matrix.

Power/dynamism matrix

Figure 5.7 shows the power/dynamism matrix on which stakeholders can be plotted. This is a useful way of assessing where the 'political efforts' should be channelled during the development of new strategies. The most difficult group to cope with are those in segment D, since they are in a powerful position to block or support new strategies, but their 'stance' is difficult to predict. The implication should be clear: a means must be found to 'test out' new strategies with these stakeholders before an irrevocable position has been established. In contrast,

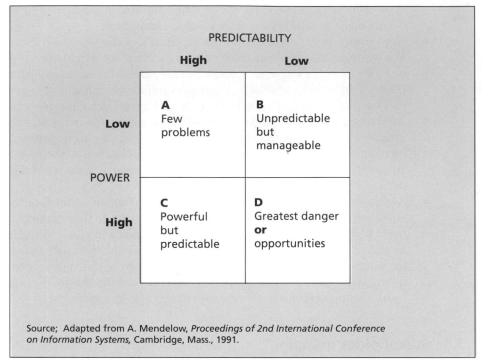

Figure 5.7 Stakeholder mapping: power/dynamism matrix

stakeholders in segment C are likely to influence strategy through the process of managers anticipating their stance and building strategies which will address their expectations. Although stakeholders in segments A and B have less power, this does not mean they are unimportant. Indeed, the active support of such stakeholders may, in itself, have an influence on the attitude of the more powerful stakeholders.

Power/interest matrix

A valuable development of the power/dynamism matrix can be seen in Figure 5.8. This classifies stakeholders in relation to the power they hold and the extent to which they are likely to show interest in the organisation's strategies. The matrix indicates the type of relationship which the organisation will need to establish with each stakeholder group. Clearly the acceptability of strategies to the *key players* (segment D) should be a key consideration during the formulation and evaluation of new strategies. Often the most difficult stakeholders are those in segment C. Although these stakeholders might in general be relatively passive, readers are reminded that stakeholder groups tend to emerge and influence strategy as a result of *specific events*. It is therefore critically important that

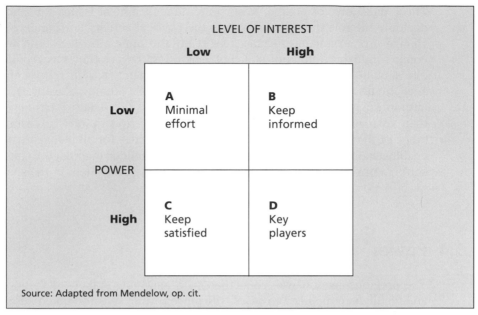

Figure 5.8 Stakeholder mapping: power/interest matrix

the likely reaction of stakeholders towards future strategies is given full consideration. A disastrous situation can arise if their level of interest is underrated and they suddenly *reposition* to segment D and frustrate the adoption of a new strategy. Similarly, the needs of stakeholders in segment B need to be properly addressed – largely through information. They can be crucially important 'allies' in influencing the attitudes of more powerful stakeholders. The value of this type of stakeholder mapping is in assessing the following:

- Whether the political/cultural situation is likely to undermine the adoption of a particular strategy. In other words, mapping is a way of assessing *cultural fit* (which will be an important consideration in strategic evaluation, as discussed in Chapter 7).
- Who the key *blockers* and *facilitators* of change are likely to be, and therefore, whether strategies need to be pursued to *reposition* certain stakeholders. This could be to lessen the influence of a key player or, in certain instances, to ensure that there are more key players who will champion the strategy (this is often critical in the public-sector context).
- The extent to which *maintenance* activities will be needed to discourage stakeholders from repositioning themselves. This is what is meant by *keep satisfied* in relation to stakeholders in segment C, and to a lesser extent *keep informed* in segment B. *Side payments* to stakeholders as a means of securing their acceptance of new strategies have traditionally been regarded as a key maintenance activity.

These questions, of course, raise some difficult ethical issues for managers in deciding the role they should play in the political activity surrounding strategic change. For example, are managers really the honest brokers who weigh the conflicting expectations of stakeholder groups? Or are they answerable to just one stakeholder – such as shareholders – and hence is their role to ensure the acceptability of their strategies with other stakeholders? Or are they, as many authors suggest, the real power behind the throne, constructing strategies to suit their own purposes and managing stakeholder expectations to ensure acceptance of these strategies? These are important issues for all managers to consider. Illustration 5.4 shows an example of a stakeholder map used to analyse the shifts in position of key stakeholders in UK local government in the second part of the 1980s.

5.4 Power

The previous section was concerned with analysing stakeholder expectations, and highlighted the need to assess the power of the various stakeholders. Power is the mechanism by which expectations are able to influence strategies. It has been seen that in most organisations power will be unequally shared between the various stakeholders. In other words, formulation of strategy tends to be dominated by one group, usually the management of the company – although they are unlikely to be a single cohesive group/stakeholder. They may need to be regarded as sub-groups or factions.

Before proceeding, it is necessary to understand what is meant here by 'power'. In particular, a distinction needs to be drawn between the power that people or groups derive from their position within the organisation, and the power that they actually possess by other means. For the purposes of strategic analysis, power is best understood as the extent to which individuals or groups are able to persuade, induce or coerce others into following certain courses of action. This is the mechanism by which one set of expectations will dominate strategic development or seek compromise with others. Analysis of power must, therefore, begin with an assessment of the sources of power.

5.4.1 Sources of power within organisations[10]

Power within organisations can be derived in a variety of ways, any of which may provide an avenue whereby the expectations of an individual or group may influence company strategies. The following are the normally recognised sources of power (see Figure 5.9):

1. *Hierarchy* provides people with formal power over others and is one method by which senior managers influence strategy. In particular, if

ILLUSTRATION 5.4
Shifts in stakeholder positioning in UK local government

A repositioning of a major stakeholder will trigger a realignment of other stakeholders as priorities and strategies are changed.

The late 1980s in the UK was a major period of change in local government as the Conservative central government attempted to exert more control and accountability over local authorities, many of which were Labour controlled. Between 1985 and 1990 this produced a significant shift in strategy at local authority level from what had been described as *policy-led* to *finance-led*. In other words, the need to define and deliver strategy within strict financial limits became the dominant consideration for those running local authorities. This change in emphasis caused – and required – some important repositioning to occur among stakeholders, as shown on the stakeholder map below, which illustrates some of the more important shifts which occurred in Sheffield during this period:

A. Central government decided to be more proactive as discussed above.
B. The private sector was actively encouraged to play a greater role in the local economy directly (B1), through new agencies such as the Sheffield Development Corporation (B2) and the Training and Enterprise Council (TEC) (B3).
C. The trade unions became less influential (C) in line with the national trend.
D. A more executive style of leadership emerged (D1), reducing the power of the Labour group as a whole (D2).

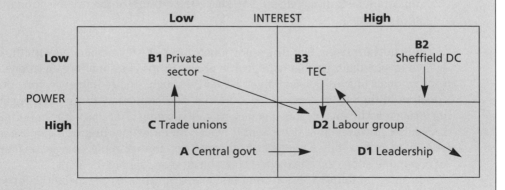

Source: John Darwin, MBA project, Sheffield Business School.

(a) Within organisations	**(b) For external stakeholders**
1. Hierarchy (formal power), e.g. autocratic decision making	1. Control of strategic resources, e.g. materials, labour, money
2. Influence (informal power), e.g. charismatic leadership	2. Involvement in strategic implementation, e.g. distribution outlets, agents
3. Control of strategic resources, e.g. strategic products (coal)	3. Possession of knowledge (skills), e.g. subcontractors
4. Possession of knowledge/skills, e.g. computer specialists	4. Through internal links, e.g. informal influence
5. Control of the environment, e.g. negotiating skills	
6. Involvement in strategic implementation, e.g. by exercising discretion	

Figure 5.9 Sources of power

strategic decision making is confined to top management, this can give them considerable power. However, it is important to remember that this type of power has a very limited effect if used in isolation. Many industrial disputes illustrate the impotence of management if they rely only on formal power.

2. *Influence* can be an important source of power and may arise from personal qualities (of leadership) or because a high level of consensus exists within the group or company (i.e. people are willing to support the prevailing viewpoint). Indeed, there is strong support for the view that the most important task of managers is to shape the culture of the organisation to suit its strategy.

It is not surprising that those individuals most closely associated with the core beliefs or paradigm are likely to accrue power. In professional organisations, key professionals have considerable power through their influence on others (doctors in the health services; accountants in accountancy firms; even engineering firms tend to have qualified engineers as managing directors). It is important to recognise, however, that the extent to which an individual or group can use influence is determined by a number of other factors. For example, access to channels of communication (e.g. the media) could be an essential requirement.

In many situations, prior commitments to principles or specific courses of action can give individuals influence. Some of these principles may be quite central to the organisation's mission. For example, following the major changes in eastern Europe in 1989, many organisations were reshaped with the explicit purpose of excluding Communist Party members from senior management positions. This led to some difficult situations in the short term, where those who had been party members for pragmatic rather than ideological reasons were sidelined while other, often less able, managers leapfrogged into senior positions.

3. *Control of strategic resources* is a major source of power within companies. It should be remembered that the relative importance of different resources will change over time, and hence power derived in this way can show dramatic shifts. The power of organised labour is most potent when demand for output is high and labour supply short. The decline in the position of car workers in the wages league during the 1970s was evidence of the erosion of this source of power. Within any one company the extent to which the various departments are seen as powerful will vary with the company's circumstances. Design or R & D departments may be powerful in companies developing new products or processes, whereas marketing people may dominate companies which are primarily concerned with developing new markets.

4. The logical extension of the previous point is that individuals can derive power from their specialist *knowledge or skills*. Certain individuals may be viewed as irreplaceable by the company, and some will jealously guard this privileged position by creating a mystique around their job. This can be a risky personal strategy, since others in the organisation may be spurred to acquire these skills or to devise methods of bypassing them. The power of many organisations' computer specialists was threatened with the advent of microcomputers, which provided others within the organisation with a means of bypassing those specialists. The rapid internationalisation of many organisations has spurred individuals to improve their language skills and international experience as key requirements in the labour market.

5. *Control of the environment* is another source of power within organisations. Most people know that events in the company's environment are likely to influence company performance. However, some groups will have significantly more knowledge of, contact with, and influence over the environment than others. This can become a source of power within the company, since these groups are able to reduce the uncertainty experienced by others. It is probably for this reason that financial and marketing managers have traditionally been seen as dominant in strategy determination, while production managers have taken a back seat. This source of power becomes most important when the environment is hostile or unpredictable. Then most of the factions will unite behind those who are considered best able to protect the company, despite the fact that the medicine which might be doled out could represent a denial of many of their expectations.

6. *Exercising discretion* is a most significant source of power within many organisations and is often overlooked. Individuals derive power because they are involved in the company's decision processes by the very nature of their jobs. The execution of strategy, by its very complexity, cannot be controlled in all its minutest detail by one person or group. Hence many other people in the company will need to interpret and execute particular parts of the strategy, and in doing so will use their own personal discretion. This is a major source of power for middle management in organisations. The extent to which discretion is allowed to influence strategy is obviously related to the types of structure and control system within the organisation. These will be discussed in Chapter 10.

5.4.2 Sources of power for external stakeholders

As with internal groups, those outside the organisation may have a number of sources of power which help them influence the organisation's strategies. These are also summarised in Figure 5.9:

1. *Resource dependence*[11] is a common source of power, as discussed in section 3.4.2. The power that buyers or suppliers exercise over an organisation is also likely to depend on the extent to which they are able to exercise control over resource provision or acquisition. Long-term dependence on a particular resource can shape the attitudes and culture of an organisation in a way which makes 'switching' very difficult. However, dependence may often be much wider than just suppliers or buyers. It may be ingrained in the organisation's routines and assumptions. This has been a problem experienced by many eastern European firms as they have switched from the state to a free-market situation.

2. *Involvement in implementation* through linkages within the value system can be an important source of power for suppliers, channels and buyers, as we saw in Chapters 3 and 4. One of the major changes since the 1960s in many industries has been a shift of power from the manufacturing sector to the distribution sector. The greater knowledge that distribution companies have of trends in consumer tastes has allowed them to dictate terms to manufacturers, rather than simply being outlets for goods designed and planned by manufacturing companies.

3. *Knowledge and skills* critical to the success of the company are another source of power. A subcontractor, for example, may derive power in this way, if it performs a vital activity in the company's value chain.

4. *Internal links* can provide a route for external stakeholders to influence company strategy. This is determined by the strategy-making processes

within the organisation. At one extreme, a highly authoritarian organisation is likely to be hostile to any attempts by outside stakeholders to be formally involved in formulation of strategy, and therefore any influence on strategy must be derived in other ways. In contrast, some organisations including the public services actively seek to involve a wide variety of stakeholders in strategic decision making.

5.4.3 Methods of assessing power[12]

Since there are many different sources of power and each is dependent upon circumstances, a good way of coping with this complex situation is by identifying *indicators of power*. There are four useful indicators of power:

- The *status* of the individual or group. One measure of status might be position within the hierarchy, but others are equally important: for example, an individual's salary, or job grades of groups. Equally, the reputation that a group or individual holds with others will be very relevant.
- The *claim on resources* as measured by the size of a department's budget, or the number of employees within that group. In particular, trends in the proportion of resources claimed by that group may be a useful indicator of the extent to which its power is waxing or waning. A useful comparison can be made with similar groups in comparable organisations.
- *Representation* in powerful positions. The best example of this is the composition of the board of directors and their particular specialisms. The weakness of the production function may result from lack of representation at board level. Within less hierarchical organisations, representation on important committees could be a measure of power, although a simple head count in this type of analysis would overlook the extent to which the individuals are influential. Here individual status should be taken into consideration.
- *Symbols of power*. Internal division of power may be indicated in a variety of ways. Such physical symbols as the size and location of people's offices and whether they have a secretary, carpets or newspapers delivered each morning are all important clues. Whether individuals are addressed by their first or second names, and even the way they dress, may be symbols of power. In more bureaucratic organisations, the existence of 'distribution lists' for internal memoranda and other information can give useful clues to the power structure. These lists do not always neatly reflect the formal hierarchical structure and may provide pointers as to who is viewed as powerful within the organisation.

It should be remembered that no single indicator is likely to uncover the structure of power within a company. However, by looking at all four it may be possible to identify which people or groups appear to have power. Figure 5.10 illustrates how such an analysis might be performed to assess the relative power of the marketing and production departments, and the Nottingham and Lincoln plants, in the previous example (Figure 5.6). It is clear that the marketing department is seen as powerful by all measures, and the production department universally weak. Equally, the Nottingham plant looks particularly powerful in relation to Lincoln.

Alongside this internal assessment of power, a similar analysis of the power held by external stakeholders needs to be carried out. The indicators of power are slightly different:

- The *status* of an external party such as a supplier is usually indicated by the way they are discussed among company employees, and whether they respond quickly to the supplier's demands.
- *Resource dependence* can often be measured directly. For example, the proportion of a company's business tied up with any one customer, or a similar dependence on suppliers, can normally be easily measured. Perhaps the key indicator is the ease with which that supplier, financier or customer could be *switched* at short notice. It might also be useful to examine the routines of the organisation – particularly the external linkages. These should indicate how dependency has been 'built in' to the organisational culture.
- *Negotiating arrangements* are another indicator of external power: whether external parties are treated at arm's length or are actively involved in negotiations with the company. For example, a customer who is invited to negotiate over the price of a contract is in a more powerful position than a similar company which is given a fixed price on a take-it-or-leave-it basis.
- *Symbols* are equally valuable clues: whether the management team wines and dines some customer or supplier, for example,' or the level of person in the company who deals with a particular supplier. The care and attention paid to correspondence with outsiders will tend to differ from one party to another.

Again no single measure will give a full understanding of the extent of the power held by external groups, but the combined analysis will be very useful. Figure 5.10 illustrates how an analysis of the power of external stakeholders can be performed using the data from Figure 5.6. This would be important data in the process of *stakeholder mapping*, since the strategic importance of power is also related to whether individuals or groups are likely to exercise their power.

Figure 5.11 maps stakeholders on to the power/interest matrix in relation to the possibility of the Lincoln plant closure. It can be seen that Lincoln's only real hope of survival is to encourage supplier A to reposition by raising its level of interest in opposition to the closure. Perhaps shareholder M could be helpful in this process.

1. Internal stakeholders

Indicators of power	1 Marketing dept*	2 Production*	3 Nottingham plant*	4 Lincoln plant*
(a) Status				
1. Position in hierarchy (closeness to board)	H	L	H	M
2. Salary of top manager	H	L	H	L
3. Average grade of staff	H	M	H	L
(b) Claim on resources				
1. Number of staff	M	H	M	M
2. Size of similar company	H	L	H	L
3. Budget as % of total	H	M	H	L
(c) Representation				
1. Number of directors	H	None	M	None
2. Most influential directors	H	None	M	None
(d) Symbols				
1. Quality of accommodation	H	L	M	M
2. Support services	H	L	H	L

2. External stakeholders

Indicators of power	Supplier A*	Customer X*	Shareholder M*
1. Status	H	H	L
2. Resource dependence	L	H	H
3. Negotiating arrangements	M	H	L
4. Symbols	H	H	L

* These are examples - the list will clearly vary from one situation to another.

H = high   M = medium   L = low

Figure 5.10 Assessing the relative power of stakeholders

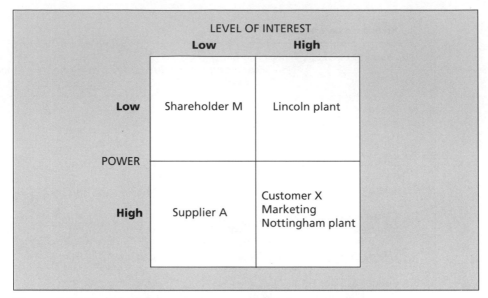

Figure 5.11 Stakeholder mapping: an example

5.5 Organisational purposes

The discussion so far has been concerned with understanding how the cultural context of an organisation influences the expectations of individuals and stakeholders. In turn these expectations influence the *purposes* of the organisation, as a result of the power which the group possesses. So the purposes tend to be shaped by those who have most power – often the organisation's management.

However, this dominant stakeholder will be influenced by the expectations of other stakeholders, and in particular by the power which they perceive these groups to have when purposes are being formulated. Some stakeholder groups do not seek to impose purposes on an organisation, but they do insist on imposing constraints. *Stakeholder mapping* (section 5.3.3) is a way of analysing the extent to which stakeholders are likely to influence the organisation's purposes.

Illustration 5.5 shows the sort of formal purposes stated by organisations, and these can be thought of as a *hierarchy* of purposes, as summarised in Figure 5.12. The important issue for managers is to recognise that these various statements of an organisation's purposes will play different roles in the strategic management process.

5.5.1 Mission

The mission of an organisation is its most generalised statement of purpose and can be thought of as an expression of its *raison d'être*. If there is substantial disagreement within the organisation as to its mission, it may well give rise to real problems in resolving the strategic direction of the organisation. If there is a mission statement and it is to be useful it should address the following issues:[13]

- It should be *visionary* and likely to persist for a significant period of time. This is important as a backcloth against which more detailed objectives and strategies can be developed, delivered and changed over time.
- It should clarify the main *purposes* of the organisation, and the reasons why the organisation exists.
- It should describe the organisation's main activities and the *position* it wishes to attain in its industry.
- There should be a statement of the key *values* of the organisation – particularly regarding attitudes towards stakeholder groups.
- The organisation should have the intention and capability to *live up to* the mission statement.

Although mission statements have become much more widely adopted in the late 1980s[14] and early 1990s, many critics would regard these statements as bland and too wide ranging. This may be necessary given the political nature of strategic management, however, since it is essential at that level to have statements to

Type of purpose	Common characteristics	
1. Mission	General Visionary Central and overriding Often unwritten	Open
2. Corporate objectives	Often expressed financially Express stakeholder expectations Formulated by senior management	Open or closed
3. Unit objectives	Specific to units of organisation Operational Often multiple	Open or closed

Figure 5.12 Organisational purposes

ILLUSTRATION 5.5
Organisational purposes

Increasingly, organisations are finding it useful to 'publish' a statement of their purposes. This is usually done at several levels of detail as the following two examples show.

ICI Agrochemicals

1. *Purposes*
   To help farmers feed the world

2. *Values*
   - Care about the environment and take active steps to lead agrochemical industry
   - Set demanding health and safety standards to safeguard colleagues, customers and public in the manufacture and use of our products
   - Have a shared business purpose
   - All participate in business and take responsibility
   - Respect, support and work for each other as an international team
   - Communicate/share relevant information
   - Encourage innovation
   - Practise highest levels of professionalism, leadership, business and people management
   - Achieve profit and customer service objectives

3. *Objectives*
   - To be number one in profit terms
   - To ensure achievement via staff, rewards, career opportunities, supportive environment, innovation
   - To operate safely with regard to employees and environment
   - High commitment to R & D
   - Relate resources to strategic priorities and performance
   - Efficient international manufacturing and operations systems
   - Relate operation to values and improve performance against the values
   - Effective international people management
   - Consistent and effective communication throughout the business
   - Involvement of all staff and recognition of their roles

which most if not all stakeholders can subscribe. The operationalisation of the mission statement is usually achieved through the more specific objectives of the organisation, which are likely to change over time.

5.5.2 Corporate objectives

Corporate objectives and unit objectives are distinguished in this chapter because there are different 'levels' of objectives with different characteristics in organisations. Corporate objectives are often expressed in financial terms. They

South Yorkshire Police

On behalf of the general public:

1. *Purposes*
    - to uphold the rule of law
    - to keep the Queen's peace
    - to prevent and detect crime
    - to protect life and to help and reassure people in need

2. *Values*
    - Act within the law, serving with integrity the ends of justice
    - Act fairly and reasonably, without fear or favour and without prejudice of any kind
    - Ensure that the rights of all citizens – especially the vulnerable – are safeguarded, regardless of status, race, colour, religion, sex or social background
    - Be courageous in facing physical danger or moral challenge
    - Be honest, courteous and tactful in all that we do and say
    - Use persuasion, common sense and good humour wherever possible as an alternative to the exercise of force and, if force is finally necessary, to use only that which is necessary to accomplish our lawful duty

3. *Objectives*
    Within five years, or as soon as practicable, to have a South Yorkshire Police Service which:

    - is more open, relaxed and honest with ourselves and the public;
    - is more aware of our environment, sensitive to change and positioning ourselves to respond to change;
    - is more clear about our role and our identity and is obviously and justifiably proud of itself;
    - is more closely in touch with our customers, puts them first and delivers what they want quickly, effectively and courteously;
    - makes its decisions at the appropriate levels;
    - is the envy of all other forces

Source: Adapted from company statements.

could be the expression of desired sales, profit levels, rates of growth, dividend levels or share valuations. Increasingly, organisations use corporate objectives of a non-financial nature, such as employee welfare or technological advance, but it is rare for these to be unaccompanied by financial objectives. They are frequently formal statements of how the organisation intends to address stakeholder expectations, as seen in Illustration 5.5. It is becoming increasingly recognised that there should be formal statements of objectives to be met on behalf of a variety of stakeholders, including customers, suppliers, employees and the community at large.

5.5.3 Unit objectives

Unit objectives are here distinguished from corporate objectives in so far as they are likely to have the following characteristics:

- They relate to the individual units of the organisation. For example, they may be the objectives of a division or of one company within a holding company. In the case of public-sector organisations, the unit could be a department of a local authority or a hospital in a particular health authority.
- They may be financial objectives stated in much the same way as corporate objectives, but at a unit level. A corporate objective of a given growth in profit after tax might be translated into an objective for each business unit. They are likely to be more operational in nature than corporate objectives. In this sense they are to do with the planning of operational activity, which is discussed in the next section.
- Multiple objectives might well be more common at the unit level than at the corporate level. This is likely to be the case if objectives are conceived of in operational terms, since the operations of a business are multi-faceted.

5.5.4 The precision of objectives

Illustration 5.5 may be looked at in another way. Some objectives can be measured: for example, 'to be number one in profit terms'. It is possible to say they can be achieved at some future time. These are *closed* objectives. Others are objectives which can never be finally achieved, since they will always persist: for example, 'to be more aware of our environment'. These are *open* objectives.

Many writers[15] have argued that objectives are not helpful unless they are capable of being measured and achieved – unless they are closed. This view is not taken here. Open statements may in fact be just as helpful as closed statements. For example, mission should be a very important influence on strategy: it may concentrate people's perception of their operation on the needs of customers and the utility of the service, for example, and at the same time set the boundaries within which they see the business developing. But statements of mission are very difficult to make in closed terms. The role of this sort of statement is very much to do with *focusing* strategy rather than deciding when it has been 'achieved'. In addition, there may be some objectives which are important but are difficult to quantify or express in measurable terms. An objective such as 'to be a leader in technology' may be highly relevant in today's technological environment, but it may become absurd if it has to be expressed in some measurable way.

However, there are times when specific objectives are required. These are likely to be when urgent action is needed, such as in a crisis or at times of major (usually strategic) transition, and it then becomes essential for management to focus its attention on a limited number of priority requirements. An extreme example would be in a *turnaround* situation. If the choice is between going out of business and surviving, there is no room for latitude through vaguely stated requirements and control.

It is also helpful to have closed objectives for planning purposes. Here the objective becomes a target to be achieved. Suppose a company is seeking to develop and launch new products: it is helpful for managers to have some yardstick, of profitability perhaps, against which to judge the success of the new venture.

5.6 Business ethics

The discussion so far in this chapter has been concerned with how societal values and individual expectations influence strategy. It has also been acknowledged that the managers of organisations have important obligations to a variety of stakeholders and not just the shareholders, and this should be reflected in the organisation's statements of purpose, such as mission statements.

This raises the question of how the activities of organisations affect the behaviour of individuals and the values of society, and concerns important ethical questions about the role of managers in the strategic management process. Much of the initial discussion on these issues centred on the *social responsibility* of organisations and was reflected in policies inclined towards corporate social responsibility. More recently, the debate has widened somewhat and is now more generally described as *business ethics*.[16]

Ethical issues concerning business and public-sector organisations exist at three levels:

- At the *macro* level there are issues about the role of business in the national and international organisation of society. These are largely concerned with assessing the relative virtues of different political/social systems, such as free enterprise, centrally planned economies, etc. There are also important issues of international relationships and the role of business on an international scale.
- At the *corporate* level the issue is often referred to as corporate social responsibility and is focused on the ethical issues facing individual corporate entities (private and public sector) when formulating and implementing strategies.
- At the *individual* level the issue concerns the behaviour and actions of individuals within organisations. This is clearly an important matter for the management of organisations, but it is discussed here only in so far as it affects strategy, and in particular the role of managers in the strategic management process.

5.6.1 The role of business in society

It is not the intention of this chapter to explore the detailed philosophical debates about the relative merits of different types of social organisation. However, at a practical level it is important when formulating and implementing strategies that managers are conscious of the circumstances in which this is occurring. This is particularly important for multinational organisations, since they will face widely differing situations in their various geographical locations. The key issue for managers is to understand and influence the social stance which the organisation is taking. Figure 5.13 outlines ten *stereotypes* within which there are four broad groupings of response:

1. At one extreme there are organisations which largely conform to Milton Friedman's maxim[17] that 'the business of business is business', and that the 'only social responsibility of business is to increase its profit'. These are in categories 1 to 3 of Figure 5.13. The holders of these beliefs argue not only that is it not the duty of business to be concerned about social issues, but that in doing so business would detract from the primary means by which it should be contributing to society: that is, by operating in an economically efficient way. Their ethical position is that it is the domain of government to prescribe, through legislation, the constraints which society chooses to impose on business in its pursuit of economic efficiency. Expecting companies to exercise these duties can, in extreme cases, undermine the authority of government and give business organisations even more power: for example, multinationals operating in developing countries are often accused of usurping the legitimate roles of government. Somewhat paradoxically, however, it is often devotees of this school of thought that most dislike government interference in business affairs.

2. The next group is in categories 4 to 7 of Figure 5.13. The ethical position of this group is similar to that of the previous group, but it is tempered with a recognition of the long-term benefit to the company of well-managed relationships with external stakeholders. Many of the social issues are therefore managed proactively and carefully as a matter of economic common sense. Sponsorship or welfare provision would be rationalised as sensible expenditures akin to any other form of investment or promotion expenditure. The avoidance of 'shady' marketing practices is necessary to prevent the need for yet more legislation in that area. Businesses in this group argue that, if managers wish to maintain discretion in the long run over issues such as marketing practices, they are wise to operate responsibly in the short term.

3. The third group (category 8), often described as *progressive* organisations, take a different ethical stance. Their view is that stakeholder interests and

Stereotype/role	Behaviour and attitude		
	Economic	Social	Political
1. Profit maximiser	Profit dominates	Regarded as an impediment to profit	Actively avoids involvement with political system
2. Profit satisficer	Growth dominates	Reacts against societal and social pressures as incursions	Avoids interaction with political system
3. Defender of free enterprise	The business of business is business	Reacts against social component as being not within firm's proper scope	Stands up for 'free enterprise'
4. The lone wolf	Prime emphasis on profit	Voluntarily but unilaterally assumes responsibility	Avoids involvement unless cornered
5. Societally engaged	Prime emphasis on profit	Interactively engaged	Engaged only in negotiation of the rules of the game
6. Societally progressive	Prime emphasis on profit	Interactively engaged	Positively involved in formulation of national industrial policies
7. Global actor	Prime emphasis on profit	Interactively engaged	Assumes a responsibility to foster a balance between national and international economic policies
8. Developer of society	Financial self-sufficiency	Produces changes in the lives of mankind through innovation	Positively involved with emphasis on planned development of social infrastructures
9. Social servant	Secondary to societal obligation	Provides essential but non-economic goods and services	Positively involved in formation of national industrial policies with emphasis on social matters
10. Employment provider	Subsidised operation	Provides jobs	Subsidised and supported by government

Source: *Facing Realities: The European Societal Strategy Project,* p. 14, summary report produced by the European Foundation for Management Development and the European Institute for Advanced Studies in Management, 1981.

Figure 5.13 Business ethics: ten roles of organisations

expectations should be more explicitly incorporated in the organisation's policies and strategies. They also argue that the performance of the organisation should therefore be measured in a much more pluralistic way rather than just by its bottom line. The Quaker companies of the last century are a good example, and to a considerable extent the attitudes of these companies have remained more progressive than others into this century. Companies in this category might argue that they would retain uneconomic units to preserve jobs, would avoid manufacturing 'anti-social' products and would be prepared to bear reductions in profitability for the social good. But to what extent would they be prepared to do so? At some point there is a conflict between social responsibility and survival, or between social responsibility and the expectations of shareholders.

Many public-sector organisations are, rightly, positioned within this group. They are subject to a wide diversity of expectations from their stakeholder groups, and unitary measures of performance are often inadequate in reflecting this diversity.

4.   The final group are those businesses which are specifically founded and run as a response to community need. Society needs are paramount and financial considerations are of secondary importance or a constraint. These are categories 9 or 10. The problem faced by these organisations is how commercial they are prepared to be in carrying out their social role. This has been an issue of major concern in the public services in the UK and many other countries, and the position of many organisations has shifted quite markedly. There is a growing recognition that the expectations of taxpayers for demonstrable value for money need to be given more prominence in strategy formulation. Inevitably, this tends to diminish the weight given to the stakeholder interests, such as those of employees and some groups of users. In terms of Figure 5.13 this represents a significant trend among public-sector organisations moving away from category 10 towards categories 9 and 8. Some charities face similar dilemmas. They are often accused of being too commercial and spending too much of their income on internal administration.

5.6.2   Corporate social responsibility

The previous section has identified the overall 'stance' which an organisation may take concerning its role in society. This still leaves the need to identify the more detailed 'agenda' of issues which an organisation may be taking into account when developing strategies. Figure 5.14 outlines a number of these issues both internal and external to the organisation, and provides a checklist against which an organisation's actions on corporate social responsibility can be assessed. Illustration 5.6 shows some of the issues faced by television news companies during the Gulf War of 1991, and the different responses made.

The difficult issue for managers to assess is the extent to which their approach will be legitimate and sustainable. The following questions need to be asked:

● What *costs* will be added by a change in approach to any issue (e.g. pollution control)? Are these costs optional, or will legislation shortly require them anyway? Are the costs likely to be borne by competitors?

● Are there any *benefits* to the organisation in this changed stance? This is

Should organisations be responsible for . . .

Employee welfare
. . . providing medical care, assistance with mortgages, extended sickness leave, assistance for dependants, etc.?

Working conditions
. . . enhancing working surroundings, social and sporting clubs, above minimum safety standards, etc. ?

Job design
. . . designing jobs to the increased satisfaction of workers rather than economic efficiency?

Internal aspects

Green issues
. . . reducing pollution below legal standards if competitors are not doing so?
. . . energy conservation?

Products
. . . danger arising from the careless use of product by consumers?

Markets and marketing
. . . deciding not to sell in some markets?
. . . advertising standards?

Suppliers
. . . 'fair' terms of trade?
. . . blacklisting suppliers?

Employment
. . . positive discrimination in favour of minorities?
. . . maintaining jobs?

Community activity
. . . sponsoring local events and supporting local good works?

External aspects

Figure 5.14 Some questions of corporate social responsibility

often a difficult question to answer with any degree of certainty. For example, sponsorship of the arts is likely to bring 'marketing' benefits to the company.

- Are the expenditures *legitimate*? This has always been an important area of scrutiny in the public sector, but an increasing emphasis on shareholder value analysis (see Chapter 8) is forcing private-sector organisations to be more explicit about the cost/benefit balance of any 'discretionary' expenditures.

5.6.3 The role of individuals/managers

It should be clear from the preceding discussion that corporate social responsibility – as part of strategic management – raises some difficult ethical issues for

ILLUSTRATION 5.6
Business ethics: the Anglo-Saxon and the French view – the case of private TV channels

In France in the early 1990s very few big companies had a formal code of ethics. The first ones were the subsidiaries of foreign groups. IBM France had a set of *règles de conduite dans les affaires* (which was an adapted translation of the original American version). For instance, precepts such as 'do not give wrong information . . ., do not look for reciprocity . . .', etc. were useful to sales people in their everyday life. The IBM code also addressed some aspects of the private lives of employees in so far as they affected the professional performance of the individual or the interests of IBM.

In some big groups like Michelin or Nestlé, top managers believed that the prestige of their company and its strong corporate culture removed the need for a written code of ethics. Moreover, codes were often considered as either too restrictive (internal administrative instructions) or too general and therefore useless or used as alibis.

Each industry or profession also had its own specific ethical problems. The war against Iraq in 1991 revealed the ethical questions that TV channels should address, particularly since more and more private TV channels were launched.

In France none of the TV channels had a code of ethics. There was a Conseil Superieur de Audiovisuel (CSA), an institution managed by the state, which was supposed to control mistakes, especially in the domain of information (news) and in relation to the specifications given to

individuals and managers within organisations. For example:

- What is the responsibility of an individual who believes that the strategy of his or her organisation is unethical? Should the individual report the organisation; or should they leave the employment of the company on the grounds of a mismatch of values? This has often been called 'whistleblowing'.
- Managers are usually in a powerful position within organisations to influence the expectations of other stakeholders. They have access to information and channels of influence which are not available to many other stakeholders. With this power comes an ethical responsibility to behave with *integrity*. Given that strategy development is an intensely political process, managers can often find real difficulties in establishing and maintaining this position of integrity. There are clear examples where this integrity falls down – such as insider trading prior to acquisitions. The international

public and private channels. Herve Bourges, president of Antenne 2 and FR3 (the two French public channels) refuted the idea of an externally imposed code of ethics. The news editor of Channel 5 argued that the Charter of Journalism written in 1918 and revised in 1939 was sufficient (even though TV was developed some twenty years later). TF1, the private channel belonging to the Bouygues group, did not answer most of the summons issued by the CSA.

The results were quite alarming when the French channels had to cover the war against Iraq, especially when film or video material were missing. Images filmed in Lebanon were shown as pro-Iraqi demonstrations in Algeria. A demonstration against the sale of chemical weapons to Iraq was presented first as taking place in Jerusalem, and then later as happening in Bonn. False 'direct-live' broadcasting, incorrect use of records and televotes, staging of reports and falsification of reporters' identities were all uncovered after the event by the CSA.

In contrast, in the USA, CBS was held up as an example of good practice as far as business ethics was concerned. Its 'CBS memorandum', the bible of American news editors, was a 50-page document which gave the ethical rules and practices to follow. The French news editors could have done a better job if they had followed some of the rules of the CBS memorandum during the Gulf War. In fact, the dissatisfaction was so great at the end of the war that the French parliament created its own Observatoire des Medias, and 80 journalists formed a group called Project Medias 92 to propose a new Charter of Information.

Source: M. Salgado, Groupe ESC Lyon.

business community was beset by a series of such cases in the 1980s. Integrity is a key ingredient of professional management and is included in the code of conduct of professional bodies such as the Institute of Management (IM).

- Perhaps the most difficult ethical problem for strategic managers is the question of *to whom* they are responsible when developing new strategies. The simplest answer in private-sector organisations is the shareholders, and in public-sector organisations the politicians as representatives of the people. However, in practical terms most managers know that it is rarely so simple. The list of items in Figure 5.14 shows just how complicated this issue can be. Perhaps the only useful guide to managers is to say that their analysis of their lines of responsibility needs to go beyond the legalistic answer. There is no question that, irrespective of the legal position, there is a clear ethical/moral responsibility to the other stakeholder groups.

5.7 Summary

This chapter has provided approaches to understanding how the expectations of individuals and groups might influence an organisation's purpose and hence its strategies. It has been shown that it is necessary to understand the cultural context within which strategies are developed. This includes external issues, such as the values of society or the influence of organised groups, and the internal factors represented by the cultural web.

Organisational culture needs to be analysed in detail in order to understand the paradigm of the organisation. This enshrines its culture and is a powerful force in preventing or facilitating change in the organisation. The most apparent expression of the paradigm is the values of the organisation – perhaps as stated in the mission. However, it is the core beliefs and assumptions which are more important to analyse, since they represent what is taken for granted within the organisation and therefore are a powerful force in shaping the organisation's actual strategies on the ground.

The expectations of individuals influence strategy because they 'belong' to one or more stakeholder groups. Understanding the expectations of both internal and external stakeholders is important. The mechanism through which stakeholders influence the organisation's purposes is power. Stakeholders acquire power in many different ways, ranging from their position in the hierarchy through to the discretion they are given over aspects of strategy implementation.

The traditional idea of strategies being developed against clear, preordained objectives 'handed down from on high' is misleading. Rather the purposes of the organisation are the product of a complex interplay of all of the factors mentioned above. These cultural and political issues pervade the organisation's structure and systems, influencing the way people behave and hence the strategies they 'favour'.

An organisation's purposes are expressed in many different ways, ranging from very broad statements such as mission, through to tightly prescribed objectives closely linked to targets and performance assessment.

Whereas most of this chapter has been concerned with how society at large and the expectations of individuals influence strategy, business ethics addresses the reverse question of how organisations affect the behaviour of individuals and the values of society.

References

1. One of the earlier works on the influence of national culture was G. Hofstede, *Cultures Consequences*, Sage, 1980. More recent work is to be found in S. Schneider, 'Strategy formulation: the impact of national culture', *Organisation Studies*, vol. 10, no. 2, (1989), pp. 149–68; S. Schneider and A. Meyer, 'Interpreting and responding to strategic issues: the impact of national culture', *Strategic Management Journal*, vol. 12, no. 4, (1991), pp. 307–20; C. Randlesome *et al.*, *Business Cultures in Europe*, Heinemann, 1990; and R. M. Kanter, 'In search of a single culture', *Business*, June 1991, pp. 58–66; R. H. Franke, G. Hofstede and M. H.

Bond, 'Cultural roots of economic performance', *Strategic Management Journal*, vol. 12, (1991), pp. 165–73.

2. E. Schein, *Organisation Culture and Leadership*, Jossey Bass, 1985.
3. J. Martin and C. Siehl, 'Organisational culture and counterculture', *Organisational Dynamics*, vol. 12, no. 2, (1983), pp. 52–64.
4. The importance of symbolic behaviour is underlined by many authors. See, for example, T. Peters and N. Austin, *A Passion for Excellence*, Collins, 1985, chapter 16.
5. D. J. Hickson *et al.*, 'A strategic contingency theory of intraorganisational power', *Administratively Science Quarterly*, vol. 16, no. 2, (1971), pp. 216–29.
6. A. L. Stinchcombe, 'Social structure and organisation', in J. D. March (ed.), *Handbook of Organisation*, Rand Mcnally, 1965.
7. R. E. Miles and C. C. Snow, *Organisational Strategy: Structure and process*, Mcgraw-Hill, 1978.
8. The early writing about stakeholders was concerned with 'coalitions' in organisations. See, for example, the seminal work by R. M. Cyert and J. G. March, *A Behavioural Theory of the Firm*, Prentice Hall, 1964. In recent years stakeholder analysis has become central to strategic analysis. See, for example, I. I. Mitroff, *Stakeholders of the Organisational Mind*, Jossey-Bass, 1983, and R. E. Freeman, *Strategic Management: A stakeholder approach*, Pitman, 1984.
9. The approach to stakeholder mapping has been adapted from A. Mendelow, *Proceedings of 2nd International Conference on Information Systems*, Cambridge, Mass., 1981.
10. J. Pfeffer, *Power in Organisations*, Pitman, 1981, and I. C. Macmillan and P. E. Jones, *Strategy Formulation: Power and politics* (2nd edn), West, 1986, both provide a useful analysis of the relationship between power and strategy. It needs to be noted that in this book the word 'power' is used in a more generic way than in the American literature, being more synonymous with their use of the word 'authority'.
11. Resource dependence as a key determinant of strategy is discussed by J. Pfeffer and G. R. Salancik, *The External Control of Organisations: A resource dependence perspective*, Harper & Row, 1978.
12. J. Pfeffer, (ref. 10 above) chapter 2, provides a useful discussion of the problems of and approaches to assessing power in organisations.
13. A. Campbell, 'Mission accomplished or ignored?', *Financial Times*, 11 January 1989.
14. See F. R. David, 'How companies define their mission', *Long Range Planning*, vol. 22, no. 1, (1989), pp. 90–7.
15. For example, I. Ansoff, *Corporate Strategy*, Penguin, 1968, p. 44, argued that objectives should be precise and measurable.
16. There is a prolific flow of literature on business ethics. Readers can gain some useful insights into the field by reading the following: J. Mahoney, 'An international look at business ethics: Britain', *Journal of Business Ethics*, vol. 9, no. 7, (1990), pp. 545–50; R. Johns, *Company Community Involvement in the UK*, R. Johns Associates, 1991; D. Clutterbuck and D. Snow, *Working with the Community*, Weidenfeld & Nicolson, 1990; S. Hamilton, 'Cashing in on good works', *Business*, July 1991, p. 99.
17. M. Friedman, 'The social responsibility of business is to increase its profits', *New York Times Magazine*, 13 September 1970.

Recommended key readings

A useful introduction to the influence of national culture on strategy can be found in G. Hofstede, *Cultures Consequences*, Sage, 1980.

R. E. Miles and C. C. Snow, *Organisational Strategy: Structure and process*, McGraw-Hill, 1978, is useful in understanding strategy as a product of culture.

Readers should be familiar with the political context of strategic decision making by reading either J. Pfeffer, *Power in Organisations*, Pitman, 1981, or I. C. Macmillan and P. E. Jones, *Strategy Formulation: Power and politics* (2nd edn), West, 1986.

For more about the stakeholder concept, see either I. I. Mitroff, *Stakeholders of the Organisational Mind*, Jossey-Bass, 1983, or R. E. Freeman, *Strategic Management: A stakeholder approach*, Pitman, 1984.

E. Schein, *Organisation Culture and Leadership*, Jossey Bass, 1985. Schein is an important book for readers wishing to understand the relationship between organisational culture and strategy.

Work assignments

5.1   Could the cultural difficulties experienced by CMB (Illustration 5.1) have been anticipated and avoided? What are the lessons for cross-national acquisitions in general?

5.2   Use the questions in Figure 5.3 to plot out a tentative cultural web for News Corporation* or an organisation of your choice.

5.3   Compare your analysis in assignment 2 with the cultural web for the regional newspaper (Illustration 5.2). What are the key differences? What would be the key management issues if your organisation from assignment 2 were to take over the regional newspaper?

5.4   Use Figure 5.4 to identify organisations with which you are familiar which are close to the three Miles and Snow stereotypes. Justify your categorisation.

5.5   *By using a number of the examples from above, critically appraise the assertion that 'culture can only really be usefully analysed by the symptoms displayed in the way the organisation operates'. Refer to Schein's book in the recommended key readings to assist you with this task.*

5.6   Use Figures 5.6 to 5.10 to identify and map out the stakeholders for the Crucible Theatre* or an organisation of your choice in relation to:
   (a)   Current strategies.
   (b)   A number of different future strategies of your choice.
   What are the implications of your analysis for the management?

5.7   In what ways would the adoption of contractual relationships in the value chain (such as the 'Target investments' in the Crucible* case) shift the stakeholder positioning on your map?

5.8   Criticise the statements of purpose presented in Illustration 5.5 in terms of their usefulness to the strategic management of those organisations. Repeat the process for one or more organisations of your choice.

5.9   For the News Corporation* or an organisation of your choice, use Figure 5.13 to establish the *overall stance* of the organisation on ethical issues.

5.10 Identify the key corporate social responsibility issues which are of major concern in an industry or public service of your choice (refer to Figure 5.14). Compare the approach of two or more organisations in that industry, and explain how this relates to their competitive standing.

* This refers to a case study in the Text and Cases version of this book.

PART III
Strategic choice

In many ways strategic choice is the core of corporate strategy. It is concerned with decisions about an organisation's future and the way in which it needs to respond to the many pressures and influences identified in strategic analysis. In turn the consideration of future strategies must be mindful of the realities of strategy implementation, which can be a significant constraint on strategic choice.

Chapter 2 showed that organisations are continually attempting to readjust to their environment, and one of the major criticisms which can be made of managers concerns their inability or unwillingness to consider the variety of strategic options open to the organisation. Rather they tend to remain bound by their paradigm and resistant to change. It is for this reason that this part of the book presents a systematic way of looking at strategic choice. The steps outlined here help to promote a wider consideration of strategy and the appropriateness and consequences of options available to the organisation.

The discussion of strategic choice has been divided into three chapters:

- Chapter 6 looks at the strategic options available to organisations, and reasons why some strategies might be viewed more favourably than others. It argues that when developing successful strategies there are *three* related aspects which must be addressed. First, the *basis* of the strategy, which relates to the way in which the organisation is positioning itself, as discussed in Chapter 3. This is connected to the issue of competitive advantage. Second, the specific *directions* in which the organisation could develop, such as new products or diversification. Lastly, the *method* of development – internally, by joint venture or through acquisition.
- Chapter 7 establishes some general criteria (suitability, acceptability and feasibility) against which strategic options might be judged. It is then argued that *suitability* is a useful starting point to judge the underlying rationale of strategies before launching into detailed analysis. It is therefore a means of *screening* options. It is suggested that this rationale is best established by building up a picture of the suitability of an option on more than one basis. Three broad areas of assessment are proposed: strategic logic, cultural fit and research evidence (linking choices of strategy to organisational performance).

- Chapter 8, entitled 'Making choices', looks at methods of assessing the acceptability and feasibility of options in more detail. It also looks at how strategies are *selected* in practice.

CHAPTER 6

Strategic options

6.1 Introduction

The purpose of this chapter is to identify the strategic options that organisations might pursue. The eventual choice between these options is, of course, dependent on the particular circumstances of the organisation, and this is discussed in Chapters 7 and 8.

In reviewing strategic options it is important to distinguish between three elements of strategy. The chapter follows a step-by-step discussion of these.

- The chapter opens with a discussion of *generic strategies*: the bases on which an organisation might seek to achieve a lasting position in its environment: for example, through competitive advantage or user benefit. This discussion acknowledges, in particular, the important work of Porter.[1] However, both theoretical and practical difficulties with Porter's work have emerged. These difficulties are explained and frameworks advanced for overcoming them.
- The chapter then goes on to discuss the alternative *directions* in which the organisation may choose to develop within its generic strategy: for example, through developing new products or markets. Here general categories in simple product/market terms, such as 'product' or 'market development', are used.
- Finally, the chapter looks at the alternative *methods* by which any direction of strategic development might be achieved: for example, through internal development, acquisition or alliances.

Figure 6.1 shows these elements of strategy and also provides a structure for this chapter. It is recognised that decisions on generic strategy, direction and method are not independent of each other. For example, an organisation pursuing a *generic strategy* of differentiation may also pursue a strategic *direction* of product or service development. However, this leaves a further choice as to the *method* by which new developments are best achieved – through the organisation's own efforts, jointly with others, or by acquisition.

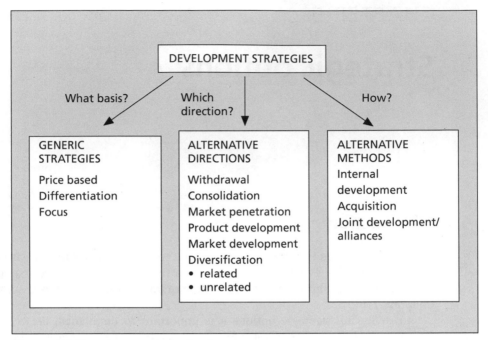

Figure 6.1 Development strategies

6.2 Generic strategies

Specific strategic options for development are most usefully considered in the context of the overall *generic* strategy which an organisation is pursuing. This section reviews these generic strategies, drawing on previous discussions concerning the competitive environment (Chapter 3) and the value chain (Chapter 4); and looks forward to the next chapter on the evaluation of strategies.

For commercial organisations the discussion in this section is concerned with establishing the basis on which a company can build and sustain competitive advantage. For public-service organisations it is concerned with an equivalent issue, the basis on which the organisation chooses to sustain the quality of its services within agreed budgets – how it provides 'value for money'.

6.2.1 Porter's generic strategies

Since the publication of *Competitive Strategy*[2] in 1980, the debate about the importance and relevance of generic strategies has become an important influence on the development of organisations' strategies. Porter's arguments have, in effect, entered the language of management. However, conceptual and practical problems in the formulation and, particularly, the operationalisation of generic strategies have become apparent.[3] This section begins by discussing the arguments advanced by Porter, some of the important principles underpinning them and some of the problems associated with them. Section 6.3 then provides a framework – the 'strategy clock' – for thinking about generic strategies, dealing with the important issues which Porter raises, but overcoming some of the problems.

Porter argued that there are three fundamental ways in which firms can achieve *sustainable competitive advantage*. These are shown in Figure 6.2 and are as follows:[4]

- A *cost leadership strategy*, where 'a firm sets out to become *the* low-cost producer in its industry ... a low-cost producer must find and exploit all sources of cost advantage. Low-cost producers typically sell a standard, or no-frills, product and place considerable emphasis on reaping scale or absolute cost advantages from all sources ... If a firm can achieve and sustain overall cost leadership, then it will be an above-average performer in its industry provided it can command prices at or near the industry average.'
- A *differentiation strategy*, which Porter defines as seeking 'to be unique in its industry along some dimensions that are widely valued by buyers ... It is rewarded for its uniqueness with a premium price ... A firm that can achieve and sustain differentiation will be an above-average performer in its industry if its price premium exceeds the extra costs incurred in being unique ... The logic of the differentiation strategy requires that a firm choose attributes in which to differentiate itself that are *different* from its rivals.'
- A *focus strategy* based on 'the choice of a narrow competitive scope within an industry. The focuser selects a segment or group of segments in the industry and tailors its strategy to serving them to the exclusion of others.' There are two variants here. 'In *cost focus* a firm seeks a cost advantage in its target segment, while in *differentiation focus* a firm seeks differentiation in its target segment.'

Porter goes on to argue that, for a firm to ensure long-term profitability, it must be clear as to its fundamental generic strategy in the terms he describes: too many firms do not make the important choice between these three strategies and end up being 'stuck in the middle'.

6.2.2 Some problems with generic strategy concepts

The generic strategy concepts are important because they have provided managers with ways in which they can think about competitive strategies and competitive advantage. However, in trying to translate the concepts into actionable strategy some significant problems have arisen. In this section some of these problems are discussed, before the strategy clock is explained in section 6.3.

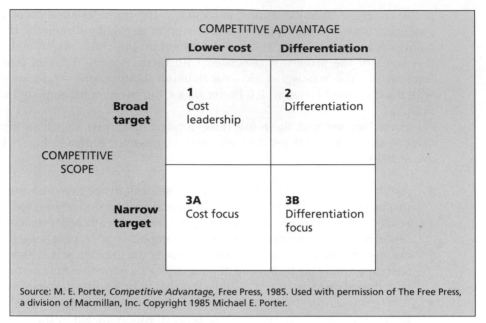

Figure 6.2 Three generic strategies

The notion of cost leadership

There are problems linked to the notion of *sustainable cost leadership*. Porter does not mean short-term cost advantage, or just low cost. Sustainable cost leadership means having the lowest cost compared with competitors over time. This is unlikely to be achieved simply by pruning costs: competitors can and will do that too. The question, then, is how competitive advantage can be achieved – if at all – through cost leadership.

It has been argued that cost leadership can be achieved by means of *substantial relative market share advantage* because this provides a firm with cost advantages through economies of scale, market power (for example, buying power) and experience curve effects (see Chapter 4). However, it is not clear what 'substantial relative market share advantage' means. Different proponents argue that it means share relative to the nearest one, two or three competitors; and there are differences in views on what level of relative share advantages might be required.[5]

In developing strategy, it is in any case dangerous to assume a direct link between relative market share advantage and sustainable advantage in the market because there is little evidence of sustainability: dominant firms do lose market share, and others overtake them. Market share itself is not what is important; but rather the advantages that it can bestow. Certainly relative share advantage can and should give cost advantages, but if managers do not manage the business to achieve these advantages, they will be lost and smaller-share businesses will catch up and overtake them.

Porter also describes the idea of cost leadership as if it is applicable across a whole industry as well as being applicable in market segments. This is a very important distinction. If the idea of cost leadership is to be taken seriously as an industry-wide strategy, it is problematic for all but a very few firms – indeed, arguably in a given industry, for all but one firm. It is therefore not a strategy which is generally applicable across an industry.

Porter has used the terms 'cost leadership' and 'low price' as though they are interchangeable. (This is shown in Illustration 6.1.) This cannot be: cost is an input measure to a firm, whereas price is an output measure. Because a firm is pursuing a cost leadership or cost reduction strategy, it does not necessarily mean that it will choose to price lower than competition. For example, it may choose to invest higher margins in R & D, or marketing – arguably what Kelloggs or Mars do, for example; and indeed, Sainsbury.

This raises one other problem with the notion of cost leadership – indeed with cost-based strategies in general. In itself, low cost gives no competitive advantage. Competitive advantage can only be achieved in terms of a product (or service) which is seen by a user (in the case of a public service also by the provider of resources) to have an advantage over the competition. Competitive advantage is therefore achieved through an organisation's output: its cost base is relevant only in so far as it may provide a means of achieving or enhancing that output in some way.

A general point arising from this discussion is that cost leadership is problematic in relation to the notion of competitive advantage. It may be more useful to think of 'cost-based' strategies, the benefits of which, such as increased margins or surpluses, low prices or efficiency, can be used to achieve competitive advantage.

Definitions of differentiation

There are also a number of definitional problems with regard to Porter's notion of differentiation. First, he defines differentiation in terms of the ability of a firm to price higher than competitors. His argument is that a product or service which offers something unique, or is of greater value than the competition, should merit a higher price. However, this neglects the possibility that a firm may choose to offer a differentiated product or service at a similar price to competitors in order to increase market share and volume.

In Illustration 6.1 Porter[6] argues that Sainsbury cannot be following a differentiation strategy because it advertises low prices. David Sainsbury finds this problematic, since his view is that Sainsbury is trying to keep down costs so that it can reinvest in unique benefits to the customer, as well as reducing price – and successfully so. This is a view increasingly supported by writers on strategy in the 1990s.[7] They argue that businesses may, by keeping down costs relative to

ILLUSTRATION 6.1

The generic strategy of Sainsbury

Michael Porter and David Sainsbury, chief executive of Sainsbury, discuss the generic strategy of the UK's largest grocery supermarket chain.

In a Thames Television programme in 1987 Michael Porter held a round table discussion of his principles of generic strategy with UK executives. In this conversation the following exchange took place between Michael Porter and David Sainsbury.

Sainsbury: I think Michael's ... discussion is enormously helpful in terms of how one looks for competitive advantage. The one bit I don't agree with is the idea that if you are stuck in the middle, that's some great disadvantage, because it seems to me that you do have customers who are only interested in price – in the food market it's quite a small bit, probably 10 per cent of the market. At the other end, you've got some people who are interested only in quality and will pay anything to get it. But the great majority of people are interested in both quality and price, which is summed up in the phrase 'really good value for money'. I think you can have a strategy which is focused, as we are, absolutely on that middle range. We're not ... interested in pure quality regardless of price, or just the price end of the market.

competition, reinvest in unique features and therefore achieve differentiation. This means that a firm could simultaneously follow a cost-based strategy, keep down prices and yet seek differentiation. Although Porter says that this is being 'stuck in the middle' and is dangerous, the evidence is that firms can do it successfully.

The final points that Porter makes in Illustration 6.1 also raise important questions. If a strategy of differentiation is to be followed then it is important to clarify the following:

- Differentiation from whom: i.e. who are the competitors? For example, who are the direct competitors of Sainsbury? It may be that Tesco is a direct competitor but Marks and Spencer do not compete on the same basis.
- Differentiation on the basis of what? Here Porter seems to judge Sainsbury on the bases of products and product quality but is that sensible? Sainsbury might argue that store ambience, location, car parks and so on are also very important and provide bases of differentiation – a point which Porter himself argues elsewhere, when pointing out that differentiation involves much more than product.

Porter: I think it's a very important point. David has shown me a model of a little truck which has the emblem of Sainsbury's on it. It says 'Good Food Costs Less at Sainsbury's'. I think that statement captures the positioning of Sainsbury's ... Now the question is, can you be low-cost and differentiated at the same time? If I read the slogan on the truck it says good food costs less. So I would say, your quality is good, but not unique. Your real strategy is low-cost, and that's your real source of advantage. You're not trying to both beat your competitors on having better quality food than theirs and be lower-cost in supplying it. Ultimately, if I read you correctly, you perceive your real advantage is going to be cost, but you're going to make sure your food is as good a quality as anybody else's ... If I went to Tesco and to Marks and Spencer and looked at their quality – I would find comparable quality. I wouldn't find better quality at Sainsbury's ... The ultimate test of differentiation, in my way of thinking, is do you command a premium price? How does Sainsbury's meet that test?

Sainsbury: I think you can make superior profits if at the same time you can keep costs down, and have prices which are competitive, and get tremendous turnover. Then you get cost advantages which enable you to actually make superior profits without commanding a premium price, because you can have the lower price.

Source: Used with permission from the *European Management Journal*, vol.6, no. 1, (1987).

These and other questions are now taken up in a framework for considering generic strategies which is based on research of managers' perceptions of competitive strategy undertaken by Cliff Bowman.[8]

6.3 Market-based generic strategies: the 'strategy clock'

Too often managers conceive of generic strategies in terms which are internal to the firm; it has already been argued that cost base – an internal measure – is not in itself a basis of competitive advantage. Similarly, and commonly, a manager may conceive of a strategy of differentiation in technical terms; for example, as a better-engineered product, or a more sophisticated service. While the uniqueness may, indeed, be real in technical terms, it is of no value in achieving competitive advantage unless it is of value to the user, so that the user has a preference for those products or services over those of competitors. This may seem an obvious point, but it is one which is often overlooked by managers who fail to address the most basic of questions, which is what the market values. Generic strategies need to be thought about in relation to this basic issue.

Assuming that the products or services of different businesses are more or less equally available, customers may choose to purchase from one source rather than another because either (a) the *price* of the product or service is lower than that of another firm, or (b) the product or service is more highly valued by the customer from one firm than another; here the term *perceived added value* is used. Though these are very broad generalisations, important implications flow from them. These are shown in Figure 6.3 and now discussed.

6.3.1 Price-based strategies (Routes 1, 2)

Route 1 may seem unattractive, but there are successful organisations which have followed it. It is the 'cheap and nasty' option which entails reducing price and perceived value added and focusing on a price-sensitive segment. It might be viable because there could exist a segment of the market which, while recognising that the quality of the product or service might be low, cannot afford or chooses not to buy better-quality goods. It is a lesson which a number of clothing retailers in the UK learned in the 1980s. As chains of stores concentrated on upgrading their merchandise, a number of other stores opened up with lower-quality merchandise at much lower prices. They were seeking not to compete in the same marketplace as the fashion chains, but rather to appeal to a market sector with low incomes.

Route 2 is one typically taken in seeking advantage over competitors. It entails reducing price, while trying to maintain the quality of the product or service. The problem here is that this is likely to be imitated by competitors who can also reduce price. Therefore, the only way competitive advantage can be achieved is if lower prices can be sustained while others are unable to do so. This does get back to the notion of cost leadership. In the end an organisation can sustain reduced prices only if it has *the lowest* cost base among competitors and is prepared to sustain a price-based battle; but it has been seen that this is very difficult to achieve (see section 6.2.2).

For a firm that does not have such leadership, but chooses to compete on price, the danger is that the result is a reduction in margins in the industry as a whole, and an inability to reinvest to develop the product or service.

It may, however, be feasible to follow a strategy of low price to achieve competitive advantage within a market segment in which (a) low price is important, and (b) a business has cost advantage over competitors operating in that segment. An example here is the success of dedicated producers of own-brand grocery products for supermarkets. They are often able to hold prices down because they can avoid the high overhead and marketing costs of major branded manufacturers. However, they can do so only provided that they focus on that product/market segment, and that others do not, or cannot, match their cost base.

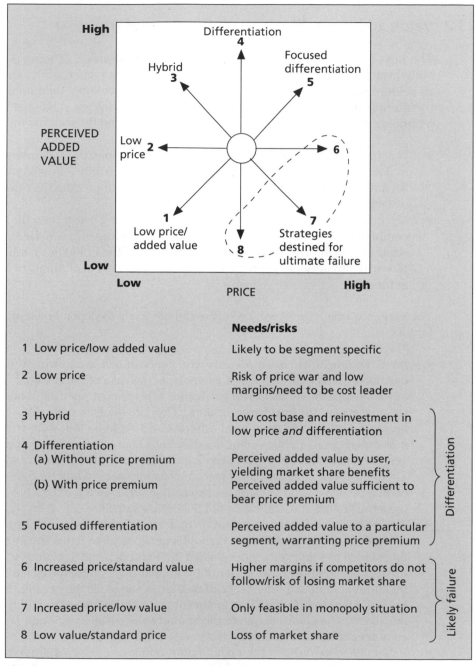

	Needs/risks	
1 Low price/low added value	Likely to be segment specific	
2 Low price	Risk of price war and low margins/need to be cost leader	
3 Hybrid	Low cost base and reinvestment in low price *and* differentiation	⎫
4 Differentiation		
(a) Without price premium	Perceived added value by user, yielding market share benefits	Differentiation
(b) With price premium	Perceived added value sufficient to bear price premium	
5 Focused differentiation	Perceived added value to a particular segment, warranting price premium	⎭
6 Increased price/standard value	Higher margins if competitors do not follow/risk of losing market share	⎫
7 Increased price/low value	Only feasible in monopoly situation	Likely failure
8 Low value/standard price	Loss of market share	⎭

Figure 6.3 The strategy clock: competitive strategy options

6.3.2   Value added, or differentiation strategies (route 4)

The next option is, in effect, a broad differentiation strategy: offering perceived added value over competitors at a similar, or somewhat higher, price. The aim is to achieve higher market share, and therefore higher volume, than competitors by offering 'better' products or services at the same price; or enhanced margins by pricing slightly higher. This strategy might be achieved through the following:

- Uniqueness or improvements in products: for example, through investment in R & D or design expertise. This strategy is successfully followed by many Japanese car firms, which have invested heavily in improving the reliability of their products.
- Marketing-based approaches, in effect demonstrating better than the competition how the product or service meets customer needs. Here the strategy is more likely to be built on the power of the brand or on uniquely powerful promotional approaches – for example, Levi in clothing, or Heinz in food.[9]

The extent to which these will be successful are likely to depend on a number of factors:

- First, the firm must clearly identify who the customer is and what the customer needs and values. For example, in the case of the regional newspaper business discussed in Chapter 5, is the customer the reader of the newspaper, the advertiser, or both? They are likely to have different needs and values. If a strategy of differentiation is to be followed, which will it be based upon? Public-sector organisations face a similar issue. It may be very important that they offer perceived added value, but to satisfy whom? There may be no market-based mechanisms for users to buy services. It may be that perceived added value is measured in terms of the extent to which pressure groups, institutions or politicians are satisfied.
- The extent to which the organisation understands what is valued by the customer, user, or perhaps a stakeholder group is often dangerously taken for granted by managers. As explained in Chapters 2 and 4, managers often drive strategy on the basis either of traditional ways of operating and their taken-for-granted experience, or of resources and skills the organisation has. Indeed, a major differentiating factor for an organisation is the ability of the managers to be close enough to the market to sense and respond to customer tastes and values.
- It is much more difficult for a competitor to imitate a basis of differentiation linked to a mix of activities or features rather than just a product or particular service. This is discussed in section 6.4 below.
- The idea that competitive advantage through differentiation can be achieved on a static basis is questionable. There are two reasons for this. In many

markets customer values change, and therefore bases of differentiation need to change. However, even if customer values can be identified which are relatively constant, over time competitors can imitate bases of differentiation. The implication is that a business following a differentiation strategy may have to review continually bases of differentiation, and keep changing its strategy.

6.3.3 The hybrid strategy (route 3)

It is possible simultaneously to provide added value in customer terms while keeping prices down: many Japanese firms have been doing this for years, and, arguably, it is the strategy pursued by IKEA (see Illustration 1.1). Here the success of the strategy depends on the ability to *both* understand and deliver against customer needs, while also having a cost base that permits low prices which are difficult to imitate.

It can be argued that, if differentiation can be achieved, there should be no need to reduce price, since it should be possible to obtain prices at least equal to the competition, if not higher. However, the hybrid strategy could be advantageous:

- If much greater volumes than the competition can be achieved, and margins still kept attractive because of a low cost base. This is what IKEA achieved.
- As an entry strategy in a market with established competitors. It is a strategic approach to new market development that Japanese firms sometimes use on a global basis. They search for the 'loose brick'[10] in a competitor's portfolio of businesses – perhaps a poorly run operation in a particular geographical area of the world. They will enter that market with a superior product, and if necessary a lower price. The aim is to take share, divert the attention of the competitor and establish a foothold from which they can move further. However, in following such a strategy it is important to ensure that (a) the overall cost base is such that low margins can be sustained, and (b) a clear follow-through strategy has been considered for when entry has been achieved.

6.3.4 Focused differentiation (route 5)

It may be that a business can compete by offering higher value to the customer at a significantly higher price. However, if this strategy is followed, it is likely to mean that the business is competing in a particular market segment – and indeed this may be a real advantage. In the market for saloon cars Ford, Rover, Peugeot, Renault, Volkswagen and Japanese competitors are all competing within the one market – trying, often with some difficulty, to convince customers that their product is differentiated from those of their competitors. A BMW is also a saloon car, but it is not seeking to compete directly with these other manufacturers. It is offering a product with higher perceived value often at a substantially higher price. It is therefore trying to attract different sorts of customers – a different market segment. However, this strategy raises some important questions and problems:

- The choice may have to be made between broad differentiation across a market or a more focused strategy. Indeed, this may take on global proportions, as managers have to decide between a broad approach in increasingly global markets, or much more selective focus strategies – as shown in Illustration 6.2.
- It is important to be clear as to which market segment the firm is competing in, defined in terms of a coherent set of customer values and needs; and this must be translated into action which consistently satisfies those customer values and needs. This may be difficult to do, particularly if the firm is attempting to compete in different market segments, with different needs.

ILLUSTRATION 6.2
Breadth or focus in European businesses

European book publishers, banks and brewers recognise the need to consider carefully the breadth of their markets.

A study of 89 European businesses showed that managers saw their strategies for 1990s as increasingly dependent on the careful choice of breadth of markets, and on the linkage of market power and market segmentation.

'I think that for breweries intermediary size will not exist any more. Either you are a small brewer, not in direct competition with the big ones, and you install yourself in market niches which are too small to interest the big companies; or you have to be big. This logic leads to two poles: on the one hand, very large companies; and on the other, small focused dynamic companies.' (French brewer)

'In the 1990s, for the big brewers, there will be more possibilities of up-scaling. I also strongly believe in the small niche breweries, either in a specific segment of the beer market, or in a specific area selling to bars. Medium-size breweries must make choice. Either they must become big, or they must aim at some precise segment of the industry.' (Netherlands brewer)

'I do not think that the universal bank, such as BNP, will be more successful than specialised banks such as La Compagnie Bancaire ... I

For example, department stores attempt to sell wide ranges of product in one store. They also may attempt to appeal to different customer types in so doing. They run into problems because the store itself, the fixtures and fittings, the décor and store ambience, and the staff may not be differentiated according to the different market segment needs. Moreover, the buying may be done centrally and fail to provide product ranges sufficiently focused on the market segments.

- Focus strategies may conflict with stakeholder expectations. For example, a public library service could undoubtedly be run more cost efficiently if it were to pull out of low demand areas and put more resources into its popular branch libraries. It might also find that an extension of its services into audio and video tapes or new forms of public information services would prove popular. However, the extent to which these strategies would be regarded as within the library's remit might be hotly debated.
- The advantages of the focused approach have to be carefully monitored because the market situation may change. For example, differences between

think there will be six to eight universal banks in Europe by the year 2000, three French banks, two British ones and a couple of German banks . . . The other ones will have to specialise.' (French retail banker)

'You have to divide the market into several segments . . . Everybody knows that a high net worth individual in general is more profitable for a bank than just a blue collar worker in any factory. And the top of the market is an opportunity to become more international.' (Netherlands retail banker)

'Our target is to get within the top six companies because we think there are going to be six major players, and then a lot of minnows swimming around the edge. We think that is the place to be successful; the time of the middle ground has been and gone. There will be no middle ground players any more. You have either got to be investing heavily in major schemes, production and marketing, or you have to go for little niche markets.' (British book publisher)

'If there is to be a European market in book publishing, it will be in the domain of heavy products (art books, encyclopaedias, etc. – or products having a high profitability threshold. On the other hand, in general literature groups do not have any European strategy; it is a more risky and fragmented business where small firms can be effective.' (French book publisher)

Source: R. Calori and P. Lawrence (eds), *The Business of Europe: Managing change*, Sage, 1991, pp. 140–7.

segments may be eroded, leaving the organisation open to much wider competition. This was a concern for the manufacturers of luxury cars such as Jaguar, as the top end of the executive car range moved closer and closer to the features of luxury cars. Or the market may be further segmented by even more differentiated offerings from competitors.

6.3.5 Failure strategies (routes 6, 7, 8)

The strategies suggested by routes 6, 7 and 8 are probably destined for ultimate failure. Route 6 suggests increasing price without increasing perceived value to the customer. Unless the organisation is in a monopoly position, it is very unlikely that such a strategy can be sustained. It is, of course, the very strategy that monopoly organisations are accused of following: in the early 1990s it was argued that the new privatised British Telecom was doing just this. Unless the organisation is protected by legislation, however, or high economic barriers to entry, competition is likely to erode market share. Route 7 is an even more disastrous extension of route 6: the reduction in value of a product or service, while increasing relative price.

Route 8, reducing value while maintaining price, is also dangerous, though firms have followed it. In the 1970s Cadbury Schweppes held the price of its basic chocolate bar, while reducing value in terms of quality, packaging, advertising support and so on, in the belief that its market share would be sufficient to preserve its position. It was not. Competitors with low market share increased their share substantially.

The strategy clock is, then, a market-based model of generic strategy options. It incorporates many of the arguments made by Porter, but crucially roots them in the question: what is of value to the user of the product or service? It does not deny that the cost base of an organisation is vitally important, but sees this as a means of developing generic strategies and not as a basis of such strategies.

6.4 Sustaining and operationalising generic strategies

In the discussion so far a recurrent theme has been how generic strategies can be put into effect so as to sustain competitive advantage. Ideally, an organisation should be seeking not just short-term advantage, but sustainable and profitable long-term advantage. Here the notion of linkages in the value chain introduced in section 4.3, combined with experience curve benefits also discussed in Chapter 4, is helpful.

6.4.1 Cost and the value chain

For reasons discussed above, most firms may not be able to achieve *cost leadership* as such. It is, however, feasible for them to achieve cost advantages or low cost which can be used to create bases of differentiation, added value or reduced prices. This is an issue which is as relevant to public-sector organisations as to businesses, as the debates in the UK National Health Service in the early 1990s showed (see Illustration 6.3).

Costs can be identified in terms of the different activities within the value chain, and experience curve benefits can apply to these activities. For example, a business purchasing large quantities of a given material through a supplier is likely to obtain better prices, have greater negotiating power to ensure that deliveries are on time, therefore able to reduce stocks, and build up knowledge and experience among its buyers that leads to greater internal efficiencies. The same business might be able to identify other activities in which it can also gain experience curve benefits, so different aspects of the value chain can be regarded as bases of efficiencies or cost reductions in which experience curve effects can be achieved. Further, it may be possible to identify where competitors are vulnerable in terms of cost within their value chain – for example, because they have a lower market share and therefore higher unit costs, or perhaps higher labour turnover because of a disgruntled workforce. It may, then, be possible for the business to drive down its costs in these areas as a further means of gaining competitive advantage.

6.4.2 Differentiation and linkages within the value chain[11]

As has been seen, crucial to a strategy of differentiation is the understanding of customer needs and values. These are unlikely to be related solely to the product and its technology. Rather the user will also value, for example, service in terms of delivery; after-sales service; the way he or she is treated; the way in which complaints are dealt with; the sort of information received from the firm; the credit policy of the finance department; and so on. The idea of value cannot be reduced to product and technology. Indeed, arguably products and technologies are the most readily imitable aspects of the strategy of a business. It is the less tangible aspects of strategy that may be more difficult to imitate.

The value chain is a useful way of thinking about how these different bases of differentiation through value creation can be made. It is also useful to consider the extent to which the different bases are mutually enhancing and supporting of each other. Often a business which claims to offer a superior quality product fails to support this by the sort of after-sales service it has, the way in which complaints are dealt with, and the off-hand attitude of personnel. In short, differentiation is likely to be achieved not by one element of the value chain, but by multiple linkages within the value chain. If these linkages can be established, a sustainable basis of differentiation may well have been found. It may be relative-

ILLUSTRATION 6.3
The search for efficiency and value added in the UK National Health Service

The policies of the Conservative government towards the UK National Health Service were seen quite differently by supporters and opponents.

Facing growing demand for its services, and the spiralling costs of those services, successive British governments wrestled with strategies to develop the British National Health Service. The Conservative government of the 1980s undertook a review of the NHS. This resulted in two strategic developments.

The first was pressure from central government from the mid-1980s to reduce costs: funding to the NHS was reduced in real terms. Second, plans were introduced to restructure the service so as to separate providers of services, such as hospitals, from purchasers of services, such as doctors and health authorities. In a letter to regional general managers of the NHS in July 1991, its chief executive, Duncan Nichol, spelled out the expectation of 'increasing activity levels' to cut waiting lists and provide better quality of service to patients, together with 'more efficient use of resources' in terms of controlling costs and capital.

There were two conflicting views of these developments.

ly easy for a competitor to imitate a product or an aspect of technology. It is extremely difficult for a competitor to imitate differentiation based on a multitude of compatible linkages throughout a value chain. For example, there is no one basis of the differentiation of Marks and Spencer. Their quality image is based on product design and selection, staff training, information systems, careful choice and control of suppliers, and so on.

6.4.3 Differentiation through linkages across value chains[12]

Businesses may improve their competitive standing by building switching costs into their products or services. By 'switching costs' is meant the actual or perceived costs for a buyer of changing the source of supply of a product or service. This might be because the buyer is dependent on the supplier for particular components, services or skills, for example. The business which can create significant switching costs is therefore achieving a differentiated position in the market.

It is important to identify bases of such switching costs. Managers might do this by considering how their own value chain might link into the value chain of

The NHS as a public service is under threat

The proponents of this view held that it was the intention of the government so to reduce funding of the health service as to persuade more and more patients to seek private health care, and to introduce, in effect, a two-tier health service in terms of quality. They argued that the reduced funding was leading to insufficient staff on hospital wards, longer waiting lists and insufficient funding to develop new hospitals and new treatments. The strategy was concerned solely with cutting costs, and not with providing services to the community.

Greater efficiency and competition will lead to improved services

The other view was that the strategy would improve services to the community. The NHS had been run as a supply-driven, not a demand-driven organisation. Hospitals had offered the services they provided, whether or not patients needed them; surgeons performed the operations they knew how to perform, whether or not these were the most efficient or the best for patients. By squeezing costs, inefficiencies would be surfaced and removed. And by separating providers and buyers, buyers would only use the services of those operators who could provide them efficiently in such a way as to meet the demands of patients. The pressure would grow for providers of the service to add value, and for buyers of the service to seek better value.

Source: Authors

buyers. For example, it could be that a manufacturing company is following a low-price strategy, and that therefore low stock levels are of significant strategic importance. A supplier might therefore choose to work closely with the manufacturer to ensure speed of delivery and information on availability of components. The supplier is seeking to build linkages between different parts of the value chain, gain experience in so doing and therefore build switching costs into the service provided.

Managers therefore need to think through how linkages between and within value chains can provide competitive advantage. Illustration 6.4 shows how a pharmaceutical company might attempt to gain competitive advantage by using information systems to provide such linkages.

6.4.4 The management challenge of generic strategies

Pulling together the various arguments made so far, they pose significant challenges to managers in the development of organisational strategy. To achieve real bases of sustainable advantage the ambitious aim is to achieve the following:

ILLUSTRATION 6.4

Information systems provide linkages within and between value chains

A partial value chain/system for an ethical pharmaceutical company shows how information systems could provide bases of competitive advantage.

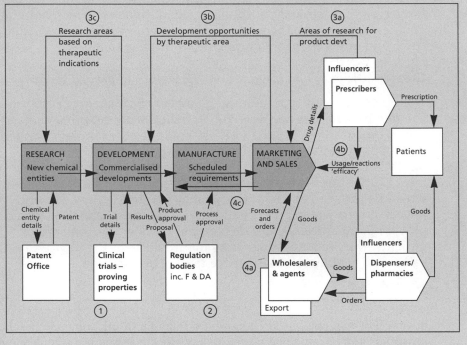

- Clearly identify customer needs and values in the marketplace, defined either broadly or by market segment.
- Given this understanding, consider and establish which of the generic strategy routes is most appropriate for the organisation.
- Operationalise this strategy in such a way that customer needs are met by a mix of activities which is distinctly different from that of competitors, and which achieves a coherent set of linkages between such activities.
- Achieve cost efficiencies or reductions through experience in these crucial activities, especially where they give cost advantages over the competition.
- Ensure that the strategic directions and methods of the organisation are in line with the generic strategy.

A strategic priority for a pharmaceutical company is to reduce the time from research to effective market launch for new drugs, thus reducing cost and potentially achieving an advantage over competitors. Information systems can help by providing more effective linkages within the organisation and between it and other organisations, e.g.:

1. External clinical trials of drugs are required during development. Getting good information on the test population and collecting and interpreting results speedily can reduce development time dramatically.
2. To produce a drug, regulatory approval must be obtained (e.g. from the US Food and Drug Administration). Proposals up to 120,000 pages long may be needed, and will result in high numbers of queries over years. Systems which allow authorities to make direct enquiries electronically are now being introduced.
3. The extent to which new drugs are developed according to market need depends on the ability of marketing to communicate effectively with researchers. Since these two groups may not share similar language or priorities, the presentation and 'translation' of information from marketplace through marketing (3a), from marketing to development (3b) and from there to the researcher (3c) becomes critical.
4. When a new drug is launched, information on likely demand is gathered by marketing from a multitude of wholesalers (4a). Making sense of this, and squaring it with feedback from pharmacies and prescribers (4b), in such a way as to provide meaningful production requirements (4c), becomes vital to the success of a launch.

Source: John Ward, Cranfield School of Management

6.5 Alternative directions for strategy development

This section sets out the strategic directions that an organisation could take. The framework takes the form of a set of 'product/market' choices[13] summarised in Figure 6.4. However, it has to be acknowledged that this is an essentially environment-led perspective: it assumes that environmental opportunities for growth exist which organisations are able to take advantage of. While this may be the case for many organisations, others may not be in such circumstances. For example, organisations in stable environments or declining market situations may be mainly concerned with the development of particular core competences of a specialist nature, or with the development of greater efficiency of resource utilisation, or even with the prospect of planning withdrawal from a market. Similarly, for public-service organisations strategy development may centre around the issue of how limited resources should best be used, since there may

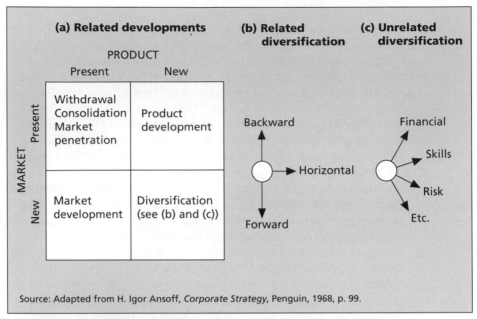

Figure 6.4 Alternative directions for development

be many more demands than can be satisfied. In these circumstances strategic choice may be dominated by resource capability (i.e. what the organisation is best at, or most efficient at providing) or by the expectation of powerful stakeholders. For these reasons it is recognised in what follows that due attention needs to be paid to strategic directions which are concerned not with growth, but rather with consolidation and efficiency.

6.5.1 Withdrawal

This is an option which is often overlooked, although there are many circumstances where complete or partial withdrawal from a market would be the most sensible course of action. Some examples make the point.

- In some markets the value of a company's products or assets is subject to considerable changes over time, and a key issue may be the astute acquisition and disposal of these products, assets or businesses. This is particularly important for companies operating in markets which are subject to speculation, such as energy, metals, commodities, land or property.
- In many public-service organisations it is important to keep under review the range of activities being provided, since withdrawal from one area would release funds to expand in others. The shifts in emphasis of a local authority's range of services over time are a good example of such a policy,

as was Richard Branson's decision in 1992 to sell his original business, Virgin Records, to concentrate on the Airlines business.

- The objective of a small entrepreneur may be to 'make a million' and then retire. Policies may therefore be followed designed to make the company an attractive proposition to buy rather than being guided by longer-term considerations.
- Large, diverse companies may view their subsidiary companies as assets to be bought and sold as part of an overall corporate portfolio.
- During the 1980s, buyouts (either complete or partial) by management and/or employees became common in the UK and to a lesser extent in France. Often they were triggered by the privatisation of companies in the public sector.
- Sometimes organisations will partially withdraw from a market by licensing the rights to other organisations. In the public sector the process of competitive tendering and separation of the roles of 'client' and provider have forced many authorities to withdraw from service provision to but remain as clients performing the roles of specifier, quality controller and 'paymaster'.
- The most extreme form of withdrawal is when an organisation's position becomes so untenable that voluntary or forced liquidation may be the only possible course of action.
- In others, declining performance may argue for the withdrawal from some activities to raise funds, or cut losses, as part of a consolidation or growth strategy for the corporation as a whole (see Illustration 6.5).

6.5.2 Consolidation

Consolidation implies changes in the ways the company operates, although the range of products and markets may remain unchanged. Consolidation takes different forms, here discussed in terms of the nature of markets:

- *Consolidation in a growing market.* A company which is operating in markets showing high levels of growth may aim to maintain market share by growing with the market. The logic of the experience curve (see Chapter 4) suggests that failure to grow in line with the competition is likely to mean that the firm ends up with an uncompetitive cost structure. When the market reaches maturity, it may be a difficult and costly task to recover market share, or achieve a competitive cost base.

    Public services trying to follow any 'natural' growth in demand for particular services can face difficult choices. Unless funds can be diverted from other areas, quality of service may decline (for example, longer waiting lists may result in health services). It may be necessary to raise funds through private sponsorship, or to introduce or increase charges (as, for example, with prescription charges for drugs in the UK).

- *Consolidation in mature markets* provides different strategic challenges. It is common for organisations to defend their position by placing an increased

ILLUSTRATION 6.5
VNU withdraws from printing

The development of strategy may require withdrawal from long-established parts of the business. A major Dutch publisher decided to sell its printing facilities.

In the early 1990s VNU was the last of the three big publishers in the Netherlands to sell its printing facilities. Elsevier-NDU had sold theirs long ago, while Wolters-Kluwer dispensed of their facilities in 1990.

VNU management gave various reasons for this step. The most important one had to do with the level of investment required: 'The printing industry requires more and more heavy investments in updating machinery. The depreciation of the old machinery is not sufficient.' There was also the threat that such investment could threaten to disturb the internal balance between the printing and publishing part of the company: 'The publishers within the company looked at all these resources which went to their printing brothers in their capital-intensive printing offices with more and more envy. As a result of this, the publishing activities were not sufficiently well motivated, while the printing activities did not get the 100 per cent attention they needed either.'

The reason VNU stuck so long with its printing operations was that it had far more frequently printed weekly and monthly magazines in its portfolio than Elsevier-NDU or Wolters-Kluwer had. Moreover, one-third of the printing capacity was being used by VNU itself, while the remaining capacity was filled up with outside customers. However, the choice was made to focus on publishing, concentrating on public and professional information. Public information included the magazines and regional newspapers, and commercial television. Professional information included professional journals, databanks for business information, and educational products. The three printing offices were to be put up for sale.

Source: *Financial Dagblad*, 13 April 1991.

Prepared by Harry Sminia, University of Groningen.

emphasis on quality (of product or service), by increasing marketing activity, or by improving cost structure through productivity gains and/or higher capital intensity. Any of these could provide barriers to the entry of new competitors. The extent to which these approaches will be appropriate will be dependent on the generic strategy the organisation adopts. The tightening of public funds available to many public services during the 1980s and 1990s required a major reassessment of these issues of quality, marketing and productivity, as Illustration 6.3 shows.

- In *declining markets*[14] consolidation may require significant changes. For example, it might be sensible to buy up the order books of companies which leave the market; distributors might need to seek new sources of supply; new internal agreements might need to be developed to ensure continuing cost competitiveness in the smaller market. In both public and private sectors, one of the most difficult decisions is whether to reduce capacity, either temporarily (moth-balling) or permanently.

- During the *transition from a mature to a declining market* an organisation may follow a strategy of harvesting: that is, gaining maximum payoff from its strong position. This might be done through the licensing of technology or distribution rights, or the leasing of facilities, for example. One of the most difficult strategic decisions is how long to remain in product markets which are in short-term decline, but where there is some hope of a market recovery. If turnaround cannot be achieved fairly quickly, exit from the product/market may well be necessary.

6.5.3 Market penetration

Opportunities may exist for gaining market share as a deliberate strategy – a strategy of market penetration. Much of the previous discussion is relevant to this option, since improving quality or productivity, and increasing marketing activity, could all be means of achieving market penetration. So too are the arguments concerning the long-term desirability of obtaining a dominant market share. However, the ease with which a business can pursue a policy of market penetration will depend on the nature of the market and the position of competitors.

When the overall market is growing or can be induced to grow, it may be relatively easy for companies with a small market share, or even new entrants, to gain share. This is because the absolute level of sales of the established companies may still be growing; and indeed, in some instances, those companies may be unable or unwilling to meet the new demand. Import penetration into some industries can be traced back to the early 1970s, when companies were unable to supply the peak demand occurring during booms and their customers had to seek alternative sources overseas. Once established with overseas suppliers, many UK users were reluctant to revert to UK sourcing. When the boom was over, the importers held on to their market share.

In contrast, market penetration in static markets can be much more difficult to achieve. The lessons of the experience curve stress the difficulty of market penetration in mature markets, since the advantageous cost structure of market leaders should prevent the incursion of competitors with lower market share. However, the complacency of market leaders may allow smaller-share competitors to catch up. Or a low-share competitor may build a reputation in a market segment of little interest to the market leader, from which it penetrates the wider market. Sometimes market penetration, particularly of mature markets, can be achieved through collaboration with others. For example, one response to tightening budgets in the UK public sector has been to reserve part of the available funding to back collaborative ventures – particularly where it is felt that value for money would be increased, for example in the recreational use of school facilities.

In declining markets the extent to which market penetration is possible will depend on whether or not other firms exit from the market. If they do, it may be relatively easy for a company to increase its share of that market.

6.5.4 Product development

A business may decide that consolidation in its present products/markets does not present adequate opportunities, and will search for alternatives which build upon the company's present knowledge and skills. In the case of product development the company maintains the security of its present markets while changing products or developing new ones. There may be many reasons why companies have a preference for product development. Companies in retailing follow the changing needs of their customers by a policy of continually introducing new product lines; and local authorities need to shift their pattern of services as local needs change. Sometimes product development is preferred because the company is particularly good at R & D, or because it has structured itself around product divisions. When product life cycles are short – as with consumer electronics – product development becomes an essential requirement of company strategy.

Nevertheless, product development raises uncomfortable dilemmas for firms. While new products may be vital to the future of the firm, the process of creating a broad product line is expensive, risky and potentially unprofitable. Most new product ideas never reach the market, and of those that do, there are relatively few which succeed.[15] For these reasons there has been a trend towards technology transfer and collaborative ventures.

There appears to be no special formula for success in product development. The most successful firms in following this strategy appear to succeed because of their approach to general management rather than to the particular activity of product development:

- They are more market focused than less successful firms in selecting opportunities for product development, and in tailoring products to market needs.
- They also concentrate on developing the products which build on core competences and skills.
- They are good at communicating the desirability and requirements of product development internally so as to avoid the disruptions that new developments can bring.

- They involve cross-disciplinary teams in such developments, as well as skills and views from outside the firm, including suppliers and customers.[16]

6.5.5 Market development

In the case of market development the organisation maintains the security of its present products while venturing into new market areas. Market development can include entering new market segments, exploiting new uses for the product or spreading into new geographical areas. Of course, market development and product development may go hand in hand, since the move into a new market segment may require developments of variants to the existing product range.

Just as some companies have good reasons to prefer product development, other companies might have preferences for market development. In capital-intensive industries a company's assets might be specifically devoted to the technology of a particular product and not easily switched to produce other products. In this situation the company's distinctive competence may lie with the product and not the market, and hence the continued exploitation of the product by market development would normally be preferred. Most capital goods companies have developed this way by opening up more overseas markets as old markets have become saturated. A similar argument applies to organisations whose distinctive competence is in R & D. The rapid world-wide exploitation of micro-electronic technology is a good example. In turn, service industries such as insurance, banking and advertising have been pulled towards globalisation, often because major customers are large multinational corporations.

Exporting is a method of market development. However, there are reasons why organisations might want to develop beyond exporting and internationalise by locating some of their manufacturing, distribution or marketing operations overseas.[17] For example, an organisation might need to do so for defensive reasons – tariff barriers might have been raised or import controls introduced in important overseas markets. There might be operational or logistical reasons which make the international option more favourable, such as changes in the relative costs of labour, transport or supplies. In contrast, other organisations might be positively seeking international markets to stave off decline in home-based demand – for example, in the capital goods industry. The way in which international expansion is pursued has significant structural implications for the firm and these are taken up in Chapter 10.

6.5.6 Diversification

'Diversification' is a term used in different ways. In this chapter the word will be used to identify directions of development which take the organisation away from both its present products and its present market at the same time.[18] However, it is convenient to divide diversification into two broad types:

1. *Related diversification* is development beyond the present product and market, but still within the broad confines of the 'industry' within which the company operates: for example, Unilever is a diversified corporation, but virtually all its interests are in the consumer goods industry. Related diversification therefore builds on the assets or activities which the firm has developed in product or market terms, and may typically take the following forms:

   (a) *Backward integration* refers to development into activities which are concerned with the inputs into the company's current business (i.e. are further back in the value system). For example, raw materials, machinery and labour are all important inputs into a manufacturing company.

   (b) *Forward integration* refers to development into activities which are concerned with a company's outputs (i.e. are further forward in the value system), such as transport, distribution, repairs and servicing.
   (Vertical integration is a broader term used to describe either backward or forward integration.)

   (c) *Horizontal integration* refers to development into activities which are competitive with, or directly complementary to, a company's present activities. A lending library's extension into tourist information or video cassette material would be an example.

2. *Unrelated diversification* is development beyond the present industry into products/markets which, at face value, may bear no clear relationship to the present product/market. For example, the portfolios of companies like Hanson or Lonrho are not linked by commonality of products or markets.

The advantages and disadvantages of developing by diversification in its different forms are discussed below. It should be remembered, however, that many organisations are already very diverse and may sensibly need to ask the reverse question: namely, how far should they specialise their activities? So readers should regard what follows as a discussion of the relative merits of specialisation and diversification.

To examine reasons for *related diversification* the case of a manufacturing company can be considered. There are many value activities both upstream and downstream of a company's operations which provide bases for related diversification. These are shown in Figure 6.5. Figure 6.6 summarises some possible advantages of such diversifications. Equally, highly diversified companies might see any of these as reasons to increase their degree of specialisation. For example, it might be decided that supplies of raw materials have become available from a reliable low-cost source, and this provides a good reason to cease the manufacture of those materials within the company.

It needs to be recognised that increased ownership of more value activities within the value chain does not guarantee improved performance for the company or better value for money for the consumer or client. Indeed, there has been some degree of disillusionment with related diversification as a strategy and more emphasis on improving performance within the value system through

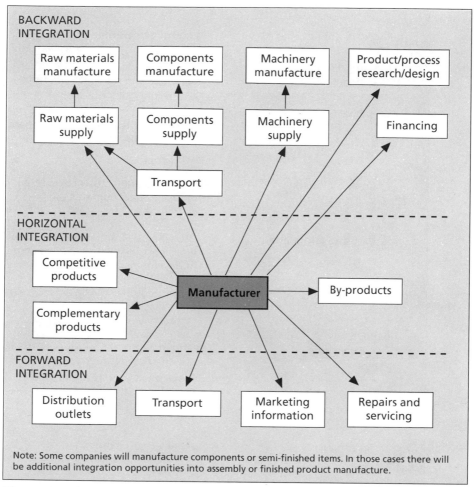

Figure 6.5 Alternatives open to a manufacturer to develop by related diversification

external linkages, relationships and management of the various parties involved.

Synergy[19] is a commonly cited reason for both *related* and *unrelated diversification*. Potentially, synergy can occur in situations where two or more activities or processes complement each other to the extent that their combined effect is greater than the 'sum of the parts'. While related diversification may build upon synergies rooted in products (for example, production processes) or markets (for example, distribution outlets), when unrelated diversification is being considered, synergyistic benefits are more likely to be based on financial synergy (e.g. the positive cash flow of one business being used for the funding requirements of another) or managerial skills (e.g. the turnaround or financial management skills of a company such as Hanson being applied to sluggish businesses in

Possible advantages	Examples/comments
1. Control of supplies	
• Quantity	Tea processors own plantations to secure continuity of supply.
• Quality	Components for motor cars may need to be manufactured by the company.
• Price	Printing facility can be cheaper if in-house.
2. Control of markets	UK shoe manufacturers own retail outlets to gain guaranteed distribution.
3. Access to information	Shoe manufacturers are involved in machinery companies to keep abreast of developments.
4. Cost savings	Fully integrated steel plants save cost on reheating and transport.
5. Building on	
• Expertise	Firm of accountants moving into tax advice or corporate recovery.
• Technology	Precision engineering equipment manufacturer in one market entering another with similar technical requirements.
6. Spreading risk	Avoids overreliance on one product/market but builds on related experience.
7. Resource utilisation	Underutilised manufacturer acquiring company for compatible products to fill capacity.

Figure 6.6 Some reasons for related diversification

mature markets). Assessing the likely benefits which synergy can bring is a method of evaluating strategy and is discussed in Chapter 7.

Other reasons for unrelated diversification may be the aspirations of corporate leaders; the opportunity to employ underutilised resources in a new field; or the desire to move into a different area of activity, perhaps because the present one is in decline. These and other reasons are summarised with examples in Figure 6.7.

Illustration 6.6 shows the different directions of strategy development discussed in this section.

Possible advantages	Examples/comments
1. Need to use excess cash or safeguard profits	Buying a tax loss situation.
2. Personal values or objectives of powerful figures	Personal image locally or nationally may be a strong motive.
3. Exploiting underutilised resources	Farmers use fields for camp sites. Local authorities use plastic waste for new materials.
4. Escape from present business	A company's products may be in decline and unrelated diversification presents the only possible 'escape'.
5. Spreading risk	Some companies believe that it is good sense not to have all their 'eggs in one basket' and so diversify into unrelated areas.
6. Even out cyclical effects in a given sector	Toy manufacturers make subcontract plastic moulded products for industry.
7. Benefit from synergistic effects	See text.

Figure 6.7 Some reasons for unrelated diversification

6.6 Alternative methods of strategy development

The previous sections have been concerned with the generic basis on which organisations might sustain competitive advantage and/or demonstrate value; and alternative directions in which organisations might develop. However, for each of these alternatives there are different potential *methods of development*. These methods can be divided into three types: *internal development, acquisition* and *joint development or alliances.*

6.6.1 Internal development

For many organisations internal development has been the primary method of strategy development, and there are some compelling reasons why this should be so. Particularly with products which are highly technical in design or method

ILLUSTRATION 6.6
Directions of growth

Strategies for growth may take different forms.

Product development

Mars is one of the most successful confectionery firms in the world with a global product range and distribution into confectioners and supermarkets. In the late 1980s it added to this product range by developing its main line confectionery products – for example, its Mars and Snickers bars – into ice-cream products. It was a major project requiring massive investment in plant, new processes and great care in product specification and design. But the new range of products was able to be introduced into the same markets in which it currently operated, and through the same distribution channels.

Market development

The opening up of eastern European markets in the early 1990s gave rise to a whole series of acquisitions and joint ventures as western European companies moved into eastern European markets. Activities were as varied as accountancy firms setting up practices, car manufacturers and airlines acquiring companies and setting up joint ventures, and industrial products companies attempting to sell into the area for the first time. Even rivals in western markets began to collaborate on market development in the East: for example, the Swiss based Nestlé and the

of manufacture, businesses will choose to develop new products themselves since the process of development is seen as the best way of acquiring the necessary skills and knowledge to exploit the product and compete successfully in the marketplace. A parallel argument applies to the development of new markets by direct involvement. For example, many manufacturers still choose to forgo the use of agents because they feel that direct involvement, gained from having their own salesforce, is of advantage in gaining a full understanding of the market.

Although the final cost of developing new activities internally may be greater than by acquiring other companies, the spread of cost may be more favourable and realistic. This is obviously a strong argument in favour of internal development for small companies or many public services, which may not have the resources available for major investment. A related issue is that of minimising disruption to other activities: the slower rate of change which internal development brings may make it favourable in this respect.

A company may, of course, have no choice about how new ventures are

French-based BSN collaborated in 1991 in a joint venture to gain control of Cokoladovny, Czechoslovakia's largest food producer.

Related diversification

Bass was once a vertically integrated group of UK brewers. It therefore had a long tradition of related diversity, particularly in its retail operations, which included catering and hotels. In the 1970s and particularly the 1980s, it concentrated on building up its hotel chains, culminating in the 1987 acquisition of Holiday Inns, and its claim in its 1991 annual report to be 'the world's leading hotel operator with more than 1,600 hotels and 325,000 guest rooms in over 50 countries'.

Unrelated diversification

Lonrho's interests include hotels in Mexico, freight forwarding and travel agencies in Canada, casinos in the Bahamas, oil and gas production in the USA, motor distribution in African states such as Kenya, Zaire and Zimbabwe; tea estates in Malawi and Tanzania; brewing in Kenya and Zambia; sugar estates in Malawi and South Africa; motorcycle distribution in Nigeria; paint manufacturing in Zambia; property development in Germany; and newspapers, refrigeration equipment and bed linen in the UK. As one former employee of Lonrho said of Tiny Rowland, head of the company: 'He just loves buying things, turning them over in his hands, making them work'.

Source: Authors

developed. Companies breaking new ground are not in a position to develop by acquisition or joint development because they are the only ones in the field. But this problem is not confined to such extreme situations. Organisations which would prefer to develop by acquisition may not be able to find a suitable target for that acquisition: this is a particular difficulty for foreign companies attempting to enter Japan, for example. Internal development also avoids the often traumatic behavioural and cultural problems arising from trying to integrate the two firms involved in an acquisition.

6.6.2 Mergers and acquisitions[20]

Development by acquisition tends to go in waves (for example, 1898–1900, 1926–9, 1967–73 and 1985–7 in the UK). It also tends to be selective in terms of industry sector. For example, in the UK the 1960s activity was particularly strong in electrical engineering and textiles, whereas between 1985 and 1987 high street retailing takeovers were common. International developments through acquisition have been critically important in some industries – such as newspapers/media, food and drink, and many sectors of the leisure industries.

A compelling reason to develop by acquisition is the speed with which it allows the company to enter new product/market areas. In some cases the product and/or market are changing so rapidly that this becomes the only way of successfully entering the market, since the process of internal development is too slow. Another reason for acquisition is the lack of knowledge or resources to develop a strategy internally. For example, a company may be acquired for its R & D expertise, or its knowledge of a particular type of production system. International developments are often pursued through acquisition (or joint development) for reasons of market knowledge.

The competitive situation may influence a company to choose acquisition. In markets which are static and where market shares of companies are reasonably steady, it can be a difficult proposition for a new company to enter the market since its presence would upset the equilibrium. If, however, the new company chooses to enter by acquisition, the risk of competitive reaction is reduced. The same arguments also apply when an established supplier in an industry acquires a competitor either for the latter's order book to gain market share, or in some cases to shut down its capacity and help restore a situation where supply/demand is more balanced and trading conditions are more favourable.

There are also financial motives for acquisitions. If the share value or P/E ratio of a company is high, then a firm with a low share value or P/E ratio may be a tempting target. Indeed, this is one of the major stimuli for the more aggressively acquisitive companies. An extreme example is asset stripping, where the main motive for the acquisition is short-term gain by buying up undervalued assets and disposing of them piecemeal.

Sometimes there are reasons of cost efficiency which make acquisition more favourable. This cost efficiency could arise from the fact that an established company may already be a long way down the experience curve, and may have achieved efficiencies which would be difficult to match quickly by internal development. In public services, cost efficiency is usually the stated reason for merging units and/or rationalising provision.

Many of the problems associated with acquisition have been hinted at in the earlier discussion of internal development. The overriding problem with acquisition lies in the ability to integrate the new company into the activities of the old. This often centres around difficulties of cultural fit – an issue which will be given fuller consideration in later chapters.

Reasons for mergers may be similar to those for acquisitions. However, mergers are more typically the result of organisations coming together voluntarily; and this is likely to be because they are actively seeking synergistic benefits, perhaps as a result of the common impact of a changing environment in terms of either opportunities or threats. An example of such a merger is given in Illustration 6.7.

6.6.3 Joint development and strategic alliances[21]

Joint development of new strategies has become increasingly popular since the early 1970s. This is because organisations cannot always cope with increasingly complex environments from internal resources alone. They may see the need to obtain materials, skills, know-how, finance or access to markets, and recognise that these may be as readily available through co-operation as through their ownership.

There are a variety of arrangements for joint developments and alliances. Some may be very formalised inter-organisational relationships; at the other extreme there can be very loose arrangements of co-operation between organisations, with no shareholding or ownership involved. The reasons why these different forms of alliances might occur are varied, but they are likely to be concerned with the assets involved in the alliance. (It should be remembered here that the assets may not just be financial or physical, but could also include access to market, skills, know-how, etc.) The form of the alliance is likely, therefore, to be influenced by:

- *Asset management*: the extent to which assets do or do not need to be managed jointly.
- *Asset separability*: the extent to which it is possible to separate the assets involved between the parties involved.
- *Asset appropriability*: the extent to which there is a risk of one or other of the parties involved appropriating the assets involved for themselves.

Figure 6.8 (see page 238) summarises the different forms of alliances that exist, and how these different factors might influence the form of the alliance. In addition, the figure shows how the same factors might also affect the decision to acquire or merge, rather than to create an alliance.[22]

Figure 6.8 is discussed below by considering, first, the differences between more and less formalised relationships. This is followed by a discussion of the reasons for some intermediate arrangements, such as licensing, franchises and subcontracting.

Joint ventures are typically thought of as arrangements where organisations remain independent but set up a newly created organisation jointly owned by the parents. The joint venture was, for example, a favoured means of beginning collaborative adventures between eastern and western European firms in the early 1990s, with eastern European firms providing labour, entry to markets and sometimes plant; and western companies providing expertise and finance.

Consortia may well involve two or more organisations in a joint venture arrangement, and would typically be more focused on a particular venture or project. Examples include large civil engineering projects such as the Thames flood barrier or major aerospace undertakings such as the European Airbus. They might also exist between public-sector organisations – for example, following the dissolution of the UK metropolitan county councils in 1986, functions

ILLUSTRATION 6.7
Why we're merging: Nationale Nederland and NMB Postbank

In February 1991 Nationale Nederland and NMB Postbank stated publicly their reasons for their planned merger.

The following are extracts from the corporate advertisement placed by Nationale Nederland, the insurance firm, and NMB Postbank announcing plans to merge.

'At heart, we are planning to merge because the market for financial services is changing rapidly. It is the companies that recognise and respond to these changes which will prosper. Our merger, therefore, is our response to the future ... These forces of change are not unique to Holland. They are happening across Europe and beyond. From Scandinavia to the Mediterranean, banking and insurance are coming together in one fashion or another.

The reasons are essentially the same: customers are becoming more demanding in the financial services they need; financial institutions are competing more vigorously for customers; and they are also looking ahead to the challenges and opportunities of the single European market ... Naturally, as personal wealth increases, what people want to do with their money, and the demands they make of financial organisations, are becoming more varied and sophisticated. In addition, the demands placed by corporate customers are becoming more complex and more international.

In order to create the services to meet these increasingly diverse needs, and provide them in the most cost-effective ways, so maximising the benefits for private and corporate customers and shareholders, banking and insurance are coming together.

such as public transport were taken over by co-ordinating consortia often involving both private- and public-sector organisations.

In such circumstances the inter-organisational relationships are likely to be formalised, in the form either of shareholding or of agreements specifying asset sharing and distribution of profits. Such formalised arrangements are likely to occur when the following conditions hold:

- The assets involved need to be jointly managed: for example, as with the setting up of a production unit.
- However, the assets can be separated from the parent companies without damaging knock-on effects in that company: for example, expertise can be specifically devoted to the joint venture without its removal harming the parent.
- At least in theory, there is a low risk that the assets could be appropriated by

Regulatory barriers to this process are coming down. In Holland, for example, the legal requirement for the separation of banking and insurance was taken away in January last year. At the same time barriers to the flow of financial services between EC countries are falling so a single European marketplace is being created ... Increasingly, we must be able to service our customers, not only in Holland but internationally, as their perspectives and needs grow.

As Holland's largest financial group, we shall have a strong home base. Our new group will have the most effective range of distribution channels to reach retail customers in our home market, via intermediaries, branches and direct marketing ... There are clear benefits in the wholesale area, too, resulting from our complementary expertise and experience, co-ordinated strategic planning and critical mass ... There will be joint functions in, for example, consumer lending and mortgages, treasury operations, trade and project finance and venture capital. In real estate, too, our expertise is extensive and complementary.

We have chosen to merge because we believe it is essential to create a single organisation, with a clear identity of purpose and a scale and range of resources that can answer our customers' needs, not only in Holland but in Europe and beyond, and can continue to grow through the 1990s.

By building on our joint international interests, we can become a powerful force in Europe and in the rest of the world ... Our new group, to be called Internationale Nederlanden Group, will be a partnership of equals; the better to serve our customers, our shareholders, intermediaries and employees'.

Source: Extracts from corporate advertisement in the *Financial Times*, 6 February 1991.

one or other party involved. Having said this, it has been argued that some firms enter joint ventures specifically to obtain know-how and expertise for their own internal development.

At the other extreme, *networks*[23] are arrangements whereby two or more organisations work in collaboration without formal relationships, but through a mechanism of mutual advantage and trust. Illustration 6.8 (see page 240) provides an example of a network arrangement in Denmark. Such networks can be enduring and provide considerable mutual benefit to the organisations involved.

More *opportunistic alliances* might also arise which are likely to be more focused around particular ventures or projects, but again may not be highly formalised. In this sense these arrangements are much nearer to market relationships than to contractual relationships. They may exist for a number of reasons:

	LOOSE (MARKET) RELATIONSHIPS	CONTRACTUAL RELATIONSHIPS	FORMALISED OWNERSHIP/ RELATIONSHIPS	FORMAL INTEGRATION
FORMS OF ALLIANCE	**Networks Opportunistic alliances**	**Subcontracting Licences and franchises**	**Consortia Joint ventures**	**Acquisitions and mergers**
INFLUENCES **Asset management**	Assets do not need joint management	Asset management can be isolated	Assets need to be jointly managed	
Asset separability	Assets cannot be separated	Assets/skills can be separated		Assets cannot be separated
Asset appropriability	High risk of assets being appropriated	Low risk of assets being appropriated		High risk of asset appropriation

Figure 6.8 Types of and motives for strategic alliances

- Because assets do not need joint management – capital, expertise, know-how and so on can come together more informally.
- Assets cannot be separated easily from the firms involved, or without harm being done: for example, it may be that one partner is providing access to distribution channels which are part of their operation as a whole.
- If the assets involved were split off into a separate organisation, there would be high risk of their being appropriated by another party involved. This would be particularly the case for the know-how and skills of the different parties involved.

There are intermediate arrangements which exist. One such is *franchising*, perhaps the best-known examples of which are Coca-Cola and McDonald's. Here the franchise holder undertakes specific activities such as manufacturing, distribution or selling, but the franchiser is responsible for the brand name, marketing and probably training. *Licensing* is common in science-based industries, where, for example, the right to manufacture a patented product is granted for a fee. With *subcontracting* a company chooses to subcontract particular services or part of a process: for example, increasingly in public services responsibility for waste removal, cleaning and so on may be subcontracted to private companies.

All these intermediate arrangements are likely to be contractual in nature but are unlikely to involve ownership. They typically arise because:

- Particular assets can be isolated for the purposes of management: for example, manufacturing under licence.
- These assets can be separated from the parent firm to their advantage: for example, by setting up distribution or manufacturing in a country in which it would find difficulty operating.

Licensing or franchising is likely to take place, however, where there is a low risk of the assets involved being appropriated: for example, if patent protection might prevent such appropriation for a licence holder. A less durable, permanent arrangement may be more appropriate if there is a risk of appropriation, as with a subcontracting arrangement, where the subcontractor may already be operating in the sphere of activity involved.

In passing it is worth noting that reasons for taking on full ownership in the form of acquisitions and mergers can also be explained in similar ways. Acquisitions and mergers are likely to take place where: (a) assets need joint management; (b) assets cannot be separated readily from either firm involved; and (c) there is a high risk of asset appropriation. Indeed, arguably the last two reasons are why an acquisition might be more attractive than a joint venture.

6.7 Summary

This chapter has looked at strategic options in terms of *generic strategies*, and *directions* and *methods* of development. The strength of a strategy is determined by the clarity of the generic strategy and how this is sustained through the combination of development direction and method.

In considering such options care does, of course, need to be taken to relate them to the context of the organisation. For example, as the life cycle for a product or service develops, the industry leaders have to make deliberate and well-planned shifts in strategy to avoid their position being undermined by the imitation of followers catching up. For example, during the introductory phase the generic strategy might have been one of exclusivity and high perceived value. This position can be eroded by new entrants and the leader may then shift to an emphasis on cost reduction to achieve low prices and volume expansion with the aim of securing market share in the growth phase. As maturity approaches, cost advantage might have been eroded and other decisions might need to be made: for example, to press cost advantage further with the purpose of encouraging withdrawals, or to concentrate on differentiated offerings as the market becomes more sophisticated and amenable to segmentation. During decline emphasis may return to cost and market share as rationalisation becomes necessary within the industry.

The identification of options is, then, only the beginning of the process of

ILLUSTRATION 6.8
A loose network aids the textile industry in Denmark

A network of co-operation between firms and local government helped textile firms in Ringkobing county, Jutland, buck the trend in the European textile industry.

In the 1980s the textile and clothing industry suffered throughout Europe. Slow growth in demand, technological improvements and intensified competition from low-wage countries led to a decrease of 50 per cent in employment from 1970.

The Danish textile and clothing industry was hit as hard as any other. In 1965 there were 53,000 employees; in 1989 just over 24,000. However, even in a small nation like Denmark the response to intensified competition had been different by area. The Danish textile industry has always had a strong basis in the Ringkobing county in Midwest Jutland. In 1965, 14 per cent of total employment in the industry was located in this county, inhabited by only 5 per cent of the Danish population; and by 1992 it was more than 40 per cent. This was due to an *increase* in employment there of 30 per cent while in the same period two out of three jobs were lost in the rest of Denmark. The concentration of employment was extremely high around Herning and Ikast. With just 78,000 inhabitants it had 25 per cent of total employment in the industry, and almost 85 per cent of total turnover in the knitwear sector.

strategic choice, since their appropriateness needs to be assessed in the light of an organisation's circumstances. The next two chapters deal with this process of evaluation in two stages. Chapter 7 establishes the broad criteria and rationale for matching options with circumstances, while Chapter 8 reviews a range of useful evaluation methods for specific options and assesses the methods by which organisations actually select strategies.

References

1. The first half of this chapter draws on Michael Porter's two books *Competitive Strategy* and *Competitive Advantage*, published by Free Press in 1980 and 1985 respectively.
2. Ibid.
3. There exist a number of papers which provide useful critiques of Porter's generic strategies: M. Cronshaw, E. Davis and J. Kay, (1990), 'On being stuck in the middle or Good food costs less at Sainsburys', working paper, Centre for Business Strategy, London School of Business; C. W. L. Hill, 'Differentiation versus low cost or differentiation and low cost: a contingency framework', *Academy of Management Review*, vol. 13, no. 3, (1988), pp. 401–12; A. Karnani, 'Generic competitive strategies: an analytical approach', *Strategic Management Journal*, vol. 5, no. 4, (1984), pp. 367–80; S. S. Mathur, 'How firms compete: a new classification of generic strategies', *Journal of General Management*, vol. 14, no. 1, (1988), pp. 30–60; D. Miller and P. H. Friesen, 'Porter's (1980) generic strategies and performance: an empirical examination with American data. Part 1: Testing Porter',

Indeed, Ringkobing county as a whole accounted for 55 per cent of total turnover in the whole clothing industry and textile firms in that area showed higher sales growth and profitability than the rest of Denmark. Yet it was an area traditionally dominated by small firms.

Looking more specifically at the Herning–Ikast area, there had always been strong co-operation between local authorities and the private sector, and the combined forces had created institutions such as the largest trade fair centre in Scandinavia, and a number of textile schools. These specialised institutions of education, not found anywhere else in Denmark, had helped create a highly skilled labour force. The concentration of activity served as a magnet: external suppliers of yarn, fabric and machinery could concentrate their selling efforts; and specialised operations such as sewing, dyeing and marketing could be carried out by the growing number of independent firms concentrated in the area.

In a small society where everyone seemed to know everybody else, a kind of collective learning developed among the firms. Due to a fairly free flow of information it was possible to learn from the successes of other firms as well as their failures. The firms saw each other as competitors; however, in periods of excess demand for the products of one firm it would place its orders with another firm which had idle capacity.

Prepared by Kent Nielsen, University of Aarhus, Denmark.

Organisation Studies, vol. 7, no. 1, (1986), pp. 37–55; D. Miller and P. H. Friesen, 'Porter's (1980) generic strategies and performance: an empirical examination with American data. Part 2: Performance implications', *Organisation Studies*, vol. 7, no. 3, (1986), pp. 255–61; R. E. White, 'Generic business strategies, organisational context and performance: an empirical investigation', *Strategic Management Journal*, vol. 7, no. 3, (1986), pp. 217–31; D. Pitt-Watson, 'Business strategy and economics', and C. Bowman, 'Managers' perceptions of competitive strategy', both in D. Faulkner and G. Johnson (eds), *The Challenge of Strategic Management*, Kogan Page, 1992.

4. These quotes concerning Porter's three generic strategies are taken from *Competitive Advantage*, pp. 12–15 (see reference 1 above).

5. The debate on the benefits of relative market share are complicated. There are perhaps three key points: (a) a firm with a high absolute market share may not have a high relative share because there may be a competitor who also has a comparable share; (b) arguments differ as

to whether relative market share should be measured in terms of the nearest individual competitor, or the nearest two or three competitors; and (c) estimates of the relative market share necessary to achieve sustainable market power advantage vary between about 40 and 70 per cent. For discussion on this debate, see, for example, R. D. Buzzell and B. T. Gale, *The PIMS Principles*, Free Press, 1987, chapter 5. See also R. D. Buzzell: 'Are there natural market structures?, *Journal of Marketing*, vol. 45, no. 1, (1981), pp. 42–51.

6. This discussion is taken from a Thames Television discussion reported in the *European Management Journal*, vol. 6, no. 1, (1987), pp. 2–9.

7. The researchers and writers who argue that cost-based strategies are not incompatible with differentiation include D. Miller 'The generic strategy trap', *Journal of Business Strategy*, vol. 13, no. 1, (1992), pp. 37–42; and Hill (see reference 3 above). Their arguments are supported by the work of PIMS (see reference 5), who argue for the benefits of a 'virtuous circle'

in strategy, by which they mean the search for low cost which provides surpluses to reinvest in differentiation and product advantages.

8. Figure 6.3 is similar to the arguments and figures which Philip Kotler employs in discussing marketing-mix alternatives in his book *Marketing Management* (6th edn), Prentice Hall, 1988, p. 519. Section 6.3 is, however, based more specifically on the work of Cliff Bowman: see 'Charting competitive strategy', in D. Faulkner and G. Johnson (eds), *The Challenge of Strategic Management*, Kogan Page, 1992. It should be noted, however, that Bowman uses the term 'perceived use value' rather than 'perceived added value'.

9. For a discussion of these two approaches, see D. Miller, 'Configurations of strategy and structure: towards a synthesis', *Strategic Management Journal*, vol. 7, no. 3, (1986), pp. 233–49.

10. See G. Hamel and C. K. Prahalad, 'Do you really have a global strategy?', *Harvard Business Review*, vol. 63, no. 4, (1985), pp. 139–48.

11. The idea of value chain linkages is discussed throughout Porter's *Competitive Advantage*, (see reference 1), but see in particular pp. 120–4.

12. Again see *Competitive Advantage*, (reference 1): in particular pp. 125–6 and 286–8.

13. For a fuller discussion of the logic of these product/market choices see H. I. Ansoff, *Corporate Strategy*, Penguin, 1988, chapter 6.

14. See Porter, *Competitive Strategy*, (reference 1), chapter 12. See also K. R. Harrigan, 'Strategies for declining businessess', Lexington Books, 1983.

15. Some of the problems of product development are discussed in P. Kotler, *Marketing Management* (6th edn), Prentice Hall, 1988, pp. 408–10.

16. A. Johne and P. Snelson, *Successful Product Development*, Basil Blackwell, 1990, is a study of UK and US firms' product development strategies.

17. See Y. Doz, *Strategic Management in Multinational Companies*, Pergamon, 1986.

18. Here the term 'diversification' is used in a similar way to that used by Ansoff in *Corporate Strategy*, op. cit. In chapter 7 Ansoff identifies general reasons why firms might choose diversification as a method of development.

19. The idea of synergy is well explained by Ansoff in *Corporate Strategy*, op. cit., and in *Implanting Strategic Management*, Prentice Hall, 1984; pp. 80–4. See also Porter's discussion of interrelationships among business units in *Competitive Advantage*, op. cit., chapter 9; and A. Campbell and K. Luchs, *Strategic Synergy*, Butterworth Heinemann, 1992.

20. A good discussion of the reasons for, and problems of, mergers and acquisitions can be found in D. Jennison and P. Haspeslagh, *Managing Acquisitions: Creating value through corporate renewal*, Free Press, 1991. See also A. Schleifer and R. Vishny, 'Takeovers in the 60s and the 80s: evidence and implications', *Strategic Management Journal*, vol. 12, Winter, (1991), pp. 51–9, for a discussion of some of the evidence for motivations in acquisitions.

21. For a discussion of the management of joint ventures, see H. R. Harrigan, *Managing for Joint Venture Success*, Lexington Books, 1986. A useful set of readings on the subject is F. J. Contractor and P. Lorange (eds), *Co-operative Strategies in International Business*, Lexington Books, 1990. See also P. Lorange and J. Roos, *Strategic Alliances: Formation, implementation and evolution*, Basil Blackwell, 1992.

22. The reasons given here for different types of alliance are derived from a paper by A. K. Gupta and H. Singh, 'The governance of synergy: inter-SBU coordination versus external strategic alliances', presented at the Business Policy and Planning Division of the annual meeting of the Academy of Management, Miami, August 1991.

23. For a discussion of networks, see H. B. Thorelli, 'Networks: between markets and hierarchies', *Strategic Management Journal*, vol. 7, no. 1, (1986), pp. 31–57.

Recommended key readings

Chapter 2 of Michael Porter's *Competitive Advantage*, Free Press, 1985, provides a succinct review of his arguments on generic strategies. Much of the book is also very useful in its discussion of the value chain and in considering bases of operationalising and sustaining competitive advantage.

David Faulkner and Gerry Johnson (eds),

The Challenge of Strategic Management, Kogan Page, 1992, contains useful papers on generic strategies and alliances.

Igor Ansoff, *Corporate Strategy*, Penguin, 1988, provides chapters on product/market options and an enduring exposition of the logic of diversification.

Work assignments

6.1 Using Figure 6.3, the strategy clock, identify examples of organisations following strategic routes 1 to 5. If you find it difficult to be clear about which route is being followed, note down the reasons for this, and consider if the businesses have a clear generic strategy.

6.2 Porter argues that a business must have a clear generic strategy. Assess the extent to which any, or all, of the following have a clear generic strategy:
(a) Peugeot*
(b) Burtons* (A, B and C cases)
(c) an organisation of your choice.

6.3 How appropriate are (a) generic strategies, (b) market-based strategic directions, as bases for considering strategies for public-sector organisations? Illustrate your arguments by reference to a public-sector organisation of your choice.

6.4 Read three of the critiques of Michael Porter's generic strategy cited in reference 3. Write a paper explaining the author's arguments and also countering as many of them as possible from Porter's point of view.

6.5 Using Figure 6.1, consider the possible combination of options in terms of generic strategies, strategic directions and strategic methods for either:
(a) Vitalograph,* or (b) an organisation of your choice.

6.6 Given incursions by Japanese firms in the automobile industry (or an industry of your choice) evaluate the strategic positions of two competing western firms (e.g. Peugeot and Rover*).*

6.7 With reference to Figure 6.5 map the directions of the diversified interests of The News Corporation,* Burtons (C)* or an organisation of your choice in terms of backward, forward and horizontal integration.

6.8 For The News Corporation, or by reference to the annual reports for the last five years of a large diversified company of your choice, explain the reasons for and evaluate its diversification strategy and methods of development.*

6.9 Referring to section 6.6 and Figure 6.8 in particular, examine the reasons for the following:
(a) the acquisition of Zanussi by Electrolux*
(b) the merger of Nationale Nederland and NMB Postbank (Illustration 6.7)
(c) the Rover/Honda* alliance
(d) two acquisitions or alliances of your choice.

* This refers to a case study in the Text and Cases version of this book.

CHAPTER 7

Strategy evaluation 1
Assessing the suitability of strategies

7.1 Introduction

The previous chapter has identified the variety of strategic options facing organisations. The purpose of this chapter and Chapter 8 is to discuss approaches to evaluating these options. However, it is first necessary to establish the criteria against which organisations might judge the merits of particular options. It will be seen that these criteria might conflict with each other, and evaluation usually requires sensible judgements on how the differing requirements should be weighed against each other.

In order to clarify how organisations might approach these difficult issues of strategy evaluation, the discussion has been divided into two parts. Chapter 7 will look at approaches to assessing the *suitability* of strategies. There will be an emphasis on how an organisation's circumstances might influence the broad types of strategy that they should follow. Chapter 8 will look at ways of evaluating *specific* strategic options at a more detailed level and the processes by which strategies are *selected* for adoption.

7.2 Evaluation criteria

A useful way of looking at evaluation criteria is to view them as falling into three categories: *suitability, feasibility* and *acceptability*.

7.2.1 Suitability

One of the prime purposes of strategic analysis is to gain a clear understanding of the organisation and the environment in which it is operating. A simple summary of this situation might include a listing of the major *opportunities* and *threats* which face the organisation, its particular *strengths* and *weaknesses*, and any *expectations* which are an important influence on strategic choice.

Suitability is a criterion for assessing the extent to which a proposed strategy *fits* the situation identified in the strategic analysis, and how it would sustain or improve the competitive position of the organisation. Some authors[1] have referred to this as 'consistency'. Suitability can also be thought of as a 'first round' look at strategies, since many of the questions below are revisited in more detail when assessing the acceptability or feasibility of a strategy. Suitability is therefore a useful criterion for *screening* strategies, as will be seen in section 7.7 below.

The following questions need to be asked about strategic options:

- Does the strategy exploit the company *strengths* – such as providing work for skilled craftsmen – or environmental *opportunities* – for example, helping to establish the company in new growth sectors of the market.
- How far does the strategy overcome the difficulties identified in the strategic analysis (resource *weaknesses* and environmental *threats*)? For example, is the strategy likely to improve the organisation's competitive standing, resolve the company's liquidity problems or decrease dependence on a particular supplier?
- Does it fit in with the organisation's *purposes*? For example, would the strategy achieve profit targets or growth expectations, or would it retain control for an owner-manager?

7.2.2 Feasibility

An assessment of the feasibility of any strategy is concerned with whether it can be implemented successfully. The scale of the proposed changes needs to be achievable in resource terms. As suggested earlier, this assessment will already have started during the identification of options and will continue through into the process of planning the details of implementation. However, at the evaluation stage there are a number of fundamental questions which need to be asked when assessing feasibility. For example:

- Can the strategy be *funded*?
- Is the organisation capable of performing to the required *level* (e.g. quality level, service level)?
- Can the necessary *market position* be achieved, and will the necessary marketing skills be available?
- Can *competitive reactions* be coped with?
- How will the organisation ensure that the required *skills* at both managerial and operative level are available?
- Will the *technology* (both product and process) be available to compete effectively?
- Can the necessary *materials* and *services* be obtained?

It is also important to consider all of these questions with respect to the timing of the required changes.

7.2.3 Acceptability

Alongside suitability and feasibility is the third criterion, acceptability. This can be a difficult area, since acceptability is strongly related to people's expectations, and therefore the issue of 'acceptable to whom?' requires the analysis to be thought through carefully. Some of the questions that will help identify the likely consequences of any strategy are as follows:

- What will be the financial performance of the company in *profitability* terms? The parallel in the public sector would be cost/benefit assessment.
- How will the financial *risk* (e.g. liquidity) change?
- What will be the effect on *capital structure* (e.g. gearing or share ownership)?
- Will any proposed changes be appropriate to the general *expectations* within the organisation (e.g. attitudes to greater levels of risk)?
- Will the *function* of any department, group or individual change significantly?
- Will the organisation's relationship with outside *stakeholders* (e.g. suppliers, government, unions, customers) need to change?
- Will the strategy be acceptable in the organisation's *environment* (e.g. will the local community accept higher levels of noise)?

Readers are referred back to the discussions in Chapter 5 on the analysis of stakeholders and, in particular, *stakeholder mapping* (see Figure 5.8). The way in which stakeholders 'line up' is dependent on the specific situation or the strategy under consideration. Stakeholder mapping is an important method of testing the acceptability of strategies. Clearly a new strategy is unlikely to be the ideal choice of all stakeholders. The evaluation of stakeholder expectations is therefore crucial and will be discussed in Chapter 8.

Illustration 7.1 shows how the criteria of suitability, feasibility and acceptability can be used to evaluate strategic options for state-owned railways in Germany and the UK

7.3 A framework for evaluating strategies

A balance needs to be struck between committing inordinate efforts to the detailed evaluation of many different strategic options and simply following a 'hunch' that a particular strategy is best. Certainly in practice the judgement of managers is an important means whereby the field of search for strategic developments is narrowed. This chapter and the next will suggest that this dilemma can be coped with in the following way (see Figure 7.1):

- Chapter 7 shows how the criterion of *suitability* can be used as a means of *screening* options. It will be argued that suitability should be assessed in a variety of complementary ways in order to build as complete a picture as

ILLUSTRATION 7.1
State-owned railways: assessment of options

Before more detailed analyses are undertaken it is useful to make a first-stab assessment of options against the evaluation criteria.

In 1992 both British Rail (in the UK) and Bundesbahn (in Germany), like many other state-owned rail services, were faced with considerable dilemmas as to the strategies they should choose for their development during the 1990s. Although there were many *specific* strategies which could be adopted, the dilemma boiled down to a choice between a more focused, profitable and probably smaller and (partially) privatised service, as against the maintenance of the existing infrastructure and range of services. The two options are assessed below as *reconfiguration* and *consolidation* strategies respectively.

Strategy	Suitability	Feasibility	Acceptability
1. Reconfigure services	Current services are merely a historical legacy of state monopoly. Efficient and effective services can best be delivered through a state-owned shareholding company – Deutsche Eisenbahn AG.	1.(+) Buyers would exist for profitable services such as Inter-City. 2.(–) Core business could be considerable and remain as 'service of last resort'.	1.(+) Saving of taxpayers' subsidy (as much as DM 400bn in Germany). 2.(–) Reduction of service levels – particularly for rural communities. 3. The relative political impact of 1 and 2 is difficult to judge.
2. Consolidate current services	One purpose of state ownership is to provide services where free market forces would eliminate them. Value for money can be imposed through emphasis on cost improvement.	1.(+) State railways own the infrastructure, which protects them from competition. 2.(–) As in many public services, capital investment for cost improvement estimated to be problematic.	1.(+) The culture and public image still remained one of 'public service' as against the profit motive. This was common in most industrialised countries. 2.(–) HIgh-profile media coverage of poor standards of service, particularly on commuter services.

Sources: *Sunday Times Special Report*, 1 December 1991; *Financial Times*, 7 January 1992.

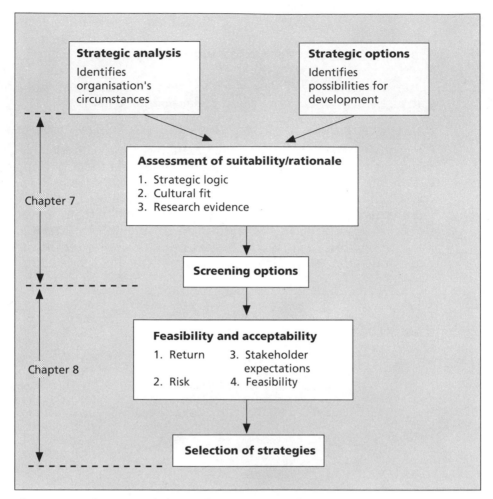

Figure 7.1 A framework for evaluating strategies

possible of the suitability of each option. Three 'tests' of the relationship between choice of strategy and subsequent performance are proposed: *strategic logic, cultural fit* and *research evidence.*

- The workable shortlist is then assessed in much more detail using the criteria of *feasibility* and *acceptability*. This is the focus of Chapter 8.
- This process is likely to be *iterative,* since options which are apparently suitable may prove less attractive after more detailed scrutiny (and vice versa).

7.4 Strategic logic

The literature on strategy evaluation has been dominated since the 1950s by rational/economic assessments of strategic logic. These analyses are primarily concerned with matching specific strategic options with an organisation's market situation and its relative strategic capabilities (or *core competences*). They attempt to establish a *rationale* as to why a particular type of strategy should improve the competitive advantage of the organisation.

Many analytical methods are useful both for understanding the current situation (strategic analysis) and for evaluating strategic options for the future. It is not the intention to provide a comprehensive treatment of all such analytical approaches, but rather to illustrate, through example, the different types of approach which might prove helpful in establishing the strategic logic, or rationale, behind a strategy. The following types of analysis will be discussed:

- *Portfolio analyses* – which help to assess how a new strategy might improve the balance or mix of activities in the organisation.
- *Life cycle analyses* – which assess whether a strategy is likely to be appropriate given the stage of the product life cycle and the relative strength of the organisation in its markets.
- *Value system analyses* – aimed at analysing how a strategic option might improve the performance of the value system as a whole. *Synergy* is a specific example of such an analysis.

Although most of the literature is concerned with private-sector profit-seeking organisations, the lessons are equally valid in the public sector. The following sections will attempt to interpret the discussion in this context.

7.4.1 Portfolio analyses[2]

Most of the discussion in Chapter 6 was concerned with the analysis of competitive strategies or activities of single organisational units. However, much of the strategy evaluation at the centre of large, diverse organisations both in the public and private sectors takes a somewhat different perspective from that at the level of the individual unit. The prime concern of evaluation at the corporate level is that of achieving a balanced range (or portfolio) of strategic business units.

Chapters 3 and 4 discussed the uses and limitations of portfolio analyses during strategic analysis. Options for the future can be plotted on to a matrix (see, for example, Figures 3.8 and 4.9) and the long-term rationale of business development can be highlighted by the matrix. For example, if the original BCG matrix were used, the following questions could be asked:

- Which strategies are most likely to ensure a move from *question marks* through to *stars* and eventually to *cash cows*? In short, will the strategy move the company to a dominant position in its markets?
- Since stars generally require an investment of funds, will there be sufficient cash cows to provide this necessary investment? A major reason for

company bankruptcies is that a firm may invest heavily in the promotion and stocking policy for products in rapid growth without profitable and well-established products from which it can fund these new ventures.

- It is important to have a *balance* of activities which matches the range of skills within the organisation, otherwise certain groups are badly overstretched while others remain underemployed. In general, question marks and stars can be very demanding on management time.
- The matrix can also help in thinking about *acquisition* strategy. Companies that embark on acquisition programmes often forget that the most likely targets for acquisition are not the stars and cash cows of the business world but the question marks or dogs. There may be nothing wrong with acquiring a question mark provided the resources are there to move it towards stardom, bearing in mind the real costs and difficulties of acquisition as pointed out in Chapter 6.

The attractiveness/strength (or directional policy) matrix shown in Figure 4.9(b) can be used for assigning development priorities among the various strategic business units: for example, by requiring managers to match competitive strategy to key forces in the environment, and perhaps concentrating resources in those SBUs that enjoy a relatively high attractiveness and can achieve a strong competitive position.[3]

7.4.2 Life cycle analyses

One particular development of the product portfolio concept has been used extensively. This is often referred to as life cycle analysis (or product/market evolution analysis). This section will review one such approach, as presented and used by the business consultants Arthur D. Little.[4] Figure 7.2 is a summary of their life cycle portfolio matrix and consists of two dimensions. The *market situation* is described in four stages ranging from embryonic to ageing; the *competitive position* in five categories ranging from weak to dominant. The purpose of this matrix is to establish the appropriateness of particular strategies in relation to these two dimensions.

Clearly, if this approach is to provide a strategic logic for the development direction of a specific organisation, the crucial issue is establishing where that organisation is currently positioned on the matrix, and therefore what types of strategy are most likely to be suitable:

- The *position within the life cycle* is determined in relation to eight external factors or descriptors of the evolutionary stage of the industry. These are: market growth rate, growth potential, breadth of product lines, number of competitors, spread of market share between these competitors, customer loyalty, entry barriers and technology. It is the balance of these factors which determines the life cycle stage. For example, an embryonic industry is

STAGES OF INDUSTRY MATURITY

	Embryonic	Growth	Mature	Ageing
Dominant	Fast grow Start-up	Fast grow Attain cost leadership Renew Defend position	Defend position Attain cost leadership Renew Fast grow	Defend position Focus Renew Grow with industry
Strong	Start-up Differentiate Fast grow	Fast grow Catch-up Attain cost leadership Differentiate	Attain cost leadership Renew, focus Differentiate Grow with industry	Find niche Hold niche Hang-in Grow with industry Harvest
Favourable	Start-up Differentiate Focus Fast grow	Differentiate, focus Catch-up Grow with industry	Harvest, hang-in Find niche, hold niche Renew, turnaround Differentiate, focus Grow with industry	Retrench Turnaround
Tenable	Start-up Grow with industry Focus	Harvest, catch-up Hold niche, hang-in Find niche Turnaround Focus Grow with industry	Harvest Turnaround Find niche Retrench	Divest Retrench
Weak	Find niche Catch-up Grow with industry	Turnaround Retrench	Withdraw Divest	Withdraw

COMPETITIVE POSITION

Source: Arthur D. Little.

Figure 7.2 The life cycle portfolio matrix

characterised by rapid growth, changes in technology, fragmented market shares and pursuit of new customers. In contrast, ageing industries are best described by falling demand, declining number of competitors and, often, a narrow product line.

● The *competitive position* of the organisation within its industry can also be established by looking at the characteristics of each category in Figure 7.2. A *dominant* position is rare in the private sector and usually results from a quasi-monopoly. In the public sector this may be a legalised monopoly status (e.g. public utilities). *Strong* organisations are those that can follow strategies of their own choice without too much concern for competition. A *favourable* position is where no single competitor stands out but the leaders are better placed (as in grocery retailing in France or the UK). A *tenable* position is that which can be maintained by specialisation or focus. *Weak* competitors are ones which are too small to survive independently in the long run.

Despite the fact that even such a detailed matrix can suggest that strategic choice is a simplistic affair, which it is not, the A. D. Little matrix can be helpful in guiding strategic choice. Given the wide variety of strategic options discussed in Chapter 6, the main value of this matrix is in establishing the suitability of particular strategies in relation to the stage of industry maturity and the organisation's competitive position.

1. Where growth is occurring and/or a favourable (or better) competitive position exists, organisations are well placed to follow the 'natural' development of the market, although this may be achieved in different ways. The extreme case is clearly a dominant organisation in an embryonic industry. The organisation is likely to be creating the natural growth through its own efforts, which it will seek to defend by moving faster than competition or by *cost leadership* (through size or experience).

2. In contrast, weak organisations are unlikely to survive through the life cycle unless they identify and exploit a market *niche* and, effectively, become a strong provider within that niche. As growth declines, organisations will need to be more selective in their choice of strategy, and this is particularly important if the organisation is not in a strong competitive position. Many of the strategies discussed in Chapter 6 allow organisations to be selective and to prosper. The concepts of *focus* as an important generic strategy (and a *niche* strategy is an extreme example of focus) are clearly of primary importance. However, in more difficult situations (towards the bottom right-hand corner of the matrix) important judgements will need to be made as to which products/markets should be pursued and which discontinued. So a strategy of *retrenchment* would normally be the first step down this road, but this may need to be followed by attempts to *turnaround* the organisation's performance, to *divest* parts of the organisation or even to *withdraw* entirely from particular products/markets.

3. It is important to recognise that some of the strategic options discussed in Chapter 6 will take on different forms depending on the position on the matrix. For example, a strategy of *market development* for a dominant company is likely to be achieved by the organisation's own stimulation of new demand. In contrast, in more mature markets and will a weaker competitive position, market development would need to be achieved much more selectively by targeting new segments or moving into new markets where the conditions were more favourable (e.g. international development).

4. Leaders[5] in an industry may choose to *consolidate* their position in a number of ways which help them gain competitive advantage by virtue of their leadership. They may exploit their superior *cost structure* through highly competitive pricing, or may attempt to raise *structural barriers* – for example through high levels of marketing expenditure, geographical spread (e.g. globalisation), blocking access to distribution channels or suppliers, or even encouraging government policies (e.g. new regulations) which would make entry more difficult. Sometimes leaders will make it *less attractive* or more risky for others to challenge their position by threatening retaliation, or by promising to match any offering of the followers. In declining markets, leaders have some difficult decisions to make: in particular, the viability of their venture is likely to be threatened unless some other organisations leave the industry. Often leaders will induce this process by *buying competitors* and closing down their capacity. In other circumstances (the steel and oil industries and agriculture are examples), leaders push hard for industry *regulation* – either voluntary or imposed. Usually the value chain will have to be reconfigured by the leaders as the economics of the chain shift with the reduction in scale.

5. Followers may enter an industry during the growth phase as a result of the leader(s) being unable (or unwilling) to cope with the potential demand. The proliferation of home computer systems in the early 1980s was a good example. Where rapid growth is occurring, the followers may well be able to develop by *imitation* of the leader's strategy – indeed, the market may be so unsophisticated as to demand imitation. Imitation can be most effective if done at lower cost (e.g. own-brand supplies).

Sometimes followers are able to enter the industry through *joint ventures* with leaders who may be hard-pressed to serve the market alone. Subcontracting is an example of such a situation, and can prove to be a low-risk way of gaining experience of the industry. Larger organisations which feel that they have missed a major development may well acquire one or more of the smaller follower organisations as a means of *catching up*.

In mature industries the most successful strategies of followers are where they are able to *differentiate* themselves from the leaders. This is usually combined with a quite deliberate strategy of *focusing* on particular parts of the market (segmentation or niche). Geographical spread on an area-by-area basis is the route whereby Japanese companies have gradually challenged and displaced the incumbent leaders in other countries (e.g. in motorbikes, cars and consumer electronics). Interestingly enough, this globalisation process was helped along by a very clear market segmentation (focus) approach. Typically, Japanese would identify what has been called the *loose brick* in a market, which was badly defended, and gradually displace the industry leaders by capturing a significant share of total industry profitability with a low-risk, low-profile strategy. This was then used as a platform to launch a drive to global brand dominance.

For followers the need to differentiate themselves continues to be of vital importance during *decline*, and it is often the case that the followers, which are more specialist, are the organisations which survive the period of decline the best. Indeed, decline usually throws up some new opportunities as the leaders shed their more peripheral activities. Many of the service elements within organisations are now provided out-of-house by thriving small businesses (e.g. design, advertising, consultancy, R & D) or through joint ventures such as consortia.

7.4.3 Value chain analyses

Chapter 4 emphasised that understanding how cost was controlled and value created within the value system is very important when assessing the strategic capability of an organisation. It was also argued that the key to sustainable success can be found in the way the value system is *configured* – that the *linkages* between value activities are just as important as the activities themselves. The logic of strategic developments can be tested by the same measure: the extent to which the strategy will change the value system and therefore the competitive position and/or value for money the organisation is able to sustain. Illustration 7.2 shows how one company viewed the strategic benefits of vertical integration within its organisation.

The concept of *synergy* is concerned with assessing how much extra benefit can be obtained from providing linkages within the value system between activities either which have been previously unconnected or where the connection has been of a different type. Synergy can be sought in several circumstances, as is illustrated by the three strategies under consideration for a grocery retailer (see Figure 7.3):

- *Market development* (buying more shops) may improve performance in the value system, since it provides a further opportunity to exploit a good corporate image, and hence 'launch costs' are minimised compared with a new entrant. Buying power should also increase.
- *Product development* (into alcoholic drinks) would improve the use of a key resource (floor space), and cash is available to fund initial stock.
- *Backward integration* (into wholesaling) may well produce cost advantage if better stock planning can be achieved between the wholesale and retail partners.

ILLUSTRATION 7.2
Making vertical integration work at Linfield

Advantages can be gained through extended ownership within the value chain. However, the benefits need to be identified and exploited as a matter of company policy.

In 1992 Linfield was a Belfast-based manufacturer of linen goods involved in spinning yarn, weaving cloth, bleaching, designing products, finishing and marketing goods. This degree of vertical integration was unusual in an industry which had become characterised by specialist companies concentrating on just one of these roles. The company believed the strength of its philosophy was that one division could help out another when times got hard, as in the recession of the early 1990s. For example, although demand for household goods made from linen had declined, cloth for apparel (clothes) had experienced strong demand (due mainly to the efforts of Italian couturiers whose marketing had made linen fashionable). As a result, the weaving division, was kept busy. But the real advantage of vertical integration was exercised when the divisions agreed to increase the percentage of in-house purchase of yarn by the weaving division. The yarn was required to meet the growing demand for apparel cloth, while the yarn division was supported in a very difficult situation of an excess industry capacity of yarn.

However, the divisional managing directors saw many more advantages of vertical integration than simply this 'backstop'. They claimed that their knowledge of the whole production process was much greater than many of their competitors, which was often valuable in discussing requirements with the end-user customers. Because the arrangements between the divisions tended not to be strictly 'contractual' but more dependent on good relationships, it allowed 'rabbits to be pulled out of the hat' from time to time. They felt it was easier and quicker to make quality improvements, and all parts of the production process (or value creation process) were under the direct control of the company. Last but not least, it had helped the company improve its on-time delivery performance from 55 to 96 per cent.

Source: *Management Today*, January 1992.

Synergy could arise through many different types of link or interrelationship: for example, in the market (by exploiting brand name, sharing outlets or pooling selling or promotional costs); in the company's operations (by shared purchasing, facilities, maintenance, quality control, etc.); in product/process development (by sharing information/know-how).

Degree of synergy with present activities	Strategy 1 Buy more shops	Strategy 2 Expand into alcoholic drink	Strategy 3 Open cash-and-carry wholesaler
1. Use cash	Produces profit from idle cash	Produces profit from idle cash	Produces profit from idle cash
2. Use of premises	None	More turnover/ floor space	None
3. Use of stock	Perhaps small gains from moving stock between shops	None	Reduction of stock in shops as quick delivery guaranteed
4. Purchasing	Possible discounts for bulk	None	Reduced prices to shops
5. Market image	Good name helps launch (i.e. cost of launch reduced)	None	Little

Figure 7.3 The assessment of synergy for a grocery retailer

Synergy is often used as the justification for *diversification* – particularly through acquisition or merger (see Illustration 7.3). It has been argued[6] firms which diversify by building on their core business do better than those who diversify in an unrelated way. However, this can be a difficult argument in practice for a number of reasons:

- The notion of a *core business* is not at all clear. Should it be defined by product or market or technology? It is often defined in terms of history, which can be misleading.
- A linked argument is that diversification may be more successful if it builds on *core competences*. These may be related to technical skills or knowledge and seen as relatively transferable. On the other hand, core competences can be regarded as much more linked to the 'tacit knowledge' and *routines* of the operation as discussed in Chapters 2 and 5. In this sense, core competences are more culturally based and are often difficult to transfer from one situation to another. This at least partly explains the difficulties that many organisations have had with diversification – assumptions are made about the transferability of core competences when, in fact, they are not transferable.
- It has been argued[7] that synergy should not be regarded as necessarily arising from horizontal linkages within the value system through the sharing

ILLUSTRATION 7.3
Synergy as a reason for mergers in the new Europe

The creation of a single market and changes in legislation have provided an impetus for restructuring in the financial services industry. Synergy is often the justification for mergers or acquisitions designed to respond to these changes.

In March 1991, the ABN bank and the AMRO bank announced a merger. The combination created the biggest bank in the Netherlands and the sixth biggest in Europe, and placed them in nineteenth position in the world. A combined statement of both executive boards claimed: 'Internationally, both as a result of Europe 1992 and developments outside Europe, a merger can provide strength, not only in pure size and capital base, but also in geographical dispersal and the bringing together of scarce experience and expertise.'

The position in the international marketplace was pressuring financial service organisations to collaborate. Both ABN bank and AMRO bank needed more and bigger international clients to be able to afford their network of branch offices outside the Netherlands. Big international operating clients needed big international banks with services available on an international scale. The ABN–AMRO combination would be one of those few banks.

Early press comment speculated that, in the home market, cost efficiency would be achieved by closing or combining branch offices which were located close together. However, AMRO bank and ABN bank stated that they did not expect to close branches in the near future, but that they would gain a bigger market share by providing more and better services to the customer in a more extended network of branch offices. Cost efficiency could be achieved, however, by office automation. The enormous costs of developing and maintaining a large computer infrastructure could be borne more easily by the bigger bank.

Source: Written by Harry Sminia, University of Groningen, from: *NRC Handelsblad*, 26 March 1991, 4 April 1991; *Financieel Dagblad*, 1 August 1991.

of activities or skills, but can also arise from a *shared strategic logic* between businesses or business units. For example, in a conglomerate like Hanson plc the centre adds value not through managing interrelationships between its businesses but because its corporate systems and managerial competences secure enhanced performances from a series of strategically similar subsidiaries.

- Figure 7.4 outlines the conditions that need to be satisfied if strategies based

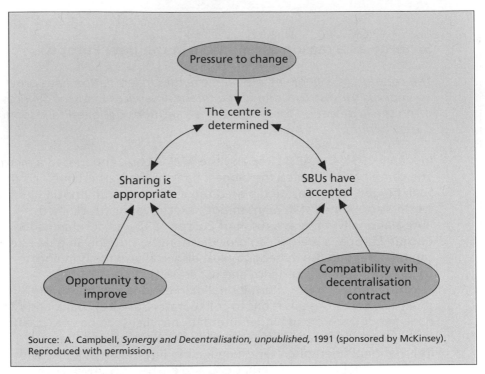

Source: A. Campbell, *Synergy and Decentralisation, unpublished,* 1991 (sponsored by McKinsey). Reproduced with permission.

Figure 7.4 Conditions for synergy

on exploiting synergy are to be regarded as suitable.[8] This provides a useful link between the logic of synergy (opportunity to move and the appropriateness of synergy) with the practical realities of adopting such a strategy (determination and acceptance and compatability with the systems and culture of the organisation).

Another area where value chain analysis can be useful to an assessment of the suitability of strategies is in the locational decisions of international companies. The logic of gaining competitive advantage through the management of individual value activities suggests that the separate activities of design, component production, assembly and marketing may be optimally located in different countries. In consumer electronics, for example, design and component manufacture tends to be located in more advanced economies (e.g. Japan) while assembly is carried out in lower-wage economies (e.g. Korea, Taiwan). This needs to be balanced against the importance of well-managed linkages, which prove more difficult to achieve the more dispersed the separate activities become internationally. The most successful international companies are those which can develop organisational arrangements to exploit the advantages of specialisation and dispersion while managing linkages successfully. These issues will be discussed more fully in Chapter 10.

7.5 Cultural fit

Although establishing the strategic logic of options is very valuable, it is also important to review those options within the political and cultural realities of the organisation. This section is concerned with how options might be assessed in terms of their cultural fit: in other words, the extent to which particular types of strategy might be more or less assimilated by an organisation. This is not to suggest that the culture of an organisation should have pre-eminence in determining strategy. Indeed, one of the key roles of the leadership of organisations is to shape and change culture better to fit preferred strategies. The tension between strategic logic and cultural fit has sometimes been described as a *head vs heart* issue.

These concerns are best understood in terms of the previous discussions (Chapters 2 and 5) about the *cultural web* of an organisation and how it legitimises and sustains the *paradigm* of the organisation. It is clear that, on the whole, organisations tend to adopt strategies which can be delivered without unduly challenging the paradigm – managers find such strategies easiest to comprehend and pursue. As explained in Chapter 2, this is why the strategies of most organisations develop incrementally. However, the key judgement is whether or not such strategies are *suitable* for the organisation's current situation – particularly if significant environmental change has occurred. The purpose of strategic logic analyses is to indicate whether or not the organisation's paradigm requires some fundamental change.

Whether paradigm change is required or not, the assessment of strategic options in terms of cultural fit is valuable. If the organisation is developing within the current paradigm, these analyses help to identify those strategies which would be most easily assimilated. In contrast, if the paradigm will need to change, the analyses help in establishing the ways in which culture will need to adapt to embrace new types of strategy. This will be valuable analysis when planning strategic change (see Chapter 11).

One of the key determinants of how culture might influence strategic choice is, again, the stage that an organisation has reached in its *life cycle*. Schein[9] provides a useful discussion of the relationship between life cycle, culture and strategy which will be summarised here, and can be linked to the life cycle models discussed in section 7.4.2 above. A combination of these two perspectives on different stages in the life cycle can prove valuable in establishing options which fit both the strategic logic and the cultural situation. The key points of the ensuing discussion are summarised in Figure 7.5.

7.5.1 Embryonic stage

The culture of an organisation in its embryonic stage is shaped by the founders. Once the organisation survives, these personal beliefs become strongly embedded in the organisation and shape the types of development which subsequently

Life cycle stage	Key cultural features	Implications for strategic choice
1. Embryonic	1. Cohesive culture 2. Founders dominant 3. Outside help not valued	1. Try to repeat successes 2. Related developments favoured
2. Growth	1. Cultural cohesion less 2. Mismatches and tensions arise	1. Diversification often possible 2. Vulnerability to takeover 3. Structural change needed for new developments 4. New developments need protection
3. Maturity	1. Culture institutionalised 2. Culture breeds inertia 3. Strategic logic may be rejected	1. Related developments favoured 2. Incrementalism favoured
4. Decline	1. Culture becomes a defence	1. Readjustment necessary but difficult 2. Divestment may prove necessary

Figure 7.5 Culture, the life cycle and strategic choices

occur. These core beliefs hold the organisation together and become a key part of its *core competence*. Organisations will typically seek out developments which fit this culture. For example, an organisation which has been founded to exploit a particular technological expertise will tend to seek further developments which fit this self-image of a technology-driven organisation. They will favour product or process development even when the economic logic would suggest they would be better advised to seek additional markets to exploit their current strengths. The strength and cohesion of culture in embryonic organisations has also frustrated the attempts of agencies established to help and advise small businesses. The internal culture may reject the idea of outside help even when it might be badly needed.

7.5.2 Growth

The growth phase of organisations involves a large variety of cultural changes in different circumstances. However, there are some commonly occurring situations which illustrate how cultural developments dictate strategic choice:

- The cohesiveness of culture seen in the embryonic stage tends to dissipate into *subcultures*, each of which may favour different kinds of development. It is at this stage, therefore, that the historical base of the company may be less of a guide to future choices. Some degree of diversification may be sanctioned in order to keep the peace between these factions.
- The growth phase also marks the introduction of significant numbers of new people into the organisation and the emergence of a middle management. This, in turn, can reinforce the *diversity of expectations* within the organisation, and the diffusion of a single dominant culture and the preference for one type of strategy.
- Some organisations in growing markets face uncomfortable dilemmas. The strategic logic may dictate that they should follow the natural growth in the market or risk being uncompetitive once growth starts to ease. However, growth may challenge many of the other beliefs of the organisation, such as the desire to maintain a family atmosphere and approach.
- Many companies and public-service organisations have decided that development strategies requiring growth are difficult to foster and deliver within the confines of a predominantly low-risk bureaucratic culture. Therefore, they either reject such developments or decide to develop them outside the mainstream structure. This issue will receive fuller discussion in Chapters 10 and 11.

7.5.3 Maturity

By the time organisations reach maturity, their culture tends to have been *institutionalised* to the extent that people are not aware of it, or even find it difficult to conceptualise culture in a meaningful way. As a general rule, mature organisations are likely to favour developments which minimise the change and are evolutionary from the current situation. However, whereas incremental developments may be easier from the cultural point of view, they may well prove wholly inadequate if environmental circumstances are changing rapidly.

It should, however, be remembered that this institutionalisation of culture can be a major strength of the organisation in terms of delivering current strategies, as shown in Illustration 7.4.

7.5.4 Decline

During decline a cohesive culture may be seen as a key defence against a hostile environment. Organisations face difficult decisions concerning retrenchment, divestment and withdrawal from products/markets which are ingrained in the culture of the organisation. Sometimes this adjustment can take many years, particularly when the external image of the organisation reinforces the dominant internal situation. In some situations the difficulties of adjustment can be so

ILLUSTRATION 7.4
Nurses show the way to total quality

When evaluating strategies it is important to assess the inherent strengths and weaknesses of the organisation's culture to ensure the strategy and culture will fit; often there are some positive outcomes to such an analysis

In the 1980s many public services had been criticised for their failure to deliver value for money and their poor quality of service. However, many of the proposed new strategies had failed to recognise that their inherent strength stemmed from the professionals' commitment to 'doing a good job' – which in itself was a sound basis for delivering quality services. Attempts to improve *customer-focus* and *quality* were often addressed through changes in systems and procedures, rather than by building on this strong cultural core of professionalism. The following extract from a newspaper article underlines the importance of understanding the real basis of quality of service.

> Imagine, if you will, an organisation where everyone works single mindedly to service the needs of the customers. Where the workers on the shopfloor have full responsibility for the quality of their work, and therefore keep a round-the-clock watch, never moving more than 10 yards from their workstation without arranging for a colleague to take their place. Where everyone has specific, well-understood responsibilities but has also been trained to do every other job in the area. Where the workers keep detailed records of their actions, and sign each of these records to demonstrate their responsibility. Where every change or adjustment to operating conditions is checked with a colleague to minimise errors. Where workers leaving a shift hand over to incoming colleagues through a detailed debriefing based on the records they have kept, a handover which is complete when the incoming worker says so, not when the clock does. Where there is no demarcation, because the workers know that satisfying the customer is the only reason their jobs exist. Where all the workers wear protective clothing to protect their product as much as themselves. Where is this industrialist's paradise? A world-class car manufacturer in Yokohama? A new-age computer facility in Silicon Valley? You may have concluded, entirely reasonably, that I have described a UK subsidiary of Sony, IBM or Hewlett-Packard, growing children now able to beat their parents. You would be wrong. I write with the authority of personal experience about the intensive-care unit in a National Health Service hospital. Your local hospital.

Source: Dr Stephen Bratt, *Sunday Times*, 16 December 1990.

great that the organisation's owners choose to sell out to another organisation, which may then be able to instigate radical changes.

7.6 Research evidence

The analyses in the previous sections have attempted to assess the suitability of strategies either by establishing the *logic* behind the strategy or through assessing the *cultural fit*. Since the major purpose of strategic change in most organisations relates to the need to sustain or improve *performance* this section will review the research evidence which is available on the relationship between the choice of strategy and the performance of organisations. In this context the continuing work of the Strategic Planning Institute (SPI) through its PIMS databank[10] is useful. This databank contains the experiences of some 3,000 businesses (both products and services). These are documented in terms of the actions taken by the business (i.e. its choice of strategic options), the characteristics of the market, competitive position, cost and investment structure, and the financial results (see Figure 7.6). Some of the more important PIMS findings, together with other research, are summarised in this section.

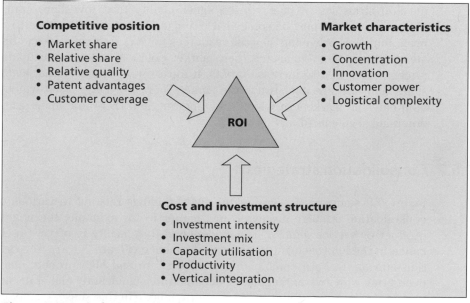

Competitive position

- Market share
- Relative share
- Relative quality
- Patent advantages
- Customer coverage

Market characteristics

- Growth
- Concentration
- Innovation
- Customer power
- Logistical complexity

ROI

Cost and investment structure

- Investment intensity
- Investment mix
- Capacity utilisation
- Productivity
- Vertical integration

Figure 7.6 Basis for assessing strategic potential

7.6.1 The importance of market share

In Chapter 3 the strategic importance of *market power* was introduced. In understanding the likely impact of the environment on any one organisation, this market power is a crucial factor to understand. Likewise, when looking at the choices open to organisations in the future, the extent to which they are likely to increase or decrease this market power needs careful assessment. Much of the research in this area has used *market share* as a measure of market power, and there is much evidence that market share and profitability are linked.

The link between performance and relative market share, which is emphasised by the experience curve work, is also supported by the findings of the PIMS study, as shown in Figures 7.7 and 7.8. Return on investment (ROI) rises steadily in line with relative market share.

A number of reasons are suggested as to why relative market share and ROI should be linked. They are largely concerned with the cost benefits which market share brings. The purchase to sales ratio differences between firms with high and low market share are startling – companies with high market share seem able to buy more competitively or to produce components economically in-house. Also some economies of scale benefit firms with high market shares. For example, marketing overhead costs tend to decline as a percentage of sales with increased share. A PIMS[11] four-year study of fast-moving consumer goods companies published in 1991 showed a strong correlation between the *brand rank*, the *mix* of advertising and promotion activities, and profitability – the conclusion being that it is difficult to make profits unless the company has one of the leading three brands. The indications are also that firms with high market share develop strategies of higher price/higher quality than low-share competitors. This phenomenon may be somewhat circular. High-share firms tend to be more profitable, thus providing the cash resources for R & D to improve and differentiate products, thus enhancing their market position and also justifying higher prices, which in turn increase profits. It must be remembered that high market share and size are not always the same. There are large firms which do not dominate the markets in which they operate; and there are small firms which dominate segments of markets.

7.6.2 Consolidation strategies

Figure 7.9 summarises some of the PIMS findings relating to various types of consolidation strategy discussed in Chapter 6: for example, the upgrading of product or service *quality*. The evidence is that quality is of very real significance in the improvement of profit performance (Figure 7.9(a)). The best situation appears to be a combination of high share and high product quality, but even firms with low market shares demonstrate significantly higher profit performance if they have products of superior quality. (In this sense, quality can be a partial substitute for market share in sustaining advantage.)

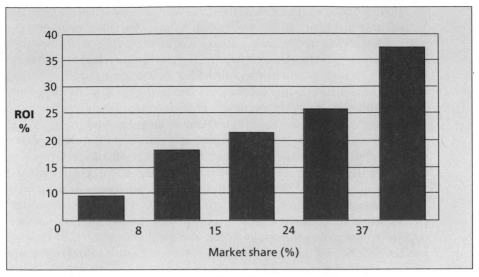

Figure 7.7 Market share drives profitability

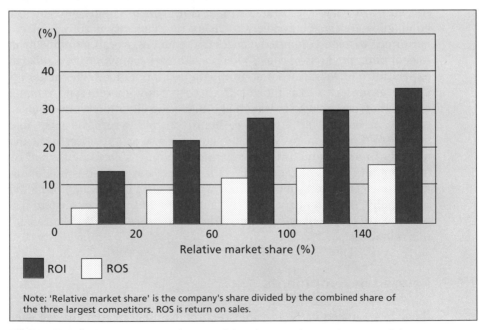

Figure 7.8 On average, market position has an important, positive influence on profits

Figure 7.9(b) suggests that a reliance on increased *marketing spending* to consolidate an organisation's position in its markets is not in itself a satisfactory way of improving performance. Heavy marketing expenditure (as a percentage of sales) may actually damage ROI for firms with low market shares. This does, of course, pose a problem for a firm that is trying to improve or maintain its standing within its existing product/market: trying to do so by increasing marketing expenditure is likely to result in reduced profitability. In other words, attempting to buy market share is unlikely to be successful.

The combined effect of marketing expenditure and product quality has also been studied. High marketing expenditure is not a substitute for quality: indeed, it appears that high marketing expenditure damages ROI, particularly when quality is low (Figure 7.9(c)). It must be concluded that simply gearing up marketing expenditure as a means of consolidating a company's position is not sufficient.

Another consolidation strategy is to seek improved productivity through *capital investment* – for example, by the mechanisation of routine tasks. This has become so much a part of accepted management wisdom that it might come as something of a shock to learn that there is evidence to suggest that increased capital intensity can damage return on investment, as shown in Figure 7.9(d). This is particularly true for companies with weak market positions (see Figure 7.9(e)).

The reasons for this are important to understand. Managers may expect reduced costs through mechanisation and reduced labour input, but assume that revenue will remain constant or rise. However, in capital-intensive industries, companies are especially keen to ensure that capacity is fully loaded, and may cut prices to keep volume, thus actually reducing overall margins; or undertake uneconomic production runs to keep customers happy; or even raise marketing expenditure to wrestle volume from competition. Since high capital investment is also a barrier to exit, those suffering from low margins are reluctant to get out so they continue to battle on and make the situation worse. Indeed, raising capital intensity in an attempt to improve profit returns is most likely to be successful for companies which already have a strong position in the market, are unlikely to meet fierce price competition, and are able to make real reductions in layout and production costs. It is for some of these reasons that many organisations have preferred subcontracting as a means of improving productivity.

Finally, the extent to which organisations are likely to sustain a profitable position is dependent on the long-term real *market growth*. Figure 7.9(f) shows this relationship.

7.6.3 Related developments

It has been argued in the previous section that high relative market share is very often of strategic advantage to organisations. However, the process of building

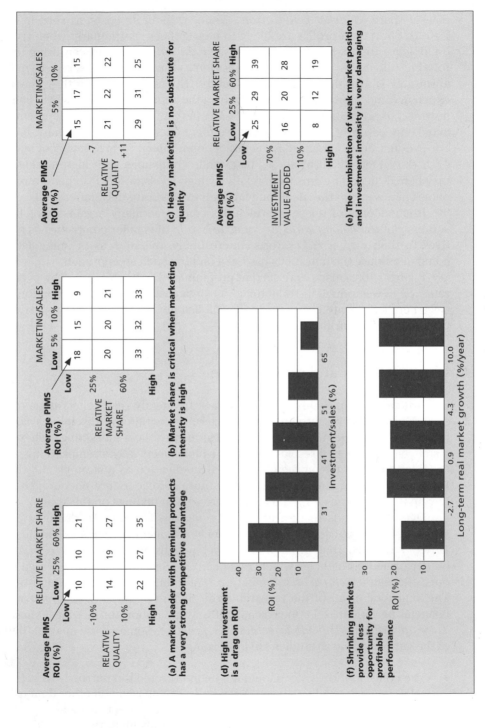

Figure 7.9 The PIMS findings relating to various types of consolidation strategy

market share – *market penetration* – is not without its costs, as seen in Figure 7.10(a). Short-term profits are likely to be sacrificed, particularly when trying to build share from a low base. Similarly, *product development* can bring uncomfortable dilemmas to many organisations. New products/services may be absolutely vital to the organisation's future. The problem is that they may prove expensive and unprofitable (particularly in the short run). This is why a balanced portfolio of products is important. *Cash cows* can fund these developments, and avoid unnecessarily increasing the investment intensity of the company.

Product development may require a commitment to high levels of spending on R & D. Figure 7.10(b) shows that, while companies with high market share may benefit in profit terms from relatively high levels of R & D expenditure, companies in a weak market position with high expenditure may suffer badly.

It is evidence of this type which has convinced many organisations to look seriously at *technology transfer*[12] or *acquisition* of smaller companies as alternatives to their own R & D efforts. Interestingly, the success of many Japanese companies since the late 1950s has been built on such an approach.

Figure 7.10(c) also confirms that profitability can be depressed by over-rapid rates of new product introductions, as organisations debug production, train sales people, educate customers and establish new channels. This is particularly problematic for market followers.

7.6.4 Diversification and performance

Diversification is probably one of the most frequently researched areas of business. Much of this research has been undertaken within the 'disciplines' adjacent to strategic management (e.g. economics, finance, law, marketing). There have also been a number of research studies which specifically attempt to investigate the relationship between the choice of diversification as a strategy and the performance of the organisation in financial terms. Readers are encouraged to follow up the references for a full review of research findings on this topic.[13]

Overall, it needs to be said that the various attempts to demonstrate the effects of diversification on performance are inconclusive. Research in the 1970s[14] suggested that firms which developed through *related diversification* outperformed both those which remained specialised and those which developed through *unrelated diversification*. These findings were later questioned.[15] The sum total of all of the research work linking patterns of diversification to financial performance is unclear apart from one important message: *successful diversification is difficult to achieve in practice*. Some of the specific findings of the various research studies are interesting:

- The concept of diversity should not be interpreted too narrowly as relatedness in product terms. Diversity is also an issue on other dimensions, such as market spread (see section 7.4.3.) There is some evidence[16] that profitability does increase with diversity, but only up to the *limit of*

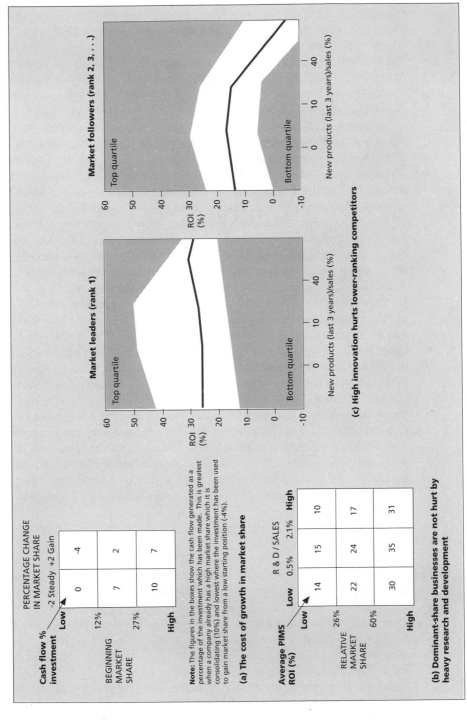

Cash flow % investment

PERCENTAGE CHANGE IN MARKET SHARE

	Low	-2 Steady	+2 Gain
		0	-4
BEGINNING MARKET SHARE	12%	7	2
	27%	10	7
	High		

Note: The figures in the boxes show the cash flow generated as a percentage of the investment which has been made. This is greatest when a company already has a high market share which it is consolidating (10%) and lowest where the investment has been used to gain market share from a low starting position (-4%).

(a) The cost of growth in market share

Average PIMS ROI (%)

R & D / SALES

	Low 0.5%	2.1%	High
Low			
	14	15	10
RELATIVE MARKET SHARE 26%	22	24	17
60%	30	35	31
High			

(b) Dominant-share businesses are not hurt by heavy research and development

Market leaders (rank 1)

Top quartile

Bottom quartile

ROI (%)

New products (last 3 years)/sales (%)

Market followers (rank 2, 3, . . .)

Top quartile

Bottom quartile

ROI (%)

New products (last 3 years)/sales (%)

(c) High innovation hurts lower-ranking competitors

Figure 7.10 The PIMS findings relating to other related strategies

complexity, beyond which this relationship reverses. This raises the issue of whether managers can cope with large, diverse organisations, a matter which will be discussed fully in Chapter 10.

● The theoretical benefits of synergy through diversification are often difficult to achieve in practice. This is particularly supported in the research on diversification through acquisition. For example, Porter concludes in his study of 33 major corporations between 1950 and 1986 that more acquisitions were subsequently divested than retained, and that the net result was usually a dissipation of shareholder value and a company often left vulnerable to corporate raiders.

● An important conclusion of many research studies is that a universal prescription of the benefits of diversification is unlikely to be found. The success of diversification is extremely contingent on the circumstances of an organisation, such as the level of industry growth, market structures and the firm's size. Some studies[17] have also demonstrated that the relationship between performance and diversity will also vary with the period of time studied (e.g. the point in the business cycle). For example, related diversification might be more suited to firms when there are opportunities for expansion in a growing economy. On the other hand, in times of little or no growth a concentration on mainline products and/or seeking more market diversity might make more sense.

● Other studies[18] argue that a key contingent factor is the resource situation of the organisation – particularly the existence of under-utilised resources. Slack in the physical resources or intangible resources (brand name, core skills, etc.) is therefore likely to encourage related developments, whereas excess financial resources may well be used to underwrite unrelated developments (e.g. through acquisition), particularly if the other resources are difficult to develop/grow quickly. This raises the question of whether successful performance is a *result* of choosing diversification or if the relationship is, in fact, the reverse. Perhaps successful organisations *choose* diversification if opportunities in their current product/market domain look are limited.

7.6.5 Public-sector strategies

Previous chapters have discussed the major changes which have taken place in the public sector in attempts to improve the performance or value for money of service organisations. A verdict on whether recent privatisations, competitive tendering, internal markets and devolved management structures have delivered what they promised will take some years to reach, and therefore research evidence of the strategy/performance relationship is very limited compared with the private-sector research studies outlined above.

However, there are some research findings on this general issue. One study[19] looked at ten organisations which had undergone a status change in the UK between 1969 and 1987. These included both moves from the public to the private sector (e.g. British Telecom, 1984) and the reverse (e.g. Rolls-Royce, 1971). In two cases (Rolls-Royce and British Aerospace) the companies experienced moves in both directions over the period. It also included changes of status within the public sector (The Post Office, HMSO, London Transport). The study was concerned with changes in productivity, employment and financial ratios. Its' conclusion is that change in status does not necessarily change the enterprise performance – even in the most sophisticated examples where change was accompanied by increased competition and managerial incentives. Importantly, in their conclusions, the authors remind readers that change has a dynamic of its own (the Hawthorn effect) which may well cloud some of the conclusions, but may in itself be a justification for new approaches to management in the public services.

In the USA[20] there is now a significant bank of data concerning the aftermath of both privatisation and deregulation in many industries, including airlines, financial services, telecommunications, railways and road haulage. The overall conclusion is that establishing a clear *positioning* strategy is the most important single issue for organisations, as undifferentiated size is no longer the basis of a sustainable strategy. Illustration 7.5 shows that privatisation programmes are common in many economies across the world.

7.7 Screening options

One of the benefits which should emerge from assessments of suitability is an understanding of the *underlying rationale* behind particular types of strategy. However, within these broad types there are likely to be a range of specific strategies which an organisation could follow, and the process of evaluation normally requires a narrowing down of these various options before a detailed assessment can be undertaken, although this is not to suggest that options eliminated at this stage will not be given further consideration later.

This section begins by reviewing the basis on which specific strategies can be assessed – whether options are to be judged on an absolute basis, against each other, or against the 'do-nothing' situation (introduced in Chapter 6). The section then outlines three contrasting approaches to the screening of options:

- *Ranking* options against a set of predetermined factors concerning the organisation's strategic situation. The extent to which specific options fit these criteria determines their position in this 'league table'.
- *Decision trees*, which also assess specific options against a list of key strategic factors. However, options are ranked by progressively eliminating others.
- *Scenarios*, which attempt to match specific options with a range of possible future outcomes and are particularly useful where a high degree of uncertainty exists (say in the environment, as discussed in Chapter 3). Scenarios provide a means of keeping many more options under consideration.

ILLUSTRATION 7.5
Privatisation

During the 1980s privatisation became a major issue in public-sector policy in many countries across the world. It was introduced in various forms and in varying degrees in both the developed and developing economies, and in both capitalist and centrally planned economies.

Privatisation as a means of improving public-sector performance was to a large extent a counterbalance to more than 50 years of growing state involvement in the provision of goods and services in many countries. One result of this extensive involvement had been to stretch the management of state enterprise too wide with resulting loss of quality and efficiency. This, in turn, created pressure on public budgets which became difficult to bear, and by the 1980s many countries started to recognise that increasing state ownership was difficult to sustain and almost certainly undesirable in its economic consequences. So privatisation was looked to as a key public-sector strategy in many countries. Three broad approaches to privatisation were adopted.

First, there was *divestment* of enterprises which had commercial potential. This was a strategy pursued aggressively in the UK from 1982 onwards. It was also seen as a key ingredient of economic reform in eastern Europe and the former Soviet states from 1989 onwards. But

7.7.1   Bases for comparison

Chapter 4 has already discussed the importance of establishing an appropriate basis for comparison (in assessing strategic capability). This is equally true during evaluation. If strategies are assessed only in absolute terms or against industry norms, this does not address a central issue in strategic evaluation: namely, the need to identify the *incentive to change* from the present strategy to a new strategy. It is often helpful to use the *do-nothing* situation to assess the company's incentive to change. The do-nothing situation represents the likely outcome if the organisation were to continue with current strategies, disregarding any changes occurring in the environment or resource position of the company. The easiest way to incorporate this situation into an evaluation is by including it as a strategic option to be evaluated alongside others. However, it must be remembered that do-nothing is not an option *per se* – it merely provides a valuable base line against which to assess the incentive to change.

A useful technique which incorporates this approach is *gap analysis*, which can be used to identify the extent to which existing strategies will fail to meet the performance objectives in the future. Figure 7.11 outlines the analysis for a

divestment programmes were also important ingredients of public-sector strategy in economies as far apart as Chile (from the mid-1970s), Kenya (from 1983), Ghana and the people's Republic of China.

Second, *contracting-out* was a key element of public policy in the UK, particularly in the health services and local authorities (through compulsory competitive tendering). Contracting-out was extensively used in the USA, and programmes were also introduced in many other countries including Indonesia, Thailand and Malaysia.

A third method of privatisation was through the use of *vouchers*. In voucher schemes the government provides eligible individuals with purchasing rights for services such as education, health care and basic social services, and allows them to buy from private-sector providers of services. In the late 1980s there was much debate about the introduction of vouchers but nervousness of the political consequences of proceeding. Voucher schemes were used extensively in the USA.

Privatisation programmes inevitably tended to be high-profile political issues, and as a result there was some noticeable 'backing-off' from previously announced programmes. Notable examples were France, Brazil and Pakistan.

Source: R. D. Utt, 'Privatisation: shifting the balance toward growth', *Economic Impact*, vol. 69, no. 4 (1989).

single product/single market situation. This is a highly simplified example and readers must bear in mind that, like any other forecasting process, gap analysis can be difficult and time consuming. In addition, it is usually necessary to apply measures other than profitability. Some of these may be easily quantifiable, such as productivity or volume of sales, whereas others may be more subjective but nonetheless very important, such as levels of quality or service.

Gap analysis is also used extensively in public-sector planning, although in a somewhat different way. Here the strategic problem is often concerned with whether the future demands on a public service are likely to change to such an extent that the current resource provision will prove wholly inadequate. This is particularly important when considering the statutory obligations of many public services such as hospitals, education or social services, and demographic information is often of central importance in attempting to assess the likely gaps in provision.

7.7.2 Ranking

Ranking is a systematic way of analysing specific options for their suitability or

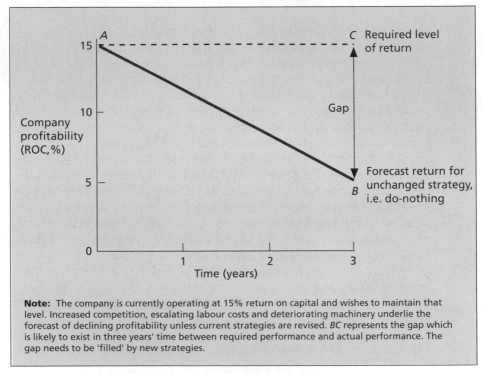

Note: The company is currently operating at 15% return on capital and wishes to maintain that level. Increased competition, escalating labour costs and deteriorating machinery underlie the forecast of declining profitability unless current strategies are revised. *BC* represents the gap which is likely to exist in three years' time between required performance and actual performance. The gap needs to be 'filled' by new strategies.

Figure 7.11 Gap analysis

fit with the picture gained from the strategic analysis. Each option is assessed against a number of key factors which the strategic analysis identified in the organisation's environment, resources and culture. Illustration 7.6 is an example of how such a ranking might be performed. One of the major benefits of ranking is that it helps the analyst to think through mismatches between a company's present position and the implications of the various strategic options. More sophisticated approaches to ranking assign weightings to each factor in recognition that some will be of more importance in the evaluation than others.

7.7.3 Decision trees[21]

Although decision trees have been widely used in operational decision making, their use in strategy formulation has not, in general, received a great deal of attention. A typical strategic decision tree is illustrated in Figure 7.12. It can be seen that the end-point of the tree is a number of discrete development opportunities, as in Chapter 6. Whereas ranking assumes that all options have equal merit (in the first instance), the decision tree approach ranks options by progressively eliminating others. This elimination process is achieved by identifying a

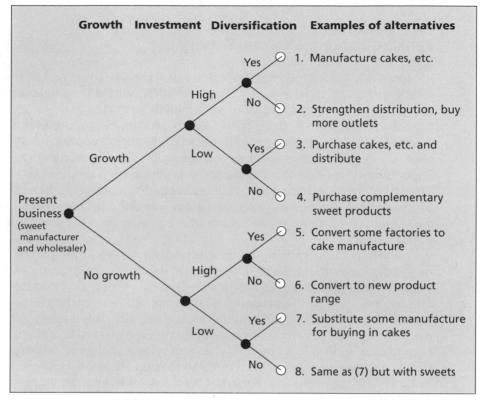

| Growth | Investment | Diversification | Examples of alternatives |

Yes — 1. Manufacture cakes, etc.

High

No — 2. Strengthen distribution, buy more outlets

Growth   Low

Yes — 3. Purchase cakes, etc. and distribute

No — 4. Purchase complementary sweet products

Present business (sweet manufacturer and wholesaler)

Yes — 5. Convert some factories to cake manufacture

No growth   High

No — 6. Convert to new product range

Low

Yes — 7. Substitute some manufacture for buying in cakes

No — 8. Same as (7) but with sweets

Figure 7.12 A simplified strategic decision tree for a sweet manufacturer

few key elements or criteria which future developments are intended to incorporate, such as growth, investment and diversification. For example, in Figure 7.12 choosing growth as an important aspect of future strategies would automatically rank options 1–4 more highly than 5–8. At the second step the need for low-investment strategies would rank options 3 and 4 above 1 and 2, and so on. Decision trees combine the identification of options with a simultaneous ranking of those options.

Perhaps the greatest limitation of decision tree analysis is that the choice at each branch on the tree can tend to be simplistic. For example, answering yes or no to diversification does not allow for the wide variety of alternatives which might exist between these two extremes (see Chapter 6). Nevertheless, as a starting point for evaluation, decision trees can often provide a useful framework.

7.7.4 Scenarios[22]

Ranking evaluates options against a specific list of items or criteria derived from the strategic analysis; decision trees achieve the same outcome by eliminating

ILLUSTRATION 7.6
Ranking options: Churchill Pottery

In 1990 Churchill Pottery, based in Stoke-on-Trent, UK, was one of the subjects of a BBC series entitled *Troubleshooter*, where the management teams of a number of companies were invited to discuss their organisation's strategic development with Sir John Harvey-Jones (ex-chairman of ICI). Like many traditional manufacturing companies at the time, Churchill found itself under increasing pressure from cheaper imports in its traditional markets, and was considering whether to move 'upmarket' by launching a new range aimed at the design-conscious end of the market. The ranking exercise below was done by a group of participants on a management programme having seen the Churchill Pottery video.

The results of the ranking are interesting. First, they highlight the need to do *something*. Second, the radical departures in strategy – such as moves into retailing or diversification – are regarded as unsuitable. They do not address the problems of the core business, do not fit the capabilities of Churchill and would not fit culturally. This leaves related developments as the frontrunners – as might be expected in a traditional manufacturing firm like Churchill. The choice essentially boils down to significant investments in cost reduction to support an essentially 'commodity' approach to the market (options 2 and 5) or an 'added value' attack on the growing 'upmarket' segments. The company chose the latter and with some success – presumably helped by their wide television exposure through the *Troubleshooter* series.

options through progressively introducing additional criteria to be satisfied. A third approach to screening is that of *scenario planning*, which was introduced in Chapter 3 as an important tool for assessing an organisation's environment in conditions of high uncertainty. It can therefore be used to screen strategic options by matching them to the possible future scenarios. The outcome of this process is not a single prioritised list of options (as with ranking and decision trees) but a series of *contingency plans* which identify the preferred option for each possible future scenario.

For example, a company planning international expansion may be uncertain about a number of key economic factors, such as exchange rates or tariff barriers. One scenario might be stable exchanges and reducing barriers. In these circumstances the company might choose to develop by manufacturing in the UK

Strategic options	Key strategic factors						Ranking
	Family ownership	Investment funds	Low price imports	Lack of marketing/ design skills	Automation low	Consumer taste (design)	
1. Do nothing	√	?	x	?	x	x	C
2. Consolidate in current segments (investment/ automation)	√	x	√	?	√	?	B
3. Expand overseas sales (Europe)	x	x	x	x	x	?	C
4. Launch 'upmarket' range	√	√	√	x	?	√	A
5. Expand 'own-label' production (to hotel/ catering industry)	√	√	√	?	x	?	B
6. Open retail outlets	x	x	?	x	?	?	C
7. Diversify	x	x	?	?	?	√	C

√ = favourable; x = unfavourable; ? = uncertain or irrelevant.

A = most suitable; B = possible; C = unsuitable.

Source: Authors based on *Troubleshooter* series, BBC, 1990.

and exporting. In contrast, a scenario of a strengthening pound and increasing barriers make a strategy of overseas-based manufacture more favoured.

Equally important is the organisation's ability to monitor the onset (or otherwise) of a particular scenario in time to implement appropriate strategies. In general, public-sector organisations have made much more extensive use of scenarios and contingency planning than the private sector.

7.8 Summary

This chapter has been concerned with reviewing ways in which the suitability of strategic options might be analysed. This is an important process, since it requires managers to be explicit as to the underlying rationale behind particular strategies and to try to understand why those strategies might succeed or fail. Rather than providing a single framework for an analysis of suitability, this chapter has suggested that a variety of different perspectives is more helpful. This relates to the central theme of this book: namely, that strategic developments within organisations are subject to a variety of different influences which, for convenience, have been grouped under three headings – the environment, resources and expectations culture.

The extent to which different types of strategy may suit an organisation's circumstances has been reviewed in relation to those various factors. It has been seen that one common thread is the stage of an organisation in its life cycle, which affects both the strategic logic of various options and the cultural climate in which strategic developments are taking place.

An assessment of the suitability of options can be used as a means of *narrowing down* to those strategies which are to be analysed in more detail. Ranking, decision trees and scenarios are useful techniques in this screening process. The next chapter considers strategic evaluation at a more detailed level, where assessments concerning the feasibility and acceptability of specific strategies need to be sharpened up.

References

1. The term 'consistency' was used by S. Tilles, 'How to evaluate strategy', *Harvard Business Review*, vol. 41, no. 4, (1963), pp. 111–21.
2. Readers are reminded of the discussion in Chapter 4 about the use and misuse of portfolio analysis. There is useful background reading in A. C. Hax and N. S. Majluf, 'The use of growth/share matrices', in R. G. Dyson (ed.), *Strategic Planning: Models and analytical techniques*, Wiley, 1990, chapter 4 Some authors have warned of the need to use portfolio matrices with care. See, for example, S. P. Slatter, 'Common pitfalls in using the BCG portfolio matrix', *London Business School Journal*, winter (1980), pp. 18–22.
3. C. W. Hofer and M. J. Davoust, *Successful Strategic Management*, A. T. Kearney Inc., Chicago.
4. The techniques built around the life cycle concept have been developed and explained by the consultants Arthur D. Little in a series of booklets, the first of which was R. V. L. Wright, *A System of Managing Diversity*, 1974.
5. M. E. Porter, *Competitive Advantage*, Free Press, 1985, chapters 14 and 15, discusses the strategies appropriate for leaders and followers at different stages of an industry's development.
6. M. E. Porter, 'From competitive advantage to competitive strategy', *Harvard Business Review*, vol. 65, no. 3, (1987), pp. 43–59.
7. A. Campbell and K. Luchs, 'Towards some new propositions on synergy', Ashridge Strategic Management Centre, 1990.
8. A. Campbell, *Synergy and Decentralisation*, unpublished work, 1991.
9. E. Schein, *Organisation Culture and Leadership*, Jossey Bass, 1985.
10. The PIMS data are collected from organisations which subscribe to the services offered by the Strategic Planning Institute. The data shown here are aggregate, but subscribers are able to access data more specific to their industry sector. More details of the PIMS methodology can be found in R. D. Buzzell and B. T. Gale, *The PIMS Principles*, Free Press, 1987.
11. PIMS, 'Marketing: in pursuit of the perfect mix', *Marketing*, 31 October 1991.
12. For discussion of technology transfer, see M. G. Harvey, 'The application of technology life cycles to technology transfers', *Journal of Business Strategy*, vol. 5, no. 2, (1984), pp. 51–60.

13. V. Ramanujam and P. Varadarajan, 'Research on corporate diversification: a synthesis', *Strategic Management Journal*, vol. 10, no. 6, (1989), pp. 523–51 is a comprehensive review article on this topic.

14. R. P. Rumelt, *Strategy, Structure and Economic Performance*, Harvard University Press, 1974.

15. C. A. Montgomery, 'The measurement of firm diversification: some new empirical evidence', *Academy of Management Journal*, vol. 25, no. 2, (1982), pp. 299–307.

16. R. M. Grant, A. P. Jammine and H. Thomas, 'Diversity, diversification and profitability among British manufacturing companies 1972–84', *Academy of Management Journal*, vol. 31, no. 4, (1988).

17. See A. Campbell and K. Luchs, 'Towards some new propositions on synergy', Ashridge Strategic Management Centre, 1990 for a summary of findings.

18. S. Chatterjee and B. Wernerfelt, 'The link between resources and type of diversification', *Strategic Management Journal*, vol. 12, no. 1, (1991), pp. 33–48.

19. A. Dunsmire, K. Hartley and D. Parker, 'Organisational status and performance', *Public Administration*, vol. 69, (1991), spring, pp. 21–40.

20. For example, see J. A. Bleeke, 'Strategic choices for newly opened markets', *Harvard Business Review*, vol. 68, no. 5, (1990), pp. 158–65; R. D. Utt, 'Privatisation: shifting the balance toward growth', *Economic Impact*, vol. 69, no. 4, (1989), pp. 73–7.

21. Decision trees are discussed in many books on management science and operational research. See, for example, P. G. Moore and H. Thomas, *The Anatomy of Decisions*, Penguin, 1976, chapters 4 and 6.

22. The use of scenarios by Shell are described in P. W. Beck, 'Corporate planning for an uncertain future', *Long Range Planning*, vol. 15, no. 4, (1982), pp. 12–21.

Recommended key readings

M. E. Porter, *Competitive Advantage*, Free Press, 1985, discusses the logic of how strategies can be chosen according to the situation of the organisation.

The work of the PIMS project and many of the findings are summarised in R. D. Buzzell and B. T. Gale, *The PIMS Principles*, Free Press, 1987.

E. Schein, *Organisation Culture and Leadership*, Jossey Bass, 1985, relates strategic choices to culture and life cycle.

Work assignments

7.1   Identify additional strategies for state railways (Illustration 7.1) and make a preliminary assessment against the evaluation criteria. Which strategy would *you* prefer? Why?

7.2   How suitable were the strategies pursued by Vitalograph* in the 1980s in terms of their strategic logic? (Refer to section 7.4 in the text.) Use more than one analysis to support your answer.

7.3   Compare the changes in strategy at Vitalograph* from 1989 with the previous period. Why did these changes occur?

7.4   Identify the strategies open to Kronenbourg* and Courage* in the 1990s and advise (and justify) the choices you think each company should make.

7.5 **Illustration 7.2 shows an organisation which is committed to vertical integration within the company. Make a critical appraisal of the advantages and disadvantages of vertical integration and explain the circumstances in which it is most likely to succeed or fail.**

7.6 *Referring to Illustration 7.3 and using additional examples of your own, criticise the argument that 'synergy is a sound basis for acquisitions'. Refer to P. C. Haspelagh and D. M. Jemison,* Managing Acquisitions, *Macmillan, 1991, to assist with this assignment.*

7.7 Choose an organisation and analyse the extent to which the dominant culture of the organisation fits the position in the life cycle (see Figure 7.5). How has this influenced the strategic choices which have been made?

7.8 **In the case of Vitalograph,* Kronenbourg,* Courage* or an organisation of your choice, write a brief for the management explaining how the PIMS findings should influence their evaluation and choice of strategies.**

7.9 *Refer to Figure 7.5 and reference 21. From the point of view of the management of an enterprise which is likely to be privatised, make a critical appraisal of the implications of privatisation to the strategy of a firm in:*
(a) a western European country
(b) an eastern/central European country
(c) a developing country.
Explain, and justify, the differences in your conclusions.

7.10 Undertake a ranking analysis of the choices available to Vitalograph* (or an organisation of your choice) like that shown in Illustration 7.6.

* This refers to a case study in the Text and Cases version of this book.

CHAPTER 8

Strategy evaluation 2
Making choices

8.1 Introduction

The previous chapter discussed evaluation criteria (suitability, feasibility and acceptability) and considered ways in which the suitability of particular types of strategy might be established in terms of their *strategic logic*, the *cultural fit* and the *research evidence* available linking the choice of strategy to organisational performance. Assessing suitability is a useful way of establishing the underlying logic of strategies and reducing the strategic options to a workable shortlist. This chapter covers the more detailed considerations which might be applied to this shortlist. It is concerned with the use of the evaluation criteria of *acceptability* and *feasibility* of strategies. Acceptability will be assessed against three broad measures: *return*, *risk* and *stakeholder expectations*. The chapter concludes with a review of how organisations select future strategies. Readers are referred back to Figure 7.1 as a reminder of how these various aspects of evaluation relate to each other.

8.2 Analysing return

An assessment of the returns likely to accrue from specific options is a key measure of the acceptability of an option. However, there are a number of different approaches to the analysis of return. This section looks at three different assessments:

- *Profitability analyses*, which are important where financial return is of central importance – the situation which prevails in most commercial organisations.
- *Cost/benefit analysis*, where the returns are more complex to assess or less tangible, as occurs in many public-service organisations, where strategies are more likely to be justified in terms of improving provision rather than financial return. The measurement of value for money is important.

- *Shareholder value analysis*, which attempts to address many of the criticisms of traditional financial assessments of strategic development by focusing more carefully on how and where real value will be created, reappraising current strategies and evaluating of new strategies.

8.2.1 Profitability analyses[1]

Traditional financial analyses have been used extensively in the evaluation of the acceptability of strategies. Three of the more commonly used approaches are as follows:

1. Forecasting the *return on capital employed* (ROCE) a specific time after a new strategy is implemented (e.g. the new strategy will result in a return on capital of 20 per cent by 1996.) This is shown in Figure 8.1(a).

2. *Payback period* has been used where a significant capital injection is needed to support a new venture. In Figure 8.1(b) the payback period is calculated by finding the time at which the cumulative net cash flow becomes zero – in the example, three and a half years.

   The judgement is then whether this is regarded as an adequate outcome and if the company is prepared to wait that long for a return. This will vary from one industry to another, and also between companies within the same industry. In capital-intensive industries, major investments normally have to be justified over a minimum of five years. In contrast, in fast-moving consumer goods and services, payback is usually required more quickly.

   Although this may imply that managers seek very different rates of return depending on the industry (which is divergent with corporate finance theory), such behaviour is better understood if payback is being used as a *targeting device*. Major public-sector ventures such as bridge building may well be assessed on a payback period of up to sixty years.

3. *Discounted cash flow* (DCF) analysis is perhaps the most widely prescribed investment appraisal technique and is essentially an extension of the payback period analysis. Once the net cash flows have been assessed for each of the preceding years (see Figure 8.1(c)) they are discounted progressively to reflect the fact that funds generated early are of more real value than those in later periods (years). In the example, the discounting rate of 10 per cent reflects the value placed on money tied up in the venture. So the projected net cash flow of £2,000 in year 2 is discounted to £1,820 and so on. The net present value (NPV) of the venture is then calculated by adding all the discounted annual cash flows (after taxation) over the anticipated life of the project. DCF analysis is particularly useful for comparing the financial merits of strategies which have very different patterns of expenditure and return. Most computer spreadsheet packages have NPV and internal rate of

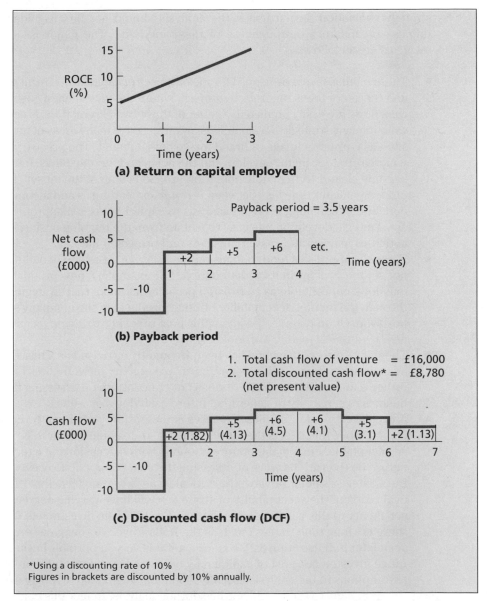

Figure 8.1 Some useful measures of profitability for strategic evaluation

return (IRR) functions available for DCF calculations. Readers are referred to the references for a fuller discussion of these financial analysis techniques.

Although the evaluation of strategies may be assisted by the use of one or more of these financial techniques, it is important to recognise some of the implicit assumptions which inevitably limit their value as comprehensive techniques of strategy evaluation. In particular, the analysis should not be misguided by the tidiness or apparent thoroughness of these methods. The major issues[2] to be aware of are as follows:

- These methods were developed for the purposes of capital investment appraisal, and therefore focus on discrete *projects* where the incremental costs and cash flows are easily predicted. Neither of these two assumptions is necessarily valid in many strategic developments, nor indeed for many areas of investment such as corporate image or brand image development. The precise way in which a strategy might develop, and the costs and income flows, tend to become clearer as the implementation proceeds than at the outset. There are often significant time lags between *revenue* expenditures and income benefits, so confining financial analysis to capital items is inappropriate. Nor are strategic developments easy to isolate from the ongoing business activities in accurately assessing costs and projected income.

- Financial appraisals tend to focus on the *tangible* costs and benefits and do not set the strategy in its wider context. For example, a new product launch may look unprofitable as an isolated project, but make real strategic sense through the market acceptability of other products in the company's portfolio. Or, in reverse, the intangible cost of losing *strategic focus* through new ventures is readily overlooked.

- The use of return on capital has been frequently criticised as a basis for evaluating strategic options since, as an *accounting* measure, it is backward rather than forward looking – it does not concentrate on assessing the business's capability of generating future cash flows or value.

- A crucial element of all these analyses is the position taken on the cost of capital, since this affects the *hurdle* which a strategy must clear to be regarded as acceptable. Financial literature abounds with discussions of a technical nature on the various ways of assessing the cost of capital. However, from the strategist's point of view, the critical issue is to recognise that the evaluation of the acceptability of strategies will have varying degrees of sensitivity to this particular assumption. For strategic investments where there are long time frames (such as the Rolls-Royce Aeroengines example seen later in Illustration 8.2), cost of capital is very important. In shorter-range investments, cost of capital may be much less important than other assumptions in the analysis. Equally, some managers may wrongly assume that it is 'safe' to set 'tough' hurdles during analysis. In fact this could tie the company to apparently low-risk strategies and miss some developments of major potential. In many cases the overemphasis on hurdles merely encourages analysts to re-do the analysis until it just satisfies the hurdle criterion – in other words, the analysis degenerates into a 'game' within the organisation.

- Overall it is advisable to use a number of financial techniques in order to build up a picture of the financial attractiveness of various strategic options. Just as important is that managers surface those assumptions with greatest uncertainty in order to perform truly testing sensitivity analysis.

Most of the discussion so far has assumed that evaluation is concerned with strategic options pursued through *internal development*. However, another common situation in which evaluation is required is strategic development through *acquisition*. Here an important additional factor is the need to assess the value of the company being acquired, cost savings which can be accomplished post-acquisition, likely proceeds from divestments or sale of assets, and the anticipated impact on the value of the merged companies. This is a crucial part of the evaluation and can often prove difficult in practice. For example, there are three main ways in which a company can be valued:[3]

1. The *balance sheet* value of the net assets. There are dangers with this approach since some key assets may not appear (e.g. goodwill) and others may be undervalued (e.g. property).

2. *Earnings potential* is probably the key strategic issue if the intention is to continue the business as a going concern or to merge the organisation's activities into the acquiring company. The methods used to make an assessment of this type are those outlined above – where the cost of acquisition is simply regarded as the 'investment' from which returns flow. There are difficulties though. Often the reason an acquisition is attractive is that the costs of the business are currently too high and the post-acquisition benefit is derived from a rationalisation of these costs (particularly overheads) and/or synergy gained from the merger of activities. Forecasting these savings and benefits can be difficult, since the analyst is unlikely to have access to 'inside' information to make such assessments. It should be remembered that the major variable determining success in acquisitions is the quality of the integration plan and the ability to implement this process.[4]

3. *Market valuation* in practice will usually represent the minimum cost to an acquirer of a publicly quoted company. During the bidding period the cost is likely to rise beyond the starting share price. Where public-sector organisations have been privatised there has been a dilemma in assessing how the market is likely to value the company. This is necessary in determining the offer price in the flotation of shares. In virtually all UK privatisations in the 1980s and early 1990s there were criticisms of overcautious valuation, leading to highly oversubscribed flotations and some considerable short-term profit taking by investors.

8.2.2 Cost/benefit analysis[5]

In many situations the analysis of profit gives too narrow an interpretation of return, particularly where intangible benefits are an important consideration. This is often the case in projects such as the siting of an airport or the sewer construction example shown in Illustration 8.1. Cost/benefit analysis attempts to put a money value on all the costs and benefits of a strategic option – including tangible and intangible returns to people and organisations other than the one 'sponsoring' the project or strategy. Although monetary valuation is often difficult, it can be done.

Illustration 8.1 is an example of the expected costs and benefits of building a sewer and shows the basis on which intangibles were quantified. The basis of quantification needs to be justified carefully and is likely to be subject to dis-

ILLUSTRATION 8.1
Sewerage construction project

Investment in items of infrastructure – such as sewers – often requires a careful consideration of the wider costs and benefits of the project.

In the early 1990s Britain's recently privatised water companies were monopolies supplying water and disposing of sewage. They needed to invest in new sewerage systems to meet the increasing standards required by law. They often used cost/benefit analysis to assess projects. The figures below are from an actual analysis carried out in 1991.

Benefits

Benefits result mainly from reduced use of rivers as overflow sewers. There are also economic benefits resulting from construction. The following benefits are quantified below:

- The multiplier benefit to the local economy of increased spending by those employed on the project.
- The linkage benefit to the local economy of purchases from local firms, including the multiplier effect of such spending.
- Reduced risk of flooding from overflows or old sewers collapsing – flood probabilities can be quantified using historical records, and the cost of flood damage by detailed assessment of the property vulnerable to damage.
- Reduced traffic disruption from flooding and road closures for repairs to old sewers – statistics on the costs of delays to users, traffic flows on roads affected, and past closure frequency can be used to quantify savings.
- Increased amenity value of rivers, e.g. for boating and fishing, can be measured by surveys asking visitors what the value is to them or by looking at the effect on demand of charges imposed elsewhere.
- Increased rental values and take-up of space can be measured by consultation with developers and observed effects elsewhere.

agreement from different interested parties. For example, the amenity benefit could be argued to be far greater than the proposed basis of assessment if the general character of the town were improved by the clean-up of the river.

One of the greatest difficulties of cost/benefit analysis is deciding on the boundaries of the analysis. For example, in Illustration 8.1 the benefits of purchases from local firms are small because most expenditure is with firms elsewhere in Britain. If the benefits had been reckoned for Britain as whole, they

- Increased visitor numbers to riverside facilities resulting from reduced pollution.

Construction cost

This is net of the cost of unskilled labour. Use of unskilled labour is not a burden on the economy, and its cost must be deducted to arrive at opportunity cost.

Net benefits

Once the difficult task of quantifying costs and benefits is complete, standard discounting techniques can be used to calculate net present value and internal rate of return, and analysis can then proceed as for conventional projects.

	£m	£m
Benefits		
Multiplier/linkage benefits		0.9
Flood prevention		2.5
Reduced traffic disruption		7.2
Amenity benefits		4.6
Investment benefit		23.6
Encouragement of visitors		4.0
Total benefits		42.8
Costs		
Construction cost	18.2	
Less: unskilled labour cost	(4.7)	
Opportunity cost of construction		(13.5)
Present value of net benefits (NPV)		29.3
Real internal rate of return (IRR)		15%

Note: Figures discounted at a *real* discount rate of 5% over 40 years.

Source: G. Owen, Policy Research Centre, Sheffield Business School.

would have been far greater than shown. In another context, a powerful argument against area-based economic development initiatives such as Urban Development Corporations or Enterprise Zones is that they displace business activity from other areas rather than encouraging new ventures.

Despite these difficulties cost/benefit analysis is an approach which is valuable if its limitations are understood. Its major benefit is in forcing people to be explicit about the various factors which should influence strategic choice. So, even if people disagree on the value which should be assigned to particular costs or benefits, at least they are able to argue their case on common ground and decision-makers can compare the merits of the various arguments. A detailed cost/benefit analysis would proceed to assign weightings to the various items in Illustration 8.1 to reflect their relative importance to the decision about whether or not to construct the sewer. This would also normally be combined with a sensitivity analysis (see section 8.3.2 below) of the key NPV and IRR outcomes in relation to the main assumptions.

8.2.3 Shareholder value analysis[6]

During the 1980s attempts were made to address many of the limitations and criticisms of financial analyses outlined above. This coincided with the growing emphasis being placed on the analysis of the value creation process through the work of Michael Porter discussed in Chapters 4 and 6. At the same time renewed attention was given to the primary legal responsibility of company directors: namely, the creation of value/benefits for the shareholders. The takeover boom of the 1980s caused both corporate raiders and victims alike to look at how corporate development strategies were, or were not, generating shareholder value.

Together these factors spawned *shareholder value analysis* (SVA). These new analytical methods are also known as value-based analyses. Although the financial technicalities are rooted in corporate finance theory, the importance of shareholder value analysis to strategic evaluation is as follows:

- It emphasises that traditional assessments such as discounted cash flow (net present value) should concentrate on strategies and not just investment projects. Ideally, the analysis should be applied to a strategic business unit (SBU). This addresses earlier criticisms about the difficulties of isolating specific developments and accurately assessing incremental cash flows. Where individual projects are under appraisal it also implies that these may be better evaluated together as *strategic investment thrusts* (i.e. a 'bundle' of related projects), particularly if there are close links between the projects.
- The financial analysis must be driven by an understanding of the value creation process and the competitive advantage which the organisation derives from this process.[7] In particular, it is critical to identify the key cash generators of the business – the *value* and/or *cost drivers* discussed in

Chapter 4. The assessment of the attractiveness (acceptability) of a strategy – say, through NPV – is likely to be critically dependent on a relatively small number of these value and cost drivers. These become the key factors which link the analysis of competitive strategy to the likely acceptability of that strategy in terms of improvements in shareholder value. For example, the ability to sustain a price premium may be directly related to the company's systems for ensuring reliable fast delivery *vis-à-vis* competitors.

- It must also be remembered that value and cost drivers often act in conjunction with each other, so managers need to make judgements on how these interdependencies may work, rather than expecting simplistic answers from precise financial measures. A view must also be taken as to whether this competitive advantage is genuinely sustainable over the period ahead and, if so, at what investment cost in business systems. In other words, the assumptions underlying the forecasts of future shareholder value are rigorously challenged against the expected competitive situation, requiring openness and realism among the management team.

Although SVA has done much to address the shortcomings of traditional financial analyses, it must be remembered that it does not remove many of the inherent uncertainties surrounding strategic evaluation. The exponents of SVA have been criticised for being heavily prescriptive in selling the virtues of SVA without necessarily highlighting the required changes in decision making, control and reward systems.[8] Nevertheless the idea of valuing a strategy may serve to give greater realism and clarity to otherwise vague strategies, as shown in Illustration 8.2.

8.3 Analysing risk

The likely return from a particular strategy is an important measure of the acceptability of that strategy. However, there is another, different, measure of acceptability against which strategic options might need to be assessed. This is the *risk* which the organisation faces in pursuing that strategy. This section outlines how this risk can be assessed as part of an evaluation of specific options.

8.3.1 Financial ratio projections[9]

A useful analysis is the projection of key financial ratios which give a measure of the risk which the organisation would be taking by pursuing various strategies. At the broadest level, an assessment of how the *capital structure* of the company would change by pursuing different options is a good general measure of risk. For example, options which require the extension of long-term loans will increase the gearing of the company and increase its financial risk.

ILLUSTRATION 8.2
Strategy evaluation at BP and Rolls-Royce

Companies need to find a use for financial analysis which reflects their specific circumstances and provides information to managers when choosing new strategies

Shareholder value at British Petroleum (BP)

Between 1986 and 1991 the BP Group shifted its corporate decision-making processes towards *value-based management* with the aim of enhancing BP's shareholder value. This change occurred because BP top management were dissatisfied with measuring performance through return on capital employed (ROCE), which was based on financial accounting measures and was backward looking.

BP looked to value-based management to:

- Align all of its financial decision-making processes with its corporate financial objective of creating value for its shareholders.
- Give management a top-down check on where BP was adding to shareholder value and also where it might be dissipating value among its business portfolio.
- Enable managers within the businesses to evaluate strategies in detail using economic bases of appraisal (looking at SBUs as projects or bundles of projects).
- Set business performance targets and indicators in a way consistent with these strategies.

Over the five-year period many major benefits had been secured. However, the process of implementation and of learning was still

---

The level of financial risk created by funding a proposed strategy from long-term loans can be tested out by examining the likelihood of the company reaching the *break-even point* (see below) and the consequences of falling short of that volume of business while interest on loans continues to be paid. In this respect there is a clear link between the assessment of risk and the feasibility of alternative strategies. The late 1980s and early 1990s proved to be an extremely difficult period for many public authorities as they struggled to cope with a financial structure which was a legacy of earlier years.

At a more detailed level, a consideration of the likely impact on an organisation's *liquidity* is important in assessing options. For example, a small retailer eager to grow quickly may be tempted to fund the required shopfitting costs by delaying payments to suppliers and increasing bank overdraft. This reduced

continuing. An important factor was that from the start the process had the firm commitment of top BP management, who refused to allow any sacred cows to dilute the changes needed.

Strategic project appraisal at Rolls-Royce Aeroengines

As a major player in a high-technology international market, Rolls-Royce Aeroengines had invested substantial sums in product development. Typically, it would take many years to recoup the value of these investments. Rapid growth in the past had resulted from airline deregulation, economic growth and changes in consumers' leisure patterns. However, this growth proved vulnerable to a variety of factors: for instance, recession, overcapacity of the airline industry and cutbacks in defence spending. In addition, Aerospace companies competed fiercely to win orders for major new projects to ensure that (a) the requirement of a single major customer could be met, (b) there would be some winners so that manufacturing capacity would be well utilised, and (c) synergies were gained in development spend where possible.

The evaluation of individual projects was thus clouded by external uncertainty and by interdependency within the product range. Financial measures of project value were therefore seen as indicative rather than precise and definitive.

Rolls-Royce had also experimented with mapping the value-creating profiles of all its major projects in order to explore the interdependency effects and key vulnerables.

Source: Research undertaken by Tony *Grundy, CAMDEV* Strategic Development Consultants, Cambridge. Reproduced with permission. Also published in A. N. Grundy, *Corporate Strategy and Financial Decisions*, Kogan Page, 1992.

liquidity increases the financial risk of the business. The extent to which this increased risk threatens survival depends on the likelihood of either creditors or the bank demanding payments from the company, and this clearly requires judgement. An increasingly important element in the assessment of risk companies intending to trade internationally is the nature of the debtors they would have to take on, and whether or not they are able or willing to take export guarantee insurance to mitigate this risk.

8.3.2 Sensitivity analysis[10]

Sensitivity analysis is a useful technique for incorporating the assessment of risk during strategy evaluation. Its use has grown with the availability of computer spreadsheet packages, which are ideally suited to this type of analysis.

The principles behind the approach are straightforward. The technique allows each of the important assumptions underlying a particular option to be questioned and changed. In particular, it seeks to test how sensitive the predicted performance or outcome (e.g. profit) is to each of these assumptions.

For example, the key assumptions underlying a strategy might be that market demand will grew by 5 per cent p.a., or that the company will stay strike-free, or that certain expensive machines will operate at 90 per cent loading. Sensitivity analysis asks what would be the effect on performance (in this case, profitability) if, for example, market demand grew by only 1 per cent, or by as much as 10 per cent. Would either of these extremes alter the decision to pursue that particular strategy? A similar process might be repeated for the other key assumptions.

This process helps management develop a clearer picture of the risks of making particular strategic decisions and the degree of confidence it might have in a given decision. Illustration 8.3 shows how sensitivity analysis can be used in strategy evaluation.

In theory, the uncertainty factor surrounding key variables in the evaluation could be assigned probability distributions, and statistical analysis used to assess how these uncertainties combine in an overall *risk analysis*[11] of the strategy. Although theoretically neater than sensitivity analysis, such an approach has proved less popular than sensitivity analysis for three main reasons:

- It is difficult to assign probability distributions to many variables. Although this is a shortcoming shared by sensitivity analysis, the worry has been that this 'inaccuracy' is forgotten in the neatness of the statistical computations. In other words, the outcome is given more status than is really warranted.
- Sensitivity analysis has proved to be a good way of *communicating* to decision-makers the areas of uncertainty underlying the evaluation, and allowing them to use their judgement in the choice process.
- In practice, managers often employ analytical tools not to seek out and explore opportunities, but to explore and *absorb uncertainty* around options which they favour.[12] Sensitivity analysis is well suited to this purpose.

8.3.3 Decision matrices[13]

There are many circumstances where *specific aspects* of strategic choice can be reduced to simple choices between a number of clearly defined courses of action. This is often the case when choosing between different development methods for a particular strategy. For example (see Figure 8.2), an organisation which has decided to expand its operations by developing a new geographical market may be faced with three different methods of achieving this: by building *new premises*; buying and *converting* existing premises; or *leasing* a purpose-

Annual sales volume (units)		
Option	**10,000**	**20,000**
1. Build new premises	£58	£35
2. Purchase and refit	£56	£33
3. Lease	£50	£40

(a) Unit cost table for the options

Annual sales volume (units)			
Option	**10,000**	**20,000**	**Maximum regret**
1. Build new premises	£8	£2	£8
2. Purchase and refit	£6	£0	£6
3. Lease	£0	£7	£7

(b) Regret table for the options

	Annual sales volume (units)		
Option	**10,000** (probability = 0.7)	**20,000** (probability = 0.3)	**Weighted average cost**
1. Build new premises	£58 x 0.7	£35 x 0.3	£51.10
2. Purchase and refit	£56 x 0.7	£33 x 0.3	£49.10
3. Lease	£50 x 0.7	£40 x 0.3	£47.00

(c) Unit costs weighted by the probability of each outcome

Figure 8.2 Decision matrices: an example

built building. It also faces uncertainty as to the likely demand, which could range from 10,000 to 20,000 units p.a.

Having analysed the costs of these various options, the likely impact on unit production costs in each case was estimated as shown in Figure 8.2(a). In deciding which option to choose it is necessary (before any detailed analysis) to be clear about which type of decision rule will be used to weigh these options

ILLUSTRATION 8.3
Sensitivity analysis

Sensitivity analysis is a useful technique for assessing the extent to which the success of a preferred strategy is dependent on the key assumptions which underlie that strategy.

In 1992 the Dunsmore Chemical Company was a single-product company trading in a mature and relatively stable market. It was intended to use this established situation as a cash cow to generate funds for a new venture with a related product. Estimates had shown that the company would need to generate some £4m cash (at 1992 values) between 1993 and 1998 for this new venture to be possible.

Although the expected performance of the company was for a cash flow of £9.5m over that period (the *base case*), management was concerned to assess the likely impact of three key factors:

● Possible increases in *production costs* (labour, overheads and materials), which might be as much as 3 per cent p.a. in real terms.
● *Capacity fill*, which might be reduced by as much as 25 per cent due to ageing plant and uncertain labour relations.
● *Price levels*, which might be affected by the threatened entry of a new major competitor. This could squeeze prices by as much as 3 per cent p.a. in real terms.

It was decided to use sensitivity analysis to assess the possible impact of each of these factors on the company's ability to generate £4m. The results are shown in the graphs.

From this analysis the management concluded that its target of £4m would be achieved with *capacity utilisation* as low as 60 per cent, which was certainly going to be achieved. Increased *production costs* of 3 per cent p.a. would still allow the company to achieve the £4m target over the period. In contrast, *price* squeezes of 3 per cent p.a. would result in a shortfall of £2m.

against each other. For example, in Figure 8.2 there are four different rules which could be applied:

1. The *optimistic* decision rule would choose the best of the best outcomes for each option. In this case the *purchase and refit* option would be chosen because at £33 it represents the lowest possible cost situation.
2. The *pessimistic* decision favours the best of the worst outcomes. In this case the option of *leasing* would be chosen, since if demand proved to be

The management concluded from this analysis that the key factor which should affect their thinking on this matter was the likely impact of new competition and the extent to which they could protect price levels if such competition emerged. They therefore developed an aggressive marketing strategy to deter potential entrants.

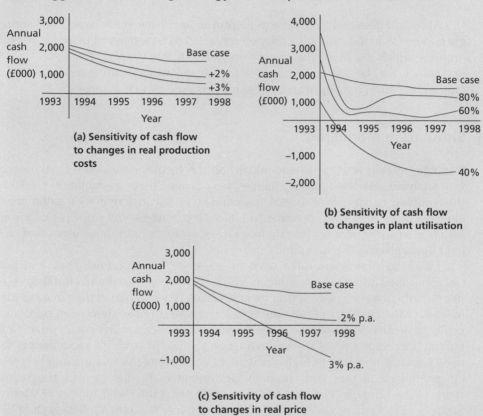

(a) Sensitivity of cash flow to changes in real production costs

(b) Sensitivity of cash flow to changes in plant utilisation

(c) Sensitivity of cash flow to changes in real price

Source: The Dunsmore example is from the authors. The calculations for the sensitivity test utilise computer programs employed in the Doman case study by P. H. Jones (Sheffield. Business School).

only 10,000 units this option would have the lowest cost at £50.

3. The *regret decision* rule would favour options which minimise the lost opportunity which might occur by choosing a particular option. So, in the example, if purchase and refit was pursued and sales turned out to be only 10,000 units then the wrong decision would have been made, since leasing would have produced a lower cost. The regret with this choice would be £6 per unit (i.e. £56 –£50). Figure 8.2(b) shows the regret table for each combination of option/outcome. The regret rule would give preference to *purchase*

and refit, since this minimises the possible lost opportunity or regret.

4. The *expected value* rule introduces an important new dimension: namely, the *probability* that each outcome (demand) would occur. This can then be used to weight the outcomes for each option, and the options can then be compared on this basis. Figure 8.2(c) shows that in this example the leasing option would be preferred, since it has the lowest weighted average cost.

Although decision matrices are helpful in analysing some aspects of strategic choice (as in the example), they clearly need to be tempered by other considerations which would not be directly included in this simplified analysis. In the example, it may be that one reason for leasing the available premises is to deny a major competitor the opportunity of setting up quickly in that location.

8.3.4 Simulation modelling

Strategic models attempt to encompass all the factors considered by the separate analyses discussed in this chapter into one quantitative simulation model of the company and its environment. It should be no surprise that such global models have been virtually impossible to build. Nevertheless, the principle of *simulation modelling*[14] is a useful one in strategy evaluation, in those aspects which lend themselves to this quantitative view.

Financial models are often used to assess strategic options. *Risk analysis* (as mentioned above) is a technique which seeks to assess the overall degree of uncertainty in a particular option by mathematically combining the uncertainties in each of the elements of the option. For example, the likelihood of a particular profit projection is governed by the uncertainties surrounding costs, prices and volume forecasts. One of the limitations on the use of strategic modelling is the need for large amounts of high-quality data concerning the relationship between environmental factors and company performance. In this respect the recent work of the Strategic Planning Institute (SPI) using the Profit Impact of Market Strategy (PIMS) database[15] has been interesting (see Chapter 7). Research at SPI has tried to build a number of quantitative causal models (using multiple regression) which explain how company performances have been influenced by up to two dozen different factors.

In general, the use of modelling in strategy evaluation is limited to well-structured problems. Particular care needs to be taken for the following reasons:

- There is a danger that the model will become a gross oversimplification of reality and fail to encompass the most important uncertainties and risks.
- Attempts to incorporate a very large number of variables make the model highly complex, and all the critical interrelationships need to be included, which is in practice very difficult, if not impossible.
- Some key data, such as competitor reactions, are difficult to assess and/or incorporate in the model. The overriding danger with models of all types is

that they can result in less insight for managers/decision-makers than much simpler techniques (such as sensitivity analysis) as they hide the analysis away in a 'black box' which managers do not feel they can open.

8.3.5 Heuristic models[16]

Many of the techniques applied to management decision making attempt to find the best or optimum solution to a problem or situation. In strategy evaluation this is invariably very difficult due to the complexities of the situation and the high levels of uncertainty involved. Many strategic decisions are concerned with finding a *satisfactory* option rather than the best option.

Heuristic models are a means of identifying 'solutions' in a systematic way, and are most valuable in complex situations where there are many options available to an organisation and many different requirements or criteria to be met. Here an analysis can be done by computer search.

This requires all of the decision criteria to be listed (e.g. *a satisfactory option must provide 5% p.a. revenue growth, labour productivity gains of 2% p.a., must avoid plant closures in Spain*, etc.). The various options are searched until one is found which satisfies all the criteria. This is not necessarily the best option. The search can be continued to provide a shortlist of options which fit the criteria and in that way could be used for screening.

With the advent of cheap and powerful computers, heuristic modelling is becoming useful as an evaluation technique, since the search process can be undertaken quickly even when many criteria need to be met and several hundred options exist.

8.4 Analysing stakeholder reactions

It was emphasised in Chapters 5 and 7 that assessing the *cultural fit* of strategies is crucial. This can be done through *stakeholder mapping*, as outlined in Chapter 5 (see Figure 5.8). Readers are reminded that stakeholder maps can only usefully be drawn in relation to specific strategic options. Stakeholder mapping is therefore a very valuable tool in assessing the likely reactions of stakeholders to new strategies, the ability to manage these reactions, and hence the acceptability of a strategy.

There are many situations where judgements on stakeholder reactions could be crucial. For example:

- A new strategy might require a substantial issue of *new shares*. This could be unacceptable to powerful groups of shareholders since it dilutes their voting power.
- Plans to *merge* with other companies or to *trade* with new countries could be unacceptable to unions, the government or some customers.

- A strategy of market development might require the cutting out of *channels* (such as wholesalers), hence running the risk of a backlash which could jeopardise the success of the strategy.

- Changes in competitive strategy in static or tight markets might upset the status quo to such an extent that competitors will be forced to retaliate in a way which is damaging to all parties, but which would undermine the assumptions on which the strategy's acceptability had been assessed. The most common example of this is a price war.

- Since the important issue is the likely reactions of competitors to particular strategic changes, *game theory*[17] should, in principle, have some use as an evaluation technique. However, the difficulties of coping with the complexity of the strategic situation have limited the use of game theory to largely qualitative applications. The biggest difficulty with using game theory lies in the assumption that the strategic competitive behaviour of companies can be predicted by using simple rules. Readers should refer to the references for a fuller discussion of this technique.

- Some very difficult (mis)judgements have been made by public-sector managers and politicians over the last few years regarding the degree of determination on the part of central government and government agencies to introduce and sustain changes in strategy. This was also a key issue for the privatised quasi-monopolies, such as British Telecom (see Illustration 8.4).

Very often the initial evaluation of a strategy using stakeholder analysis will identify critical mismatches with the expectations of some stakeholders. The evaluation might then proceed to the next stage of analysis, where the following issues need to be addressed:

- Whether the strategy should/can be amended better to fit the expectations of all the stakeholders without unduly sacrificing acceptability as assessed by the other measures of risk and return. It is unlikely that an optimum strategy exists, so successful strategies are those which seek an acceptable compromise between the conflicting interests of the various stakeholders. Stakeholder mapping allows appropriate weights to be given to these interests depending on their level of power and/or interest.

- How successful the management of stakeholder expectations is likely to be during implementation. In particular, there may be key *maintenance* activities required with some stakeholders to ensure their acceptance of the strategy, as discussed in Chapter 5.

- Similarly, there may be some stakeholders who need to be encouraged or persuaded to shift their *position* in order to give the strategy a chance. This could occur in two ways: by lessening their opposition to the new strategy; or by persuading powerful but disinterested stakeholders to become key players and to put their weight behind a new strategy.

ILLUSTRATION 8.4
Power struggle in the UK telecommunications industry

Developing strategies to respond to changing stakeholder expectations may be a key part of an organisation's development strategy.

Although British Telecom (BT) had been hailed as one of the great successes of the UK privatisation programme by the 1990s, there was growing concern that its impressive financial performance was strongly influenced by its near-monopoly situation. The UK government – although a 49 per cent shareholder – was under pressure to increase competition within the industry, either by direct action or through extending the powers of the regulatory body (OFTEL). Ian Vallence, BT's chairman, was waging a fierce defence of the company's position and resisting any suggestions that they should voluntarily give up part of their market to competition. They were aware of the fact that *equal access* legislation – which would give customers the right (and equipment) to pick the carrier of their choice – had resulted in a 23 per cent loss in market share for their American equivalent, ATT, when introduced in the USA in 1984.

Some critics believed that such an aggressive defensive strategy was not the best tactic on the grounds that BT was unlikely to defeat the government's wishes. Perhaps a better tactic would have been based around a political strategy to ensure that the expectations of the major stakeholders were accommodated. BT could have taken the initiative and pre-empted the government's reforms by announcing its own price-cap on international calls (a major source of criticism of BT). This would have taken the wind out of OFTEL's sails. Perhaps the best way of changing the government's view was by bashing it publicly and then arguing and bargaining privately. Indeed, BT could afford to take a relatively pragmatic short-term view because the threat of equal access was not immediate: fewer than half of their customers were serviced by switches which could readily provide equal access. So at the end of the day none of the stakeholders needed to feel unhappy. The government would get more competition without dissolving its shareholding in BT. OFTEL's role would expand. BT itself – recognising the inevitability of increased competition – would have developed a strategy for introducing that competition on *its own terms*.

Source: *Independent on Sunday*, 3 February 1991.

The accurate assessment of those political activities which will be needed to support a new strategy is an important aspect of strategy evaluation which is often neglected in favour of the more numerical and 'rational' analyses discussed above. Both are necessary.

8.5 Analysing feasibility

The previous two sections have been concerned with the *acceptability* of strategic options. This section looks at ways of assessing the *feasibility* of options, which is concerned with whether strategies are achievable in resource terms. It should be remembered that many approaches combine a parallel assessment of both feasibility and acceptability.

8.5.1 Funds flow analysis[18]

The assessment of financial feasibility would normally be an important part of any strategy evaluation. A valuable piece of analysis is a funds flow forecast, which seeks to identify the funds which would be required for any strategy and the likely sources of those funds. For example, in Figure 8.3 the evaluation of a proposed strategy (X) might proceed by the following steps:

1. An assessment of the *capital investment* needed (e.g. new buildings, machines or vehicles). This amounts to £13.25m.
2. A forecast of the *cumulative profits* earned over the period 1988–90. 'Funds from operations' of £15m are calculated from an estimate of future profits plus the adding back of any non-fund items such as depreciation, and represents the real flow of funds into the company forecasted for that period.
3. An estimate of the necessary increases in *working capital* required by the strategy can be made by the separate consideration of each element of working capital (stock increases, increased creditors, etc.), or by using a simple pro rata adjustment related to the forecasted level of increase in sales revenue. For example, if the present revenue of £30m requires a working capital level of £10m then a forecasted increase in sales revenue to £31.65m would account for anticipated increase in working capital of £0.55m. This type of pro rata adjustment would be valid only when looking at future strategies which are similar in nature to the present company activities.
4. *Tax liability* and expected *dividend* payments can be estimated (in relation to the anticipated profitability), in this case at £1.2m and £0.5m respectively.
5. The calculation so far leaves a *shortfall* in funds of £0.5m. The forecast is then finalised by looking at alternative ways of funding the shortfall and this is where the critical appraisal of financial feasibility occurs. In Figure 8.3 this shortfall is to be funded by an additional short-term loan of £0.9m (which in

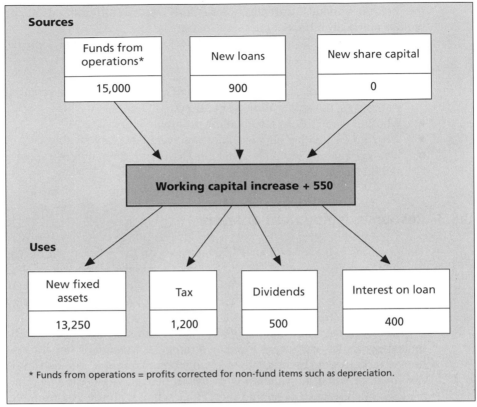

Figure 8.3 A funds flow forecast for strategy X (1988–1990), (£000)

its turn will incur interest payments of $0.4m over the three-year period, assuming simple interest at 14.8 per cent p.a.).

It should be remembered that funds flow analysis is a forecasting technique and is subject to the difficulties and errors of any method of forecasting. Such an analysis should quickly highlight whether the proposed strategy is likely to be feasible in financial terms, and could normally be programmed on to a computer spreadsheet should the model be required repeatedly during evaluation. This would also assist in identifying the *timing* of new funding requirements.

8.5.2 Break-even analysis[19]

Break-even analysis is a simple and widely used technique which is helpful in exploring some key aspects of feasibility. It is often used to assess the feasibility of meeting targets of return (e.g. profit) and, as such, combines a parallel assessment of acceptability. As mentioned above, this also provides an assessment of the risk in various strategies, particularly where different strategic options require markedly different cost structures.

Illustration 8.5 is an example of how break-even analysis can be used to investigate such issues as:

- The likelihood of achieving the levels of market penetration required for viability (in the static market situation).
- Whether competitors would allow profitable entry.
- Whether cost and quality assumptions are, in fact, achievable.
- Whether funding would be available to provide the required capacity and skilled labour to operate the plant.

8.5.3 Resource deployment analysis[20]

The previous two methods have concentrated on the assessment of feasibility in *financial* terms. It is often helpful to make a wider assessment of the resource capability of the organisation in relation to *specific* strategies. This can be done through a resource deployment analysis, which is a way of comparing options with each other (see Figure 8.4).

The resource requirements of alternative future strategies should be laid out indicating the key resources for each strategy. For example, an extension of the home market would be critically dependent on marketing and distribution expertise together with the availability of cash to fund increased stocks. The resource analysis of the company should then be matched with the resource requirement for possible strategic options. In the example it is clear that the company's resources are specifically geared towards the current product/market strategy and may represent a constraint to any change. This analysis can be closely linked to the competitive strategy by focusing the analysis on those *value activities* which most strongly underpin the cost advantage or value creation process and in this way could be part of a shareholder value analysis, as described in section 8.2.3 above.

There is a danger that resource deployment analysis will simply result in organisations choosing strategies which most closely fit the configuration of their present resources. It should be remembered that the real benefit of such an analysis should be the identification of those necessary changes in resources which are implied by any strategy, and an analysis of whether these changes are *feasible* in terms of scale, quality of resource or timescale of change. This relates to resource planning, which needs to take place during strategy implementation and will be discussed in Chapter 9. For example, in Figure 8.4 both strategies B and C will require quite significant changes in resources.

ILLUSTRATION 8.5
Using break-even analysis to examine strategic options

A manufacturing company was considering the launch of a new consumer durable product into a market where most products were sold to wholesalers who supplied the retail trade. The total market was worth about £4.4m (at manufacturer's prices) – about 630,000 units. The market leader had about 30 per cent market share in a competitive market where retailers were increasing their buying power. The company wished to evaluate the relative merits of a high-price/high-quality product sold to wholesalers (strategy A) or an own-brand product sold directly to retailers (strategy B). The table below summarises the market and cost structure for the market leader and these alternative strategies. The important conclusion is that the company would require about 22 per cent and 13 per cent market share respectively for strategies A and B to break even.

Market and cost structure	Market leader	Strategy A	Strategy B
Price to retail	£10	£12	£8
Margin to wholesaler	30%	30%	–
Wholesaler buys at	£7	£8.40	–
Variable costs/unit			
Raw material	£2.50	£2.90	£2.50
Marketing/selling	£0.50	£0.60	£0.20
Distribution	£0.20	£0.20	£0.20
Others	£0.30	£0.30	£0.20
Total	£3.50	£4.00	£3.10
Contribution/unit	£3.50	£4.40	£4.90
Fixed cost	£500,000	£600,000	£400,000
Break-even point (units)	£500,000	£600,000	£400,000
	3.50	4.40	4.90
	= 142,857	= 136,363	= 81,633
Market size	630,000	630,000	630,000
Break-even point (market share)	22.6%	21.6%	13%
Actual share	30%	0	0

Source: Authors

(a) Key resource areas	(b) Present company situation	Resource implications (c)		
		Strategy A (extend product range)	Strategy B (extend home market)	Strategy C (sell overseas)
Financial				
Available cash	2	3 (1)	4 (2)	4 (2)
High stocks	3	2 (1)	4 (1)	4 (1)
Physical				
Modern machines	5	5 (0)	3 (2)	3 (2)
Distribution network	0	1 (1)	5 (5)	5 (5)
Human				
Skilled engineers	5	5 (0)	1 (4)	2 (3)
Marketing expertise	0	2 (2)	5 (5)	5 (5)
Other				
Reputation for quality	5	5 (0)	5 (0)	5 (0)
Overseas contacts	0	0 (0)	0 (0)	4 (4)
Degree of mismatch		(5)	(19)	(22)

(a) This would be produced from a strength and weakness analysis (see section 4.6 of Chapter 4).
(b) From previous resource analysis 0 = major weakness, 5 = major strength.
(c) 0 = unimportant, 5 = critical to success of strategy.

Figure 8.4 Resource deployment analysis

8.6 Selection of strategies

The discussion in Chapter 7 and so far in this chapter has been concerned with how evaluation of strategic options can be undertaken in terms of both the suitability of particular *types* of strategy and also the merits of *specific* strategic options. However, it is important to recognise that these evaluations do not by themselves determine which strategies should be or are *selected* for implementation. Readers are reminded of the discussions in Chapter 2 about the process of strategy development. There are several different ways in which strategies are selected.

8.6.1 Selection against objectives

This is a widely accepted view of how a 'rational' choice of future strategies should occur. Here the organisation's objectives, quantified where possible, are used as direct yardsticks by which options are assessed. Evaluation methods are therefore central to the decision-making process and are expected to provide quantified 'answers' regarding the relative merits of various options and to indicate the 'right' course of action. In practice, however, even where this type of selection process occurs, it is very often the case that objectives need to be adjusted as the evaluation proceeds, and they then become what is often called *post-rationalised*. The objectives fit the strategy and vice versa. In general, it is a sound discipline to assess the extent to which strategic options might fit specified objectives of the organisation, provided it is also recognised that there are likely to be other ways in which strategies will be selected.

8.6.2 Referral to a higher authority

A common way in which the selection of strategies occurs is by referring the matter to a higher authority, as mentioned in Chapter 2. Those managers responsible for evaluation may not have the authority to give the go-ahead to the 'solution'. Equally, those senior managers who must decide on strategy may not have participated in the evaluation of options. This is a very important observation which should have a strong influence on how the results of evaluation are conveyed to senior management. In particular, it is unlikely that senior managers will have the time or inclination to unravel all the detailed ramifications of an evaluation. They are more concerned with using their *judgement* of the situation on the available facts, and also with seeing how different strategies will fit the overall mission of the company. Thus the evaluation process can be seen as a means of *raising the level of debate* which occurs among senior managers when they are using judgement on the selection of strategy.

In large diversified organisations (including the public services) there will be different types of evaluation occurring at the centre from those in the divisions, subsidiary companies or (in public services) the various service departments. The board of a holding company, for example, might look at its businesses using product portfolio analysis, and the issue of a balanced portfolio might be at least as important a selection criterion as the more specific business criteria of one of the businesses. At the same time the management of the different businesses will be evaluating their alternative strategies to convince their corporate masters that they should be given more resources to support new developments.

8.6.3 Partial implementation

There are many circumstances where the uncertainties which an organisation faces are such that evaluation processes leave the choice of directions for the future very finely balanced. Nevertheless some organisations will need to come off the fence and commit their resources and efforts to a particular strategy. This would be true for manufacturing companies if strategic developments required significant capital investment. Others, particularly service organisations (public or private), may be more favourably placed and able to cope with these uncertainties by *deferral* of an overall 'final' decision on strategy while committing some resources to the partial implementation of one or more strategies. This allows the organisation to gain more experience on the ground, to improve its understanding of the suitability of each strategy and, at a later date, to make a more informed decision on which strategies to pursue. This also fits the incrementalist view of strategic development discussed in Chapter 2.

An added virtue of partial implementation is that it can usually be authorised at lower levels within the organisation. So this 'testing and learning' becomes an important precursor to the bid for resources to higher authorities which might follow.

From the senior managers' viewpoint there are some dangers in allowing too much freedom for such unauthorised experimentation within the organisation. In the extreme case it could result in the organisation only ever developing by tinkering around at the edges in a very minimalist way, and never really making fundamental reassessments of its present situation and future opportunities. This would be incrementalism at its worst.

In large organisations, such as multinationals, there is a need to plan how new developments which emerge through such a testing and learning process might proceed to more widespread adoption across the organisation. The process by which this wider selection of strategy occurs is illustrated in Figure 8.5. New developments are encouraged within local (national) divisions and the corporate centre is monitoring these local initiatives for ones which might be potential winners internationally. This could then be followed by encouraging two or more divisions regionally (e.g. Europe) to test the wider acceptability of the product or strategy and/or any modifications or variants which might be required. If this proves successful, the product or strategy is adopted by all European divisions. The same process is then repeated internationally, culminating in a formal acceptance of a new international product or strategy.

8.6.4 Outside agencies

There are often disagreements on strategy between stakeholders who have similar power within the company. This may be between management and unions, or between two different managers. In these circumstances it is not unusual for an outside agency, such as a consultant, to evaluate the situation for the company. Often this process of evaluation is described as objective and rational by virtue of the consultant's detachment from the situation. In practice, of course, consultants are aware of the political reasons for their involvement. To a large extent their role may be one of arbitrator and the evaluation must reflect those circumstances. In multinational ventures, particularly where government is involved, it is likely that consultants will be employed to assess the merits of the various strategies or at least to act in an advisory role to the decision-makers – as happened, for example, in the case of the Channel Tunnel bids in 1986.

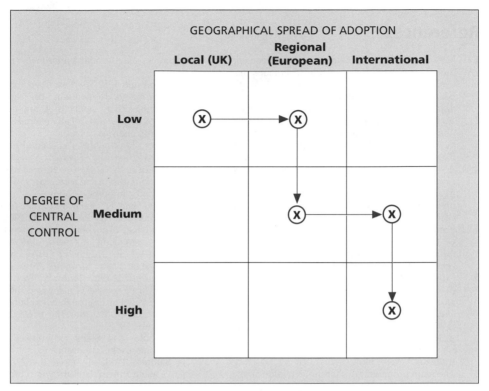

Figure 8.5 'Rolling-out ' strategies in a multinational

8.7 Summary

Strategy evaluation has often been presented as an exact science – a way of deciding what organisations should do. In fact, the analytical methods discussed in Chapters 7 and 8 are only useful as a source of information to strategic decision-makers. It has been seen that the contributions which various analytical methods make to improving the quality of strategic decision making will differ quite considerably. Some methods of analysis are valuable because they are eye-openers – they help managers to see the logic or rationale behind strategies, rather than assessing those strategies in detail. Other methods are more detailed and are useful ways of understanding how acceptable or feasible a specific strategy might be.

However, even the most thorough strategy evaluation cannot possibly anticipate all the detailed problems and pitfalls which might be encountered in the implementation of a strategic change. So it is necessary to recognise that strategic decisions will be refined or even reversed as part of their implementation, and this process is discussed in the final part of the book.

References

1. Most textbooks on financial management include sections relating to the techniques discussed in the text. See, for example, M. W. E. Glautier and B. Underdown, *Accounting Theory and Practice* (4th ed), Pitman, 1991.
2. An in-depth appraisal of the applicability of financial techniques to the evaluation of strategy can be found in C. Tomkins, *Corporate Resource Allocation*, Basil Blackwell, 1991, and A. N. Grundy, *Corporate Strategy and Financial Decisions*, Kogan Page, 1992.
3. Again see M. W. E. Glautier and B. Underdown, op cit., for a fuller discussion of the valuation of companies.
4. For a strategic discussion of acquisitions, see P. C. Haspelagh and D. B. Jemison, *Managing Aquisitions: Creating value through corporate renewal*, Macmillan, 1991.
5. Cost/benefit analysis is discussed in chapter 9 of A. Rowe, A. Mason and K. Dickel, *Strategic Management and Business Policy: A methodological approach* (2nd edn), Addison-Wesley, 1985. It is also included as a computer model in A. Rowe, R. Mason, K. Dickel and P. Westcott, *Computer Models for Strategic Management*, Addison-Wesley, 1987.
6. The main proponent of shareholder value analysis was A. Rappaport, *Creating Shareholder Value: The new standard for business performance*, Free Press, 1986. An interesting article is H. Kay, 'More power to the shareholders', *Management Today*, May 1991.
7. The management consultants Braxton Associates emphasise the need to analyse the value creation process and link it to competitive advantage. See their in-house publication, *Managing for Value*, 1990.
8. See Grundy, reference 2 above
9. Financial ratio analysis is covered by many books on management accounting. See, for example, Glautier and Underdown (reference 1 above).
10. B. Taylor and J. R. Sparkes, *Corporate Strategy and Planning*, Heinemann, 1977, discuss the use of sensitivity analysis. Computer spreadsheet packages are ideally suited for simple sensitivity analysis.
11. D. Hertz, 'Risk analysis in capital investment', *Harvard Business Review*, Sept./Oct. 1979; reprinted in R. G. Dyson, *Strategic Planning: Models and analytical techniques*, Wiley, 1990.
12. See Grundy, reference 2 above
13. S. Cooke and N. Slack, *Making Management Decisions* (2nd ed), Prentice Hall, 1991.
14. T. H. Naylor, 'A conceptual framework for corporate modeling', *Operational Research Quarterly*, vol. 27, no. 3, (1976), pp. 671–82; reprinted in Dyson, *Strategic Planning: Models and Analytical Techniques*, Wiley, 1990.
15. The PIMS data base is discussed more fully in Chapter 7. Their approach is explained in R. D. Buzzell and B. T. Gale, *The PIMS Principles*, Free Press, 1987.
16. See Cooke and Slack (reference 13) Rowe, Mason and Dickel (reference 5).
17. G. Saloner, 'Modeling, game theory and strategic management', *Strategic Management Journal*, vol. 12, (1991), pp. 119–36, discusses the uses and limitations of game theory in strategic evaluation.
18. See reference 1 above.
19. Glautier and Underdown (reference 1 above)
20. This relates to the idea of 'Resource-based strategies' discussed in Chapter 4. Useful references are B. Wernerfelt, 'A resource-based view of the firm', *Strategic Management Journal*, vol. 5, no. 2, (1984), pp. 171–80, and an example given by D. J. Collis, 'A resource-based analysis of global competition', *Strategic Management Journal*, vol. 12, summer (1991), pp. 49–68.

Recommended key readings

S. Cooke and N. Slack, *Making Management Decisions* (2nd edn), Prentice Hall, 1991, is a useful text on decision-making techniques.

M. W. E. Glautier and B. Underdown, *Accounting Theory and Practice* (4th edn), Pitman, 1991, covers most of the financial techniques underpinning strategic evaluation.

A. N. Grundy, *Corporate Strategy and Financial Decisions*, Kogan Page, 1992, is a review of the ways in which financial analysis can contribute to strategic evaluation and some of the pitfalls.

A. Rowe, R. Mason, K. Dickel and P. Westcott, *Computer Models for* *Strategic Management*, Addison-Wesley, 1987, provides some useful computer routines.

Work assignments

8.1 Choose a specific strategy for Vitalograph,* Kronenbourg,* Courage* or an organisation of your choice, and explain which financial measures you would regard as most appropriate in assessing the anticipated return.

8.2 Criticise the cost/benefit analysis in Illustration 8.1 by commenting on:
(a) the appropriateness of the listed benefits
(b) the ease/difficulty of assigning monetary values to these benefits.

8.3 Compare the approach to financial evaluation in BP, Rolls-Royce Aeroengines (Illustration 8.2) and an organisation of your choice. What are the main differences in approach, and why do they exist? How would you change any of these approaches?

8.4 Using Illustration 8.3 as an example, what would you propose as the most important parameters to include in a sensitivity analysis in the case of each of the following organisations:
(a) News Corporation*
(b) Crucible Theatre*
(c) Kronenbourg*
(d) Peugeot*
(e) Burton (B)* and (C)*
(f) An organisation of your choice
What general conclusions can you draw about the use of sensitivity analysis by comparing your answers for each organisation?

8.5 Referring to Illustration 8.4, plot out a stakeholder map for British Telecom and make your assessment of whether or not the organisation's evaluation of its stance in relation to its major stakeholders is appropriate in supporting the competitive strategy of the organisation. What changes would you suggest and why?

8.6 *Using examples from your answers to previous questions, make a critical appraisal of the statement that 'strategic choice is, in the end, a highly subjective matter. It is dangerous to believe that analytical techniques will ever change in reality.' Refer back to the key readings by Johnson (chapter 2), Schwenk (chapter 2) and Stacey (chapter 3) who between them contend that strategic decision making neither is, nor should be, driven by analysis.*

* This refers to a case study in the Text and Cases version of this book.

PART IV
Strategy implementation

Strategic analysis and choice are of little value to an organisation unless the strategies are capable of being implemented. Strategic change does not take place simply because it is considered to be desirable; it takes place if it can be made to work. Part IV deals with the vital problems of implementing strategy and with the planning of that implementation. Chapter 1 made it clear that one of the major characteristics of strategic decisions is that they are likely to give rise to important changes. It is therefore vital to consider the types of change required and how they can be managed.

- Chapter 9 is concerned with planning how resources will have to be reallocated given strategic change. It does this at two levels: at the corporate level, where the problem is the allocation of resources between different parts of the organisation (e.g. between different businesses in a conglomerate); and at the operating unit (or business) level, where the problem is the provision and allocation of resources between departments, functions or projects, such as the phasing-in of production, the addition or deletion of new products, the raising of finance or the development of people. Strategic changes usually affect many resource areas: they may be implemented on a day-to-day basis through the operating functions of the organisation, but they need to be thought through as a whole to see how they form a coherent package. This overall strategic planning of resources is the theme of Chapter 9.
- A major resource of any organisation is the people who work for it. How they are to be managed is obviously important: it is also clear that changes in strategy are likely to give rise to the need to reorganise how people are managed. The last two chapters of the book examine this problem. Chapter 10 concentrates on how people are to be organised in terms of who will be responsible for what: it is therefore concerned with questions of structure and control. What shape should the organisation take? At what level should different sorts of decision be taken? What systems of control and regulation are available? The chapter also considers the conditions under which different organisational forms might be more or less appropriate.
- Chapter 11 examines more specifically how strategic change might be managed. This is done by considering different explanatory models of

change; means of diagnosing blockages to change; and different approaches to managing change, including the role, styles and tactics of managers as change agents. The chapter concludes by linking its contents to other issues raised in the rest of the book.

Throughout Part IV it is important to remember the distinction between the planning of implementation and actually carrying out the tasks of implementation. As the three chapters proceed they move progressively from planning to the often problematic day-to-day activities of managing change.

CHAPTER 9

Planning and allocating resources

9.1 Introduction

The successful implementation of strategies will invariably require some degree of change in the organisation's resource profile. The careful planning of these resource changes is therefore important. The discussions in Chapter 4 (resource analysis) highlighted the fact that the resource issues which need to be considered differ with the level in the organisation at which the analysis is focused. This is equally true when detailed *resource planning* is being undertaken.

Resource planning usually entails two levels of consideration. First, there are the broader issues of how resources should be *allocated* between the various functions, departments, divisions or separate businesses. These considerations should be aided by the analysis of the *balance* of an organisation's resources referred to in Chapters 3, 4 and 7 – in particular, *portfolio analysis*. Second, the more detailed issue of how resources should be *deployed* within any one part of the organisation best to support the strategies is concerned with the operational aspects of resource planning and is supported by the detailed assessment of strategic capability discussed in Chapter 4 – in particular, *value chain analysis*. The chapter concludes with some practical advice on how organisations might develop resource allocation plans in a systematic way.

It is also important to emphasise again that, in thinking through how strategy will be put into effect, detailed thought is in fact being given to the *feasibility* of its implementation. As such, the planning of resource allocation is also part of the evaluation of strategy. There is no sense in proceeding with the implementation of a strategy if, in planning how it should be done, it becomes clear that it is unrealistic. Indeed, given the often generalised nature of strategic decision making as it occurs in reality, it may be that really detailed consideration of a strategic course of action does not actually take place until the planning of implementation begins. Managers should then realise that they are not simply planning how something is to be done, but also deciding whether it is possible or sensible to do it.

9.2 Resource planning at the corporate level

At the corporate level in an organisation, resource planning is mainly concerned with the *allocation* of resources between the various parts of the organisation, whether those be the business functions (marketing, finance, etc.), operating divisions or geographical areas (e.g. in a multinational), or service departments (e.g. in public services). This process needs to be understood in the context of how these separate parts of the organisation support the overall strategies. Readers are reminded of the discussions in Chapters 3, 4 and 7 about *portfolio analysis* and the *balance* of an organisation's resources. In large organisations the allocation process and issues of balance could involve several layers or stages of resource allocation.

This section looks at how these broader issues of allocation might be tackled in order to support the implementation of strategies. Figure 9.1 illustrates some stereotypes of how allocation occurs in practice. These relate to two important factors which determine the overall approach to allocation:

- The *perception of the degree of change* required in the resource base if strategic change is to be achieved successfully. This could be the extent to which the aggregate level of resources might need to change (e.g. growth or decline) or where significant shifts are required between resource areas within an unchanged overall resource.

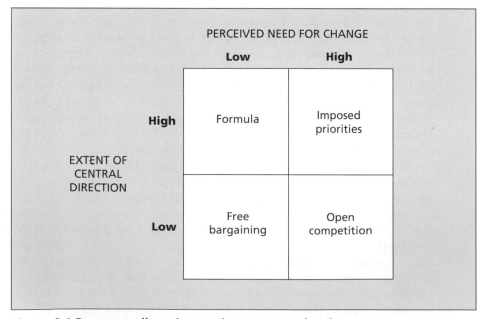

Figure 9.1 Resource allocation at the corporate level

- The extent of *central direction* of the allocation process – whether detailed allocations are dictated from the corporate level or are in response to the detailed plans and aspirations of the various units of the organisation. This relates to how the organisation is structured and where, within the structure, strategic decisions are made. This issue is discussed more fully in Chapter 10.

To illustrate these general approaches to resource allocation the following three situations will be discussed:

- *Few changes* in overall resources or in the deployment of resources.
- *Growth* in the overall resource base.
- *Decline* in the overall resource base, or significant *reallocations* within a static resource base.

In each case the contrasting approaches of centralised or decentralised control of resource planning will be considered. It should be remembered that the stereotypes represented by the four boxes in Figure 9.1 rarely exist in a pure form. Resource allocations in practice are usually tempered by varying degrees of *bargaining* or *bidding*. Nevertheless these stereotypes are useful in understanding the *dominant philosophy* underlying resource allocation in different circumstances.

9.2.1 Few resource changes

If the managers in an organisation perceive strategic development as requiring few changes in the level or deployment of resources, they are likely to manage resource allocation in ways which reflect this perception. In Figure 9.1 this is represented by the two extreme stereotypes of *formula*-driven allocations (where central direction is high) and *free bargaining* (where allocation is decentralised). A criticism of many organisations in these circumstances is that they adopt resource allocation methods which are too rigid, creating problems in making the incremental adjustments to strategies which are important to the organisation's development.

Many organisations will use a *formula* as the starting point in establishing allocations. For example, the advertising budget might be 5 per cent of sales, or in the public services revenue might be allocated on a per capita basis (e.g. doctors' patients). There will then be some room for *bargaining* and fine tuning around this historical position – for example, in *redefining* the formula or the way in which resources are measured.

There are several shortcomings of formula-driven processes even as a starting point. First, there are usually disagreements about the *validity* or fairness of the formula. Often the response is to amend the formula by making it more complex – by weighting, or introducing additional factors, etc. This rarely solves the disagreements and if anything can make them worse because there will always be some degree of arbitrariness about this type of formula. *Zero-based budgeting*[1] (discussed later in the chapter) could be a means of putting some check on this process and relating allocations to client needs or demand.

The opposite extreme – *free bargaining* between the centre and departments/divisions perhaps around a zero-based budgeting scenario – is rarely seen in its 'pure' form. If the degree of change is low, it is probably undesirable for senior management to be involved in extensive bargaining processes about marginal shifts in resources. What is really required is some degree of discretion about how resources are allocated by a department or division itself within its global sum. This space can be created through relaxing the rules on *virement* between budget heads. The issue of how the centre of an organisation can retain control of the overall strategies while providing more freedom within departments or divisions will be discussed more fully in Chapter 10.

Finally, readers are reminded that it is the *perception* of the degree of change which will determine approaches to resource allocation. Consequently, the *defender*[2] organisation discussed in Chapter 5 is likely to operate closer to the formula end of the spectrum as it tries to minimise the changes experienced by the organisation by seeking out strategic developments which require few shifts in resource allocation. In contrast, *prospector* organisations are likely to encourage the active search for new opportunities by a resource allocation regime which discourages the status quo. So even in situations of little change they are likely to operate closer to the *free bargaining* approach.

9.2.2 Allocations during growth

Where organisations are implementing strategic changes which require significant changes in resources, different approaches to resource allocation may be necessary (see Figure 9.1). For example, during growth resources can often be reallocated in relative terms without any particular area of the organisation suffering a reduction in resources – simply by directing new resources selectively across the organisation.

Again, extreme stereotypes exist of how this reallocation could occur. Priority areas could be established centrally and the resource allocations could be *imposed* from the centre. At the other extreme, the centre could allocate resources through a process of *open competition*. This could be done through operating an internal *investment bank*[3] from which divisions or departments can bid for additional resources. Most organisations during growth will follow a middle path between these two extreme approaches. This would be described as *constrained bidding*, where the departments or divisions of the organisation are able to bid for additional resources but within defined criteria and constraints.

Illustration 9.1 shows how the resource allocation methodology in the funding of higher education in the UK changed radically in the early 1990s in an attempt to achieve both growth and improved cost efficiency without sacrificing quality.

9.2.3 Allocating resources in static or declining situations

Many of the same issues faced by organisations experiencing growth also apply in static or declining situations, but there are important differences. In particular, resource reallocation will require some areas to reduce in absolute terms to maintain other areas and/or to support new developments.

There are differing approaches to these (often difficult) reallocation problems. In some organisations the reallocation is simply *imposed* centrally – for example, there may be some plant closures. In other circumstances the reallocation may be achieved in an *openly competitive* way – for example, a freeze may be imposed on replacement of staff; instead, as vacancies arise they are made subject to open competition and go to those units with the most pressing case. Again there is a middle road – *constrained bidding* for resources. In this case resources will be diverted from one area to another. This is often achieved by earmarking a proportion of the total organisational resources for reallocation to new ventures ('top-slicing').

Many companies and public-service organisations experienced the difficulties of reallocating resources during the 1980s and early 1990s. Some of the ways in which this was achieved illustrate these general points:

- Often reductions were achieved by *amalgamating* related areas or activities. For example, within a hospital two related specialisms might be merged under the same consultant. Although resulting resource savings were often explained by 'cutting out overlap' or 'economies of scale', usually neither of these was as important as the opportunities that arose to *prioritise* within the new unit rather than favouring one unit against another.
- Another common solution was the creation of new units *outside* the normal structure. The unit is resourced by the marginal paring back of all other areas (hence maintaining 'equality of pain'). Eventually, the unit is reassimilated back into the mainstream structure and by this obtuse process resource reallocation has occurred – often to a substantial degree.
- There are some circumstances where resource allocation is achieved by a more overt and less subtle process – by simply closing down one part of the organisation. Such extreme forms of central direction are tolerated in organisations facing crisis as a necessary evil to ensure survival.

9.2.4 Allocating shared resources

One of the particularly difficult aspects of resource allocation at the corporate level in large organisations is the extent to which overlap, sharing or duplication of resources should occur between the various parts of the organisation. This arises in many different ways, from the extent to which services (e.g. secretarial) should be shared between departments to bigger issues such as whether two divisions

ILLUSTRATION 9.1
Changing approaches to resource allocation in UK higher education

As the UK government's approach to the management of public services changed from one of a centrally determined masterplan to the progressive introduction of competition and market forces, so the methods of allocating public funds to the providers of services needed to shift too.

By the late 1980s the UK government was concerned about the cost efficiency, vocational relevance and low participation rates which higher education was achieving in the UK compared with other western economies. It therefore introduced several major changes including making polytechnics independent of their local authorities and introducing new funding councils for the university and polytechnic/college sectors (UFC and PCFC respectively), which were charged with delivering *growth* and *improved unit costs*, while maintaining quality. (These two bodies were subsequently merged in 1992 when universities and polytechnics became a single sector.)

An important issue for the funding councils in achieving these stated purposes was the resource allocation mechanisms to institutions. So, in their first year (proper) of operation (1990/91), the PCFC introduced the following major changes from the way that the previous system had operated:

● Historically, institutions received their public funds through two routes: The *block grant* from the funding council and the *student fee* which was paid for the student by his or her local authority. The former had been much bigger than the latter. The government switched this balance and attempted to make the student fee about the level of the *direct costs* (staffing and materials) which an efficient institution might incur. So the block grant came more into line with the central costs of an institution. The logic was to reflect market pressure – for example, cost-efficient institutions were allowed to take *fees-only* students on a marginal cost basis.
● The allocation of block grant funds to an institution became a *contract*, i.e. the funds were against agreed performance measures

should share their production capacity or have a common salesforce. Issues of this type are very closely tied to the structure and systems of the organisation and will be discussed in Chapter 10. It is important to recognise that the extent to which the centre of the organisation is willing to release control over the resource allocation process will be determined at least partly, by these issues of sharing and overlap.

So strategies which are dependent on high degrees of co-ordination or co-as outlined in the institution's strategic plan. Initially, the key measures were the number and mix of students the institution planned to educate.

- Subject to satisfactory performance, 95 per cent of the institution's previous block grant (as related to student numbers) was rolled forward as *core* funding.
- The remaining 5 per cent of all funding for the sector was made available to institutions through *competitive bidding*.
- Success in bidding was dependent on the *price* (i.e. the funds per student that institutions were prepared to accept). The bidding process also included a weighting given to institutions which were deemed to be *quality* providers in a particular subject (i.e. if they bid at higher prices they could still 'win' student numbers).

The important outcomes and subsequent changes to the resource allocation process up to 1993 were interesting:

- The initial bids from institutions were very rough and ready, since they had no reliable information on *unit costs*. However, they quickly developed cost analysis.
- The *core* was reduced to 90 per cent in 1991/92 and quality premiums were increased to make the methodology 'tougher'
- An absolute limit on student numbers was imposed on those institutions which had used the fees-only student option to grow rapidly. The limit was determined by a judgement on the *physical capacity* of the institution.
- Many institutions claimed to have done well through the bidding process – largely because they defined success by their own very *varied criteria* (growth, unit costs, etc.).
- After three years there was a feeling that the bidding had become very *tactical*, e.g. institutions were attempting to exploit the weaknesses of methodology, rather than bidding in line with their strategic plan.
- There was increasing pressure to take *quality* more seriously as a criterion for resource allocation – a noticeable weakness of the methodology linked to price.

Source: Bernard Jones, Sheffield Business School, 1992.

operation between departments/divisions (e.g. gaining advantages through synergy) will need to have more central direction over detailed resource allocations to underpin strategies. In contrast, where divisions or subsidiaries are largely independent, such detailed direction from the centre is less important. Where sharing or overlap does exist there are choices of the process by which these shared resources can be allocated. There are three main ways:[4]

- *Indirectly* by an overhead recovery charge from the centre to the division.
- *Directly* by charging-out for services taken (either from central services or from other divisions).
- *Directly* by passing managerial responsibility to a designated division which then cross-charges other users.

The direct methods keep accountability and responsibility for resource management in the same hands, but run the risk of creating a new bureaucracy to administer the charging-out system. Many organisations therefore confine charging-out to two main areas:

- Internal services which can be delivered in a genuine supplier–customer relationship (e.g. computer services, personnel), for example through *service-level agreements*.
- Major items of overhead where an incentive is needed to encourage divisions/departments to think more strategically (e.g. floor space).

9.3 Resource planning at the business level

In the discussion of resource analysis (Chapter 4) the idea of the *value chain* was introduced as a means of analysing the way in which an organisation's strategic capability can be understood. It was emphasised that an organisation needs to understand which particular *value activities* most contribute to the success of the organisation's strategies: for example, through cost advantages or differentiation from competitors (or in the public services through cost efficiency or service enhancement). Moreover, strategic capability is often determined by the way in which linkages between these value activities are managed.

When planning the implementation of new strategies these same issues are of central importance in the resource planning:

- Planning must establish which value activities are of greatest importance to successful implementation of the selected strategies and ensure that these are planned with particular care (see section 9.4.1 below).
- Planning must address resource requirements throughout the value chain, including linkages between value activities and with the value chains of suppliers, channels or customers.

Although resource planning at this level is necessarily detailed, it is nonetheless important to conceive it in a strategic manner. In particular, it is important to understand how the detailed *operational resource plans* underpin the strategies of the organisation. It is therefore helpful to put the detailed plan in a strategic framework by ensuring that three central questions are addressed (see Figure 9.2):

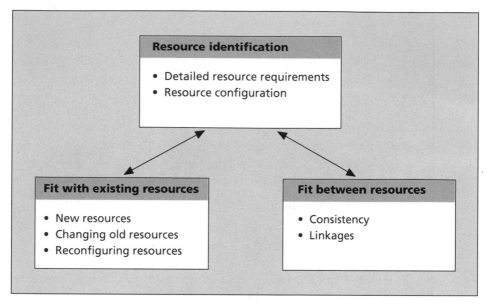

Figure 9.2 Matching operational resource plans to strategies

- *Resource identification* – exactly what resources will a strategy require, and how should these resources be configured?
- *Fit with existing resources* – to what extent do these resources build on or are they a change from existing resources?
- *Fit between resources* – can the required resources be integrated with each other?

Figure 9.3 illustrates how the value chain can be used as a checklist in planning the resource requirements to deliver the strategy successfully.[5] This checklist should be used to identify those value activities which are of critical importance to the strategy and the related issues of fit – both with existing resources and between the separate resources and activities.

9.3.1 Resource identification

Effective planning of resources depends on the extent to which the planner is clear about the detailed resource needs. It has already been pointed out that, both at an individual level and at a corporate or even industry level, managers manage very much on the basis of past experience. Therefore, there is a danger that new strategies will be considered in the context of old expectations or existing bases of operating, rather than in terms of what is required in the future. Illustration 9.2 also shows that detailed resource planning may be forced on organisations in a period of crisis.

SUPPORT ACTIVITIES	LINKS WITH SUPPLY CHAIN	Inbound logistics	Operations	Outbound logistics	Marketing and sales	Service	LINKS WITH DELIVERY CHAIN
			PRIMARY ACTIVITIES				
Procurement	Sources of supply • Cost • Quality • Location	Transport Warehousing Capital	Machines Consumables	Transport Warehousing	Product/service Patents/licences Brand names	Guarantees Credit facilities	Channel choice • Type • Cost • Location • Performance
Technology development	Sources of technology (incl. funding)	Know-how Design Technology transfer (in)	Process development	Shipments	Network of contacts Information systems	Fault diagnosis	Delivery system Display EPOS
Human resource management	Training TQM	Recruitment Shareholders Creditor relations Image in City	Team development Job satisfaction Subcontractors Training	Subcontractors	Agents Salesforce Goodwill	After-sales staff Reputation Maintenance staff	Franchisees Merchandising Training
Management systems	Supplier vetting Just in time Quality control	Purchasing systems Vehicle scheduling Materials handling	Production planning Quality control Cash management Stock control Facilities layout	Delivery scheduling	Order processing Debtor control	Customer service system	EPOS Market research

Figure 9.3 Some resource implications of strategic change

Although the resource requirements of specific strategies will inevitably vary in detail, there are some useful observations which can be made about the resource requirements of different types of strategy. Figure 9.4 compares two examples:

1.   A low-price strategy will require an emphasis on *cost-efficient* plant and processes, with an ability to renew investment to maintain advantage in these areas. It is also likely that particular attention will be paid to achieving simplicity of operating processes and low-cost distribution systems. An organisation following a strategy of *differentiation*, on the other hand, is likely to require different sorts of skills and resources. In particular, there is likely to be a need for strengths in marketing, research and creativity, with an emphasis on product development and engineering. So an important need is to identify those value activities which are critical to the success of particular types of strategy. This process will be described more fully in section 9.4 below.

2.   The competitive position of an organisation is not only determined by how well it plans the resource requirements of the separate value activities. It is also dependent on how well matched are the *management systems* and approach to support the strategies being pursued. Figure 9.4 also identifies the key requirements which are likely to be necessary to support different types of strategy. So cost-efficiency is not only underpinned by planning the processes, labour supervision, etc. appropriately, but also by ensuring that these plans are supported by management systems which will ensure that cost efficiency is actually delivered.

LOW-PRICE STRATEGY	DIFFERENTIATION STRATEGY
Key skills	**Key skills**
'Process' design	'Product' design
Labour supervision	Marketing
Easily produced 'products'	Creative flair
Low-cost distribution	Research capability
	Corporate image
Requiring	**Requiring**
Tight cost control	Looser control
Detailed reporting	Simpler reporting
Highly structured	Strong co-ordination
Quantitative targets	Market-based incentives

Figure 9.4 Key skills and resources to support different strategies

ILLUSTRATION 9.2
Resource identification: adjusting to crisis

Resource planning has to cope with unexpected and unwanted strategies as well as the organisation's preferred strategies.

In August 1990 Iraq invaded Kuwait and triggered off a period of considerable difficulty for the world's airlines. Not only was there an immediate price increase in fuel, but many large corporations – particularly the Americans – banned all but vital journeys for their executives because of the fear of terrorism. Although neither of these issues proved to be problematic (fuel prices declined again and there were no terrorist acts in support of Iraq), the fear of their occurrence reduced the business class traffic, which most airlines relied on to subsidise the economy-class passenger. In these circumstances all of the major international airlines had to change their resource plans. This required a clear identification of resource reductions which would ensure that they could cope with the crisis with the minimum long-term damage to the business. A newspaper report summarised some of the measures taken by international airlines.

Airlines tighten their belts

AIR FRANCE
Flight capacity is being cut by at least 6% in the first quarter of this year. There is a freeze on the hiring of staff, other than cockpit crew. Nine smaller European routes have

This is likely to involve tight cost control, detailed reporting and so on. In contrast, strategies of differentiation are likely to require 'looser' systems of reporting and control, but a strong emphasis on *co-ordinating* the separate value activities to ensure that they are genuinely adding value in the process of creating and delivering the product or service.

This process of understanding how the planning of value activities and management systems support strategy implementation is made difficult in practice for three reasons:

- New strategies may require organisations to shift their approach. In the example given in Figure 9.4 this would not be an easy transition to make – in either direction – since the planning and control of resources is geared to support old strategies and not new ones.
- It was emphasised in Chapter 6 that generic strategies are not absolute choices in the sense that, for example, pursuing a differentiation strategy

already been axed and capacity transferred from loss-making sectors like the Middle East

BRITISH AIRWAYS
Cuts of at least 10% are planned in the workforce – about 5,000 jobs. Other staff have been offered unpaid leave or shorter working hours. The £1.5 billion replacement of TriStars has been deferred and other capital spending has been cut

KLM ROYAL DUTCH AIRLINES
1,100 workers have been axed. Another 2,000 will go as the airline contracts out non-core activities such as staff canteens. Delivery of Boeing 747–400s has been postponed. The aim is to slash costs by £300m

LUFTHANSA
Staff have been asked to take holidays and may have to take unpaid leave. Transatlantic services and flights to Britain have been cut. 50 jets will be put in storage

PAN AM
6,000 redundancies in total. Capacity cut by 7.5%. There are plans to sell London routes to United for $400m. The IGS operation has already been sold to Lufthansa for $150m. The airline is in Chapter 11 protection against bankruptcy

SAS
Productivity improvements will cut $180m in operating costs. European services have been reduced, and flights to Istanbul stopped. The management has been restructured

TWA
Heathrow and Gatwick routes will be sold to American Airlines for £230m. Then it wants to take over Pan Am. The airline is cutting 1,500 jobs and making big reductions in services

Source: *Sunday Times*, January 1991.

absolves management from any need to plan cost efficiency or vice versa. In reality both would be important in underpinning a successful strategy.

- Diverse organisations are likely to position different products and businesses in different ways. This requires specific configurations of resources for each market or client group, and may prove difficult for an organisation with plant, labour and management held in common across products and services. For example, products sold on the basis of quick response to customer orders may require some slack in the production system, cutting across the pressures to achieve high capacity fill – and cost efficiency – for other products.

9.3.2 Fit with existing resources

One of the pitfalls in resource planning of new strategies is to prescribe the *ideal* resource configuration. However, few strategic changes are introduced in a greenfield site situation, and therefore the second central question in resource planning is how the required resources fit the *existing* resource configuration of the organisation. A key task in planning implementation is how the organisation will change or *reconfigure* its current resources to support new strategies, and how new resources will be fitted in. Indeed, a company may choose to manufacture and market a new product range through a new division or even a new company to avoid problems of conflict or incompatibility with existing operations. So the planning of resources also leads into structural considerations and issues of managing change, which will be discussed more fully in the next two chapters.

An assessment of this fit with existing resources begins to establish the extent to which implementation is likely to require major changes within the organisation or is achievable by an adjustment of the current resource base and organisational arrangements.

9.3.3 Fit between required resources

One of the critical ingredients of successful strategies is the way in which the linkages work between the important value activities, including those with suppliers, channels and customers. There must be *consistency* in the way that the various value activities are planned in order to support the strategy. Figure 9.5 illustrates the large number of linkages which need to be planned in the case of a new product launch.

This often causes difficulty for managers in deciding where within such a complex situation resource planning should start. In some senses it does not really matter, since the planning of a product launch will require several iterations around the various linkages shown in the figure. In this way, the need for a new product may have been triggered by the underutilisation of manufacturing capacity. In turn this required detailed analysis of the types of new product the plant was capable of producing, whether there was a place in the market for them, if the workforce had the right skills, etc. This issue of planning priorities will be discussed more fully in section 9.4.2 below.

The problems of establishing a workable plan for the launch are not only created by the inherent complexity of these linkages. They are often made worse by the political dimension which arises because the responsibility for managing the separate activities identified in Figure 9.5 is divided within the company – probably between different departments. The different perceptions and objectives of these departments need to be reconciled in the planning process too, since their involvement in implementation is crucial.

9.4 Preparing resource plans

So far this chapter has dealt with some of the underlying principles behind the planning of resources at both corporate and business levels, and has discussed

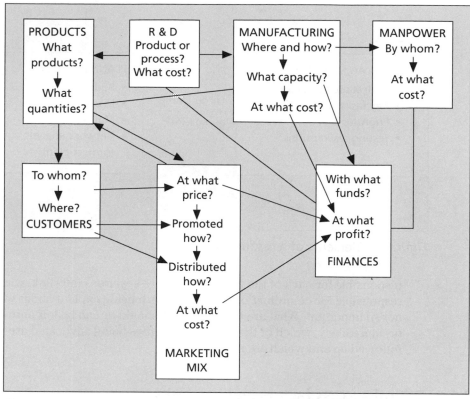

Figure 9.5 Resource integration in a product launch

some of the detailed resource issues which need to be resolved during implementation. This final section is concerned with the *process* of resource planning
and considers ways in which resource plans can be prepared. Figure 9.6 identifies the main issues which a resource plan should address, and some of the planning tools which are commonly used:

- *Critical success factors*[6] are those factors on which the strategic change is
  fundamentally dependent for its success: for example, the need to improve
  customer care or reduce product cost.
- A resource plan should also itemise the *key tasks* which need to be
  undertaken to ensure that the critical success factors are actually achieved.
  This may require the creation of new value activities or the development of
  new linkages within the value chain, or with suppliers, channels or customers.
- *Priorities*, on the other hand, are more to do with timing. They are the
  actions that need to be tackled to get the project under way: designing and
  commissioning of plant or ensuring that financial resources are available
  might be priorities in this sense. The identification of priorities and key tasks
  also provides a basis for the allocation of responsibilities. Who is to be

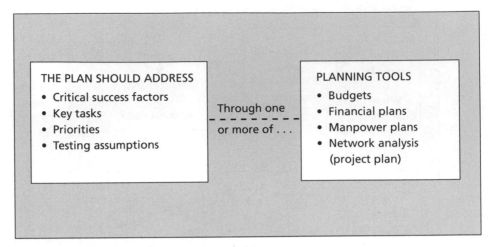

Figure 9.6 Elements of a resource plan

responsible for each of the key areas? Where key areas interlink, who is responsible for co-ordination? It is also worth being explicit about what is not so important. What are the things that should or can be left until later, or, more likely, which of the different priorities being advocated are to be followed up and which are not?

9.4.1 Critical success factors and key tasks

One of the major shortcomings of strategy implementation in many organisations is a failure to translate statements of strategic purpose – such as market share targets – into a practical statement of those factors which are critical to achieving these targets, and the key tasks which will ensure success. Illustration 9.3 shows how one company had built its success around a clear understanding of this issue.

It is therefore valuable as part of the resource-planning process to ensure that these issues are addressed systematically. This can be done using the value chain as a framework (see Figure 9.7):

- Agree the critical success factors for the specific strategy, attempting to keep these to a manageable list (no more than six). In the example these range from product features (software) to the performance of suppliers.
- Scrutinise the list to ensure that all factors are genuinely *necessary* and that the list is in fact *sufficient* to underpin success.
- Identify the *key tasks* which are essential to the delivery of each critical success factor. These may relate to individual value activities, improvements in support activities or changes in linkages within the value system. In the example, the critical success factor of *customer care* is underpinned through the three key tasks of responding to *enquiries*, supplying accurate

ILLUSTRATION 9.3
United Stationers turn distribution into a fine art

Intermediaries in a supply chain must ensure that they are adding value through their activities and that they have planned their resources to achieve this.

How does an office products distributor get retailers to buy such a simple, undifferentiated item as paper clips from them rather than from their competitors? The answer for United Stationers, one of the USA's biggest office products distributors, was the quality, speed and reliability of the service. The company's investment strategy and resource planning were entirely geared to ensuring that it could provide unparalleled standards of service and still make profits. In 1992 it sold products from 400 manufacturers to about 10,000 retailers in the USA via 14 regional distribution centres. The company invested some $200m in computing and telecommunications networks to underpin its strategy.

United's customers could obtain information on their inventory by access to the network, and entered about 70 per cent of the orders directly themselves. Ultimately they were planning to apply the same links to *their* suppliers and to connect the two ordering systems. There were other aspects of their value-added service too. The retailer could bill its customers as soon as it knew that goods had been dispatched from United – it also had access to up-to-date manufacturer prices to help manage its own pricing decisions.

Giving customers access to the ordering and inventory system had required the company to rethink entirely the logic of the binning system in its warehouses to ensure rapid turnaround of orders. For example, it ensured that fast-moving ('hot') products were binned in accessible locations, and the list of hot products was updated by the computer. The next planned development to keep ahead of competition was to produce an *electronic catalogue* with colour pictures, dimension data and moving price information. The company had also been able to reduce the minimum order quantity that it could handle profitably, which was seen as a significant benefit to many customers. The only downside it saw to this process of improving customer service was that it simply changed the expectations of what 'normal service' meant. And competitors were keen to observe and imitate. So in order to *sustain* competitive advantage, United had to continue to innovate and develop to ensure that it remained the easiest company to do business with.

Source: *Financial Times*, 23 April 1991.

CRITICAL SUCCESS FACTORS	KEY TASKS UNDERPINNING SUCCESS					
	Inbound logistics	Operations	Outbound logistics	Marketing and sales	Service	Support activities
1. Software features	Royalty payments (5% above norm)			Customer feedback (monthly)		
2. Customer care		Responding to enquiries (within 24 hours)		Accurate information (all customers)	Speed of response (3 hrs) (maintenance)	Installations Database
3. Systems design	Recruitment campaigns (high profile)	Responsibilities and work planning (per-formance indicators)				Training (all staff)
4. New business opportunities				Salesforce reports (monthly)		Competitor profiling (top 10)
5. Excellent supply	Supplier vetting Supplier award scheme (annually)					Supplier profiling (top 50)

Figure 9.7 Critical success factors and key tasks: an example – office systems supplier

information and speed of breakdown *maintenance* service. In turn these are dependent on the firm's infrastructure, particularly its data base on customer installations.

- Allocate management responsibility for each of the key tasks. In the example, the area where this could go badly wrong is data base maintenance. Although this responsibility is assigned to the customer maintenance department, the linkages they have established with both the sales and software systems departments are crucial in ensuring accurate information. This is a reminder that, since strategy implementation is likely to require changes to the organisational *routines*, this will require a shift in culture. In this case collaboration will be required between departments which had been used to operating independently.

- Some key tasks may be *symbolic* in order to assist in the organisation's paradigm. For example, the supplier award scheme is designed not only to reward suppliers, but also to symbolise to internal groups the critical part which suppliers play in the strategy.

9.4.2 Planning priorities[7]

A resource plan is the output of the series of questions raised so far in this chapter.

It sets out what resources need to be obtained and which disposed of. This may well be in the form of a budget, but might also be usefully expressed as a sequence of actions or a timetable of *priorities* in a written plan. For example, in Figure 9.5 an organisation introducing a new product line would need a plan of action to co-ordinate the various aspects of its resource planning. On-the-job production line retraining cannot begin until a production facility exists. Until the company has examined in detail the timing of development, installation, commissioning and completion of plant, it is not possible to examine fully the flow of funds required to finance the venture. Until it knows at what rate production is to be geared, it cannot take a sensible view about the extent of the product launch; and that in turn means that it will not have a clear idea of expected revenue flow, so again it cannot think sensibly about the requirement for funds.

The circularity of the problem is quite usual in developing a plan of action and raises the question of where to start – with a market forecast, an available level of funds, a production-level constraint, or what? The answer is that it may not matter too much where the starting point is, since the plan will have to be reworked and readjusted several times. A useful guideline is to enter the problem through what appears to be the major change area. An organisation planning new strategies of growth may well start with an assessment of market opportunity. Someone starting a new business may well begin with a realistic assessment of how much capital he or she might have available. Many public services have been compelled to replan their resources to achieve particular levels of cost savings.

Planning priorities will require consideration of how activities need to be *sequenced* and *scheduled*. There can be conflict between these two planning tasks, since the schedule of when particular activities need to be completed may not be consistent with the best sequence of activities to put the plan in place. The way in which the resource plan balances these conflicting pressures must relate to the key elements of the strategy concerned, and not to a predetermined set of rules and procedures to be used in all cases. For example, the sequence of activities may be determined by any of the following factors:

- Some activities must precede others because they are *prerequisites* for later activities. For example, a motor car cannot be assembled unless all components have been manufactured or purchased. Sometimes the sequence of activities is dictated by the *ease* with which tasks can be done. This is particularly important where the strategy requires a creative element, such as design or product development. The learning process which is involved in such activities means that later activities can be built on this experience. Often new products or services are introduced into the most receptive parts of the market first.
- Because some value activities are *more important* than others, the planning of the other activities is regarded as subsidiary to these major tasks. For example, in the building industry priority will be given to outdoor jobs during periods of good weather to minimise the risk of later delays.

- In many public services there is a core of mandatory services to be provided together with a range of services offered at the department's discretion. In these circumstances the tasks needed to deliver the mandatory services may need to take priority.

In contrast, the scheduling of when activities should be completed may be determined by any of the following factors:

- The *efficient* running of the organisation's operations requires proper scheduling of resource utilisation to avoid periods of overuse followed by low utilisation. For organisations operating in highly seasonal markets, this is an important part of their planning.
  The extent to which efficient scheduling should be a priority is related to the type of strategies being pursued as discussed in section 9.3.1 above.
- Some activities occur infrequently, but must occur at precisely the right time. The timing of a major television advertising campaign must match the market conditions and the company's readiness to supply the product. Correct timing might also mean a specific day or even the right time-slot within a day.
- *Customer service* is very strongly affected by the scheduling of tasks (such as orders) within companies. This is most clearly illustrated in terms of the delivery times.

One specific approach to activity scheduling which has received considerable attention and proved to be of strategic importance to many manufacturing companies is *just in time*.[8] This technique has revolutionised the way in which some companies plan the acquisition of resources, with a resultant reduction in costs or improvement in lead times and, at least in the short run, the potential of gaining competitive advantage on that basis.

9.4.3 Testing key assumptions

All plans are based on assumptions. They may be assumptions about resource availability, or the capacity of the organisation to adapt existing resources or co-ordinate the resource requirements of a new strategy. Assumptions may also be to do with the environment – that a market will grow, that funds can be raised or that suppliers will deliver on time.
  The danger is that, when a plan is drawn up, the assumptions built into it take on the appearance of fact and become unquestioned. This means that the vulnerable areas of the plan are disguised and reasons for shortfalls or failures may not be recognised. If assumptions are made explicit, the plan can be used as a model to help both in the evaluation of strategy and also in the investigation of alternative means of implementation of strategy. Different assumptions about market conditions, price acceptability, competitive action, cost levels and so on,

can be tested out to see how vulnerable plans of action are to different assumptions. So, too, can different assumptions about timing be tested out: the effect that delays in a construction programme would have on capital requirements, for example. *Sensitivity analysis* and *break-even analysis* – both of which were discussed in Chapter 8 – are two methods which can be used to test assumptions. For example, the best, worst and most likely assumptions can be built into budgets. The resulting plans can be examined to see the implications of these differing assumptions.

Referring back to Figure 9.6, these various elements of a resource plan can be put together by the use of one or more of the following *planning tools.*

9.4.4 Financial planning and budgeting[9]

Financial planning is concerned with translating the resource implications of decisions into financial statements of one sort or another. This is most commonly done through the various types of budget that managers use. Budgets have many uses and perform different roles in organisations. The concern here is with budgets as plans and as models.

A budget may take the form of a *consolidated* statement of the resource position required to achieve a set of objectives or put into effect a strategy. To achieve such a statement it is necessary to identify and think through the required resource position of the organisation. A budget expresses these in a monthly or yearly form, perhaps split down by departments in the organisation. At both an organisational and a departmental level, a budget is in effect a model of required resources. A model can be examined, tested and adjusted to see the implications of changing assumptions about the future, or about the progress that might be achieved in a project. This can be achieved if the budget is set up on a computer spreadsheet package.

The following types of budget or financial plan might typically be used in resource planning of strategy implementation:

- *Capital budgeting* is concerned with generating a statement of the flow of funds related to a particular project or decision. A company may decide to invest in new plant or acquire a new business. A capital budgeting exercise might well seek to determine: (a) what the outflow and inflow of funds associated with that project will be; (b) what the implications of different means of financing the project would be (for example, how an acquisition financed by increased loan capital would differ from one financed by increased equity capital); or (c) some assessment of how worthwhile the project is through some measure of return on investment. Readers are reminded of some of the shortcomings of these analyses from a strategic viewpoint, as discussed in section 8.2. In particular, capital budgeting often relates to specific strategies but neglects the impact on overall organisational performance.

- *Annual revenue budgets* are commonly used to express the detailed resource plan in financial terms. They are also used as a means of measuring and controlling performance against the plan.
- *Financial plans* and projected profit and loss accounts may well be useful in projecting, perhaps over a period of years, implications of decisions on an organisation's overall performance. They are usually less detailed than annual budgets. They are particularly useful in highlighting potential shortfalls in resources – or the impact of a changing mix of resources in terms of the overall performance of the company rather than simply of the new strategy in isolation.

One of the very real difficulties experienced in budgeting is the extent to which the process actually helps the reallocation of resources to fit future strategies. This is because the budgeting process is usually tied into the power structure in the organisation. The types of reallocation which may be necessary at both the corporate and operational level may well prove extremely difficult due to historical vested interests. This has been shown to be particularly problematic in public-service organisations, where spending is justified against 'need' rather than income and is often subject to approval through a political process. The outcome is often that the strong remain strong even where there is agreement to a changing strategy.

In order to address these budgeting difficulties some organisations have attempted to adopt a *zero-based budgeting*[10] approach, where the historical size of the various budgets is given no weight in establishing the future deployment of resources. On the whole this process has been unsuccessful unless tempered with some short-term pragmatism. The most effective use of zero-based budgeting occurs where a safeguard is used whereby any individual budget will not vary by more than an agreed percentage from the previous year (this is the *constrained bidding* or *constrained bargaining* referred to earlier). There are often good practical reasons for this. For example, the redeployment of resources from one area to another may be achievable, and even universally supported, if the pace of change does not lead to an unmanageable period of transition. *Base budget reviews*[11] have been used in many organisations as a way of using the zero-based philosophy selectively (see Illustration 9.4).

9.4.5 Manpower planning[12]

Strategic change invariably has a significant impact on the people within the organisation. Manpower planning attempts to anticipate these changes in several respects. Three important issues are *manpower configuration, recruitment* and *training/development*.

ILLUSTRATION 9.4
Base budget reviews at Cheshire County Council

Many organisations have found that the philosophy behind zero-based budgeting is most likely to pay practical benefits if applied selectively. Base budget reviews are one example of such an approach.

Zero-based budgeting (ZBB) requires managers to propose and justify their budgets in relation to cost/benefit and alternative uses of that resource. The existence of a budget in the previous year is not an acceptable basis of justification. In practice many organisations, in both the public and private sector, found ZBB difficult to implement in a comprehensive way. Some organisations, such as Cheshire County Council, decided to implement it selectively through a programme of *base budget reviews*.

The programme was started in early 1991 with a stated purpose: 'to ask and answer challenging questions about the rationale for providing a particular service at all, for choosing a particular level of provision and the arrangements for delivery'.

The reviews were started on a pilot basis and undertaken by mixed teams of officers – usually one from the service under review, one from another front-line service and one from a central support service department. There was also an opportunity to involve external members if appropriate. The results were submitted to the appropriate service committees. The business planning process was expected to provide a considerable amount of the background material and data.

There were two important features of Cheshire's approach to base budget reviews. First, the council saw the process as a long-term continuing activity and had developed a rolling programme of reviews covering a five-year period (budgets totalling about £40m were to be reviewed each year). Second, the initial reviews were concentrated on *undelegated revenue budget items*. So, for example, within Education Services, reviews were to cover careers service, student awards, youth and community services, in-service teacher training, etc., but not the delegated budgets of schools. It was intended that each service department would pick up the base budget philosophy in terms of the management tasks for which the officers in that department were specifically and personally responsible.

Source: Authors (with permission of Cheshire County Council).

1. *Manpower configuration.* An important part of resource planning is to work through *in detail* the manpower requirements of particular strategies. This will include a specification of the *number* of people required, and the types and levels of *skill* required. This could, in turn, require a detailed plan of how the new configuration of manpower is to be achieved. For example, a strategy to introduce a new product by building new plants and converting some of the current plants is likely to have the following effects. Some staff may need to be *redeployed* or *transferred* to new plants. There may be some *redundancies* which will require *consultation* with the unions. There may also be issues about *job grades and rewards*. All of these factors are important aspects of a resource plan.

2. *Recruitment and selection.* These also need to be linked to the strategic direction of the organisation and the type of change being experienced. Incremental change may be possible by working largely with existing staff and developing them. The greater the need for global change, the more likely it is that 'new blood' will be required. This could be either because of the need for new skills or as an important means of challenging the *paradigm*. This is not just a matter of planning for senior executive changes; it may be that the blockages on change are lower in the hierarchy.

In effect, the recruitment and training policies of many years have left an organisation peopled by those comfortable with the dominant paradigm. To change this it may be necessary to bring in people with different experience. For example, many public-sector organisations have recruited from the private sector in areas such as finance, personnel and information technology. It may be that more general recruitment policies need to change. For example, it was not until the 1980s that many retail organisations started to recruit graduates as a means of changing the mechanistic and hierarchical organisation. *Methods* of selection may also need to change, even in quite simple ways. For example, the new personnel director of a firm trying to develop away from its traditional base in heavy chemicals noticed that recruitment practices were biased towards chemical engineers. He reduced the space available on application forms to do with past career and qualifications and introduced a new section requiring applicants to write about possible future strategies. He also changed the journals in which vacancies were advertised and involved more outsiders in interviews.

3. *Training and development.* Figure 9.8 shows that approaches to training and development need to vary with circumstances. The greater the degree of strategic change, the more likely it is that training will need to provide a basis for understanding and internalising change. Such aims are unlikely to be achieved through programmed learning techniques, but rather through discussion work and particularly by on-the-job, practical and project-based experience. Some organisations rightly regard this as an issue of *career planning* and ensure that managers get a broad experience of managing change during their careers in different parts of the organisation.

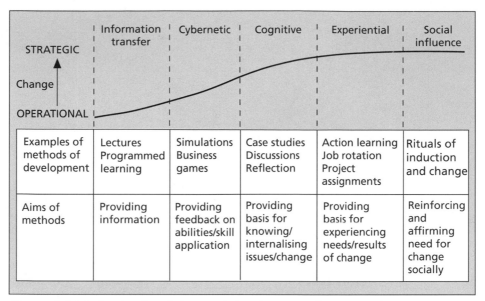

STRATEGIC ↑ Change OPERATIONAL	Information transfer	Cybernetic	Cognitive	Experiential	Social influence
Examples of methods of development	Lectures Programmed learning	Simulations Business games	Case studies Discussions Reflection	Action learning Job rotation Project assignments	Rituals of induction and change
Aims of methods	Providing information	Providing feedback on abilities/skill application	Providing basis for knowing/ internalising issues/change	Providing basis for experiencing needs/results of change	Reinforcing and affirming need for change socially

Figure 9.8 Methods of training and development for managing strategic change

There has also been an increased use of *strategy workshops* or similar events which involve managers, as teams, in planning the implementation of new strategies for their organisation.

9.4.6 Network analysis[13]

Network analysis, also known as *critical path analysis*, is a technique for planning projects by breaking them down into their component activities and showing these activities and their interrelationships in the form of a network. By considering the times and resources required to complete each of the activities, it is possible to locate the critical path of activities which determines the minimum time for the project. The network can also be used for scheduling materials and other resources and for examining the impact of changes in one sub-area of the project on others. The technique is particularly relevant to projects which have a reasonably definite start and finish.

It has been used very effectively in new product or service launches, construction of plant, acquisitions and mergers, relocation and R & D projects – all the sorts of activity relevant to strategy implementation. Figure 9.9 is an outline network analysis diagram for a customer survey project which was of major importance in underpinning a drive for improved customer service standards. It can be seen how this type of analysis can help in resource planning:

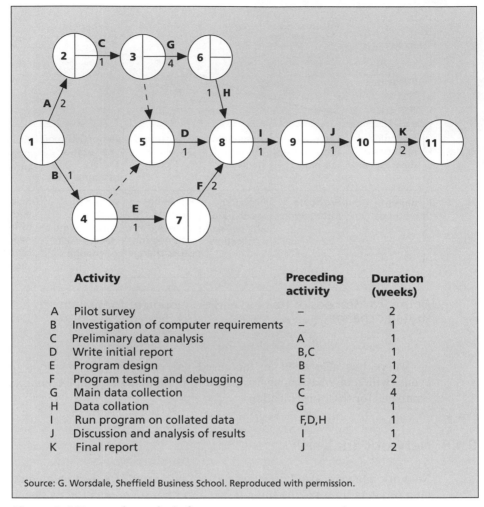

Activity		Preceding activity	Duration (weeks)
A	Pilot survey	–	2
B	Investigation of computer requirements	–	1
C	Preliminary data analysis	A	1
D	Write initial report	B,C	1
E	Program design	B	1
F	Program testing and debugging	E	2
G	Main data collection	C	4
H	Data collation	G	1
I	Run program on collated data	F,D,H	1
J	Discussion and analysis of results	I	1
K	Final report	J	2

Source: G. Worsdale, Sheffield Business School. Reproduced with permission.

Figure 9.9 Network analysis for a customer survey project

- It demands the breakdown of the programme of implementation into its constituent parts by activity. It is therefore easy to build onto the value chain analyses discussed earlier.
- It helps to establish priorities by identifying those activities upon which others depend. For example, the network identifies that the main data collection cannot start until the pilot survey is completed, whereas the identification of computer requirements can proceed in parallel.
- A network represents a plan of action. It enables the analyst to examine the implications of changes in the plan or deviations from the plan. Questions can be asked and followed through to assess the implications to the whole programme of any aspect of the plan taking a longer, or shorter, time than

expected. So a network is of particular value in thinking through the timing implications of a plan.

The network itself may be drawn up at several levels. The network shown in Figure 9.9 may be fine as a generalisation of a plan of action; however, there would also need to be much more detailed planning at a departmental level. There might be subnetworks for marketing and computer departments or, indeed, a much more detailed overall network.

A common alternative or addition to a network is some form of departmental or project plan which details activities within the network, sets target dates for completion and locates clear responsibilities for completion of specific tasks. This is a practical means of ensuring that key tasks are implemented on the basis of the principles discussed in section 9.4.1.

There are a number of developments of network analysis methods which readers may find of interest. *Programme evaluation review technique* (PERT) allows uncertainty about the times of each activity in the network to be taken into account. For example, in Figure 9.9 steps 8 to 11 would be so dependent on the outcome of the initial report that, in reality, it might be difficult to make a precise estimate of the time needed for these activities at the outset. PERT would be a useful refinement in such circumstances.

Network analysis can be very valuable in establishing the sequence in which tasks need to be planned. A good network should also assist in drawing up a time schedule (i.e. the precise time when each task should start and finish). There are other techniques which can also be helpful in scheduling activities, such as *Gantt charts* or *route planning*.[14] One specific approach to activity scheduling which has received considerable attention and proved to be of strategic importance to many manufacturing companies is *just in time*.

Many organisations are now realising that the quality of their resource planning will have a major impact on their competitive position in the market through reductions in costs or improvements in lead times[15] as seen in Illustration 9.5.

9.5 Summary

Resource planning is an important aspect of strategy implementation and needs to occur at two levels within most organisations. First, there are the broad issues of resource allocation between different divisions, service departments, functions or businesses. This has been referred to as resource planning at the *corporate level*, where the focus is one of deciding how resources should be allocated to the various parts of the organisation in order to support the overall strategies of the organisation. There are many different approaches to corporate allocation; the choice depends on the degree of change envisaged in the resource base and the extent to which priorities are to be dictated centrally. This in turn is strongly

ILLUSTRATION 9.5
Shortening the development cycle: the Land Rover Discovery

When cost and quality become taken for granted among competitors, speed of developing new products becomes a key competitive weapon.

As world-acclaimed experts in four-wheel-drive vehicles, Land Rover was undeniably late into the mid-range market. By the mid-1980s Land Rover's confidence was at an all-time low. The original Land Rover, launched in 1948, had been a real world-beater. However, following the golden era of the 1960s and 1970s, the company entered a period of real difficulty. It had become overcommitted to Third World countries for sales of the standard vehicle. These economies were badly hit by world economic factors including the oil crisis and growing national debts. The company's other product, the Range Rover, was a top-of-the-market vehicle, and sales volumes in no way compensated for the fall-off in the workhorse Land Rover range. Meanwhile the Japanese, led by Mitsubishi's Shogun model, aimed at the middle leisure sector.

Having established through market research that this sector was likely to remain in 1986, Land Rover made the decision to enter the market as quickly as possible with a new vehicle entitled the Discovery. There were several critical changes in the management of the development process which ensured that the overall time to market was significantly shortened.

related to issues of organisational design, which are discussed fully in Chapter 10.

Second, the success of a strategy is also dependent on a detailed consideration of the resources required at the *operational level*. The organisation's value chain is a useful framework for identifying the resource requirements of any strategy. The way in which resources need to be deployed and managed through the value chain will differ considerably depending on the type of generic strategy being pursued by the organisation. Understanding these requirements in detail, the linkages which will be required between separate resources, and how new requirements will relate to the current resource position are all important ingredients of a resource plan. A resource plan should therefore ensure that the *critical success factors* which underpin the strategy are clearly identified, and that the *key tasks* required to deliver the plan are properly prioritised. Given the uncertainty surrounding the development of strategies, it is also important that the plan assesses the likely impact of any changes in the key assumptions underlying the plan.

There are a number of planning tools available to address these issues – the most commonly used ones being budgets, financial plans and network analysis. It should be remembered that the successful implementation of resource plans is

- A multifunctional project team was created. Traditionally, development had been done in a sequential process starting with the designer's drawing. This project team undertook their tasks simultaneously – a more risky approach, but one ensuring considerable time saving.
- Suppliers were brought in at an early stage again to cut development time at their end.
- A major advantage of the project team was the reduction in time spent in 'referring queries for answer'. With all the experts there in the team, these queries got answered immediately.
- Because the manufacturing function had been properly involved in the project team, their commitment to the (major) changes required in their production methods was very high.

These efforts paid off. In 1990, the first full year of sales, the Discovery left its competition standing, outselling the Shogun by two to one in the UK. Significantly, a large part of sales went to buyers switching from two-wheel-drive vehicles (such as the Volvo estate car) and interested in the higher-quality internal fittings which the Discovery offered compared to its Japanese competitors. So, although Land Rover was late to enter this mid-market, its speed of development meant that the company was able to have a product available during the crucial growth phase.

Source: *Management Today*, October 1991.

fundamentally dependent on people within the organisation. The next two chapters look at the role of people in the implementation of strategy, and the implications for organisational design and the management of change.

References

1. Zero-based budgeting is discussed in detail in P. A. Phyrr, *Zero-Based Budgeting: A practical management tool for evaluating expenses*, Wiley, 1973. A useful critique can also be found in S. Eildon, 'Zero-based budgeting: promise or illusion?', *Omega*, vol. 9, no. 2, (1981), pp. 107–12.

2. For an explanation of defenders, prospectors and analysers, see R. E. Miles and C. C. Snow, *Organisational Strategy: Structure and process*, McGraw-Hill, 1978.

3. For example, the operation of an 'Investment Bank' in the 3M company is discussed in T. Peters and R. Waterman, *In Search of Excellence*, Harper and Row, 1982.

4. The issue of 'charging-out' was of central importance to the operation of 'internal markets'. For example, see K. Scholes, 'Learning to live with devolution', *Sheffield Business School*, 1991.

5. Detailed resource identification is often started by looking at the implications of each functional area of the business. G. A. Steiner, *Strategic Planning*, Free Press, 1979, is a useful guide.

Readers who are unfamiliar with resource analysis in any functional area may wish to consult one of the following standard texts: P. Kotler, *Marketing Management: Analysis, planning, implementation and control* (7th edn) Prentice Hall, 1991; R. Wild, *Production and Operations Management* (3rd edn), Nelson, 1984; M. W. E. Glautier and B. Underdown, *Accounting Theory and Practice* (4th ed), Pitman, 1991; D. Torrington and L. Hall, *Personnel Management: A new approach*, Prentice Hall, 1986; C. Fombrun, N. Tichy and M. Devanna, *Strategic Human Resource Management*, Wiley, 1990.

6. See M. Hardaker and B. K. Ward, 'Getting things done', *Harvard Business Review*, vol. 65, no. 6, (1987), pp. 112–20, for a fuller discussion of how critical success factors can be identified and used.

7. For a fuller discussion of the planning of priorities, see K. Scholes and M. Klemm, *An Introduction to Business Planning*, Macmillan, 1987, chapter 5.

8. 'Just in time' is explained in T. Hill, *Manufacturing Strategy*, Macmillan, 1985.

9. As a general introduction to budgets and budgetary control, see Glautier and Underdown (reference 5 above). More details on capital budgeting can be found in S. Lumby, *Investment Appraisal and Financing Decisions: A first course in financial management* (4th edn), Chapman and Hall, 1991.

10. See reference 1.

11. Base budget reviews have been used by a number of public-sector organisations in an attempt to take on board the philosophy of zero-based budgets (see D. Wise, *Management Today*, July, 1986) in a way that could be worked in practice.

12. C. Fombrun, N. Tichy and M. Devanna, *Strategic Human Resource Management*, Wiley, 1990.

13. Network analysis is explained in Wild (reference 5) or K. Howard, *Quantitative Analyses for Planning Decisions*, Macdonald and Evans, 1975.

14. See Wild (reference 5), M. Christopher, *Effective Logistics Management*, Gower, 1986; or M. Christopher, 'Logistics and competitive strategy', *Logistics World*, Dec. 1988.

15. Time as a key strategic resource is discussed in T. K. Das, 'Time: the hidden dimension in strategic planning', *Long Range Planning*, vol. 24, no. 3, (1991), pp. 49–57, and J. T. Vesey, 'The new competitors: they think in terms of speed to the market', *Academy of Management Executive*, vol. 5, no. 2, (1991), pp. 23–33.

Recommended key readings

G. A. Steiner, *Strategic Planning*, Free Press, 1979, chapter 11–13, is a useful guide on translating strategic plans into functional plans.

M. Hardaker and B. K. Ward, 'Getting things done', *Harvard Business Review*, vol. 65, no. 6, (1987), pp. 112–20, is an excellent guide to how critical success factors can be identified and used.

M. W. E. Glautier and B. Underdown, *Accounting Theory and Practice*, (4th edn), Pitman, 1991, covers most of the financial techniques which underpin resource planning.

M. Christopher, *Effective Logistics Management*, Gower, 1986, is useful for its consideration of many of the practicalities of making strategies work.

Work assignments

9.1 By referring to Figure 9.1, characterise how corporate allocation of resources works in an organisation of your choice. Assess whether or not you would regard the current approach as appropriate.

9.2   Compare your answer to assignment 1 with the way you would characterise other organisations in the same industry. What differences do you observe and why do they occur?

9.3   Explain the changes that had occurred in the methods of resource allocation in higher education in the UK from 1989 (Illustration 9.1).
(a) Why were these changes occurring?
(b) Assess the importance of the changes in underpinning strategic development *for the sector.*
(c) in what ways would individual institutions and departments/schools within those institutions need to respond to this changed approach?

9.4   Choose two strategic developments for an organisation with which you are familiar and compare the resource planning implications (Figures 9.2 and 9.3). How would this analysis influence your choice of strategy?

9.5   (a) Choose an organisation which is shifting its generic competitive strategy from low price to differentiation (or supplementing the former with the latter). Describe any resource planning difficulties which are occurring as a result of these changes and how they are being tackled. (Refer to Figure 9.4.)
(b) Choose an organisation which is attempting the opposite shift (differentiation to low price) and undertake the same analysis.

9.6   By referring to Figure 9.7 undertake an analysis of the critical success factors and the associated key tasks for an important strategic development in an organisation of your choice, or for KMPG* or United Stationers (Illustration 9.3).

9.7   Criticise the usefulness of zero-based budgeting as a strategic approach to resource planning by referring to the base budget review process in Cheshire County Council (Illustration 9.4). What improvements would you make to its approach, and how applicable is it to other organisations?

9.8   Draw up a network analysis for a strategic development in an organisation of your choice (refer to Figure 9.9). How could the 'time to market' be shortened, and what risks would the organisation be taking (compare Illustration 9.5)?

9.9   *Choose an important strategic development for an organisation of your choice and draw up a detailed resource plan for implementing the strategy. Refer to section 9.4 of the text to assist with your answer.*

9.10 'Resource allocation to support new strategies is tied up with issues of organisational design and the management of change. Therefore, these implementation factors must be considered *together* and not separately.' Discuss the validity of this statement by using examples from your answers to previous questions.

* This refers to a case study in the Text and Cases version of this book.

CHAPTER 10

Organisation structure and design

10.1 Introduction

One of the most important resources of an organisation is its people; so how they are organised is crucial to the effectiveness of strategy. The previous chapter dealt with how resourcing aspects of implementation might be planned. Chapters 10 and 11 are primarily concerned with how implementation is effected through the people in the organisation.

Traditional views about regulation through organisation can be traced back to early twentieth-century management scientists and beyond.[1] These approaches are commensurate with a view of strategy making which is essentially top-down. Strategy is formed at the top and the rest of the organisation is seen as a means of implementation; so organisation design becomes a means of top-down control. Such principles of control are known as *bureaucratic* or *mechanistic*.[2] As was seen in Chapter 2, however, the idea that strategy is formulated in a top-down way is questionable, and the extension of this, that mechanistic structures and controls are necessarily appropriate, is therefore also questionable.

This chapter considers organisational structure/design in the context of the strategic management of organisations. It is accepted that there is a need to regulate the implementation of strategy, but this needs to take account of many influences. For example, what are the *types* of problem that the organisation faces in constructing strategy? Is it in a highly *complex* or *changing* environment, or a fairly *stable* environment? How *diverse* is the organisation: for example, the needs of a multinational company are different from those of small local firm. To what extent is the organisation reliant on simple or complex technologies? How answerable are the top executives to *external influences*: for example, is the organisation a public body, perhaps answerable to a government minister; is it a privately owned firm; or perhaps a charity or a co-operative? All these different influences must have a bearing on the way the organisation needs to be designed. It is not possible to have a simple set of rules which can prescribe organisational structures and systems.

This chapter examines these issues, first, by reviewing *basic structural forms* of organisations; second, by looking at different types of *organisational design*; and finally, by considering how organisational *systems* of control influence strategy implementation.

10.2 Structural types

Managers asked to describe their organisations usually respond by drawing an organisation chart, in an attempt to map out its structure. These structures are like skeletons: they define the general shape and facilitate or constrain certain activities. This chapter begins with a review of these basic structural types, and their advantages and disadvantages.

10.2.1 The simple structure

A simple structure could be thought of as no formal structure at all. It is the type of organisation common in many very small businesses. There may be an owner who undertakes most of the responsibilities of management, perhaps with a partner or an assistant. However, there is little division of management responsibility and probably little clear definition of who is responsible for what if there is more than one person involved. The operation is then run by the personal control and contact of an individual.

The main problem here is that the organisation can only operate effectively up to a certain size, beyond which it becomes too cumbersome for one person alone to control. This threshold size will depend on the nature of the business: an insurance broker may personally handle a very large turnover, whereas a similarly sized business (in terms of turnover) manufacturing and selling goods may be much more diverse in its operations and therefore more difficult to control personally.

10.2.2 The functional structure

A functional structure is based on the primary tasks that have to be carried out, such as production, finance and accounting, marketing and personnel. Figure 10.1 represents a typical organisation chart for such a business. This structure is typically found in smaller companies or those with narrow, rather than diverse, product ranges. However, within a multidivisional structure, the divisions themselves are likely to be split up into functional management areas.

Figure 10.1 also summarises the basic advantages and disadvantages of a functional structure.[3] There are advantages, mainly in so far as it allows greater operational control at a senior level in an organisation; and linked to this is the clear definition of roles and tasks. However, there are disadvantages, particularly as organisations become larger or more diverse. In such circumstances, senior managers can be burdened with everyday operational issues, or rely on their specialist skills, rather than taking a strategic perspective on problems. Such organisations are also likely to require greater co-operation between different functions, since they cannot rely on lengthy vertical chains of decision making.

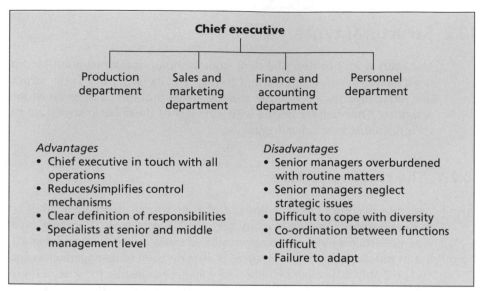

Figure 10.1 A basic functional structure

10.2.3 The multidivisional structure

The main characteristic of a multidivisional structure (Figure 10.2) is that it is subdivided into units; these divisions may be formed on the basis of products, services, geographical areas, or the processes of the enterprise. Divisionalisation often comes about as an attempt to overcome the problems that functional structures have in dealing with diversity.[4] Its main advantage is that each division is able to concentrate on the problems and opportunities of its particular business environment. The products/markets in which the company operates may be so different that it would be impractical to bring the tasks together in a single body. It makes more sense to split up the company according to the different products/markets or operations and then to ensure that the needs of each division are met by tailoring the operations within the division to the particular business needs. A similar situation exists in many public services, where the organisation is structured around *service departments* such as recreation, social services and education.

The result can, of course, be a complex organisation: for example, a company may decide that it needs a number of levels of divisions in order to break up business activities sensibly. Figure 10.3 shows this. The company might be broken into a first level of divisions based on broad products/markets. Within each of these divisions there may be separate businesses, which may in turn have their own divisional structure. At some level in the organisation a division will then be split into functionally based departments dealing with the specialist tasks of that business.

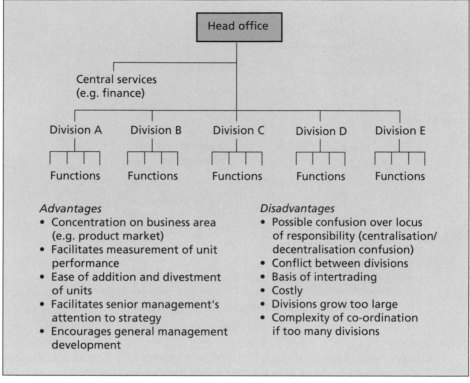

Advantages
- Concentration on business area (e.g. product market)
- Facilitates measurement of unit performance
- Ease of addition and divestment of units
- Facilitates senior management's attention to strategy
- Encourages general management development

Disadvantages
- Possible confusion over locus of responsibility (centralisation/ decentralisation confusion)
- Conflict between divisions
- Basis of intertrading
- Costly
- Divisions grow too large
- Complexity of co-ordination if too many divisions

Figure 10.2 A multidivisional structure

This raises another problem. Which functions are to be included at what level of divisionalisation; and which functions are properly placed within the corporate head office rather than within any one of the divisions? For example, in Figure 10.3 where should a function such as financial planning be placed? Presumably this is required both at a corporate level and at some level within an operating business, but should this be at level one, two or three, for example? This issue will be discussed in detail in section 10.4 below.

The advantages of divisional structures mainly centre on the ability to operate and monitor the activities of a division as a separate business (or business unit) and if necessary to divest that business unit. There are, however, disadvantages and difficulties, since the operation and control of multidivisional organisations is often far from straightforward. These issues are discussed more fully in section 10.6 below. Figure 10.2 also summarises the advantages and disadvantages of a multidivisional structure.

10.2.4 The holding company structure

In its most extreme form, a holding company is really an investment company. It

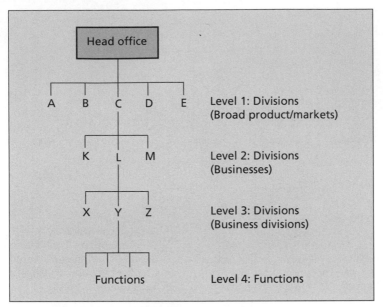

Figure 10.3 Levels of divisions

may simply consist of shareholdings in a variety of individual, unconnected business operations over which it exercises little or no control. However, the term is also applied to an enterprise which, itself, operates a portfolio of virtually autonomous business units. Although part of a parent company, these business units operate independently and probably retain their original company names. The role that the parent company takes may be limited to decisions about the buying and selling of such companies, with little involvement in their product/market strategy. Arguably, this is the situation as far as Lonrho or BTR is concerned. However, the holding company may argue that in doing this it has a corporate strategy and approach which achieves a synergistic effect, as discussed in Chapter 7.

An example of a holding company structure is given in Figure 10.4. The business interests of the parent company are likely to be varied: some of them may be wholly owned and some not, and there may be many business units within the group. To a large extent, the business units retain their own identity and perhaps their own individual structures. Central corporate staff and services may be very limited. The essential differentiating feature for a holding company is, then, the extent of the autonomy of the business units, particularly over strategic decisions. The advantages that a holding company can offer are based on the idea that the constituent businesses will operate to their best potential if left alone, particularly as business environments become more turbulent.

There are other organisational advantages and disadvantages of the holding company structure. For example, the organisation does not have to carry the

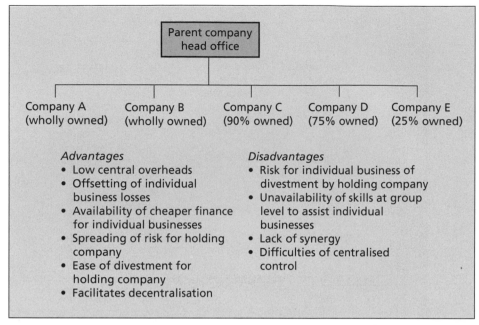

Figure 10.4 A holding company structure

burden of a high central overhead, since the head office staff of the parent is likely to be small. However, the business units can benefit from their membership of the group in such ways as offsetting profits against others' losses, and obtaining cheaper finance for investment from the parent company. The holding company itself may also claim benefits, such as the spreading of risk across many business ventures and the ease of divestment of individual companies. Perhaps the greatest weakness of this structure is, however, the risk of a lack of internal strategic cohesion and duplication of effort between business units. It is one thing to say that business units operate better if they are given the profit responsibility to do so on their own; but in a large, perhaps multinational, operation there may be very considerable payoffs from having some sort of overall logic to the activities – some sort of horizontal integration[5] in the group.

10.2.5 The matrix structure

A matrix structure is a combination of structures. It often takes the form of product and geographical divisions, or functional and divisional structures, operating in tandem. Figure 10.5 gives examples of such a structure. Matrix structures are often adopted because there is more than one factor around which a structure could be built, so that pure divisional structures would be inappropriate. For example, if a company extends its operations on a multinational scale and devel-

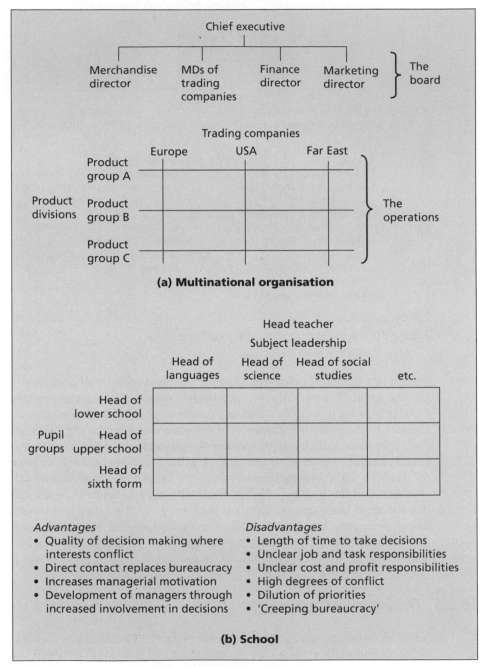

Figure 10.5 Two examples of matrix structures

ops new product interests, it may regard geographically defined divisions as the operating units for the purpose of local marketing and product divisions as responsible for the central worldwide co-ordination of product development, manufacturing and distribution to the geographical divisions. Illustration 10.1 shows that in some organisations the matrix structure reflects more than two dimensions.

Matrix structures do not occur only in large, complex organisations; they are sometimes found in quite small organisations and are very common in professional service organisations (both public and private sector).

It is claimed that matrix structures[6] improve the quality of decision making in situations where there is a risk of one vital interest of the enterprise (e.g. a geographical area) dominating strategy at the expense of others (e.g. worldwide co-ordination of manufacturing). Formal bureaucracy is replaced by direct contact between individuals. It is also supposed to increase managerial motivation and development because of wider involvement in strategies.

However, matrix structures have some very real problems associated with them:

- There is a high risk of a *dilution of priorities*, whereby the message to those in the organisation is that everything matters equally and deserves equal debate.
- The *time* taken for decisions to be made may be much longer than in more conventional structures.
- It can be unclear who is *responsible* for what; while the idea of joint responsibility may be conceptually laudable, it can give rise to problems.
- Organisations with matrix structures may have to cope with a good deal of *conflict* because of the lack of clarity of role definition and responsibility.

A summary of advantages and disadvantages is provided in Figure 10.5. The critical issue with any organisation structure in practice is the way in which it is operated. This is particularly important in the case of matrix structures, and the following guidelines should be considered:

- One arm of the matrix should *lead* in order to minimise the risk of paralysis.
- The allocation of workloads and/or duties for individuals should not normally be spread evenly across the matrix. So, for example, within the personnel function there should be some degree of matching of individuals with the geographic divisions to provide the *ownership* which can be lost in a matrix structure. In the extreme form, the matrix structure will shade through into project teams of dedicated individuals from central functions seconded semi-permanently to divisions.
- Senior managers must be capable of *collaborating* across the matrix. The structure does not suit managers who are fiercely competitive (internally) and who do not like *ambiguity*.

ILLUSTRATION 10.1
Matrix structure at Shell

Sometimes a matrix structure will need to reflect more than two dimensions

In the early 1990s Shell was a major international corporation operating around the world, having diversified during the 1980s from its traditional base of oil, gas and petrochemicals into coal, metals and chemicals. The core of business activities was vested in the separate *operating companies*, but the need to co-ordinate their efforts, geographically, functionally and also by business sector, had led the organisation to develop a matrix structure with *four* dimensions: business sectors; business functions; geographical regions; and operating companies. This structure required a high degree of collaboration across the arms of the matrix: for example, a new development in technology developed in one operating company would be made available – via the research function – to other operating companies in all appropriate business sectors.

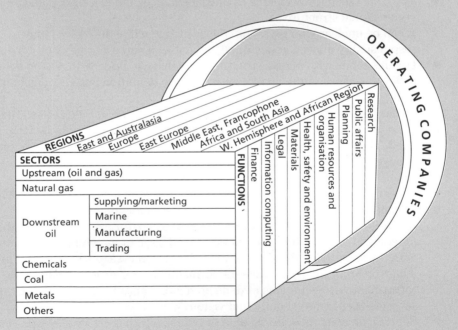

Group organisational matrix

Source: The figure is from the case study 'Planning in Shell' by Julie Verity.

10.2.6   Intermediate structures and structural variations

Few organisations adopt one of the pure structural types discussed above. The skill is in blending structure to the organisation's circumstances. There exists a whole range of 'shades of grey' between these pure types of structure. For example, a company may move from a functional structure to a divisional structure by a series of smaller incremental changes. Problems first arise within the functional structure as new products/markets compete for resources. Initially these conflicts might be resolved by pushing the decision upwards until a sufficiently *senior executive* makes the decision. When too many conflicts need to be resolved in this way, new *rules*, guidelines and procedures may develop to guide how resources are to be shared between products. The next step may be to *formalise* these procedures in the planning process by, for example, allocating a budget to the new products/markets.

Up to this stage the problem has been dealt with by manipulating methods of control and operation rather than by structural changes. As the new products/markets become more important and create competition for resources, it may be necessary to create *interdepartmental liaison roles*: for example, a committee or a temporary taskforce may be set up to advise on priorities. This may lead to either permanent teams of co-ordinators or special *co-ordinating jobs* (the product manager is a good example). Another step which may prove necessary to maintain the functional structure is the creation of departments with the sole function of co-ordination: *centralised planning departments*, for example. Ultimately, the organisation will divisionalise as the diversity increases and the 'costs' of maintaining the functional structure become unacceptably high.

It is also common to adopt a *mixed* structure to address such problems as a *functional structure with subsidiaries.*[7] The main business, which employs the majority of employees, might have a functional structure, with more peripheral business interests organised as divisions or subsidiaries. The converse of this is the company that is divisionalised except for certain key functions which remain at the centre and which have responsibilities across all the divisions.

Another way of coping with the need for organisational change, without fundamentally affecting what already exists, is to *externalise* the change by moving the responsibility for it outside the enterprise or into a *joint venture*, as discussed in Chapter 6.

10.2.7   Structural types in multinational companies[8]

The growth in the size and importance of multinational businesses warrants some special mention of the structural implications for them. A basic form of structure for a multinational is the retention of the 'home' structure and the management of whatever overseas subsidiaries exist through *direct contact* between the manager of the subsidiary and the chief executive of the parent company. This is most common in single-product companies or where the overseas interests are relatively minor. Beyond this simple structure the critical issue is the extent to which local independence or responsiveness should take precedence over global co-ordination (see Figure 10.6). This balance will vary with circumstances and over time:

1.   A common form of multinational structure is the *international division*. Here the home-based structure may be retained at first – whether functional or divisional – but the overseas interests are managed through a special international division. The international subsidiaries will draw on the products of the home company and gain advantage from this technology transfer. The disadvantage is a lack of local tailoring of products or technology. Such structures tend to work best where there is a wide geographical spread but quite closely related products.

2.   The logical extension of this structure is that geographically based *international subsidiaries* evolve which are part of a multinational whole, but which operate independently by country. In these companies virtually all the management functions are nationally based, allowing for higher degrees of local responsiveness. In such circumstances the control of the parent company is likely to be dependent on some form of planning and reporting system and perhaps an ultimate veto over national strategies, but the extent of global co-ordination is likely to be low.

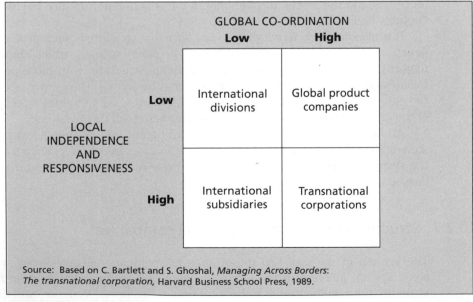

Source: Based on C. Bartlett and S. Ghoshal, *Managing Across Borders: The transnational corporation*, Harvard Business School Press, 1989.

Figure 10.6 Structural types in multinational companies

3.   In many industries there has been a move away from the international divisional or subsidiary structure to what has become known as a *global product* or integrated structure. Here the multinational is split into product divisions which are then managed on an international basis. The logic of such an approach is that it should promote cost efficiency (particularly of production) on an international basis, and should provide enhanced transfer of resources (particularly technology) between geographical regions. The network of plants, each one in a separate country, may be making parts of cars, for example, which are assembled in yet another country, and this manufacturing network may be supported by an international research and development network. The international development of many Japanese companies, for example in electronics, has been managed in this way.

A key requirement to support this structure is planning mechanisms to co-ordinate the various operations, and it is in these organisations that the planning and control systems are likely to be most sophisticated. Research has shown that the theoretical benefits of the global product structure are not always realised. Although cost efficiency is improved, it does not appear that technology transfer is necessarily enhanced. Also, while the structure is well suited to promoting defensive or consolidation strategies, it does not seem to meet the expected benefits of better strategic planning and is not suited to the promotion of aggressive or expansionist strategies. These difficulties may be accounted for in part by the senior management of the global division becoming mainly concerned with central co-ordination and thus losing their sensitivity to local needs, particularly in terms of marketing and competitive activity.

4.   Recently, some organisations have developed structures which attempt to combine the local responsiveness of the international subsidiary with the advantages of co-ordination found in global product companies. These have been called *transnational corporations.*[9] The key lies in creating an integrated *network* of interdependent resources and capabilities. Specifically, the transnational exhibits the following features:

- Each national unit operates independently, but is a source of ideas and capabilities for the whole corporation.
- National units achieve global scale through specialisation on behalf of the whole corporation.
- The centre manages a global network firstly by establishing the role of each subsidiary and then by sustaining the culture and systems to make the network operate effectively.

The global role of subsidiaries is largely determined by their capabilities and the nature of their national markets (see Figure 10.7):

- *Strategic leaders* are capable subsidiaries with key national markets and play a leadership role for the company as a whole.

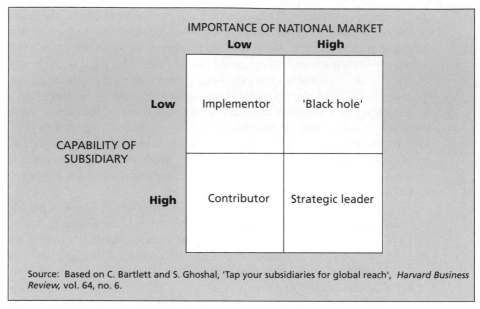

Source: Based on C. Bartlett and S. Ghoshal, 'Tap your subsidiaries for global reach', *Harvard Business Review,* vol. 64, no. 6.

Figure 10.7 Role of subsidiaries in transnational corporations.

- *Contributors* have high capability but weak national markets and their ideas and products are exploited in other markets.
- *Implementors* have weak national markets and little to contribute globally. Their main role is often the local marketing of products from other subsidiaries.
- The *black hole* represents an undesirable position of a weak subsidiary in a key market. Joint ventures or acquisitions may be necessary to convert the black hole into a leader.

This discussion of multinational organisation has illustrated that the basic structures of organisations are less important than the organisational design built around this structure. Indeed, as Illustration 10.2 shows some companies were prompted to review their design alongside the development of new strategies for the single European market. The next four sections will look at these issues of organisational design in more detail, since they apply to all organisations and not just multinationals.

10.3 The elements of organisational design

It should be clear from the previous section that the structure of an organisation is a skeleton on which the flesh can be hung. Structure in itself will not ensure the success of strategy, although an inappropriate choice of structure could

ILLUSTRATION 10.2
ICI's structure for Europe

Many major companies were reviewing their organisation's structure alongside developing strategies for the single European market.

In the late 1990s the European market will effectively consist of some 440 million people in 21 countries – or even more if the Balkan states and the western republics of the former Soviet Union are included. Multinational managers will therefore have to cope with a plethora of different markets, all comparatively prosperous, and all with some similarities and some differences. For most purposes the markets will need to be treated separately, but for some purposes they can be treated alike.

Against this background ICI decided to change from its traditional matrix structure of functional, product and geographic responsibilities. The reshuffling of the traditional product divisions into 15 'businesses' and the cutting back of head office had happened some years previously. However, European operations had remained as a hybrid around a *Europa* regional office near Brussels, which had been established in the 1970s to encourage product divisions to take an interest in the emerging EEC. Europa sought to act as a bridge overcoming some of the difficulties of the fragmented presence of the 15 divisions. However, by 1990 the degree of customer responsiveness through the matrix was not really adequate to service European markets against competition.

It was therefore decided to make the product divisions responsible for their own marketing and sales in continental Europe, but *simultaneously* to raise Europa's status by appointing a chairman, David Beynon, based in Brussels, who reported to the central ICI Executive just like the heads of ICI Americas and Asia-Pacific. He did not have profit responsibility but had to develop a European strategy in a forum consisting of the European marketing directors of each business. Importantly, the UK became just one of seven regions each with its own manager, reporting to Beynon, and charged with maintaining close contact with the group's major customers and spotting the potential for new ICI business – whatever the product. ICI regarded as a critical part of change the fact that French would deal with French, Italians with Italians. The contact would be as strong as ever – but better and faster.

Source: *Management Today*, January 1991.

impede success. Developing the flesh on this structure is the province of organisational design and consists of three elements:

- *Centralisation/devolution* – deciding where within the structure the responsibility for operational and strategic decision making should lie.
- *Organisational configurations* – the need to match the detailed structure with the context which the organisation is operating.
- *Management systems* – how systems relate to the structure and influence the behaviour of people.

These three elements of organisational design will be discussed in the sections which follow.

10.4 Centralisation vs devolution

One of the most important recent debates in both public- and private-sector organisations has been concerned with *devolution*.[10] This is the extent to which the centre of an organisation releases its control of decision making to units and managers lower down in the hierarchy. This raises the question: control over what? Goold and Campbell,[11] through their work on management styles in diversified organisations, have provided some stereotypes of possible relationships between the centre and the parts of an organisation, and how responsibilities for decision making can be divided. Each provides a valuable checklist of the key features of the different relationships and is useful when considering the links between strategy and organisational design. The three stereotypes are *strategic planning, financial control* and *strategic control* – and the key features of the centre/division relationship in each case are shown in Figure 10.8.

10.4.1 Strategic planning

Figure 10.9 shows a typical relationship between the centre and the divisions which would be found in an organisation whose approach is described as *strategic planning*. Goold and Campbell cite BOC, Cadbury, Lex and STC as examples of this stereotype. This has also been the dominant approach in most public-sector organisations. The centre operates as the *masterplanner* developing a detailed central plan and prescribing detailed roles for divisions and departments. They are seen as the *agencies* which deliver parts of the plan, and their role is confined to the operational delivery of the plan. The following features are likely to be emphasised:

- The *annual budget* as the key control mechanism.
- *Detailed item-by-item control* within the budget.

	Key features	Advantages	Dangers	Examples
STRATEGIC PLANNING	• 'Masterplanner' • Top-down • Highly prescribed • Detailed controls	Co-ordination	Centre out of touch Divisions tactical	BOC Cadbury Lex STC Public sector pre-1990s
FINANCIAL CONTROL	• 'Shareholder/banker' • Financial targets • Control of investment • Bottom-up	Responsiveness	Lose direction Centre does not add value	BTR Hanson plc Tarmac
STRATEGIC CONTROL	• 'Strategic shaper' • Strategic and financial targets • Bottom-up • Less detailed controls	Centre/divisions complementary Ability to co-ordinate Motivation	Too much bargaining Culture change needed New bureaucracies	ICI Courtaulds Public sector post-1990

Source: After M. Goold and A. Campbell, *Strategies and Styles*, Basil Blackwell, 1987.

Figure 10.8 Centre–division relationships

- *Capital allocations* to support the strategy determined by the centre.
- *Detailed procedures* and rule-books.
- *Imposed* infrastructure and central services.

The main benefits of operating in this way are the high levels of control and co-ordination which the centre is able to exert over strategy. McDonald's, the fast-food chain, used such an approach which allowed them to internationalise while maintaining consistent product quality and company image. It had the added benefit of achieving this alongside low cost, since the bureaucratic systems allowed the use of unskilled labour. However, there can be major problems with operating in this way if the managers of divisions come to see their relationship with the centre as entirely tactical and devote much of their management time to special pleadings and item-by-item bargaining. The quality of strategic thinking at the centre can become very limited through the lack of involvement of divisional management.

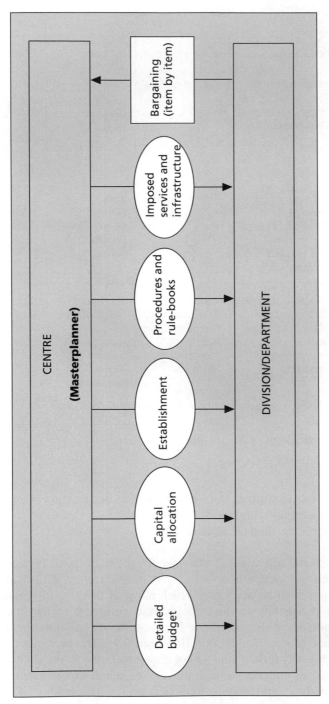

Figure 10.9 Strategic planning

10.4.2 Financial control

Almost the opposite extreme from strategic planning is *financial control,*
where the centre sees itself as a *shareholder* or a *banker* for the divisions (see
Figure 10.10). Goold and Campbell's examples were BTR, Hanson Trust and
Tarmac. There is little concern for defining the product/market strategy for divisions. It is quite possible that a business unit within a company such as Lonrho
might take decisions about entering new markets or developing new products
independently, and might even have the facility to raise funds to support new
developments from outside the parent group. The main roles of the centre are as
follows:

- Setting *financial targets.*
- Performance *appraisal* of divisions.
- Appraising *capital bids* from divisions.

Perhaps the most important question which needs to be asked about this
type of relationship is why the centre is needed at all. Indeed, it has been
argued[12] that, unless the centre is demonstrably adding value, the performance
for shareholders would be better if the company were dismembered into its
constituent parts with the stock market then taking over the role of sharehold-

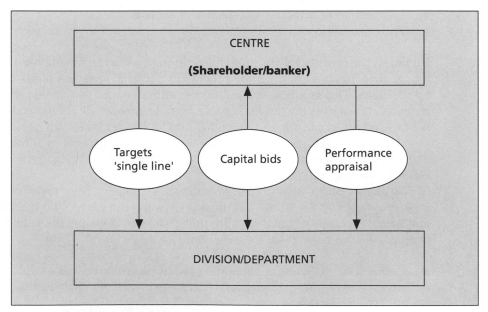

Figure 10.10 Financial control

er/banker. The ways in which the centre of such a devolved organisation can add value are as follows:

- *Bargaining power* with other stakeholders such as bankers, suppliers and customers.
- *Management skills*, particularly in financing and control.

10.4.3 Strategic control

One of the concerns about the devolution debate in both the public and private sectors has been a mistaken belief that devolution means complete independence of divisions from the centre. Such extreme forms of devolution are rarely found – even in the private sector – and are totally inappropriate for most public-sector organisations for reasons of public accountability and political control. In fact during the late 1980s and early 1990s, changes in the centre/division relationship[13] – in both the private and public sectors – were mainly concerned with a move from the tightly prescribed relationships of strategic planning to those of *strategic control* (see Figure 10.11). Goold and Campbell's examples included ICI and Courtaulds. Here the centre is the *strategic shaper*, so unlike in the case of financial control the centre is concerned with the following:

- The *overall* strategy of the organisation.
- The *balance* of activities and the *role* of each division.
- The organisational *policies* (on employment, market coverage, etc.).

However, the centre's role is not fulfilled through a masterplan imposed from the top. Rather it is built through the process of agreeing *business plans* produced by divisions. This is a bottom-up process within central guidelines. The centre remains responsible for assessing the *performance* of divisions against their business plan, within which the annual *budget* has an important part. Another key difference from strategic planning is that certain aspects of infrastructure and central services may be *optional* rather than imposed (e.g. personnel services, IT, floor space).

Strategic control requires organisations to establish a clear understanding of how responsibility for strategy is divided between the centre and the divisions, and hence the tasks which the centre undertakes. In principle the guidelines are simple – the centre must have the capability to do its job of:

- Defining *key policies* (or supporting politicians to do so in the public sector).
- *Allocating resources* to divisions – as a key means of influencing the balance of the organisation.
- Assessing the *performance* of divisions.

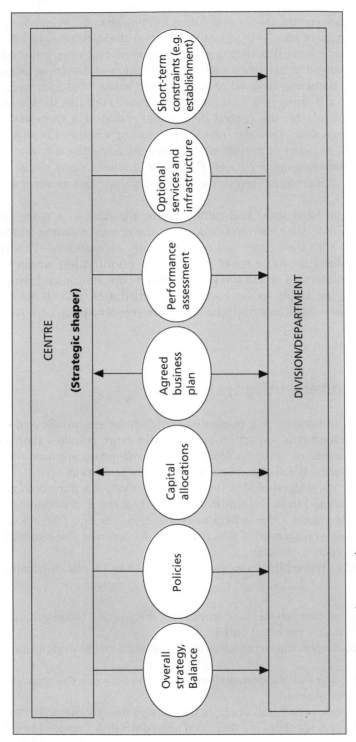

Figure 10.11 Strategic control

All other tasks are candidates for devolution to divisions. For example, a central personnel department should legitimately assist in the development of employment policies and ensure that they are being followed. However, whether or not it is directly involved in activities such as recruitment and training is questionable. Of course, there may be good reasons why divisions would not wish to take on recruitment or training (e.g. cost, lack of expertise) but this then results in a different type of role for the central department – that of a *specialist agency* within the organisation. This also raises the issue of whether the organisation should establish an *internal market* where divisions relate to each other and the centre on a customer–supplier basis. Figure 10.12 shows some of the benefits and difficulties of increasing devolution within organisations as compared with central control.

Managers can have some real difficulties in adjusting to a more devolved regime. For example, they need to break out of the special pleading and bargaining relationship with the centre and become more self-sufficient. This requires more management time to be spent on issues of prioritisation within the division. Devolution can also create too much internal competition and rivalry – the casualty can be the ability to act corporately. Illustration 10.3 shows how one local authority attempted to strike a balance between devolution and overall corporate purpose.

10.5 Organisational configurations

The discussion in section 10.2 presented structure as essentially synonymous with levels in a hierarchy. Structure is in practice more complex than this and consists of a number of *building blocks* and *co-ordinating mechanisms* which together make up the detailed *configuration* of an organisation.

Mintzberg[14] has suggested that there are essentially six pure configurations which can be adopted to fit the context that different types of organisation face. A seventh configuration – the network organisation – is also discussed. Before considering these configurations it is necessary to describe the building blocks which make up each configuration.

Figure 10.13 shows Mintzberg's six basic building blocks of organisational design:

- The *operating core* where basic work is produced – the factory floor, the operating theatre, the retail outlet.
- The *strategic apex* where the general management of the organisation occurs.
- The *middle line* – all those managers who stand between the strategic apex and the operating core.
- The *technostructure* – staff analysts who design the systems whereby the work processes of others are delivered and controlled. Included here are

	Benefits	**Difficulties/problems**
Centralisation	• Ability to achieve and control consistent strategy • Co-ordination of activities • Simpler control systems • Allocation of resources facilitated • Speedier strategic decision making	• Failure to achieve response to local conditions • Difficulties in developing general management capabilities • Cumbersome and costly central overheads
Devolution	*Operational* • Rapid response to specific or local problems • Improved motivation/ commitment *Strategic* • When environmental or decision-making complexity too great to be dealt with at apex of the organisation	• Definition of split of operational and strategic responsibilities • Excessive internal competition • Loss of corporate purpose • Lengthy referral processes and delayed decisions • Frustrated management • Complicated control procedures/new bureaucracies

Figure 10.12 Some benefits of centralisation and devolution

    engineers, accountants and computer specialists.
- The *support staff* – those who support the work of the operating core, such as secretarial, clerical and technical staff, catering.
- The *ideology* – which was referred to in Chapter 5 as the paradigm – consisting of the organisation's values and core beliefs.

The relative size and importance of these building blocks will vary with circumstances (see below), as will the methods by which work is *co-ordinated* within the organisation. The following methods of co-ordination exist:

ILLUSTRATION 10.3
Centralisation and devolution in Sheffield City Council

Many local authorities have been searching for structures which simultaneously give the advantages of devolution – particularly improved quality of services – while building a stronger corporate purpose. This is a difficult formula to find.

In 1990 the recently appointed chief executive of Sheffield City Council, Pamela Gordon, announced a major reorganisation of the management structure in order to meet five principles approved by the Council's Policy Committee:

- Ensuring the effective delivery of good-quality, value-for-money services.
- Operating within frameworks that promoted corporate working.
- Providing the advice which councillors needed.
- Cost-effective use of resources.
- Effective delivery of equal opportunities.

The existing senior management team of seventeen chief officers of service departments was to be trimmed (provisionally to eleven) and responsibilities allocated in new ways:

- A new central team was created, consisting of the chief executive, city treasurer (also acting as deputy), assistant director (responsible

- *Mutual adjustment* through informal contact between people in the operating core. This is very common in small, simple organisations where people work closely and informally together. It is also common in very complex situations, such as research and development projects.
- *Direct supervision* through the hierarchy. Work is supervised by instruction from the strategic apex, through the middle line to the operating core.
- *Standardisation of work processes* through systems which specify how work should be undertaken. It is usually the job of the analysts in the technostructure to design and develop these system of work standardisation.
- *Standardisation of outputs* – for example, through product or service specifications – is another means of co-ordination. This is particularly important where responsibility for separate value activities is divided within the organisation. Many organisations are now developing *service-level agreements* between departments in order to clarify the parameters of

for policy co-ordination and human resources) and city solicitor (also acting as head of administration).
- Working with this group was a new team of six directors responsible for planning, developing and co-ordinating the activities of their 'directorate' in line with overall corporate strategy.
- The directorates of education, housing and social services remained largely unchanged. A new area of operational services was created by combining cleansing and works departments. Arrangements for two other areas were on a temporary basis to allow a review of responsibilities. An existing chief officer was to co-ordinate the work of three previous departments (land and planning, employment/economic development, and environmental health), while another would co-ordinate arts/leisure and recreation services.
- Day-to-day management of departments was to be carried out by a second tier of management known as heads of service.

The overhaul was prompted by the chief executive's view that the existing management team was seriously inadequate in the way it operated. In particular, it had not provided a robust and co-ordinated lead to the work-force or an integrated view to members on key policy issues such as equal opportunities or resource allocation. She did not see this as the fault of individuals but the result of management structure. Chief officers had faced practical problems in trying to adopt a corporate and strategic role while coping with day-to-day management problems in their own departments.

Source: *Working for Sheffield*, September 1990.

service expected from, say, computer services, credit control, etc.
- *Standardisation of skills* – including knowledge – is an important co-ordinating mechanism in many professional activities (private and public sector). So the operating core of a professional service, such as a hospital or an architect's practice, functions smoothly because the operators share the same core knowledge and skills.
- *Standardisation of norms* – where employees share the same core beliefs – is particularly powerful in many voluntary organisations.

10.5.1 Choosing a configuration

The choice of configuration to support an organisation's strategies can best be thought of in terms of matching the organisation's configuration to its strategic situation through the choice of the two design parameters discussed above: namely, the *building blocks* and *co-ordinating mechanisms*.

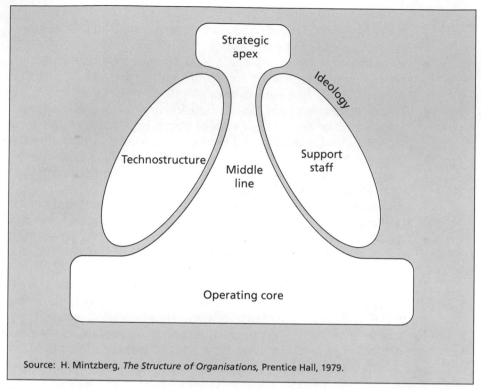

Source: H. Mintzberg, *The Structure of Organisations*, Prentice Hall, 1979.

Figure 10.13 The six basic parts of an organisation

Figure 10.14 summarises the key features of Mintzberg's six configurations, in terms of both the circumstances or situations to which each is best suited and also the 'shape' and *modus operandi* of the organisation – its building blocks and co-ordinating mechanisms. This relationship between organisational design and the situation in which the organisation is operating will be discussed in more detail in section 10.7 below.

One important addition to Mintzberg's organisational configurations which is increasingly found in practice is the *network organisation*,[15] and this has been included in Figure 10.14. This type of organisation has many similarities with the adhocracy, the major difference being the use of networking as the key co-ordinating mechanism, which is stronger and often more extensive than the mutual adjustment usually found in the adhocracy.

Although few organisations will fit neatly into just one of these stereotypes, they can be used to think through some important issues concerning the structure/strategy fit in an organisation:

● Managers can check out in Figure 10.14 which stereotype their current structure most resembles. More importantly, they can then describe the

	SITUATIONAL FACTORS		DESIGN PARAMETERS	
	Environment	Internal	Key part of organisation	Key co-ordinating mechanism
SIMPLE STRUCTURE	Simple/dynamic Hostile	Small Young Simple tasks CEO control	Strategic apex	Direct supervision
MACHINE BUREAUCRACY	Simple/static	Old Large Regulated tasks Technocrat control	Technostructure	Standardisation of work
PROFESSIONAL BUREAUCRACY	Complex/static	Simple systems Professional control	Operating core	Standardisation of skills
DIVISIONALISED	Simple/static Diversity	Old V. large Divisible tasks Middle-line control	Middle line	Standardisation of outputs
ADHOCRACY	Complex/dynamic	Often young Complex tasks Expert control	Operating core Support staff	Mutual adjustment
MISSIONARY	Simple/static	Middle-aged Often 'enclaves' Simple systems Ideological control	Ideology	Standardisation of norms
NETWORK ORGANISATION	Dynamic	Often young Professional control	Strategic apex or support staff	Networking and relational contracts

Source: Based on H. Mintzberg, *The Structuring of Organisations*, Prentice Hall, 1979.

Figure 10.14 Mintzberg's six organisational configurations, plus network organisations

situational factors (both external and internal) for their own organisation and see how closely these match the situation for which that particular configuration is best suited, as listed in Figure 10.14. For example, the simple structure is particularly appropriate for small companies in simple but dynamic environments.

● It is quite likely that changing circumstances will have created a mismatch between the configuration and the situation. This is where many difficulties occur in practice. For example, the small company may have grown and diversified so that the simple structure can no longer cope. Many public services had taken on features of professional bureaucracies during a period of little change and experienced considerable difficulty in adjusting parts of their organisation towards an adhocracy as a necessary response to a dynamic environment that required more flexibility and customisation of services.

● It should be remembered that the strategy/structure relationship operates both ways. So the configuration will influence how an organisation perceives its circumstances – both internal and external – and how it positions itself in terms of seeking out (or avoiding) particular types of strategic development. For example, the *machine bureaucracy*, which is characterised by high levels of work standardisation – usually contributing to cost competitiveness – will often regard segments of a market with high added value as undesirable, since they do not easily fit into current methods of work organisation. In this way, the paradigm of the organisation is protected by the organisational configuration. Figure 10.14 can be used as a checklist to challenge the paradigm and ask whether the current configuration really is appropriate to the situation the organisation faces.

10.6 Management systems and control

The discussion so far has looked at some of the parameters which can be used to match the organisational design with strategies. A key ingredient in this organisation design process is the *management systems*, particularly those relating to information, control and rewards. Illustration 10.4 shows that even in centrally planned economies there has been an increasing recognition of the importance of these issues to company performance. Often managers have too narrow a view of what constitutes management control in the strategic context. It is useful to think of control systems in two broad categories:

- Systems of *information and measurement*. This category would include financial systems such as budgets and variance analysis. However, other organisational objectives may need to be measured and controlled in different ways. Many organisations are attempting to develop a wider range of *performance indicators* which relate to the purposes identified in their strategic plan. Some of these may lend themselves to quantified measurement, such as sales targets or staff turnover. Others have to be dealt with more subjectively, such as some aspects of quality, ethical standards or competitive standing. It is important to recognise that measurement of strategic performance will almost certainly require a *mixture* of measures, only some of which will be genuinely quantifiable.
- Systems which *regulate* the behaviour of people rather than simply measuring the end result of their efforts. Reward systems are the most important example of this type of system.

10.6.1 Control through information and measurement[16]

The successful implementation of strategy will require that managers find ways of identifying how implementation is proceeding and the extent of variance from

ILLUSTRATION 10.4
State/company relationship changes in China

Even in centrally planned economies there is a growing recognition that the central planning authorities must develop frameworks and control mechanisms which encourage improved economic performance.

In 1991 the Guangdong provincial government in China published guiding principles aimed at invigorating state-owned large and medium-sized enterprises during the Five-Year Plan period (1991–5):

- The government will use laws and economic means, rather than administrative orders, to manage and supervise enterprises.
- Enterprises will keep at least 10 per cent of their profits to supplement their funds.
- To encourage enterprises to develop new products, profitable manufacturers may retain 1 per cent product sales, with hi-tech firms keeping 1.5 per cent.
- In adopting new technologies and developing new products, enterprises will be allowed to include instruments and equipment worth up to 50,000 yuan (about £5,000) in their production costs.
- The enterprises will have the right to sell certain quantities of their products that are under government control, with profits to be used only to expand production.
- Firms will be allowed to set prices on their products – except those goods directly under the state price control.
- Each city may choose two or three enterprises to experiment with the management styles of rural firms and foreign-invested firms. They will have the right to decide their own methods of payment, to employ and fire workers, and to use funds for technological renovation. They may also calculate their own production costs following international accounting practices.
- State-owned enterprises should try to improve their product quality and economic performance while strictly following government policies and financial regulations.

Source: *China Daily*, 11 August 1991.

what is expected. The underlying notion in such forms of control is that, if people are clear what is expected of them, and are provided with information that shows the extent to which these expectations are, or are not, being met, they will change their behaviour, or redirect their energies or attention, to remedy the situation. Although the overall design of such controls needs to be considered in terms of the strategic direction and context of the organisation, there are perhaps some general guidelines for the design of control systems.

- *Distinguish between various levels of control.* It has been suggested that control needs to take place at three levels: strategic, management and operational. For example, a venture into new overseas markets would require controlling at the strategic level through an overall budget, at the management level by monitoring expenditures and motivating employees, and also at the operational level by ensuring that routine tasks are properly performed.
- *Create responsibility centres.* The complexity of strategic change usually requires the subdivision of control within a company. These smaller units can be regarded as responsibility centres. They are identifiable parts of the whole organisation and are responsible for a certain aspect of the business; their performance is measured and controlled accordingly. There are a number of bases on which this responsibility can be apportioned, as shown in Figure 10.15. The choice of responsibility centre must be in line with the degree of devolution within the organisation, as discussed in section 10.4. In this way, investment centres are appropriate for financial control and so on.
- *Select key factors and collect relevant information.* It is crucial to identify factors critical to the success or failure of the strategy, and to develop performance indicators for these factors. Value chain analysis should assist with this process.
- *Allow diversity in control.* There is a temptation in many organisations to simplify control systems to the extent that they do not adequately reflect the degree of diversity in the organisation's activities. An obvious example is the lack of profitability of new products during their early days. The profitability of *cash cows* and *stars* would not be expected to be the same, since the strategic purpose of those two groups of products is different. Their contribution to the company may have to be measured and controlled differently.
- *Avoid misleading measurements.* Many aspects of strategy are difficult to measure quantitatively. This can lead to situations where the pressure to produce quantitative measures distorts the process of control and, in some cases, leads to poor performance. The police force has a problem in this respect as the assessment of how well law and order is being maintained is very difficult. In the absence of any precise measures there is a tendency to develop *surrogate measures*, such as the number of arrests or convictions, or the proportion of cases solved. A police force which had extremely good relations with its local community might score badly by these measures.
- *Beware of negative monitoring.* There is a danger that systems will be concerned with purely negative monitoring of performance: for example, with highlighting variances which are below plan. The result can be that departments and individuals become overconcerned with minimising the risk of such negative variances.

Type	Examples	Control exerted over	Typical controls
1. Revenue	Sales department	Income	Sales targets
2. Cost centre (a) Standard cost centres (b) Discretionary expense centres	Production dept (manufacturing) R & D Administrative dept.	Cost of labour, materials, services, etc. Total expenditure	Detailed budgeting Standard product costing Budget
3. Profit centres	Internal services (e.g. design) Product or market division Subsidiary company	Profit	P & L accounts
4. Investment centres	Subsidiary company	Return on capital	Complete financial accounts

Figure 10.15 Different types of responsibility centre

10.6.2   Control through reward systems[17]

Control of strategy implementation is not only pursued through systems of information and measurement. The design of *reward systems* is also a key element in creating a climate for strategic change. The need is to decide what the most important issues are for the reward system to deal with in order to influence the behaviour of people within the organisation. Reward systems are also important through their symbolic impact, since they are a visible signal of the types of behaviour which is to be encouraged in the organisation. Rewards include both monetary reward systems, such as graded pay schemes, bonuses, profit-sharing schemes and productivity schemes, and also non-monetary reward systems, such as promotion and increased status.

It is also important to remember that reward systems have both positive and negative impacts. The failure to achieve rewards, or the withdrawal of rewards, may be perceived as punishment. So rewards also need to be tied into the organisation's *appraisal system* both as a means of linking rewards to personal targets and as a basis for identifying personal development needs.

In addition, the *nature* of the rewards needs to be considered in terms of the objectives to be achieved: for example, if long-term growth of profits is the aim then rewards based on short-term achievement of sales targets are not likely to be helpful. Illustration 10.5 shows how one company attempted to relate rewards to the changing nature of its business.

This section considers how reward systems might affect the behaviour of people and therefore be an important design feature in supporting strategic change. This is done by considering some of the key issues that are likely to arise in implementing strategy, and how reward systems might relate to these issues:

- *Short- versus long-run perspectives.* As has already been indicated, the nature of rewards needs to vary according to the time horizons. In general, the shorter the time horizons, the more important it is that any incentives such as bonuses should be based on clear quantitative measures of performance relating to the short term. On the other hand, the longer the time horizon, the more likely it is that more qualitative measures may be appropriate, unless quantitative measures can be made relevant to long-term performance.

- *Risk aversion and risk taking.* Organisations wishing to encourage greater risk taking are likely to find that developing qualitative measures of performance upon which to base bonus awards or share options is beneficial. Quantitative measures of performance may result in behaviour which avoids failure rather than risk-taking behaviour to achieve results.

- *Rewards for individuals.* An important issue to consider is how reward systems can or should reflect individuals' *capabilities, effort and job satisfaction.* The Human Resources Movement of the 1930s[18] saw job performance as primarily related to job satisfaction. Others have seen rewards and payment as a major stimulus to effort and the emphasis has been placed on payment by results (e.g. piecework, sales commission). In other organisations, rewards tend to reflect capability: for example, where skilled workers are paid more than unskilled workers. It is important to bear in mind that reward systems which are geared to only one aspect, such as effort, can have a negative effect on people's performance in other ways.

- *Individual or group rewards.* Rewarding individuals for effort and performance can prove difficult unless the organisational structure and the systems of control allow an individual's performance to be isolated from the efforts of others. From a strategic point of view, therefore, it may be an important consideration whether reward systems should seek to influence the behaviour of individuals or groups[19]. Figure 10.16 summarises some of the pros and cons of each system. This list is useful in choosing reward systems, since it helps in matching the conditions described in the table with the type of strategic change being undertaken.

- *Business unit versus corporate perspective.* Care has to be taken to balance the corporate interest against the business-unit interests. The greater the independence of the units from the centre or from each other, the more likely it is that unit-based reward systems are sensible. Similarly, the more removed the individual manager or group within the unit is from influencing corporate performance, the more sensible it is to have unit-based reward systems. However, real problems occur in the case of divisional or unit-based general managers and directors. Such managers typically have dual

ILLUSTRATION 10.5
Changes in reward systems at ICL

Reward systems may need to change in order to support a new emphasis in an organisation's strategies.

During the latter part of the 1980s ICL, like many other computer manufacturers across the world, faced a rapidly growing market but one which was fiercely competitive and where major structural changes were occurring as smaller and cheaper computing equipment became available. As part of its approach to meeting this challenge, the organisation was keen to introduce a reward system which – at least partly – related pay to performance.

However, this was a major change from the reward systems it inherited as a result of multi-mergers during the 1960s and 1970s. In the early 1980s pay determination was through an annual salary review negotiated by unions for all employees and awarded across the board. Pay scales were adjusted upwards and individuals retained their position within the scale. *Separately*, and at a different time of year, managers would allocate a *merit* fund to progress individuals through their grade. This system was seen to have several major problems as a basis for relating pay to performance. First, the merit fund (typically 3 per cent of salaries) was not large enough to provide *significant* discrimination, and second, managers found it difficult to refuse some staff an award because it was undertaken as a separate exercise.

The first change was to combine the two systems into a single annual pay award which helped in eliminating the latter difficulty. However, in 1986 it was decided not to negotiate a general increase but to move to an annual review of salaries based on management discretion and related to performance, commitment and contribution of the individual employee. The unions would not agree to this change but, significantly, did not refuse the go-ahead.

The change proved to be critical in integrating a number of elements of the human resource strategy – objective setting, appraisal and pay – with the overall strategy of ICL. These links became an important part of the management agenda in many organisations in the late 1980s and early 1990s.

Source: D. F. Beattie and F. M. K. Tampoe, 'Human resource planning for ICL', *Long Range Planning*, 23 (1), pp. 17–28.

influences: both on their unit performance and in contributing to the corporate well-being. Care has to be taken to develop a sensible balance of rewards.

Aspects to be considered	Schemes based on individual performance	Schemes based on group performance
Managerial contribution to company performance	(a) Appropriate where individual's contribution is relatively independent (b) Appropriate where performance standards are relatively variable, i.e. some managers at much higher standard than others	(a) Appropriate where individuals' contributions are relatively interdependent (b) Appropriate where performance standards are relatively uniform
Type of behaviour	Encourages entrepreneurial, self-reliant or creative types of behaviour	Encourages greater co-operation, co-ordination and team management
Flexibility of scheme	Scheme can be negotiated individually, or can be uniform	Scheme can be negotiated individually, but is more likely to be standard or uniform
Administration	Administrative requirements relatively great	Administrative requirements relatively slight
Discrimination	Relatively easy to achieve high discrimination between different levels of performance	Discrimination can be achieved between different groups or teams, but not so easily between individuals

Source: Angela M. Bowey (ed.), *Handbook of Salary and Wage Systems* (2nd edn), Gower, 1982, p. 254.

Figure 10.16 Individual or group incentives

10.7 Influences on organisational design[20]

The previous section has discussed the elements of organisational design: namely, *centralisation/devolution*; organisational *configurations* and *systems* of control/reward. These elements need to work collectively to support the organisation's strategies. Typical styles of organisation develop to support particular strategies: for example, the long-standing stereotypes of *mechanistic* and *organic* organisations (see Figure 10.17). However, the most important issue is how this style should be matched to the organisation's circumstances. This section will briefly outline those factors which should influence organisational design and will relate back to the organisational stereotypes outlined in Figure 10.14 above.

10.7.1 Type of strategy

The discussion of organisational configurations in section 10.5 acknowledged the importance of matching organisational design to the types of strategy which the organisation is pursuing. It also pointed out that this is a two-way process: organisational configuration also influences preferences for particular types of strategy.

Mechanistic	Organic
1. Specialised differentiation and definition of tasks in the organisation	1. Contributive nature of special knowledge to the total concerns of the organisation
2. Hierarchical supervision and reconciliation of problems	2. Redefinition of tasks and responsibilities through interaction with others
3. Precise definition of job responsibilities, methods, rights and obligations	3. Commitment to the organisation beyond any technical/precise definition; such commitment more valued than loyalty
4. (Perceived) location of superior knowledge at the top of the hierarchy	4. Network structure of control, authority and communication
5. Vertical interaction of individuals between subordinate and superior	5. Omniscience not imputed to senior executives; knowledge located anywhere in the organisation and this location may become centre of authority for given issue
6. Insistence on loyalty to organisation and obedience to superiors	
7. More prestige attached to job (and local) than to more general knowledge, experience and skills	6. Lateral rather than vertical direction of communication
8. Formalised systems, rules and communications	7. Communication consists of information and advice rather than instructions and decisions

Figure 10.17 Characteristics of mechanistic and organic systems in organisations

So different generic strategies will often require different forms of organisational design. The organisation following a low-price strategy will need to find means of ensuring a cost-efficient operation with an emphasis on cost control; whereas the organisation following a differentiation strategy may need higher degrees of creativity and, probably, a rapid response to problems and opportunities.

The likelihood is that the low-price strategy will require a more mechanistic system of control, with clear job responsibilities, frequent and detailed reports on organisational efficiency and cost, and a clear delineation of responsibility for budgets and expenditure. The structure for an organisation following a differentiation strategy, on the other hand, might need to be more organic in nature, with looser controls, a greater encouragement of informality and creativity within a more decentralised structure, but a good deal of co-ordination between its various functions. The emphasis is likely to be more on groups of managers relating to problems and opportunities than individual managers or departments being concerned with specific job functions. An organisation that seeks to follow differentiation and low-price strategies for different parts of its business is likely to experience conflicts in terms of organisational design.

10.7.2 Operational processes and technology

The nature of the tasks undertaken by the operating core of an organisation has an important influence on the various aspects of organisational design. It is known that there are links between the type of production process and the approach to management.[21] Mass production systems require the standardisation of process (i.e. the *machine bureaucracy*) and result in greater direction and control by senior managers; there is also a tendency towards centralisation. Firms with a less standardised manufacturing process are more likely to have more devolved and informal decision-making processes.

The more sophisticated and complex the technology of an organisation, the more elaborate the structure becomes for a number of reasons. First, it is likely that a good deal of responsibility and power will devolve to those specialists concerned with the technology itself. The organisation tends to operate as an *adhocracy*. In turn this may create the need for liaison between such specialists and the operating core of the business, giving rise to an increase in integrating and co-ordinating mechanisms, such as committees, joint working groups, project teams and so on.

More sophisticated technology can give rise to increases in centralisation or devolution. For example, in some organisations the advent of more sophisticated information technology has allowed the operating core to cope with far more complex problems than hitherto; in retailing, the ability to record sales by electronic scanning in the store (EPOS) has provided retailers with greatly enhanced knowledge of rates of sales and stockturn by product. This has facilitated tighter central decision making on merchandise planning and store layout. On the other hand, the same technology might also allow devolution by providing systems which can be used locally.

10.7.3 Organisational type

Other influences on organisational design stem from the size, accountability and culture of organisations:

- It is inconceivable that all aspects of a *large* and *diverse* corporation could be organised except by splitting the tasks of management. The larger the corporations, therefore, the more likelihood there is of *divisionalisation.*[22] The large corporation is also likely to move towards some form of devolution, as discussed in section 10.4.
- The nature of an organisation's *accountability* will also affect organisational design. This is well illustrated by nationalised industries and other public-sector bodies. Where government involvement is high, the issue of public accountability becomes an important influence: it is likely to give rise to a centralised structure of decision making where both power and accountability are in the hands of an easily identifiable team or individual at the centre. As a result, public authorities have tended to operate through *strategic planning*. However, the price that has often been paid for this ease of public accountability is an inability to respond quickly to market and other environmental changes.
- In commercial enterprises where there is pronounced dependency on some *external body*, such as a parent company or a powerful shareholder group, the same sort of result comes about. There is a tendency towards centralisation of decision making and, because external standards of performance are imposed, a more mechanistic style of management.
- *Owner control* may also be an important influence on structure. For example, many companies which are owner-controlled operate a *simple* structure and retain a high degree of centralisation, even when they grow quite large, as the influence of the owner-manager continues.
- The importance of organisation culture has already been discussed in Chapters 2 and 5, and reference has been made to the *cultural web*. Organisational structures over time come to reflect and support the organisational *paradigm*.
- The *defender*[23] organisation referred to in Chapter 5 tends to specialise rather than diversify in terms of strategy. Structurally, it is likely to be functional, permitting an emphasis on specialisation at most levels and emphasising efficiency. Commonly, defenders will operate as *machine bureaucracies*.
- The *prospector*, on the other hand, seeks actively for new opportunities so as to be first in the market. Here there is likely to be much less emphasis on control and efficiency and more on innovation. There may well be a tendency to devolve and minimise top-down control. The style of management will be organic, encouraging flair and risk taking, and there may be complex systems of co-ordination with, for example, specialist co-ordinating roles. Typically, prospectors would configure the organisation

like an *adhocracy*. Influence and power are likely to be lodged primarily in development areas of the business, such as marketing and R & D.

10.7.4   The environment

The importance of the nature of the environment to the choice of an organisation's configuration has already been outlined in Figure 10.14. It is also influential on the other design factors of centralisation and control systems (see Figure 10.18):

- In an environment which is simple and static, organisations gear themselves to operational efficiency. They standardise their operations and their management. Management styles tend to be mechanistic and centralised. Mintzberg[24] calls this type of organisation *centralised bureaucratic*. Examples are some mass production companies or raw material producers.
- Increasing complexity is handled by devolving decision responsibility to specialists. This means that organisations in complex environments tend to be more decentralised at least for operational purposes. Hospitals and universities are good examples of those organisations that have traditionally been in fairly stable or predictable environments, but ones of a complex nature. They are *decentralised bureaucratic* organisations.
- In dynamic conditions the need is to increase the extent to which managers are capable of sensing what is going on around them, identifying change and responding to it. It is unlikely that bureaucratic styles of management will encourage such behaviour, so a more organic style is likely to be adopted. Mintzberg calls this type of organisation *centralised organic*.
- However, this may not be the only response to dynamic conditions. In situations of high levels of competition – which require a rapid response but also overall control at a strategic level (the extreme example being a *crisis*) – it may be necessary to revert to highly centralised decisions by a dominant leader, if only temporarily.
- Where the environment is both complex and dynamic, Mintzberg suggests that *decentralised organic* organisations may be found. Some of the firms operating at the frontiers of scientific development are in these conditions. Their environment is changing so fast that they need the speed and flexibility that organic styles of management provide; and the level of complexity is such that they must devolve responsibility and authority to specialists.

Illustration 10.6 shows how a major change in the financial services industry – the so-called Big Bang – had significant implications for the way in which companies were structured and managed.

	Stable	**Dynamic**
Complex	Decentralised bureaucratic, e.g. hospitals	Decentralised organic, e.g. advanced electronics
Simple	Centralised bureaucratic, e.g. mass production	Centralised organic, e.g. retailing *or* Decentralised bureaucratic

Source: Adapted from H. Mintzberg, *The Structuring of Organisations,* Prentice Hall, 1979, p. 268. Reproduced with permission.

Figure 10.18 Environmental influences on organisational structure

10.8 Summary

This chapter has concentrated on structural and design implications of strategic change. It has been argued that strategy implementation is effected through the people in the organisation, and that the way in which those people are organised is of key importance. To help readers understand how this might be accomplished, the chapter has reviewed the various forms of structure in common use, together with their advantages and disadvantages. It then examined the sorts of influence from inside and outside the organisation that may affect organisational design.

Given conflicting influences on organisational design, how is it sensible to set about dealing with the problem? There is no formula for doing this, no right answer. It is again a question of analysis and, in the end, judgement. However, it might be useful to ask these questions:

● What are the influences inside and outside the organisation which affect how it should be structured? The influences discussed in this chapter should provide a basis for answering this question.

ILLUSTRATION 10.6
Coping with 'Big Bang' in the investment banking industry

Major changes in an organisation's environment require a fundamental rethink of structures and systems and not just quick-fix solutions.

In 1987 the computerisation and reform of the UK stock exchange – referred to as 'Big Bang' – was designed to attract internationally mobile investment money to London. The reforms allowed banks and other outsiders into the stock market for the first time. Commercial banks, which had little or no experience of securities and investment banking, attempted to catch up quickly by paying huge salaries to attract experienced staff and acquiring broking and jobbing firms at high cost. As a result many banks ended up with an unsustainably high cost structure and no real depth of underpinning to this new area of business. Eventually banks had to accept the reality that their new investment banking subsidiaries were complex multiproduct, international businesses which needed skilled management and sophisticated control and information systems. Four types of change were introduced in many banks:

- The traditional commercial banking managers had to become more experienced at managing in a trading situation. Equally, the stockbrokers – who had been used to managing their own small

- Of these, which are the critical influences – that is, those that will affect performance more than the others, or those that simply override all others?
- Given the identification of these critical influences, it may be that some clear structural implications emerge, or it could be that there are options. If there are options, what are the advantages and disadvantages of each, in the context of the strategy that the organisation wishes to follow?
- The final point is too often overlooked. No matter how elegant a structure is, the most important point is that it has to be workable. How will the structure be put into effect? If divisionalisation of a holding company is recommended, exactly what is going to happen to the chairs of the many virtually autonomous businesses that are to be rationalised into a few divisions? Who is to report to whom in this new organisation? Where will decisions of what sort be taken? If substantial decentralisation is to take place in the divisions, will senior management accept it and will junior management be able to handle it? Part of the evaluation of structural alternatives, just as for strategic options, is to consider feasibility.

businesses – had to develop skills of management in the much larger business situation. Both of these were achieved through a combination of on-the-job experience, training and bringing in some new blood from outside the industry.

- As competition for staff diminished, remuneration policies were shifted. The golden packages available immediately after 'Big Bang' disappeared. Although payment by results remained a key aspect of pay, there was a move away from rigid formulae-driven bonuses to the use of discretionary bonuses. Some firms also experimented with equity schemes as part of the remuneration package.
- Piecemeal systems developed immediately after 'Big Bang' were drawn together and integrated as management demanded better information to help them to assess and control the risk profile of their investment strategies.
- Major structural changes occurred in many organisations. Immediately following 'Big Bang' the component elements (functions) of investment were left alone to trade as they had in the past. But slowly these functions were integrated as part of the need to reduce cost and cut out duplication. This philosophy had also started to break down the barriers between trading and other aspects of traditional banking – for example, drawing together securities and corporate finance functions.

Source: *Financial Times*, 4 November 1991.

It should be clear that organisation design will not in itself ensure the successful implementation of strategy. The way in which strategic change is managed – in particular, the management of people – is the most important ingredient and will be discussed in Chapter 11.

References

1. Some of these early writings are to be found in D. Pugh, *Organisation Theory*, Penguin, 1984.
2. These definitions come from T. Burns and G. Stalker, *The Management of Innovation*, Tavistock, 1968.
3. The advantages and disadvantages of functional structures are discussed in T. Peters and R. Waterman, *In Search of Excellence*, Harper and Row, 1982, and H. Mintzberg, *The Structuring of Organisations*, Prentice Hall, 1979.
4. This view of divisionalisation as a response to diversity was put forward by A. D. Chandler, *Strategy and Structure*, MIT Press, 1962, and supported by others such as D. Channon, *The Strategy and Structure of British Enterprise*, Macmillan, 1973.
5. The benefits of horizontal integration are discussed in M. Porter, *Competitive Advantage*, Free Press, 1985.
6. Matrix structures are discussed in K. Knight, 'Matrix organisation: a review', *Journal of Management Studies*, vol. 13, May, (1976), pp. 111–30.
7. 'Functional with subsidiaries' is a category used by R. Rumelt, *Strategy, Structure and Economic*

Performance, Harvard University Press, 1974.

8. A good general text on multinational corporations is Y. Doz, *Strategic Management in Multinational Companies*, Pergamon, 1986.
9. C. Bartlett and S. Ghoshal, *Managing Across Borders: The transnational corporation*, Harvard Business School Press, 1989; C. Bartlett and S. Ghoshal, 'Tap tour subsidiaries for global reach', *Harvard Business Review*, vol. 64, no. 6, (1986), pp. 87–94.
10. See K. Scholes, 'Learning to live with devolution', *Sheffield Business School*, 1991.
11. M. Goold and A. Campbell, *Strategies and Styles*, Basil Blackwell, 1987.
12. See H. Mintzberg and J. B. Quinn, *The Strategy Process*, (2nd edn), Prentice Hall, 1991, p. 672.
13. This issue of the centre/division relationship has had a good deal of debate, particularly in the public-sector context of the early 1990s. See, for example, K. Scholes, 'Learning to live with devolution', *Sheffield Business School*, 1991, M. Clarke and J. Stewart, *The Enabling Council*, Local Government Management Board, 1988; *The Role of the Centre*, Local Government Management Board, 1991.
14. Mintzberg, *The Structuring of Organisations*, Prentice Hall, 1979. These configurations are also discussed fully in Mintzberg and J. B. Quinn, *The Strategy Process*, 2nd Edition, Prentice Hall, 1991.
15. Network organisations as an important configuration are discussed in R. E. Miles and C. C. Snow, 'Fit, failure and the hall of fame', *California Management Review*, vol. 26, no. 3, (1984) pp. 10–28; R. E. Miles and C. C. Snow, 'Organisations: New concepts for new forms', *California Management Review*, vol. 28, no. 3, (1986), pp. 62–73; and J. Naisbitt, *Megatrends*, Futura, 1984.
16. R. N. Anthony and J. Deardon, *Management*

Control Systems: Text and cases (3rd edn), Irwin, 1976, remains a useful reference text on management control systems. Other references which discuss control and information systems in a strategic context are S. Bungay and M. Goold, 'Creating a strategic control system', *Long Range Planning*, vol. 24, no. 3, (1991) pp. 32–9; A. Gupta and V. Godvindarajan, 'Knowledge flows and the structure of control within multinational corporations', *Academy of Management Review*, vol. 16, no. 4, (1991) pp. 768–92; and J. Ward, 'Information, management and organisational strategy' in D. Faulkner and G. Johnson (eds), *The Challenge of Strategic Management*, Kogan Page, 1993.
17. A discussion of the relationship between rewards and strategy can be found in J. R. Galbraith and R. K. Kazanjian, *Strategy Implementation: Structure, systems and process*, West, 1986.
18. See F. J. Roethlisberger and W. J. Dickson, *Management and the Worker*, Wiley, 1964, p. 517.
19. A. Bowey (ed.), *Handbook of Salary and Wage Systems* (2nd edn), Gower, 1982.
20. Mintzberg, op. cit., and Mintzberg and Quinn (both reference 14) provide the most comprehensive discussion of the relationship between organisational design and situational factors (both internal and external).
21. See J. Woodward, *Industrial Organisation: Theory and practice*, Oxford University Press, 1965.
22. See Chandler (reference 4) and P. Lawrence and J. Lorsch, *Organisation and Environment*, Irwin, 1969.
23. See Chapter 5 and R. E. Miles and C. C. Snow, *Organisational Strategy: Structure and process*, McGraw-Hill, 1978.
24. See reference 14.

Recommended key readings

The different organisational structures are clearly explained in J. R. Galbraith and R. K. Kazanjian, *Strategy Implementation: Structure, systems and process*, West, 1986.

The centralisation/devolution considerations are discussed in M. Goold and A. Campbell, *Strategies and Styles*, Basil/Blackwell, 1987.

Organisational configurations are covered comprehensively in H. Mintzberg, *The Structuring of Organisations*, Prentice Hall, 1979, and H. Mintzberg and J. B. Quinn, *The Strategy Process*, (2nd edn), Prentice Hall, 1991.

Organisational design issues in multinational corporations are covered in C. Bartlett and S. Ghoshal, *Managing Across Borders: The transnational corporation*, Harvard Business School Press, 1989, and Y. Doz, *Strategic Management in Multinational Companies*, Pergamon, 1986.

Work assignments

10.1 Draw up organisation charts for a number of organisations with which you are familiar and/or any of the case studies in the book. Why are the organisations structured in this way?

10.2 Compare the structure of Shell (Illustration 10.1) and ICI (Illustration 10.2). To what extent do you think they are in line with current thinking on organisational structure for multinational corporations (see Figures 10.6 and 10.7). Would you recommend any changes in approach?

10.3 *Make a critical appraisal of the importance of the centre/division relationship in underpinning the strategic development of organisations (see Figures 10.8 to 10.11). Illustrate your answer by describing (with justification) the relationships which you feel would be most appropriate for the following organisations:*

(a) News Corporation*   *(d) Sheffield City Council (Illustration 10.3)*
(b) Burton*   *(e) an organisation of your choice.*
(c) Peugeot*
Refer to Goold and Campbell in the recommended key readings to help with your answer.

10.4 By referring to Figures 10.13 and 10.14 which of Mintzberg's organisational configurations best fits the situation of each of the organisations in assignment 3. To what extent is the actual configuration of the organisation in line with this expectation, and what are the implications of any mismatches?

10.5 From the point of view of a manufacturing company in China, how important are the changes in regulations and control described in Illustration 10.4 in supporting a more entrepreneurial strategy and moving towards international competitiveness? What other changes would you recommend?

10.6 Compare the reward systems in an organisation of your choice with the system in ICL described in Illustration 10.5. What are the main differences, why do they exist and how appropriate is each reward system to the strategic development of the organisation?

10.7 *By using specific examples from your answers to the previous assignments explain how the various aspects of organisational design need to fit together to support an organisation's strategies. How close are theory and practice? Refer to Mintzberg and Quinn in the recommended key readings to assist with your answer.*

10.8 By referring to the issues of organisational design in this chapter and resource allocation in Chapter 9 compare and contrast the key differences you would expect to find between the approach of an organisation operating in a relatively stable environment as against another organisation operating in a turbulent environment.

* This refers to a case study in the Text and Cases version of this book.

CHAPTER 11

Managing strategic change

11.1 Introduction

Much of this book has been concerned with concepts of strategy, and with tools for analysing and evaluating strategic issues. However, strategic management, and strategic change in particular, is also concerned with the *process* of management and the *action* of managers. Building on the mechanisms for managing change in such areas as recruitment and training, introduced in Chapter 9, and the importance of organisational design and organisational behaviour, discussed in Chapter 10, this chapter concentrates on the activities of managers in *managing strategic change*.

Managing strategic change has been written about in various ways. Some writers have taken a rather mechanistic approach, suggesting that there are a set of 'levers' for change which managers can employ. Other writers have emphasised the role of the individual as change agent, sometimes laying particular stress on the charisma and vision of the leader. In this chapter both the role of the leader and the role of the mechanisms he or she can employ are reviewed. However, the central argument here is that such action as is taken must address the powerful influence of the *paradigm* and the *cultural web* on the strategy being followed by the organisation.

Figure 11.1 provides a structure for the chapter. The chapter begins by revisiting some of the arguments in Chapter 2, building on these to explain two frameworks for understanding the processes of managing strategic change, one of which is more appropriate for helping to explain incremental change, and the other for explaining more fundamental strategic change.

Section 11.3 then considers how the need for strategic change can be diagnosed. The problems of managing strategic change occur because organisations tend to be resistant to change for at least three, often linked, reasons:

- As shown in Chapter 2, the strategic direction of an organisation builds up a *momentum* of its own which may be reinforced by success.
- The *culture* of the organisation is likely to support this momentum of strategy. These two linked factors may result in organisational inertia when it comes to change.

- Faced with change there may also be political resistance within and around the organisation (see Chapter 5).

In this context, section 11.4 considers change processes in terms of the role of change agents and the action they might employ to overcome resistance and manage successful change. The term *change agent* is used rather than leader because, although it may be that one individual takes the lead in effecting change, this is not always the case. Change agency is reviewed in terms of tactics and styles of managing change, and also the characteristics of successful change agents.

The chapter concludes with an integrating section which pulls together the arguments in this chapter, and links them to some of the themes running through the book.

11.2 Understanding processes of strategic change

Chapter 2 showed that organisations change in different ways. In the main, strategic change in organisations is *incremental*, with occasional more *transfor-*

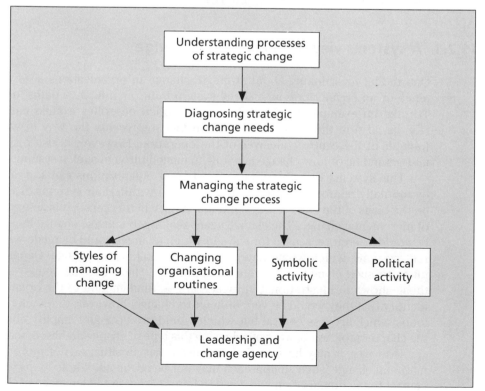

Figure 11.1 A framework for managing strategic change

mational changes. Arguably, it is beneficial for an organisation to change incrementally. In so doing it will build on the skills, routines and beliefs of those in the organisation, so change can be efficient, probably smooth and most likely win the commitment of those in the organisation. However, Chapter 2 also pointed out that such incremental change may well take place *because* it is within the paradigm and routines of those in the organisation, even if environmental or competitive pressures would suggest the need for more fundamental change. There is then a risk of strategic drift and deteriorating performance.

More *transformational* change may come about either because the organisation is faced with major external events that demand such large-scale change, or because the organisation anticipates such changes and therefore initiates action to make major shifts in its own strategy, or because the cumulative effects of strategic drift lead to deteriorating performance and require transformational strategic change.

In considering different means of managing strategic change, thought needs to be given to which approaches reviewed in this chapter are more or less appropriate to incremental or transformational change. Comments on this are made as the chapter progresses. However, it is also useful to consider two frameworks which help explain incremental and transformational change processes, and allow the reader to consider appropriate action for each.

11.2.1 A systems view of incremental change

One model for thinking about strategic change in organisations sees the existence of an organisation as a social system built on 'influence paths' or 'loops'. To take an example see Illustration 11.1, which describes a child care centre (Kindercare) in the USA. The model, in fact, represents the way in which the founder of the centre conceives of the operation. However, it also provides an understanding of how change might be managed through such a system.

This systems view therefore suggests that organisations can and do change by mutually reinforcing and amplifying stimuli within their systems. It is change on the basis of the current ways of doing things: in this sense, it is an explanation of incremental change. The change agent seeking to manage change incrementally would, therefore, search for ways in which changes could be made within current systems, which would have the effect of amplifying change. Gauging resistance to such change is, of course, important. There may be 'loops' similar to those shown in Illustration 11.1, which are so fundamental to the organisation's identity that they would be very difficult to change; however, there may be other loops which are less central but which would promote and amplify change.[1] As the chapter progresses, ways of achieving this type of change are discussed further.

However, it may have to be recognised that, in situations of more transformational change, such an approach may not be adequate. Whole loops which are central to the organisation may need to be replaced: in the language of this book, change may need to be outside the paradigm and the current routines, rather than within them.

11.2.2   Unfreezing and the management of strategic change[2]

Other explanations of change suggest that it takes place by more substantial shifts resulting from an unfreezing of the paradigm. Figure 11.2 shows how such change might take place through challenge, information building and experimentation. However, it needs to be recognised that, at the different stages described in Figure 11.2, there is a likelihood that the powerful effect of the paradigm will act to promote conformity around the existing strategy. The stages in the model can be related to change processes as follows (and it can be seen that a number can be related to styles in the strategic decision making discussed in section 2.4.1):

- A deteriorating market position may act over time as an *unfreezing* mechanism and lead to a growing sense of anticipation, in which people try to make sense of rumours and signals, which may contribute to an ill-defined but *felt need for change*. At this early stage, however, problems may be made sense of within the paradigm, thus contributing to further strategic drift.
- This may lead to a situation of *flux* or *crisis* in the organisation, in which competing views of causes of, and remedies for, the problems surface.
- This debate gives rise to and is fed by *information building* as executives attempt to check, test or find means of supporting their position, a stage which is likely to be a lengthy, iterative process (see section 2.4.1). Again, however, it may be that this information building is driven by the organisational paradigm – that information is deemed meaningful because it 'makes sense', or is overlooked because it is outside the experience of people in the organisation.
- Conflict and new information may contribute to individuals or groups questioning fundamental assumptions and arguing for quite different strategic concepts. These may then be tried out in practice – a process of *experimentation* – and, if successful, this could lead to the emergence of a new paradigm.
- Members of the organisation, faced with such disruption, are likely to require a 'safety net' for the future. It may be that they will be ready to relate to the emerging new paradigm, but it may be that they revert to the old. In either event, *refreezing* processes, which will be discussed later in this chapter, are then likely to occur. These confirm the organisation validity of the changed or existing paradigm.

The framework suggests that, for strategic change to take place, unfreezing mechanisms or triggers for change may be necessary; that discord or flux, as well as information collection and experimentation, can be productive in so far as they help challenge the paradigm; and that there need to be means of refreezing or consolidating a changed paradigm. There will, however, also be pressures,

ILLUSTRATION 11.1
Managing change at Kindercare

Mapping the system of loops that makes up the functions of a child care centre can help us see how change can be managed.

Kindercare is a child care centre in the USA, founded by Perry Mendel, which approximately doubled in size every three years for fifteen years. The map drawn here displays the system of loops that, in Perry Mendel's mind, explains how Kindercare operated to meet customer needs.

Several loops responsible for the rapid growth of Kindercare are built around the concept of 'innovative child care': for example, more innovative child care leads to more teacher satisfaction, which leads to more retention of motivated ex-schoolteachers, which leads to even more innovative child care.

Or, considering one of the major loops responsible for rapid growth: providing innovative child care gives parents good feelings that make them eager to pay for services that result in revenues, which invite entrepreneurial opportunities, which demand the development of professional management and financial resources, which result in both retaining motivated ex-schoolteachers and acquiring land and buildings required for providing innovative child care.

Thus, a little increase in innovative child care results in continuously more innovative child care and, at the same time, in continuously more Kindercare revenue. Once such loops are identified, they provide a means of managing strategy development and change in an organisation.

Source: Adapted from M. G. Bougon and J. Komocar, 'Directing strategic change: a dynamic holistic approach', in Anne Huff (ed.), *Mapping Strategic Thought*, Wiley, 1990.

perhaps even a natural tendency, in the stages of flux, information building and experimentation, for existing assumptions and routines to exert pressures for conformity. The extent to which this occurs is likely to depend both on the strength of stimulus for change and the effectiveness of the levers and mechanisms for change employed to achieve the sort of challenge and questioning required within the organisation.

11.3 Diagnosing strategic change needs

There is, then, a need to assess what type and magnitude of change is appropriate in an organisation. There are two key requirements of such a diagnosis. The

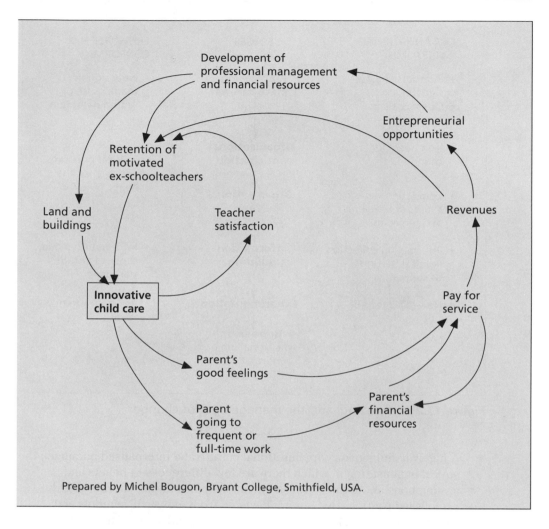

Development of
professional management
and financial resources

Entrepreneurial
opportunities

Retention of
motivated
ex-schoolteachers

Land and
buildings

Teacher
satisfaction

Revenues

**Innovative
child care**

Pay for
service

Parent's
good feelings

Parent
going to
frequent or
full-time work

Parent's
financial
resources

Prepared by Michel Bougon, Bryant College, Smithfield, USA.

first is to assess the extent to which incremental or transformational change is required. The second is to identify the specific barriers to change that exist.

11.3.1 Detecting strategic drift

Incremental strategic change is more typical within an organisation, and much less disruptive, than transformational change. However, it is important to gauge when incremental change has given rise to strategic drift and therefore in what circumstances more fundamental change may be required. Determining this is problematic because there is no absolute set of conditions which describe a state of strategic drift: in the end this is a matter of managerial judgement. However, some of the symptoms might be as follows:

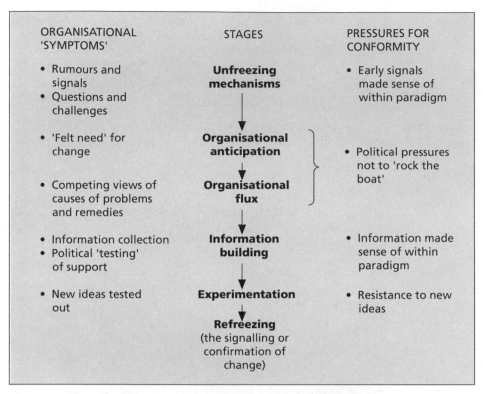

Figure 11.2 'Unfreezing' and the management of change

- A highly homogeneous organisational culture and internalised paradigm: the sort of organisation in which there are few differences of beliefs and assumptions about the organisation and its place in the external world; established routines that are not deviated from; powerful symbols and stories of a historical and conservative nature; and so on. Particularly if there is little toleration of questioning or challenge in the organisation and a readiness to dismiss new ideas with 'we've tried this before and it didn't work', the observer might well be seeing signs of drift.
- Major power blockages to change, either because of resistant dominant leaders or because some group or layer of management is resistant to change. As one executive in a major manufacturing company put it: 'Our problem is our senior managers: they've been there years and most of them are going nowhere and know it; but they can block anything if they choose. They are our "concrete ceiling".'
- An organisation with little focus on its external environment, particularly its markets, might also face a risk of drift. This might take the form of a lack of market information in a company; a reliance on competing based on price or cost control, rather than delivering added value to customers; or a bias

towards 'selling what we make' rather than responding to market and customer requirements. Such organisations are likely to be building their strategy on internalised views of the world and skill bases. This can, of course, be checked by means of research comparing managerial and customer perceptions of the organisation.

- Finally, deteriorating relative performance is a sign of strategic drift: for example is the performance of a business unit keeping pace with or outstripping its rivals, or has there been a gradual decline in relative performance?

11.3.2 Identifying barriers to strategic change

It is useful to identify the barriers to strategic change in order to decide what levers and mechanisms of change are likely to be useful. Here the cultural web can be useful in providing a framework for identifying the aspects of the organisation that will tend to preserve the current assumptions and ways of doing things. Illustration 11.2 shows the sort of situation which emerged in eastern European countries in the early 1990s, but it also illustrates more general problems of barriers to strategic change. The new CEO's intended strategy for Zolotoy Kolos was clear enough, but no doubt he would be able to see some of the barriers to achieving this – and very likely the potential western partner, as an outsider, would see still others.

Apart from the product itself, very clearly the controls on quality were quite inappropriate. However, these in turn reflected the less formalised, but probably deeply entrenched production routines, rooted in the past command economy: the workforce and the supervisors were not concerned with sales, or markets, but were trying to maintain output. The old ways of doing things were further enshrined in the very product itself: beer was seen not so much as a product for a market, but as the output of production useful for bargaining with other firms and providing bonuses to the workforce. The old routines of central planning and negotiating inputs from government might have gone, but there remained the assumption that some other agency – in this case a western partner – would solve the problems: an assumption the CEO himself appeared to share. All of this was taking place within a structure which remained hierarchical, with little involvement of junior management or the workforce, who believed that their product could only sell locally and clung to the assumption that they could sell everything they could produce. No doubt all this was reinforced by the symbolism of the historic buildings, and perhaps by stories of how much better things were in the past – and might be again in the future with western help.

Routines, control systems, structures, symbols and power or dependency relationships can therefore be important blockages to change. However, the identification of such blockages can help to provide an agenda for considering appropriate mechanisms for change. In sections 11.4 and 11.5 processes for managing change are discussed. Changes in the structure, design and control sys-

---

ILLUSTRATION 11.2
Blockages to change in Zolotoy Kolos

The new-found independence of Russian enterprise may lead to bold new strategies – but the legacy of the past was a severe blockage to change.

Zolotoy Kolos brewery produced beer mainly for the St Petersburg area. Its site had not changed much in the past 150 years, and most of the buildings had never been refurbished; in fact one red-brick tower had been declared of historic interest.

Before 1989 Zolotoy Kolos was simply a production unit taking output quotas from the ministry, as well as the necessary raw materials and equipment from the government supplies agency Gossnab. Its products were sold through government wholesalers at prices determined by the government pricing committee. The CEO was mostly involved in negotiating lower output targets and higher inputs with government officials. The employees' aim was to produce as many units as possible in order to obtain bonuses in kind – usually the beer itself.

Zolotoy Kolos was considered low priority for government funding and low prestige to work for. Its only advantage was that it produced a highly sought-after product: after strict licensing laws were introduced in 1985, alcohol became an important bargaining tool for those who had access to it.

The 1989 law on enterprise activity granted the firm a measure of independence, and the CEO decided that it had to undergo radical change. His aim was to sell abroad and generate hard currency profits. However, by 1992 the production process remained primitive and the beer was considered unsuitable by westerners who tried it. The CEO

---

tems of organisations have already been reviewed in Chapters 9 and 10. This chapter focuses on the style and role of the change agent, and the way in which he or she can employ changes in organisational routines and political and symbolic aspects of management as means of overcoming blockages to change and promoting challenge, question or change to the paradigm. These mechanisms and processes are summarised in Figure 11.3.

11.4 Managing the strategic change process

This part of the chapter deals with the processes, or approaches, which need to be considered by the change agent. These include the *style* of managing change;

recognised that it would be necessary to improve the production process, to purchase brewing and bottling equipment and to retrain employees. This transformation had to be financed in hard currency. Since there was no possibility of obtaining a loan, the CEO decided to seek a western partner. At the time (1989), there were many western European and US companies willing to enter the Soviet market.

An executive from one western firm visited the plant in the spring of 1990. He found the brewing department housed in an ill-lit, crumbling building. The passages overlooking the vats were covered in thick dust. Although the shop floor had never been tiled and the walls were plain unpainted brick, the bottling department had been supplied with automatic equipment which filled and capped the bottles. However, the means of controlling the level of fill was manual: if a bottle was overfull, the tester picked it off the line and drank some!

The engineer in charge seemed to resent the CEO's drive to better quality: 'My opinion is never even asked. How can they expect me to improve quality when the beer we receive is brewed in such filthy conditions? The people who work here aren't interested in improvement: all they want is as much beer to take home as possible.' Another manager considered any change pointless: 'We sell everything we produce and there is demand for much more. We could never make the kind of beer which would sell abroad anyway.'

The CEO received the prospective partners with great hospitality. He was sure an agreement could be reached and that the right western partner would solve Zolotoy Kolos' problems.

Prepared by Eleonora Cattaneo, IMISP (International Management Institute of St Petersburg: a joint venture between Bocconi University, Milan, and Leningrad State University).

and the *tactics* of change management, discussed here in terms of changes in organisational *routines* and *symbolic* and *political* activity.

11.4.1 Styles of managing strategic change

A number of writers[3] have discussed more or less appropriate styles of management for those faced with managing change. These styles are summarised in Figure 11.4, with examples shown in Illustration 11.3.

- *Education* and *communication* might be appropriate if there is a problem in managing change which is based on misinformation or lack of information. It requires an atmosphere of mutual trust and respect between managers and

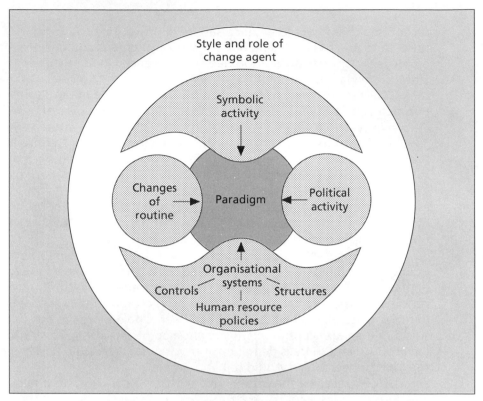

Figure 11.3 Mechanisms and processes for managing strategic change

employees, and might well be time consuming if large numbers are involved in the change since it is unlikely that mass briefings of people will be sufficient to communicate effectively. Many organisations now realise that such situations are likely to require small group briefings and debate if the communication is to be effective. However, often the direction or process of strategic change lacks clarity, so relying on processes of communication alone is problematic.

● *Participation* in the change process can be helpful in increasing ownership of a decision or change process and strengthening commitment to it. This may entail the setting up of project teams or task forces; those involved are then able to make a meaningful contribution to the decision-making process, the outcome of which may be of higher quality than decisions taken without such an approach. However, there is the inevitable risk that solutions will be found from within the existing paradigm. The change agent who sets up such a process may well, therefore, need to retain the ability to intervene in the process.

● With the *intervention* approach the change agent retains the co-ordination of and authority for such processes, but delegates aspects of the change

Style	Means/context	Benefits	Problems	Circumstances of effectiveness
Education and communication	Mutual trust/respect Small group briefings	Overcoming lack of (or mis) information	Time consuming Direction or progress may be unclear	Incremental change or global change with long time horizon
Participation	Small group/task force involvement	Increasing ownership of a decision or process May improve quality of decision	Time consuming Solutions/outcome within existing paradigm	
Intervention	Change agent retains co-ordination/control, delegates aspects of change	Process is guided/ controlled but involvement takes place	Risk of perceived manipulation	Incremental or non-crisis global change
Coercion/edict	Exploit power through edict or imposition of change	May be successful in crises or states of confusion	Least successful unless crisis	Crisis, rapid global change or change in established autocratic cultures

Figure 11.4 Styles of managing strategic change

process. For example, it might be that particular stages of change, such as idea generation, data collection, detailed planning, the development of rationales and norms of change, are delegated to project teams or task forces. However, the sponsor of the change maintains overall control and ensures that progress is monitored and improvement demonstrated.[4] There is, however, the risk with this approach that those taking part in the process may see themselves as being manipulated, and may withdraw co-operation.

- However, on occasions it might be necessary to *manipulate* the context of change: for example, to present an apparent crisis or a favourable picture for change. Certainly, the evidence is that some form of *trigger* is necessary for change to occur, and especially if transformational change is required, a clear crisis or opportunity is likely to be needed. The change agent may need either to create such a context or perhaps to dramatise circumstances in such a way as to establish conditions for change.

- *Coercion* or *edict* is the imposition of change or the issuing of directives about change. It is the explicit use of power. The evidence is that coercion and edict is the least successful style of managing change unless time is short or, perhaps, there is such a crisis or state of confusion in the organisation that people welcome it as a way of clarifying and smoothing the situation.

Figure 11.4 also suggests some circumstances in which different styles might be effective:

- *Education* and *communication* and *participation* are likely to be best suited to incremental modes of change, or to situations of transformational change in which time horizons are long.

- *Coercion* and *edict* are likely to be effective only if there is a crisis or need for rapid transformational change, unless change is taking place in an established autocratic culture.

- It may be that *intervention* provides an intermediate style of management in which more transformational change can be achieved with less risk, but it is a style which can also be effective in incremental change.[5]

11.4.2 Changes in organisational routines

Routines are the institutionalised 'ways we do things around here' which tend to persist over time and guide how people do their jobs. As has been seen in discussion on the value chain in Chapters 4 and 6, it may be that an organisation which becomes especially good at carrying out its operations in particular ways achieves real competitive advantages, but there is also the risk that the same routines act to block change and lead to strategic drift (see Chapter 2).

The power of such routines is clear enough when they are required to be

ILLUSTRATION 11.3
Styles of managing change

Executives use different styles of managing change.

Education, communication and participation in the electrical industry

In the early 1990s Jan Timmer, the chief executive of Philips NV, was seeking to move the company from its cumbersome technologically focused, organisationally complex past to a more market, customer-focused future. A 'customer day' was organised in January 1992 on which Timmer communicated by satellite with 80,000 Philips employees throughout Europe. He spoke to every employee in their local workplace for an hour. This was followed by groups of employees locally identifying what a customer-oriented organisation and a customer-responsive employee should be like. Views on these local deliberations, together with questions for Timmer, were sent to the Eindhoven head office that same day. In the afternoon Timmer again spoke to employees by satellite, answering the questions, commenting on the views and taking live questions from an audience in Eindhoven.

Intervention in the oil industry

A Dutch executive of an oil company was appointed as chief executive in a national subsidiary in southern Europe which had long been subject to government regulation on prices. 'I faced a sleepy management team which had simply managed the distribution of oil products; there was no thought about competition. Within a year we had to face a free market and all that meant in competitive terms. It was tempting to try and tell them what to do, but it would not have worked. They knew they had to change, but they did not know what it meant or how to do it. I set up project teams to tackle some of the major issues. I gave them the questions; they had to come up with the answers. I made it clear that the questions were based around the performance levels achieved in other companies in the group, so they knew they could be achieved. For example, how do we reduce costs by 30 per cent; how do we increase share by 50 per cent; and productivity by a similar amount? Members of the project team visited companies in other countries to see what they were doing; they came to me and asked questions and I offered some suggestions; consultants I brought in argued with them and challenged them. Their task was to come up with recommendations for the future within a six-month period. This they did and we debated them. I then led a team to pull it all together and identify specific plans of action to make it happen.'

Source: Authors

changed in order to accommodate some new strategy. Managers often make the mistake of assuming that because they have specified a strategy which requires operational changes in work practices, and have even identified to more junior management what such changes are, the changes will necessarily take place. They may well find that the reasons which emerge as to why such changes should be delayed or cannot occur are to do with the persistent influences of long-standing routines.

Chapter 9 argued that it is important to drive the planning of strategic change down through the identification of critical success factors to key tasks. In this way the planning of the implementation of the intended strategy is being driven down to operational levels, and it is likely that there will then be changes required in the routines of the organisation. It is at this level that changes in strategy become really meaningful for most people in their everyday organisational lives. Moreover, as was seen in Chapters 2 and 5, routines are closely linked to the taken-for-grantedness of the paradigm, so changing routines may well question and challenge deep-rooted beliefs and assumptions in the organisation.

It is therefore important that managers, trying to effect strategic changes, take personal responsibility not only for identifying such changes in routines, but also for ensuring they actually occur. The changes may appear to be mundane, but they can have significant impact. To take a few examples:

- Buyers in a major retailer had always 'bought long' to obtain the greatest discounts; a new managing director wanted a more responsive fashion-oriented operation and insisted on cutting buying lead times by half.
- The new chief executive of an engineering firm, appointed to turn round the business, found an unacceptably high level of stock, particularly in small items. These were kept in 'bins' in the stock room. He required the bins to be replaced with smaller ones and the size of the stock room to be reduced.
- The management of a transport and distribution firm, seeking to emphasise rapid response to customer needs, established a routine of telephone answering in the head office: no phone was allowed to ring more than twice before being picked up by someone; and no one was allowed to ignore a ringing phone – 'it might be a customer'.
- Public-sector organisations have been obsessed with the stewardship of public funds – often resulting in very risk-averse cultures. Some have tried to break this by setting up internal 'investment banks' so that staff can 'bid' for the funding of new ventures.
- The activities of branch personnel in many UK banks were dominated by manual form-filling procedures; the effect was that these procedures were often seen as more significant than dealing with customers. In the 1980s the banks moved rapidly to computerised systems. This was not just to reduce staff costs but also to remove the paperwork from remaining staff. As one manager put it: 'If you haven't got a form to fill in, you have to attend to customers, and that is at the heart of our strategy.'

11.4.3   Symbolic activity in managing change[6]

Change processes are not always of an overt, formal nature; they may also be symbolic. Chapter 2 explained how symbolic acts and artefacts of an organisation help preserve the paradigm, and Chapter 5 explained how their relationship to culture and strategy can be analysed. Here the concern is how they can be managed to signal change.

There is a need to understand that the 'mundane tools that involve the creation and manipulation of symbols over time have impact to the extent that they re-shape beliefs and expectations'.[7] Managers need to understand that, for change to be meaningful to individuals, that meaning must be apparent in the day-to-day experience of those individuals in the organisation; and day-to-day 'reality' is represented by the many mundane aspects of organisational life that come to take on symbolic significance. This is one reason why changes in routines are important. Other such 'mundane' aspects include the stories that people tell, status symbols such as cars or sizes of office, and the type of language and technology used. Many of the *rituals* (or rites) of organisations are also implicitly to do with effecting or consolidating change. Figure 11.5 identifies six different rites of this sort.[8]

Symbolic significance is also embedded in the *systems* discussed elsewhere in this chapter and in Chapter 10. For example, reward systems, information and control systems, and the very organisational structures that represent reporting relationships and often status are also symbolic in nature. Indeed, even the budgeting and planning systems discussed in Chapter 9 come to take on symbolic significance in so far as they represent to individuals the everyday reality of organisational life.

To take an example of such systems, the way selection interviews are conducted is likely to signal to those being interviewed the nature of the organisation and what is expected of them. A highly formal interview procedure may signal a mechanistic, rather hierarchical organisation; whereas a more informal dialogue, perhaps preceded by open questioning of potential colleagues, is likely to signal an environment and expectation of challenge and questioning. Moreover, the fact that selection processes are changed, different types of manager appointed, and challenge and questioning visibly encouraged can signal within the organisation the commitment to strategic change. In this sense, selection processes are symbolic in nature.

The most powerful symbol of all in relation to change is the *behaviour of change agents* themselves. This is discussed further in section 11.5, but it is sufficient to point out here that the behaviour, language and stories associated with such executives can signal powerfully the need for change and appropriate behaviour relating to the management of change. It must also be pointed out that the behaviour of executives can also severely undermine change processes. Too few senior executives understand that, having made pronouncements about the need for strategic change, it is vital that their behaviour is in line with such change.[9] It is one thing for the leader, as strategist, to analyse the strategic position carefully, or to conceive of a strategic way forward, but the organisational

Types of rite	Social consequences	Role in promoting/ consolidating culture change	Examples
Rites of passage	Facilitate transition of people into social roles and statuses that are new for them	Consolidate ways people carry out social roles Promote new ways of social interaction	Induction of new recruits
Rites of degradation	Dissolve social identities and their attendant power	Provide public acknowledgements that problems exist Defend group boundaries by redefining who belongs and who does not Reaffirm social importance and value of role involved	Firing and replacing top executives
Rites of enhancement	Enhance social identities and their attendant power	Spread good news about the organisation Provide public recognition of individuals for their accomplishments and motivate others to similar efforts Emphasise social value of performance of social roles	Award ceremonies at company conferences
Rites of renewal	Refurbish social structures and improve the ways they function	Reassure members that something is being done about problems Focus attention on some problems and away from others Legitimate systems of power and authority	Problem-centred/ project taskforces Appointment of consultants on specified projects
Rites of integration	Encourage and revive shared feelings that bind people together and keep them committed to a social system	Permit venting of emotion and temporary loosening of various norms Reassert and reaffirm, by contrast, moral rightness of usual norms	Office Christmas parties
Rites of conflict reduction	Reduce conflict and aggression	Re-establish equilibrium in disturbed social relations Compartmentalise conflict and its disruptive effects	Internal appeal systems Union–management committees

Source: Adapted from H. M. Trice and J. M. Beyer, 'Using six organizational rites to change culture', in R. H. Kilman et al. (eds), *Gaining Control of the Corporate Culture*, Jossey Bass, 1985, pp. 374–5.

Figure 11.5 Types of rite (ritual) and their roles in culture change

world of most people is one of deeds and actions, not of abstractions.

It is of vital importance, therefore, that the visible actions of the change agent are in line with the strategic thrust he or she is trying to advance. In one major retail business with an espoused strategy of customer care, the chief executive, on visiting stores, tended to ignore staff and customers alike; he only seemed to be interested in the financial figures he examined in the store manager's office. It was not something he was aware of until it was pointed out, and his change in behaviour afterwards, insisting on talking to staff and customers on his visits, became a 'story' which spread around the stores and substantially supported the strategic direction of the firm.

Also important in effecting change is the *language* used by change agents.[10] Change agents use metaphor and symbolism in their language of change. Some examples are included in Illustration 11.4. In this context, language is not simply to do with communicating facts and information. Language is also powerful because it is symbolic, and it is simultaneously able to carry several meanings at once. For example, it may link the past to the future; it may attach or undermine an image of the past, and therefore carry a very serious message, yet it may do so in a playful way; and it may evoke emotional feelings as strongly as rational understanding.

Either consciously or unconsciously, change agents may therefore employ language and metaphor to galvanise change. Of course, there is also the danger that change agents do not realise the power of language and, while espousing change, use language that signals the importance of the status quo, or their personal reluctance to change. In short, those involved in change need to think carefully about the language they use, and the symbolic significance of their actions.

Building on the 'unfreezing' model (see Figure 11.2), Illustration 11.4 gives examples of how the symbolic activity and language of change agents can advance procedures of *questioning, challenging, experimentation* and *confirmation* of change. The examples show that powerful signals to promote change can exist within the day-to-day aspects of organisational life. The change agent needs to be sensitive to what these might be, and must learn to employ them to aid the change process. For example, using the sort of terminology introduced in Figure 11.5 concerning the rituals of organisations, *rites of enhancement* might include spreading 'good news' of transformation and rewarding those contributing to it. There could be *rites of integration,* such as conferences which applaud change and 'change heroes', or involve or associate members of the organisation with new approaches, activities or belief systems. And *rites of conflict reduction* can minimise or contain disunity; these often take the form of structural change or personnel appointments which demonstrate which executive groups have significant influence and which have been marginalised.

Rites of passage, to signal change from one stage of the organisation's development to another, may be seen in the steps taken to implement strategy. For example, the departure of the old and the introduction of new and often younger management, perhaps the replacement of senior board members or even a whole board, signifies much more than personnel changes; it is a typical signal of passing from one era to another. Other rites of passage may be less structurally

ILLUSTRATION 11.4
Symbolic activity and strategic change

Symbolic aspects of management, including the action and language of change agents, can aid the change processes in organisations.

1. In 'unfreezing', challenging and questioning will occur.

    A new CEO in a transport company ordered that the liveries of vehicles be removed. When managers then asked how they should repaint the vehicles, his answer was to request proposals. In effect he was challenging them to rethink what the business was about without preconceptions rooted in history.[11]

    The CEO of a retailing firm facing a crisis addressed his board: 'I suggest we think of ourselves like bulls facing a choice: the abattoir or the bull ring. I've made up my mind: what about you?'

    In another company the CEO described the threat of a takeover in terms of pending warfare: 'We've been targeted: they've got the hired guns (merchant bankers, consultants, etc.) on board. Don't expect chivalry: don't look for white knights and safe harbours: this is a shoot-out situation.'

2. Signalling the legitimacy of new ideas and experimentation.

    In the ANZ Bank in Australia a central component of change was a 'customer care' programme. Informal networks of 'diagnostic groups' were set up across levels of management to search for service quality changes. Their activities were legitimised through well-presented programme guides, certificates of merit, formal presentation ceremonies to regional managers for discussing results achieved in service quality improvement, and rituals which provided a sense of identity, such as a 'groupie handshake' and a special way of sitting on chairs.[12]

3. Confirmatory signals of change.

    These may be very dramatic. In a textile firm in Scotland, equipment associated with the 'old ways of doing things' was taken into the yard at the rear of the factory and physically dismantled in front of the workforce. In other cases the signals might be more subtle. For example, shop staff in a clothing retailer whose strategy was to move from a down market, staid product range to more fashionable merchandise were required to wear merchandise from the new fashion shops which had been launched. This move was potent: as one executive remarked, 'We did not realise the significance; you see, they had to *wear* the new strategy.'

Source: Authors

formal but nonetheless powerful. When the new president of Asaki Breweries in Japan introduced Koku-Kire beer, he signalled a fundamental shift in product policy and a required commitment to the new product, not only with a publicity launch and a change in company logo, but also by dumping all stocks of the old product and recalling it from 130,000 stores.[13]

11.4.4 Political processes[14]

It is likely that there will be a need for the reconfiguration of *power structures* in the organisation, especially if transformational change is required. This may well go hand in hand with the legitimising of dissent from those in the organisation who are questioning the existing ways of operating. In order to effect this reconfiguration of power it is likely that the momentum for change will need *powerful advocacy* within the organisation, typically from the chief executive, a powerful member of the board or an influential outsider.

However, political activity is not only relevant at the chief executive or senior executive level. Any manager faced with managing change needs to consider how it might be implemented from a political perspective. Managers also need to realise that analysis and planning may themselves take on political dimensions. A new marketing director of one company commissioned market research on customer perceptions of service and found the results were highly critical. The director found that the presentation of the findings to the board gave rise not to analytical debate, but to systematic 'rubbishing' of the research report. As he later stated, he failed to realise that his work had been seen as 'not so much an analytical statement, as a statement of political threat'. The analysis had threatened the very bases of the business upon which many on the board had built their authority and power in the organisation.

So managers need to be sensitive to the political dimensions of their activities: not just because there might be blockages to apparently rational behaviour, but also because political activity might itself help to effect change.

Power and the management of strategic change

Chapter 5 showed the importance of understanding the political systems of the organisation. Having established this understanding, there is also a need to plan the implementation of strategy within this political context. The approach developed here draws on the content of Chapter 5 and also some of what has been discussed in this chapter to provide a framework for considering such political activity.

Figure 11.6 summarises some of the political mechanisms in organisations.[15] These include the manipulation of *organisational resources*; the relationship with powerful groupings and/or *élites*; activity with regard to *subsystems* in the organisation; and again *symbolic activity*. All of these may be used to (a) build a

Activity areas	Mechanisms				Key problems
	Resources	Élites	Subsystems	Symbolic	
Building the power base	Control of resources Acquisition of/identification with expertise Acquisition of additional resources	Sponsorship by an élite Association with an élite	Alliance building Team building	Building on legitimation	Time required for building Perceived duality of ideals Perceived as threat by existing élites
Overcoming resistance	Withdrawal of resources Use of 'counter-intelligence' information	Breakdown or division of élites Association with change agent Association with respected outsider	Foster momentum for change Sponsorship/ reward of change agents	Attack or remove legitimation Foster confusion, conflict and questioning	Striking from too low a power base Potentially destructive: need for rapid rebuilding
Achieving compliance	Giving resources	Removal of resistant élites Need for visible 'change hero'	Partial implementation and participation Implantation of 'disciples' Support for 'young Turks'	Applause/ reward Reassurance Symbolic confirmation	Converting the body of the organisation Slipping back

Figure 11.6 Political mechanisms in organisations.

power base, (b) encourage support or overcome resistance, and (c) achieve commitment.

1. The control and manipulation of organisational *resources* was shown in Chapter 5 to be a source of power. For example, acquiring additional resources or being identified with important resource areas or areas of expertise, and the ability to withdraw or allocate such resources, can be a valuable tool in overcoming resistance or persuading others to accept change. And the careful use of information or news to counter the information being used to justify opposition to change can also be important.

2. Powerful groupings (or *élites*) in the organisation are of crucial importance and may, of course, correspond to stakeholder groups (discussed in Chapter 5). Association with such groupings, or their support, can help build a power base, and this may well be necessary for the change agent who does not have a strong personal power base from which to work. Similarly, association with a change agent who is respected or seen to be successful can help a manager overcome resistance to change. However, this is likely to be a gradual process of influence, perhaps more suited to adaptive change.

    It may, of course, be necessary to remove individuals or groups resistant to change. Who these are can vary from powerful individuals in senior positions to loose networks with powerful influence – sometimes referred to in organisations as 'the mafia' – to whole layers of resistance perhaps in the form of senior executives in a threatened function or service – the sort of 'concrete ceiling' referred to earlier in the chapter.

3. The main vehicles for implementing change are to do with communicating and consolidating its acceptance throughout the organisation. It is vital that processes are under way which achieve acceptance of change throughout the organisation. How the *subsystems* of organisations are handled will therefore be important. Building up alliances and a network of contacts and sympathisers, even though they may not be powerful themselves, may be important in overcoming the resistance from more powerful groups.

    Attempting to convert the whole organisation to an acceptance of change is difficult; it is likely that there will be parts of the organisation or individuals in it more sympathetic to change than others. The change agent might more sensibly concentrate on these to develop momentum for change, building a team or network strongly supportive of the activities and beliefs of the change agent. The danger is that existing élites in the organisations may regard the building of such a team as a threat to their own power, and this may lead to further resistance to change. An analysis of power and interest similar to that described in Chapter 5 might, therefore, be especially useful to identify bases of alliance and likely political resistance.

4. Finally, as has been seen, the conscious employment of *symbolic mechanisms* of change is likely to be useful. From a political point of view this

may take several forms. To build power, the manager may initially seek to identify with the very symbols which preserve and reinforce the paradigm – to work within the committee structures, become identified with the organisational rituals or stories that exist, and so on. On the other hand, in breaking resistance to change, removing, challenging or changing rituals and symbols may be very powerful means of achieving the questioning of what is taken for granted. Third, symbolic activity can be used for consolidating change: by concentrating attention or 'applause' and rewards on those who most accept change, its wider adoption is more likely; and there may be means of confirming through symbolic devices such as new structures, titles, office allocation and so on that the change is to be regarded as important and not reversible.

Problems with managing political systems

Political aspects of management in general, and change in particular, are unavoidable; and the lessons of organisational life are as important for the manager as they are, and always have been, for the politician (see Illustration 11.5). However, the political aspects of management are also difficult and potentially hazardous. Figure 11.6 summarises some of the problems.

The problem in building a power base is that the manager may have to become so identified with existing power groupings that he or she either actually comes to accept their views or is perceived by others to have done so, thus losing support among potential supporters of change. Building a power base is a delicate path to tread.

In overcoming resistance the major problem may simply be the lack of power to undertake such activity, since attempting to overcome resistance from a lower power base is almost certainly doomed to failure. There is a second major danger: that in breaking down the status quo, the process becomes so destructive and takes so long that the organisation cannot recover from it. If the process needs to take place, the replacement of the status quo by some new configuration of beliefs and the implementation of a new strategy is vital and needs to be speedy. And, as already identified, in implementing change the main problem is likely to be carrying the body of the organisation with the change. It is one thing to change the commitment of a few senior executives at the top of an organisation; it is quite another to convert the body of the organisation to an acceptance of significant change. The danger is that individuals are likely to regard change as temporary: something which they need to comply with until the next change comes along.

Change agents also have to cope with the tactical political manoeuvring of other managers resistant to change. The sort of tactics typically employed to counter change are identified in Figure 11.7. The figure also identifies some of the moves that might be taken in countering such countermoves: many of these build on the discussion in this chapter about styles of managing and symbolic and political aspects of management.

ILLUSTRATION 11.5
Machiavelli on political processes

It should be borne in mind that there is nothing more difficult to handle, more doubtful of success, and more dangerous to carry through, than initiating changes in a state's constitution.

`The innovator makes enemies of all those who prospered under the old order, and only lukewarm support is forthcoming from those who would prosper under the new. Their support is lukewarm partly from fear of their adversaries, who have the existing laws on their side, and partly because men are generally incredulous, never really trusting new things unless they have tested them by experience. In consequence, whenever those who oppose the changes can do so, they attack vigorously, and the defence made by the others is only lukewarm. So both the innovator and his friends come to grief.' (*The Prince*, Penguin, p. 51; OUP, p. 22.)

Machiavelli's Prince is precariously balanced between four interest groups: the army, the nobility, the populace and the state. Gauging the relative power of these and devising strategies which take this into account become crucial, as Machiavelli illustrates.

Scipio's *army* rebelled against him in Spain for allowing too much licence. Commodus and Maximinus (two Roman emperors) both exhibited excessive cruelty, and both were killed by their armies.

The *nobility*'s desire is to command and oppress the people. Bentivogli, Prince of Bologna, was killed by the Canneschi (nobility) who conspired against him. However, after the murder the people rose up and killed the Canneschi. The Canneschi misjudged the popular goodwill of the people toward Bentivogli.

It is necessary for a prince to possess the friendship of the *populace*, particularly in times of adversity. Nabis, prince of the Spartans, sustained a siege by the rest of Greece and a victorious Roman army, defended his country against them, and maintained his own position through unifying the populace.

Machiavelli commends three principles:
- Establish whether you are in the position, in case of need, to maintain yourself alone, or whether you need the protection of others.
- Esteem your nobles, but don't make yourself hated by the populace.
- Follow the example of Ferdinand, King of Aragon and Spain, who 'continually contrived great things which have kept his subjects' minds uncertain and astonished, and occupied in watching their result'.

Source: Machiavelli, *The Prince*, Penguin, 1961.

Prepared by Roger Lazenby, Cranfield School of Management.

Countermoves to change

- *Divert resources.* Split budget across other projects, give key staff other priorities/other assignments.
- *Exploit inertia.* Request everyone to wait until a key player takes action, read a report, or make an appropriate response; suggest the results from another project should be assessed first.
- *Keep goals vague and complex.* It is harder to initiate appropriate action if aims are multidimensional and specified in generalised, grandiose or abstract terms.
- *Encourage and exploit lack of organisational awareness.* Insist that 'we can deal with the people issues later', knowing this will delay or kill the project.
- *'Great idea – let's do it properly.'* Involve so many representatives or experts that there will be so many different views and conflicting interests it will delay decisions or require meaningless compromise.
- *Dissipate energies.* Conduct surveys, collect data,prepare analyses, write reports, make overseas trips, hold special meetings . . .
- *Reduce the change agent's influence and credibility.* Spread damaging rumours, particularly among the change agent's friends and supporters.
- *Keep a low profile.* Do not openly declare resistance to change because that gives those driving change a clear target to aim for.

Countering countermoves to change

- *Establish clear direction and objectives.* Goal clarity enables action to proceed more effectively than ambiguity and complexity, which can slow down action.
- *Establish simple, phased programming.* For the same reasons as having clear goals.
- *Adopt a fixer–facilitator–negotiator role.* Resistance to change can rarely be overcome by reason alone, and the exercise of these interpersonal skills is required.
- *Seek and respond to resistance.* Take a proactive approach to resistance in order to overcome, mitigate or block it: appeal/refer to high values/standards or powerful authorities; warn them off; use influential intermediaries; infiltrate meetings and supporters; wait them out or wear them down.
- *Rely on face to face.* Personal influence and persuasion is usually more effective in winning and sustaining support than the impersonal memo or report.
- *Exploit a crisis.* People will often respond more positively to a crisis which they understand and face collectively than to personal attempts to change behaviour.
- *Co-opt support early.* Build coalitions and recruit backers; of prior importance to the building of teams: co-opting opponents may also be tactically useful.
- *The meaningful steering committee/ taskforce/ project team.* Include in its membership key players in the organisation who carry 'weight', authority and respect.

Source: Adapted from D. Buchanan and D. Boddy, *The Expertise of the Change Agent: Public performance and backstage activity*, Prentice Hall, 1992, pp. 78–9.

Figure 11.7 Political manoeuvres and change

11.5 Leadership and change agency

While it is very important to identify blockages to change and understand the sort of mechanisms of change which exist, it is also necessary to examine the nature of change agency at an individual level to understand the characteristics of an effective change agent.

A good deal of the literature on leadership emphasises the personal, individualistic aspects of change management in organisations. Such literature sometimes suggests that strategic change is heavily dependent on the activities of charismatic leaders[16]. These views can be misleading because they fail to identify the context in which change agency occurs, or the extent to which change agency skills can be developed. The manager faced with managing change needs to consider carefully the extent to which various components of change agency are in place, or can be developed. A number of these components have already been discussed:

- First, does the change agent have a *clarity of direction* or *vision* which can be communicated clearly to others? Clear objectives or mission may be very important here, and these were discussed in Chapter 5. Indeed, much of this book has been concerned with developing a clarity of strategy.
- Second, the importance of *context* needs to be emphasised. The change agent needs to be especially sensitive to the type of change required (see section 11.2), the nature of the blockages that exist (section 11.3.2) and therefore the opportunities for change. It may be that even relatively weak opportunities or threats can be transformed into triggering mechanisms. The successful change agent, then, is someone who can perceive the nature of required change and the opportunities for change, and turn these into triggers for change.
- Third, as discussed in section 11.4.1, the successful change agent will be able to employ an appropriate *style* of managing change, adapting that style to the circumstances rather than imposing his or her style without regard to the specific context of change.
- Linked to this is the ability to use the political and symbolic processes that provide the levers and mechanisms of change.

In a study carried out on the perceived effectiveness of change agents,[17] many of these aspects of managing change were shown to be important, and these are reflected in fifteen key competences identified in that study (see Figure 11.8).

However, there are two further aspects of change agency that need to be considered:

1. *Endowed authority.*[18] It would be incorrect to conceive of a change agent as someone who necessarily achieves change by imposing that change on others. It is likely that the successful change agency builds largely on the extent

Goals

1. Sensitivity to changes in key personnel, top management perceptions and market conditions, and to the way in which these impact on the goals of the project in hand.
2. Clarity in specifying goals, in defining the achievable.
3. Flexibility in responding to changes without the control of the project manager, perhaps requiring major shifts in project goals and management style, and risk taking.

Roles

4. Team-building abilities, to bring together key stakeholders and establish effective working groups, and clearly to define and delegate respective responsibilities.
5. Networking skills in establishing and maintaining appropriate contacts within and outside the organisation.
6. Tolerance of ambiguity, to be able to function comfortably, patiently and effectively in an uncertain environment.

Communication

7. Communication skills to transmit effectively to colleagues and subordinates the need for changes in project goals and in individual tasks and responsibilities.
8. Interpersonal skills, across the range, including selection, listening, collecting appropriate information, identifying the concerns of others and managing meetings.
9. Personal enthusiasm, in expressing plans and ideas.
10. Stimulating motivation and commitment in others involved.

Negotiation

11. Selling plans and ideas to others, by creating a desirable and challenging vision of the future.
12. Negotiating with key players for resources, or for changes in procedures, and to resolve conflict.

Managing up

13. Political awareness, in identifying potential coalitions and balancing conflicting goals and perceptions.
14. Influencing skills, to gain commitment to project plans and ideas from potential sceptics and resisters.
15. Helicopter perspectives, to stand back from the immediate project and take a broader view of priorities.

Source: Adapted from D. Buchanan and D. Boddy, *The Expertise of the Change Agent: Public performance and backstage activity*, Prentice Hall, 1992, pp. 92–3.

Figure 11.8 Fifteen key competences of change agents

to which those influenced by or following the change attribute the authority for change to the change agent, or endow him or her with the qualities of leadership.

The extreme view would be that leadership or change agency is placed upon someone by those around him or her. Another view would be that change agents actively seek to understand, or readily relate to, the values and beliefs of others in and around the organisation (see Chapter 5), and build their position upon this. The important lesson is that the successful change agent needs to relate to and be very sensitive to the values of those in the organisation who will be supporting the change, and will only in exceptional circumstances be able to effect lasting change if their needs and values are ignored.

2. The final component is the *personal traits* of change agents. To what extent do successful change agents demonstrate special or different personal traits from others? Though much of the literature on leadership is highly anecdotal, it does suggest that leaders have special qualities. It is argued that they have visionary capacity; they are good at team building and team playing; they are self-analytical and good at self-learning; they have mental agility and 'constructive restlessness', while also being able to concentrate for long periods; and they are also self-directed and self-confident.[19]

    However, perhaps one of the more telling commentaries on strategic change agency is Peters and Waterman's[20] perceptive argument that the successful manager of change in organisations is a 'master of two ends of the spectrum'. By this they mean that the change agent is simultaneously able to cope with potentially conflicting ways of managing. Consider these requirements of the successful manager of strategic change:

- In strategy creation, an ability to undertake or understand detailed analysis, while at the same time being visionary about the future.
- In achieving organisational credibility for a strategy, being seen as insightful about the future, and yet action orientated about making things happen.
- In challenging the status quo in an organisation, an ability to maintain credibility and carry people with the change, while attacking the taken-for-granted and current ways of doing things.
- In communicating strategic intent, an ability to encapsulate often quite complex issues of strategy in everyday ways which people can understand. Indeed, clarity of communication of strategy is especially important: some writers have argued, for example, that successful change agents employ the tactic of delivering no more than three strategic messages – the 'three themes' approach.[21]
- In achieving commitment to a change in strategy, an ability to achieve a focus and clarity sufficient to overcome ambiguity and complexity.
- In consolidating a strategy, and making it happen, an ability to maintain performance of the organisation while breaking down old assumptions, old

ways of doing things and practices which jeopardise the efficiency of the organisation.

It is a challenging task which requires a degree of flexibility, insight and sensitivity to strategic context, together with an ability to relate to others. Such qualities are not common.

11.6 Conclusions

In their study of firms which had managed change successfully, Pettigrew and Whipp[22] summarise their findings in a way which usefully integrates much of the material in this chapter with other chapters in this book. They use Figure 11.9 to draw together the main points. Their argument is that organisations which manage change successfully demonstrate five important characteristics.

11.6.1 Environmental assessment

Chapter 3 explained the importance of understanding the business environment for the management of strategy. However, this does not mean simply employing techniques of analysis, or hiring analysts to do this. Those organisations that manage change effectively are more like open learning systems: the sensitivity to the environment is organisation-wide; it is not dependent on a set of techniques or specialists. Managers and staff in the organisation see their role as keeping close to, being sensitive to, and responding to signals in the environment. The external orientation is, therefore, part of the culture of the organisation: it is 'taken for granted' that this is an important orientation, and this view is championed visibly by senior management. Furthermore the structural characteristics of the organisation are such that there is an emphasis on external rather than internal orientation (see Chapter 10).

11.6.2 Leading change

It is dangerous to think of the management of change as a prescribed set of activities. The way in which change is led by change agents must depend on contexts which will differ by organisation, or perhaps by market. However, the ability of the change agent to establish or develop a context for change is crucial, both in cultural terms and also in terms of the capabilities of the organisation. It is also necessary to tailor the agenda for change specifically to the organisational context and the values and beliefs of those in the organisation.

This chapter has emphasized this point and has also discussed ways of managing strategic change. However, the important message is that these need to be

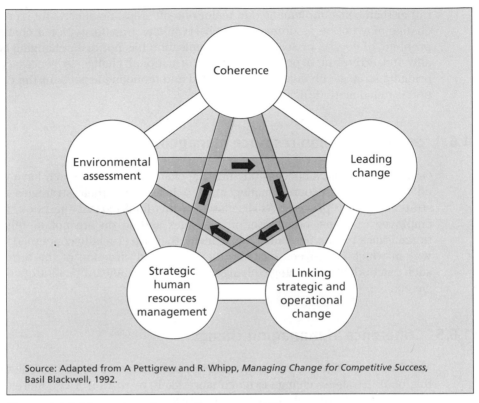

Source: Adapted from A Pettigrew and R. Whipp, *Managing Change for Competitive Success,* Basil Blackwell, 1992.

Figure 11.9 Managing change for competitive success:
the five central factors

drawn upon in ways which are specific and relevant to a particular context. They are not capable of being prescribed as appropriate in all situations. The successful change agent is therefore one who is especially sensitive to context, and who can adapt his or her approach to change in that light.

11.6.3 Linking strategic and operational change

In organisations which have successfully managed change, the change agents have been able to link strategic change with operational change and the everyday aspects of the organisation. This emphasises the importance not only of translating strategic change into detailed resource plans, critical success factors and key tasks (Chapter 9), and the way the organisation is managed through control processes (Chapter 10), but also of how change is communicated through the mundane and symbolic aspects of the organisation discussed in this chapter.

This is more likely to be effective if change can be continual and incremental: if change is continually occurring in the everyday aspects of the organisation, rather than being implemented in major one-off steps. So successful incremental change may not be as dramatically observable as transformational change. The problem, of course, arises when an organisation has not been changing continually and arrives at a point when transformational change is necessary. Then bridging strategic change and operational and mundane aspects of the organisation is much more difficult.

11.6.4 Strategic human resource management

Organisations which successfully manage change are those which have integrated their human resource management policies with their strategies and the strategic change process. As discussed in this final part of the book, training, employee relations, compensation packages and so on are not merely operational issues for the personnel department; they are crucially concerned with the way in which employees relate to the nature and direction of the firm, and as such can both block strategic change and also be significant facilitators of strategic change.

11.6.5 Coherence in managing change

The final point that needs emphasising in a sense summarises the whole thrust of this book. Strategic change is much more likely to work if it is coherent across all aspects of the organisation. By this is meant that:

- There is a consistency between the intended strategy, the stated strategic objectives, their expression in operational terms and, very important, the behaviour of executives in reinforcing the strategy.
- The direction of strategic change is consistent with what is happening in the environment, and the way in which this is understood in the organisation; and that it is also managed with due regard to stakeholders, including suppliers and customers, on whom the organisation is critically reliant.
- The strategy is feasible in terms of the resources it requires, the structuring of the organisation and the changes that need to occur in organisational culture and operational routines.
- Overall, the strategic direction is clearly related to achieving competitive advantage or excellent performance, and internally it is understood how this is so.

Such coherence means that there needs to be an ability to hold the organisation together as an efficient, successful entity, while simultaneously changing it. Illustration 11.6 gives an example of this.

11.6.6 Pulling it all together

There are a growing number of studies on the reasons why some organisations are more successful than others. All make it clear that the clarity of strategy direction and its relevance to a changing environment is crucial. The wiser researchers and writers realise, however, that it is not possible to reduce the explanations of how this is done to simple do's and don'ts. Rather, successful organisations are those that are able to sense the critical forces at work around them and change by building a capability for organisation-wide learning and adaptation.[23]

This book has aimed to provide an insight into some of the ways in which managers might contribute to this. It has done so by describing research which tries to explain success; by explaining techniques of analysis, evaluation and planning which can help to provide bases of success and to plan for the future; but most of all by stressing that it is the processes of management, the skills of managers and the ability of managers to relate to their external environment, their internal culture and the people around them, that will ensure success.

References

1. Michel Bougon and John Komocar discuss a systems view of learning in 'Directing strategic change: a dynamic wholistic approach', in Anne S. Huff (ed.), *Mapping Strategy Thought*, Wiley, 1990.

2. This framework of 'organisational learning' builds on the work of K. Lewin, *Field Theory in Social Science*, Tavistock, 1952. The framework is used by a number of writers to discuss strategic change. See, for example, L. A. Isabella, 'Evolving interpretations as a change unfolds: how managers construe key organisational events', *Academy of Management Journal*, vol. 33, no. 1, (1985), pp. 7–41; and E. H. Schein, *Organisational Culture and Leadership*, Jossey Bass, 1985.

3. See, for example, J. P. Kotter and L. A. Schlesinger, 'Choosing strategies for change', *Harvard Business Review*, vol. 57, no. 2, (1979), pp. 106–14.

4. The intervention style is discussed more fully by P. C. Nutt, 'Identifying and appraising how managers install strategy', *Strategic Management Journal*, vol. 8, no. 1, pp. 1–14.

5. P. C. Nutt has also explored the links between styles of managing change and their effectiveness in 'Selecting tactics to implement strategic plans', *Strategic Management Journal*, vol. 10, no. 2, (1989), pp. 145–61.

6. For a fuller discussion of this theme, see G. Johnson 'Managing strategic change: the role of symbolic action', *British Journal of Management*, vol. 1, no. 4, (1990), pp. 183–200.

7. This reference is taken from one of Tom Peters early papers: 'Symbols, patterns and settings: an optimistic case for getting things done', *Organisational Dynamics*, vol. 7, no. 2, (1987), pp. 3–23.

8. See H. M. Trice and J. M. Beyer, 'Studying organisational cultures through rites and ceremonials', *Academy of Management Review*, vol. 9, no. 4, (1984), pp. 653–69; and H. M. Trice and J. M. Beyer, 'Using six organisational rites to change culture', in R. H. Kilman *et al.* (eds), *Gaining Control of the Corporate Culture*, Jossey Bass, 1985.

9. This is a point made forcibly by Andrew Kakabadse, *The Wealth Creators*, Kogan Page, 1991.

10. The importance of the language used by corporate leaders has been noted by a number of writers, but see particularly L. R. Pondy, 'Leadership is a language game', in M. W. McCall, Jr and M. M. Lombardo (eds), *Leadership: Where else can we go?*, Duke

ILLUSTRATION 11.6
Longman

Longman's successful development of new areas of publishing on an international scale was achieved through a mix of management actions.

Environmental assessment

Cherished strategic formulae were challenged by the relentless inquisitorial role adopted by the chief executive with his board colleagues. Management also ensured that shifts in the environment were understood within the companies through an extensive communication network. The UK company became but one unit (albeit large) among the collection of international subsidiaries – knowledge was not assumed to flow only from the UK. The strength of local publishing overseas was impressive, and from this the whole company derived market knowledge. Longman Hong Kong had its own sales and production operation, yet Longman UK's English language teaching (ELT) division used such local knowledge in selling their own specialist books in the Far East. Moreover, management further challenged views of the market by recruiting marketing staff from outside the industry.

Leading change

Longman's strategic changes were linked to the personal development of the chief executive, Tim Rix. Rix's extensive international publishing experience gave him an insight into the growth possibilities inherent in the USA, Europe and the Far East. What was commonly referred to as 'Tim's vision' did not appear overnight but developed over ten years, and provided the basis for collective action first at board and then at divisional level.

The keynote was Rix's development of his own understanding of the need for change, followed by his inculcation of a collective capacity among senior management. This he did in a number of ways: by creating a relatively stable board of eleven in the 1980s, where individual members were at first educated by Rix of the international market possibilities and then led their sectors accordingly; by combining diverse talents, unseen elsewhere in UK publishing, such as human resources management (HRM) and computing directors at board level in order to supply the capacity to change; and by developing the finance committee from its early budgeting duties in the 1970s to performing an educative role for the top teams of each division in producing and executing their business plans.

Linking strategic and operational change

Longman's ability to translate strategic initiatives into operational form was shown in the development of its US market. In the late 1960s Longman decided to expand in the developed world, particularly North America, and opened a small import house in New York in 1973. This was used to sell UK books in the USA while building up Longman's own commissioning from New York on three fronts: medical, college and ELT.

There was no attempt to achieve major changes in one jump: less risky, more manageable steps were tried, gradually turning strategic market choices into operational forms. In the medical field, for example, the Churchill Livingstone imprint was used to sell UK texts to the USA. Subsequently, books by American medical and scientific authors were published; the added benefit was that they in turn could be sold in the UK. In college publishing Longman tried to publish across too wide a band of subjects in the 1970s. From this they learned that they could not cover the market as a whole, as did US publishers. Instead they exploited their strengths within specialist niches. The success is shown by the contribution of US sales to Longman: 2.7 per cent in 1975, 28.5 per cent in 1985 and 35 per cent in 1990.

Managing human resources

By the mid-1980s Longman's strategic position was underpinned by a growing HRM approach. During the 1970s centralisation of negotiation and information, together with the attempt to develop a new salary structure based on job evaluation, gave rise to rigidity of work practices, the post-entry closed shop and restrictive management. From 1983 most of the existing structure and practices had been changed. Weak supervisory systems had been overhauled, the bonus scheme revised and a new agreement negotiated with SOGAT, which led to Longman leaving the Publishers' Association's national negotiations.

The appointment of the director of personnel to the board from 1982 saw a new phase initiated. The aim was to diffuse the commitment to HRM beyond the senior management and to develop human resource plans for each division. The potential benefits were considerable, given the slowness of other major publishers to move to such orientations. However, the HRM approach was not allowed to become a programme for itself. Its relevance had been shown in the contribution to commercial performance. Nowhere was this better demonstrated than in Longman's need to alter its knowledge base. Senior management and personnel staff worked from 1982 to alter editorial techniques, values and standards of professionalism, to align them more closely with the

(Continued on p. 420)

requirements of diversification. Without such a shift, Longman's activities in the USA and the Far East would not have been possible.

Coherence

The development of coherence in such a change process required a range of management action. This included generating a coherence of purpose and belief among the senior management team, even though individual styles and methods differed. Similarly, inter-organisational complementarity was established across the range of customers, suppliers, distributors and collaborators upon which the firm relied. This required breaking with suppliers and distributors who failed to meet requirements; educating authors so that they met specific market demands; using contract sub-editors to meet fluctuations in the publishing process; and forging new links with computer hardware and

University Press, Durham, NC. See also J. A. Conger and R. Kanungo, 'Toward a behavioural theory of charismatic leadership in organisational settings', *Academy of Management Review*, vol. 12, no. 4, (1987), pp. 637–47.

11. This example is taken from one given by Edgar Schein (see reference 2).

12. The ANZ example is taken from D. Ballantyne, 'Management of the diagnostic review process in service quality management', Cranfield School of Management Working Paper, SWP 3/90.

13. The paper by T. Nakajo, and T. Kono, 'Success through culture change in a Japanese brewery', *Long Range Planning*, vol. 22, no. 6, (1989), pp. 29–37, is an interesting account of strategic change in a quite different culture, but draws many lessons parallel to this chapter.

14. This discussion is based on observations of the role of political activities in organisations by, in particular, Henry Mintzberg, *Power In and Around Organisations*, Prentice Hall, 1983, and Jeffrey Pfeffer, *Power in Organisations*, Pitman, 1981.

15. Figure 11.8 is based on advice given by P. Keen, 'Information systems and organisational change', in E. Rhodes and D. Weild (eds), *Implementing New Technologies: Choice, decision and change in manufacturing*, Basil Blackwell/Open University Press, and R. M. Kanter, *The Change Masters: Corporate entrepreneurs at work*, Unwin, 1983. Both are reported in D. Buchanan and D. Boddy, *The*

Expertise of the Change Agent, Prentice Hall, 1992, pp. 78–80.

16. Much of the writing of Tom Peters (for example, *In Search of Excellence*, with R. H. Waterman, Harper and Row, 1982, and *A Passion for Excellence*, with N. Austin, Collins, 1985) tends to emphasise the central role of the leader or 'champion' of change. However, for a useful and balanced review of the notion of charismatic leadership, see H. M. Trice and J. M. Beyer, 'Charisma and its routinisation in two social movement organisations', *Research in Organisation Behaviour*, vol. 8, (1986), pp. 113–64.

17. See D. Buchanan and D. Boddy, *The Expertise of the Change Agent: Public performances and backstage activity*, Prentice Hall, 1992.

18. The notion of endowed leadership is discussed by Trice and Beyer (see 16 above) pp. 124–6.

19. For a review of the characteristics and traits of successful corporate leaders, see C. Garfield, *Peak Performers: New heroes in business*, Hutchison Business, 1986; but also see the work by Kakabadse (see reference 9).

20. Peters and Waterman argue that 'An effective leader must be the master of two ends of the spectrum: ideas at the highest level of abstraction and actions at the most mundane level of detail'. See *In Search of Excellence*, (reference 16), p. 287.

21. The importance of limiting messages to 'three themes' is discussed by D. A. Nadler and H. L. Tushman, 'Organisational frame bending: prin-

software houses to develop products which exploited new technology.
While the experience of the 1980s generated certain shared assumptions within Longman, almost equal attention was given to the contradictions which arose. They were acted upon and the new knowledge built in to the cycle of strategic thinking and action. What stands out was the use of modest islands of progress, such as the finance committee's techniques, or the use of local publishing cells. The trying out of such responses to a problem was non-threatening and did not raise expectations unduly. The consequent solution was more amenable to diffusion and invaluable in sustaining the momentum of a complicated set of changes.

Prepared by Richard Whipp of Cardiff University Business School. A fuller account of Longman's experience appears in A. Pettigrew and R. Whipp, *Managing Change for Competitive Success*, Basil Blackwell, 1991.

ciples for managing, reorientation', *Academy of Management Executive*, vol. 3, no. 3, (1989), pp. 194–204.
22. This integrating framework is taken from the research on strategic change undertaken by Andrew Pettigrew and Richard Whipp. See *Managing Change for Competitive Success*, Basil Blackwell, 1991.

23. This conclusion is, of course, closely aligned to the views of those who advocate an organisational learning view of change. See, for example, P. Senge, *The Fifth Discipline: The art and practice of the learning organisation*, Century Business, 1992.

Recommended key readings

Chapter 14 on 'Managing change' in *The Strategy Process* edited by Henry Mintzberg and James B. Quinn, provides useful reading on some processes of managing strategic change.

For a fuller discussion of symbolic aspects of change management, see Gerry Johnson, 'Managing strategic change: the role of symbolic action', *British Journal of Management*, vol. 1, (1990), pp. 983–200.

There are surprisingly few readings which focus on aspects of political management. H. Mintzberg, *Power In and Around Organisations*, Prentice Hall, 1983, is probably the best book; but Machiavelli's *The Prince*, Penguin, 1961, remains the most compelling reading.

For a review of change agency, see D. Buchanan and D. Boddy, *The Expertise of the Change Agent: Public performance and backstage activity*, Prentice Hall, 1992.

For an integrating discussion of the management of strategic change, see A. Pettigrew and R. Whipp, *Managing Change for Competitive Success*, Basil Blackwell, 1991.

Work assignments

11.1   Based on cultural webs you have drawn up (e.g. see assignments 2 and 3 in Chapter 5) or on the basis of the cultural web in Illustration 2.6, identify the main blockages to change in an organisation?

11.2   With reference to section 11.4.1 and Figure 11.4, identify and explain the styles of managing change employed by different change agents, e.g. Ralph Halpern in Burton (B)* and (C)*; Rupert Murdoch in The News Corporation,* or a chief executive whose work you are familiar with.

11.3   *In an example of change management with which you are familiar, e.g. Burton (A)* or the Crucible Theatre* identify political blockages to change; and building on section 11.4.4 and Figures 11.6 and 11.7, suggest how a change agent might overcome such blockages.*

11.4   Using Figure 11.5, give examples of rituals which do (or could be used to) signal change in an organisation with which you are familiar.

11.5   **Using the frameworks for managing strategic change discussed in Part IV of the book, and Chapter 11 in particular, compare and evaluate the approaches to strategic change followed by two change agents, e.g. Ralph Halpern of Burton* and Tim Rix of Longman or two others of your choice. Bear in mind their strategic and organisational contexts in your evaluation.**

11.6   *There are a number of books by renowned senior executives who have managed major changes in their organisation (e.g. by Lee Iacocca, John Harvey-Jones, Michael Edwardes). Read one of these and appraise the approach taken and the abilities of that change agent, in the context of this book and writers on change agency (e.g. refer to Buchanan and Boddy in the recommended key readings and to Kakabadse's The Wealth Creators; See reference 9).*

11.7   *Using the Longman illustration (11.6), Burton (B)* or an organisation of your choice, identify the reasons for the success of a strategy in terms of:*
   (a) competitive positioning
   (b) organisation structure and control
   (c) management style
   (d) processes of strategic change.
   To what extent are any of these elements more or less significant in the success of the organisation?

* This refers to a case study from the Text and Cases version of this book.

Index of companies and organisations

ABN (bank), 257
Air France, 324–5
Albani, 98
American Airlines, 325
AMRO (bank), 257
Amstrad, 128, 129
Antenne 2, 197
ANZ Bank, 404
Arthur D. Little, 250, 252
Asaki Breweries, 405
Association of British Travel Agents, 160
ATT, 299

Bass, 96, 98, 233
BBC, 122
Benetton, 128
Black and Decker, 124
BNP (bank), 214
BOC, 358
Boston Consulting Group, 130–1, 144, 145, 249
Braxton Associates, 25
British Aerospace, 271
British Airways, 14–15, 116, 119, 122, 325
British Insurance Brokers Association, 160, 162
British Petroleum, 290–1
British Rail, 25, 92, 247
British Telecom, 216, 271, 298, 299
Brother, 124
BSN, 233
BTR, 348, 361
Bundesbahn, 247

Cadbury Schweppes, 216, 358
Carnaud, 161,
CBS, 197
Cheshire County Council, 335
Chrysler, 67
Churchill Livingstone, 419
Churchill Pottery, 276–7
Clydesdale Bank, 81
CMB Packaging, 161
Coca-Cola, 238
Cokoladovny, 233
Companiex, 126–7
Conseil Superieur de Audiovisuel, 196–7

Courtaulds, 362

Degussa, 80
Deutsche Babcock and Metallgesellschaft, 81
Deutsche Eisenbahn AG, 247
Digital Equipment Corporation, 66
Dunsmore Chemical Company, 294–5

Elsevier–NDU, 224
Europa, 357

Ford, 27, 37

GEC, 98
General Motors, 27
Gossnab, 394
Guinness, 98, 117, 119

Hanson Trust, 229, 257, 361
HMSO, 271
Holiday Inns, 233
Honda, 89

IBM France, 196
ICI, 122, 188, 357, 362
ICL, 375
IKEA, 3–11, 17, 19–21, 23–4, 32, 213
Institute of Management, 197
Internationale Nederlanden Group, 237
ITT, 66–7

Kelloggs, 89, 207
Kia, 37
Kindercare, 388, 390–1
KLM, 325
Kronenbourg, 98

La Compagnie Bancaire, 214
Land Rover, 340–1
Lex, 358
Linfield, 255
London Transport, 271
Longman Publishing, 418–21
Lonrho, 233, 348, 361
Lufthansa, 325

McDonald's, 238, 359
Marks and Spencer, 89, 98, 208–9, 218
Mars, 101, 207, 232
Mazda, 37
Medic Aid, 24
Metal Box, 161
Michelin, 196
Midland Bank, 81, 122
Mitsubishi, 340
Monopolies and Mergers Commission, 89
Motorola, 80

National Australia Bank, 81
National Health Service, 81, 140–1, 217–19, 262
National House Builders Registration Council, 160
Nationale Nederland, 236–7
Nestlé, 101, 196, 233
NFC, 106, 108–9
NMB Postbank, 236–7

OFTEL, 299
OPEC, 87, 162
Opportunity 2000, 122

Pan Am, 325
Philips, 80, 399
Polytechnic and College Funding Council, 318–19
Post Office, 271
Project Medias 92, 197
Publishers' Association, 419

Reed International, 122
Rolls-Royce, 67, 80, 271, 284, 291

Royal Dutch Airlines, 325

Sabena World Airlines, 15
Sainsbury, 91, 122, 207–8, 209
SAS, 325
Savoy Hotel, 170
Sheffield City Council, 366–7
Sheffield Development Corporation, 179
Shell, 86–7, 352
SOGAT, 419
South Yorkshire Police, 189
STC, 358
Strategic Planning Institute, 263, 296

Tarmac, 361
Tesco, 208–9
TF1, 197
Training and Enterprise Council, 179
Trusthouse Forte, 170
TWA, 325

Unilever, 101, 227
United Stationers, 330
University Funding Council, 318

Vickers, 80
Virgin Records/Airlines, 222
VNU (publisher), 224
Volkswagen, 37

Wolters-Kluwer, 224

YMCA, 25

Case Studies

Case Studies

A guide to using the case studies

The main text of this book includes about 60 short illustrations which have been chosen to enlarge specific issues in the text and/or provide practical examples of how business and public-sector organisations are managing strategic issues. The case studies which follow allow the reader to extend this linking of theory and practice further by analysing the strategic issues of specific organisations in much greater depth – and often providing 'solutions' to some of the problems or difficulties identified in the case.

The case studies are intended to serve as the basis for class discussion and not as an illustration of either good or bad management practice. They are *not* intended to be a comprehensive collection of teaching material. They have been chosen (or specially written) to provide readers with a *core* of cases which together cover most of the main issues in the text. As such they should provide a useful *backbone* to a programme of study, but can sensibly be supplemented by other material.

Some cases are written entirely from published sources, but most have been prepared in co-operation with and have the approval of the management of the organisation concerned. Case studies can never fully capture the richness and complexity of real-life management situations and we would encourage readers and tutors additionally to take every possible opportunity to explore the live strategic issues of organisations – both their own and others.

A new feature of this edition is the inclusion of *work assignments* at the end of each chapter. These relate issues in the text to illustrations and the readers' own experience or choice of organisations but also to the case studies in this section of the book. The format of work assignments is explained in the preface.

The following brief points of guidance should prove useful in selecting and using the case studies provided:

- The summary table which follows indicates the main focus of each of the chosen case studies – together with important subsidiary foci (where appropriate). In general, the sequence of cases is intended to mirror the chapter sequence. However, this should not be taken too literally because, of course, many of these cases cover a variety of issues. The 'classification' provided is therefore for guidance only. We expect readers to seek their own

Guide to main focus of cases

		TEXT CHAPTERS						Strategic choice							
No.	Case	Page no.	All Intro-duction	2 Strategic Management Process	3 Industry Analysis/ Business Environment	4 Resource Analysis	5 Expect-ations Objectives	3-5 Overall Strategic Analysis	6 Generic Strate-gies	6 Strategic Options	7 & 8 Strategic Evalua-tion	6 Diversi-fication	9 Resource Planning	10 Struc-ture & Sys-tems	11 Man-aging Change	All Integra-tive Case
1	British Steel	431	**													
2	Planning in Shell	435	**	**												
3	European Brewing Industry	444			**											
4	Courage	475						*	*		**					
5	Kronenbourg	482						*	*		**			*		
6	Laura Ashley	495				**	*									
7	Crucible Theatre	526				*	**						*			

No.		Page
8	World Automobile Industry	558
9	Peugeot	571
10	Rover/Honda	591
11	Vitalograph	603
12	The News Corporation	623
13	Electrolux	651
14	KPMG	676
15	Burton 'A'	686
16	Burton 'B'	697
17	Burton 'C'	710

Note: ** = Major focus
* = Important subsidiary focus

lessons from cases, and tutors to use cases in whichever way and sequence best fits the purpose of their programmes.

- Where cases have been chosen to illustrate the issues of strategic choice and implementation covered later in the book, it will normally be a prerequisite that some type of strategic analysis of the case material is undertaken. When planning the use of these cases within programmes, care needs to be taken to balance the time taken on strategic analysis so as to allow the time required to analyse the main issues for which the case has been chosen.

- Where the text and cases are being used as the framework for a strategy programme (as we hope they will), it is essential that students are required to undertake additional reading from other sources and that their 'practical' work is supplemented by other material as mentioned above.

- While many of the cases can play an integrative role within a strategy course, we have a series of cases on the development of corporate strategy in Burton specifically as an integrative set. It has proved particularly useful to round off a strategy course by examining the extent to which different issues interrelate over time in the complex process of strategy formulation and implementation: Burton (A), (B) and (C) can be used for this purpose.

British Steel

Kevan Scholes

In January 1992 British Steel announced that it was closing its last remaining steel-making facility in Scotland – the Ravenscraig plant – with the loss of 1,220 jobs. The facilities were to be split up and sold to operators outside the European Community (EC), probably in eastern Europe or Asia. Critics were complaining that this decision flew in the face of the pledge made at the privatisation of British Steel (in 1989) that the plant would remain open until 1994 or be sold as a going concern. However, the state of the national and international markets for steel had proved worse than anyone had predicted, with UK output in 1991 – 16.5 tonnes – 8 per cent lower than in 1990, which in turn had been 4 per cent below 1989. In addition, European Steel prices were as much as 20 per cent below levels of 1990.

This was a far cry from March 1990 when British Steel stood on top of the world. It had become the most profitable steel company in the world with pre-tax profits of £733m. It was hailed as nothing short of an industrial miracle. In ten years the near-bankrupt state-owned British Steel Corporation (BSC), which made cumulative losses of £7,000m between 1975 and 1984, had been transformed into the super-fit, privatised British Steel.

At the time of privatisation in 1989 the ingredients of BSC's transformation could be clearly seen. For example, labour costs had fallen from 31 per cent to 20 per cent of total costs since 1980 as the workforce was reduced from 140,000 to 51,000; and in terms of productivity, by 1987 the UK steel industry produced around 320 tonnes per man year against West Germany's 279 – a remarkable change from 1981 when Germany led the UK by 227 tonnes to 167. These improvements in performance were dependent on a number of important changes and management decisions made during that period:

- An investment programme of £985m for modernisation and re-equipping was undertaken. For example, by early 1989, the Corporation produced about 80 per cent of its output by the efficient continuous casting method rather than the ingot method. This represented savings of about £14–18 per tonne.

This case study was prepared by Professor Kevan Scholes, Sheffield Business School, from published sources. It incorporates information from the previous British Steel case study (1988). It is intended as a basis for class discussion and not as an illustration of either good or bad management practice. © Kevan Scholes, 1992.

However, the French, Italian and West German industries were all nearly 90 per cent committed to continuous casting by 1988. The Corporation itself believed that it needed about £250m annually to maintain the necessary investment programme.

- The Corporation had completely revamped its management structure, reducing central overheads considerably and devolving responsibility for operations and profit to a substantial degree.
- There was a revolution in working practices. Up to 18 per cent of pay became bonus-related, giving BSC room to curb its wage bill during fluctuating demand.

Despite the impressive results which these changes achieved, there were also grounds for caution. Many observers felt that operating five integrated steel plants was overcomplicated and costly. There were elements of cost where BSC compared poorly against international competition. The Corporation itself had been telling analysts that its use of energy was perhaps 20 per cent more than it should be – other sources regarded that as an underestimate. It also had some way to go on process control and continuous production monitoring to reduce defects.

Other factors, largely outside their control, also affected their performance. The speed at which other European producers were reorganising and improving efficiency, and the movement of the more aggressive producers such as South Korea into higher value-added products, and Europe, were both important.

The period immediately prior to and following privatisation was one of growing international demand and impressive financial performance from British Steel, as shown in the Appendix. However, by 1991 the recession and overcapacity in Europe had forced both prices and volumes down by more than 10 per cent. The economics of British Steel's position were harsh. A 10 per cent reduction in price took some £300m off profits; and 10 per cent off volumes reduced profits by a further £500m, transforming a healthy profit of £773m in 1989/90 to an anticipated loss of some £100m in 1991/92.

However, some analysts felt that there were longer-term changes already occurring in the international steel markets which British Steel and others would need to take on board. More steel was crossing borders in Europe as the 1992 single market approached. British Steel's profitable dominance of its own national market was no longer assured. Market share in the UK had fallen from 62 to 57 per cent during 1990. European rivals – such as the state-owned French giant Usinor Sacilor – were buying up distributors in Britain. At the same time, Britain's entry into the exchange rate mechanism of the European Monetary System (in 1990) had minimised the currency risk that always made stockholders reluctant to buy foreign steel in case a fall in sterling sent its price soaring.

However, open European markets worked both ways, and British Steel was hitting back. In 1990 its exports rose 10 per cent to a record 39 per cent of the group's £5 billion sales. But increasing market share on the continent was a long haul and not a very profitable one at that. British Steel had only 2.5 per cent of the fragmented European steel market. Moreover, prices were such that British Steel had to export almost three tonnes of steel to make the same profit as it did on one tonne in Britain. Cost cutting was one way to relieve the pressure on margins. British Steel might have lost its top spot in the global profitability league, but it remained alongside the South Koreans as the world's lowest-cost manufacturer.

A two-year programme to cut 6,000 jobs from its 53,000-strong workforce was accelerated to fight the profit slump, culminating in the announcement of the Ravenscraig closure in 1992. British Steel was also investing heavily to increase efficiency through closures, rationalisation and building modern plants.

However, efficiency was not the only strand of British Steel's international strategy. Its main aim was to become a genuine multinational business rather than a UK-based exporter with 60 per cent of its sales in the home market. This international development was being pursued with an emphasis on the core business of steel – a contrast with Japanese and some German steelmakers which had diversified into many other areas, including silicon chips and lap-top computers.

The international steel market in the early 1990s remained nationalistic with many political barriers to takeovers. A number of potential joint ventures in Europe and the USA had stalled as trading conditions worsened towards the end of 1991. A proposed joint venture with Bethlehem Steel in the United States was scuppered by opposition from American unions. German steelmakers united to slam the door on British Steel's attempts to buy into Europe's largest market. Talks to buy a large chunk of Aristrain, one of Spain's leading construction steel makers were deadlocked over price. There was also speculation that British Steel might link up with a Japanese producer to gain global coverage in a core business such as automotive steel. During the same period Usinor (France's largest producer) had enjoyed considerable success with takeovers and joint ventures in Germany, Italy, Luxembourg, Britain and USA, spending £1.6 billion of state money on acquisitions in 1989/90. However, British Steel turned down a proposal from Usinor to form a joint venture in the production of steel plate. Although on the face of it this seemed a good way of reducing losses, it was rejected because Bob Scholey (British Steel chairman) appeared to have an aversion to linking with state-owned companies, the reason being that politics were liable to pre-empt commercial considerations.

In July 1992 British Steel announced that they were to merge their stainless steel operations – mainly based in Sheffield – with the Swedish steel producer Avesta. The new company would have a turnover in excess of £1 billion, 9,300 employees (one third in the UK) and a capacity of some 800,000 tonnes. Nonetheless with pending losses of £100m, analysts were asking whether this was the end of the miracle. Would British Steel, which had become one of Britain's truly world-class businesses, be overtaken by foreign rivals?

Appendix Pre-tax profits (£m)

1980/81	−1,800	1986/87	177
1981/82	−492	1987/88	419
1982/83	−866	1988/89	593
1983/84	−253	1989/90	733
1984/85	−378	1990/91	254
1985/86	−42	1991/92	−100
			(forecast)

Planning in Shell
Julie Verity

Background The Royal Dutch/Shell Group

The Royal Dutch/Shell Group operates in more than 100 countries worldwide and employs 130,000 people in the oil and gas, chemicals, coal, metals and forestry business sectors. The size of the group is substantial. Net income in 1991 amounted to £2.4 billion, capital employed £33.1 billion and capital expenditure £6.8 billion. The origins of the group extend back to 1907 when the Royal Dutch Company (based in the Hague) and the Shell Transport and Trading Company (based in London) made an alliance whereby the two companies agreed to merge their interests while keeping their separate identities. Over 80 years later, the two public companies were still separate with their own boards of directors, responsible to their own shareholders: Royal Dutch with a 60 per cent interest and Shell Transport a 40 per cent interest in the group.

The group organisation was decentralised in nature, each operating company being responsible for the performance and long-term viability of its own operations, usually geographically defined. Service companies, based in London and the Hague, provided advice and services to group operating companies outside the USA (Exhibit 1). These were not corporate headquarters or central management offices and had no stated 'corporate' decision-making responsibility.

In the service companies there was a matrix of group regions, business-sector organisations and functions (Exhibit 2). The interests of the group shareholder, on behalf of the parent companies, were served by regions which examined plans, aired support for capital expenditure, made key personnel appointments and appraised operating companies' performance. Group functions ranged from finance, HR, public affairs and marketing to technical functions such as research. These functions had the job of keeping up to date with professional and technical knowledge and disseminating it throughout the group, giving advice and setting standards, guidelines and procedures. The business sectors (chemicals, upstream oil, etc.) existed to take a global perspective of the businesses: primarily their job was to provide operating companies with insights into the commercial global environment, to help with strategic thinking and to give whatever professional support was required. However, this global overview did not extend to power over the local operating company:

This case study is drawn from an interview in 1991 conducted with Graham Galer, who is head of planning support within Shell's Group Planning function in London. It is supplemented by his comments and from published literature of Shell. It is intended for classroom discussion and not as an illustration of good or bad management practice. © Cranfield School of Management, 1992.

Exhibit 1 **Structure of the Royal Dutch/Shell Group**

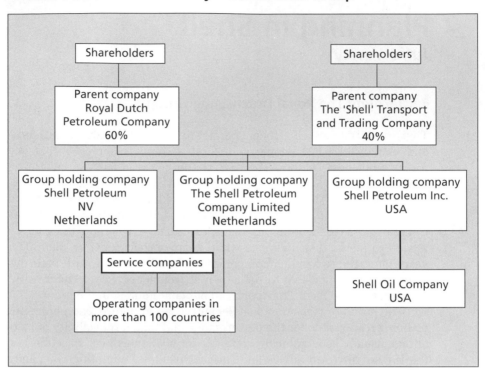

No matter how important the global overview and the amount of advice and service a local operating company chooses to request, the Shell approach is that nothing is allowed to detract from the basic principle of local accountability. This emphasis on decentralised 'bottom line' accountability ensures that the group can evolve with changing times . . .
(*The Organisation of International Business: the Shell approach*, 1990)

Group planning

The group planning function was part of the London Service Company and comprised about 32 people (Exhibit 3). The role of this department was given as to:

- Ensure that the group adopts appropriate planning processes and criteria.
- Scan and monitor the global business environment.
- Co-ordinate periodic reviews of group strategies and resources.
- Act as a centre of expertise for the group in planning matters.
- Provide support services and training in planning to group management.

Exhibit 2 **Group organisational matrix**

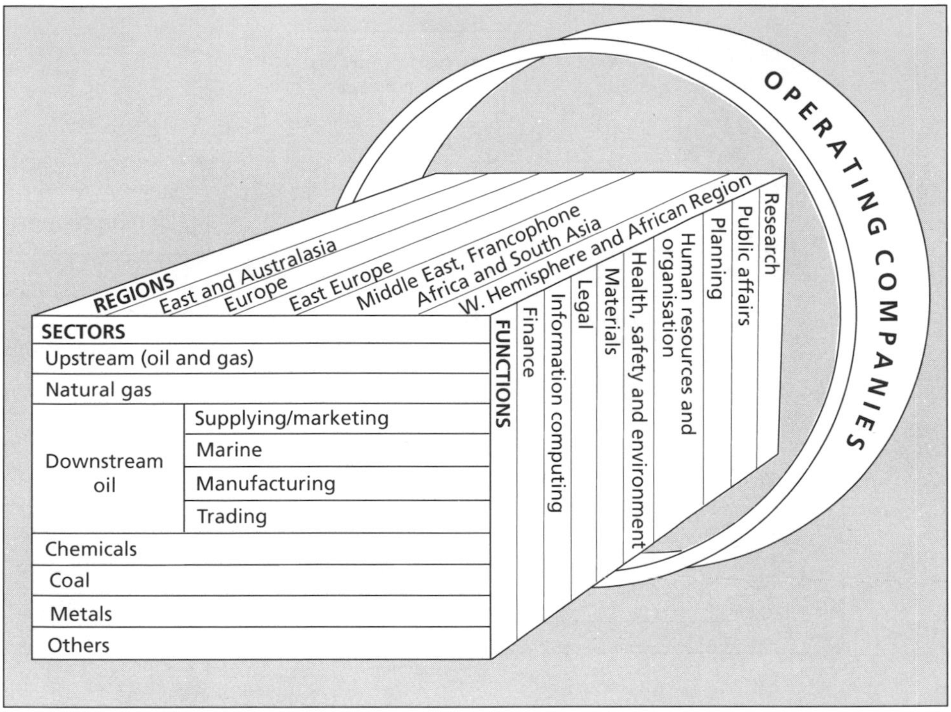

Planning activities were described in three parts: the planning cycle, planning processes and planning methods.

The planning cycle

The planning cycle provided a framework for periodic overview of the operating companies' strategies, plans and resource requirements. It comprised three main elements: strategic planning, which formed the basis for the next element, which was business planning, and appraisal. This system and its timing is summarised in Exhibit 4.

Strategic planning was done at the country and business-sector level, and from the group perspective was a 'bottom-up' exercise conducted by the major operating companies. Input from the central planning group was the presentation of scenarios (revised on a 2–3-year cycle), the purpose of which was to provide a background for strategic thinking within the operating companies and business sectors. The group strategy review compiled all the strategy thinking into a periodic overview for the group as a whole.

Business planning was done on an annual basis and took a shorter-term view (five years forward) of the business. The whole was brought together in the

Exhibit 3 Group Planning organisation – London

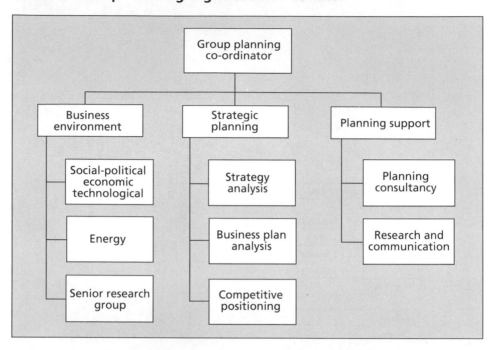

group resources review, which essentially presented financial and human resource requirements called for by the sum of operating company plans.

The annual appraisal process of performance against plan consisted of a series of reviews carried out by operating company managements with teams from the service companies who acted as 'shareholders' representatives'.

The planning process

Group scenarios, produced by Group Planning, were an important part of the strategic planning process. They were alternative, long-term (twenty years) views of the future produced by a methodology devised within Shell (described in more detail below). They were global in nature and raised general, but potentially key issues for the future. It was regarded as essential that the scenarios were 'owned' by group senior management and not imposed by Group Planning. This ownership was gained by a process of discussion/interview and iteration, leading to a consensus between managers and central group planners that there was a robust logic behind the scenarios, deeming any of them probable. The scenarios were disseminated (by presentation, visits and in written form) to major operating companies and business sectors by Group Planning personnel.

Scenarios, adopted by 'strategic thinkers' (key decision-takers and planners) in sectors, regions and operating companies, were sometimes elaborated

Exhibit 4 **The group planning cycle**

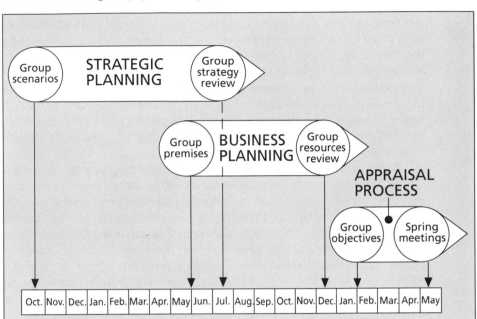

Group planning – 1991

or translated into a form which suited the local environment, focusing on local issues and producing 'focused scenarios'. This process was one which entailed testing the global logic against what was occurring locally, the objective being to bring the global picture to credible reality. For example, if a global scenario assumed a world where free-market forces were increasingly the political choice, translation to the local scene would mean less industry regulation, more privatisation and increasing competition. Local implications would be added into the focused scenario and tested with current trends and indicators. Responsibility for providing focused scenarios fell to different personnel depending on the operating company, business sector or region, but was likely to be shared between planners and key decision-makers in the local organisation.

From scenarios and/or focused scenarios, the strategic planning process followed various routes according to the participating organisation. Larger operating companies were likely to follow more sophisticated processes. Smaller parts of the business would undertake a much simpler process which involved fewer people and less time. Some operating companies would not follow any formal procedure, although all would include a statement of strategic direction in their business plans (see below).

The recommended strategic planning process (usually facilitated by Group Planning) was essentially one of manager participation in a series of strategy meetings or workshops. The latter provided a structured framework to consider the implications of the scenarios, to develop a strategic vision of the future for the business and to identify key issues and strategic options. Discussion also took place on the nature of competition, the critical success factors required and the distinctive competences (for the company relative to the competition). Workshops were held offsite in an informal atmosphere and emphasis was put on brainstorming and creative thinking. An 'external' facilitator was used during the workshops who might be a representative from Group Planning. Representation from the local organisation would again vary, but was likely to include the senior management team (including CEO, where appropriate) and their senior planners (if they existed).

A report of the outcome of the strategic planning process was submitted to Group Planning for the purpose of the group strategy review (Exhibit 4). In this exercise, sector, regional and operating country strategies were compiled into a single report, by Group Planning, for consideration by the Committee of Managing Directors (CMD) and other senior group management. As well as presenting the total of the group's strategic thinking, it tried to assess what the aggregation meant for the group. It also reported progress on special strategic studies and identified new issues for future study. Like scenarios, the group strategy review was typically undertaken every two or three years as events required.

The strategic planning process was not highly formalised; it was a process which was done as and when it was seen as necessary. Graham Galer, head of planning support, commented:

A lot of people [within the organisation] think you cannot systematise strategic planning – you will stifle creativity. There are others who feel it is not really necessary, but then there is a substantial body of people who see value from devoting effort to it . . . I think strategic management is an aspect of management and I think that a company that is managed well will be strategically managed well – it all goes together. In one of our operating companies for instance they certainly have followed all the procedures religiously, but their results are not very good. In another example, they have a rather heavyweight planning system, nevertheless their performance is mediocre to say the least, but I would not blame the processes – maybe the quality of thinking, the implementation, bad luck or a strategic block they cannot overcome?

The business planning process was highly systematised when compared with strategic planning. Every operating company (even very small ones) had to produce an annual business plan which looked forward five years. The degree of sophistication and standardisation was consistent across all operating companies.

The process was supported by Group Planning, which supplied 'premises' to the operating companies as a set of assumptions which should be used as a common basis of quantification in all plans. These included examples such as oil price, exchange rates and economic growth rates. The plans themselves gave an account of current and anticipated business and what each company was planning to do, especially in terms of resources. The process was essentially 'bottom-up' (from the group and operating company perspective), starting at the operating company level between June and September. These were reviewed with central offices during October and November and the process culminated in the group resources review in December. The group resources review was prepared by Group Planning and Group Finance and was presented to CMD and other senior management.

The actual process was largely one of consensus building. Graham Galer gave the example of Shell Australia:

> Shell Australia has got businesses in virtually everything the group does, so its plan will include: exploration, production, downstream, chemicals, metals, coal. In bringing the plan here [London] for support it comes to a series of two or three meetings at various levels. At one of these the managing director responsible for the Far East will ask (for example) the representative from Chemicals if they support the plan from Shell Australia. And the Chemicals man will normally be able to say yes, because before this meeting, Chemicals Australia will have discussed their plans with Chemicals Sector which ensures, ahead of time, that the Australian plan was acceptable. This is important because, for example, both Shell Australia and Shell Singapore might decide they want to build a polypropylene plant to supply markets in the Far East. This would be a waste of group resources, so this sort of argument has to be sorted out before it goes into the Australian plan.

The spring appraisal process consisted of a review of performance against plan for the previous year (plans prepared in the autumn of 1989 would be discussed in the 1991 spring appraisal). Both the business plan and strategy were reviewed, Galer commented: 'some people have a problem handling appraisal and strategy review together. Among regions there are different degrees of commitment and understanding. But in the bigger companies it is mostly run very well.'

Planning methods

A major role of Group Planning and group functions has been to supply useful planning tools and techniques to operating companies to assist in this process. The approach used is the '4 box' approach which is shown in Exhibit 5. The boxes – analysis of the business environment (scenarios are used here), competitive positioning, the development of strategic vision and option management – are interrelated, and may be seen as a set of handles with which to grasp a strategic business problem, or alternatively as a kit of tools for its analysis.

Exhibit 5 The '4 box' approach

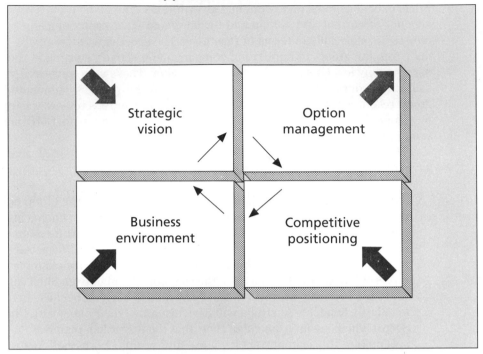

'Strategic planning is about managing options, creating them, identifying them, selecting the right ones, against a background of knowing what you want to do, i.e. the strategic vision, within the business environment.'

Scenario methods were used to make assessments of the future business environment. Experts from many areas (external and internal to the business) assess macro- and micro-environmental forces in order to gain alternative long-term views of the future based on current observable trends (albeit small or unimportant at the present). A critical role of this thinking process was to surface different perspectives and different mental maps with which to challenge conventional thinking and encourage debate in a learning process. There was no simple formula for generating useful scenarios: the methodology depended on the use of multidisciplinary teams and open, free-thinking brainstorming sessions.

Techniques used for competitive analysis and positioning were largely those available from the academic and consulting spheres, which have been adopted in various degrees throughout the group. This analysis was designed to create a better understanding of the nature of competition and the factors which affected the ability to sustain profits. These elements, together with an analysis of the business itself, formed the basis for a review of the strategic vision for an operating company (what the company would like to be by the end of the twenty-year period). Here a standardised format was used so as to pull out the key components of a vision statement. In this format the notion of 'distinctive competences', in which an effort was made to identify the ways of securing competitive advantage, played a vital part. As a consequence, options could be generated and assessed which would lead to a strategic plan.

A group planning perspective on planning in Shell

Graham Galer's overall view about planning in Shell could be summarised as follows:

> Planners have moved in recent years from being experts and number crunchers to being facilitators of processes. . . . We have been encouraging people working in planning to take more responsibility for the planning processes, to see themselves as facilitators of a management process. We put the emphasis here for two reasons. First, is to get management ownership of the plans they make and second, to encourage matching scenario work to strategy, to make links between a scenario and what it means to the business.
>
> To many managers in Shell, planning is a bit of a distraction to their day-to-day operations. Especially strategic planning. Business planning is very well established, everybody knows they have to do them. In the major operating companies, these business plans are well accepted and seen as a management tool.

The approach to planning, as a part of the group's management system, has changed over the years so that now the objective is to subsume planning activities into the practice of 'strategic management', effected by local management teams. The role of Group Planning has evolved to be one of developing useful tools and techniques which can help managers cope profitably with the uncertainties and difficulties of the modern business world.

The European brewing industry 1992

Murray Steele

In 1992 Europe was the major centre of beer consumption and production in the world. The output of *Europe as a whole* was more than 50 per cent greater than that of the USA, the world's largest beer-producing country. However, significant differences existed from country to country, in terms of both industry structure and market characteristics. As a Dutch brewer put it:

> The Americans or the Japanese, they see the unification of Europe as an imminent thing, Europe is a new market of 320 million consumers. They do not realise, like we do, that it is a multi-local market. In Italy there has to be a different approach from Spain.

Industry Structure

Table 1 shows the output of the top fifteen European brewers in 1990. It can be seen that the European market was not very concentrated, the top five brewers having a combined market share of 31.2 per cent. The European brewers were relatively insular. Only five of the top fifteen had sales of any significance, i.e. over 1 million hectolitres per annum, outside Europe. Similarly, for the majority of them, the bulk of their output was produced in their country of origin.

On a global comparison, only two of the brewers listed in Table 1 were in the top ten brewers of the world. Heineken was number three, and BSN was number six. To put this further in context, Anheuser–Busch of the USA, the largest brewing company in the world, had an annual output of the order of 102 million hectolitres, almost double that of Heineken, Europe's largest brewing group.

Industry Concentration

In 1992 individual European countries had substantially different industry struc-

The author acknowledges the assistance of his colleagues Gerry Johnson and Bridget Garnish, and also of the MODEM Research Group, who provided the quotations from their book, *The Business of Europe: Managing change*, Sage, 1991, which punctuate this case study. It is intended as a basis for class discussion and not as an illustration of either good or bad management practice.

Table 1 Top fifteen brewers in Europe, 1990

	Estimated European sales	European market share (%)	Estimated rest of world sales	Total sales
1. Heineken (Holland)	28.9	9.2	24.6	53.5
2. BSN (France)	24.2	8.2	1.5	25.7
3. Carlsberg (Denmark)	15.2	5.1	3.8	19.0
4. Guinness (Eire)	14.4	4.8	4.4	18.8
5. Bass (UK)	13.9	4.6	0.3	14.2
6. Courage (UK)	13.5	4.5		13.5
7. Allied (UK)	11.5	3.8	0.5	9.0
8. Interbrew (Belgium)	9.8	3.3	5.6	15.4
9. Whitbread (UK)	8.3	2.8	0.1	8.4
10. Oetker (Germany)	7.8	2.7	0.1	7.9
11. S & N (UK)	7.0	2.4		7.0
12. Marz (Germany)	6.5	2.3		6.5
13. Brau & Brunnen (Germany)	6.5	2.3		6.5
14. Grolsch (Holland)	4.6	1.5	0.2	4.8
15. Holsten (Germany)	4.6	1.5	0.4	5.0

Notes
1. All figures are in millions of hectolitres.
2. Volumes include those companies in which the relevant brewer has an interest in excess of 30%.
Source: Annual reports, trade sources and ERC data bases.

tures. They varied from the highly concentrated to the highly fragmented. Some countries, e.g. the United Kingdom, had regulations which limited the degree of concentration allowed in industries. Other countries did not have these rules, and in fact may have encouraged concentration to help the creation and development of significant international competitors. Table 2 shows the varying degrees of concentration in the principal European brewing countries.

> Concentration will certainly continue, to improve industrial efficiency, to face the growing power of retail chains and to achieve the conquest of European markets in the 1990s. (French brewing manager)

Ownership

There was much variation in ownership patterns across Europe. There was little ownership of breweries by other European companies in West Germany, and none in Denmark and the United Kingdom. On the other hand, significant proportions of the Italian and Spanish industries were in the hands of foreign brewers.

These ownership structures were created during the 1970s and 1980s when there were significant cross-border acquisitions. These moves were driven by small domestic markets, causing ambitious brewers to seek international expansion opportunities.

European brewers did not wait for 1992, 'l'Acte Unique', before moving into different countries. Our international development strategy, including acquisitions, started in 1978.   (French brewing manager)

1992 started ten years ago for us, because at the end of the 1970s we saw that the home market was too small, if we wanted to expand on a global scale. So the board of directors decided as a policy to make Europe our home. Since then we have made a lot of acquisitions in other European countries.   (Dutch brewing manager)

Table 3 shows the major European cross-border ownership stakes in 1992.

There was little ownership in Europe by non-European brewers. The largest example was Courage of the United Kingdom, which was owned by Fosters

Table 2 Industry concentration by country, 1990

Country	Industry situation	Number of competitors	Degree of concentration (%)
Denmark	Monopoly	1	75
Holland	Monopoly	1	65
Italy	Monopoly	2	57
Belgium	Monopoly	2	72
France	Monopoly	2	71
United Kingdom	Concentrated	5	80
Spain	Concentrated	5	87
West Germany	Fragmented	5	28

Note The degree of concentration relates to the combined market share held by the stated number of competitors.

Table 3 Cross-European ownership stakes

	Heineken	BSN	Carlsberg	Stella-Interbrew
France	*	**		*
West Germany			*	
Belgium		*		**
Holland	**			
Denmark			**	
Spain	*	*	*	
Italy	*	*	*	*
United Kingdom				
Ireland	*			

Notes *   denotes an ownership presence.
         ** denotes country of origin.

Brewing Group of Australia. The only other examples were Labatts of Canada, which owned two small breweries in Italy, and Stroh of the USA, which had a minority stake in Cruz del Campo, the leading Spanish brewer.

In addition to cross-border ownership stakes, there were licensing arrangements whereby brewers in one country brewed a particular brand from another country. This principally took place in the United Kingdom. A good example was Whitbread, which brewed and sold both Stella Artois and Heineken under licence in the UK. This provided it with an expanded portfolio of brands.

Consumption

Table 4 shows the consumption per capita in litres per annum for the major European and eastern European markets in the 1980s.

Brands

With low growth, or declines, in consumption in the European markets, brewers intensified their brand development policies to strengthen their positions in the marketplace. One British brewing manager stated the point succinctly:

> My success factor is that you have got to own your own brands, and they have got to be good brands, or else you are going to be dead in the water.

Table 4 Consumption (litres per capita)*

	1989	*1988*	*1987*	*1985*	*1980*
West Germany	143	143	144	146	146
East Germany**	147	143	143	142	139
Czechoslovakia**	132	130	130	133	138
Denmark	127	126	125	130	131
Belgium	115	119	121	121	131
Austria	119	118	118	119	102
United Kingdom	110	111	110	108	117
Hungary**	103	101	100	99	86
Ireland	90	94	94	105	122
Holland	88	83	84	85	86
Spain	72	69	67	61	53
Portugal	64	53	47	38	38
Greece	39	40	36	34	26
France	41	39	39	40	44
Italy	22	23	23	22	17

Notes *   including low-alcohol beers.
      ** denotes eastern European.

Source: UK Brewers' Society.

Consumers were seen as identifying with the image of a product, and strong branding was essential to take advantage of this.

Figure 1 shows the top ten selling beer brands in Europe in 1990. Not surprisingly, the top three brands were marketed by the three largest companies, which had the most extensive operations across Europe. Heineken had two of the top five brands – Heineken and Amstel – and Carlsberg had two of the top ten brands – Carlsberg and Tuborg.

Market segmentation

For the same reasons as branding had intensified, i.e low growth or declining consumption patterns, clear segments of the market, with different characteristics, were beginning to develop.

> We notice that in a saturated market there is segmentation. In a growing market beer is beer, in a segmented market this is not the case. (Dutch brewing manager)

A good example of a growing segment in a mature market was the increase in lager sales in the United Kingdom. During the twenty years up to 1990, the total volume of beer sold in the UK had not changed substantially, but in that period lager's share of the market increased from 7.5 to 55 per cent.

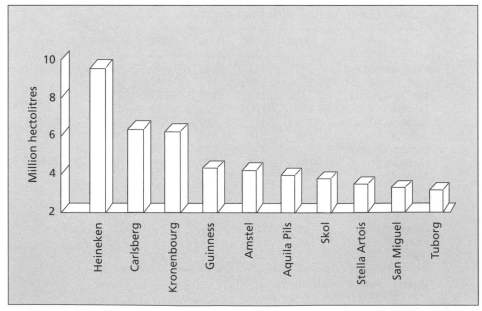

Figure 1 Top ten European brands

Distinct segments of the European market had developed (see Table 5). The segments which had been growing and were expected to continue to grow were the low-alcohol and alcohol-free beers, and particularly the premium and speciality beers. Also seen as having growth potential were the supermarket chain own-label beers. This was a function of their low price and the distribution power of the supermarket chains.

> The beers selling increasingly are the premium beers, specialities and non-alcoholic beers which have doubled their sales. This is the tendency for several years now.   (French brewing manager)

> Because of the anti-alcohol lobby and drink-driving, people will drink less but demand better products. Hence premium products will grow, they are growing all over the world. The growth in premium beer sales is even higher than the growth in supermarket own labels.   (British brewing manager)

Different brands in their segments were viewed differently from country to country. Brands which did not have their origin in a country, i.e. which were 'foreign', were often viewed as premium segment products. However, potential hazards existed for brewers in pursuing this policy:

> In Great Britain, Stella Artois is a premium beer, one of the most expensive beers you can get there, and people buy it because it is expensive. It is marketed and promoted that way. The British are travelling people, now when they come to Belgium, they discover that Stella Artois is a cheap beer, so they ask themselves if it is justified to pay so much for it in Great Britain.
> (French brewing manager)

Another diversity existed in price relationships between premium and ordinary beers and by European geographic region:

> There is another interesting difference between countries. In southern Europe the price differential is high between the premium/speciality

Table 5 European market segments

Segment	Estimated market share (%)
Low and no alcohol	7
Premium or strong	25
Speciality – aperitif or special occasion beers	5
Ordinary – the major volume sector	63
of which:	
Branded products	50
Supermarket chain low-price, own-label beers	13

segment and the ordinary segment – of the order of 40 per cent. In northern Europe the difference is much lower, only 15 per cent.

(French brewing manager)

A possible explanation for this wide discrepancy lies in the widely differing duty and taxation rates on beer across Europe.

Duty

Not only did the rates of duty vary across Europe, but also the method of calculating them. Two methods existed: the wort system, and at the brewery gate (BG). The latter, as its name implies, means that was levied at the 'brewery gate' on point of shipment to the next stage in the distribution channel. The wort system was more complex and dated from the last century. Duty was calculated during the brewing process, at the point of fermentation. Table 6 shows the different methods of duty calculation, the duty rates and also sales tax rates across Europe.

This variation in duty rates had some clear impacts on the economics of brewing. In the UK, for example, raw materials, salaries, packaging, etc. were one-third of total manufacturing costs; the other two-thirds was duty. One British manager summed up the duty situation thus:

Table 6 European duty and tax rates and calculation methods

	Duty system	Duty	Sales tax (%)
West Germany	BG	6.87	14
Denmark	BG	60.82	22
Belgium	Wort	11.39	19
United Kingdom	Wort	51.80	17.5
Ireland	Wort	85.37	25
Holland	Wort	20.38	20
Spain	BG	3.31	12
France	BG	2.78	18.6
Italy	Wort	20.17	9

Notes
1. A standard measure was used to ensure consistent comparison.
2. BG = brewery gate.
3. Duty is measured in ECU per hectolitre.
4. Belgium has a lower rate of sales tax of 17% on beer consumed in cafés and bars.
Source: Various national trade associations.

The harmonisation of duty is a mess in Europe, frankly. There are very wide duty differences across Europe. You have the situation where there is a potential price difference between France and the UK of 25 per cent in a very saleable commodity.

The UK government are saying that there won't be any need to harmonise duty, because they will be able to control it one way or the other, they will capture it at the border. I really don't think that is realistic, because if you can make £25,000 profit bringing a tanker of beer across the Channel, you will bring a tanker of beer across the Channel, whether it is legal or illegal, and if you get caught once or twice it is probably still worth it.

Distribution

European consumers purchased their beer in two principal ways. The difference between the two was the place of consumption. They either purchased beer in supermarkets to be transported to their home and drunk there, or they purchased it, principally on draught, and consumed it simultaneously in a bar, pub, café, restaurant or hotel. Table 7 shows the percentage of beer purchased on draught during the 1980s in the major European markets.

The type of container in which beer was purchased also varied significantly from country to country. The four principal types were: draught beer, where the beer was served from a container to a glass and drunk immediately, normally in a bar; returnable bottles, where the bottle was returned to the point of sale or some other point after the beer had been drunk; non-returnable bottles, where the bottle could be discarded after consumption of the beer; and cans, which were also normally discarded after consumption of their contents.

Table 7 Percentage of beer consumed on draught by country

	1989	1988	1987	1985	1980
West Germany	28	28	29	29	40
Denmark	5	4	4	3	23
Belgium	44	45	40	40	48
United Kingdom	72	73	75	77	88
Ireland	86	86	88	88	94
Holland	29	30	31	31	40
Spain	40	40	n/a	35	n/a
Portugal	25	25	24	19	n/a
Greece	3	3	n/a	n/a	n/a
France	25	25	24	22	n/a
Italy	16	16	16	16	n/a

Source: CBMC.

Table 8 shows the percentages of consumption by the different types of container for the major European countries in 1989. With the exception of the United Kingdom, beer sold in cans was not a significant feature of the European market: in fact, beer could not be purchased in cans by law in certain European countries, e.g. Denmark.

Channels of distribution also varied, which was to be expected given the different consumption characteristics of each market. Figure 2 describes the channels of distribution which existed in most mainland European countries, i.e. France, Holland, Spain, Italy, Belgium and Denmark. The proportion of beer sales which flowed through each channel varied from country to country.

Since the brewing companies owned a very small percentage of the retail outlets in these countries, they did not distribute directly to them. Distribution took place through wholesalers, which might or might not have been owned by the brewers. It would have been uneconomic for the brewers to distribute beer direct to thousands of small bars, restaurants and hotels.

The supermarket chains had substantial power in the distribution channels. They offered the brewing companies attractive economies of scale. Brewers could deliver large volumes to a central point in the supermarket chain distribution system. This power was growing across Europe as greater proportions of beer were sold through supermarkets.

Figure 3 depicts channels of distribution which had a different structure. This was the situation in the United Kingdom and to a lesser extent in West Germany. In both these countries, the brewing companies owned a significant proportion of the retail outlets – 59 per cent in the United Kingdom and 22 per cent in West Germany. Hence the brewers distributed direct to the pubs and bars in these two countries.

Table 8 Consumption patterns by country, 1989 (%)

	Draught beer	Returnable bottles	Non-returnable bottles	Cans
West Germany	28	72	0	0
Denmark	5	95	0	0
Belgium	44	47	5	2
United Kingdom	72	8	3	17
Ireland	86	8	4	2
Holland	29	68	0	3
Spain		Not available		
Portugal	25	68	5	2
Greece		Not available		
France	25	27	44	4
Italy	16	25	54	5

Source: CBMC.

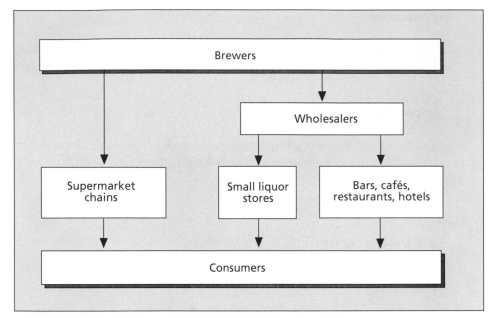

Figure 2 Typical channels of distribution in most European countries

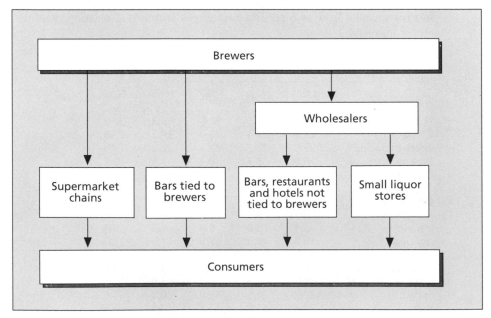

Figure 3 UK and West German channels of distribution

Production

Table 9 shows the production outputs of the major European and eastern European beer-producing countries during the 1980s in millions of hectolitres.

Imports and Exports

Tables 10 and 11 show imports as a percentage of consumption and exports as a percentage of production respectively for the major European brewing countries during the 1980s.

Brewing by countries

Denmark

Beer in Denmark was dominated by Carlsberg, which had 75 per cent of the market and was a major global competitor, being the thirteenth largest brewing company in the world. Its brand, Carlsberg, was the second most popular beer brand in Europe, selling over 6 million hectolitres annually. Carlsberg was owned by a charitable trust.

Table 9 Brewing output by country (million hectolitres)

	1989	1988	1987	1985	1980
West Germany	93.0	92.6	92.8	93.3	92.3
East Germany*	24.8	24.4	25.0	24.3	23.6
Czechoslovakia*	22.8	22.7	22.2	22.3	23.4
Denmark	8.8	8.7	8.2	7.9	8.2
Belgium	13.2	13.8	14.0	13.9	14.2
Austria	9.2	9.0	8.9	8.7	7.5
United Kingdom	60.0	60.2	59.9	59.7	64.8
Hungary*	9.7	9.5	9.1	8.7	7.9
Ireland	5.1	5.0	5.4	5.5	6.1
Holland	18.8	17.5	17.5	17.5	15.7
Spain	27.3	26.6	25.8	23.4	20.0
Portugal	6.8	5.5	5.0	3.7	3.6
Greece	3.9	4.1	3.8	3.0	2.5
France	20.9	20.1	19.9	20.3	21.6
Italy	10.4	11.3	11.1	10.3	8.5
Total	334.7	331.0	328.6	322.5	319.9

Note * Eastern European.
Source: UK Brewers' Society.

Table 10 Imports as a percentage of consumption

	1989	1988	1987	1985	1980
West Germany	1.7	1.5	1.5	1.2	0.8
Denmark	0.3	0.3	0.3	0.3	0.1
Belgium	5.6	4.5	4.6	5.1	7.5
United Kingdom	7.2	6.9	6.5	5.9	3.9
Ireland	13.3	14.8	12.5	4.7	0.9
Holland	4.5	5.6	4.3	3.4	2.8
Spain	3.3	2.8	2.8	1.5	0.5
Portugal	1.5	0.7	0.7	0.1	0.1
Greece	3.6	3.8	1.2	0.9	1.0
France	12.0	11.2	11.3	11.1	11.2
Italy	16.4	13.3	16.4	17.6	11.1

Source: UK Brewers' Society.

Table 11 Exports as a percentage of production

	1989	1988	1987	1985	1980
West Germany	5.7	6.1	6.1	5.4	3.2
Denmark	23.7	23.8	23.4	19.4	15.8
Belgium	18.2	19.1	18.1	18.9	17.7
United Kingdom	2.2	2.0	1.9	1.6	1.2
Ireland	46.3	43.2	41.6	34.1	31.1
Holland	34.0	33.1	32.6	31.5	23.7
Spain	0.7	0.5	0.5	0.4	n/a
Portugal	2.8	2.2	1.5	1.9	2.4
Greece	0.4	0.5	n/a	n/a	n/a
France	4.0	3.6	3.4	3.3	2.8
Italy	0.9	0.5	0.7	0.7	0.4

Source: UK Brewers' Society.

There were twenty breweries in Denmark, almost all of which were controlled by the three major competitors in Denmark – Carlsberg, Albani and Faxe-Jyske. Danish brewers were also the largest producers of soft drinks in Denmark. This had been useful in gaining access, for beer, to channels of distribution.

Danish beer drinkers were by nature conservative. Most of the beer sold in Denmark was brewed domestically. There had been some attempts to introduce foreign beer, but they had not been very successful. Even foreign beer brewed under licence by a Danish brewery had been unsuccessful. In the mid-1980s Carlsberg brewed Budweiser under licence in Denmark, but it was not a success.

A particular feature of the Danish beer market was the 'border trade' on the German–Danish border. Many Danes drove across the border into West

Germany, filled their petrol tank with cheap German petrol and bought cheap beer. What was interesting was that they bought Danish beer, supplied by Danish breweries to German retailers. The Danish brewers did not lose any production, but the Danish government lost tax revenue and Danish retailers lost sales income. It was estimated that the border trade accounted for 10–20 per cent of all beer sold in Denmark.

The beer market was dominated by the brewers' individual brands. However, the big supermarket chains had introduced their own brands which had been sold as cheap discount beers. These beers were also brewed by Danish brewers and were estimated to have 10–20 per cent of the market. Approximately 70 per cent of beer was sold through retailers, while the rest was sold through restaurants, bars, hotels, etc. The big supermarket chains were therefore extremely important customers of the brewing companies.

An interesting feature of the Danish beer market was the bottle reuse system. It was not legal to sell beer or soft drinks in Denmark in one-way packaging such as cans. Beer had to be sold in reusable bottles, for which there existed standard sizes determined by the Danish Association of Brewers. It was claimed that this bottle reuse system was a major entry barrier preventing foreign brewers from entering the Danish market. However, there had been a ruling by the European Court allowing Denmark to keep its bottle reuse system for environmental reasons.

Until 1987 the Danish beer industry was regulated by the members of the Danish Association of Brewers. The regulations fixed minimum prices for beer, prohibited discounts, limited the form of advertising and regulated the distribution system. Post-1987 the market and industry were basically unregulated.

Holland

Similar to Denmark, Holland was dominated by one brewery, Heineken, which was the largest in Europe and the third largest in the world. Although Heineken produced only 7.1 million hectolitres of beer in Holland, it produced 53.5 million on a world-wide basis. Heineken also had ownership stakes in brewing companies in Spain, France, Italy and Ireland. The only major European countries it did not have ownership stakes in were the UK and West Germany, although it had a licensing agreement with Whitbread in the UK to brew Heineken for sale in the UK market. Heineken was the largest imported beer brand in the USA, with 1.5–2 per cent of the total market. The company had been exporting its beer to the USA since 1928, when prohibition ended. The brand Heineken could be purchased in 145 countries world-wide.

There were three other Dutch brewing companies with outputs of approximately 2 million hectolitres of beer per annum. One of these, Verenigde BV, was owned by Allied-Lyons of the UK, the only brewery to be owned by a British company outside the UK. The other was Grolsch BV.

Grolsch, despite its relatively small output of only 1.9 million hectolitres of beer per annum, had been able to carve out for itself a strong market position in many of the world's major beer markets. The company had only one brand, but it had a strong brand image, promoted by its unusual shape of bottle and 'swing top' which allowed the bottle to be resealed. In 1991 it exported to 35 different countries and from 1985 to 1989 its export sales grew as a proportion of total revenues from 14 to 31 per cent with a future target of 50 per cent. Grolsch's main export markets were the USA and the UK.

Holland was a major exporter of beer, probably the largest exporting country in the world. The countries exported to are too numerous to list. Its proportion of production exported grew from 23.7 per cent in 1980 to 34 per cent in 1989. Imports had doubled from 2.8 per cent to 5.6 per cent since 1980. Ninety per cent of imports came from Belgium.

Beer was mainly purchased in supermarkets in Holland for consumption at home. This accounted for 70 per cent of all beer sales, the remaining 30 per cent being sold through bars, cafés, hotels and restaurants.

Belgium

A feature of the Belgian brewing industry was the large number of beers produced: 420 different brands of eighteen different types. It was claimed by the Belgians that no other country could offer such a wide choice. The trend had been towards more expensive beers in a market which was in overall gentle decline. These more expensive beers tended to be drunk in bars, which accounted for the decline of drinking of beer in the home.

Belgium was also a large exporter of beer. It exported approximately 18 per cent of production, whereas imports amounted to less than 6 per cent of consumption. Exports had remained relatively static in the latter half of the 1980s, while imports had fallen steadily. Over 95 per cent of Belgian beer exports were to other EC countries. This was a function of Belgium's central geographic location in Europe and the problems of transporting beer over long distances while still maintaining quality. The biggest export market by far was France, which took 63 per cent of Belgian exports. Other major export markets were Italy, the Netherlands and the UK.

The Belgian beer industry was dominated by two competitors, Stella-Interbrew and Alken-Maes, which between them had 85 per cent of the Belgian market. Stella-Interbrew was formed in 1986 by a merger of the two leading Belgian brewers, Artois and Piedboeuf. As well as beer the company was a significant producer of soft drinks. The company had its own production and bottling units in France and Italy and in a number of African countries; licensing agreements in the UK and Canada; and distribution companies in the Netherlands, France, Italy and the USA. Stella-Interbrew had approximately 65 per cent of the Belgian market.

In August 1988 Alken-Kronenbourg and Maes Breweries merged to form a new company, Alken-Maes, in which the French company BSN had a 50 per cent shareholding. Alken-Maes had subsidiaries in France, Italy, Spain and the Netherlands, and sales organisations in many other countries. The company had a 20 per cent share of the Belgian market. The remaining 15 per cent of the market was shared between nine other smaller breweries, which mainly focused on their local or regional markets.

Beer was distributed in Belgium through various channels. Principal among these was the specialised dealer or *negociant*, who provided the following services: home delivery of beverages, a beverages discount outlet, delivery to the hotels, restaurants, cafés and bars sector, and dealing as a wholesaler.

The home delivery of beverages was a typically Belgian approach to distribution and highlighted the importance of drinking to the Belgian consumer. For many years the role of the *negociant* was to deliver beer to the home, and subsequently other beverages were added. Home delivery had, however, been declining slowly over the previous twenty years, due to the growth of supermarkets which could offer a wider range of beers at lower prices, and to changes in lifestyle, e.g. an increase in car ownership leading to greater consumer mobility, an increase in real disposable income and more working women, who were therefore unable to take deliveries during the day time. Home delivery was expected to decrease further in the future, but at a slower rate than over the previous two decades.

Discount outlets for beverages were a recent development. The first was opened in 1974 by the Artois brewery and there were now around 1,000 in Belgium. This type of outlet combined the advantages of home delivery and supermarkets. These included a large choice of products offered, fast service and lower than average prices.

The hotels, restaurants, cafés and bars sector represented a large part of the market. In this sector the *negociant* played a key role, offering a large choice of products and adding a certain number of services to the delivery of products, such as taking care of refrigerators.

The *negociant* had had to adapt to changing market conditions and had kept its important role in the distribution of beer in the Belgian market. It was estimated that 49 per cent of beer sales were distributed through *negociants*, 27 per cent through supermarkets and 6 per cent through direct sales in cafés and bars.

In January 1991 Belgium's Interbrew announced that it was planning a major investment programme to challenge Europe's leading brewers in the single European Community market after 1992. To improve profitability and catch up with competitors, privately owned Interbrew would invest $650 million in two new breweries. Each would have a capacity of four million hectolitres, and most of the production would be earmarked for export as the domestic market was already heavily supplied. The likely target was southern Europe where consumption per capita was rising. Interbrew had recently been outbid by Guinness for Spain's leading brewer, Cruz del Campo, but was still looking for possible acquisitions.

Italy

As a product, beer had not enjoyed a tradition in Italy as a popular, widely consumed drink. Italy had the lowest consumption per capita of all European countries. Production of beer in Italy began on an industrial scale only in the nineteenth century, and consumption was not as well developed there as in the rest of Europe, being concentrated primarily in the north of the country. After 1960 beer began to gain popularity among all the social classes of Italy, whereas previously it had been a drink of the rich. Beer was popular with the younger sections of the population, with limited sales to those over the age of 60.

The consumption of beer in Italy was very different from that in the rest of Europe. In Italy, beer was drunk primarily as a refreshing drink with low alcohol content, and at times other than meal times. However, there had been an increase in the consumption of beer drunk with meals. In the rest of Europe beer was regularly drunk as part of a meal. Italian beer drinking frequently occurred as an accompaniment to snacks, sandwiches, pizzas and fast-food meals. The growth of snack meals had consequently stimulated the growth of beer consumption.

As beer was taken mainly as a refreshing drink, it was drunk above all in the warm summer months. Over half the total beer sales were made in the period June to September. The most popular type of beer in Italy was the light, low-alcohol product. This type of beer accounted for over two-thirds of total sales. However, its share of the market was declining as Italian brewers were making products of a higher alcoholic strength, which were considered 'special' beers. Foreign beers were almost all classified as special beers. It was expected that the market share of special beers would steadily rise.

Imports, which had been very small, doubled from 1970 to 1980. In 1989 they accounted for 16 per cent of total consumption, an increase of 50 per cent on 1985, and this rose to 22 per cent when foreign beer brands brewed under licence in Italy were included. The principal importing countries were West Germany, the Netherlands, Belgium and Denmark, whose products were considered to be higher-quality types and constituted the upper segments of the market. Exports were negligible, being less then 1.0 per cent of production.

Since 1970 there had been much concentration in the Italian beer industry. In that year there were 34 beer producers, but by 1992 their number had been reduced to nine. The market was dominated by Peroni and Dreher, which between them controlled 57 per cent of the market. A feature of the Italian industry was the relatively high degree of foreign ownership. In 1990 the main competitors and their annual domestic outputs were as shown in Table 12.

Peroni was a family enterprise established in 1846 and 80 per cent of the company was still owned by the family. In 1989 it merged with Wuhrer, which was owned by the BSN Group of France. BSN then became a 20 per cent shareholder in Peroni. The company had six breweries located in different parts of the country, giving it national coverage. It produced a wide range of beers, including special and non-alcoholic beers, and also brewed the Dutch beer Amstel under

Table 12 Domestic output of main
Italian beer producers in 1990
(million hectolitres p.a.)

Peroni	4.8
Dreher	3.9
Moretti and Prinz	1.1
Poretti	0.9
Wunster	0.8

licence. It had a strong sales network of over 3,000 distributors and was well established in all categories of retail outlets and the catering trade.

Dreher, the second largest brewer in Italy, was 85 per cent owned by the Heineken Group of Holland. It had five breweries and 1,200 distributors. Moretti and Prinz were formed from two small brewing companies which were bought in 1989 and merged by Labatt of Canada. Poretti was half-owned by the Italian Group, Bassetti and Carlsberg of Denmark. It had two breweries and brewed Tuborg under licence and imported Carlsberg. Wunster had only one brewery and was bought from the von Wunster family in 1987 by Stella-Interbrew. The company had been making losses and this was one of the reasons for its sale.

Distribution was similar to that in most European countries. Hotels, restaurants, cafés and bars accounted for 50 per cent of sales, supermarkets and hypermarkets for a further 34 per cent and traditional grocery outlets for 16 per cent. The traditional independent grocers were losing market share to the supermarkets. Door-to-door distribution was growing in importance in Italy. Traditionally, this system had been used by wholesalers of soft drinks, and since beer was assimilated to soft drinks in the consumer's mind, it could be readily included in this distribution system.

There were about 10,000 of these wholesale drinks distributors in Italy. They worked on a very localised basis and in some cases covered only a limited area of a town or city. They were ideally suited to supplying small restaurants, cafés and bars, offering frequent deliveries and enabling small businesses to avoid tying up capital in stock. Only the large supermarket chains bought directly from the brewers, and not all of them did so. For supermarkets located far from a brewery or for smaller self-service operations, the wholesale distributor was often a preferable source of supply.

France

Beer was not a mainstream consumption product in France. Only Italy of the major European countries had a lower annual consumption per capita. Wine had a firm grip as the French national drink, and consumption of beer had been declining slowly but steadily during the 1980s. This trend was in the opposite direction to the other warm, southern European 'sunbelt' countries where consumption of beer per capita had been steadily growing in the same period. Despite this, the French industry leader, BSN-Kronenbourg, was the second largest brewing company in Europe and the sixth largest in the world.

At the end of the Second World War, there were 1,000 breweries in France. Since then much concentration had taken place. In 1992 there were three main brewing companies, which had 82 per cent of the market. The remaining 18 per cent was held by approximately 30 small specialist brewing companies. The principal companies with their domestic outputs in 1990 were as shown in Table 13. Française de Brasserie was wholly owned by Heineken of Holland, and Artois-Interbrew by Stella-Interbrew of Belgium.

France was not a major exporter of beer. It exported only 4.0 per cent of its output, principally to its neighbours Italy and Spain. Eleven and a quarter per cent of its consumption was imported, again principally from its neighbour Belgium.

Brewing and the drinking of beer in France were essentially northern activities. BSN's main brewery was in Strasbourg. Consumption patterns varied substantially across the country. In the north, average consumption was 80 litres per capita compared to the French national average of 41 litres. In the south average consumption was only 20–5 litres.

Distribution patterns had remained static throughout the 1980s, with supermarkets and hypermarkets selling 60 per cent of all beer, and bars, cafés, hotels and restaurants the remaining 40 per cent. Breweries did not own bars or cafés, but would provide them with finance at preferential rates of interest in return for selling their beers under contract for five to ten years. The market was segmented similarly to other European countries, with light or low-alcohol beers, ordinary beers and strong or speciality beers. The low-alcohol and strong/speciality beers were the faster-growing segments.

The five countries already discussed, i.e. Denmark, Holland, Belgium, Italy and France, had much in common in their brewing industries. They had similar degrees of industry concentration and distribution systems. The countries still to be discussed – Spain, the United Kingdom and West Germany – exhibited considerably different characteristics from the first five. West Germany and the UK, in

Table 13 Domestic output of main
French beer producers in 1990
(million hectolitres p.a.)

BSN	10.3
Française de Brasserie	6.0
Artois-Interbrew	1.4

particular, could be considered out of step with the rest of the European brewing community.

Spain

The brewing industry in Spain was not dominated by any one company. The major brewing companies with their domestic outputs in 1990 were as shown in Table 14. There were three other small breweries with a local focus and small production outputs.

The Spanish market was regionally orientated with three very strong regional groups which had been able to develop strong production economies of scale and distribution power. These three were Cruz del Campo, Mahou and Damm. Only San Miguel marketed its brand successfully nationally at the time, although this was expected to change as the international brewers took more interest in the Spanish market.

An interesting feature of the Spanish industry was the high degree of foreign ownership compared to other European countries. Cruz del Campo, the largest beer producer, was a southern-based company which was 25 per cent owned by the Stroh company of the USA, the seventh largest brewing company in the world. Mahou, the third largest producer, focused its efforts on Madrid and was 33 per cent owned by the BSN Group of France. The fourth largest brewer, Damm, was based in Barcelona and was 18 per cent owned by Oetker of West Germany. El Aguila was 51 per cent owned by Heineken of Holland, San Miguel was affiliated to the San Miguel Corporation of the Philippines, the sixteenth largest brewing group in the world, and Union Cervecera was 60 per cent owned by Carlsberg.

The Spanish market was not as well developed as other European markets. It was almost entirely satisfied by domestic production. It exported only 0.7 per cent of its output and imported 3.3 per cent of its consumption. Importation from any country other than France was difficult due to the distances involved with Spain being on the edge of Europe.

It was only in the late 1980s that the market segments, well established in

Table 14 Domestic output of main Spanish beer producers in 1990 (million hectolitres p.a.)

Cruz del Campo	5.1
El Aguila	4.6
Mahou	4.2
Damm	4.1
San Miguel	3.5
Union Cervecera	1.9

other European countries, had begun to develop in Spain. There were three basic market segments – ordinary, special and strong beers. However, the consumer's perception of these segments could vary from region to region, so strong were the three regional brewers. In 1992 the market was developing rapidly, forced mainly by the foreign brewers such as Carlsberg and Heineken through strong advertising and brand development campaigns. The 'new' market segments, i.e. special, strong and a small non-alcoholic segment which could not be called beer in Spain, were the fastest growing.

Distribution in Spain was split into 25 per cent through supermarkets and 75 per cent in cafés, bars, hotels and restaurants. However, there was a definite move towards increased sales through supermarket grocery chains, as in the rest of Europe. This development was related to the changing lifestyles of the Spanish. More of them were buying beer in supermarkets to take home to drink while watching television. The quality of Spanish television had been increasing during the 1980s, encouraging this trend. Packaging trends were also changing, from returnable bottles to non-returnable bottles and cans.

During 1991 Guinness, the Irish brewer, moved to further consolidate the Spanish industry. At the beginning of the year, Guinness spent US$875 million to buy an 88 per cent stake in Cruz del Campo, Spain's largest brewer. It followed this in July with a bid worth US$47 million for Union Cervecera. Union Cervecera was a loss-making subsidiary of Carlsberg. As part of the deal Carlsberg purchased 10 per cent of the newly enlarged Cruz del Campo for US$96 million and its brand Carlsberg was to be distributed by the new group. Carlsberg also took the right to increase its shareholding in Cruz del Campo.

United Kingdom

The UK brewing industry was very different from that in the rest of Europe. A major difference was the type of beer consumed. In Europe, virtually all beers drunk were of a light texture and colour, and consumed after chilling – the type of beer generally defined as lager. In the UK there were three principal types of beer drunk – lagers, ales and stouts. Ales were dark, brown beers which were generally drunk warm. Stouts were heavy, dark-coloured beers, which could be drunk chilled or warm – principal among these was Guinness.

In 1970 ales dominated the beer market, being 85 per cent of the total market. Stouts and lagers each had a 7.5 per cent market share. Since 1970 the market had changed dramatically. In 1991 lager had 55 per cent of the market, ales 40 per cent and stouts the remaining 5 per cent. This trend occurred due to changing consumer tastes, caused by increased foreign travel and large brand and advertising campaigns by the major brewers to promote lager. Lagers tended to be brands with national coverage, while ales were sold more on regional loyalty. The trend towards lager was expected to continue.

The UK brewing industry was not as concentrated as other European countries. In 1990 there were six large brewing companies which had 80 per cent of the market, eleven regional brewers which had 13 per cent of the market, and over 50 local brewers which had the remaining 7 per cent.

British brewing companies were highly vertically integrated. They owned not only the breweries, but also many of the outlets through which beer was sold to the consumer, and even in some cases the sources of raw materials – hops, barley and yeast. In outlets not owned by breweries, a supply agreement known as a 'tie' might exist. This meant that the outlet could sell only the beer products of the brewing company to which it was 'tied'. In return for this arrangement the owner of the outlet received a preferential loan from the brewing company.

This situation arose because of the historic development of the UK brewing industry. In the nineteenth century breweries only supplied pubs which they owned in a small geographic locality. Gradually they expanded to cover wider areas, some establishing breweries away from their place of origin in an attempt to gain national coverage for their products and to take advantage of economies of scale in distribution and production.

In the 1950s, 1960s and 1970s there was a wave of mergers which led, in 1990, to the industry structure shown in Table 15. There were 78,600 pubs in Great Britain and a further 61,400 clubs, hotels and restaurants. The brewers directly controlled 46,000 pubs, equivalent to 59 per cent of the total number. The six largest breweries controlled 43 per cent of the pubs.

However, the UK government took a keen interest in the brewing industry. During the 1970s and 1980s there had been two major government investigations into the industry, and five relating to specific merger and acquisition situations. This may not seem many given the timescale involved, but it was substantially more investigations than any other British industry had been subjected to. No other European government had subjected its brewing industry to the same degree of scrutiny.

Two reports were published in March 1989. One concerned the general state of the industry and had taken over two years to prepare. The other report barred Courage, a subsidiary of the Australian Fosters Brewing Group, from acquiring Scottish & Newcastle, the fifth largest UK brewer, despite the fact that the newly merged business would not have had a market share in excess of that of Bass, the market leader.

Table 15 Structure of the UK brewing industry in 1990

Brewer	Market share (%)	No. of pubs owned	% of total pubs
Bass	22	7,200	9.2
Allied-Lyons	13	6,700	8.5
Grand Met	13	6,400	8.1
Whitbread	12	6,500	8.3
Scottish & Newcastle	11	2,300	2.9
Courage	9	5,000	6.4

The findings of the 500-page general report were damning about the industry. The principal conclusion was that a complex monopoly existed, which restricted competition at all levels of the industry. The investigation concluded that the results of this had been as follows:

- The price of a pint of beer in a public house had risen too fast in the few years before the report.
- The high price of lager was not justified by the cost of producing it.
- The variation in wholesale prices between regions of the country was excessive.
- Consumer choice was restricted because one brewer did not usually allow another brewer's beer to be sold in the outlets which he owned. This restriction often happened in loan-tied outlets as well.
- Consumer choice was further restricted because of brewers' efforts to ensure that their own brand of cider and soft drinks were sold in their outlets.
- Tenants of pubs were unable to play a full part in meeting consumer preferences, both because of the tie and because the tenant's bargaining position was so much weaker than the landlord's (the brewer's).
- Independent manufacturers and wholesalers of beer and other drinks were allowed only limited access to the on-licensed market (pubs).

The investigating commission recommended some strong measures to increase competition. Principal among them were the following:

- No brewer should own more than 2,000 pubs. This restriction was later eased, after substantial lobbying of the British government by the brewers, to 2,000 pubs plus 50 per cent of their original holding. This means that the six largest brewers had to divest themselves of 11,000 pubs by the deadline of November 1992.
- The loan tie to be eliminated.
- Tenants of pubs to be allowed to buy at least one brand of beer from a brewery other than the tenant's landlord.
- The tie for non-alcohol or low-alcohol beers, wines, spirits, ciders, soft drinks and mineral waters to be abolished.

The report concluded with the following statement: 'If no changes are made we believe it is inevitable that a very small number of brewers will increasingly dominate the supply of beer in the United Kingdom.' What this statement by the UK government meant was that it would closely scrutinise any future takeover or merger in the UK industry.

The UK was not a significant exporter of beer, just over 2 per cent of output being exported. Imports in 1989 were 7 per cent of consumption, up from 4 per cent in 1980.

A trend in the UK brewing industry which was similar to Europe was the increased sale of beer from grocery supermarket chains. This grew from 12 to 18 per cent during the 1980s and was predicted to be 25 per cent of all beer sales by the year 2000.

In October 1990 the UK government allowed a merger between the brewing interests of Courage and Grand Metropolitan. Under the terms of the arrangement Courage would focus on brewing and distribution, and the development of brands – it would acquire Grand Met's breweries. Grand Met would focus on retailing and property management, assuming control for Courage and Grand Met pubs. The property aspect of the pubs would be owned 50/50 on a joint venture basis. After the arrangement had been fully implemented Courage would be the UK's second largest brewer in terms of market share with 18 per cent, behind Bass with 22 per cent. This merger would create in Courage the first European-style brewer in the UK.

In October 1991 further consolidation of the UK brewing industry took place when Carlsberg (UK), the British subsidiary of the Danish brewer, announced that it was forming a 50/50 joint venture with Allied-Lyons, the third largest UK brewer. The company, to be called Carlsberg-Tetley, would be in place by March 1992, would have an 18 per cent UK market share and would be the third largest UK brewer. Carlsberg would invest £245 million in the project, its biggest overseas investment. The new company would supply all Allied's pubs. The market share forecast had been boosted by Allied's agreement with Greenalls, a major regional brewer, to supply it with beer. Greenalls intended to cease brewing, to concentrate on its pub retailing activities, as had several other regional brewers.

West Germany

West Germany had the highest consumption of beer per capita in the world in 1992, was the second largest market in the world after the USA, and was the largest beer-producing nation in Europe. However, the structure of its beer industry was very different from that of the rest of Europe. The industry had not experienced industrial concentration on the same scale as the rest of Europe. There were approximately 1,200 breweries in West Germany, producing an average of less than 80,000 hectolitres per annum. In Bavaria there were 800 breweries, equivalent to one brewery for every 14,000 people. The Bavarians drank an average of 225 litres of beer each year compared to the national average of 143 litres. The West German brewing industry produced 5,000 different brands of beer. These accounted for nearly half the world's total.

Some signs of concentration were beginning to appear. In the 1970s and 1980s the five largest West German brewers had increased their combined market share from 6 to 28 per cent, and the number of breweries had fallen from 3,000 to 1,200. However, in 1992 there were still nearly 30 breweries with annual production over one million hectolitres. West German drinkers were very conservative and loyal to their favourite beer, normally a beer brewed locally. Ninety per cent of breweries sold their products within a 30-mile radius. This conservatism and loyalty was encouraged by a feature of the German market not found anywhere else in the world. This was the *Reinheitsgebot* or 'purity laws'. The strength of this loyalty and the prospects of it changing in the future can be seen in quotations from two German brewing company managers:

> The consciousness of the consumer of the *Reinheitsgebot* is very high. Ninety to ninety-five per cent of consumers say they will only buy beer which has been brewed in accordance with the *Reinheitsgebot*.

> The Germans will still cling to the *Reinheitsgebot* in ten years' time. It is a matter of marketing. Even if the Federal Government were to allow additives as in other European countries, the German brewers would not do it and the customers would not accept it.

The 'purity laws' were first introduced in 1516 and ultimately became federal law in 1919. The law stated that only malted cereals, hops, yeast and water could be used in the brewing process. Artificial additives were not allowed to improve quality or extend shelf life, thus clearly inhibiting imports or the transportation of local products over any significant distance.

In 1987, following complaints by the French government and European brewers, the European Court of Justice ruled that the *Reinheitsgebot* could not be used to prevent the sale of imported beers in West Germany, provided that they met the laws of their country of origin. West Germany adopted a compromise law, allowing beers with additives to be sold, but they had to be clearly labelled and could not be called beers. This was clearly prejudicial to importers of beer and may have been in contravention of the 1987 ruling by the European Court of Justice. Despite this ruling, only a few foreign companies had entered the German market. These were Carlsberg, Heineken, Guinness, Grolsch and Fosters, the Australian beer producers. Fosters was to be brewed in Germany, in accordance with the *Reinheitsgebot*, by Holsten.

As a result of the 'purity laws', imports were not a major feature of the West German market. During the 1980s the proportion of beer consumption that was imported doubled to 1.7 per cent. The proportion of beer production exported grew during the 1980s from 3.2 to 5.7 per cent. The principal countries exported to were the UK, France, Italy, Spain, Austria and Switzerland. The UK was West Germany's largest export market by far, where many of the successful lager brands were of West German origin.

Another feature of the West German brewing industry was the low profitability of the brewing companies. The manager of one brewing company summarised the situation thus:

> There are very large breweries in the Federal Republic of Germany which earn less than the hot-dog stand at the corner. They have not paid dividends for ten years and they say there will be no dividends for the next five years.

Many of the German brewing companies were privately or family owned and enjoyed significant support from the banking institutions. They did not have, and did not need to have, the same commercial thrust or ambition as publicly owned companies, particularly in other countries. The profit margins of German brewing companies were very much lower than elsewhere in Europe. One German brewing company manager highlighted the position:

> The margin in Germany amounts to about 1 per cent. In the United Kingdom, it amounts to 10 per cent. The difference is that the British want to earn 10 per cent and the Germans are very pleased with 2 per cent.

This low profitability was another factor contributing to the low importation of beer brands.

Distribution channels had some similarities to the rest of Europe, but also some differences. The major similarity was that 60 per cent of beer sales were made through supermarkets for consumption in the home. It was estimated that 60 per cent of all beer sales across Europe were made through supermarkets in 1992. The German brewers sold and delivered direct to the supermarket chains. The remaining 40 per cent of German beer sales was sold through cafés, bars, hotels and restaurants. Where Germany differed from the rest of Europe, with the exception of the UK, was that about 22 per cent of cafés and bars were owned by the breweries. In addition, many cafés and bars not owned directly by the breweries had 'arrangements' with breweries to sell only their products. This supply arrangement could be for as long as 25 years and usually involved the brewery making cheap loans to the café or bar. It was a strategy for breweries to maintain a strong hold in their local marketplace.

There had been some changes in consumer tastes in the 1970s and 1980s. There had been a trend towards lighter and less sweet beers, and Pils types of beer had increased their share of the market from 20 to 60 per cent. In the early 1990s, similar market trends to the rest of Europe began to appear, with the growth in sales of both low-alcohol beers and speciality beers.

The brewing companies

Heineken

In 1992 Heineken was essentially a family controlled business with 51 per cent of its shares being held by a holding company which was controlled by the family. It was the third largest brewer in the world and the most international, in terms of the number of countries in which it operated. It was possible to buy its principal beer brand, Heineken, in 145 countries. Table 16 gives a geographic breakdown of its sales.

Beer was produced in Holland, France and Greece; exported, particularly from Holland to the USA; brewed under licence, notably in the United Kingdom, Nigeria and Japan; and produced by partly owned, company-managed sub-

Table 16 Heineken sales by geographic area (million hectolitres)

	1990	1989	1988	1987	1986	1985
Holland	7.1	7.0				
Rest of Europe	21.8	20.6	26.5	25.2	25.5	24.8
Western hemisphere	13.3	11.6	10.3	8.5	7.7	6.2
Asia/Australia/Oceania	3.4	2.7	2.5	2.4	2.4	2.4
Africa	7.9	7.6	7.7	6.9	6.5	6.2
Total	53.5	49.5	47.0	43.0	42.1	39.6

Table 17 Heineken's European operations

Country	Situation	No. of breweries	Sales (million hl)	Market share (%)
France	100% ownership of second largest brewery	3	5.9	24
Spain	51% stake in El Aquila, second largest brewery	4	4.9	18
Italy	95% stake in Dreher, second largest brewery	6	3.7	29
Greece	100% ownership of largest brewery	3	3.2	65

sidiaries in Italy and Spain. In 1990 Heineken's sales breakdown was: beer, 84 per cent; soft drinks, 11 per cent; wines and spirits, 4 per cent; and others, 1 per cent.

Due to the limited size of its home market, Heineken began international operations as early as 1928 when it began exports to the United States. It was estimated that the USA accounted for 6 per cent of total production and 30 per cent of profits in 1990. The major moves in terms of internationalisation took place in the 1980s with a series of acquisitions in France, Spain, Italy and Greece. Table 17 summarises Heineken's European position in 1992. In the UK, Whitbread brewed 3.2 million hectolitres of Heineken beer under licence. Heineken owned 1 per cent of Whitbread and had a seat on the board.

Table 18 gives a financial summary for Heineken from 1985 to 1990.

Heineken announced in August 1991 that it was acquiring a 50.3 per cent stake in a Hungarian brewery near Budapest. The brewery was only three years old and would need no investment. It had a production capacity of 340,000 hectolitres, which would be expanded to 500,000 to increase the brewery's market share from its then 4 per cent.

Table 18 Heineken's financial summary

	1990	1989	1988	1987	1986	1985
Sales income	8,210	7,820	7,291	6,659	6,684	6,402
Operating profit	613	572	537	511	513	454
Net profit	366	325	291	287	285	265
Capital employed	7,484	7,122	6,540	6,051	5,781	5,250

Notes 1. All figures are in millions of guilders.
      2. Exchange rate, February 1992: £1 = 3.15 guilders.
Source: Company annual reports.

In December 1991 it was announced that Heineken had signed a joint venture agreement to become the first foreign beer producer in Vietnam. By late 1993, Vietnam Brewery Ltd would produce beer under the Heineken and Tiger labels from a new US$42.5 million brewery near Ho Chi Minh City. The brewery would have an initial output of 300,000 hectolitres per annum.

The company also announced that it was considering selling one or two of its Spanish breweries due to falling demand.

Carlsberg

In 1992 Carlsberg was one of the most international brewers in the world, with 28 breweries in eleven different countries. Its Carlsberg brand was the second best selling in Europe, with sales of 6.3 million hectolitres, and Tuborg was tenth with 3.2 million.

Carlsberg began international expansion for the same reasons as Heineken, i.e. its domestic market was too small to allow further expansion. Sales of beer outside of Denmark continued to rise and in 1990 accounted for 72 per cent of total beer sales.

Its most successful overseas operation was in the UK where it had a 3.0 million hectolitre brewery, which partly supplied the free trade, and also Grand Metropolitan, which itself brewed 1.2 million hectolitres of Carlsberg Pilsner. Carlsberg had a 5.6 per cent share of the UK market, but this contributed an estimated 50 per cent of its total profits. In Spain Carlsberg owned 60 per cent of Union Cervecera, a company with six breweries despite sales of only 1.9 million hectolitres. In Italy it owned 50 per cent of Poretti, which had sales of close to 1.0 million hectolitres. Financially, Carlsberg was the first foreign brewer to have a stake, 83 per cent, in a German brewer, Hannen Braueri, which had sales of around 850,000 hectolitres. Carlsberg was also one of the major exporters of beer to Germany – around 500,000 hectolitres. Tuborg and Carlsberg were the largest German imported brands. Although Carlsberg was distributed by

Anheuser-Busch in the USA, it was not one of the top ten imported beers. Carlsberg's most significant businesses outside Europe were in Hong Kong, where it had 15–17 per cent of the market, and Malaysia, where its share exceeded 50 per cent. Exposure was also strong in the remainder of the Far East, with breweries in Thailand and China. Carlsberg brewed about 0.5 million hectolitres in Africa. Table 19 shows the development of Carlsberg's sales from 1985 to 1990.

The ownership of Carlsberg was unusual. Its shares were quoted on the Copenhagen Stock Exchange and held by some 7,000 shareholders, many of whom were employees, but the largest single shareholder by far was the Carlsberg Foundation, which was pledged to possess a minimum of 51 per cent of the shares of Carlsberg A/S. Only one other shareholder, the Danish Labour Market Supplementary Pension Scheme, accounted for more than 10 per cent of the shares, although the Tuborg Foundation was also an important shareholder with 6 per cent. The Carlsberg Foundation was established by Carlsberg's founder, brewer J. C. Jacobsen, in 1876 and its income supported Danish natural and social sciences as well as the humanities. In December 1991 the Carlsberg and Tuborg Foundations announced that they had agreed to merge in order to improve Carlsberg's ability to raise new capital.

In 1992 Carlsberg derived approximately 30 per cent of sales from non-beer-related activities. These included wines and spirits, soft drinks, supplying complete processing plants to the beverage and food industries, and Royal Copenhagen A/S which manufactured and sold porcelain, glassware, silverware and plastic and glass packaging. Royal Copenhagen had 15 subsidiaries in export markets and 35 retail shops worldwide.

Table 20 gives a financial summary of Carlsberg from 1985 to 1990.

Grolsch

Grolsch, until the early 1990s, had been a one-product company selling its Grolsch product on draught, principally in Holland, and in the very distinctive swing-top resealable bottle which had made it an easily identifiable drink in its

Table 19 Carlsberg's sales (million hectolitres)

	1989/90	*1988/89*	*1987/88*	*1986/87*	*1985/86*
Outside Denmark	12.5	12.4	11.9	11.2	10.6
In Denmark	5.0	5.0	4.9	4.8	4.8
	17.5	17.4	16.8	16.0	15.4
Associated companies	1.8	1.7	1.0		
Group total	19.3	19.1	17.8		

Table 20 Carlsberg's financial summary

	1989/90	1988/89	1987/88	1986/87	1985/86
Sales income	10,482	10,215	10,002	9,122	9,076
Operating profit	952	843	773	729	719
Net profit	719	632	540	438	375
Capital employed	13,391	12,485	11,204	10,086	8,953

Notes 1. All figures are in millions of Danish kroner.
    2. Exchange rate, February 1992: £1 = 10.87DKK.
Source: Company annual reports.

markets. However, early in the 1990s it launched two new products – Grolsch Amber, a dry beer, and an alcohol-free beer.

Grolsch began exporting in the mid-1970s for two reasons: the small size of the Dutch market and its dominance by Heineken. Tourists visiting Holland were surprised that they rarely found Grolsch in Dutch bars, such was the strength of Heineken. In 1990 Grolsch had a market share of 17 per cent in Holland and produced 1.9 million hectolitres per year. During the latter half of the 1980s Grolsch increased its exports as a percentage of turnover from 14 per cent in 1985 to 31 per cent in 1989. However, export sales represented only 20 per cent of Grolsch's volume, showing the higher price premium it commanded in overseas markets. Its principal foreign markets were the USA and the UK, estimated at 25 and 40 per cent of its export volume respectively, and it was available in a total of 35 markets worldwide. Duty-free sales were estimated to account for another 25 per cent of sales by volume.

In 1992 it started to expand into Germany and was planning to brew Grolsch in accordance with the old law of *Reinheitsgebot*. It also had plans to move into southern Europe.

The company was floated on the Amsterdam Stock Exchange in the mid-1980s by its then owners the Groen family, who still had a 40 per cent ownership stake and hence a strong defence against any unwelcome takeover bids. However, the family members had recently retired from the board and this heralded a possibly more aggressive stance by the management team.

Table 21 gives financial details of Grolsch's development in the latter half of the 1980s.

In February 1991 Grolsch announced that it had acquired Germany's Rheinisch-Bergischen Brauerei, also known as the Wickuler Group. The Wuppertal-based company, only 100 km south of Grolsch's headquarters at Enschede on the Dutch–German border, was owned by the Wehahn family and was purchased for cash. It had a brewing capacity of 2 million hectolitres and thus doubled Grolsch's sales. Wickuler brewed several well-known brands including Wickuler Pilsener. The acquisition made Grolsch only the second foreign brewer, after Carlsberg, to own a German brewer. Grolsch saw opportunities for developing the brands on an international basis. The purchase was part of a strategy to provide Grolsch with access to the tradition and experience of German brewers and an opportunity to increase its volume via existing distribution channels. It also provided opportunities to gain access to markets in eastern Europe and the former East Germany.

Grolsch confirmed in July 1991 that it intended to buy a British ale brewer sometime during 1992. It already had trading links with two regional brewers, Wolverhampton and Dudley, and Fullers. The move was part of a strategy to create a 'Europe of Brands', as opposed to one pan-European brand, and to develop a strong north-west European group of individual names. They would have in common 'a strict quality philosophy, long family tradition and cultivated brewing', said a Grolsch spokesperson.

In February 1992 Grolsch announced that it was purchasing the Ruddles real ale brand and brewery, in the United Kingdom, from Courage for £40 million. The purchase was funded from cash flow. Ruddles had estimated sales of 490,000 hectolitres per annum, and this boosted Grolsch's sales by 15 per cent to Fl800m. The UK markets for premium lager and real ale were both growing.

Bass

In the early 1990s Bass was the UK's largest and most profitable brewer. The company had a strong brand range, was highly successful in free trade sales (approximately 60 per cent of total beer sales) and owned the largest number of pubs – 2,405 managed pubs and 4,373 tenancies. However, by 1992 it was in the process of reducing its number of pubs in line with the Monopolies and Mergers Commission (MMC) directives. It announced in 1990 that it would free 2,680 pubs before November 1992 to comply with the directives. To facilitate this, Bass reorganised in 1989 to a divisional structure separating brewing and pub retailing.

Bass had a production volume of 14 million hectolitres from thirteen breweries and its UK market share was 22 per cent. It was number one in the UK

Table 21 Grolsch's financial summary

	1990	*1989*	*1988*	*1987*	*1986*
Sales income	472	414	380	345	342
Operating profit	43	36	34	31	30
Net profit	35	29	26	23	22
Capital employed	459	427	406	376	396

Notes 1. All figures are in millions of guilders.
        2. Exchange rate, February 1992: £1 = 3.15 guilders.
Source: Company annual reports.

lager market with its national brands Tennents and Carling Black Label. Its national ale brands were Stone's and Toby, as well as Bass Ale, which was also distributed in the United States. Bass was alone among the big UK brewers in owning all its brands. It was estimated that ale accounted for 45 per cent of sales and lager the remainder, and that exports were less than 5 per cent of production.

The company was also the number two soft drinks manufacturer and combined with wines and spirits these accounted for 20 per cent of Bass sales. The other main group activity was hotels. Bass owned the world's largest hotel chain, Holiday Inns. Other leisure activities included the UK's third largest bookmaker; the Toby chain of restaurants; the branded retail chains Kelly's Kitchens and Drummonds Café Bars; and the Augustus Barnett chain of off-licences.

By 1991 trading profits were about 56 per cent brewing and pubs; 25 per cent hotels and restaurants; and 19 per cent leisure and other. Table 22 gives a financial summary of Bass's development from 1987 to 1991.

In December 1991 Bass announced a series of moves designed to streamline its operations. Two breweries were closed in May 1991 and it was planned to close two others in 1992, reducing the number of Bass breweries to nine. Earlier in 1991, Bass had raised £558 million through a rights issue, to be used for future investment, principally in Holiday Inns, in which Bass had made a commitment to invest $1 billion from 1991 to 1993.

Table 22 Bass's financial summary

	1991	1990	1989	1988	1987
Sales income	4,383	4,461	4,036	3,734	3,213
of which:					
Brewing	1,056	929	868		
Pub retailing	1,173	1,089	1,050		
Operating profit	616	673	526	459	386
of which:					
Brewing	148	177	121		
Pub retailing	238	245	214		
Net profit	452	470	382	323	262
Capital employed	6,397	5,790	4,682	4,107	3,673

Note All figures are in £ millions.
Source: Company annual reports.

Courage Ltd

Murray Steele

Courage's development as a brewer epitomised that of the UK brewing industry. However, by 1992 it had developed into a business which was very different to its UK brewing rivals.

Brief history of Courage

Courage was the outcome of a series of mergers over 200 years. The following is a brief chronology of its development:

1787   Founder John Courage, a Scot who came to London to work as an agent for a Scottish shipping company, in 1787 diversified his interests by purchasing a brewhouse in Southwark for £616.

1888   Courage & Co. Limited formed and was the largest brewer in London, brewing 1,600 barrels of beer per day.

1903   Courage made its first acquisition, G. & E. Hall's brewery at Alton in Hampshire to acquire supplies of pale ale.

1920s Expansion across the Thames with the acquisition of the Camden brewery. Further acquisitions took place during this period.

1955   Courage merged with Barclay Perkins, a friendly rival. The merged company had 2,500 tied pubs and extensive free trade interests.

1961   Acquisition of Simonds Brewery based in Reading, with four breweries and 1,400 pubs, and Bristol Breweries, based in the West Country.

1971   The public company John Smiths of Tadcaster, Yorkshire, merged its 1,800 pubs, spread mainly over the north of England, with the expanding Courage.

1972   Courage was acquired by Imperial Group, the cigarette manufacturer.

1986   Imperial Group was acquired by Hanson Trust, but Courage remained part of Hanson Trust for only nine months before it was sold to the Australian group Elders IXL, brewers of Fosters lager.

Appendix 1 gives financial information on Courage.

This case study was prepared by Murray Steele. It is intended as a basis for class discussion and not as an illustration of either good or bad management practice.

Fosters Brewing Group

At the 1990 annual general meeting the shareholders of Elders IXL voted to change the company's name to the Fosters Brewing Group. This change reflected the concentration on the company's brewing interests.

At its peak in 1989 Elders had sales of A$17.6 billion, and had major businesses in brewing, agribusiness, finance, investments and natural resources. By 1991 sales had fallen to A$10.3 billion, reflecting the withdrawal from non-brewing interests after asset disposals to the value of A$1.7 billion. Group operating profits had more than doubled to A$234 million from A$104m. However, due to the recession, the core brewing division had cut its contribution to A$488m from A$513m. Fosters losses at the bottom line totalled A$1.3 billion. In 1992 it was still seeking to make further disposals of its remaining agricultural and finance activities. This would be difficult until the Australian economy revived.

Elders IXL had entered brewing in 1983 with the acquisition of Carlton United Breweries (CUB) of Melbourne. In 1986 it acquired Courage in the UK, and in 1987 Canada's third largest brewing company, Carling O'Keefe. In 1989 it merged Carling O'Keefe in a 50/50 joint venture with Molsons. These acquisitions were part of a global strategy to make Fosters a major international beer brand. At the time of the Courage acquisition, Elders top management stated that they viewed Courage as a potential springboard into the rest of Europe.

Fosters' brewing activities made it the fourth largest brewer in the world, behind Anheuser-Busch, Miller and Heineken. Worldwide it brewed 36 million hectolitres per annum and was the market leader in Australia and Canada and number two in the UK.

The Courage merger with Grand Metropolitan

In February 1991, Courage announced that it had completed a pubs-for-breweries swap with Grand Metropolitan, the UK-based international brewing and foods group. The merger had first been announced almost exactly a year before, but had been delayed while the UK Monopolies and Mergers Commission carried out an investigation into the effects of the transaction.

Under the terms of the agreement Courage would focus on brewing, distribution, brands marketing and sales. Grand Metropolitan would cease all brewing activities and concentrate on retailing and property management. Courage acquired all Grand Metropolitan's breweries and beer brands. The pubs of both parties were merged into one company, which was owned on a 50/50 basis by Courage and Grand Metropolitan, but managed by the latter.

After completion of the merger, which, it was believed, could take as long as two years, Courage would have strong lager brands, an effective distribution network and efficient breweries. It would be the UK brewer which most closely resembled its continental European competitors. It would also be unique among British brewers in that its only business activity would be brewing, unlike its major UK competitors which had diversified into other areas of activity, such as hotels and restaurants. The following sections give fuller details about the impact of the merger.

Market Shares

Table 1 shows the brewing market shares of the leading UK brewers before and after the Courage–Grand Met merger. After the merger there was some rationalisation. Courage sold the Trowbridge brewery and 450 pubs to its management, and in February 1992 it announced that it had concluded a deal with Grolsch, the specialist Dutch brewer, for the sale of Ruddles, receiving £40 million for the real ale brand and brewery.

Brewing

After the merger and the sale of the Trowbridge and Ruddles breweries, Courage would have five modern and efficient breweries with an annual capacity of 11 million hectolitres, the sixth largest in Europe.

The merger of the Courage and Grand Met brewing interests would create the opportunity for cost reduction. For example, one brewery could be dedicated to brewing one type of beer or even just one brand. Industry analysts estimated that a cost reduction of £10 per barrel could be achieved (1 barrel = 1.6 hectolitres). This reduction would give Courage a considerable advantage over its competitors.

Table 1 Brewing market shares of leading UK brewers before and after merger

| | Total (%) | | Ale (%) | | Lager (%) | |
	Before	After	Before	After	Before	After
Bass	22	22	20	20	24	24
Courage	**9**	**18**	**9**	**17**	**10**	**23**
Allied-Lyons	13	13	12	12	13	13
Grand Met	13		9		13	
Whitbread	12	12	12	12	12	12
Scottish & Newcastle	11	11	13	13	7	7

Source: Monopolies and Mergers Commission, Beer Report on Courage/Grand Met Merger.

Brands

The merger gave Courage an extensive range of brands. Grand Met's ales complemented existing Courage ale brands, but the combination of lager brands would be particularly strong, although not without some difficulties. Grand Met brewed under licence Budweiser, Holsten and Carlsberg. However, Courage brewed Miller Lite, the arch rival of Anheuser-Busch's Budweiser. After lengthy negotiations Courage was able to retain all the former Grand Met licensing agreements, making it the only brewer in the world to have the rights to brew Budweiser and Miller simultaneously.

Courage's list of brands would put it equal with Bass in market share for lager. Its range of brands would include Fosters, Carlsberg, Holsten, Budweiser, Miller, Kronenbourg and Molson – all well-known international brands. Table 2 shows the market shares of leading lager brands in the UK.

Pubs

Under the terms of the merger Grand Metropolitan would manage, initially, 9,700 public houses. However, before November 1992, 3,500 pubs would be either freed from the beer tie by 'arm's-length' operation, to comply with government orders, or sold.

Courage would have a supply agreement to provide beer to the Grand Met pubs and also its take-home and free trade customers. This agreement would give Courage access to a significantly greater number of customers. The government forced some changes to the supply agreement before approving the merger. Courage and Grand Met had originally wanted the supply agreement to be for ten years. The government suggested five years and agreement was finally reached at eight years.

Table 2

	Market share (%)	Brewer	Ownership situation
Carling Black Label	11	Bass	Owned
Fosters	**8**	**Courage**	**Owned**
Heineken	8	Whitbread	Licence
Carlsberg	6	Carlsberg & **Courage**	Owned **Licence**
Tennents	5	Bass	Owned
Castlemaine XXXX	4.5	Allied	Licence
Skol	4.5	Allied	Owned
Harp	3	Guinness/Greene King	Owned

Source: Various estimates.

Distribution

The merger offered Courage the opportunity to reap benefits of economies of scale in sales and distribution. After the merger Courage would have 45 secondary distribution depots nationwide. There would be much overlap, and rationalisation would be inevitable. However, after rationalisation was completed Courage would have a low-cost distribution service. As customer service became increasingly important, the effectiveness of distribution would become a powerful competitive weapon.

Courage in Europe

As with many other UK brewers, Courage had traditionally practised little sales activity in Europe. However, when acquired by Fosters Brewing Group, Courage had access to its first truly global beer brand, Fosters lager. Licensing agreements were concluded with Pripps of Sweden to gain access to the Scandinavian market, and with Holsten in Germany, Europe's largest market. Holsten was to brew Fosters under the German *Reinheitsgebot* or purity laws, and also to market it alongside its own brand range. Fosters was also distributed nationally in Italy, Greece and Spain. Under these agreements the licensors distributed Fosters alongside their own products through their channels of distribution, normally wholesalers and supermarkets.

The director responsible for Courage's European operations, Rick Scully, described their approach:

> You cannot Fosterise Europe overnight with a blanket. It has to be a bit of a quiltwork, patch by patch, territory by territory. It's not an overnight job, it is a multi-year job.
>
> We have to adjust and become a European brewer, European focused with a European mentality, European market-orientated production and marketing.
>
> With the 1992 freeing of trading barriers in Europe, Courage is in a good position to attack new market opportunities.

Appendix 1 Courage Ltd Financial History

Profit and loss account (£ million)

	1990	1989	1988
Sales	762.7	694.5	638.9
Gross profit	166.1	144.1	230.3
Net operating profit	64.0	61.6	146.3
Profit before tax	109.4	105.7	144.0
Profit after tax	89.0	80.6	120.0
Net profit	99.7	104.6	224.0
Operating cash flow	122.6	127.2	245.2
Employees	9,717	9,469	9,527

Source and application of funds (£ million)

	1990	1989
Net income	99.7	104.6
Depreciation	23.0	22.6
Change in non-trade current liabilities	14.3	64.4
Change in long-term liabilities	(73)	(75.5)
Share issue	0	36.8
Total funds generated	63.9	152.8
Net capital expenditure	15.5	55.9
Dividends	0	41.0
Change in net working capital	43.6	57.1
Change in liquid assets	4.8	(1.2)
Other	0	0.0
Total funds used	63.9	152.8

Balance sheet (£ million)

	1990	1989	1988
Land and buildings	136.3	126.7	109.5
Plant and equipment	188.0	205.1	189.0
Intangibles	120.0	120.0	120.0
Other non-current	142.3	142.3	142.3
Total fixed	586.6	594.1	560.8
Inventories	56.2	60.0	51.7
Trade debtors	98.8	66.9	65.7
Other debtors	754.6	757.5	716.8
Cash	8.6	3.8	5.1
Other current	15.2	4.3	9.0
Total current	933.4	892.7	848.3
Total assets	1,520.0	1,486.7	1,409.0
Trade creditors	44.2	51.9	63.4
Bank loans/overdrafts	0.0	0.0	0.0
Taxation	29.3	47.5	52.7
Loans payable	509.8	477.0	433.4
Other current	75.8	76.0	50.1
Total current liabilities	659.1	652.5	599.6
Share capital	8.3	8.3	8.3
Retained earnings	465.9	362.2	291.1
Reserves	250.6	254.7	225.4
Deferred taxation	120.4	75.1	74.0
Long-term liabilities	15.7	134.0	210.7
Total liabilities and equity	1,520.0	1,486.7	1,409.0

Source: Company annual reports.

Brasseries Kronenbourg
Roland Calori

The company

Kronenbourg SA is the holding company of the beer branch of the BSN Group; and Brasseries Kronenbourg the main department of the beer branch based in Alsace, a region with a strong brewing tradition. In the 1990s Brasseries Kronenbourg produced and distributed two main product ranges under the generic names of Kronenbourg and Kanterbraü, each of which had several brands. Brasseries Kronenbourg had a strong leadership position in the French market in 1990 with a 48 per cent market share. The number two was the Société Française de Brasserie – a 100 per cent subsidiary of Heineken – with 28 per cent, and number three was the Belgian Interbrew-Stella with 11 per cent of the market. Brasseries Kronenbourg also exported a growing share of its production and Kronenbourg beer was produced under licence in the UK (by Courage) and in Nigeria.

Through Kronenbourg SA, BSN was also represented in several other European markets and its beer brands were distributed in 70 countries in the world. BSN owned Henninger Hellas, a brewery in Greece (80 per cent of the equity); had a joint venture with Alken-Maes in Belgium (50 per cent of the equity); and owned 33 per cent of Mahou, a Spanish brewery, and 20 per cent of Peroni in Italy. Altogether, in 1990, the volume sold by the breweries in which the BSN Group had dominant or significant stakes was around 24.8 million hectolitres and the sales turnover about Ffr10.5 billion.

The sales of Brasseries Kronenbourg itself were about Ffr5,329 million in 1989 and Ffr5,637 million in 1990. From 11.4 million hectolitres in 1989, they had increased to 11.6 million hectolitres in 1990 (including a small percentage of soft drinks: 0.5 per cent). The sales of Brasseries Kronenbourg in France were about 10.7 million hectolitres in 1990 (compared to 10.67 million in 1989), of which 6.8 million hectolitres were for Kronenbourg and 3.9 million for Kanterbraü. The exports had increased more rapidly: from 695,000 hectolitres in 1989 to 873,000 in 1990; in addition, production under licence was about 1 million hectolitres.

The author would like to thank the Brasseries Kronenbourg for their support in the writing of this case study. It is intended as a basis for class discussion and not as an illustration of either good or bad management practice.

Table 1 gives simplified balance sheets and statements of income of Brasseries Kronenbourg for 1988, 1989 and 1990; Table 2 breaks down the data on volumes sold by Brasseries Kronenbourg and the foreign breweries controlled by the BSN Group. During this time Kronenbourg 1664 (*bière spéciale* competing with Carlsberg, Tuborg or Heineken) and Kronenbourg Light, a low-alcohol beer (3°) experienced high sales growth. Among the Kanterbraü beers the Tourtel – a non-alcoholic beer – was also particularly successful with a 30 per cent average annual increase in sales, establishing itself as the market leader in non-alcoholic beers in France, Spain, Belgium and Switzerland. Kronenbourg believed this segment could soon represent 5 per cent of the beer market.

In 1990 Brasseries Kronenbourg invested Ffr330 million in industrial plant and equipment (to compare with Ffr310 million in 1989), Ffr98 million in com-

Table 1 Kronenbourg SΛ: Balance sheets and statements of income (simplified)

(Simplified) balance sheets (Ffr 000)

	1990	1989	1988
Assets			
Net property plant, equipment and intangible assets	2,135,008	2,148,015	2,230,659
Financial assets	2,329,486	2,296,542	699,822
Current assets	1,553,447	1,594,371	1,653,514
Miscellaneous	7,418	10,135	2,895
Total assets	6,025,359	6,049,063	4,586,890
Liabilities			
Equity	1,885,870	1,810,278	1,770,932
Provisions	126,601	171,068	278,506
Debts	3,920,870	3,976,018	2,464,093
Miscellaneous	92,018	91,699	73,359
Total liabilities	6,025,359	6,049,063	4,586,890

(Simplified) statements of income (Ffr 000)

	1990	1989	1988
Net sales	5,766,750	5,493,780	5,211,960
Operating costs and expenses	4,864,065	4,655,523	4,486,990
Operating profit*	902,685	838,257	724,970
Net profits	262,219	331,114	324,138

Note * Before financial revenues and expenses, before extraordinary items and before income tax.
Source: Annual reports, 1989, 1990.

Table 2 Volumes sold by Brasseries Kronenbourg and other companies under control of Kronenbourg SA

Brasseries Kronenbourg

	1988	*1989*	*1990*
France (beer)			
Kronenbourg	6,493,000	6,703,000	6,769,000
Kanterbraü	3,835,000	3,969,000	3,929,000
Total	10,328,000	10,672,000	10,698,000
Direct export sales	534,000	695,000	873,541

Foreign sales subsidiaries
Gastrodrink: Switzerland; Kronenbourg Vertriebsgesellschaft: Germany;
Interali: Italie; Kanterbraü Italia: Italy; Paybesa: Spain.

Production under licence

	1988	*1989*	*1990*
In the UK	432,000	490,000	530,000
In Nigeria (starting from 1990)			500,000

Subsidiaries and companies in which Kronenbourg was a significant stakeholder

	1989	*1990*
Europe	11,698,000	12,679,000
Africa	1,049,000	368,000
Total	12,747,000	13,047,000

Alken-Maes: Belgium (2,377,000 hl in 1990); Peroni: Italy (5,369,000 hl in 1990); Mahou: Spain (4,316,000 hl in 1990); Société Congolaise des Brasseries Kronenbourg: Congo (368,000 hl in 1990); International Beer and Beverage Industries and Sona Breweries: Nigeria (until 1990); Henninger Hellas: Greece was acquired in 1989 (617,000 hl in 1990).

Sources: Annual reports, 1989, 1990.

mercial investments, mainly in equipment in cafés and restaurants linked to exclusive distribution contracts (compared to Ffr109 million in 1989), and Ffr170 million in acquisitions and shares of other companies (to compare with Ffr1,608 million in 1989 when Kronenbourg SA took over Henninger Hellas in Greece).

Kronenbourg, the Beer Branch and the BSN Group

BSN was mainly a glass manufacturer when it acquired Kronenbourg in 1970.

The BSN Group then began a radical change from glass making to the food and drinks industries: in 1973 it acquired Gervais Danone, a major dairy product business, followed by other food companies. From Ffr300 million in 1966, the turnover of the group went up to about Ffr53 billion in 1990 (among which packaging represented only 10.9 per cent).

In 1990 the sales turnover of the group was Ffr52,897 million (Ffr48,669 million in 1989) and its consolidated net profits reached Ffr3,091 million (Ffr2,698 million in 1989). The branches in food and drinks became the core businesses (see Table 3). More precisely, the sales revenue of the Beer Branch of the group was about Ffr6,188 million in 1989 and about Ffr6,598 million in 1990. The operating profit of the Beer Branch of the group was about Ffr806 million in 1989 and about Ffr843 million in 1990.

The goal of Antoine Riboud, président directeur général of the group, was to become the leader or the number two in each area of busines, first at the European level, then at the world level. At the end of 1990, BSN sold its champagne business, Lanson and Pommery, to LVMH for Ffr3.1 billion, in order to focus on the businesses in which the leadership or number two positions could be reached. By 1991 BSN was the third leading food marketer in Europe, challenging Nestlé and Unilever. It was also the world's largest seller of dairy products and mineral water. At the beginning of 1990 it was the second in the world for pasta sales and biscuits (number one in Europe); and number two in Europe in the beer industry.

Between January 1989 and June 1990 BSN acquired fifteen food and drinks concerns in Europe, among which were the five European subsidiaries of R.J.R. Nabisco (for $2.5 billion). The group was also looking at the USA and South-East Asia; it bought Nabisco subsidiaries in New Zealand, Hong Kong, Singapore and Malaysia in March 1990, then took 50 per cent of Associated Biscuits International, which also gave it a share in Britannia Industries Ltd, the first biscuits marketer in India. In March 1990 Antoine Riboud declared that BSN would also seek to invest in eastern Europe.

Belonging to a large, diversified group meant shared responsibilities between the headquarters and the companies. Antoine Riboud explained the relationships in *Le Figaro* (9 September 1991):

> You have to limit the number of hierarchical levels, avoid complicated procedures, avoid barriers to the free circulation of information, cash flow

Table 3 BSN: % of sales turnover by product type

	1990	1989	Example
Dairy products	24.5	25.4	Gervais Danone
Epicerie, pasta	19.6	20.1	Panzani
Biscuits	23.6	22.2	Lu and Belin
Beer	12.2	12.4	Kronenbourg and Kanterbräu
Champagne and mineral waters	9.2	8.7	Evian

and people. You have to delegate operational decisions. At BSN the managers of branches and departments are free with regard to the management of operations, but each one knows his limits. On the other hand, strategy must be centralised, it is the responsibility of the 'Premier Rond' of BSN.

The 'Premier Rond' of BSN consisted of Antoine Riboud (president), the vice-president, the chief executive and the vice-chief executive. The 'Deuxième Rond' consisted of the managers of the seven branches (among whom was the manager of the Beer Branch), the manager of the International Branch of Dairy Products, the manager of the Asia and Pacific Branch, and two functional managers (Finance and Human Relations). The 'Troisième Rond' included 80 general managers of the departments and of the subsidiaries of the group, among them the managing director of Brasseries Kronenbourg.

Each year, the managing director of each department/company in the group presented the previous year's results and the future scenarios for the company to the Premier Rond. The Premier Rond responded with general objectives for the year coming. It was then the responsibility of the manager of the corresponding branch to monitor the achievement of the objectives of the department. The headquarters left the managing directors of departments/companies free to manage their businesses, as long as the objectives were achieved. In the Beer Branch, each company was a department: Brasseries Kronenbourg in France, Alken-Maes in Belgium, Henninger Hellas in Greece, Mahou in Spain, and Peroni in Italy.

Even the companies in which BSN did not have a dominant financial stake were participating in the BSN planning system. The branch level helped restructuring companies joining the group when needed and was also in charge of transferring skills between the departments.

The management style of the BSN Group, personified by Antoine Riboud, also influenced Kronenbourg. The cornerstone of this philosophy was a double economic and social intent: '*Pas d'économie sans social, pas de social sans économie*'. Indeed, the group won the Palme d'Or for the best corporate institutional image among managers in an Ipsos-L'Expansion study conducted in 1990 in France. 'Dialogue' at work and with strong unions, 'participation of the personnel in the profits of the firm' and 'mutual support' were the key characteristics of the management at BSN. Personnel training expenses represented 3.65 per cent of the wages and participative management was the norm.

The strategy of Brasseries Kronenbourg

The top management of Brasseries Kronenbourg saw brewing as a 'heavy industry' with the emphasis on the capacity of production units and increasing capital intensity due to the development of automatic processing. They therefore believed there were three key success factors for the business:

- Managing the high level of investments with a tight control of the debt/equity ratio.
- The achievements of economies of scale – the high level of fixed costs required a focus on lower production costs through larger units to cover bigger geographical areas (up to 1,000 km for mass-market beer).
- Improvements in productivity and quality through effective human resource management to keep up with new techniques (e.g. automation and quality control).

The management of inventories and production planning were also seen as critical functions, as beer consumption was seasonal, especially in southern Europe.

Compared to many other food-processing businesses, the beer industry dealt with two distinct distribution channels: cafés and restaurants; and food retailing for home consumption. Each distribution channel required a specific approach (e.g. to sales packaging). Selling to cafés and restaurants required investments in the place of consumption, and long-term contracts were concluded with cafés. However, the food channel was taking a bigger share of the market: for instance, in France the food channel accounted for 58 per cent of the volumes of beer, 70 per cent of which was through the major retail chains. Dealing with the food channel, especially with large retail chains, demanded both high expenditure and management skills in advertising and merchandising. Brasseries Kronenbourg aimed to improve its position in both distribution channels and to tailor its marketing strategy to each.

In both channels the image of the product and the brand name were viewed as key success factors, and marketing skills and financial support critical to strengthen and expand the brand image. Finally, in order to grow in a mature market and to cover the company's high fixed costs, international development was viewed as crucial.

Productivity, quality and human resource development

One of the objectives of Brasseries Kronenbourg was to be among the best brewers in the world in terms of productivity; this was vital given overcapacity of around 30 per cent in the industry. High investments in automation were made during the 1980s. Between 1989 and 1991 a *restructuration* plan was implemented to improve productivity. The manpower was reduced by 570 jobs during this period,[1] mostly by voluntary departures (an agreement was signed between the top management and the unions to organise the re-employment of the workers).

Personnel training was increased to keep up with new techniques and to improve quality control – it represented 5.23 per cent of the wages in 1990. New modes of management were also being developed: consultation with all the

---

[1] In 1990 Brasseries Kronenbourg employed 2,674 persons (56 per cent in production; 29 per cent technicians, supervisors and administrative staff; and 15 per cent managers).

employees in 1988 led to the establishment of participative *groupes de réflexion*. These made recommendations to the executive committee on professional development, improvement of information systems and communication and reward systems. The implementation started at the beginning of 1990 and was planned to go on for some time.

In 1990 Brasseries Kronenbourg distributed Ffr128 million to the personnel *au titre de la participation* (shares) and Ffr58 million *au titre de l'intéressement* (bonuses of the profits of the company). The rate of absenteeism, 3.5 per cent, was among the lowest in the industry.

Marketing, innovation and image

The company strategy was to develop both the Kronenbourg and Kanterbraü generic brands, under which different product ranges would be marketed to address all the market segments according to quality and alcohol levels.

- *Bières de luxe* for the mass market, from lower-priced products sold under retailers' names to higher-priced branded beers under the Kronenbourg and Kanterbraü labels. This segment represented about 59 per cent of the French market.
- *Bières spéciales*, more upmarket with 1664 from Kronenbourg, the development of which was seen as a priority, and Gold from Kanterbraü. *Bières spéciales* represented about 24 per cent of the French market. Brasseries Kronenbourg also imported Carlsberg in France.
- *Spécialités* even further upmarket, representing about 5 per cent of the French market, with high growth, and including beers with higher levels of alcohol and imported foreign beers. Here Brasseries Kronenbourg distributed foreign brands such as Grimbergen (from Alken-Maes, the Belgian partner) and, in France, Guinness and Kilkenny.

According to the top management of Brasseries Kronenbourg, there was a particular phenomenon in the brewing industry: a beer positioned in the segment of *spéciales* in its country of origin tended to become a *spécialité* in the foreign countries to which it was exported. For instance, 1664 was seen as a *spécialité* beer in Italy and in the UK.

- Non-alcoholic beer was a particular segment which had developed rapidly in Europe in the late 1980s (above 30 per cent a year) and occupied about 5 per cent of the market. Here Kanterbraü was the leading brand in France, Belgium and Italy with Tourtel, which had 73 per cent of the French market segment. Kronenbourg had also launched Silver, a new brand of non-alcoholic beer in 1990. This segment was characterised by being more international or pan-European, and Brasseries Kronenbourg competed with the Buckler brand from Heineken.
- Low-alcoholic beer or 'light beer' could also be considered as a separate

segment. Here Brasseries Kronenbourg successfully launched Kronenbourg Light and sales were growing quickly. However, this segment represented less than 4 per cent of the market.

- *Panachés* were a mix of beer and lemonade and they represented about 3.8 per cent of the French market. Kronenbourg had the Force 4 brand, and Kanterbraü the Chopp brand; they competed with the Panaché from Société Française de Brasserie (Heineken). Kronenbourg had also created new niche products such as Krony, a very light beer mixed with raspberry, peach or kiwi.

Table 4 summarises the main products and brands of Brasseries Kronenbourg.

Product innovation was seen as important in the company. Tourtel was the first non-alcoholic beer launched in the European market, and Kanterbraü was the first to expand the range of non-alcoholic beer to dark beer in 1989 with Tourtel Brune and Tourtel Ambrée (1990). The successful 1664 pils was also

Table 4 Main product lines and brands of the Brasseries Kronenbourg

Main product lines brands sold on the French market

Segment	Kronenbourg	Kanterbraü
Bières de luxe (mass market)	Kronenbourg	Kanterbraü
Bières spéciales	1664 – Blonde – Brune	Gold
Spécialités	(Imported Belgian beers from Alken-Maes and other imported beers)	
Non-alcoholic beer	Silver	Tourtel – Blonde – Ambrée – Brune
Light beer	Kronenbourg Light Obernai	Valstar Wilfort
Other niche products	Force 4 (panaché) Krony Kronen-Pils	Chopp (panaché)

Main products/brands sold on foreign markets by direct exportation or through the foreign companies owned or controlled by the group

Kronenbourg	(spéciale)
1664	(spécialité)
Tourtel	(non-alcoholic beer)

complemented by a dark 1664 in 1990. Kronenbourg launched Bière de Mars, brewed traditionally and sold only in March, in the same way as the beaujolais nouveau; this was marketed under the Obernai Primeur brand. The whole idea was to satisfy more and more diverse customer tastes, to sell a diversity of products and to 'de-banalise' beer by enhancing its image, especially in France.

In the same way, innovations in packaging were also seen as important. Kronenbourg and Kanterbräu had improved the design of their logo and developed a variety of product presentations (bottles and packaging) for the French market and for the international market. Indeed, Kronenbourg had won an award for packaging in France with its 'prestige' new 33 cl bottle for cafés and restaurants, thin, with angles and an encrusted label, and preserving the brilliance of the glass after several re-uses.

The advertising campaigns of Brasseries Kronenbourg were based on conviviality. As TV advertising for beer was forbidden in France, several other media were used, such as the press, sponsorship and street advertisement. Moreover, in France, the *Loi Evin* would limit possible themes for advertising alcoholic drinks in any media. Most of the other markets targeted by the company in Europe, however, had less strict limitations.

The international strategy of Brasseries Kronenbourg and the Beer Branch of BSN

Given high relative costs of transportation and logistics and high marketing expenses, the geographical scope of the market was seen as limited around a production unit. The case of upmarket beers (at the top of the pyramid) was different: the higher margins of the premium products would cover the costs of distribution logistics and marketing. So the Brasseries Kronenbourg started to export its premium products in the 1960s, selling to local importers and distributors, completing its range of drinks to be sold mainly in the cafés, hotels and restaurants. This export mode was still employed in 1990 in the case of distant foreign countries such as Japan, Hong Kong, Australia, Canada and Sweden.

However, this strategy would not lead to high volume, and volume sales required a significant position in a foreign market, a broader range of products, including lower-priced beers, and therefore higher costs of distribution and marketing. Given the overcapacity in the beer industry, the executives from Brasseries Kronenbourg believed that partnerships and acquisitions were the best way quickly to achieve a significant position in a foreign market.

As far as licences were concerned, Brasseries Kronenbourg had already taken a position in the United Kingdom by a production licensing agreement with Courage (a ten-year contract, worth 530,000 hectolitres in 1990) when the British market started to consume more and more continental/international lagers and reduce their consumption of traditional ale.

However, the top management of the Beer Branch of BSN believed that the best way to take a significant position in a new targeted market was to take over the local number one or number two brewery in that market. As the owners of the target firms were not always ready to sell, another more patient way was to take a minority participation and then to increase it and conclude partnerships with other stronger local breweries. This type of solution was implemented in Italy, Belgium, Spain and Greece. Several criteria were considered to select the priority countries for international development:

- A permeable upmarket segment.
- Growing demand for beer.
- Signs that the competitive structure of the industry might be beginning to concentrate.

The Mediterranean countries typically were in this situation at the end of the 1970s, and it was regarded as urgent to establish a position in these countries before other international competitors did so.

The selection of the brands that Brasseries Kronenbourg would make international was based on the success of the brand in its home market. The leading brands in France were selected: namely, Kronenbourg, 1664 and Tourtel. Selectivity was crucial because it was recognised that developing an international brand would require very high marketing investments. As beer consumers travelled more and more for work or holidays across Europe, it was critical that they could find their favourite beer everywhere. The formula applied to dealing with the product range overseas was to keep the local brands of the partner (or the acquired company), but to add the Kronenbourg, 1664 and Tourtel brands from Brasseries Kronenbourg to the product range of the local partner, positioning them as upmarket beers.

In *Italy*, Kronenbourg SA first took control of Wührer, which had a 10 per cent market share and was particularly well established in the north of Italy. However, Peroni was the market leader and well established in the south. BSN arranged the merger of Wührer and Peroni, Kronenbourg SA having a 20 per cent stake in the company. In 1990 Peroni sold 5.4 million hectolitres (90 per cent beer and 10 per cent soft drinks); its sales turnover was 478 billion lire (+ 19.5 per cent compared to 1989) and Peroni was the leader in the Italian beer market with a 40 per cent market share. By 1990 Peroni sold five main brands: Peroni, Wührer, Nastro Azzuro (an Italian premium beer), Kronenbourg and Tourtel (which were increasing rapidly).

The market in *Belgium* was nearly as big as the Italian market, due to a high consumption of beer per capita, but it was slowly decreasing. Kronenbourg SA first took control of Alken and of Anglo Belge, which together held 10 per cent of the market, then a joint venture with Maes gave a 25 per cent share of the market to Alken-Maes, in which Kronenbourg SA had 50 per cent of the capital). In 1990 Alken-Maes was number two in Belgium after Interbrew, which had 60 per cent of the market (merger of Stella Artois and Jupiter). In 1989 Alken-Maes sold 2.3 million hectolitres of beer (and 253,000 hectolitres of soft drinks), an increase of 9 per cent compared to 1988; its sales turnover was Bfr5,854 million. The main brands of the company represented a wide range of products: Maes Pils, which was experiencing growth, Cristal, Kronenbourg, Tourtel, which had become the leader in the non-alcoholic beer segment in Belgium, and several Belgian traditional specialities (e.g. Grimbergen, Cuvée de l'Ermitage). In 1990 the turnover of Alken-Maes reached Bfr5,954 million.

In *Spain*, Kronenbourg acquired 33 per cent of the capital of Mahou, the number three in the market. Spanish consumption had regularly increased by 3–4 per cent a year in the 1980s. From 72 litres per person per year in 1989, experts forecasted a 100 litres per person per year consumption by the end of the century. Mahou sold 4.4 million hectolitres of beer in 1989 (+ 5 per cent compared to 1988) and had regularly increased its market share (17 per cent); its sales turnover was around pta29 billion. Since the capacity of the Paseo Imperial brewery of Mahou in Madrid was saturated, the group decided to invest in a new plant to produce, at first, 1 million hectolitres starting from 1992. However, as the Spanish market was attractive, other European competitors had entered. The number two, El Aguila, was controlled by Heineken, and in 1990 Guinness acquired Cruz del Campo (the market leader with a 22 per cent market share) for £500 million the highest bid from a foreign company in Spain. In 1990 Mahou sold 4.3 million hectolitres but its sales turnover increased by 9.6 per cent to pta31.8 billion and its profits also increased. However, as Mahou did not accept distribution of the international brands of Brasseries Kronenbourg in Spain, Brasseries Kronenbourg had to continue parallel distribution through a sales subsidiary, Paybesa.

In July 1989 Kronenbourg acquired 80.3 per cent of the equity of Henninger Hellas, the number two Greek brewery, which had a 30 per cent market share and a sales turnover of Ffr250 million. It then began a commercial and industrial restructuring. During the restructuring, in 1990, the sales went down by 4.9 per cent compared to 1989. However, it was planned that from 1991 the introduction of the Tourtel and Kronenbourg brands in Greece would improve the competitiveness of Henninger Hellas.

With strong bases in southern Europe, Kronenbourg therefore planned to develop both local brands and the international brands of Brasseries Kronenbourg.

In Switzerland, Brasseries Kronenbourg had a sales subsidiary, Gastrodrink, and was the leader among imported beers. The leading Swiss brewer, Feldschlösschen, preferred to conclude a distribution agreement with Brasseries Kronenbourg and took 50 per cent of the sales subsidiary at the beginning of 1991.

Organising for acquisitions

Brasseries Kronenbourg itself had direct control of its sales subsidiaries and of the partnerships for the production of Kronenbourg under licence in the United Kingdom and in Nigeria. But the other companies linked to the group – Alken-Maes, Henninger Hellas, Peroni and Mahou – reported directly to the Beer Branch of BSN, which had been directly involved in the decisions on acquisitions and partnerships. The extent of integration of acquisitions was carefully pre-planned.

> A constant effort is made to rationalize the industrial process. Before each acquisition the specialists from BSN analyse the commercial value of the potential acquisition (brands, market shares, distribution network); but they also analyse the potential productivity gains after the integration into the BSN industrial network. (*Le Figaro*, 9 September 1991)

The Beer Branch would transfer skills in R & D, production and marketing, and if necessary help the restructuring of the company. Brasseries Kronenbourg also played an important role in the process of international acquisitions and joint developments: by signalling opportunities to the Beer Branch, by providing cash and by transferring its distinctive skills.

Brasseries Kronenbourg also retained marketing control on its international brands which were distributed by Alken-Maes, Peroni and Henninger. European marketing co-ordination functions were established at Brasseries Kronenbourg – one for Kronenbourg and one for Tourtel – in order to support the international development of these brands. However, the packaging of Kronenbourg, 1664 and Tourtel on foreign markets was slightly different from the packaging of these products in France, and pricing policy was different between countries for a given product.

The future

It was the view of the top management of Kronenbourg that, considering the positions taken by major competitors such as Heineken, Kronenbourg and to a lesser degree Interbrew and Carlsberg, and considering the constraints of anti-monopoly institutions, it would be hard for any major brewer to achieve any new significant acquisition in the EC. The major uncertainties concerned the British brewing industry and the German brewing industry, the latter still highly fragmented with customers giving the preference to German local brands.

The executives of Brasseries Kronenbourg believed that it was too early in 1990 to try to move into the German market. It was impossible then to find a partner of a national level. In order to take a significant share, a foreign brewer would have had to take over five or six breweries, manage the diversity of the resulting product range and probably close some of the breweries. The idea was to let the Germans first restructure their industry.

Kronenbourg believed that the European single market would not bring radical changes, especially for the major brewers already established in several countries. However, the pricing policy would probably have to change across countries. The level of taxes (excise duties and VAT) were very different across Europe (for instance, high in the UK and low in France) and the same brand was often positioned differently in different countries: for example, a *bière spéciale* in its home market was often seen as premium-priced *spécialité* in another. In consequence the differences in pre-tax prices could reach 50 per cent between European countries. The expected progressive harmonisation of taxes and duties across European countries and the free circulation of goods would lead international breweries to harmonise their prices across Europe, probably at a lower level. Then international logistics would also have to be revised and the co-ordination of marketing across Europe would become crucial.

The management of Brasseries Kronenbourg were confident of their European strategy, and concluded the 1990 annual report with the following:

> In a context of a stable market for beer, Brasseries Kronenbourg will continue building on its strengths: strong brands, an extensive range of non-alcoholic beers and international development.

Laura Ashley Holdings plc
John L. Heath

Laura Ashley became a public company in November 1985. It was floated on the stock market to a rapturous City, and such was the enthusiasm for the company that the offer was oversubscribed 34 times. The company had grown from its origins in a flat in Pimlico, London, in 1953 to become an international group manufacturing and retailing its own range of clothes, home furnishings and related products through 219 shops world-wide. It was generating annual profits of £14m and the flotation valued the Ashley family's 70 per cent stake at £292m.

Five years later the group was facing considerable difficulties. In the year to January 1990 it lost £4.7m, and by August of that year it had debts of around £100m. In the year to January 1991 it managed to reduce its debts but lost a further £6.7m. Some of Laura Ashley's difficulties were shared with other companies similarly hit by high interest rates and a significant downturn in retail business. Other problems had their roots in the history, development and nature of the Laura Ashley Group itself.

The development, activities and organisation of the Laura Ashley Group to November 1985, when it 'went public', are described in Part 1 of the case, and the group's subsequent performance as a public company and its further development over the period 1986 to 1991 are described in Part 2.

Part 1 The Laura Ashley Group to November 1985

Background

In 1953 Bernard and Laura Ashley started printing tea towels and scarves to their own design in their flat in Pimlico, London. The success of these designs led the Ashleys to form their first company, Ashley, Mountney Ltd in 1954. In 1954 Bernard Ashley, whose particular interest was in printing and dyeing, developed for £200 his first continuous textile printing machine and a curing oven to fix the dyes. This enabled the Ashleys to expand the business of wholesaling furnishing

This case was prepared by John L. Heath and is a revised and updated version of the 1988 case. It is intended as a basis for class discussion rather than to illustrate either effective or ineffective handling of management situations. Extracts from annual reports and accounts are included by kind permission of Laura Ashley. © J. L. Heath, 1991.

and dress fabrics mainly to department stores. In the years that followed, sales continued to grow and the first export orders were obtained.

The expanding scale of the business led to the decision by the Ashleys in 1960 to move the business to Wales, where Laura Ashley was born. The business was established at the old railway station at Carno in Powys, which remains the site of the headquarters of the manufacturing division. The Group HQ relocated to Maidenhead in October 1990. During the early years, when resources were inadequate to fund the purchase of purpose-built machinery, Bernard Ashley used his skills as an innovator to modify and adapt second-hand equipment to the needs of the business.

In 1966 the group had a staff of nineteen and sales of around £1,000 a week. At about this time Laura Ashley designed the first clothing items, two house-dresses retailing at around £2 each. These were not originally intended as fashion items, but the move into clothing was of profound significance to the subsequent development of the group.

Encouraged by the success of their exports and a small retail selling operation near Carno, the Ashleys became convinced that their products had a wider market than they had been able to reach by selling to department stores and speciality shops. They therefore opened the first Laura Ashley retail shop in South Kensington, London, in 1968.

For the first six months sales in the shop were slow. Bernard Ashley therefore decided to put posters advertising £6 dresses in the London Underground. Sales at the shop increased dramatically and attention was drawn for the first time to the highly individual design and style of Laura Ashley. The subsequent growth and development of the group stems from the move into direct retailing. Demand was such that within two years the group had withdrawn from wholesaling to concentrate on producing goods for sale in its own shops. The basic structure of Laura Ashley as a vertically integrated business embracing design, fabric printing, clothing manufacture and retailing was thus established.

In the next few years more shops were opened, and in 1973 the first overseas shop was opened in Geneva, quickly followed by shops in Amsterdam, Paris and Düsseldorf. In late 1974 the group opened its first shop in the United States, and the remainder of the 1970s saw rapid retail expansion. By the end of 1980 the number of shops world-wide had risen to 71 and total sales exceeded £25m. To meet the growing demand in the shops, production capacity for textiles and wallpaper was steadily expanded.

In 1974 John James joined the group as financial controller, and his appointment in 1976 as joint managing director in the United Kingdom enabled Bernard Ashley to concentrate on the expansion of the business overseas.

Laura Ashley died in September 1985, an event which greatly shocked and saddened staff and customers. Her interests covered a wide range of matters including design, the needs of the market and, in particular, the welfare of Laura Ashley staff. Commenting on Laura Ashley's contribution to her company's growth, *The Economist* noted that:

Her popularity lay in the taste she stamped on her international empire, not so much for the elegance and smartness as for the prettiness and comfort. Nobody was intimidated by the look or the price of a Laura Ashley design. Her home furnishings offered a cheap and feminine alternative to the drab, the posh, and the sternly post-war Habitat Scandinavian. She made it possible to look smart without paying Liberty prices.

Her company's success has been the acceptable face of British capitalism in the past two decades. She was deputy chairman to her husband and her power had been considerable. She prized the loyalty of her staff and cared for their welfare; there was no smoking and no fried fish in the canteens, no night shift in the factories.

Design

Laura Ashley's design philosophy, deeply rooted in traditional English country values, remained as the foundation for the group's designs, their serenity, charm and colours partly explaining the nostalgia for the past that Laura Ashley evoked. The fundamental image remained consistent, but to keep the ranges fashionable, innovative and competitive, new products were introduced and existing lines regularly updated and improved. The marketing and design strategy of the group was aimed to appeal to a customer's lifestyle.

In 1982 Nick Ashley succeeded his mother as design director, and she concentrated on research and on designing prints for the home furnishing ranges in particular. Laura Ashley created and trained teams of designers to continue and develop her work, and her design concepts were thoroughly absorbed and understood throughout the group.

Clothing collections

There were two major clothes collections each year, for the spring/summer and autumn/winter seasons. The development of a collection started some eighteen months before it reached the shops, with discussion between retail divisions, members of the design team and central marketing. A portfolio of fabrics and patterns was brought together, and designers prepared a range of clothing styles that could be used for the collection. Samples were made up of fabrics and styles in a full range of colours, and these were presented to a series of meetings culminating in the Group Collection Meeting, at which the final selection was made.

The group's other divisions played a significant role in the development of the collections. Merchandisers from each of the three retail divisions contributed to the selection of colours, prints and garment styles, while the involvement of members of the product division in each stage of the development of a collection ensured that selected designs could be produced in an efficient and cost-effective manner.

Home furnishing collections

The furnishing collections were based originally on small, precise designs combined with bold colours. Matching reversals were then introduced. Later collections contained a much broader selection of designs, small and large, including stripes, geometrics and florals. Wallpaper and furnishing fabrics were at the heart of the furnishing collections, around which a wide range of products were duly added, including tiles, lamps, upholstered furniture and bed linen. These allowed the customer to create a fully co-ordinated style in the home.

Production

As a vertically integrated group, Laura Ashley manufactured a substantial majority of its products itself. This enabled it to respond rapidly to changes in demand from the retail divisions, to compete more effectively with other retailers on price and quality and to retain control over the group's design quality. The production facilities of the group were organised to produce relatively short production runs, which enabled the retail divisions to offer a wide choice of design and colour. The product division aimed to ensure that prices charged to the retail divisions were competitive with those which would be available to them if they purchased outside the group.

In 1985 the group and its subcontractors manufactured around 85 per cent by value of the products sold by the group. The group used outside manufacturers to produce items, such as ceramic tiles, which it did not manufacture itself. It also had a policy of enabling periodic increases in production demand to be met outside the group, thereby not impairing operational efficiency or the continuity of group employment.

Fabric production started with greige cotton cloth, the principal raw material used by the group. This passed through a series of production processes for conversion into finished cotton fabric. In-house printing of both textiles and wallpaper was considered to be of great importance in preserving the design quality of Laura Ashley products, and this was reflected in the product division's considerable investment in production machinery. Fabric for clothes was cut according to patterns developed from final designs. The cut fabric, ready for sewing, was then supplied to one of the group's making-up plants. The group historically operated the 'make through' process which, although more costly, enabled the product division to respond rapidly to changes in orders from the retail divisions. Subsequently, some plants were organised into 'high productivity units', whereby each person was responsible for part of the garment only. This facilitated the production of simple garments in large numbers.

The group aimed to protect its manufacturing from variations in demand by setting in-house production levels at slightly less than the minimum forecast weekly demand, at about two-thirds of total sales. This enabled the group to minimise production costs and to maintain the level of service and quality of product.

By 1985 the group had eight garment making-up plants within a radius of about 80 miles of Carno, employing some 1,200 people. It also had a plant in Dublin of some 180 employees making up cloth for export. Fabric was also supplied to a third-party manufacturer in Kentucky, USA, where garments were made up under contract for Laura Ashley Inc. Two further plants in the United Kingdom were used for making up home furnishing accessories and made-to-measure curtains and blinds.

The group also manufactured Laura Ashley wallpapers and by 1984 was producing approximately 16 million metres per annum. Around 20 per cent of Laura Ashley wallpapers were purchased outside the group in order to smooth production volumes or because Laura Ashley did not have the appropriate printing facilities for certain wallpapers.

Clothing and home furnishing products were supplied directly to each shop in the United Kingdom, principally by the group's own lorries. Clothing and home furnishings for continental Europe were distributed either by group transport or through arrangements with local carriers. Clothing for North America was dispatched weekly by airfreight to each shop.

In 1985 the group had two major warehouses in the United Kingdom, one at Carno with 30,000 square feet for home furnishings, and one at Newtown with 34,000 square feet for clothing. Modern computer systems were used to control the flow of stock from production to the shops world-wide and to ensure optimum stock levels. All products were housed on one site in Newtown at the end of 1985 with the establishment of a centralised distribution centre.

Production planning

The development and consolidation of forecasts for retail demand and the preparation of long-term plans for the group's material and product requirements was the responsibility of a production planning director. Overall demand for clothing was forecast sixteen months forward. From this, a six-month short-term clothing plan was developed and reviewed weekly. The relatively short making-up cycle and a four-week stock of cloth enabled planners and merchandisers to adjust manufacturing programmes so that production was concentrated on best-selling styles. Home furnishing products were also produced on the basis of a sixteen-month forecast updated three monthly for all products and further reviewed monthly for best sellers.

Retailing

Laura Ashley shops were designed to create the same look and atmosphere throughout the world and played an important part in projecting the image of Laura Ashley. Their 'Paris Green' shop fronts were instantly recognisable. High-quality wooden fittings were a standard feature and great attention was paid to the pre-planning of window and in-shop displays. The presentation of merchandise within each shop was carefully balanced to reflect local customers' preferences.

The group sought wherever possible to obtain prime retail locations for its shops. Many of the shops were free-standing, but there were also standard units within shopping malls, particularly in the United States, and concessions in the stores of other companies, notably Sainsbury's Homebase in the United Kingdom and Au Printemps and Galeries Lafayette in France.

In its shops the group was an early adopter of electronic point-of-sale (EPOS) systems whereby sales figures from each shop were analysed daily by product line. These figures were automatically collected by the group's computers and enabled it to respond quickly in the areas of stock control and production planning.

An important role in the group's marketing was played by its catalogues, which were also used for mail order. Catalogues were produced for the home furnishings and clothing collections and special collections such as bridal. The catalogues were not fully identical between national markets as the emphasis was varied to reflect local market needs.

The group's advertising was largely in magazines with some additional newspaper advertising. It was primarily concerned to communicate innovation in the product ranges within the collections. Point-of-sale material was extensively used by the shops, often to support particular promotions. Such in-shop promotions were co-ordinated with window displays, press advertising and the timing of the catalogues. The printed materials produced by the group were carefully designed to ensure consistency with the style of all Laura Ashley products.

United Kingdom

In the United Kingdom priority was originally given to the selection of sites in retail areas which were considered harmonious with the traditional country image of Laura Ashley, such as Bath and Winchester. This factor was considered important particularly in the choice of buildings, many shops being of historical interest in themselves. However, in some places – for example, Peterborough and Brent Cross – the best sites were in new shopping precincts rather than in the High Street and this influenced the choice of location.

In 1981 the group was invited to open a 'shop-in-shop' within J. Sainsbury's first Homebase home and garden centre. Laura Ashley shops within the Homebase centres sold only home furnishing merchandise and were separate and clearly differentiated shops in prime positions within each store, operated and staffed by the group. The Homebase shops proved to be highly successful and by 1985 accounted for about 20 per cent of the group's UK home furnishings sales. The representation in all Homebase centres gave the group access to an increasingly important do-it-yourself market served by out-of-town sites.

Mail order accounted for about 3 per cent of UK sales and was handled by the mail-order centre in Newtown. The centre also distributed and processed pre-paid orders taken in shops: for example, for made-to-measure curtains and upholstered furniture.

In September 1985 the Laura Ashley chargecard was launched in association with Welbeck Finance plc. The group believed that the introduction of the chargecard would be an important factor in increasing average transaction values, particularly of home furnishing products.

North America

In the United States, Laura Ashley was seen by the customer as a high-quality exclusive designer label with a special English and romantic appeal. In the period to 1985 sales of clothing represented around two-thirds by value of total Laura Ashley sales in the United States, a much higher proportion than elsewhere in the group. This reflected a difference in consumer habit in the United States, where a higher proportion of furnishing consumers than in the United Kingdom use the services of professional interior designers and decorators. The group responded to this difference by establishing decorator collection showrooms, which sold to the interior designers in specialist centres. Consultancies were also established to provide a complete interior design service for clients in their own homes.

Rapid expansion in the United States was facilitated by the relatively low capital costs of establishing shops compared with the United Kingdom. More than two-thirds of Laura Ashley shops were located in modern shopping malls. Rentals were generally turnover related, and Laura Ashley was attractive to mall developers as a tenant because of its high sales per square foot.

The catalogues used in the United States were similar to those issued in the United Kingdom. They were made available to generate interest in the shops and also to increase general consumer awareness of the Laura Ashley name. The catalogues were also used for mail order activity in the United States.

The group granted a number of licences to United States manufacturers. The major licence was with Burlington Domestics, which had exclusive rights in the United States to manufacture and sell bed linen and bathroom accessories, the design of which was under the full control of the group. These products were sold in major department stores throughout the United States as well as in Laura Ashley shops. Other licences were arranged with Henredon Furniture Industries Inc., which manufactured and sold in the United States a range of furniture upholstered in Laura Ashley fabrics, and with Raintree Designs Inc., which produced a range of furnishing fabrics, vinyl and other wall-coverings sold through interior design stores in the United States, Puerto Rico and Canada. The group also had an agreement with the McCall Pattern Company for the production of dress patterns to Laura Ashley designs which were sold world-wide by the group.

Pacific Basin

Within the Pacific Basin the group had, by 1985, eleven shops in Australia and one shop in Japan. Until that year the Australian operations were a joint venture with local partners, but then they became wholly owned and managed by the group. The group believed that there were significant opportunities to expand sales in the Pacific Basin area and intended to increase the number of shops in this region.

The group had a joint venture with Japan United Stores Company (JUSCO) under which a shop was opened in Tokyo in February 1985, selling home furnishings and clothing made up locally from printed cloth supplied from Carno.

Continental Europe

By late 1985 there were 46 Laura Ashley shops in seven countries in continental Europe. Of these, twelve were 'shops-in-shops' and two were decorator collection showrooms. The divisional headquarters was at Helmond, Netherlands, the site of the group's continental Europe manufacturing operations.

The major contributors to the division's sales in the year to January 1985 were France, 38 per cent; West Germany, 20 per cent; and the Netherlands, 17 per cent. Sales were almost equally divided between garments and home furnishings during the 1980s. Generally there were higher garment sales in the Netherlands, Switzerland and West Germany, and higher home furnishings sales in France and Italy.

Mail-order operations had been conducted on a small scale in continental Europe for some years, and in 1984/85 mail-order sales represented 9 per cent of the division's turnover.

The group had a licensing agreement with Bassetti Spa for the manufacture and sale of bed linen, which was also stocked by the group's shops.

Other retailing

In addition to its major retailing areas, the group also had a number of arrangements with retailers, either as franchisees or designated stockists, in countries where Laura Ashley was not otherwise represented.

Organisation

Laura Ashley Holdings plc was the parent company of all operating subsidiaries throughout the world trading under the name of Laura Ashley. In 1980 the group was reorganised on a divisional basis, and with minor modifications this was the structure at the time of the offer for sale in November 1985. There were six divisions as outlined below.

- *Laura Ashley Design Services* was responsible for the design and development of Laura Ashley products.
- The *product division* was responsible for all the group's manufacturing activities, for the purchase of products obtained from outside the group and for the distribution of products to the shops.
- The *three retail divisions*, the United Kingdom, North America and continental Europe, were responsible for all sales in their regions. The local retail management of the Pacific Basin area reported to the group managing director.
- *Laura Ashley Group Services* was responsible for group finance, accounting, legal and secretarial matters, as well as for group informatics.

Each division had a managing director who was also on the board of the parent company. The other members of the divisional boards were the senior management of each division together with some main board directors. The retail and product divisions had, within the constraints of the group's marketing and design policy, the greatest possible trading autonomy. The group structure was designed to allow effective communication between the six divisions and provided a responsive and market-sensitive management control system.

The role of the merchandisers was central to the system. As members of the retail divisions, they were responsible first for interpreting customers' demands and reactions to assist the designers to respond to market trends, and second for informing the product division in order to permit close control over stock levels and any adjustments necessary to production planning.

Information technology

A vital element in the group's organisation was its major commitment to information technology in all areas of its operations. Group informatics covered information technology, data processing and telecommunications, and by 1985 its three main computer centres – in Carno (Wales), Helmond (Netherlands) and Mahwah (New Jersey, USA) – all using the same IBM technology, were linked through a communications network. The computers in Carno and Mahwah interfaced with the electronic point-of-sale (EPOS) systems in the shops.

The product division made extensive use of on-line data-processing systems in such areas as control of work in progress and stock management, as well as computer-aided design and computer-aided manufacturing.

This extensive use of computers enabled the group to operate efficiently and at the same time enabled the design and product divisions to respond quickly to the needs of the retail divisions. The informatics capability was regarded by management as a crucial element in the effectiveness of the group's vertically integrated structure.

The 1985 offer for sale

The offer for sale of 46.5 million ordinary shares (23.3 per cent of share capital) in Laura Ashley Holdings plc in November 1985 attracted great interest and was heavily over subscribed. The issue raised £62.8m, of which £36.8m went into family and charitable trusts, and £23m was new money for the group to support growth through store openings and the expansion of design and production facilities. Employees were offered £50 worth of shares free and preferential rights for up to 10 per cent of the shares on offer.

At the time of the offer, the pre-tax profit forecast for the year to 26 January 1986 was 'not less than £17m'. At the issue price of 135p per share, this indicated a prospective P/E ratio of 23. Immediately following the share offer the Ashley family and the Ashley Foundation (a registered charity established by Laura and Bernard Ashley in 1983) held approximately 72 per cent of the issued share capital of the company and it was their stated intention to remain as major share-holders on a long-term basis.

Although the share offer was widely endorsed by the business press as an attractive investment, there were some notes of caution amidst the general euphoria.

'Although storming ahead in the USA, European performance is at best luke-warm. Mrs Ashley's death will be a severe loss.'

'Expansion in Europe, notably France, has not been a success.'

'Does a mish-mash of designing, manufacturing and retailing warrant a premium store rating?'

Part 2 Group activities and development, 1986–91

Acquisitions

In 1986 the group began a series of acquisitions with the purchase of Sandringham Leather Goods Ltd of Llanidloes and Bryant of Scotland Ltd, a high-quality knitwear company.

Two further acquisitions were made in 1987 of small businesses, considered to have strong brand identification which the group could develop internationally. In August, Willis and Geiger, a traditional outdoor clothing specialist with both wholesale and retail business in the USA, was acquired for $3 million. In November, Penhaligons Ltd, an old established perfumery business holding royal warrants from both HRH The Duke of Edinburgh and HRH The Prince of Wales was acquired for £1 million. Penhaligons had developed an exclusive range of gentlemen's fragrances and operated from five distinctive shops in London. It was intended to develop the Penhaligon range of products and extend its business internationally. The first shop outside London opened in Bath in April 1988, followed by two further shops in York and Chester at the end of that year. The Laura Ashley Group had since 1979 produced its own unique range of women's fragrances through its Swiss-based subsidiary, Parfums Laura Ashley.

The group intended to extend the product ranges and shop openings of its acquisitions in their base countries and later internationally.

In March 1989 the purchase of Revman Industries Inc., a US home furnishings marketing company, was announced, and it was established as an important source of quality designer bed linen selling to major department stores, specialist chains and catalogue houses across the United States.

Design protection

During the period the group vigorously protected its designs from infringement. In 1986 a Tokyo shop, Check Out, merchandising and selling products similar to those of Laura Ashley, agreed to stop the infringement, scrap one of its logos and offending catalogues, and pay Laura Ashley compensation. Later that year a case was brought against Coloroll whose symbol of open lettering and floral sprigs was similar to Laura Ashley's own oval symbol, but this case was unsuccessful.

In 1989 Laura Ashley was in dispute with Victoria's Secret Inc., whom it alleged was infringing Laura Ashley packaging by selling its perfume in bottles that were direct copies of Laura Ashley designs used for its own Penhaligon-branded products. A settlement was reached after a one-day hearing in New York.

Manufacturing investment

In August 1985 work commenced on Texplan, a new textile factory in Wales. The factory building covered an area of 135,000 square feet (approximately three football pitches). The following year on an adjacent site the construction of a new vinyl wallpaper plant began that would have a capacity of two million rolls per annum. Some 6,300 trees and shrubs were used to landscape the area, and land surrounding the Texplan building was reserved for future expansion if required. When these plants became operational, textile and fabric production would cease at Carno after nearly twenty years and the Carno factory would be used for centralised garment cutting and administration.

These facilities represented an investment of some £7.5 million, a significant part of the cost of which was offset by a grant from the Development Board of Rural Wales, which supervised the development and construction on behalf of Laura Ashley. This state-of-the-art facility became operational progressively from 1987 and increased production capacity by 50 per cent.

In 1987 a £1.3 million computer-aided design system was installed in the textile design studios at Carno, and in the following year a computerised garment cutting room was opened at Carno at a cost of £1.75 million. Other investments in manufacturing included a computerised handling system installed in the Newtown garment factory in 1988 at a reported cost of £670,000. This was designed to reduce garment throughput times from several days to a few hours, and thereby to allow more rapid response to retail demand.

Reorganisation in 1988

Early in 1988 the group was restructured into seven divisions in order to facilitate its growth over the next five years. Each division had a managing director separately accountable to the main board for his division's profit performance. The reorganisation was reported to reflect, in part, the group's decision to break away from the vertically integrated structure that had been a distinctive feature of the Laura Ashley organisation almost since its inception. The new divisions were as follows:

- Laura Ashley Group Services – responsible for finance, legal work, informatics and strategic planning.
- Laura Ashley Brand Management Group – responsible for design, sourcing, image protection and licensing.

- Laura Ashley Industries – responsible for textile, wallpaper and garment manufacture and distribution, together with leather goods and knitwear subsidiaries.
- Laura Ashley UK Retail – responsible for retail operations in the UK.
- Laura Ashley Continental Europe Retail – responsible for retail operations in continental Europe.
- Laura Ashley Inc. – responsible for retail operations in the USA and Canada.
- Laura Ashley Pacific Basin – responsible for retail operations in Australia and Japan.

Mike Smith was appointed managing director of Laura Ashley Industries following the resignation of Adam Lofthouse in September 1989, a post he held in addition to that of chairman of Laura Ashley UK Retail. Group chief accountant in 1985 at the time of flotation, Mike Smith moved up to managing director of UK Retail prior to the 1988 restructuring.

Major cost-cutting, restructuring and quality improvement initiatives were introduced by Mr Smith within the industries division as the group gradually reduced its dependence on its own manufacturing activities. Whereas around 85 per cent of products sold in 1985 were manufactured in-house, by 1988 this was down to 60 per cent and falling.

Retail developments

In 1987 the group took a 'major step towards segmentation' with the opening of six Laura Ashley Mother & Child shops in the USA. These sold a co-ordinated range of clothes and bedroom furnishing products for babies and children up to twelve, and dresses for their mothers. Mother & Child collections were also launched in the UK and continental Europe the following year.

In 1989 Laura Ashley Home shops were launched to sell a wider range of furniture than was available in existing Laura Ashley outlets. The range featured Laura Ashley designed furniture carrying the Laura Ashley brand name but manufactured outside the group. This, together with the home furnishing range, offered customers a complete Laura Ashley lifestyle package.

Also in 1989 Laura Ashley's first Units shop was opened, the first of 50 such shops Laura Ashley planned to open in the UK by 1992. Units stores were operated under licence from the Stinu Corporation. This Dallas-based subsidiary of the J. C. Penny retailing group operated a franchised chain of 150 Units shops in the USA, and offered a range of unsophisticated women's clothing items made from knitted fabric, which could be co-ordinated into several different garments.

In the UK and Ireland the number of Laura Ashley outlets increased from 87 in 1986 to 182 by early 1991. UK turnover in this period rose from £56.4m to £143.6m.

An enlarged mail-order centre was opened in Newtown in December 1987. Mail-order sales grew steadily over the period, increasing by 50 per cent in 1988, 45 per cent in 1989 and 40 per cent in 1990 to overtake the turnover performance of Laura Ashley's most successful UK store.

Laura Ashley's international expansion continued and by early 1991 there were over 500 outlets world-wide (Appendix 9). Expansion in continental Europe, slow at first, gathered pace towards the end of the period. In the year to January 1991 turnover increased by 19 per cent, largely as a result of a repricing policy, and the number of outlets rose from 65 to 95. European expansion was primarily through shop-in-shops, eleven such outlets opening in Spain and two in France during the year.

In North America, garments and home furnishing sales accounted for 70 per cent and 30 per cent respectively of 1990/91 turnover of £136.2m. During the year, six 'main-line', three Laura Ashley Home and seven Mother & Child shops were opened, and turnover reached an average $642 per square foot in established stores.

In the Pacific Basin, Laura Ashley's principal markets were Australia and Japan. In the latter part of the period, sales in Australia were hampered by depressed trading conditions, but in Japan Laura Ashley's joint venture with the Aeons Company (formerly Jusco) saw substantial growth. The number of outlets in Japan doubled from 12 to 24 in the year to January 1990, a further 13 were opened by January 1991 and 12 more were planned for the following year.

Part 3 Difficult Times: 1989–91

Background

By the end of the 1980s Britain's economy was causing increasing concern in government and business circles alike. The trade deficit in 1989 exceeded £20 billion, second in absolute terms only to that of the USA, and despite a series of interest rate increases sterling was under almost continuous attack on foreign exchanges. Reliance solely on the interest rate mechanism to control inflation had pushed interest rates up to what was probably the maximum level politically acceptable. Within the government disagreement over economic policy, particularly over Britain's membership of the European Monetary System, saw the departure of Chancellor Nigel Lawson in October 1989.

Overall, British business was bracing itself for a difficult start to the 1990s. High interest rates, combined with new restrictions on mortgage interest tax relief, brought a virtual standstill in the housing market. There were serious knock-on effects in the construction industry, and in home furnishing and home improvements markets.

Among the casualties of the recession were a number of well-known competitors of Laura Ashley. At Next, the retail group that George Davies had made a High Street star, the tide had already turned. Many of the group's acquisitions were sold to reduce its debts and in December 1988 Davies was ousted. New chief executive David Jones acknowledged that Next had grown too quickly and would now concentrate on its core businesses.

In March 1990 John Ashcroft resigned as chairman of Coloroll, the Lancashire mill that in twelve years he had turned into a major fabrics, bedding, carpets, china and wall coverings group. Affected by high interest rates and falling property prices, profits at the group had slumped. In November 1990 Sir Ralph Halpern's departure from the Burton Group after a 39 per cent fall in profits marked the end of a colourful twelve-year reign.

By mid-1991 it was still not clear whether the UK recession had bottomed out and few analysts were forecasting any recovery before the end of the year.

Laura Ashley, 1988/89

In the year to January 1989 Laura Ashley reported its first fall in profits, down to £20.26m from the previous year's figure of £23.08m. This was blamed on a £1m start-up loss at Willis & Geiger, higher interest charges and the strength of sterling, which cost the company £3m in reduced margins and a further £0.75m in translating US earnings. Chief executive John James said that, in spite of the exchange rate problems, the company had adopted an expansionist policy in the USA which it saw as its biggest potential market. Some press comments on the year's results suggested that manufacturing rather than retailing was at the heart of the group's problems.

1989/90

The following year, to January 1990, was a difficult one for the group and it reported a net loss of £4.7m before tax, despite sales increases across all divisions. In his report for the year Sir Bernard Ashley pointed to cost-cutting and quality improvement initiatives within the UK apparel division which he said were already showing results and would yield further benefits over the next two years. He acknowledged the need to reduce the group's high borrowing levels, and in response a major rationalisation programme was being implemented. This, Sir Bernard warned, might include disposals of businesses and restrictions on new shop openings.

Press comment on the group's losses highlighted a series of problems. These included a £2m loss on overproduction of Laura Ashley catalogues, a £0.9m trading deficit at Willis & Geiger (sold during the year at a book loss of £1.4m after tax), and severe production difficulties, particularly over supplies to the USA. 'The 1989 autumn range arrived three months late in the shops long after everyone's thoughts had turned to spring'.[1] Results were also hit by exceptional costs of £3.1m, comprising £1.5m for a management consultancy project at Laura Ashley factories, a £1m bill for ending a licensing agreement in the USA and £0.6m redundancy costs following the dismissal of 100 white-collar and production workers.

However, production efficiency was reported to have improved significantly, with production up by 19 per cent, a 4.3 per cent reduction in labour, and 'seconds' down from 5.1 to 1.6 per cent of output.[2]

[1] *Sunday Times*, 4 February 1990.
[2] *Independent*, 26 April 1990.

Some commentators wondered whether Laura Ashley was becoming dated. The editor of *Homes and Gardens* suggested that Laura Ashley had lost its youth market – the middle classes setting up home – and was failing to find a new one. 'What has happened is that the typical buyer has simply grown up. Laura Ashley has failed to provide for the more discerning sophisticated 30-plus consumers – who don't want their homes or their clothes to evoke the design team of a chain store.'[1]

1990/91

In June 1990, after protracted and difficult refinancing negotiations involving the Bank of England and fifteen banks, it was agreed to increase the group's loan facility from £75m to £115m.

Press reports indicated that following a consultant's report into the company, and in order to secure the long-term support of its bankers, the company had agreed to recruit two new non-executive directors and strengthen its top management. John James acknowledged that the company had been overstretching the executive talent it had, and intended to reverse the decision whereby directors had doubled up their responsibilities to cover some of the departures that had occurred since the flotation in 1985.[2] The appointment of Andrew Higginson in May 1990 came more than a year after the resignation of Peter Phillips, the previous finance director. In the intervening period Mr James had covered this responsibility in addition to his role as chief executive.

In July 1990 the group disposed of Penhaligon's for £7.5m, a price reflecting a substantial premium on the company's assets of £235,000. In the previous year Penhaligon's suffered a reported loss of £0.92m on sales of £1.6m.

Chief executive John James ended a long association with the group when he resigned on 1 September, 1990. His place was taken, on a temporary basis, by Mike Smith pending the appointment of a new chief executive 'in due course'. Press reports suggested that John James's attempts to reorganise the group had been hindered by the company's somewhat insular family culture and a very conservative board. The Ashley family's 70 per cent stake in the company led one writer to comment: 'the upheavals at Laura Ashley must take investors wonder whether companies should ever be floated with such dominant shareholdings'.[3]

At the end of August 1990 it was announced that the Aeon Group (formerly Jusco), Laura Ashley's partner in Japan, would inject £39m into the group. The Japanese company was to acquire a 15 per cent stake at 85p per new share and also take 48 per cent of Laura Ashley's US subsidiary, Revman, for $16.8m (£8.6m). Revman's management were to take a further 5 per cent, making it an associate company of Laura Ashley and allowing the group to take $27m of debt off its balance sheet. As part of the deal, Jusco secured exclusive rights to both sales and manufacture of Laura Ashley goods throughout Asia, with Laura

[1] Quoted in the *Sunday Times*, 4 February 1990.
[2] *Retail Week*, 4 May 1990.
[3] *Independent*, 25 August 1990.

Ashley retaining brand control and receiving increased royalty. The Jusco deal reduced Laura Ashley's gearing down to 30 per cent from more than 100 per cent and Sir Bernard Ashley's holding and that of his family trusts fell from 69.7 to 59.2 per cent. Sir Bernard said he would allow his stake to fall below 50 per cent in the future as the company expanded.

In September, the forthcoming closure of seven of the group's UK factories was announced with a potential loss of 1,500 jobs world-wide. 'It is no longer viable to source current levels of garments world-wide from our British factories when products of a similar quality can be bought at significantly lower cost from suppliers abroad', said Sir Bernard.

Laura Ashley's Report and Accounts for the year to January 1991, published in April, summarised a troubled period as Sir Bernard reviewed another 'eventful and challenging year' in which widespread discounting and high interest charges contributed to a group net loss of £6.7m. Among the few bright spots were a 175 per cent increase in sales from Parfums Laura Ashley after its continued expansion in USA, South America and other markets, and 88 per cent increase in sales in Japan when the number of stores increased from 24 to 37.

During the year, the group was able to reduce net borrowings from £87m to £23m, principally as a result of the Aeon Group transactions which reduced Group borrowings by £45m, and a reduction in stocks by £65m to £40m. In the 1991 Report and Accounts the actions taken to strengthen the group's financial position were highlighted as follows:

> The short term priorities of the business during the year have centred on strengthening the financial position of the Group with a clear focus on the balance sheet and stronger central control. The Group's financial management was strengthened through a combination of selected internal promotion coupled with external recruitment. Central controls over profit and cash management were implemented and new policies were introduced on capital expenditure and investment appraisal. A stringent stock control programme was implemented to reduce lead times, eliminate buffer stock and dispose of slow selling lines.
>
> The businesses that were not core to the Laura Ashley brand were divested or closed. These included the sale of Penhaligon's, Bryant of Scotland, Sandringham Leather Goods and the closure of the UK 'Units' franchise.
>
> The decision to protect profit by the reduction of in-house manufacture and general overheads was swiftly implemented. The Helmond print factory was purchased by its management team, and the Oswestry soft furnishing factory was sold as a going concern. Those sewing factories which were being divested ceased operations at the end of March 1991.
>
> Following the implementation of the agreement with the Aeon Group a second re-financing was arranged to replace the June facility. An unsecured £60m loan facility with a smaller number of relationship banks was implemented in November 1990.

Finally, a programme to improve relations with the City, investors and the financial press was instigated to develop a better understanding of the company's plans and actions.

Reorganisation in 1991

In his 1991 report, Sir Bernard highlighted the international brand name 'Laura Ashley' as the company's most valuable asset, and in order to develop and exploit the Laura Ashley brand more effectively world-wide, a new corporate structure was put into place with effect from February 1991.

The Group Marketing division is responsible for all aspects of marketing the brand, and for designing and sourcing products to satisfy consumer expectations.

The UK and continental Europe retail divisions have been amalgamated with the objective of obtaining synergies from shared marketing and a reduction of overheads. The intention is to retain regional marketing focus. The retail divisions use their knowledge and experience of their own markets to maximise opportunities for Laura Ashley branded products.

The Group Operations division is responsible for co-ordinating the logistical aspects of the business, moving products from the suppliers into retail and other distribution outlets. It accommodates the in-house manufacturing facilities, which now comprise the print factories in Newtown, the Welsh-based garment operation (four factories) and one home furnishing factory.

In 1991 a group marketing planning director, Glenne Gibson, joined the company from Coopers and Lybrand Deloittes retail group, where a year earlier she had been asked to undertake an assessment of Laura Ashley viability. Among her findings was that Laura Ashley designs needed a major revamp. Recognition of this was reflected in the autumn 1991 clothing collection, which displayed the new design aim of 'simple, well-made, versatile clothes the customer can make sophisticated, youthful, or traditional to suit herself'.[1]

Results of the company's retrenchment began to emerge with the publication of first-half results for 1991. Sales for the six months to the end of July 1991 fell from £174m to £132m, and the group expected no improvement in sales during 1992. Trading conditions in Britain and America were reported to have been very difficult and only Japan saw strong growth in the period. However, the 1990 refinancing deal with the Japanese helped to reduce net interest from £7m to

[1] Reported in the *Daily Telegraph*, 2 September 1991.

£1.4m and the company was able to announce slightly improved pre-tax profits of £530,000 for the six-month period.

In July 1991 the company announced the appointment of a new group chief executive, Dr Jim Maxmin, aged 48, to take effect from 16 September 1991. Jim Maxmin was born in the United States and lived in the UK from 1964 to 1988. After completing a PhD in Philosophy at King's College, London, he joined Unilever plc, working primarily in marketing roles. In 1971 he joined Lex Service Group plc, rising to chief executive and joint chairman of Volvo Concessionaires UK by 1979. In 1983 he moved to Thorne-EMI as chief executive of television rentals. In 1988 he moved to Boston to oversee the acquisition of Rent-a-Center Inc. and was also appointed president of Thorne-EMI Inc. Commenting on the appointment, Sir Bernard Ashley said:

> I am delighted to announce the appointment of Jim Maxmin as Chief Executive. After a thorough search we are delighted to have found the right candidate who will help us exploit the very real potential of the Laura Ashley brand, and who is totally sympathetic to the core Laura Ashley values. Jim Maxmin has that unique blend of international brand development and retailing experience that we are looking for.

Appendix 1 Group financial record, 1986–91

	1991 (£)	1990 (£)	1989 (£)	1988 (£)	1987 (£)	1986 (£)
Profit and loss accounts						
Turnover	327.5	296.6	252.3	201.5	170.9	131.5
Operating profit	5.3	6.1	23.6	23.8	21.4	16.7
Royalty income	0.3	1.1	1.6	1.7	1.6	2.1
Profit/(loss) from associated undertakings	0.1	(0.2)	–	–	–	–
Net interest payable	(12.4)	(8.6)	(4.9)	(2.4)	(0.5)	(0.9)
Exceptional items	–	(3.1)	–	–	–	–
Profit/(loss) on ordinary activities before taxation	(6.7)	(4.7)	20.3	23.1	2.5	17.9
Taxation	1.3	(2.0)	(7.2)	(8.5)	(8.0)	(6.4)
Profit/(loss) on ordinary activities after taxation	(5.4)	(6.7)	13.1	14.6	14.5	11.5
Extraordinary items	(2.1)	(1.4)	–	–	–	1.8
Profit/(loss) for the financial year	(7.5)	(8.1)	13.1	14.6	14.5	13.3
Dividends	(0.1)	(1.7)	(4.7)	(4.7)	(4.5)	(2.0)
Retained profit/(loss) for the year	(7.6)	(9.8)	8.4	9.9	10.0	11.3
Balance sheets						
Fixed assets	67.1	81.5	80.2	70.7	57.8	40.9
Net current assets/(liabilities)	66.9	(2.2)	46.5	14.3	22.2	28.1
Long-term creditors	(41.4)	(3.5)	(44.7)	(9.1)	(11.1)	(10.3)
Provisions for liabilities and charges	(0.4)	(2.9)	(2.2)	(2.1)	(0.5)	(1.5)
Net assets	92.2	72.9	79.8	73.8	68.4	57.2
Issued capital	11.7	10.0	10.0	10.0	10.0	10.0
	80.5	62.9	69.8	63.8	58.4	47.2
Shareholders' funds	92.2	72.9	79.8	73.8	68.4	57.2
Statistics						
Earnings/(loss) per share after tax	(2.60)p	(3.38)p	6.57p	7.30p	7.24p	6.29p
Dividend per share	0.10p	0.85p	2.35p	2.35p	2.25p	1.00p
Operating profit/sales	1.6%	2.1%	9.3%	11.8%	12.5%	12.7%
Profit/(loss) b.tax/net assets	(7.2%)	(6.4%)	25.4%	31.3%	32.9%	31.3%
Net asset value per ordinary share	39.3p	36.5p	40.0p	37.0p	34.4p	31.2p
Gearing	25.0%	119.0%	57.6%	49.3%	16.1%	(8.9%)

Appendix 2 Group profit and loss accounts, 1981–85

Date	31/12/81	31/12/82	28/1/84	26/1/85	31/7/85
No. of weeks	52	52	56	52	26.5
	(£000)	(£000)	(£000)	(£000)	(£000)
Turnover	34,153	44,556	66,701	96,448	59,840
Cost of sales	14,671	17,921	26,188	36,700	24,582
Gross profit	19,482	26,635	40,513	59,748	35,258
Other operating expenses	15,189	22,475	34,789	46,715	28,301
Operating profit	4,293	4,160	5,724	13,033	6,957
Royalty income	287	642	1,369	1,975	1,101
Profit before interest and tax	4,580	4,802	7,093	15,008	8,058
Net interest payable	1,043	830	735	866	434
Profit before taxation and extraordinary items	3,537	3,972	6,358	14,142	7,624
Taxation	552	723	1,841	5,336	2,715
Profit attributable to ordinary shareholders before extraordinary items	2,985	3,249	4,517	8,806	4,909
Extraordinary items	–	(518)[1]	–	–	(131)[2]
Ordinary dividend	106	–	–	–	–
Retained profit	2,879	3,249	3,999	8,806	4,778
Earnings per ordinary share of 5p	1.66p	1.80p	2.51p	4.89p	2.73p

Notes
[1] Deferred taxation.
[2] Employee share scheme £225, deferred taxation £(94), net £(131).
Source: Offer-for-sale documents, 1985.

Appendix 3 Group balance sheets, 1981–85

Date	31/12/81 (£000)	31/12/82 (£000)	28/1/84 (£000)	26/1/85 (£000)	31/7/85 (£000)
Fixed assets	9,298	12,347	15,651	20,874	31,678
Current assets					
Stocks and work in progress	8,880	10,652	17,053	22,732	27,665
Debtors	2,173	3,340	5,446	9,129	8,199
Short-term deposits	–	–	–	895	92
Cash at bank and in hand	421	652	643	4,054	2,283
	11,474	14,644	23,142	36,810	38,239
Creditors: Amounts falling due within one year					
Borrowings	2,883	2,844	4,498	2,059	8,115
Bills of exchange	535	1,093	1,204	3,142	3,638
Taxation and social security	433	2,075	2,413	4,318	4,479
Other creditors	6,029	5,415	11,052	14,797	14,804
	9,880	11,427	19,167	24,316	31,036
Net current assets	1,594	3,217	3,975	12,494	7,203
Total assets less current liabilities	10,892	15,564	19,626	33,368	38,881
Creditors: Amounts falling due after more than one year					
Borrowings	1,888	2,835	2,583	2,476	8,341
Taxation	–	–	–	2,701	1,321
Other creditors	72	27	106	219	1,006
	1,960	2,862	2,689	5,396	10,668
Provisions for liabilities and charges	820	751	1,382	1,881	1,835
	8,112	11,951	15,555	26,091	26,378
Financed by: Capital and reserves					
Called-up share capital	32	32	160	160	333
Reserves	8,080	11,919	15,395	25,931	26,045
	8,112	11,951	15,555	26,091	26,378

Source: Offer-for-sale documents, 1985.

Appendix 4 Source and application of funds statement, 1981–85

	Year to 31/12/81 (£000)	Year to 31/12/82 (£000)	Year to 28/1/84 (£000)	Year to 26/1/85 (£000)	6 mths to 31/7/85 (£000)
Sources of funds:					
Profit b. tax and extraordinary items	3,537	3,972	6,358	14,142	7,624
Adjustments: non-cash items:					
Depreciation	1,614	2,095	2,495	3,467	2,489
Profit on sale of fixed assets	131	(358)	(50)	(78)	–
Exchange differences	259	183	8	2,092	(2,054)
Funds generated from operations	5,541	5,892	8,811	19,623	8,059
Funds from other sources					
Sale of fixed assets	38	543	401	546	260
Loans	299	1,345	871	2,012	13,204
Government grants	63	640	555	489	59
Issue of shares	–	–	–	–	173
Total sources of funds	5,941	8,420	10,638	22,670	21,755
Application of funds:					
Capital expenditure	2,027	5,349	6,870	8,367	14,858
Increase in investments	–	–	–	71	268
Purchase of goodwill: subsidiaries	–	–	–	–	1,691
Repayment of loans	485	461	1,269	2,666	2,195
Taxation	444	432	1,132	2,625	3,686
Dividend	106	–	–	–	–
Increase/(decrease) in w. capital:					
Stocks and work in progress	1,655	1,772	6,401	5,679	4,933
Debtors	942	1,167	2,106	3,683	(930)
Creditors	(948)	(1,165)	(5,332)	(7,201)	(1,053)
Total application of funds	4,711	8,016	12,446	15,890	25,648
Net movement	1,230	404	(1,808)	6,780	(3,893)
Movement in liquid funds:					
Cash at bank and in hand	74	231	(9)	3,411	(1,771)
Short-term deposits	–	–	–	895	(803)
Bank loans and overdrafts	1,156	173	(1,799)	2,474	(1,319)
	1,230	404	(1,808)	6,780	(3,893)

Appendix 5 Consolidated profit and loss accounts, 1987–91

Date	31/1/87	30/1/88	28/1/89	27/1/90	26/1/91
No. of weeks	53	52	52	52	52
	(£000)	(£000)	(£000)	(£000)	(£000)
Turnover	170,892	201,477	252,431	296,608	327,533
Cost of sales	65,624	78,214	108,044	136,042	158,680
Gross profit	105,268	123,263	144,387	160,566	168,853
Other operating expenses	83,862	99,486	120,820	154,428	163,479
Operating profit	21,406	23,777	23,567	6,138	5,374
Share of (loss)/profit					
from related company	87	(45)	42	(177)	98
Royalty income	1,563	1,709	1,610	1,091	293
Net interest payable	(606)	(2,363)	(4,963)	(8,635)	(12,435)
Profit/(loss) on ordinary activities					
before taxation and exceptional items	22,450	23,078	20,256	(1,583)	(6,670)
Exceptional items	–	–	–	(3,070)[1]	–
Profit/(loss) on ordinary activities					
before taxation	2,450	23,078	20,256	(4,653)	(6,670)
Taxation on ordinary activities	7,993	8,511	(7,135)	(2,096)	(1,315)
Profit/(loss) on ordinary activities					
after taxation	14,457	14,567	13,121	(6,749)	(5,335)
Extraordinary items	–	–	–	(1,391)[2]	(2,114)[3]
Profit/(loss) for the financial year	14,457	14,567	13,121	(8,140)	(7,469)
Dividends	4,491	4,691	(4,691)	(1,697)	(102)
Retained (loss)/profit for the					
financial year	9,966	9,876	8,430	(9,837)	(7,571)
Earnings/(loss) per share	7.24p	7.30p	6.57p	(3.38)p	(2.60)p

Notes [1] Reorganisation costs £2,081, licence termination payment £989, total £3,070.
   [2] Losses on discontinued operations £2,672, taxation credit £(1,281), total £1,391.
   [3] Cost arising from fundamental reorganisation of the business: disposal of shares in associated
      undertakings £(5,725), disposal of businesses £179, restructuring costs £6,683, refinancing costs
      £2,192, tax credit £(1,215), total £2,114.
Source: Annual reports.

Appendix 6 Consolidated balance sheets, 1987–91

Date	31/1/87 (£000)	30/1/88 (£000)	28/1/89 (£000)	27/1/90 (£000)	26/1/91 (£000)
Fixed assets					
Tangible assets	57,292	70,241	79,734	80,784	60,983
Investment in related company	452	423	460	682	6,074
Loans to related company	53	45	–	–	–
	57,797	70,709	80,194	81,466	67,057
Current assets					
Stocks	45,521	66,824	75,790	104,804	64,642
Debtors	12,148	15,340	20,970	27,550	33,106
Short-term deposits and cash	5,507	4,448	4,336	1,947	17,137
	63,176	86,612	101,096	134,301	114,885
Creditors: Amounts due within one year					
Borrowings	7,864	34,240	8,155	85,741	807
Bills of exchange	745	1,128	2,326	–	
Taxation and social security	11,014	12,133	5,038	978	
Proposed dividend	2,994	2,994	2,994	–	102
Trade and other creditors	18,292	24,982	36,122	49,779	47,042
	40,909	75,477	54,635	136,498	47,951
Net current assets/(liabilities)	22,267	11,135	46,461	(2,197)	66,934
Total assets less current liabilities	80,064	81,844	126,655	79,269	133,991
Creditors: Amounts due after one year					
Borrowings	8,670	6,555	42,112	2,958	39,390
Taxation	1,394	545	949	6	{
Trade and other creditors	1,053	2,062	1,636	534	{1,992
	11,117	9,162	44,697	3,498	41,382
Provisions for liabilities and charges	512	(1,119)	2,172	2,853	430
Net assets	68,435	73,801	79,786	72,918	92,179
Capital and reserves					
Called-up share capital	9,980	9,980	9,980	9,980	11,740
Share premium account	21,440	21,440	21,440	21,440	48,710
Profit and loss account	37,015	42,381	48,366	41,498	31,729
Shareholders' funds	68,435	73,801	79,786	72,918	92,179

Source: Annual reports.

Appendix 7 Consolidated statement of source and application of funds, 1987–91

	Year to 31/1/87 (£000)	Year to 30/1/88 (£000)	Year to 28/1/89 (£000)	Year to 27/1/90 (£000)	Year to 26/1/91 (£000)
Sources of funds:					
Profit/(loss) b. tax and extraordinary items	22,450	23,078	20,256	(4,653)	(6,670)
Adjustment: non-cash items:					
Depreciation	7,142	11,447	13,708	16,382	16,952
Profit on sale of tangible assets	(1,262)	(310)	(244)	(267)	129
Increase/(decrease) in provisions	40	(242)	255	84	52
Exchange differences	1,183	(554)	(1,093)	1,825	564
Profit/(loss) retained in related co.	(34)	53	(39)	188	(98)
Funds generated from operations	29,519	33,472	32,843	13,559	10,929
Funds from other sources:					
Sale of tangible assets	2,041	1,987	1,432	2,343	12,002
Loans	4,204	1,584	39,165	24	–
Government grants	–	310	–	–	–
Issue of shares	–	–	–	–	29,030
Total sources of funds	35,764	37,353	73,440	15,926	51,961
Applications of funds:					
Increase in tangible assets	24,417	28,836	25,254	17,019	12,104
Dividends paid	3,493	4,691	4,691	4,692	–
Goodwill arising on acquisitions	17	1,520	527	869	–
Loans to related company	53	–	–	–	–
Repayment of loans	3,036	2,287	3,038	679	–
Taxation	7,611	9,629	10,790	5,391	1,860
Increase in investments	–	–	–	448	5,404
Extraordinary item	–	–	–	2,672	3,329
Increase/(decrease) in w. capital:					
Stocks	9,918	21,303	8,966	29,014	(40,162)
Debtors	1,943	3,192	5,630	6,580	(238)
Creditors	60	(6,670)	(11,429)	(10,230)	5,972
Total application of funds	50,548	64,788	47,467	57,134	(11,731)
Net movement	(14,784)	(27,435)	25,973	(41,208)	63,692
Decrease/(increase) in net borrowings:					
Short-term deposits and cash	(15,797)	(1,059)	(112)	(2,389)	15,190
Bank loans and overdrafts	1,013	(26,376)	26,085	(38,819)	48,502
	(14,784)	(27,435)	25,973	(41,208)	63,692

Source: Annual reports.

Appendix 8 Geographical analysis of trading 1986–91

Turnover by country of operation

	1986/87 (£m)	1987/88 (£m)	1988/89 (£m)	1989/90 (£m)	1990/91 (£m)
UK and Ireland	77.2	94.2	125.9	142.6	143.6
North America	66.5	74.9	90.1	117.2	136.2
Continental Europe	21.6	26.1	28.5	28.6	40.7
Other	5.5	6.2	7.8	8.2	7.1
Total	170.9	201.5	252.4	296.6	327.5

Operating profit/(loss) by country of operation

	(£000)	(£000)
UK and Ireland	917	(931)
North America	4,577	6,638
Continental Europe	926	347
Other	(282)	(680)
Total	6,138	5,374

Source: Annual reports.

Appendix 9 World-wide retail outlets, January 1991

Country	Group	External
European Division		
Austria	2	0
Belgium	4	0
Denmark	0	1
Finland	0	1
France	24	2
Germany	16	0
Greece	0	3
Holland	8	0
Iceland	0	1
Ireland	2	0
Italy	1	7
Norway	0	2
Middle East	0	2
Portugal	0	1
Spain	0	12
Sweden	0	3
Switzerland	5	0
UK	177	3
North American Division		
Canada	11	0
Mexico	0	1
USA	190	11
Pacific Basin		
Australia	24	0
Hong Kong	0	1
Japan	37	0
Korea	0	1
Malaysia	0	1
Singapore	0	1

Source: Annual report, 1991.

Appendix 10 Retail outlets and retail space, 1985–90

Retail outlets

	1985/86	1986/87	1987/88	1988/89	1989/90
UK and Ireland	87	109	140	164	184
North America	84	113	140	151	185
Continental Europe	47	53	61	66	65
Other	13	17	24	37	47[1]

Retail Space (000 sq. ft)

	1985/86	1986/87	1987/88	1988/89	1989/90
UK and Ireland	155.6	233.1	302.7	344.2	393.7
North America	115.6	161.2	197.6	235.6	255.6
Continental Europe	72.7	77.5	99.5	110.7	99.0
Other	13.1	20.3	34.0	57.0	68.1[2]

Notes: [1] Australia 23, Japan 24.
   [2] Australia 34.8, Japan 33.3.
Source: Annual reports.

Appendix 11 Directors, October 1985

Bernard Ashley (aged 59). Chairman of the Group. During the Second World War, he was commissioned into the Royal Fusiliers and also served with the Gurkha regiment. From 1947 to 1953 he worked in the City of London. Since 1953 he has been the driving force behind the international success of the Laura Ashley Group. In 1977 he became a Fellow of the Society of Industrial Artists and Designers.

Emlyn Hooson (aged 60). Non-executive director. He was called to the Bar in 1949, becoming a QC in 1960. He was Liberal MP for Montgomery from 1962 to 1979 and was created a life peer in 1979. He joined the group as a non-executive director in April 1985.

John James (aged 46). Group managing director. He was a chartered accountant and joined the group in 1974 as financial controller and company secretary, having previously worked with Unilever plc and Fitch Lovell plc, where he was divisional finance director. He was appointed joint managing director with Bernard Ashley in 1976. He was also a non-executive director of Control Techniques plc.

Adam Lofthouse (aged 43). Managing director, product division. He joined the group in 1984 after previous experience as a divisional director with Courtaulds plc, and with Coats Patons plc where he was managing director of a number of operating subsidiaries.

Peter Phillips (aged 43). Group finance director and managing director of Laura Ashley Group Services. He was a chartered accountant and joined the group in 1982 after previous experience with the Marley Tile Company, RCA Corporation, Celanese Corporation and the Plessey Company plc where he was a divisional finance director.

Peter Revers (aged 40). President of Laura Ashley Inc. He joined the group in the United Kingdom in 1970 as marketing manager. He opened the group's first shop in the United States in 1974 and was responsible for the group's retailing activities there.

Alphons Schouten (aged 42). Managing director, continental Europe. He was a Dutch citizen. He joined the group in 1981 from the Bluebell Corporation where he was a marketing director. He spoke the languages of the major countries in which the Continental Europe division operates.

John Winter (aged 45). Deputy group managing director. He was also the managing director of the United Kingdom retail division and of Laura Ashley Design Services. He joined the group in 1984. Prior to this he was a partner in the management consulting division of Deloitte Haskins & Sells, and from 1980 had been advising the group.

Notes
John Winter resigned in August 1987.
Peter Phillips resigned end 1988.
Adam Lofthouse resigned in September 1989.
John James resigned in September 1990.
Peter Revers resigned in November 1990.
Source: Offer-for-sale documents, 1985.

Appendix 12 Directors, January 1991

Sir Bernard Ashley	*Chairman*
Emlyn Hooson	*Non-executive director*
Hugh Blakeway Webb	*Non-executive director, deputy chairman*
Takuya Okada	*Non-executive director*
Iwao Matsuoka	*Alternate director*
Mike Smith	*Chief executive (acting) and managing director operations*
Andrew Higginson	*Finance director*
Alphons Schouten	*Managing director Europe*
Terry Smith	*Chairman and CEO North America*

Notes

Bernard Ashley was knighted in 1987 for his contribution to British industry. In May 1990 he remarried Mme Regine Buruell of Brussels.

Hugh Blakeway Webb was appointed in January 1991. He is a barrister called to the Bar in 1975. In 1978 he joined Coopers & Lybrand Deloitte, becoming a partner in 1983. He resigned his partnership on joining the board.

Takuya Okada, president of Laura Ashley Japan Co. Ltd, was appointed in December 1990, and Iwao Matsuoka was appointed as his alternate on the same date.

Andrew Higginson was appointed in May 1990.

Terry Smith was appointed in November 1990.

Source: Annual reports and company sources.

Appendix 13 Principal Subsidiaries, January 1991

Company	Country of incorporation and operation
Laura Ashley Ltd	England and Wales*
Laura Ashley BV	Netherlands*
Laura Ashley Manufacturing BV	Netherlands
Laura Ashley Distribution BV	Netherlands
Laura Ashley Investments BV	Netherlands
Laura Ashley Trading BV	Netherlands
Laura Ashley SA	France
Laura Ashley SA	Switzerland
Parfums Laura Ashley SA	Switzerland
Laura Ashley NV	Belgium
Laura Ashley GmbH	Germany
Laura Ashley GesmbH	Austria
Laura Ashley Srl	Italy
Laura Ashley (Ireland) Ltd	Ireland
Ashley Shops (Ireland) Ltd	Ireland
Laura Ashley (Australia) Pty Ltd	Australia
Laura Ashley Shops Ltd	Canada
Laura Ashley Inc.	United States

All subsidiaries are wholly owned.
*Held directly by Laura Ashley Holdings plc

Associated Undertakings

Laura Ashley Japan Co. Ltd 40% issued share capital 400bn yen	Japan
Revman Industries Inc. 47.5% issued common equity stock $9.8m 100% issued 8% cumulative preferred stock $8.1m	United States

Source: Annual report, 1991.

The Crucible Theatre

Kevan Scholes

The Artistic Director has resigned, attendances are down by 50%, productions planned for the new year are cancelled, the Company is heading for a £250,000 deficit – but there is no crisis at the Crucible, said Stephen Barry, Chief Executive of Sheffield Theatres.

So read the article in the *Sheffield Weekly Gazette* in early October 1991. The declaration came after an emergency meeting of the directors of Sheffield Theatres Ltd to discuss the drastic fall in Crucible box office receipts following the opening of the refurbished sister theatre (the Lyceum), adjacent to the Crucible, in December 1990. Stephen Barry, the chief executive of both the Crucible and the Lyceum – a new appointment made in 1990 – insisted that changes would have to be made at the Crucible:

> The theatre is 75% empty. We are not asking for more money nor are we trying to take audiences away from the Lyceum. We are seeking to grow our overall audience and have been very successful at that. There are many different types of audience out there and we must look at ways of attracting them to the Crucible. We are also discussing new ways in which our funding arrangements with Sheffield City Council might change in order to clarify the contribution the theatres are making to the city and the local community.

This was not the first crisis faced by the Crucible Theatre over its twenty-year history, but to many people it came as something of a surprise given the growing investment in and support for theatre and the arts in Sheffield.

The theatre in Sheffield

The foundation of the Sheffield Repertory Company dates back to around 1923,

This case study was prepared by Professor Kevan Scholes, Sheffield Business School, with the assistance of the theatre management, Sheffield City Council and Crispin Raymond Associates. It incorporates information from the previous case studies (1976 and 1988). It is intended as a basis for class discussion and not as an illustration of either good or bad management practice. © Kevan Scholes, 1992.

being renamed 'The Playhouse' in 1938. The 1960–1 season was the most signifi-cant one for Sheffield theatre, being the first year that the Arts Council of Great Britain awarded a grant: 'to allow the Playhouse to undertake more prestigious productions than their own resources allow'. This grant of £5,000 marked the change from commercial to subsidised theatre, a transition which was complet-ed in April 1963 when the Playhouse became one of only eight theatres outside London to be taken into formal association with the Arts Council.

In August 1966 Sheffield Council announced its intention to sponsor the building of a £700,000 theatre to house 800 to 900 people, and a board of trustees was appointed consisting of representatives of Sheffield Council, the University, the Trades and Labour Council, and the Playhouse itself. The board was respon-sible for organising the public appeal and all other decisions concerning the building of the new theatre. After some controversy final designs were agreed – the theatre was to have 1,000 seats round three sides of a thrust-stage (which critics complained limited its use for large-scale opera and ballet). In addition, provision was made for a 'studio theatre' with a capacity of approximately 250 and variable seating arrangements.

By the time the project was completed in 1971, the cost of the building alone had risen to £884,000. Sheffield Corporation agreed to lease the site (valued at £250,000) and in addition contributed £350,000 to the capital cost. The Arts Council granted a further £300,000 from its 'Housing the Arts' fund. The public appeal reached £150,000 with a further £55,000 from other bodies (primarily £50,000 from the Gulbenkian Foundation – for the studio theatre). In October 1970 it was announced that the new theatre was to be called 'The Crucible Theatre', a name reflecting both the design of the building and Sheffield's histori-cally famous steel industry. Building work proceeded to schedule, the Playhouse held its last season in 1970/1.

In November 1971 the Crucible Theatre opened in a great blaze of local and national press coverage – yet by September 1972 the Crucible found itself head-ing for unprecedented losses and the centre of a public storm. Leaks from a con-fidential report on the theatre by the city treasurer, Mr Jones, claimed that the theatre should slash costs and attract bigger audiences in order to improve its financial position. The Crucible was criticised for not staging enough popular shows, for inadequate use of the building and for 'having too many chiefs and not enough Indians'. Sheffield Corporation was offering to bail out the Crucible providing it agreed to put its house in order in line with Mr Jones' report. The theatre administrator, David Brayshaw, however, was resisting the Council's terms, claiming that many of the savings urged would endanger vital artistic standards. The following sections describe the ways in which the theatre devel-oped over the period from 1971 to 1992. Appendix 1 provides some general back-ground to the arts and professional theatres in Great Britain.

Crucible Theatre Trust and theatre management

Following its formal association with the Arts Council in 1963, Sheffield theatrical activity had tended to reflect the philosophy of the Arts Council. The Memorandum of Association of the Crucible Theatre Trust stated the primary objects of the company as:

- 'To promote, maintain, improve and advance education, particularly by the production of educational plays and the encouragement of the arts of drama, mime, dance, singing and music . . .'
- 'To receive, educate and train students in drama, dancing, music and other arts, and to promote the recognition and encouragement of special merit in students . . .'

The company was directed by a board of trustees or directors consisting of elected members (mainly local dignitaries) together with representatives of Sheffield District Council, Sheffield University, and Sheffield Trades and Labour Council. The company was registered as 'limited by guarantee' in May 1968.

The directors met twice yearly but also operated via a Management Committee consisting of some directors, the theatre management and representatives from the local authorities (Sheffield MDC and South Yorkshire County Council). This committee met every two months and was responsible for advising on policy and reviewing performance. A financial sub-committee met monthly to review the company's financial position and report back to the Management Committee. When the theatre opened in November 1971 it operated with two directors – David Bradshaw (administrative) and Colin George (artistic) – both of whom had been heavily involved in the process of establishing the new theatre.

New directors

Colin George resigned in 1974 after nine successful years in Sheffield theatre and was replaced by Peter James, who, at 34, was already a name in the theatrical world due to his involvement in establishing the Everyman Theatre in Liverpool. Shortly after his appointment Peter James gave a clue to his approach to theatre management in an interview for the *Guardian*:

> What I'd like to have is a permanent grant to cover the theatre's running costs – management, front of house, cleaning, etc., and then a different grant to cover the production side. I'd like to make the plays pay for themselves and, if they make a profit, for the actors and directors to take a cut.

When David Brayshaw retired in October 1975, Peter James was redesignated 'the Director' largely in response to people outside the theatre who had failed to comprehend the concept of the dual leadership.

In 1981 Clare Venables was appointed director in succession to Peter James. She had previously been at the Theatre Royal, Stratford East (London). In an interview shortly after her arrival she commented on the role of theatre in the city: 'A theatre that isn't controversial is dead. If people aren't talking about it, thinking about it and getting excited about the theatre, even if it includes criticism, then you are having no impact.'

The 1982 crisis

A major financial crisis in 1982 led to changes in these structures following an investigation by the Arts Council and Sheffield City Council reported by the *Sheffield Star*.

> The Board, then with 12 members, met only twice a year – not enough to even fit in with the Arts Council's rules for theatres which they subsidise . . . The Management Committee did not manage at all – it was a general debating group. The Arts Council investigators suggested it should be abolished altogether . . . But by far the most scathing comments were levelled at the Finance Committee. The Arts Council report comments: 'In our opinion the role of the present Finance Committee is ill-defined and its performance ineffective. It has failed to recognise that the theatre's inability to attain its financial targets ought perhaps to mean a radical change of approach to the theatre's pattern of activity. Even now, when the Company is passing through the most critical period of its existence, there is little evidence of the committee urgently seeking a resolution to the present problems, and there is almost an air of complacency which we find both surprising and disturbing'.

Following these criticisms the chairman of the board of trustees (Anthony Hampton) resigned and was replaced by Tony Thornton (from the famous chocolate company family). The Finance and Management Committees were disbanded and replaced with a single Executive Committee. The board met bimonthly and the Executive Committee monthly. A 'Theatre Council' was proposed in the Arts Council report (to replace the old Management Committee). This was to be used as a sounding board on artistic policy. In fact this proposal was never implemented – instead the board of management was extended to give wider representation to both internal and external interests. For example, in 1986 Sheffield City Polytechnic was represented on the board for the first time. Also an elected representative of the theatre staff attended the meetings as an observer, as did the Yorkshire Arts Association.

After the financial crisis of 1982 it was also decided to plan the budget on the assumption of an average 50 per cent capacity fill and not 70 per cent – the figure which had been used since the early 1970s despite the fact that 70 per cent had only ever been achieved once (1974). It was planned to open the theatre for more weeks in the year, although in practice the number of active weeks continued to vary from year to year as previously. Overall there was a much more careful planning of the year's activities and spending in relation to detailed forecasts of box office revenue show by show. There were implications for the artistic policy of the theatre as Clare Venables commented at the time:

> I was told to cut down gambling what we, as a theatre, do. In a high risk business like this, it's hard. I have to cut an enormous amount of the good things we're doing artistically. We cannot cut any further without ruining the theatre – I couldn't do that . . . If the Theatre Board had decided it wanted to control artistic policy as well as finances, I would have resigned.

During Clare Venables' period as artistic director, Geoffrey Rowe was the Crucible Theatre's administrator. He commented on the realities of managing subsidised theatre in the mid-1980s:

> What is certainly true is that life is lived more on a knife edge these days than even the early '80s. There is no chance the Arts Council could give such a large grant, or indeed, local authorities would loan large sums of money to get a theatre out of its problems as happened in 1982. The continuing deficit of the Crucible in the '70s was run up in an atmosphere where it was likely that you would be bailed out by the local authorities. It is an indication of the kind of money that was around at that time. The Arts Council no longer has reserves, does not have guarantees against loss and the atmosphere in the Arts is that you dare not run up a deficit which pushes one to be more conservative both financially as well as artistically.

Sheffield Theatres Ltd

In 1987 Sheffield City Council decided to redevelop the Lyceum Theatre which had stood derelict next door to the Crucible for many years. This redevelopment, costing £12.4m, was part of the decision to build a number of first-class sporting and leisure facilities for the 1991 World Student Games. It was decided that, in order to achieve greater economies of scale and prevent management overlap, a new company to run both theatres would be established. This was named Sheffield Theatres Ltd. However, the two theatres maintained their own separate trusts in order to preserve their charitable status. There were therefore three boards, and initially John Cornwell chaired all the boards. However, in May 1990 Councillor Mike Pye was appointed chairman of the Crucible Theatre Trust.

In late 1989 a new post of chief executive Sheffield Theatres was advertised, and in January 1990 Stephen Barry was appointed to manage the Crucible/Lyceum complex. His previous appointment was with the Theatre Royal, Bath – one of the few provincial touring theatres in the UK to be financially viable without revenue grants from public funds. Geoffrey Rowe, the Crucible's administrator, resigned in February 1990 and Clare Venables completed her final season as director in 1990. Stephen Barry commented on the operation of the trusts by 1992:

> The exact roles of the Crucible and Lyceum Trusts are still being established although the Lyceum's custodian role is easier to define while the Crucible's role as a former policy-maker is more difficult to redefine. The Board of Sheffield Theatres is clearly perceived as the senior partner in the new structure. The new organisation structure therefore reflects this development and is likely to develop still further.

Details of membership of the three boards and the management structure in early 1992 are shown in Appendices 2 and 3 respectively.

Employees

Despite the vast changes in the theatre which had occurred in Great Britain since the war, there was still a high level of vocation among actors, management and employees alike. In 1992 the Crucible employed approximately 230 people. Since the mid-1960s the actors' union, Equity, had grown in strength and operated a closed shop in most theatres, including the Crucible. Minimum rates of pay and working conditions were agreed between Equity and theatre management on a national basis. As a general rule the actors were recruited for each play, although in casting their own plays each of the directors would bear in mind the possibility of cross-casting for the next play.

Rates of pay for employees and management were appreciably lower than equivalent jobs in local industry and local government, yet despite this low pay and also unsocial hours people tended to stay within the theatre. Staff turnover at the Crucible was very low – partly due to the excellent working conditions and the good technical facilities.

Productions

Until the opening of the Lyceum in December 1990, Sheffield had only one theatre. As a result the Crucible tended to offer a wide variety of entertainment. Nevertheless the theatre remained largely committed to the production of plays. Well over 70 per cent of all performances in the main theatre were the Crucible Theatre's own produced plays. Appendices 4 and 5 show details of productions and attendances. The studio theatre was also used for a variety of activities, although a much greater proportion of plays were touring companies (including many 'fringe' groups).

In an interview with the *Sheffield Star* in December 1975, Peter James spelt out his policy in choosing plays:

There is a wealth of difference between what an audience thinks they want and what contemporary writers want to write about. The problem is trying to strike a balance. We want to have quality artists coming up to Sheffield and we don't get them unless we're putting on exciting new things like *Bomb in Brewery Street*. The same applies to directors – no director wants to do endless productions of *Habeas Corpus*. This place is for everyone and we can't please all the people all the time – what we do, however, is satisfy everybody at least once a year.

His first season was a classical one which played to less than 50 per cent capacity. After three years of trying to revive a flagging box office he hit on the idea of staging blockbusters and both the audiences and the national press came running. He commented on this in 1981:

As long as you surround an idea with enough razzmatazz you're OK – for example hustling for the rights of something off Broadway, or bringing in a Russian Director for *The Government Inspector* . . . I don't think there were many people sitting on the doorstep waiting for the next review of that play, but they came. The whirlpool brings in people with it.

Under the directorship of Clare Venables the theatre continued to enjoy a considerable reputation – at least among its regular audiences. To many observers the 1982 financial crisis appeared to be part of the regular blood-letting which seemed the hallmark of the subsidised arts in the UK. The years following the crisis were characterised by what could be called 'balanced programming' – the philosophy expressed by Peter James in 1975. However, the balance of the theatre's own productions and tours did fluctuate from year to year as seen in Appendix 4.

By 1987 the theatre had reached a capacity fill of 74 per cent – a figure which had only previously been bettered once (in 1974). An article in the *Sheffield Telegraph* in November 1991 to mark the 20th anniversary of the Crucible looked back on the latter part of the 1980s under Clare Venables:

During that time the theatre was probably at its most controversial and challenging artistically. People walked out of plays like *The Park* and *Passion in Six Days*. There were some memorable productions and generally there was a buzz about the place. Then attention began to focus on the Lyceum and suddenly the Crucible started to take a back seat.

From December 1990 the Crucible and Lyceum were operating in tandem. The Lyceum was entirely devoted to touring productions and the Crucible was mainly a producing house (repertory theatre). Stephen Barry commented on the artistic policy of the two theatres in his first two seasons (1990/2):

In retrospect we were too defensive about the Crucible – narrowing our market appeal and attempting an over specialist role. We did not capitalise on the single site thinking brought about by the management structure. We knew the Lyceum would inevitably have an initial effect on the Crucible audiences – which no doubt was deepened by the recession. However, by the end of year 1991/92 a balance between the two theatres' programmes had begun to emerge and box-office turned upwards again. For example, we relaxed our attitude towards touring productions in the Crucible and the traditional Christmas pantomime in 1991 was staged in the Lyceum. In times of recession – when people are paying good prices – there needs to be a 'guarantee element'. So, well known plays or actors familiar from television help considerably. Interestingly enough the familiarity which can be built with a repertory company through a season also works – but of course it takes a few productions to build this up. Perhaps we should have staged *As You Like It* to open the season and had *The Government Inspector* later.

Other activities

One of the most notable differences between the Crucible Theatre and the old Playhouse was the range of activities which were undertaken. Apart from the productions staged in the two theatres, there was a restaurant, coffee bar, shop and licensed bar. Most of these services were operated throughout the day on the principle that the more people who could be enticed through the doors for whatever purpose, the stronger the theatre-going community would become. The town centre site lent itself admirably to this concept of the theatre as a social centre. The foyer/bar in the theatre was exceptionally large by most standards and was often used for ad hoc lunchtime or late evening performances of folk music. The use of this area for exhibitions was increased considerably from the mid-1970s onwards.

The Crucible also had the 'Theatre in Education' (previously Vanguard) – a travelling production unit which performed in schools, community centres, prisons and pubs, and sometimes in the open air. The theatre also had a limited number of plays transfer to the West End of London, including *Golden Pathways Annual*, *The Wiz* and *Lennon*. Many of the touring productions in the Lyceum were pre-West-end runs.

Snooker

To many people in the UK the Crucible became synonymous with the World Snooker Championships – staged at the theatre every year from 1977. Snooker had hitherto been a cinderella sport played in smoke-filled rooms above Burtons tailors. But the advent of colour TV popularised the game in the early 1970s and the move to the Crucible Theatre, together with big sponsorship money, revolutionised the sport. By the 1980s it was one of the most popular spectator sports in the UK and the Crucible World Championships marked the pinnacle of the year's events.

However, bringing snooker to the Crucible was not without its critics. Many serious theatre-goers felt that this three-week period (April/May) broke up the theatre season. Others complained about the poor financial deal they felt had been struck with the promoters. By 1987 it was estimated that the snooker earned about £100,000 for the theatre, including extra catering profits. Successive contracts had been signed guaranteeing the championship up to and including 1996.

Attendances

Attendances varied considerably depending on the type of production being staged. 'Stars' tended to boost attendances, although the familiarity of the play was probably the most important factor. There were certain plays which were absolute winners – *The Stirrings in Sheffield*, a musical steeped in local tradition, drew almost 40,000 people in 47 performances in 1973. *It's a Bit Lively Outside*, the story of the Sheffield Blitz, was also popular in 1987. The theatre regularly produced plays in the autumn which were 'set books' for local school-children. The Christmas entertainments also proved highly successful, returning to a traditional pantomime format from the late 1970s onwards, and drawing audiences of some 60,000 each year.

The normal pattern of production was one of single runs varying from two weeks to four weeks, interspersed with short tours and one-night stands. The studio theatre was a different picture – with a maximum capacity of 250, and six performances per week, average attendances increased from around 40 per performance in 1972 to over 100 in 1987. Short tours were an important part of the Crucible's activities in both the main theatre and the studio, and tended to attract larger audiences than the theatre's own productions, often due to the stars concerned, but perhaps also because they ran for a shorter period (typically seven performances). From December 1990 the majority of tours were staged in the Lyceum.

Theatre audiences

Broadly speaking, the theatre scene in Sheffield was very similar to that in other provincial cities. A report published by the Yorkshire Arts Association in 1974 sketched out the pattern of theatre-going in Sheffield (see Appendix 6). They were also typical of audiences in other provincial cities. A fair proportion of theatre-goers attended with some measure of regularity. In 1974 it was estimated that 70 per cent of attendances were accounted for by some 19,000 people (approximately 20 per cent of attenders). The average theatre-goer attended some 10–15 per cent of all performances.

The relatively low levels of attendance at the theatre were not due to lack of awareness of the presence of the Crucible, since almost 95 per cent of the local population were aware that the theatre existed. The majority of people who had never attended the theatre had not done so because they did not see themselves as theatre-goers, preferring cinema, TV or other activities. The theatre policy towards productions, prices, booking, etc. was of secondary importance in this respect. This situation – which was typical of theatres in general – was often referred to as 'threshold fear'.

Although such an extensive exercise had not been repeated, smaller surveys suggested that audience characteristics were still broadly in line with these findings. Details of a market survey among the Crucible mailing list and Crucible Card holders in 1990 are also included in Appendix 6.

Prices

Price levels were determined annually as part of the budgeting process. With a knowledge of the expected income from grants, and estimates of likely expenditures needed for the type of programme to be given, the balancing figure needed to be taken at the box office. This revenue target formed the framework within which the pricing of individual seats was decided.

Over the years many different approaches to seat pricing had been used. In 1991/2 three basic prices were used (£6.50, £8.00 and £9.00) with higher prices for Friday and Saturday (£7.50, £9.50 and £11.00). These prices compared favourably with those for touring productions in the Lyceum, with prices ranging from £4 to £30. A sophisticated concession policy was operated for over-60s, children, students, UB40s, disabled and groups – except for Saturday evening. From 1985/6 the theatre introduced a 'Crucible Card' which provided seats at five shows for the price of four. Sales in 1991/2 had been disappointing at only 900 compared with a peak of over 4,000.

The theatre's revenues

Since the beginning of subsidised theatre in Sheffield (1960/1), the raising of revenue had moved steadily away from the purely commercial sources of the old theatre towards a heavy dependence on grants, primarily from the Arts Council of Great Britain and the local authorities. By 1976/7 some 63 per cent of income was in the form of grants, although this declined to about 55 per cent by the 1980s and 50 per cent by 1991 (see Appendix 7).

Following an Arts Council report in 1984 entitled *Glory of the Garden*, there was a significant shift in policy regarding the funding of regional theatre in two respects. The Arts Council instigated a policy of diverting more funds to provincial theatre (as against the national companies) and this was linked to the designation of thirteen regional theatres (including the Crucible) which would be the major beneficiaries. This was an attempt to build up genuine 'centres of excellence' in the regions. The Crucible received significant increases in its Arts Council grant from 1985 onwards. For example, in 1986/7 the theatre received an additional £100,000 which covered inflation but also allowed a relaunch of the 'Theatre in Education' programme and a genuine 52-week operation of the theatre. As a matter of policy the Arts Council did not provide revenue grants to touring theatres (such as the Lyceum) – instead it funded selected touring companies.

Another important change in policy was the introduction of the concept of parity funding. The Arts Council aimed to agree that the total public funding to any one theatre should be shared equally between themselves and the local authority. However, over the period of the late 1980s Sheffield City Council failed to reach agreement with the Arts Council concerning parity. Together with the increasing financial pressure on local authorities the effect of this was a significant decline in the real value of public funding received by the Crucible from a peak in 1986/7 (see Appendix 8). Although Sheffield City Council's grant had stayed steady in real terms, the Arts Council's move towards parity meant a meeting at this lower level. (see Appendices 9–11). David Patmore, Director of Arts for Sheffield City Council, commented on this position in 1992:

> There are a number of reasons why the City Council found it difficult to provide the higher levels of funding for the Crucible but the most important was that our overall commitment to the theatre in Sheffield was increasing with the Lyceum project. This is where we tend to get caught out by the Arts Council's structure and internal rivalries. Their drama department fund repertory theatre, like the Crucible, and the touring department supports the companies which are now being attracted to the Lyceum. From our point of view in Sheffield we'd prefer to talk to the Arts Council about our theatre policy as a whole – but their structure gets in the way of this.

Although comparison with other provincial repertory theatres needs to be done with care, the £1.1 million received in 1991/2 was about 7 per cent below the average for large provincial repertory theatres (see Appendix 12). The Crucible had lost ground in terms of the Arts Council 'pecking order'. In 1987/8 only the Manchester Royal Exchange received more than the Crucible. By 1991/2 the Crucible (£609,000) had been overtaken by the Leicester Playhouse (£771,000) and the West Yorkshire Playhouse (£713,000).

New funding possibilities

In September 1991 a consultant's report was commissioned by Sheffield City Council to make proposals concerning the funding of Sheffield Theatres up to 1994/5. The report recommended that the council should reaffirm its commitment to the vital role which the theatres played in the city in relation to the strategy for regeneration based on a growth in its leisure network and increases in tourism. The theatres were seen as a primary focus for the city centre, and a contribution to the new image of the city.

The two major recommendations were: first, that the basis of the council's financial support should change from the traditional *deficit funding* to one of *target investments* – funding only those aspects of the theatres' operations which were of key importance to the objectives of the city; and second, that the council should assist the theatres in reducing further their dependence on public funding – by creating a more entrepreneurial culture and encouraging them to operate as a community-orientated business.

Target investments

The report identified six key areas which Sheffield City Council could justify as investments in the theatre in terms of real benefit to the city. These were:

- *Building maintenance* – since they were a focal point of the city centre.
- *Production support* – to ensure that enough productions were produced in Sheffield to maintain a centre of artistic excellence.
- *Programme support* – for touring productions in the Lyceum.
- *Theatre in Education* – traditionally supported by the Education Department.
- *Priority audience development* – to encourage the broadening of the theatre's audience.
- *Staff development and training* – as a key investment to underpin the professional excellence of the theatre.

David Patmore, the Director of Arts of Sheffield City Council, commented on these proposals:

> In principle we are very much in favour of this shift to a more contractual basis with an emphasis on the outputs we can expect for our money. The old method of setting funding levels in relation to the previous year's grant is all very well providing it's keeping pace with inflation. Of course these proposals reflect the mood of the 1990s as regards Local Authority involvement in 'sharp end services'. Legislation is now imminent to require compulsory competitive tendering for Local Authority run Arts venues. It's all part of the process of turning the Authority into a 'client' organisation rather than a direct provider of many services. So, if we adopt the concept of Target Investments for our funding of the Crucible we'll probably find ourselves as a sort of pilot nationally. I must say that the Arts Council are unenthusiastic about this whole issue. They have argued for many years, and with some success, that the need for the Arts is almost limitless and that outputs are difficult to quantify – Target Investments would challenge this approach.

The test of whether we can move in this direction will be the next 15 months where we will get down to the detailed specification of each 'contract'. We know that this will be difficult. One thing we are absolutely clear about is that the contracting process must not stray into the area of artistic judgement. What goes on in the theatre must remain the province of the theatre board.

Dependence on public funding

The final part of the consultant's report commented on some of the changes which might be necessary to allow a more entrepreneurial and business-like approach to management. In particular there were issues of the membership of the board – the majority of whom were nominees from public organisations – and the ambiguity of the role of three boards. It was suggested that only building maintenance moneys should go directly to the Crucible Trust; the other target investments should go to Sheffield Theatres, in order to encourage a feeling of one company not three.

A crucial proposal was that Sheffield City Council should cease to regard itself as the watchdog of the theatre's financial affairs and move its relationship on to a contractor–supplier basis through the device of target investments. The theatre should be encouraged to seek similar funding from other sources without the fear that Sheffield would then reduce its own commitment. Stephen Barry commented on these proposals:

> Generally I welcome what I regard as an interesting set of proposals which introduce a new language into the funding debate. Many of the concepts appear in line with performance indicators introduced into the public sector recently. What must be remembered is that we are a creative organisation involved in a risk-taking business. I'm not certain you can always measure such important qualities. Of course it will start to compartmentalise our resource which would be quite a problem if all our public funding came through Target Investments. But a combination of a more general 'pool' from the Arts Council and the more targeted use of City Council funds would be quite acceptable. One practical implication of this new approach is the need for better information. For example, audience profiles will clearly be needed to assess our achievements on Priority Audience Development.

Expenditure

Appendix 7 shows the details of both income and expenditure from 1972/3 to 1990/1. The most important factor influencing the level of expenditure was the policy on the type of productions to be undertaken. The expenditure incurred and the income-earning potential was substantially different from one production to the next. Peter James was questioned about this issue by the *Sheffield Star* in December 1975 and said:

If you look back at previous seasons you can see that the public wants big lavish shows. You could put on *Calamity Jane* and pack it out but you'd still lose out in the long run, because of the money you've spent putting it on. We've also tried to have longer runs but in the case of *Mrs Warren's Profession* we spread it too thin and the numbers dropped. You also have to be careful that when cutting back you aren't forfeiting quality.

The theatre management planned the programme in four-month blocks. The Planning Committee, together with the directors of plays, would draw up a programme which was influenced by a review of the latest financial position on the one hand, and the particular plays the directors wanted to stage on the other. Once this programme was agreed, each play was allocated a budget and brochures were printed and released to the public. Each director would then hold a production meeting with the production manager and head of design to decide exactly how the play was to be staged within the agreed budget.

Following the poor audiences at the beginning of the 1991/2 autumn season, the theatre took the unusual step of cancelling a number of plays in the programme and replacing them with alternatives. For example, Ibsen's *Hedder Gabler* was dropped and the traditionally popular *Stirrings in Sheffield* was introduced. Stephen Barry explained why:

We were heading for a deficit of around £250,000 by the year end (March 1992). This would have severely restricted creative potential in the coming year and would undoubtedly have had an influence on our funders' thinking in what is a difficult time – especially the City of Sheffield.

These programme changes achieved the planned financial result, with the Crucible reaching break even by the end of the financial year in March 1992.

The future

In November 1991 an article in the *Sheffield Telegraph* commented on the future against the background of the latest crisis:

History has a habit of repeating itself. In the Crucible's case, about once every six or seven years. Today the Crucible is holding a 20th birthday party. It will be a low key affair in keeping with the theatre's current mourning for a season that promised so much yet delivered so little. But is there really a need to worry? The 20 year history is peppered with crises . . . but every time the theatre bounces back . . . The current predicament should not have come as any surprise. Now that the Lyceum has settled down the Crucible needs to regain its own niche in a changed situation. But the key to success will be doing what it has always been best at over the years – strong, creative, sometimes controversial, but always challenging theatre. Happy Birthday!

Appendix 1 The arts and professional theatre in Great Britain

Since 1945 the government had given funds for sponsoring the arts. The Arts Council of Great Britain was the body primarily responsible for the allocation of these funds to the many diverse activities included under the heading of 'the arts'. This body made policy independent of government. The amounts of money granted by the Government were as follows:

	£m
1971/72	11.1
1976/77	38.1
1981/82	83.0
1986/87	128.1
1987/88	134.5
1988/89	141.3
1989/90	155.5
1990/91	175.8

In 1990/1 the Arts Council expenditure was divided into 83 per cent for England, 11 per cent for Scotland and 6 per cent for Wales. A large slice of the English expenditure went to the national companies (English National Opera, Royal Opera (including Dance), Royal National Theatre and Royal Shakespeare Theatre), taking 24 per cent although this proportion had declined from a level of 35 per cent in 1974/5. The remainder was divided among drama (10 per cent), music (7 per cent), art (7 per cent) and dance (4 per cent). In addition, touring companies received 5 per cent and English Regional Arts Associations 20 per cent.

Professional theatre

In the early 1990s Britain was one of the world's major centres of theatrical activity. In London and Stratford during the summer season, theatres were packed with foreign visitors. In the provinces there was enthusiastic support for the work of local repertory companies. Britain was also famous for its playwrights and directors, many of whom had international followings.

The theatre scene had changed considerably since the Second World War. The most significant change had been the decline of commercial theatre in the provinces. Whereas London had managed to hold on to most of its commercial theatres, by 1975 the provinces had less than a quarter of the commercial theatres which existed in the 1930s. As the commercial theatre declined, so the number of subsidised theatres grew from twelve in 1939 to sixty in 1970.

By 1990 there were over 300 theatres in professional use in Britain. Most were owned or rented by non-profit-distributing companies, about 30 of which were receiving Arts Council subsidies, while the remainder were operated commercially or owned by local authorities. There were also about 25 touring companies receiving subsidy.

The centre of theatrical activity was in London where there were some 100 principal theatres in or near the West End or in the suburbs. Most of the theatres were let to producing managements on a commercial basis for each production, but twelve were occupied by important subsidised companies, including the Royal National Theatre and Royal Shakespeare Companies. The former staged classical and modern plays from all countries; the latter presented Shakespearean plays in Stratford-on-Avon and a mixed repertoire in London.

Outside London there were a number of theatres, which accommodated pre- and post-West End tours of the major London productions and performances by companies specially formed for touring. These theatres had been declining in numbers, and several had been purchased by local authorities. Many non-repertory theatres outside London presented all kinds of drama, and many also put on variety shows and other entertainments. There had, however, been a growth in the activities of some 30 repertory companies (including the Crucible Theatre, Sheffield), which received financial support from the Arts Council and the local authorities. The repertory companies employed many leading producers, designers and actors, and standards were high. Some companies had the use of their own theatres, while others rented from local authorities.

Sources: *'Britain 1991: An official handbook'*; Arts Council 46th annual report, 1990/1.

Appendix 2 Theatre trust memberships, January 1992

SHEFFIELD THEATRES LIMITED

Nominated by Sheffield City Council
Councillor Michael Pye (*deputy chairman*)
Prof. Roy Bailey
Andrew Holt

Nominated by Crucible Theatre Trust Limited
John Elliott MBE
David Brown
Maureen Whitebrook
Brian Wrigley (*company secretary*)

Nominated by Lyceum Theatre Trust Limited
John Cornwell (*chairman*)
David Heugh
Julian Paul
Norman Adsetts OBE

Observers
David Patmore (*Arts Dept, Sheffield City Council*)
Arts Council of Great Britain
Roger Lancaster (*Yorkshire and Humberside Arts*)
Shea Connolly (*Yorkshire Arts*)

Appendix 2 (*continued*)

CRUCIBLE THEATRE TRUST LIMITED

Roy Bailey (*chairman of TIE Advisory Panel*)
David Brown
John C. Cornwell
Councillor Don Gow
John Elliott MBE
Brian Wrigley (*company secretary*)

Nominated by Sheffield City Council
Lord Morris of Castle Morris
Councillor Stuart Dawson
Councillor Peter Price
Reginald Munn
Councillor Vivienne Nicholson
Councillor Michael Pye (*chairman*)
Mary Sharrock
Dr Maureen Whitebrook

Nominated by Lyceum Theatre Trust Limited
Alan Aikin
David Heugh
Councillor Peter Horton
Norman White

Nominated by Rotherham District Council
Councillor T. R. Sharman

Nominated by Sheffield Trades Council
Blanche Flannery

Nominated by University of Sheffield
Professor Philip Roberts

Nominated by Sheffield City Polytechnic
Dr Clive J. Sutton

Nominated by Barnsley District Council
Councillor Don Ramsden

Observers
Arts Council of Great Britain
Yorkshire Arts
David Patmore
Yorkshire and Humberside Arts

Officers in attendance
Stephen Barry (*chief executive*)
Mark Brickman (*Crucible director*)
William Farr (*financial director*)
Dulcie Scott (*staff representative*)

Appendix 2 (*continued*)

SHEFFIELD LYCEUM THEATRE TRUST

Norman Adsetts OBE
John Cornwell (*chairman*)
Julian Paul
Andrew Holt
Penny Allen

Nominated by South Yorkshire Opera (founding members)
Alan Aikin
David Heugh (*vice-chair*)
Albert Uttley
Norman White

Nominated by Sheffield City Council
Councillor Peter Horton (*vice-chair*)
Councillor Michael Pye
Martin Flannery MP

Nominated by Crucible Theatre
John Elliott MBE
Prof. Philip Roberts
Blanche Flannery
Brian Wrigley (*secretary*)

Nominated by Sheffield MPs
Lillian Munn
Chandran Owen
David Blunkett MP

Observers
Malcolm Newman (*city treasury*)
David Patmore (*Director of Arts, Sheffield City Council*)
Shea Connolly (*Yorkshire Arts*)
Peter Johnson (*Lyceum Theatre Appeal*)
Roger Lancaster (*Yorkshire and Humberside Arts*)

Source: Theatre records.

Appendix 3 **Organisation chart: Sheffield Theatres Ltd (STL), January 1992**

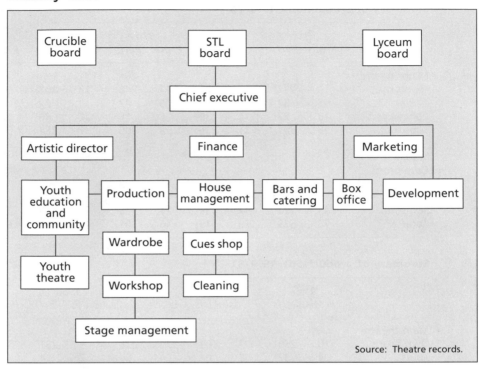

Source: Theatre records.

Appendix 4 Summaries of productions

Summary of productions, 1972–76

	1972		1973		1974		1975		1976	
	Prods	Perfs	Prods	Perfs	Prods	Perfs	Prods	Perfs	Prods	Perfs
Main theatre										
Own prods	13	237	11	243	11	248	12	307	12	324
Tours	5	37	6	42	6	42	3	29	7	56
Concerts	10	27	14	30	6	15	22	46	20	20
Sub-total	28	301	31	315	23	305	37	382	39	400
Studio										
Own prods									11	173
Tours		n/a		n/a		n/a		n/a	9	70
Concerts									5	11
Sub-total	45	222	47	198	23	196	7	309	25	254
Total	73	523	78	513	46	501	44	691	64	654

Summary of productions, 1977–81

	1977		1978		1979		1980		1981	
	Prods	Perfs	Prods	Perfs	Prods	Perfs	Prods	Perfs	Prods	Perfs
Main theatre										
Own prods.	10	235	7	181	9	238	9	251	7	228
Tours	4	32	8	64	4	56	2	4	8	52
Concerts	15	20	19	22	26	30	25	30	25	35
Sub-total	29	287	34	267	39	324	36	285	40	315
Studio										
Own prods.	13	211	10	178	7	113	6	94	4	75
Tours	5	40	8	47	8	77	16	103	16	129
Concerts	1	1	0	0	5	7	2	2	4	6
Sub-total	19	252	18	225	20	197	24	199	24	210
Total	48	539	52	492	59	521	60	484	64	525

Appendix 4 (*continued*)

Summary of productions, 1982–86

	1982		1983		1984		1985		1986	
	Prods	*Perfs*	*Prods*	*Perfs*	*Prods*	*Perfs*	*Prods*	*Perfs*	*Prods*	*Perfs*
Main theatre										
Own prods.	6	203	7	212	6	216	5	171	7	212
Tours	4	46	1	9	7	55	7	87	6	58
Concerts	18	22	13	16	20	21	7	7	12	14
Sub-total	28	271	21	237	33	292	19	265	25	284
Studio										
Own prods.	5	98	9	163	4	80	5	90	7	147
Tours	9	68	2	13	0	0	13	80	14	67
Concerts	0	0	0	0	0	0	0	0	0	0
Sub-total	14	166	11	176	4	80	18	170	21	214
Total	42	437	32	415	37	372	37	435	46	498

Summary of productions, 1987–91

	1987		1988		1989		1990		1991	
	Prods	*Perfs*	*Prods*	*Perfs*	*Prods*	*Perfs*	*Prods*	*Perfs*	*Prods*	*Perfs*
Main theatre										
Own prods	7	201	8	236	7	217	7	214	9	217
Tours	6	63	1	22	5	53	4	47	5	28
Concerts	10	12	11	11	9	9	6	7	7	7
Sub-total	23	276	20	269	21	279	17	268	21	252
Studio										
Own prods	6	133	4	102	4	85	4	64	8	112
Tours } Concerts	8	51	10	61	14	57	0	0	8	35
Sub-total	14	184	14	163	18	142	4	64	16	147
Total (Crucible)	37	460	34	432	39	421	21	332	37	399
Lyceum	–	–	–	–	–	–	4	52	50	114

Source: Theatre records.

Appendix 5 Summary of attendances

Summary of attendances, 1972–76

| | 1972 | | 1973 | | 1974 | | 1975 | | 1976 | |
	No.	% full	No.	% full	No.	% full	No.	% full	No.	% full
Main theatre										
Own prods	145,000	52	157,000	69	185,000	77	143,000	45	164,139	52
Tours	30,000	58	44,000	76	39,000	74	28,000	74	27,672	49
Concerts	2,100	48	5,100	52	1,600	54	12,200	73	12,781	64
Sub-total	177,100	52	206,100	69	225,600	76	183,200	49	204,600	51
Studio										
Own prods ⎫									15,395	
Tours ⎬	n/a		n/a		n/a		n/a		6,386	
Concerts ⎭									616	
Sub-total	13,400		15,300		20,200		32,200		22,400	
Total	190,500		221,400		245,800		215,400		227,000	

Summary of attendances, 1977–81

| | 1977 | | 1978 | | 1979 | | 1980 | | 1981 | |
	No.	% full	No.	% full	No.	% full	No.	% full	No.	% full
Main theatre										
Own prods	142,889	61	98,356	54	113,502	48	163,875	65	126,703	56
Tours	22,622	71	47,860	75	25,675	46	1,128	28	26,871	52
Concerts	13,720	69	16,156	73	19,776	66	22,570	75	20,095	57
Sub-total	179,200	62	162,400	61	159,000	49	187,600	66	173,700	55
Studio										
Own prods	14,864		16,724		6,432		4,381		5,813	
Tours	3,225		3,937		8,030		8,798		12,986	
Concerts	21		0		874		257		632	
Sub-total	18,100		20,700		15,300		13,400		19,400	
Total	197,300		183,100		174,300		201,000		193,100	

Appendix 5 (*continued*)

Summary of attendances, 1982–86

	1982		1983		1984		1985		1986	
	No.	% full	No.	% full	No.	% full	No.	% full	No.	% full
Main theatre										
Own prods	133,473	66	150,631	71	119,750	55	94,440	55	155,531	73
Tours	14,093	31	8,240	92	33,240	60	67,731	78	44,771	77
Concerts	12,123	55	9,889	62	14,956	71	5,558	79	10,047	72
Sub-total	159,700	59	168,800	71	167,900	58	167,700	63	210,300	74
Studio										
Own prods	9,282		11,958		8,023		9,236		14,192	
Tours	7,352		972		0		8,722		6,986	
Concerts	0		0		0		0		0	
Sub-total	16,600		12,900		8,000		18,000		21,200	
Total	176,300		181,700		175,900		185,700		231,500	

Summary of attendances 1987–91

	1987		1988		1989		1990		1991	
	No.	% full	No.	% full	No.	% full	No.	% full	No.	% full
Main theatre										
Own prods	149,335	74	148,016	62	116,530	54	129,101	60	78,276	36
Tours	49,066	78	18,510	84	37,382	71	40,080	86	18,386	70
Concerts	8,468	71	8,538	84	6,054	67	6,254	89	4,145	59
Sub-total	206,869	75	175,064	65	159,966	58	175,435	65	100,807	40
Studio										
Own prods	9,797	61	11,091	65	9,257	75	4,903	64	6,799	39
Tours } Concerts	5,105	70	5,442	52	4,234	47	0	–	2,711	56
Sub-total	14,902	64	16,533	60	13,491	63	4,903	64	9,510	43
Total (Crucible)	221,771	74	191,597	65	173,457	58	180,338	65	110,317	41
Lyceum	–	–	–	–	–	–	50,819	91	315,598	77

Source: Theatre records.

Appendix 6 Demographic characteristics of theatre-goers and local population

	Total population (Yorkshire and Humberside, 1974)[1]	Crucible audiences (1974)[1]	Crucible mailing list 1990[2]	Crucible Card holders 1990[2]
1. *Social class*				
% A, B, C1	29%	80%	50%	71%
2. *Education*				
% completing full-time education Age 19 or over	3%	50%	n/a	n/a
3. *Age*				
% under 35	37%	Main theatre 55% Studio theatre 75%	25%	17%
4. *Sex*				
% females	51%	Main theatre 60% Studio theatre 50%	66%	64%
5. *Sheffield post code*	n/a	80% (est.)	70%	91%

Notes
A – Higher executive, professional.
B – Middle management, lesser professions.
C1 – Lower management, semi-professional, technicians, office workers.

Sources: [1] *The Potential for the Arts in Sheffield*, Yorkshire Arts Association, 1974; [2] Sheffield Theatres Ltd: Market Study Report (McCann, Matthews, Millman), August 1990.

Appendix 7 Summaries of revenue accounts

Summary of revenue accounts, 1972/73–1976/77

	1972/73 £	%	1973/74 £	%	1974/75 £	%	1975/76 £	%	1976/77 £	%
Income										
Box office	89,251	37	118,881	41	142,399	41	152,037	38	208,728	40
Grants	167,053	64	168,665	58	190,750	56	242,061	60	364,875	63
Catering	3,048	1	2,199	1	6,944	2	5,133	1	(3,284)	(1)
Other	2,599	1	2,911	1	3,591	1	5,915	1	9,631	2
Total	261,951	100	292,656	100	343,684	100	405,146	100	579,950	100
Expenditure										
Production	162,651	62	176,629	60	206,843	60	251,134	62	298,242	51
Admin. and O/H	110,964	42	118,422	40	144,579	42	197,086	49	228,184	39
Total	273,615	104	295,051	101	351,422	102	448,220	111	526,426	91
Surplus (deficit)	(11,664)	(4)	(2,395)	(1)	(7,738)	(2)	(43,074)	(11)	53,524	9

Summary of revenue accounts, 1977/78–1981/82

	1977/78 £	%	1978/79 £	%	1979/80 £	%	1980/81 £	%	1981/82 £	%
Income										
Box office	225,961	37	255,795	36	342,634	40	379,501	38	399,453	40
Grants	349,200	58	412,391	58	458,778	53	519,716	53	576,184	58
Catering	401	0	12,598	2	15,038	2	23,433	2	(22,940)	(2)
Other	29,203	5	36,145	5	46,480	5	64,974	7	33,354	3
Total	604,765	100	716,929	100	862,930	100	987,624	100	986,051	100
Expenditure										
Production	352,924	58	463,868	65	514,033	60	633,879	64	610,697	62
Admin. and O/H	256,939	42	332,631	46	387,255	45	464,602	47	545,411	55
Total	609,863	101	796,499	111	901,288	104	1,098,481	111	1,156,108	117
Surplus (deficit)	(5,098)	(1)	(79,570)	(11)	(38,358)	(4)	(110,857)	(11)	(170,057)	(17)

Summary of revenue accounts, 1982/83–1986/87

	1982/83 £	%	1983/84 £	%	1984/85 £	%	1985/86* £	%	1986/87* £	%
Income										
Box office	388,995	38	454,236	35	486,214	35	1,144,522	55	1,306,058	55
Grants	628,450	55	711,703	55	776,074	55	926,808	45	1,072,925	45
Catering	16,646	1	43,680	3	50,239	4	n/a		n/a	
Other	105,438	9	86,646	7	88,344	6	n/a		n/a	
Total	1,139,529	100	1,296,265	100	1,400,871	100	2,071,330	100	2,378,983	100

Appendix 7 (*continued*)

Summary of revenue accounts, 1982/83–1986/87

	1982/83		1983/84		1984/85		1985/86*		1986/87*	
	£	%	£	%	£	%	£	%	£	%
Expenditure										
Production	576,456	51	733,139	57	775,073	55	999,538	48	1,127,604	47
Admin. and										
O/H	522,645	46	570,846	44	647,696	46	1,017,805	49	1,169,643	49
Total	1,099,101	96	1,303,985	101	1,422,769	102	2,017,343	97	2,297,247	97
Surplus (deficit)	40,428	4	(7,720)	(1)	(21,898)	(2)	53,987	3	81,736	3

*Catering revenues and costs included *within* the revenue and cost figures from 1985/86 onwards.

Summary of revenue accounts, 1987/88–1991/92

	1987/88		1988/89		1989/90		1990/91*	
	£	%	£	%	£	%	£	%
Income								
Box office	1,330,054	56	1,445,978	57	1,596,245	60	1,117,856	50
Grants	1,054,096	44	1,095,294	43	1,065,193	40	1,103,449	50
Total	2,384,150	100	2,541,272	100	2,661,438	100	2,221,305	100
Expenditure								
Production	1,200,337	50	1,179,283	46	1,416,880	53	891,421	40
Admin. and								
O/H	1,202,592	51	1,321,774	52	1,414,334	53	1,294,857	58
Total	2,402,929	101	2,501,057	98	2,831,214	106	2,186,278	98
Surplus (deficit)	(18,779)	1	40,215	2	(169,776)	6	35,027	2

(*continued*)

	1991/92	
	£	%
Income		
Box office	1,172,071	50
Grants	1,157,066	50
Total	2,329,137	100
Expenditure		
Production	932,104	40
Admin. and		
O/H	1,391,114	60
Total	2,323,218	100
Surplus (deficit)	5,919	0.3

*Accounting practices changed for 1990/91. The trading activities (other than productions) are *excluded*.
Source: Theatre records.

Appendix 8 **Real value of the Crucible's total public funding**

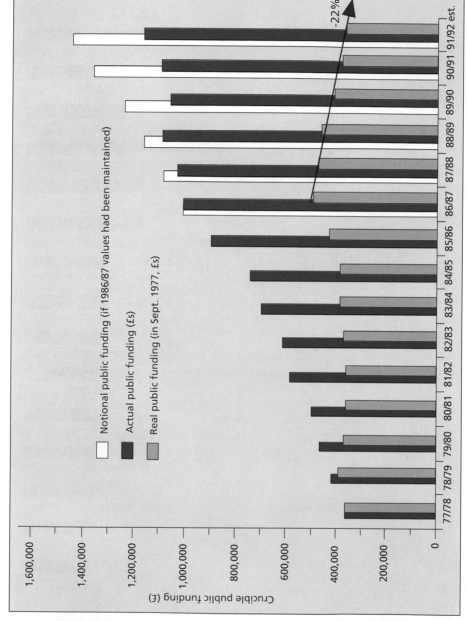

Legend:
- Notional public funding (if 1986/87 values had been maintained)
- Actual public funding (£s)
- Real public funding (in Sept. 1977, £s)

Crucible public funding (£)

-22%

Note The real value of the Crucible's total public funding has fallen each year since its 1986/87 peak and would now be £1.47m if this peak value had been maintained. Source: Crucible Theatre Trust Ltd.

Appendix 9 Real value of Sheffield City Council's grants to the Crucible

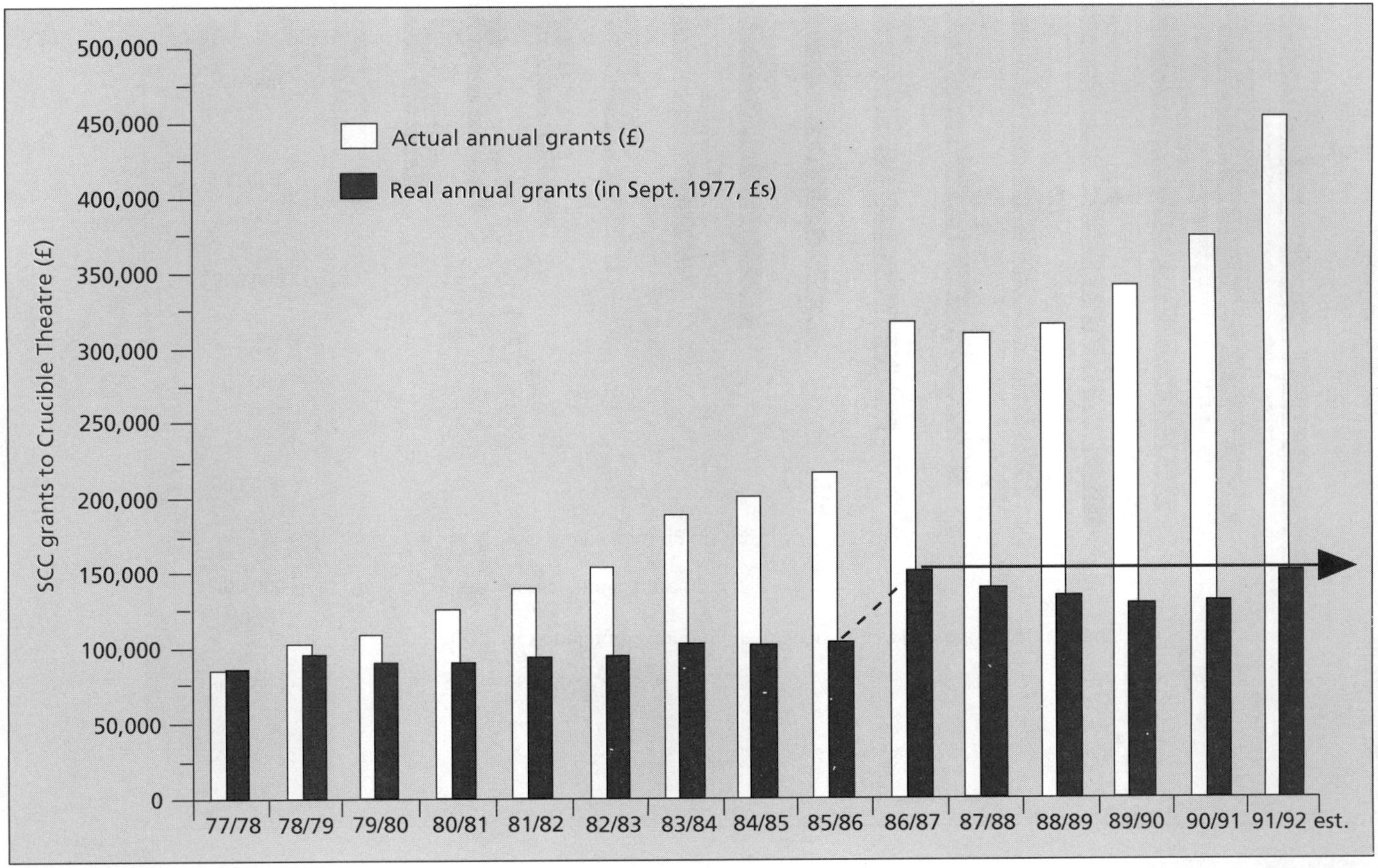
SCC grants to Crucible Theatre (£)
500,000
450,000
400,000
350,000
300,000
250,000
200,000
150,000
100,000
50,000
0
Actual annual grants (£)
Real annual grants (in Sept. 1977, £s)
77/78
78/79
79/80
80/81
81/82
82/83
83/84
84/85
85/86
86/87
87/88
88/89
89/90
90/91
91/92 est.

Note The real value of Sheffield City Council's grants to the Crucible surged following the demise of South Yorkshire but remains the same as five years ago.
Source: Crucible Theatre Trust Ltd.

Appendix 10 Real value of the Arts Council of Great Britain's grants to the Crucible

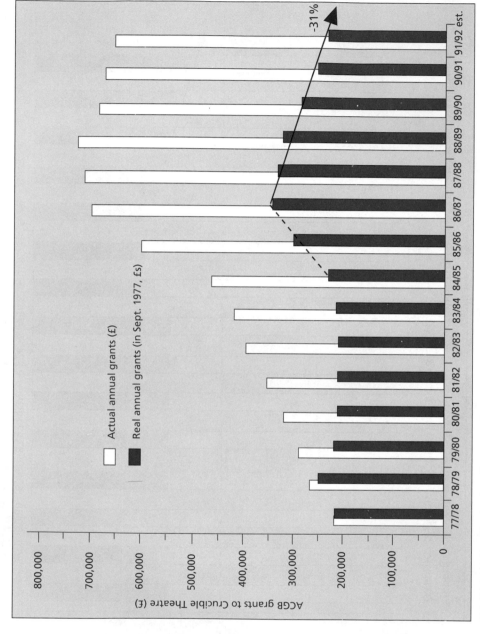

-31%

Actual annual grants (£)

Real annual grants (in Sept. 1977, £s)

ACGB grants to Crucible Theatre (£)

0 100,000 200,000 300,000 400,000 500,000 600,000 700,000 800,000

77/78 78/79 79/80 80/81 81/82 82/83 83/84 84/85 85/86 86/87 87/88 88/89 89/90 90/91 91/92 est.

Note The real value of the Arts Council's grants to the Crucible surged following the 'Glory of the Garden', but has fallen back over the last five years.
Source: Crucible Theatre Trust Ltd.

Appendix 11 Crucible funding and the achievement of parity

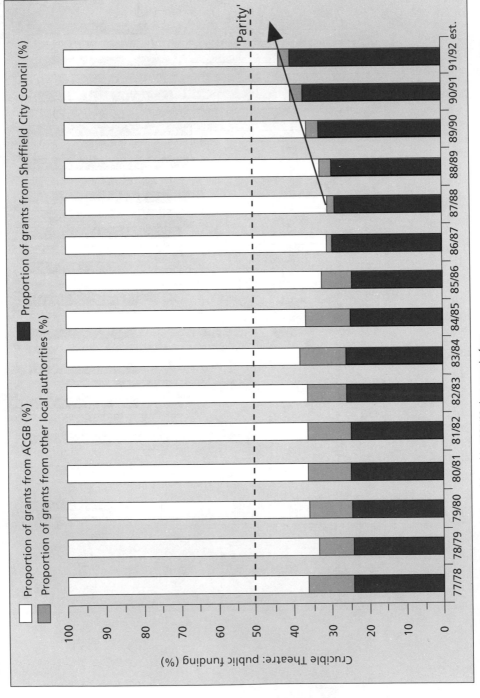

Note At first sight, parity is closer to being achieved in 1991/92 than ever before.
Source: Crucible Theatre Trust Ltd.

Appendix 12 Public funding of selected repertory theatres

Theatre	Seating capacity	Local authority and Arts Council funding (excluding debt charges)				
		1987/88 (£, actual)	1988/89 (£, actual)	1989/90 (£, actual)	1990/91 (£, actual)	1991/92 (£, estimate)
Birmingham, Rep*	900 seats	n/a	n/a	n/a	n/a	1,210,000
Coventry, Belgrade	866 seats	866,760	907,590	936,970	1,009,430	1,090,388
Nottingham, Playhouse	766 seats	820,066	996,328	883,163	980,550	1,118,419
Leicester, Haymarket	750 seats	1,194,800	1,246,600	1,321,800	1,364,470	1,452,600
Leeds, Playhouse	750 seats	544,500	596,000	854,650	1,063,500	1,426,000
Plymouth, Theatre Royal*	1,296 seats	n/a	n/a	n/a	n/a	1,135,300
Average (excluding Sheffield)		856,532	936,630	999,146	1,104,488	1,238,785
Sheffield, Crucible	1,000 seats + studio	1,054,096	1,095,244	1,065,193	1,103,449	1,147,853

Note
These comparisons should be viewed with great caution because: the figures exclude any grants from RAAs, which may vary widely; public funding is used to support a range of other activities within the venues (e.g. studio productions, TIE) and the extent of these may also vary; and comparable figures were not available for the Manchester Royal Exchange. As the rep with the highest level of public funding in Britain, its figures, if included, would have increased the average considerably.
Sources: The theatres themselves, except* provided by the Arts Council.

A note on the world automobile industry

Philippe Very, Michel Berthelier and Roland Calori

This note provides information on developments in the world automobile industry, and particularly the growing significance of Japanese competition.

The market and competitors

By the end of the 1980s, Europe had become the biggest market for automobiles, ahead of North America. Table 1 summarises demand in the main geographical zones; and Table 2 gives information about the demand for cars in the main countries.

The market could be segmented according to power and size: mini, supermini, low medium, upper medium, executive, luxury cars and small utility vehicles.[1] In North America, the higher-powered segments still represented a high share of

Table 1 Demand for cars and small utility vehicles by geographical zone (million vehicles)

	1988	1989	1990[1]
United States and Canada	17.4	16.4	15.5
Western Europe	14.9	15.4	15.3
Eastern Europe	3.1	3.2	3.2
Middle East	0.4	0.3	0.4
Latin America	1.7	1.8	1.7
Africa	0.6	0.6	0.6
Asia	9.8	10.8	11.8
Total	47.9	48.5	48.5

[1] Figures for 1990 are estimations.

[1] The category 'utility vehicles' embraces vans and other vehicles which are semi-commercial in nature.

This case was prepared by Philippe Very, Michel Berthelier and Roland Calori. It is intended as a basis for class discussion and not as an illustration of either good or bad management.

Table 2 Demand for cars in the main countries and zones (000 vehicles)

	1989	*1990*[1]
Germany	2,831	3,064
France	2,274	2,309
United Kingdom	2,301	2,009
Italy	2,362	2,347
Spain	1,085	945
Netherlands	496	500
Belgium and Luxembourg	474	512
Other EC countries	433	479
Total EC	12,256	12,165
Sweden	307	229
Switzerland	323	330
Other western Europe	511	493
Total western Europe	13,397	13,217
Total eastern Europe[2]	1,969	?
United States	9,903	9,121
Canada	975	868
Total North America	10,878	9,988
Japan	4,404	4,844
Korea, Hong Kong, Singapore, Taiwan	949	?

[1] Figures for 1990 are estimations.
[2] The USSR market represented about 50% of the market in 1988.
Source: DRI.

Table 3 Demand by segment and by country in western Europe (%)

Segment	Country				
	Germany	*France*	*UK*	*Italy*	*Spain*
Utility	2.22	4.06	2.30	16.50 ⎫	43.00
Super mini	14.46	40.31	25.51	38.94 ⎭	
Lower medium	35.62	23.03	34.41	27.37	37.10
Upper medium	22.92	22.25	25.48	8.06	13.90
Executive	24.76	10.35	12.31	9.14	6.00

Source: DRI, 1989.

the market, but there was a tendency for growth in mid-range cars. Table 3 contrasts the demand by segment in Europe between countries.

A number of developments were clear. Customers wanted a greater choice; in consequence, a given model had more and more versions (28 versions of the Peugeot 205, for instance), and manufacturing processes were therefore becoming more and more flexible. Some niches were developing quickly, such as four-wheel-drive vehicles and 'monocorps' cars (such as the Renault Espace or the Chrysler Voyager); according to experts, altogether, niches would come to represent more than 5 per cent of the market in the mid-1990s (in terms of number of vehicles).

Other trends were noticeable: more and more sophisticated equipment in cars; a growing need for passengers' safety; and a tendency towards environmentally friendly automobiles. These improvements would require more electronics in the cars of the 1990s. In 1987 there were Ffr235 of electronics in an American car, Ffr160 in a Japanese car and Ffr90 in a European car (on average). It was expected that these figures were likely to increase dramatically in the 1990s.

The supply of cars was concentrated in the three zones of the 'Triad', with a growing share for Japanese manufacturers, as shown in Table 4. In the US market the 'big three' (General Motors, Ford and Chrysler) were losing share to Japanese manufacturers. Between 1980 and 1990 the market share of General Motors, the world leader, declined from 45 to 35.7 per cent in the USA. Table 5 shows the US shares at the end of the 1980s. In 1990 GM lost a colossal $4.6bn in the USA (including a $2bn provision for plant closure) and reduced manpower by 15,000 jobs (15 per cent of the workforce). Honda/Acura, Toyota/Lexus, Nissan/Infiniti, Mazda and Mitsubishi together held 27 per cent of the US market by 1990; over 30 per cent when Japanese-engineered cars sold by GM, Ford and Chrysler under their own badges were taken into account. Japanese transplants in the USA represented 22 per cent of the market (17 per cent in 1989). From

Table 4 Production of vehicles by geographical zones and main countries (cars and small utility vehicles, 000s)

	1989	*1990*[1]
Europe	15,468	15,435
Japan	13,025	13,495
USA and Canada	12,877	11,900
USSR	2,018	2,080
Other eastern Europe	1,327	1,260
South Korea	1,130	1,280
Rest of the world	3,040	2,950

[1]Figures for 1990 are estimations.
Source: DRI.

1.32 million vehicles in 1990 their production was expected to increase up to 2.4 million units in 1992.

Industry experts were wondering what would happen in the European market in the 1990s; especially since the automobile manufacturing industry represented 1,800,000 direct jobs, and 4,000,000 jobs and about 7 per cent of the GNP of the EC when all the related businesses were included.

For a long time American automobile manufacturers had taken significant positions in Europe by direct investment: together they held about 25 per cent of the European market. Indeed, Ford Europe and GM (the latter under the names Vauxhall in the UK and Opel on the continent) were considered as European manufacturers. However, the Japanese had only about 11.6 per cent of the European market in 1990. This was not least because Italy, Spain and France were still protected by limitations on the importation of Japanese automobiles.

Table 6 gives the estimated market shares of the main competitors in Europe as a whole. However, the market shares differed across European countries, as shown in Table 7. In particular, the market shares of the Japanese competitors differed across European countries because of differences between government policies towards imports from Japan. The situation was as follows in 1991:

- Free entry to Japanese automobiles in the Netherlands, Denmark, Belgium, Luxembourg, Greece and Ireland.
- Agreement around 12 per cent of the market in the UK (but openness to direct Japanese investments).
- Agreement around 15 per cent of the market in Germany.
- Quota limiting importations in Portugal.
- Quota limiting importations around 1 per cent of the market in Spain.
- Quota limiting importations around 3 per cent of the market in France.
- Quota limiting importations around 1 per cent of the market in Italy.

In spite of the possibility of a decrease in demand in western Europe, most of the main competitors were investing heavily and planning to increase their

Table 5 Market shares in the US market (%)

	1989	1990
General Motors	35.2	35.7
Ford	22.3	21.0
Chrysler	10.4	9.3
Honda	8.0	9.2
Nissan	5.1	4.8
Toyota	6.9	8.4
Others	12.1	11.6

Source: DRI.

production capacity. Some were also investors in eastern Europe, where car manufacturers were not efficient and where it was estimated the market could double in the 1990s. It seemed that the opening of eastern Europe and in particular the unification of Germany benefited Opel GM and the Volkswagen Group, which had also strengthened its position by taking over Skoda in Czechoslovakia.

In the third zone of the 'Triad', Japanese automobile manufacturers (and to a lesser degree Korean ones) dominated the market. US exports to Japan and south-east Asia were very low (19,080 vehicles sold to Japan in 1989). The only significant exporters from Europe to Japan were the German manufacturers, who exported 120,300 units in 1989 (mainly BMW and Mercedes with their luxury cars, but also the Volkswagen group with its Golfs and Audis). The rest of the European-based manufacturers exported only 39,316 cars in 1989. The total imports of cars in Japan represented about 4 per cent of its market in 1989. The top ten companies in the world market according to the number of cars and small utility vehicles sold in 1989 are listed in Table 8.

The appendix briefly presents the key characteristics and strategies of the indigenous competitors in Europe: the Volkswagen Group, the Fiat Group, GM Europe, Ford Europe and Renault-Volvo. (For Peugeot and Rover, see the

Table 6 Sales volumes and market shares of the main competitors in Europe

	Company	Sales volume (000 vehicles)		Market share (%)	
1.	Volkswagen (including Audi and Seat)	2,031	(+1.5%)	15.4	(+0.4)
2.	Fiat (including Lancia, Alfa, Ferrari, Innocenti and Maserati)	1,874	(−5.6%)	14.2	(−0.6)
3.	PSA Group	1,708	(+0.6%)	12.9	(+0.2)
4.	General Motors (including Opel, Vauxhall and Saab)	1,554	(+1.6%)	11.8	(+0.4)
5.	Ford (including Jaguar)	1,529	(−3.2%)	11.6	(−0.2)
6.	Renault	1,295	(−6.3%)	9.8	(−0.5)
7.	Total Japanese car manufacturers	1,535	(+5.6%)	11.6	(+0.8)
	Among which:				
	Nissan	381	(−4.1%)	2.9	(−0.1)
	Toyota	351	(+1.1%)	2.7	(+0.1)
	Mazda	274	(+16.3%)	2.1	(+0.3)
	Mitsubishi	173	(+4.7%)	1.3	(+0.1)
	Honda	159	(+4.3%)	1.2	(+0.2)
8.	Daimler-Benz	431	(+1.2%)	3.3	(+0.1)
9.	Austin Rover	390	(−5.6%)	2.9	(−0.2)
10.	BMW	362	(−4.4%)	2.7	(−0.1)
11.	Volvo	234	(−12.0%)	1.8	(−0.2)
12.	Other competitors	263	(−7.4%)	2.0	(−0.1)

Note Between brackets the evolutions between 1990 and 1989.
Source: AID/industry estimates.

Table 7 Market shares by country in Europe, 1990 (estimation, %)

Company	Country								
	D	F	UK	I	SP	NL	BL	SWE	CH
VW Group	27.08	10.25	6.23	12.85	20.04	11.86	17.38	12.11	15.15
Fiat Group	4.96	7.07	3.08	52.53	8.55	6.47	5.10	1.58	9.87
PSA Group	4.35	33.14	9.19	7.72	18.63	12.82	14.90	5.16	8.24
GM Europe	17.34	5.03	16.71	4.46	13.53	14.61	12.18	16.94	14.24
Ford Europe	9.93	6.98	25.78	7.78	14.82	9.58	9.32	10.10	6.75
Renault	3.50	27.69	3.36	6.64	16.76	5.38	10.50	2.58	5.06
Japanese companies	15.76	3.30	11.69	1.94	1.55	26.36	19.60	24.84	28.25

Source: PSA.

Table 8 Top ten producers of cars and small utility vehicles, 1989 (000 vehicles)

Car manufacturers	1983	1989
1. General Motors	7,769	8,064
2. Ford	5,001	6,128
3. Toyota	3,183	4,396
4. Nissan	2,462	3,111
5. Volkswagen Group	2,116	2,936
6. Fiat Group	1,465	2,711
7. PSA Group	1,680	2,235
8. Chrysler	1,494	2,203
9. Renault	2,072	2,049
10. Honda	1,122	1,859

Source: CCFA.

respective case studies.) Background to the Japanese competitors is given later in the note.

Supply and distribution

A quick analysis of the production–distribution chain shows the importance of suppliers and subcontractors of components and systems, which manufactured about 50 per cent the value of cars. In Germany (Bosch) and in the UK (Lucas), components manufacturers were more concentrated. In France, Michelin and Valeo were of world size, but in general supply was more fragmented. The fragmentation was even more pronounced in Italy and Spain. The tendency was for car manufacturers to reduce the number of suppliers and develop closer partnerships with them to improve quality and to systematise 'just-in-time' practices in order to reduce inventories.

The European automobile manufacturers had preserved exclusive distribution channels and after sales services. This system of franchising was protected by a European regulation (réglement 12/85) at the EC level. Such control over the distribution of cars was radically different from the North American system of megadealers, which sell cars of diverse origins, therefore increasing the competition among manufacturers. By 1990, with the decrease of sales combined with various forms of competition, the margins of the exclusive dealers had shrunk and the future of the whole system in Europe was uncertain.

Japanese competitors

Among the nine Japanese manufacturers which competed against each other in east Asia, five had taken significant positions in western markets: Toyota, Nissan, Honda, Mazda and Mitsubishi. Table 6 shows the market shares of the Japanese competitors in Europe. As already mentioned, imports from Japan were limited by quotas or agreements in the main European countries, which sought to protect their national manufacturers or to stimulate direct investments. Since sales volumes were constrained, the Japanese kept prices relatively high, so actual sales figures did not reflect their competitive potential.

Beside imports, Nissan had been producing cars in the UK since 1986 (120,000 units in 1990) and 4×4 in Spain; in 1992 production was scheduled to begin at Toyota's and Honda's European assembly plants, both in the UK. By 1990 Honda also had a 20 per cent stake in the British company Rover; and Honda cars were coming off Rover's UK assembly lines at the rate of 40,000 a year. In 1991 Toyota was planning to sell cars shipped from one of its US assembly plants. Mazda and Mitsubishi Motors were seeking ways to establish their

Table 9 Comparisons of productivity between Japanese, American and European companies: number of work hours to make a car

	The best performing plant	Average	The worst performing plant
Japanese plants in Japan	13	17	27
Japanese plants in North America	19	21	26
American plants in North America	19	25	31
Japanese and American plants in Europe	22	35	57
European plants in Europe	22	35	55

Source: International Motor Vehicle Programme (Dynasteurs).

first European car production, other than from existing assembly lines in Portugal. Moreover, a sixth Japanese car manufacturer – Suzuki – was getting more active in Spain, Germany and the UK.

It was in the late 1970s that Japanese automobile manufacturers started to be competitive on costs. By 1990 their productivity was higher than the productivity of their American or European counterparts (see Table 9). The average absenteeism rate was about 5 per cent in Japan compared to about 13 per cent in Europe. During this period the Japanese also developed just-in-time systems and improved radically the quality of cars at the production level (see Table 10). In a 1990 survey, British car buyers rated 21 makes on such criteria as number of breakdowns and frequency of repairs: Honda, Mazda, Mitsubishi, Nissan and Toyota shut out the European manufacturers by taking the top five spots.

By the end of the 1980s the Japanese had also shortened the life cycle and the development phase of new vehicles: in 1990 the average development phase lasted for about five years in European companies compared with 3.5 years in Japanese companies; the average life cycle of European cars was about 6 years as against 4.5 years for Japanese cars.

Top managers in many of the European firms agreed with industry experts that a quick renewal of models was a condition to gain market share. Here design capacity was critical; but in 1990 there were 280 designers at Toyota compared to 70 at Peugeot SA and 108 at Volkswagen.

Moreover, at the end of the 1980s, Toyota with Lexus, Honda with Acura and Nissan with Infiniti entered the top segment of the market to compete with BMW and Mercedes, first on the North American market with a relative low-price strategy. The financial power of companies like Toyota had increased dramatically during the previous ten years (estimated at around Ffr80bn in cash in 1989), giving more strategic freedom to gain more market share. Several western companies preferred to conclude alliances with Japanese car manufacturers. Rover in the UK and North American competitors were active in alliances. For example, in 1983 General Motors entered a 50/50 joint venture with Toyota in the USA; it also took shares in Isuzu (38 per cent), Suzuki (5 per cent) and the Korean Daewo (50 per cent). Ford US took 24 per cent of Mazda. In 1989 Volkswagen

Table 10 Comparisons of quality and reliability of vehicles: number of defects during the first three months after the acquisition (per 100 cars)

	1987	*1988*	*1989*	*1990*
Europeans	195	255	200	180
Americans	170	175	160	150
Japanese	125	145	105	110

Source: Dynasteurs.

started to manufacture small utility vehicles with Toyota (15,000 a year at Hanover), and the two companies concluded a reciprocal distribution agreement at the beginning of 1991. Volvo signed an agreement with Mitsubishi concerning the Volvo plant in the Netherlands; and Mitsubishi also had a distribution agreement with Mercedes. Figure 1 shows the different joint developments that existed around the world.

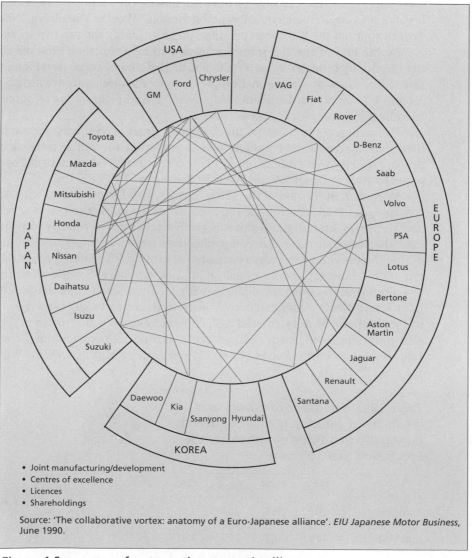

- Joint manufacturing/development
- Centres of excellence
- Licences
- Shareholdings

Source: 'The collaborative vortex: anatomy of a Euro-Japanese alliance'. *EIU Japanese Motor Business*, June 1990.

Figure 1 Summary of automotive strategic alliances

Appendix Strategies of the main competitors in Europe

(For Peugeot and Rover, see the respective case studies.)

Volkswagen Group

The Volkswagen Group was the leader in the European market (15.4 per cent of the market in 1990); its sales turnover was about DM68 billion in 1990 (DM 63.35bn in 1989), and its net profits DM1 billion in 1990, which was stable compared to 1989.[1]

The group was mainly involved in the automobile industry. In 1990 it had four main companies (and marques):

- Volkswagen (Polo, Golf-Jetta, Passat, Corrado, Scirocco and Voyage), the most important one (sales DM44 billion in 1989, profits 520 million DM).
- Audi (80/90, 100, 200, Quattro).
- Seat (Ibiza, Marbella, Malaga, Toledo).
- Skoda.

The Spanish government sold loss-making Seat to VW in 1986, and it moved into profits in 1988. Seat manufactured its own models and some Polos.

The east German market increased the home territory of VW by up to 2.7 million vehicles in 1989, to 3.1 million in 1990 and an expected 3.25 million in 1991 (considering the boom of second-hand car sales from the west to the east). The Volkswagen Group was also targeting the other east European markets. It was planning to buy a 31 per cent stake in Skoda, the Czechoslovakian car manufacturer, turn this into a joint stock company in 1991 and increase its share-holding to 70 per cent by 1995. VW plans were to invest over DM9.5 billion in Skoda in the 1990s. In 1989 Skoda sales were around 183,000 units (of which 50,000 were exported to western Europe). The objective was to sell 400,000 Skoda cars a year by 1997. Skoda would retain its identity and its own dealer networks, which would also be extended. Volkswagen also had a position in South America (a joint venture with Ford: Auto Latina),[2] in China, and in Japan where the Japanese subsidiary of VW Audi planned to invest 1.4 billion yen to build an import centre. The objective was to sell 100,000 vehicles in Japan by 1995, compared to 53,000 units in 1990. From 1989 Volkswagen and Toyota had a joint venture in manufacturing utility vehicles at Hanover; at the beginning of 1991 the group made an agreement with Toyota on reciprocal distribution of cars (Europe/Japan).

The Volkswagen Group invested DM4.25 billion in 1989, and the *extra*

---

[1] These figures do not include Skoda.
[2] VW also had another joint venture with Ford: a $3 billion plan to build a multipurpose mini van in Europe.

investments in Spain, east Germany, Czechoslovakia, China and Japan would represent about DM25 billion in the 1990s.

The priorities were the following: development in central and eastern Europe, improvements in production methods, improvements in the quality of vehicles, training the workforce, and R & D on an environmentally friendly car. The major problem of VW was the cost of labour in Germany with an increase of 6 per cent in wages and a 35-hour week from October 1993. Labour costs were higher than in France and 40 per cent higher than in Spain; in consequence the group envisaged the possibility of gradually delocalising the manufacturing.

Fiat Group

The Fiat Group is diversified: in the 1980s only about 50 per cent of its sales turnover came from automobiles (and small utility vehicles). The other businesses included industrial vehicles, tractors, aeronautics, engineering, chemicals, publishing, insurance and financial services, and retailing. In 1989 turnover of the automobile branch was just above 50,000 billion lire; sales increased in 1990 up to 52,000 billion lire, but this was less than the president, Gianni Agnelli ('l'Avvocato'), was expecting; and profits went down – gross profits on turnover decreased from 9.3 to 4.3 per cent. Moreover, the market share of Fiat in Italy reduced from 57 to 52.4 per cent. The only exception was Lancia, which also made advances in Germany and France.

Ford, with an aggressive pricing policy, gained share against Fiat. German cars also gained share of the Italian market in the upper segments and with the VW Golf. This evolution was particularly problematic because 60 per cent of the sales of Fiat were in Italy. The Fiat Group (Fiat, Lancia, Alfa-Romeo, Autobianchi and Ferrari) held 14.2 per cent of the European market; the Fiat brand itself had a 10.4 per cent share.

Two brands in the group had an extensive range of models: Fiat with Panda, Uno (Ritmo), Tipo, Regata and Croma; and Lancia with Y10, Delta, Thema and Prisma. Alfa-Romeo had three models in the medium and upper segments.

The Italian market was still protected by quotas (1 per cent of the market), limiting the importation of Japanese cars, and the group was lobbying at the EC level (together with French car manufacturers) to limit the competition with the Japanese after 1992.

Between 1987 and 1990 most of the investment of Fiat was in the area of productivity improvements, to reduce the gap between the group and other European and Japanese competitors: in industrial organisation, process innovation, logistics and distribution network. The priority for the beginning of the 1990s was total quality control.

Another priority was to become more international, particularly to develop in eastern Europe. Fiat had always had an active strategy in eastern Europe – USSR, Poland and Yugoslavia. It planned to take a 30 per cent stake in the first phase of the Yelabuga project (a joint venture with USSR), which was expected to produce about 300,000 cars. The whole project, of which there were three phases, had been valued around $7 billion. Fiat was also active in joint R & D programmes at the EC level. It had a joint venture (Sevel) with the PSA Group to manufacture small utility vehicles, and there had been rumours about a closer alliance with PSA, but it seemed that PSA was not favourable to the idea. Discussions were also going on with Chrysler about an alliance, but after the problems of Chrysler the discussions ended with an agreement to distribute Alfa-Romeos in the United States.

GM Europe: Opel

The Opel Group is the European branch of General Motors, focused on manufacturing two brands of automobile: Vauxhall in the United Kingdom and Opel in the rest of Europe. In 1990 GM Europe overtook Ford as the leading US car maker in Europe with an 11.8 per cent market share. It sold 1,561,000 cars on the European market and made about DM2 billion net profit in 1989 and 1990.

As General Motors was having problems in North America, the European market became a priority for the group. GM bought first Lotus (a UK sports car maker) in 1986, then Saab in Sweden in 1989, with a 50 per cent stake and management control. The aim was to get classier brand names and to sell upmarket cars. Saab lost $787 million in 1990 and a plant had to be closed, but the company did have a strong image in Europe. As Opel's headquarters and a high share of its manufacturing was based in Germany, it benefited from the growth of this market in 1990 and turned to eastern Europe. Opel was committed to building a DM1 billion plant at Eisenach in east Germany to make 150,000 cars a year, and it was building an engine plant, a small volume car assembly plant and a component operation in Hungary.

In 1989 Opel invested DM750 million in rationalising the product range, reducing production costs, reorganising manufacturing plants and protecting the environment. The technical centre which designed and developed new models was common to Opel and Vauxhall. Improvements in costs and quality were the two priorities of the company for the 1990s.

Ford Europe

The headquarters of Ford Europe and its main production sites were in the United Kingdom. It was composed mainly of Ford Motor Company Ltd, Aston Martin Lagonda (a small UK sports car manufacturer acquired in 1985) and Jaguar (acquired in 1989 for $2.5 billion). Ford had an extensive product range: Fiesta, Escort-Orion, Sierra, Granada, Scorpio and the Transit; the acquisition of Jaguar added the luxury cars segment.

As Ford was facing tough Japanese competition in the USA (the group lost $17 million in 1990), increased efforts were made in the European market. However in 1990 Ford lost market share in Europe, and at the end of 1990 it was number five with sales of 1.534 million cars and decreasing profits.

In 1989 Ford invested heavily in R & D, the development of new cars, motors and manufacturing. Besides, Ford Europe started to develop its distribution network, creating 181 'Ford Shops' first in the UK. In some countries like Italy, Ford started an aggressive pricing policy. The stated priority for the early 1990s was cost reductions.

Renault

The second French automobile manufacturer, Renault, was once the European leader in the industry; it lost market share at the end of the·1980s. In 1990 its sales turnover decreased by 5 per cent compared to 1989, falling to Ffr166 billion, 76 per cent of it coming from the automobile branch; and its Mack Trucks subsidiary in the USA lost Ffr1.5 billion. As a consequence, the net debts of the group went up again. In the car industry, Renault had an extensive product range of cars with the (R4), R5, Clio, (R9–R11), R19, R21 and R25, and with the monocorps Espace it had created a new market niche. It also had a range of utility vehicles.

The French state, owning the company, had to strengthen the equity of the Regie Renault in the 1980s, in order to reduce the very high level of debt. In the late 1980s Renault invested primarily in renewing the models, manufacturing organisation and processes, and long-term R & D programmes. By the early 1990s the priority was given to total quality control and improving the flexibility of the structure of the group.

At the beginning of 1990 the efforts of Renault to strengthen its position led to an alliance with the Swedish car (and trucks) manufacturer Volvo. In 1989 the turnover of Volvo was Sk91 billion and its net profits were about Sk4.8 billion; in 1990 the turnover of Volvo went down to Sk83 billion with losses of Sk287 million, partly due to a restructuring plan. The alliance included share swaps between the two companies – Renault took 25 per cent of Volvo cars and 45 per cent of Volvo trucks, and Volvo took 25 per cent of Renault and paid an additional Sk6.5 billion to Renault. Several improvements were expected from the alliance: to reach a critical mass in R & D, to achieve a geographical complementarity of sales (Volvo being strong in northern Europe and exporting to the USA, and Renault having strong positions in southern Europe), and to reduce purchasing costs.

Peugeot SA Group
Roland Calori, Philippe Very and Michel Berthelier

The PSA Group was the foremost French private industrial group in terms of sales turnover (Ffr160 billion) and manpower (159,100 persons) in 1990. It was also the leading French exporter and the highest French taxpayer, with net profits of Ffr9.3 billion in 1990. It also had the highest profits among European car makers in 1989 and 1990. In 1990 it had 12.9 per cent of the European market, after the Volkswagen Group (15.4 per cent market share) and the Fiat Group (14.2 per cent market share). At that time about 95 per cent of the sales turnover of the group was in the car industry.

After a favourable period of growth of the European car market, from 1985 to 1989, demand started to decrease in 1990 (see Figure 1). Most competitors had invested heavily to gain market share. Among them, the Japanese car manufacturers, after taking more than 30 per cent of the US car market, were targeting the European market and the 13 to 14 million cars sold each year in western Europe. Given existing protective measures in some countries in the EC, it was unclear how successful the Japanese would be, but it was widely expected that the market share of the Japanese would increase in the 1990s, especially after the single European market came into being in 1993. The opening of eastern Europe was also an important event for the car makers, with a market of 2 million units in 1990 and a possible 4 million units forecast for the year 2000. Many experts believed that the European market, which accounted for over 90 per cent of Peugeot's sales, would be the most important battleground for the car industry in the 1990s.

The PSA Group

In 1976 Peugeot, a family owned company, took over Citroën. Then in 1978 it took over the European subsidiaries of Chrysler. By 1990 the group (Peugeot and Citroën) was controlled by the Peugeot family, who owned 22.7 per cent of the equity, the largest other shareholder being Michelin with 5.8 per cent. The rest of the equity was held by financial institutions and individual stockholders.

The authors would like to thank the PSA Group for its support in writing this case study. It is intended as a basis for class discussions and not as an illustration of either good or bad management practice.

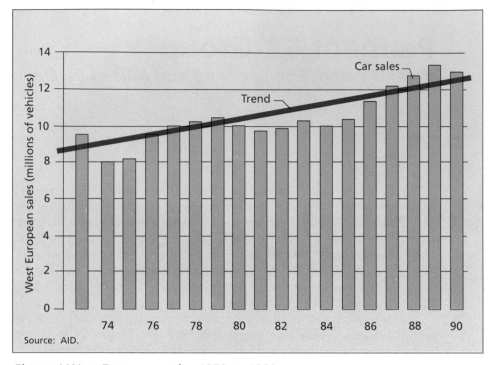

Figure 1 West European sales 1973 to 1990

From 1980 to 1984 the PSA Group went through financial difficulties, its net debts rising to Ffr33.1 billion and its equity dropping to Ffr5.3 billion in 1984. In 1983 the group lost Ffr2.6 billion. The renaissance of PSA came with the hiring of a new top manager, Jacques Calvet, and with the growth in the European market (+ 4 per cent year on average) between 1985 and 1989 (see Figure 2).

Jacques Calvet became president directeur general of Peugeot, then president directeur general of Citroën in 1983 and president du directoire of the holding company in 1984. Formerly he had been directeur du trésor at the French Ministry of Finance and president of the Banque Nationale de Paris. Experts believed that his skills and the rigour of his management were at the centre of the recovery of the PSA Group. Losses were cut as early as 1984 and debts were reduced starting from 1987. At the end of 1989 the company announced net profits of Ffr10.3 billion (a net margin of 6.7 per cent of the turnover); the sales turnover was about Ffr153 billion and debts had been reduced to Ffr1.9 billion (compared with the debt of Renault, for example, standing at Ffr17 billion in 1989).

Substantial progresses in production methods were also achieved: productivity improvements were about 72 per cent between 1982 and 1987 (the best European performance according to the consulting company Luvigsen Associates), and 50 per cent during the period 1985–9. High investments were

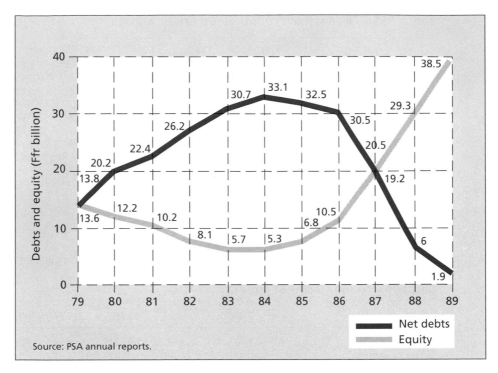

Figure 2 The renaissance of the PSA Group

made to rationalise manufacturing and to develop the company's range of products.

In 1986 Jacques Calvet announced an ambitious goal for PSA: to become the leading car manufacturer in the European market in terms of number of vehicles sold. The aim of dominant market share was postponed with the recession of the west European market and the unexpected opening of the eastern European market, which was more favourable to the Volkswagen Group, the current leader. However, PSA did become the most profitable western car manufacturer in 1989 and 1990.

Table 1 gives the main financial indicators of the group between 1986 and 1990; Table 2 gives the consolidated statements of income and the consolidated balance sheets (years 1986 to 1990); Table 3 shows the evolution of manpower for 1987 to 1990; and Table 4 gives information on the two main companies of the group, Automobiles Peugeot and Automobiles Citroën.

In 1990 the world market stagnated around 48.4 million vehicles. Demand increased in Asia (+ 22 per cent) and in Japan (+ 7.2 per cent), but it decreased in Europe (– 1.5 per cent) and in the USA (– 5.3 per cent). More precisely, in Europe: the German market increased (+ 7.4 per cent) as well as the Belgian market (+ 8 per cent), whilst demand decreased in France (– 1.6 per cent estimated), in Spain (– 12.9 per cent) and in the United Kingdom, (– 12.7 per cent).

Table 1 PSA Group: main consolidated financial data

	1990	1989	1988	1987	1986
Net sales	159,976	152,955	138,452	118,167	104,946
Cash flow	16,157	18,553	16,017	13,562	7,169
Investments (tangible assets)	15,139	12,235	11,951	8,835	7,350
Net profit	9,258	10,301	8,848	6,709	3,590
Shareholders equity	47,166	38,530	29,263	20,528	10,535
Net financial debts	8,278	1,911	5,956	18,643	29,874
Earnings per share (Ffr)	185	206	177	156	113

Note Figures in million French francs unless stated.
Source: Adapted from annual report, 1990.

Table 2 PSA Group: consolidated statements of income and balance sheets

Consolidated statements of income

	1990	1989	1988	1987	1986
Net sales	159,976	152,955	138,452	118,167	104,946
Other revenues	815	602	475	522	644
Purchases and other expenses	(111,981)	(101,914)	(89,359)	(77,503)	(69,763)
Staff	(30,031)	(28,789)	(26,915)	(25,880)	(25,534)
Other operational expenses	(3,078)	(4,375)	(5,006)	(3,851)	(2,707)
Operational margin	15,701	18,479	17,647	11,455	7,586
Rationalisation expenses	(197)	(160)	(847)	(326)	(772)
Net financial expenses	(969)	(556)	(1,874)	(3,012)	(3,492)
Other net revenues and expenses	(1,598)	(2,512)	(1,215)	(577)	(486)
Pretax profits of companies in equivalence	1,140	1381	1,164	1,043	1,007
Operating income before tax	14,077	16,632	14,875	8,583	3,843
Income tax	(4,638)	(6,068)	(5,683)	(3,420)	(1,476)
Net income of the group (Before former deficits)	9,439	10,564	9,192	5,163	2,367
Income paid to minority shareholders	(181)	(263)	(344)	(247)	(98)
Former deficits	–	–	–	1,793	1,321
Net income of PSA	9,258	10,301	8,848	6,709	3,590

Note Figures in million French francs.

Table 2 (*continued*)

Consolidated balance sheets

	1990	*1989*	*1988*	*1987*	*1986*
Assets					
Tangible assets					
Land, plant and equipment					
Gross book value	72,660	62,197	53,767	46,424	41,670
Depreciation	(27,032)	(23,436)	(20,354)	(18,482)	(17,106)
	45,628	38,761	33,413	27,942	24,564
Specific equipments	7,135	6,503	6,624	5,790	5,009
Net tangible assets	52,763	45,264	40,037	33,732	29,573
Other fixed assets	10,956	8,784	7,062	5,943	5,545
Net deferred charges	28	64	1,350	1,614	2,845
Receivable/state	–	–	–	–	772
Inventories	24,128	19,762	17,544	17,756	17,437
Net accounts receivable	11,357	10,889	10,164	9,246	9,531
Other quick assets	7,579	6,433	4,680	5,124	4,355
Cash assets	8,712	16,109	17,020	3,642	2,030
Total assets	115,523	107,305	97,857	77,057	72,088
Liabilities					
Capital	1,748	1,747	1,746	1,746	1,135
Premiums	5,195	5,190	5,175	5,174	2,037
Retained earnings	40,223	31,593	22,342	13,608	7,363
Stockholders' equity	47,166	38,530	29,263	20,528	10,535
Minority interests	928	1,048	1,021	633	375
Securities	693	775	–	–	–
Debenture loans	1,975	2,546	4,252	4,441	6,159
Other long-term loans	3,876	4,009	9,969	11,275	15,972
Long-term loans	5,851	6,555	14,221	15,716	22,131
Deferred taxes	4,841	3,834	2,630	539	133
Other reserves	2,400	2,693	2,078	1,817	1,639
Accounts payable	23,667	24,349	21,261	18,621	16,177
Other current liabilities	29,977	29,521	27,383	19,203	21,098
Current liabilities	53,644	53,870	48,644	37,824	37,275
Total liabilities	115,523	107,305	97,857	77,057	72,088

Note Figure in million French francs.
Source: Adapted from annual report, 1990.

Table 3 Employees of the PSA Group

	1987	1988	1989	1990
Peugeot branch				
Automobiles Peugeot	60,300	57,200	56,300	56,200
French subsidiaries	7,300	7,600	7,600	7,500
Foreign subsidiaries	16,900	18,000	18,400	17,500
Total	84,500	82,800	82,300	81,200
Citroën branch				
Automobiles Citroën	33,900	33,100	34,200	34,500
French subsidiaries	11,400	11,200	11,100	10,900
Foreign subsidiaries	12,900	13,400	13,500	13,300
Total	58,200	57,700	58,800	58,700
Other companies	2,400	2,500	2,700	2,900
Total	145,100	143,000	143,800	142,800
Division des Activités Mécaniques et de Services	15,200	14,800	15,000	16,000
Peugeot SA	300	300	300	300
Groupe PSA	160,600	158,100	159,100	159,100
France	130,300	126,300	126,700	127,700
Foreign countries	30,300	31,800	32,400	31,400

Source: Annual reports, 1988, 1989, 1990.

In this context, the sales turnover of the PSA Group increased by 4.6 per cent up to Ffr160 billion and its share of the European market went up to 12.9 per cent (compared to 12.7 per cent in 1989). 2,194,300 cars (and small utility vehicles) were sold.

Table 5 shows the breakdown of the sales of the group in the world, and Table 6 gives the breakdown of sales of the group in Europe. Two factors explain the increase of sales in value: PSA did not follow the reduction in prices started by some competitors; and the sales of its new top segment models – the 605 and the XM – increased significantly. The PSA annual report of 1990 summarised the position as follows: 'Altogether, these performances, below the ambitions announced at the beginning of the year, are the consequence of the shrinking of the European markets during the year 1990. Nevertheless they allowed the PSA group to improve its relative position in Europe.'

As PSA went on investing in 1990 – about Ffr15.1 billion – net debts went up again to Ffr8.3 billion. The equity also rose to Ffr47.1 billion and the net profits were maintained at the highest level in Europe, Ffr9.258 billion (compared with

Table 4 The two main companies of the PSA Group: Automobiles Peugeot and Automobiles Citroën

AUTOMOBILES PEUGEOT (PARIS)	AUTOMOBILES CITROËN (NEUILLY)
Share of the group: 99.99% (by Peugeot SA)	Share of the group: 100% (by Peugeot SA)
Production centres in Sochaux, Montbéliard and Mulhouse; plants in Dijon, Lille, Saint Etienne, Vesoul, Valencienne, La Rochelle, Sept-Fons.	Production plants in Aulnay, Rennes, Paris (and area), Caen, Charleville and Reims

	1990	1989		1990	1989
Production (000 vehicles)	1,407	1,311	Production (000 vehicles)	812	905
Sales (000 vehicles)	1,378	1,318	Sales (000 vehicles)	816	883
Manpower of the company	47,200	47,600	Manpower of the company	34,500	34,200
Manpower of the branch	81,200	82,300	Manpower of the branch	58,700	58,800
Consolidated financial data (Ffr million)			Consolidated financial data (Ffr million)		
Sales (before tax)	99,205	94,567	Sales (before tax)	68,828	65,909
Cash flow	10,000	10,663	Cash flow	4,699	6,673
Net profit (to Automobiles Peugeot)	6,397	7,126	Net profit (to Automobiles Citroën)	1,438	2,052
Shareholders' equity (before appropriation)	25,805	20,229	Shareholders' equity (before appropriation)	9,468	8,299
Investments (tangible assets)	6,500	5,545	Investments (tangible assets)	7,644	5,945
Dividends	997	903	Dividends	–	196

Source: Adapted from annual report, 1990.

Ffr.10.3 billion in 1989). The ratio of net profits to turnover (5.8 per cent for PSA) remained much higher than that of other competitors in Europe (in general between 0.2 and 2.8 per cent). The productivity gains were around 5.2 per cent in 1990 (compared to 4.7 per cent 1989).

However, by mid-1991 the situation had changed. With unification the German market had grown dramatically – up 37 per cent for the first five months of 1991 – but other markets were in decline. Some such as the UK, were dramatically so, falling 24 per cent, and France 17.1 per cent for the same period. As Jacques Calvet remarked in June 1991:

> Since PSA's market share is greatest in the countries where demand was the weakest, the sharply contrasting trends could not help but erode the group's overall European position. Diminished demand in France and two of our major export markets – the UK and Spain – was therefore only partially offset by Peugeot's and Citroëns remarkable 60 per cent surge in Germany. These shifts in the geographic mix of European demand accounted for about one point of overall decline of PSA's year-to-date European market share,

Table 5 Sales of the PSA Group by geographical zone (including small utility vehicles)

	1987	*1988*	*1989*	*1990*
France				
Automobiles Peugeot	508,900	552,500	574,300	571,000
Automobiles Citroën	338,000	348,500	375,000	346,500
Groupe PSA	846,900	901,000	949,300	917,500
Europe: Other countries				
Automobiles Peugeot	519,400	621,800	631,200	674,800
Automobiles Citroën	394,600	425,300	466,600	431,000
Groupe PSA	914,000	1,047,100	1,097,800	1,105,800
Africa				
Automobiles Peugeot	20,100	31,600	30,000	31,100
Automobiles Citroën	4,700	4,500	5,800	6,500
Groupe PSA	24,800	36,100	35,800	37,600
America				
Automobiles Peugeot	14,700	20,300	13,500	11,400
Automobiles Citroën	3,400	3,600	4,500	3,300
Groupe PSA	18,100	23,900	18,000	14,700
Asia-Oceania				
Automobiles Peugeot	36,100	46,700	47,500	65,800
Automobiles Citroën	13,800	15,700	19,700	12,000
Groupe PSA	49,900	62,400	67,200	77,800
Sous-Immatriculation (Special)				
Automobiles Peugeot	19,100	20,300	21,200	24,100
Automobiles Citroën	11,200	11,700	11,200	16,800
Groupe PSA	30,300	32,000	32,400	40,900
Total				
Automobiles Peugeot	1,118,300	1,293,200	1,317,700	1,378,200
Automobiles Citroën	765,700	809,300	882,800	816,100
Groupe PSA	1,884,000	2,102,500	2,200,500	2,194,300

Source: Annual reports, 1988, 1989, 1990.

which at the end of May had slipped to 11.5 or 11.6 per cent compared with 12.9 per cent for all of 1990.

The strategy of PSA

Jacques Calvet was known for his perseverance, the rigour of his management and his personal involvement in the management of Peugeot and Citroën. His vision of the future of the group could be summarised in seven strategic thrusts.

Table 6 Sales of Peugeot and Citroën in the main European
countries (registrations, *not* including small utility vehicles)

	1987	1988	1989	1990
Automobiles Peugeot				
France	440,700	491,800	473,100	498,500
Germany	79,900	70,500	62,100	84,800
Belgium–Luxembourg	34,300	42,500	42,700	43,900
Netherlands	34,500	35,100	35,900	39,500
United Kingdom	101,300	126,800	139,000	123,700
Italy	79,700	97,900	103,400	111,200
Spain	95,300	113,600	114,900	101,300
Automobiles Citroën				
France	262,800	265,900	273,000	266,800
Germany	43,400	38,100	40,400	46,600
Belgium–Luxembourg	27,300	26,900	29,700	32,400
Netherlands	30,400	23,400	23,000	24,700
United Kingdom	46,000	66,900	66,400	60,900
Italy	69,100	70,700	79,200	70,100
Spain	54,900	80,100	83,900	74,800
Automobiles PSA				
France	703,500	757,700	746,100	765,300
Germany	123,300	108,600	102,500	131,400
Belgium–Luxembourg	61,600	69,400	72,400	76,300
Netherlands	64,900	58,500	58,900	64,200
United Kingdom	147,300	193,700	205,400	184,600
Italy	148,800	168,600	182,600	181,300
Spain	150,200	193,700	198,800	176,100

Source: Annual reports, 1988, 1989, 1990.

The attitude towards the Japanese

Jacques Calvet presented his arguments in an article he wrote in *Le Monde*
(January 1990). They are summarised here:

- The Japanese had a skilled workforce working at least 20 per cent more than
  the workforce in Europe (2,300 hours per person per year in Japan against
  1,600 h/p/y in Europe). Moreover, the social expenses of the firms were
  about three times lower in Japan than in France.
- The distribution of cars in Japan was controlled by the local manufacturers,
  and the competitors targeted foreign markets while maintaining high
  consumption prices on their domestic market.
- Japanese consumers preferred to buy Japanese products.

Such cultural, economic and social differences with western countries had to be
considered before any liberalisation of trade. On the other hand, the arguments

for free trade did not hold in the long term, as had been demonstrated in the USA.

- Japanese investments in Europe would not really improve technological learning; the best European competitors matched the Japanese in this respect.
- Prices might be lowered in the short term, but as soon as the Japanese took a significant share of the market they would raise their prices.
- Even in the case of Japanese investments in Europe the level of employment would be dramatically reduced (one new job gained against two jobs lost).

In *European Motor Business* (November 1989) Jacques Calvet stated:

> We must develop a common foreign policy towards Japan. We must limit the imports of Japanese cars as long as we do not sell a significant number of cars in Japan, that is to say a ratio of at least one [European car sold to Japan] for two [Japanese cars sold in Europe]. We must also have a common policy concerning the Japanese transplants in Europe . . . We need a significant proportion of local content [in Japanese transplants in Europe] – namely 80 per cent – because this relates to the problem of employment and to sustaining technological capabilities in Europe . . . We should examine the suggestion made by Gianni Agnelli [president of the Fiat Group] who says that there should be an overall quota on the importations of Japanese cars – wherever they come from – and a limitation to the manufacturing of Japanese cars in Europe.

As far as the strategy of the PSA Group was concerned, he also stated in *Le Figaro Economie* (April 1991): 'As long as I am President of the Group, I will never accept an agreement with the Japanese.'

The PSA Group was actively lobbying at the EC level to defend the argument of protection against the Japanese, as stated in the annual report of the group in 1990:

> The group will continue its efforts of persuasion in order to avoid dangerous drifts in building Europe and in the negotiations, which are badly opened, between the twelve states of the EC and Japan . . . Do we make Europe for the Europeans, for employment, for technology, for European wealth and power or do we abandon ourselves to a competition which is not truly based on free trade and which would lead to a weaker Europe?

With the exception (to some extent) of the Fiat Group, the other European car manufacturers had less intransigent positions towards Japanese competition. However, the attitude of the German companies and of the subsidiaries of the North American companies in Europe evolved towards more protectionism between 1989 and 1990. The attitude of the EC Commission also changed in this direction during the same period. The decrease in demand for cars in 1990 and the crisis of North American car manufacturers in the USA probably influenced this evolution.

Investment and productivity

The PSA Group had invested about Ffr35 billion from 1987 to 1989 (compared to some Ffr25 billion at Renault or Fiat) to become the leader on the European market and to respond to the Japanese challenge. In 1990 the investments increased to Ffr15.1 billion, about 9.5 per cent of the sales turnover, one of the highest ratios of the industry. They were financed internally rather than through borrowing. High profits were a condition of such a policy: 'Investments are aimed to renew the product range. They are also aimed to continue the modernisation of the industrial assets of the group, in order to improve productivity, flexibility, efficiency and the quality of the products' (annual report, 1990).

One of the priorities of the top management was to increase *productivity* by 50 per cent during the period 1990–5 (progress comparable to the group's performance during the previous five years). A better organisation of work and increased automatisation would also be achieved. The group had 200 robots in 1982, 1,300 in 1988 and planned to have about 2,000 in 1992. The company saw robotisation as necessary to improve the *flexibility* of the plants and to adapt to market fluctuations of each model. The aim was that a given plant should be able to change quickly from one model to the other, or even assemble different models simultaneously (for instance, the 205 and 405). Another decision was taken to improve productivity: the assembly of subsystems beside the main line, which would also help to improve quality control.

Reductions in costs were also vital. Jacques Calvet stated that the market reversals in 1990 and 1991 made this even more so:

> Under the circumstances, the group must not only pursue but intensify across-board cost-cutting even as we maintain – if not speed up – our investments for the future . . . Investment commitments must be made at the least possible cost and with increased simplicity and reliability. We must foster productivity enhancement and technological advances by intensifying our policy of partnerships with suppliers.

Investments in *renewing models* and in quality were other stated priorities. PSA was planning to launch 1.4 new models a year to catch up with the Japanese – a major challenge, since launching a new car would cost around Ffr8 billion.

In order to achieve those goals it was planned to increase personnel training expenses as well as research and development expenses. From 1988 to 1990 PSA spent 3.5 per cent of its turnover on R & D. In 1990 the budget for R & D was Ffr6,100 million, representing 3.8 per cent of the consolidated turnover, high compared to other European competitors but lower than the Japanese Toyota and Honda (both around 5 per cent). Some of the R & D projects were developed

jointly with other firms. PSA had agreements with Renault to develop environmentally friendly cars and was actively involved in several long-term Eureka EC
programmes: for instance, Carmat, on the use of composites and new metallic
materials; Ceramique, for the industrial development of new ceramic and metallic components of engines; and Prometheus, to improve road traffic in Europe.

Two marques

Another main element of the strategy of PSA was to keep and develop *two marques* – Peugeot and Citroën – both with a range of cars, since both were involved
in the four main segments of the market (see Table 7).

Some other competitors also had more than one marque. The Volkswagen
Group had several, with Seat and Skoda at the low end of the market,
Volkswagen as a generalist and Audi at the top end of the market. The Fiat
Group had Ferrari at the very top of the market, Alfa-Romeo, Fiat itself and
Lancia. Other car manufacturers such as Renault or Rover only had one marque.

At PSA, the standardisation of vehicles was relatively high between the two
product lines, about 50 per cent of the components being common to the two
marques. There were the non-visible components – engines, gearboxes, etc. –
while the elements of the car that could be seen were different. Joint purchasing
of components through Sogedac, a company of the group, was seen as a source
of competitive benefit by the company.

Part of the R & D expenses were also shared: thanks to the two parallel
model ranges, synergies in R & D were about 20 per cent and increasing. A priority was seen as the 'implementation of single computer systems and closer co-

Table 7 Models of Peugeot and Citroën, production of the group in Europe
(number of vehicles)

	Peugeot			**Citroën**		
	Models	*1990*	*1989*	*Models*	*1990*	*1989*
Super Mini	205	605,100	565,800	AX	327,900	390,200
				2 CV	9,900	19,100
Lower Mini	309	245,700	239,500	(ZX to be		
	305	4,200	9,700	launched in 1991)		
Upper medium	405	349,700	378,300	BX	236,900	290,300
	504	23,700	23,800			
Executive	505	24,800	32,400	CX	2,100	7,000
	605	80,700	12,600	XM	96,200	46,300
Utility and miscellaneous	P4, J5, J9	73,600	48,900	C15, C25, C35	139,400	152,200
Total		1,407,500	1,311,000		812,400	905,100

Source: Annual report, 1990.

operation between the engineering, methods, production, quality and management control teams of PSA's two automobile companies'. However, there was no intention to merge the two distribution networks, since executives believed the weaker marque could be disadvantaged (a problem which occurred when Peugeot took over Chrysler-Simca in 1979). Besides, the view was that merging the two independent distribution networks could give an opportunity for foreign competitors to take over dealer networks.

Such a strategy required an important effort to renew the range of models of the two companies. In order to renew eight basic models (four Peugeot and four Citroën) every six years, the PSA Group would have to launch 1.4 new models every year (actually one or two). In 1989 the PSA Group had launched two models in the 'executive' segment: the 605 and the XM; no new model was launched in 1990; and two new models were planned to be launched in 1991: the ZX (Citroën/lower medium) and the 106 (Peugeot/mini).

One of the consequences of the investment in developing the two marques was that PSA had not entered niches such as 4×4 and 'monocorps' cars. 4×4 leisure cars, such as the Land Rover or the Renault Jeep Cherokee manufactured by Chrysler, represented 1 per cent of the European market in 1990, with a growth of 100 per cent since 1985. Monocorps cars, such as the Renault Espace with 60 per cent of this niche in Europe in 1990, represented a potential market of 250,000 units in 1994 (four times more than in 1989). There were discussions on a possible joint project for a monocorps car in association with Fiat, but the model would not be launched before 1995. According to experts, it would cost about Ffr5 billion to develop such a car, and the manufacturing would have to be adapted to short production runs. However, PSA was actively involved in one niche, the electric car, a point which will be discussed later.

Improving the development of models

Improving the *development of models* was seen as a key success factor. The case of the Citroën ZX showed the efforts of the group in this respect.

The Citroën ZX would compete in the lower-medium segment with the Peugeot 309 (with 5.4 per cent of the European market in this segment), the Fiat Tipo (8.9 per cent), the Opel Kadett (15.3 per cent), the Ford Escort (12.7 per cent), the Renault 19 (10.6 per cent), the VW Golf (18.5 per cent), the Toyota Corolla and the Mazda 323. This segment represented 30 per cent of the European market, and the success of the ZX was seen as a major challenge for the whole group at the beginning of the 1990s. The objective was to sell 186,000 ZXs in 1991, including in foreign markets. The plan was to manufacture in France (Aulnaye and Poissy), in Spain (Vigo) and probably in China in 1993. The cost of development studies alone amounted to Ffr1.75 billion, the investment amounted to Ffr5.8 billion and the development of industrial processes took about 3.4 million hours of work.

Development methods of Peugeot and Citroën had already been revised with an earlier collaboration between manufacturing, designers and the main subcontractors in order to match style, engineering and production feasibility. For instance, in the case of the ZX the project started in 1985; at the end of 1985 the pilot production phase of the first vehicle began; several versions were presented in March 1988; then a project leader was named, and the designers also participated in the final phase of the master model. It was planned that the new organisation of product development would be applied to the next model (which would replace the AX) to shorten again the lead time for the development and the industrialisation from five years to three years. A project manager would be named from the beginning, to be in charge of quality, cost, scheduling and specific performance targets. The aim was to extend the co-operation between designers, process engineers and the manufacturing function from the beginning to the end of the project.

A new marketing policy was also introduced for the ZX. Until 1990 Citroën used to market many 'special' versions of a given basic model; with the ZX, the product line was to have four brand identities: Reflex (young, modern), Avantage (family), Aura (men, older people) and Volcane (higher social levels). The launching of the ZX in 1991 benefited from the victory of a rally version of the car, driven by Ari Vatanen, in the Paris–Dakar rally in January 1991. To strengthen its image and differentiate its cars, PSA participated actively and successfully in international car competitions: for example, first with the 205 in the world rally championship; then with the 205 and 405 in the Paris–Dakar; and finally in the world championship for sports cars, where it won the Suzuki race for the first competition of the Peugeot 905, against Jaguar and Mercedes at the beginning of 1991.

The international strategy of the PSA Group

At the beginning of 1990, PSA had industrial units in several countries in Europe: France (Sochaux, Mulhouse, Aulnay, Poissy and Rennes), United Kingdom (Ryton), Spain (Villaverde and Vigo) and Portugal (Mangualde); and three main companies abroad: Peugeot Talbot Motor (United Kingdom), Peugeot Talbot Espana and Citroën Hispania SA (Spain). The group also manufactured small utility vehicles in Italy, in joint venture with Fiat. Table 8 gives an overview of the industrial and commercial units of PSA throughout the world.

Automobiles Peugeot and Automobiles Citroën had 92 per cent of their sales in Europe; and the European market was seen as a priority for the PSA Group: 'The European market, which attracts the world car manufacturers, is both more promising in terms of volume and less vulnerable to cyclical variations than the North American market' (annual report, 1990).

Among European countries, the German market was seen as particularly attractive for its importance and growth. PSA was strengthening its positions there, particularly with the models of the top segment – the 605 and the XM. A network of about a hundred dealers was being set up in east Germany. The market of the United Kingdom was also important for PSA; Peugeot Talbot UK was one of the companies of the group, producing the 405 at Ryton. Peugeot had

Table 8 Industrial and/or commercial units of the PSA Group in the world (automobiles, 1990)

	Industrial units	Commercial units
Europe		
France	•	•
United Kingdom	•	•
Spain	•	•
Portugal	•	•
Italy	• (small)	•
Germany		•
Austria		•
Belgium		•
Denmark		•
Greece		•
Iceland		•
Norway		•
Sweden		•
The Netherlands		•
Switzerland		•
Israel		•
Turkey	•	•
Yugoslavia	• (small)	•
Romania		•
Other developed countries		
USA		•
Canada		•
Japan		•
Australia		•
South America		
Argentina	• (small)	•
Chile	• (small)	•
Uruguay	• (small)	•
Africa		
Centrafrique, Kenya, Morocco, Nigeria, Zaire, Zambia, Zimbabwe	• (small)	•
Algeria, Ivory Coast, Senegal, Tunisia		•
Asia (other)		
China, India, Indonesia, Iran, Malaysia, Taïwan, Thaïland	• (small)	•

Source: Annual report, 1990.

taken over the chronically loss-making UK operations of Chrysler in 1978. The production rose for five years in succession from about 20,000 units in 1985 up to 116,500 in 1990. In 1990 the turnover rose by 8 per cent to £1.6 billion, but pre-tax profits fell by 11 per cent to £109 million. Considering the steep decrease of the British market, it was expected that the production and sales would decrease in 1991. However, the production of a second model was planned for 1992 at Ryton, and PSA was planning to increase its market share anyway. The Spanish and Portuguese markets, where PSA had several plants, and the Italian market, where the group had a strong position, were also priorities.

The sales of the PSA Group outside Europe increased by 11.5 per cent between 1989 and 1990:

> The industrial projects target countries with a real potential of development for the group, considering the situation of the economy of the country, its industrial base, and the perspective of growth of the automobile market. Important progress has been achieved in this direction, in China, in India, in Iran and around the Mediterranean basin, particularly with a common project between Peugeot and Citroën in Turkey. (Annual report, 1990.)

Peugeot also had a strong position in Africa, where it was market leader with 39,000 vehicles. However, growth in Africa was seen as limited.

PSA executives also believed that they could not neglect the Japanese market, comprising 123 million sophisticated customers with high purchasing power. The sales of Peugeot and Citroën in Japan had increased regularly since 1986, up to 6,117 Citroën and 5,414 Peugeot cars in 1990 (altogether 0.25 per cent of the market). In particular, Peugeot had experienced success with the 205 GTI. Peugeot Japan was created in 1989 with a number of partners: in 1990 PSA had 67 per cent of PJ, Rover Japan had 11.5 per cent, Suzuki Motor had 11.5 per cent and Seibu and Nisho Iwai had 5 per cent each. It was felt that sales could reach 20,000 cars in 1992/3, especially if the 605 was successful.

In eastern Europe, by 1990 the group had established a distribution network in most of the countries and the manufacturing of the 605 in Russia was being considered.

The relationships between the corporate centre in France and the foreign subsidiaries were becoming more complex as the international strategy developed. Research and development were centralised in France; product marketing, pricing and communication policies were also decided in France; but some adaptations to some particular important foreign markets were negotiated between the headquarters and some subsidiaries.

Peugeot Talbot Motor Company Ltd (UK) also had a higher degree of autonomy than most of the Peugeot operating businesses. From 1982 onwards PSA took over the marketing and design decisions for the UK, and disbanded the Ryton design centre. However, PSA Centre did realise the differences in the UK market, especially because of the importance of the fleet market (cars purchased centrally by companies for company personnel). There was, then, a marketing director in the UK, but with a strong functional reporting link through to marketing and design in PSA Centre. The degree of autonomy was less than had been expected by George Turnbull, the chief executive from 1978 to 1985, and he had left. The increasing autonomy of the later 1980s had been 'earned' not only by the UK company delivering against its business objectives and the improvements made in industrial relations and productivity, but also because of the 'diplomatic' style of the chief executive at that time, Geoffrey Whalen, towards the corporate centre.

The 'clean' car

The PSA Group had its own point of view about reducing pollution by cars: consume less fuel to pollute less. It was different from the German position based on catalytic converters, which had strongly influenced regulations at the EC level. PSA argued that heavier cars with catalytic converters consume more fuel than lighter cars with more efficient engines. So PSA had tried to champion low petrol consumption. On average its cars consumed less petrol than Fiats and VWs. By 1991 the stated aim was to 'reduce average fuel consumption of all vehicles to 6 litres per 100 kilometres, even with the use of catalytic converters'. As diesel engines consumed less (about – 25 per cent) and as diesel fuel cost less than petrol, PSA had become the European leader in diesel cars and had a significant competitive advantage in this domain. It sold diesel engines to Rover, Ford and Daf, and 37 per cent of the Citroën cars and 32.3 per cent of the Peugeot cars were diesel.

PSA was also an active developer of electric cars. Indeed, it aimed to be the first car manufacturer to sell electric vehicles at the beginning of 1991 (first to Electricité de France and then to local government authorities and public institutions) for urban use. The market was estimated by executives to be around 250,000 vehicles in Europe by 1995. At that time PSA would target more than 20 per cent of the market and the use of the electric car would be extended to the second car of the family to drive for short distances, mainly in towns.

The social policy of the PSA Group

After the strikes at Mulhouse and Sochaux in 1989, a more active policy of human resource management, particularly with regard to training and quality circles, was developed and a wages agreement was reached with the unions in 1990; on average wages increased by 5 per cent between 1989 and 1990, which was relatively high compared to the average in France and compared to previous years at PSA. However, as Jacques Calvet explained repeatedly, the competition with the Japanese did not leave much freedom to increase salaries; the Japanese worked more hours per year per person than the Europeans and the social security system was much lower cost in Japan. An agreement on a clearer definition of jobs and careers paths was also reached in 1990. The training of the workforce was seen as a priority for the group, about 4.3 per cent of the wages being spent on training to help adapt people to new technologies and processes.

An innovation was to be tried at the Poissy plant in 1991 – the four-day week. The number of hours a week would not change for a person (38.5), but each one would have a free Saturday and Sunday plus another free day during the week. This solution would increase the operating time of the machines from 77 to 96 hours a week (two shifts). In addition, Ffr1.7 billion would be invested in the plant, 1,100 new employees would be hired, 706,000 hours of training would be added and a Ffr700 bonus per person would be paid. With this approach, it was expected that the Poissy plant could increase its capacity by 25 per cent

Challenges for the 1990s

In the short term (1991 and 1992) the fluctuation of demand in Europe was considered an important issue by the top management of the PSA Group: it was expected that there would an average decrease of the western European market and divergent trends in demand between European countries; There would be growth in Germany, and an expected decrease in other countries, particularly Spain and the UK: 'This divergent evolution of demand between European countries affects the position of the PSA Group in Europe, considering our stronger market share in France, Spain and Great Britain than in Germany' (Jacques Calvet, annual report, 1990).

It was felt that the 3 per cent decrease of the European market expected in 1991, and the small increase expected in 1992, could influence the attitude of some car manufacturers, who might cut prices in order to maintain sales volume; and that this would have a severe impact on profitability: 'Under such circumstances, the efforts of the whole group must not only continue, they must be increased to reduce costs in all possible domains, while maintaining and sometimes accelerating the preparation of the future' (annual report, 1990).

The single European market starting on January 1993 was not considered as an important event by the top management of the group. Nevertheless some uncertainties were of concern. In 1991 the prices of a given car were very different from one country of the EC to another (high in countries where taxes on cars were low and where the competitive position of the firm was strong; low in countries where taxes on cars were high and the competitive position of the firm was weaker). Differences in pre-tax prices of the same car could reach 60 per cent between countries. Starting from 1993 it was recognised that the free circulation of goods would probably lead to harmonisation of prices in Europe, probably downwards. The more and more severe environmental protection regulations which would harmonise progressively – lowering exhaust emissions, fuel economy and recycling of old cars – would require higher investment from car manufacturers. The future of the 'block exemption' system, which protected the exclusive franchises of dealers, was uncertain; it was supposed to run out in 1995. If this happened, dealers could progressively distribute several marques, and megadealers (such as in the USA) could develop, putting more pressure on the car manufacturers. However, it was more probable that the block exemption system would survive 1995.

The top management of the PSA Group considered that the future of the EC was most unclear, its frontiers not delineated, and other challenges much more important, such as the group's attitude towards Japanese competitors.

The position of the EC towards the Japanese importations and transplants in Europe had varied, from being liberal in 1989 to imposing limitations at the beginning of 1991. The decrease of the European market in 1990, the active lobbying of European car manufacturers and pressure from some national governments explained some of these developments.

The EC and the CCMC (the European car manufacturers association, which later became the ACEA) started negotiations with the Japanese government (MITI) in 1991. An agreement was reached on the following basis: Japanese imports into Europe would be limited to their 1990 level – that is to say, 1.23 million vehicles a year – during a transitory period until the end of 1999.

More precisely, in the EC countries previously protected by quotas, the volume of Japanese imports would be limited:

- Under 150,000 vehicles in France (compared with 76,000 in 1990).
- Under 138,000 vehicles in Italy (compared with 44,000 in 1990).
- Under 79,000 vehicles in Spain (compared with 15,000 in 1990).

With regard to Japanese transplants in Europe (not the subject of the above limitations), there seemed to be a misunderstanding after the negotiations. Frans Andriessen (vice-president of the Commission for Trade of the EC) affirmed that both parties had agreed to limit the production of Japanese transplants to under 1.2 million vehicles until the end of 1999. On the other hand, Japanese officials from the MITI affirmed that the sales from their transplants in Europe were not limited in the agreement. Anyway nothing had been written and signed on this question; and these was nothing either concerning the sales of 'Japanese' cars manufactured in the USA and shipped to Europe. Experts estimated that the ambitions of the Japanese were to sell about 2 million vehicles in Europe, from their transplants, by the end of 1999. Starting from the year 2000 the entry to the European market would be free.

Jacques Calvet gave his opinion on this 'pseudo agreement' as 'a slice of Swiss cheese full of holes' (*Liberation*, November 1991). As a consequence, PSA executives saw another challenge as overcapacity, even in a scenario of limited Japanese competition. The political and economic developments in eastern Europe were uncertain. Experts saw Hungary, Czechoslovakia and Poland as the less risky markets, but limited in their size because of low purchasing power. In consequence, the forecasts concerning the market for cars in eastern Europe diverged. A decrease in demand in Europe was expected in 1991 partly because of the Gulf War. According to the French Bureau d'Information et de Prevision

Economiques, the European market should be about 15.2 million vehicles in 1995 (14.2m in western Europe and 1m in eastern Europe, not including the former USSR and the former East Germany). This meant an average annual growth of about 2 per cent.

The additional market of 2 million cars had to be considered in relation to the high investments most of the competitors were making: VW, General Motors, Ford, PSA and the Japanese (who would sell about 400,000 units more in 1995 and 1.2 million units more in 1999 in the most optimistic scenario). Altogether the overcapacity could reach 2 million vehicles in 1995, with a high risk of a price war and decreasing margins. All the European-based competitors, including PSA, would certainly suffer from that.

In the interim annual report in June 1991, Jacques Calvet stated:

On balance are we optimistic? No – not if we consider the confusion that has taken hold of Europe's political leaders just as we are facing ever-increasing dangers. But yes – if we consider the determination of the men and women at PSA to work harder, more intelligently, and each year with greater solidarity.

The Rover/Honda alliance
David Faulkner

The strategic alliance between the Rover Group and Honda was embarked upon after a meeting between the two companies at the Fairmont Hotel, San Francisco, in September 1978. From that time it evolved from a limited licensing agreement into a multi-functional relationship including joint development and production and a 20 per cent share exchange between the two companies.

Background

At the time of the approach to Honda, Rover was an ailing car manufacturer owned reluctantly by the British government, and still making large losses despite attempts by its then chief executive, Michael Edwardes, to modernise it through a major rationalisation plan, and a determination to curb the trade union power that had contributed in a major way to making BL an example of failing British industry.

By 1979, despite the rationalisation plan, the company was still losing money (£46 million in 1979), and was facing the prospect of a Tory government less likely to continue to finance unprofitable development. The world automobile market, after a number of years of growth, had shown signs of becoming less attractive. Rover had been pinning its hopes on the Metro, the Maestro and the Montego, but none of these models was reaching its targeted sales figures. The major problem seemed to be Rover's poor reputation for quality.

At the very least Rover needed a new product in the 'lower-medium' sector to plug a gap in its product range, but it lacked both the time and the finance to do this unaided. Still named the British Leyland Motor Corporation (BLMC), the company was facing a declining market share and had poor financial results. The world automobile industry was dominated by the multinational giants, and entry to this exclusive club did not seem to be available to Rover.

Furthermore, the Japanese were beginning to make their presence felt on the world automobile stage with their emphasis on quality, reliability, robotic methods of manufacture and fuel economy.

Among the Japanese car makers, Honda was something of a maverick. Having started its international life as predominantly a motor-cycle manufacturer, it did not develop a presence in the car market until 1963. In automobile company terms Honda was a medium-sized organisation, with a very high reputation for sound engineering, high quality and high productivity. It had a philosophy based on customer satisfaction and customer improvement, and aspired to be a global player.

Honda was a successful company, but in world automotive industry terms it was still regarded as principally a motor-cycle manufacturer. Honda's image was not sufficient at the time of the alliance formation for it to take its place naturally among the General Motors or even, in its own country, the Toyotas.

Honda had established itself well in the USA, but of the three legs of the Triad, the European leg was to Honda almost entirely undeveloped in 1979. Also Honda felt insecure in this area as it knew European tastes differed from American ones, but it did not trust its understanding of them. Furthermore, Honda did not believe it had the time to set up in Europe, and develop its own European arm from scratch. The development costs of new European models would be too great at that stage of Honda's development, and the time scale too long to be acceptable. As Mr Hayashi, managing director of Honda UK commented:

> At that time there were restrictions on exports to Europe, therefore there was no way to increase our exports there . . . Europe was suffering from over-capacity, so we had no chance to build our own factory there . . . We thought the Rover approach might help in Europe. It was company policy to be flexible with people who approached us, and to have international collaboration, so we agreed to license Rover to manufacture Honda products from knock-down kits.

However, they covered any reservations they might have had by limiting the first deal to an arm's length licensing arrangement, and some time later embarked on the building of the Honda Swindon factory to maintain their flexibility.

In 1978 Rover and Honda were approximately the same size, in terms of world sales, at about £4 billion turnover. Honda was profitable and growing fast, however, and Rover was loss making and possessed factories operating at a level substantially below capacity.

Development of the alliance

The 1978 meeting in San Francisco came about because BLMC had recognised that, if it wanted a successful future in the world automobile industry, it needed a partner. Roland Bertodo, Rover's strategic planning director, described how the BLMC top management tackled the problem:

We consciously sat down and wrote down all the automotive companies and listed the pluses and minuses against each one. Honda was the one that came out top purely because it was a similar size to us, it had growth ambitions, and a reputation for high quality at a time when quality for us was the biggest problem. It was renowned for its management at a time when we were struggling for management know-how. We were therefore attracted to Honda.

Rover lacked the financial resources and the time to produce market-acceptable new models after the lack-lustre performance of the Maestro and the Montego. It also lacked a self-confident company culture after years of loss making, union restrictive practices disputes, and poor press. It knew that it was regarded as one of the major 'lame ducks' of British industry.

Rover had access to an acceptable UK and European network of component suppliers and subcontractors. It had ample spare capacity in its factories, and could manufacture as many cars for Honda as the Japanese company could manage to sell. Rover also had an understanding of European tastes, and it could contribute to the development costs of new models to make this necessary factor come within the financial reach of both companies.

Rover was a little concerned at the outset that Honda would absorb its know-how and then walk away. As Bertodo noted:

We took steps to limit transparency and minimise informal transfer of knowledge by circumscribing a partner's opportunity to learn in an uncontrolled manner . . . The challenge is sharing sufficient skill to create a competitive advantage for both partners while avoiding wholesale transfer of core abilities.

The risk from Rover's viewpoint was at shopfloor level where close discipline in relation to information transfer was unlikely to prevail. Honda faced little risk in this area since, as John Bacchus, Rover's director of collaborative strategy, commented, the Japanese are traditionally secretive and do not seem to feel the need to demonstrate their knowledge to show their abilities.

Rover was the driving force in bringing about the alliance, and was subsequently the active partner in proposing new avenues for collaboration.

Honda responded positively to Rover's initiative, and the first deal was signed in December 1979, which was a limited licensing arrangement for BLMC to manufacture the Triumph Acclaim from Honda 'knocked-down' kits at the BLMC factory in Longbridge in Birmingham. The Triumph Acclaim was based on the Honda Accord and filled the vacant position in Rover's product range. 130,000 Acclaims were manufactured at Longbridge, and the brand achieved a regular position in the top ten UK sellers list, although it was in reality no more than a rebadged Honda.

The next phase of the partnership was the Rover 200 launched in 1984, of which 175,000 were built. This was the 'sister' model to the Honda Ballade. The

200 was a Japanese-designed car, but with Rover fenders, wheels, bumpers and interiors. Both the 200 and the Ballade were produced at Longbridge and equipped with different badges. The agreement was more than a simple licence this time. Rover had the right to change the basic design if it wished to do so for its version of the car, and there was also a manufacturing agreement to make cars for Honda. For the Ballade, Rover provided the missing European values in terms of styling that Honda needed.

In 1985, however, Honda announced its intention to build a factory in Swindon. This concerned the British press; *The Times* warned of a possible Rover takeover by stealth, and questions were asked in the House of Commons on the issue of whether this move heralded the decline of the alliance with Rover. This proved not to be the case. Honda proposed only to make engines in Swindon at first, and subsequently to make both Rovers and Hondas there. On the question of whether Honda might be in the market to buy Rover, Honda's president Mr Tadashi Kume claimed it lacked the resources. *The Times* concluded also that this was not generally how Japanese companies behaved. Organic development was much more the rule than acquisition. By 1985 Honda was still a very small player on the British market. It sold 19,000 cars in the UK that year for 1 per cent market share.

In 1986 the partnership evolved further with the launch of the Rover 800 and the Honda Legend. This was the first car that was the product of a joint develop-

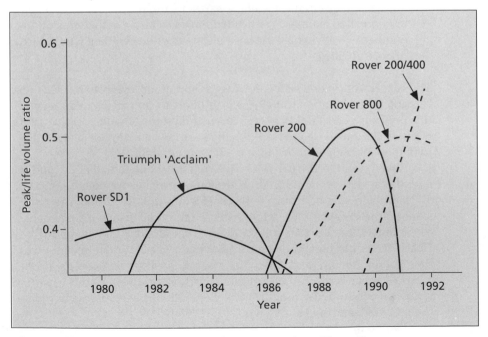

Figure 1 Progressive shortening of Rover product life cycle

ment effort. The experience of working closely together on design made the relationship between the two companies much closer, and led to a substantial improvement in Rover's understanding of quality standards. At this time Rover and Honda signed a statement of understanding to extend the partnership, which dealt with the principles of the relationship. However, it was felt that the mutual trust that had developed during the work on Project XX, as the 800 was called, was much more important than any legal document.

By this time Rover's product life cycle for new models had become considerably shorter than it had traditionally been. Figure 1 illustrates this reduction from about seven years to nearer five. Rover's productivity was also on a steeply improving curve (see Figure 2), with average costs moving rapidly towards Japanese levels. These improvements followed from absorbing the Honda philosophy that it was not in the business of making excellent cars. Its aim was to make *perfect* cars!

A further maturing of the relationship occurred in 1988. Rover and Honda agreed to stop making the Rover 800 and the Honda Legend for each other at their respective factories. It was claimed by both companies that this was because both parties wanted to make refinements that could not be easily carried out at each other's factories. However, Honda had built only 1,600 Rover 800s at its Suyama works in Japan, and Rover only 3,500 Legends in Cowley, and these low volumes were probably a major factor behind the move. The decision did not appear to damage the relationship in any way.

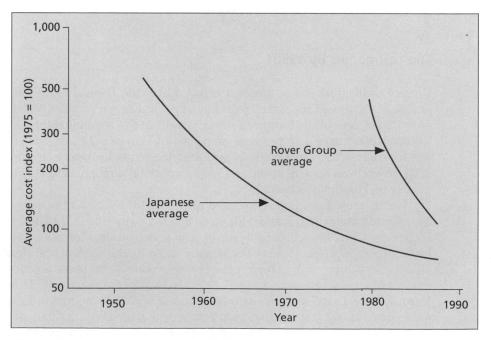

Figure 2 Comparative productivity experience

1989 saw the next project, the Rover 200/400 with its twin the Honda Concerto. This heralded a further development, in that it was the product of joint development and co-production plus the cross sourcing of components. In 1990 Rover built more than 40,000 Concertos for Honda for sale in the UK and EC to a quality standard acceptable to the Japanese.

By 1990 Rover and Honda were engaged on a further collaborative venture involving integrated development and production, and demonstrated their further confidence in the future potential longevity of the alliance by concluding a 20 per cent share exchange between Rover and Honda Manufacturing (UK) Limited.

Thus from an arm's length licensing agreement in 1979 the alliance had progressed a long way in terms of mutual development and production, and had even reached the point of minority share exchange. However, there was no attempt to collaborate in merging marketing identity, or in management off the shop floor.

Honda was still clearly a Japanese company with its own aims and ambitions. Its objectives were wider than Rover's. It sought to provide a range of cars to meet all quality segments save the top and bottom, and to become a true global player. It had a distinct strategy and Rover featured in this only as a European partner. At the time the alliance was concluded, Honda were strong in the USA and a medium-sized player in Japan. Its European presence was negligible.

Rover was fairly strong in the UK, had 2.9 per cent share of the European market and had little presence anywhere else. In fact 95 per cent of its production in 1980 was for Europe, including the UK. Similarly, Rover had its distinct identity and showed no sign of losing it.

The companies by 1990

Despite trebling its size in turnover terms during the 1980s, Honda was still not among the giants of the motor world by 1990. In Europe its sales accounted for only 1.2 per cent of the European market, and Rover's accounted for 3.1 per cent against Volkswagen's 15 per cent and Ford of Europe's 14 per cent. However, much progress had been made in performance terms for both companies since 1979. Rover was back in profit and with a coherent strategy, and Honda had an established foothold in Europe.

Honda grew from a medium-sized player in 1978 with a turnover of around £4 billion to one with a world-wide sales level of more than £12 billion, of which 66 per cent was earned outside Japan, and a net profit after tax of more than £500 million in 1990. Honda was already large in the USA at the time of the alliance formation, and motor cycles, power products and parts accounted for a quarter of total revenue, as was still the case in 1990 (see Figure 3). However, in Europe, Honda's sales of cars increased from a negligible amount in 1978 to £700 million or 191,000 units in 1990 (see Figure 4 on page 599). Not only had Honda raised its European direct sales, but it also benefited from part of Rover's sales of approximately 450,000 units.

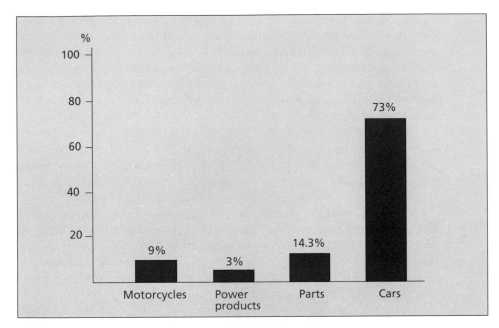

Figure 3 Percentage of total Honda sales by volume (1990)

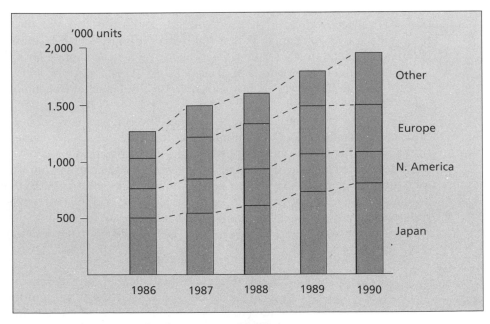

Figure 4 Honda car sales by geographical area

Honda had the characteristic Japanese total quality control attitude to manufacturing, which by lengthy tuition had been able to elevate Rover into a quality performer. It had a pragmatic attitude to design that facilitated the creation of reliable marketable cars. It had the robotics-dominated methods of manufacture that could gain the necessary cost economies in unit terms. Also it had sufficient finance to collaborate with Rover in the production of new models and this was an important attraction.

Rover aimed to become an upmarket quality executive marque with a high reputation for style, quality and reliability; and priced at a level to make the senior management fleet buyer its natural customer. It now became unashamedly a niche marketeer under its chairman Sir Graham Day, and was no longer the largest UK car producer, coming third behind Ford and Vauxhall.

However, from its position as a regular loss-maker, Rover moved steadily into profit from 1986 onwards, and in 1990, as a subsidiary of British Aerospace plc, it contributed an annual profit in excess of £50 million to its parent. But that was not the whole of the picture. Rover's overall financial performance through most of the 1980s was pretty dismal. It only became profitable with financial restructuring after its acquisition by British Aerospace (Table 1).

Sales turnover remained on a plateau at £3–4 billion and not growing, and in terms of assets Rover contracted dramatically from its bloated 1970s size. Rover's export sales were pretty stable in the late 1980s, and its UK sales showed little growth either (Tables 2 and 3).

But if quality and a regenerated reputation were prime objectives, these seemed to be established. The 800, the 200 and the 400 series were all generally acknowledged to be first-class cars from a quality viewpoint, and Rover's reputation was reflected in its profit figures. It was estimated also that the business between the two companies at that time was currently worth in the region of £500,000 annually. However, the Honda-related models accounted for only about a quarter of total Rover production (see Table 4). The much maligned Metro, Maestro and Montego were still responsible for a substantial tranche of Rover's sales.

The 20 per cent share exchange between the companies was intended as a positive demonstration of commitment. On this issue Hayashi commented that the share exchange was most important for the manufacturing and development staff, since it engendered trust, in that it showed that the partnership was for the long term. Of course, the trust had not been naive. Rover only released information on a 'need to know' basis; the Japanese likewise, and the two teams did not fraternise greatly at a social or shopfloor level. However, trust did develop as the two sides grew used to working together. Matters moved on successfully and as Hayashi said:

> The Legend, the joint Honda–Rover product, cleared the way for Honda to enter into the executive car sector of the market. Rover's interior design and European taste contributed to the success of the Legend . . . Now Rover is a truly integral part of Honda's strategy in Europe.

Table 1 Summary of Rover Group results,* 1983–7

	1983	1984	1985	1986	1987
Turnover		£ mn			
UK	1,935	1,987	2,353	2,228	1,827
Overseas	1,486	1,415	1,062	1,184	1,269
Total	3,421	3,402	3,415	3,412	3,096
Exports from UK (including above)	917	827	764	768	1,042
Profits and losses					
Operating profit (loss)	4.1	(11.7)	(34.6)	(246.4)	16.8
Exceptional losses	–	–	(15.0)	(109.2)	
Share of profits of associated companies, formerly subsidiaries	–	–	–	–	11.1
Profit (loss) before interest and taxation	4.1	(11.7)	(49.6)	(355.6)	27.9
Interest	(71.2)	(61.6)	(75.7)	(100.0)	(49.5)
Loss on ordinary activities before taxation	(67.1)	(73.3)	(125.3)	(455.6)	(21.6)
Taxation on ordinary activities	(7.2)	(7.7)	(4.1)	(6.5)	(5.2)
Loss on ordinary activities after taxation	(74.3)	(81.0)	(129.4)	(462.1)	(26.8)
Minority share of profits of subsidiaries	(3.8)	(1.8)	(1.4)	–	–
Loss before extraordinary items	(78.1)	(82.8)	(130.8)	(462.1)	(26.8)
Extraordinary profits (losses)	(64.8)	163.4	(7.2)	(430.0)	
Profit (loss) after extraordinary items	(142.9)	80.8	(138.0)	(892.1)	(26.8)
Loss on translation and other movements	(8.6)	(6.7)	(25.8)	(6.9)	(0.1)
Transfer to (from) reserves	(151.5)	73.9	(163.8)	(899.0)	(26.9)
Balance sheets					
Fixed assets	1,014.6	908.5	939.2	772.8	703.7
Other net assets	500.2	434.7	447.1	26.3	190.2
Total	1,514.8	1,343.2	1,386.3	799.1	893.9
Net borrowings	(796.5)	(571.9)	(790.5)	(1,108.7)	(560.2)
	718.3	771.3	595.8	(309.6)	333.7
Called up share capital	2,139.5	2,139.5	2,139.5	2,139.5	2,762.2
Reserves	(1,463.2)	(1,389.3)	(1,553.1)	(2,452.1)	(2,428.5)
	676.3	750.2	588.4	(312.6)	333.7
Minority interests in subsidiaries	42.0	21.1	9.4	3.0	–
	718.3	771.3	595.8	(309.6)	333.7
			Pence		
Net asset value per share	15.8	17.5	13.7	–	6.0
			£ mn		
Capital expenditure including tooling	247.7	234.2	231.5	172.8	119.8
Depreciation and amortisation	177.9	147.2	154.5	160.3	135.7
Vehicle unit sales ('000)	564	511	542	494	513
Weekly average number of employees ('000)	103	96	78	73	49
Ordinary shareholders (year end) ('000)	67	65	63	62	60

Note * These figures include all divested businesses up to their effective date of leaving the group, including Jaguar to July 1984, and Unipart, Leyland Vehicles and Freight Rover to December 1986.
Source: Rover Group.

Table 2 Total Austin Rover retail export sales, 1982–9 (units)

	1982	1983	1984	1985	1986	1987	1988	1989[*]
Passenger cars	110,328	100,165	89,709	101,821	117,963	139,289	132,720	130,500
Car derived vans	1,582	856	412	566	388	388	1,312	1,500
Total	11,910	101,021	90,121	102,387	118,351	139,677	134,032	132,000
[*] EIU estimates.								

Source: Rover Group.

Table 3 Development of the Rover Group's car sales in the UK, 1980–9

		Change on previous year			Market share	
					% change on previous year	
	Units	Units	%	%		
1980	275,798	−61,186	−18.2	18.2	−1.4	
1981	285,071	9,273	3.4	19.2	1.0	
1982	277,260	−7,811	−2.7	17.8	−1.4	
1983	332,725	55,465	20.0	18.6	0.8	
1984	312,054[*]	−20,671	−6.2	17.8	−0.8	
1985	327,955	15,901	5.1	17.9	0.1	
1986	297,466	−30,489	−9.3	15.8	−2.1	
1987	301,811	4,345	1.5	15.0	−0.8	
1988	332,607	30,796	10.2	15.0	−	
1989	312,306	−20,301	−6.1	13.6	−1.4	

[*]Excludes Jaguar.

Source: SMMT.

Thus the alliance with Honda had had a dramatic effect on Rover's quality performance, and as John Bacchus said, it no longer saw itself as a 'loser'.

The future

It was one thing to form an alliance; quite another to make it work. Two separate studies, one by Mckinsey, and one by Coopers and Lybrand showed that more than 50 per cent of alliances foundered within five years. Rover also had some experience of disappointing alliances. As Bertodo recounted, they had been in fifteen previous alliances since 1921 with, among others, Isuzu, BMW, Ferguson, Hindustani, AMC, Perkins and, at the time of the Honda negotiations, Nissan.

Table 4 Production of the Rover Group by model, 1985–9 (units)

	1985	1986	1987	1988	Jan–Nov 1989
Mini	34,974	33,720	37,210	36,574	37,193
Metro	174,466	158,546	161,285	144,701	128,930
Rover 200/Honda Ballade	65,844	63,167	80,263	95,859	84,355
New Rover 200 series	–	–	–	–	8,105
Maestro	88,848	63,722	58,280	67,406	56,032
Montego	95,874	70,623	73,447	79,316	71,221
Rover SDI	15,916	2,870	–	–	–
Rover 800 Series/ Honda Legend	–	16,029	57,111	49,894	36,787
Land Rover	23,772	19,195	20,475	22,229	17,160
Range Rover	13,314	14,494	20,815	24,021	25,962
Discovery	–	–	–	–	2,632
Total	513,008	442,366	508,886	520,000	468,377

Source: Rover Group.

Only seven could be judged successful, he commented, and only four outstandingly so.

In Bacchus' view if Honda were to exit the alliance, Rover would be unlikely to maintain the quality standards it had learned to achieve under Honda's discipline. Furthermore, Rover was still small in global terms, and its only hope would be to find another partner or establish a defendable niche. Also, some major issues appeared in 1990: Rover was losing market share in Europe and even in the UK, and the technological and financial power of Honda threatened to turn the alliance into one dominated by the Japanese company.

Hayashi saw it differently: 'If we broke apart, we would be in competition with the same technology, the same components, the same suppliers, and the same products: a duplicate of ourselves.' But an EIU article in *European Motor Business* in 1990 suggested that:

> model development in the car programme has been shifted over largely to Honda, with Rover manipulating the available hardware to encompass its upmarket and niche model ambitions. This compromise will permit a more rapid updating of the model range than Rover could otherwise contemplate, but this attachment to Honda has also given rise to uninspired styling and uncompetitively bland designs.

If there were any validity to this criticism, the joint enterprise would need some rejuvenation to succeed in the next round of competition. Hayashi was confident however:

We have strong commitment to the alliance. Even when we start production in Swindon we will still benefit from the joint supply network, and Rover is still in need of Honda's capability in product development, and quality standards. In that sense both companies have a management policy of strong commitment, because competition in Europe is very keen, and since we are already established in the UK with suppliers and co-operation with Rover this confirms our commitment.

The inevitable early problems with contrasting cultures seemed to have been largely successfully handled, as Hayashi commented:

Much endeavour and patience were needed to overcome many barriers . . . in language, culture, ways of thinking and sense of value to name just a few. By overcoming these barriers, the people of Honda and Rover were able to generate mutual understanding and trust, which eventually led to close friendship.

Bertodo confirmed his belief in the future of the alliance similarly: 'Honda have compressed our learning curve and given us better value for money by sharing resources on R and D.'

There were joint design teams working on new models. Both companies' factories produced for the other partner. There was joint sourcing of components, and many compromises were made to accommodate the respective manufacturing needs of the two partners. However, from the outset the marketing arms of the two companies remained separate. Entry into Europe by Honda did not mean the use of Rover's sales network.

Bertodo saw the alliance as requiring constant refreshening, by both sides being ready with something extra to trade at each crucial point in what he called the 'collaboration vortex' to prevent the alliance flying off centrifugally into independence, or centripetally into one-sided dependency. He saw a key part of his job as preventing Rover, in particular, from doing the latter.

Some key issues remained however: What would happen if a beleaguered British Aerospace decided to put Rover on the market? In the existing world automobile industry, was a strategic alliance a secure way to achieve competitive advantage that could be sustained in the face of keen competition by integrated corporations? And finally, do the undoubted costs involved in co-ordinating alliances lead to a competitive cost advantage in relation to the major world players in the global marketplace? Only the future would answer these questions.

Vitalograph
Chris Carr and David Lethbridge

In the summer of 1991 Norman Burden, Vitalograph's chairman and chief executive, was considering the company's strategic options. He had taken over the
chairmanship of the company in 1989 from Bernard Garbe, the son of the
founder. Vitalograph was a small, family owned, internationally based company,
manufacturing and marketing products, principally spirometers, for health-care
applications. A typical Vitalograph spirometer, illustrated in Exhibit 1, produces
a graphical analysis of a patient's breath, enabling diagnosis of any lung-function
problems. Less than a quarter of their company's sales were accounted for by the
UK, other major markets being Germany and the USA, and its main manufacturing operation was now located in Ireland. Since Norman Burden's arrival two
years previously, the company had substantially restructured and had attempted
to become more market orientated. With overheads streamlined and profits
recovering, a number of options seemed open.

Early company background

Vitalograph's success in spirometers dated back to its entrepreneurial founder
Dietmar Garbe following the Second World War. Born in Germany in 1924, Mr
Garbe had been in physical education prior to the war. Indeed, he had been in
the national gynastic team! Shortly after the war, he met and married an English
girl and came to the country, adopting British citizenship. Together they set up a
German translation service and were commissioned to translate technical manuals for importers of German high-tech medical respiratory equipment. This
equipment included blood gas analysers, ventilators, iron lungs and resuscita-
tors, and was new to the British market. The companies involved needed a UK
distributor and the opportunity was seized by Mr Garbe. Having acquired some
technical understanding from the manuals, he brought in a third partner and
formed a new company which then specialised in importing German respiratory
and anaesthesiology equipment, and also provided a bespoke service to UK hospitals.

This case was prepared by Chris Carr and David Lethbridge of Manchester Business School and is intended as a basis for class
discussion and not as an illustration of either good or bad management practice.

Exhibit 1 **The Vitalograph R-Model Spirometer**

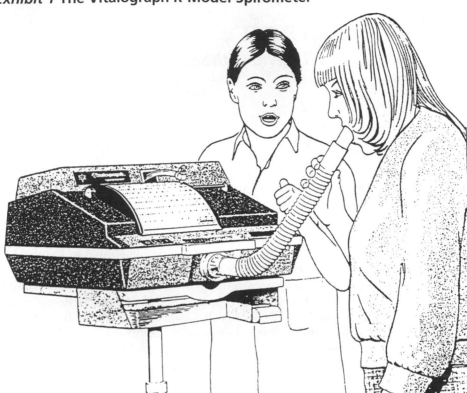

Only the Vitalograph Spirometer offers you so many diagnostic advantages for such a low investment.

In 1960 they identified the need for a simple, inexpensive and portable spirometer which could be marketed to the medical profession. A machine was developed cheaply, literally in the stables of the family house just outside Buckingham. Sales did not come easily at first, but the breakthrough came in March 1963 when the first 'Vitalograph' spirometer was delivered to a hospital in a snowstorm, just beating the hospital's 5 April budget deadline. With orders flowing in, the present company, Vitalograph Ltd, was founded at the end of the year, to concentrate on manufacturing and marketing the new machines.

By the time of the founder's death in 1980, the company had expanded considerably and its spirometers were being used in 114 countries around the world in hospitals, general practices, company health-care services and specialist testing laboratories. Though still small in terms of its 150 or so employees, Vitalograph had also become internationally based. More routine production had been relocated to a new factory on the west coast of southern Ireland in 1976 in response to local planning restrictions, and for many years it benefited from low wage rates and tax concessions. No tax was payable for the first ten years, after which the rate was only 10 per cent. The Irish factory initially cost £0.17m, plus an equal sum provided by the Irish government.

Extracts from Vitalograph's 1980 accounts are shown in Exhibit 2. These need to be interpreted carefully. Vitalograph UK accounts were consolidated to include overseas marketing subsidiaries in Germany and the USA, but accounts for Vitalograph Ireland were quite separate, even though most directors and shareholders were the same, and the vast majority of sales of products produced in Ireland were handled through Vitalograph UK.

Vitalograph's strategy 1980–89

Company structure and culture

Bernard Garbe took over as managing director and chairman following his father's death in 1980. Having served an apprenticeship with another local company, he had graduated in engineering and then gone on to work for British Aerospace, but he had also been acting as Vitalograph's R & D director at the time. His father had always run the company on a tight rein, with a somewhat autocratic management style, and the family still retained control. Mrs G. Garbe

Exhibit 2 **Extracts from Vitalograph UK and Vitalograph Ireland accounts, year ended 31 December 1980**

	Vitalograph UK (£000)	Vitalograph Ireland (IR£000)
Turnover	2,084	662
Operating profit	18.2	140.3
after charging/(crediting)		
depreciation	26.3	7.8
directors' remuneration	194.8	4.5
net interest paid	39.1	5.3
grant amortisation	–	1.0
Tax charge/(credit)	(92.4)	0.2
Profit after tax	110.6	140.1
Profit retained for year	110.6	140.1
Fixed assets	167	162
Current assets	1,294	220
Less current liabilities	1,068	52
Capital employed	393	329
Operating profit/sales	0.9%	21.2%
Operating profit/capital employed	4.6%	42.6%

was also on the board. Two non-family executives, Peter Mitchell, marketing director, and Peter Henry, production director, were joined a year later by Mike Lindsay, finance director, but these three held only a minority shareholding.

The culture was very much that of a family firm. The firm provided a comfortable source of occupation to family members, though of course its continued development and growth were also important aims. Directors (with the exception of the new finance director) and employees tended to be local, often having worked with the company or at least in the small local town all their lives. The production director had worked his way up the company having joined at the age of 21. Similarly, the marketing director had begun his career as a technician and had no outside marketing experience. Bernard Garbe was proud that his company was able to fill senior positions internally, and considerable loyalty existed between the company and its staff: 'Corporate culture is something that Vitalograph pays great attention to. Perhaps too much. However, I think that our success in achieving an unusually healthy corporate culture and "family feeling" is remarkable in view of the fact that we have such widespread facilities.'

The Irish plant proved successful and was expanded. By 1986 it employed 45 people, compared to 73 in Vitalograph UK, and capacity had doubled to a level similar to the UK operation while still offering plenty of space for expansion. Vitalograph Ltd purchased products from Vitalograph Ireland, fully packaged and ready for shipping to the international distributor. Products for the UK market, representing a little under 20 per cent of turnover were, however, modified in the manufacturing facility situated on the same site as the head office in Buckingham. There was a packaging facility and a printing unit which undertook outside work as well as handling the company's own needs for brochures, etc. The UK head office also retained responsibility for all product development and marketing. By 1986 Vitalograph UK had a turnover of £5.3m and a pre-tax profit of £77,000, and a larger profit was being generated in the Irish subsidiary. As a family company it had accumulated fairly healthy financial reserves.

Vitalograph's international position had also developed substantially by this time. West Germany and the USA each accounted for about 20 per cent, the balance being split between over 100 different countries. The organisation of selling varied by country. The UK position was strong and was handled direct from head office. In Germany, the company maintained a fairly autonomous marketing subsidiary and its agents successfully maintained its position of market leadership. A marketing subsidiary in the USA covered Canada as well. This employed eight full-time staff, handling marketing and a small distribution facility which included a warehouse. In the main, however, the company made use of the independent distribution system, which comprised about a hundred medical dealerships, serviced by about twenty commission agents. In Italy it enjoyed an excellent, exclusive arrangement with a distributor which commanded a high percentage of the market. Vitalograph also had a substantial position in the Australian market.

Exhibit 3 shows Vitalograph's accounts and international structure in the two following years, 1987–8.

Exhibit 3 Extracts from Vitalograph accounts, year ended 31 December 1988 and 1987

	Vitalograph UK		Vitalograph Ireland	
	1988 (£000)	1987 (£000)	1988 (IR£000)	1987 (IR£000)
Turnover	5,765	5,368	–	–
Operating profit (loss)	277.3	311.8	(0.5)	(14.0)
after charging/(crediting)				
depreciation	126	127		
staff costs	1,094	879		
materials, etc.	2,807	2,962		
Net interest payable	(69.5)	(68.4)	0.7	0.4
Pre-tax profit	207.8	243.4	0.2	(13.6)
Tax charge	(84.2)	(106.0)	(0.1)	(0.4)
Profit after tax	123.5	137.4	0.1	(14.0)
Dividend	(59.6)	(54.1)	–	–
Profit retained for year	140.7	95.7	0.1	(14.0)
Fixed assets	682	682	1,226	1,226
Current assets	1,826	1,967	38	18
Less current liabilities	1,511	1,667	34	18
Capital employed	997	981	1,230	1,227
Less loans and deferred tax	404	433	500	497
Equity	593	548	730	730
Operating profit/sales	4.8%	5.8%		
Operating profit/capital employed	27.8%	31.8%	0.0%	1.1%
Geographical split of sales				
UK	16%	18%	n/a	n/a
USA	18%	17%	n/a	n/a
Rest of world	66%	65%	n/a	n/a
Number of employees				
Office and management	45	45	n/a	n/a
Production and R & D	43	37	n/a	n/a
Total	88	82	n/a	n/a

Product developments

The basic Vitalograph product had remained virtually unchanged in terms of basic function and design, right up until the founder's death in 1980. Machines were extremely reliable and very accurate, and had established themselves as almost the generic name in the business, particularly in European and Commonwealth markets: the medical profession would commonly refer to a 'Vitalograph' rather than a spirometer. Of course, doctors did not necessarily buy the Vitalograph model, but the company was extremely well established in the market. Indeed, in some countries the medical profession was suspicious of modifications, and in the very conservative German market it was believed that it was better *not* to draw attention to any new features that were added, but rather to stress the reliability and long service that could be anticipated from the product.

In the early 1980s, the known manufacturers of spirometers were relatively few in number, and at the annual trade fairs some eight firms would have representatives, all of whom were on first-name terms. Competition, however, was increasing, particularly in the USA which accounted for half of the total world potential market. For example, the Japanese exhibited at trade fairs for the first time in 1981. Their models were so inferior that Vitalograph expected they would be out of the marketplace within a year, but by 1982 they had improved considerably. The increasing importance of electronics also attracted new entrants and substantially increased technological demands.

A programme to develop new technology was undertaken. Since Vitalograph's own development department at that time comprised of only one engineer and half of a draughtsman and lacked electronics skills, it came to an arrangement with London University under which a new part-electronic spirometer would be developed. Convinced it had a world-beater on their hands, the company commenced marketing with considerable confidence. Such high hopes were soon dashed, however, when the new model proved relatively unreliable and of questionable increased accuracy. To protect the company's name it was withdrawn from the market.

A crash programme was introduced to develop a more acceptable product. The UK development team expanded to just over twenty staff, taking on additional electronic engineers and people with associated software skills, drawing on other company staff or those from neighbouring companies. Utilising bought-in electronic chips, it was possible to respond to a growing trend in the marketplace for machines which could handle a greater range of parameters and measurements. For example, typical healthy comparison measurements vary according to sex, nationality, weight, etc. and such allowances were incorporated in a more advanced model. Even Chinese characters were built in! The development programme precipitated a considerable cash flow problem, which peaked in 1984, but by the end of 1987 new models were being introduced, such as the Vitalograph-Alpha which took only a year from original design to market launch.

By 1988 Vitalograph had a range of eight different spirometry systems. Some were still based on the original wedge-type bellows designs, with or without electronics or computerisation. These were 'volume displacement' or 'mechanical' type spirometers. Other spirometers supplied were the more modern 'flow sensing' or 'electronic' types. In contrast to sturdier, electro-mechanical machines which provided the core of the company's product range until the 1970s, these were more compact and were based on quite different technology. The essential task, however, still involved similar measurements and tests on air expired from the lungs, enabling the detection of a range of ailments. More expensive machines offered more substantial computational capacity, and both graphical and digital displays and print-outs. Associated instruments were also available and employed similar principles: an example being a carbon monoxide monitor, a simple instrument for home use by asthma patients. Prices of products generally ranged between £700 for small 'open-system' flow sensing models to over £5,000 for larger models at the top of the range, though the variation in manufacturing costs was much less marked.

Markets and competition

Market segmentation in spirometers was very similar in every country of the world, and fell neatly into three main user groups: hospitals, which was really a distribution classification, since there were many departments within hospitals using spirometers; occupational, which usually had special requirements often arising out of legislation, including large companies and specialist medical services for corporate health programmes; and finally, general practitioners (GPs). This latter segment displayed much greater variability by country because of different methods of payment for health care. Large GP practices were sometimes almost indistinguishable from small hospitals and clinics. There had been a strong trend in favour of occupational and GP segments, both of which tended to demand modern, more portable products which were cheaper and easier to use.

The USA was the largest world market, but it was fragmented with no competitor being able to take much more than about 15 per cent. There were many small players and frequent new entrants. One of the keys to success lay in overcoming an almost inherent difficulty of efficient distribution in such a large country. Some large companies with multiproduct lines addressed the problem using direct selling. However, local market territories were frequently too small to justify a sales person, and in recent years direct selling had proved no more successful than indirect – a trend which was expected to continue. Vitalograph was one of the largest companies in the USA in its chosen field, and it was confident that its approach, using mainly independent distributors, would continue to serve it well against other large rivals.

The USA was becoming fiercely competitive. From the mid-1980s prices had been driven down, cutting margins wafer-thin. By late 1987 there were over eighty manufacturers of spirometers showing at the American trade fairs, and any cosy marketing arrangements had certainly disappeared. Some precipitation of weaker companies was expected. Certainly at this time, however, Bernard Garbe did not perceive Vitalograph as threatened, given its size and the success of its distribution approach; indeed, it was in a 'position to significantly improve its market share over the next few years . . . provided it was strong enough to "hang on" these few years, probably carrying losses, while weaker manufacturers and distributors went to the wall. This was already starting to happen, although the writing had been on the wall for several years.'

Japanese manufacturers accounted for about 25 per cent of the world spirometer market, but Bernard Garbe did not regard them as a major threat. Their home market had been small, although this was likely to change during the next ten or fifteen years. It had also been extremely fragmented, and there was no single Japanese manufacturer with a leading presence in any of the world's major markets. He accepted, however, that some threat was posed by the number of such companies that were producing spirometers for overseas distribution. Most had almost identical equipment, and watched each other like hawks: where one was successful, it was expected that others would follow. Japanese spirometers were sophisticated in terms of data presentation and analysis, and could eventually pose some threat in Europe also, once they decided to enter.

Vitalograph's position in Europe was quite strong. Not only did it dominate the UK market, but it was also one of the leaders in Germany, though here there were two or three other formidable rivals.

Strategic choices in the 1980s

Bernard Garbe felt that 'Vitalograph's great strength historically had always been *marketing*'. He conceded that some loss of marketing focus had occurred during the later 1970s and early 1980s, due to having to set up adequate manufacturing and development facilities, but by late 1987 Vitalograph was 'strongly focused towards marketing again'. The company saw itself as the Volvo of the spirometry industry – producing lung function products that were solid and reliable, if a bit unexciting. A natural development, once the market moved towards saturation, might be just to move further upmarket, sticking to the same field. An obvious option would be to move into big box lung-testing machines. Such machines involved chambers large enough for people to go into, as opposed to them just blowing into a machine.

Niche strategy was something that the company was 'geared for', but which Bernard Garbe felt it had 'not seriously started to use yet': indeed, the simple spirometer could be viewed as being its own special niche, and on this basis the company dominated the market in most countries, though national requirements varied. Niching implied potentially better prices, high quality, but lower volumes. Numerous niches could be identified which neither Vitalograph not its competitors had yet addressed; but the necessary product development and distribution strategies would take time and tie up limited resources. Such an approach would also address the issue of indirect competition: 'The physician or hospital budget is today being allocated towards vascular dopplers (devices for analysing blood), ambulatory electro-cardio-graphical (ECG) monitors, nuclear magnetic resonance (NMR) scanners, and all kinds of other high-tech equipment which together is far greater competition than any of the direct competition that Vitalograph has (or ever will have).'

Bernard Garbe accepted that market research had 'never been one of Vitalograph's strong points'. It kept closely in touch with customers, whose repeat orders would generally only be necessary every fifteen years, and several devices were used to keep the company name in front of them; but no formal market research had been carried out to define customer needs. There were *new* products that could be sold to *existing* users, particularly with their good name and reputation, and market research might prove useful in guiding them towards these products.

Another alternative was to go for the much larger market for easier-to-use, highly portable, low-cost units. In 1985 Bernard Garbe persuaded his board to invest more in a cardio-pulmonary-resuscitator (CPR) product range. Although the initial product was poorly received, subsequent designs improved considerably and the company received national design awards. In 1971 CPR products represented less than 7 per cent of total group turnover, but were now growing at nearly twice the rate of spirometers. It was still early days, but Bernard Garbe believed these products could ultimately account for an amount of profit equal to the spirometry product range. In many ways the marketplace addressed was different, involving different specialities and entirely different distribution systems. Subsequently, the board backed a plan by Bernard Garbe to form a separate CPR division, to be headed by Marcus Garbe, the company founder's younger son.

The board also then backed another plan, aimed at a radically more decentralised organisational approach. This involved identifying profit centres to be run as autonomously as possible by managers, to allow the board to direct the company objectively and, if necessarily, ruthlessly. Bernard Garbe regarded the sales organisation as 'stronger than ever', both at home and overseas, but he was similarly keen to adopt a separate UK selling organisation. More contentiously, he was also interested in supporting US operations with a local manufacturing base, and indeed a high proportion of his own time was now being spent in the USA.

Given that Vitalograph's penetration of the potential market was low, Bernard Garbe was not keen on any less related forms of diversification. Complementary products to their main line were already being sold and others were being developed, but these activities were likely to remain limited for some years to come. Joint ventures had been attempted in a small way on several occasions, but without too much success. Although joint venture opportunities were a possibility in the marketing area, with non-competitive companies offering complementary product ranges, Bernard Garbe considered that the joint venture option really 'would be second choice'. Inward licensing, on the other hand, was being increasingly used with some success. Make-or-buy decisions were handled pragmatically, with artful marketing rather than product innovation and manufacturing being regarded as critical to success.

Bernard Garbe's policies and plans did not, however, prove popular. According to one director on the board at the time, organisational changes had been 'forced through without any great enthusiasm'; his desire for a US plant was also controversial. Both executives and other shareholders became concerned about increasing overheads and declining profitability in 1989. As a result Norman Burden, who had been taken on as a marketing consultant by the company early in 1989, was asked to take on the chairmanship. Bernard Garbe was persuaded to stand down and to take over instead as production manager of the Irish plant – a position which he was still holding in 1991.

Strategic changes under Norman Burden (1989–91)

The question of market orientation

Taking over in 1989, Norman Burden held a very different view to Bernard Garbe on the company's strategy. He did not consider that Vitalograph's response had measured up to major shifts in the market. By 1991 electronics-based products accounted for two-thirds of the market, compared to one-third ten years earlier, and even traditional products, on which the business had been built up, now had electronic add-ons. This accelerating trend had fundamentally altered the nature of the business, as products could now be introduced much more quickly due to the faster pace of change in software. Non-spirometry companies had entered the business.

There had also been a tremendous shift, particularly in Britain, from selling to the health service to selling to private industry, due partly to tighter European legislation on occupational health and other government policies. Previously, three-quarters of the market had been accounted for by hospitals, with about a quarter taken by company health care; but by 1991 this position had been reversed. The former health service market had become more commercially orientated. General practitioners, who would never previously have purchased spirometry equipment, now had more responsibility for patient testing and, thus, a need for simpler, cheaper instruments. Competition had also further intensified, particularly in the US market which was now growing at only about 4–5 per cent per year. Japanese companies still had only a modest presence there, but they had made significant entries into Europe in some market segments.

Norman Burden felt that Vitalograph had been 'really a bit complacent'. 'To say we made strategic choices then was putting on a grander title than was really justified. We still didn't attack the competition at all . . . It was very much we will continue in the same vein and, because it's a Vitalograph product, it will sell.' While the company had professed itself market-led, in reality it was not. Seeing itself essentially as a spirometry company, it had relied on sales reorganisations the effects of which had been largely confined to the UK, and on product upgrades. Until recently, no formal market research had been carried out, nor any really new product ideas introduced. In Norman Burden's view, the problem was 'a matter of corporate culture', rather than a deficiency of ideas. Product development, though sometimes successful, had been too detached from the market – an approach 'not based on hunger, but on contentedness'. Over eight years the development department had grown from 'a man and a dog' to over twenty people; but without adequate controls, its efforts had been dispersed over some 25 to 30 products, on an undifferentiated basis with ideas pursued almost as they arose. Products developed sometimes meshed poorly with production processes in Ireland.

Under Norman Burden, however, strategic planning received fresh impetus, and such exercises led to a distinctive and much sharper view of the business that the company should really be in. This thinking crystallised in the mission statement shown in Exhibit 4, and provided a framework against which more immediate rationalisation and restructuring decisions could be taken.

Rationalisation and restructuring

Norman Burden's main aim initially was to 'make the company as competent as it can be in its chosen field of endeavour'. The company's organisation was streamlined, stripping out the separate UK sales organisation previously introduced and reincorporating the CPR division. CPR products still represented only a little over 8 per cent of turnover, but were found to have been absorbing almost half of the company marketing and product development efforts – a level of commitment Norman Burden considered unjustified by market research or the company's newly emerging mission.

One priority was to improve radically Vitalograph's product development approach. Its UK development team was replaced by a smaller, much higher calibre team located on the Irish site – several with doctoral-level qualifications. Their new mandate was to contract out a substantial amount of development work. One product, developed in the USA, was now ready for launching.

Secondly, new skills were introduced into the marketing function to increase customer orientation. Moving their own technical staff into marketing functions proved a false start. A new group marketing manager recruited in mid-1989 failed to make it to board level as was hoped, and left, his task having been made slightly more difficult in a culture where outsiders were rare. Some less qualified staff left of their own volition and the company recruited a new sales manager and also a new marketing services manager, both with professional marketing backgrounds. This represented a major change in a culture proud of self-reliance.

The small production unit in the UK was closed, with the work transferred to the Irish plant. This saved four production staff directly and a further eight on related tasks, compared with only two extra production people subsequently taken on in the Irish plant. The space released was now intended for a small business park. On investigation, the small printing unit proved highly capital intensive with printing presses costing £30,000 a time; cost control was poor and it was absorbing disproportionate management time and effort. This was sold off to its management early in 1991.

Partly because of opportunities arising, the company has tended to focus more on UK and German markets, which each moved up appreciably to some 25 per cent of turnover, at the expense of the US market which fell to around 17 per cent.

Extracts from Vitalograph's accounts for the years 1989 to 1990 are shown in Exhibit 5. Profits had remained poor initially, reflecting costs borne from tackling necessary rationalisation and restructuring. However, the company now faced the future with a more streamlined organisation and a more competitive cost base, particularly in respect to overheads. Total employment fell some 20 per cent following the rationalisation programme, and the balance also altered considerably. Employment on the head office site halved; US marketing staffing was slightly trimmed; but by 1991 more people were employed in Ireland. 1991 figures suggested sales up by 40 per cent and that Vitalograph was back to making healthy profits.

Exhibit 4 **Mission statement**

The paragraphs that follow describe the long-term role of Vitalograph. They define our business; they show the main elements of how we intend to develop; and they set out the responsibilities we aim to fulfil.

Our Business

Vitalograph is an engineering-based company which manufactures and markets products internationally for healthcare applications.

Vitalograph's products are essentially simple to use and are easily transported. They adapt proven technology in an innovative way to serve the medical and allied professions and the general public.

Our Approach

1. We apply proven technology in an innovative way, with the aim of being the first to use it in our defined markets.
2. We are adaptors not inventors.
3. We are always one of the top three companies in our defined markets and never have less than 20% market share.
4. We are a manufacturer, and preserve that image for all items in our product range.
5. We stay close to our customers and have a better understanding than our competitors of the future development of demand.

Our Responsibilities

We see ourselves as being responsible to three groups of people:
Customers, by
– our closeness to them and our understanding of their needs
– our flexibility and speed of response
– our consistent and reliable quality standards in everything we do
– our genuinely international outlook
– our high level of product knowledge throughout the company
Employees, by
– making them part of the company's success
– providing them with a rewarding job in a successful company
– offering opportunities for training and for career progression.
Shareholders, by
– increasing the capital value of their investment
– providing acceptable annual dividends

Exhibit 5 **Extracts from Vitalograph accounts, years ended 31 December 1990 and 1989.**

	Vitalograph UK		Vitalograph Ireland	
	1990 (£000)	*1989 (£000)*	*1990 (IR£000)*	*1989 (IR£000)*
Turnover	6,509	5,681	3,707	2,694
Operating profit (loss)	(48.4)	3.6	550.8	286.4
after charging/(crediting)				
depreciation	78.4	124.3	78.1	89.2
staff costs `	1103	869		
materials, etc.	3,953	3,184		
Net interest payable	(110.3)	(77.4)	34.9	21.5
Pre-tax profit	(158.8)	(73.8)	349.0˙	264.9
Tax charge	11.6	17.3	54.5	1.9
Profit after tax	(170.3)	(91.1)	294.5	262.9
Dividend	–	(24.6)	591.2	88.0
Profit retained for year	(132.7)	65.6	(296.7)	175.0
Fixed assets	458	629	1,322	1,106
Current assets	2,102	1,880	1,806	1,239
Less current liabilities	1,857	1,579	1,264	234
Capital employed	703	930	1,864	2,111
Less loans and deferred tax	384	412	375	332
Equity	319	518	1,489	1,779
Operating profit/sales	(0.7%)	0.1%		
Operating profit/capital employed	(6.9%)	0.4%	29.5%	13.6%
Geographical split of sales				
UK	27%	22%	n/a	n/a
USA	14%	20%	n/a	n/a
Rest of world	59%	58%	n/a	n/a
Number of employees				
Office and management	45	48	n/a	n/a
Production and RD	21	39	n/a	n/a
Total	66	87	n/a	n/a

Note £ = IR£1.08 in 1990.
After deducting for exceptional items of IR £166,900.

Strategic choices in 1991

The market outlook in the UK and West Germany

This section describes the market situation in the UK and West Germany, Vitalograph's two most important markets, in early 1991.

In the UK spirometry end users were principally hospital specialists (both private and National Health Service) and to a more limited, but increasing, degree occupational health specialists in both the NHS and commercial employment sectors (e.g. large companies in potentially hazardous industries). The usage of these latter groups was expected to increase considerably in the future, as the COSHH regulations became more established and demanding. General practitioners in the UK were not expected to be a worthwhile target group for Vitalograph, as they generally used only less elaborate equipment such as peak flow meters. There was some potential in the longer term, in the health and leisure sector, for low-cost, easy-to-use machines.

Promotion in the UK was felt to be best targeted towards the physician-user, via regular sales representative contacts, advertising in journals recognised by physicians, and trade fairs. Wall charts and patient leaflets were also felt to be helpful.

The market potential for a hand-held spirometer was good, particularly in the UK among hospital specialists, where there was an acknowledged need for such equipment. Portability was important, but accuracy and reliability could not be compromised. A price break of £400 was likely to facilitate fast take-up, as in many cases this eliminated the need for formal purchasing authorisation. Compatibility with other Vitalograph computer peripherals was likely to enhance value perception. Increasing product sophistication could require increased training of doctors.

In West Germany there were fewer spirometers and peak flow meters per establishment than in the UK (half as many spirometers, one-third as many peak flow meters); but spirometers tended to be very much more sophisticated. However, in terms of numbers of physicians to whom it was appropriate to market spirometry equipment, West Germany represented the greater potential, since family practitioners and physicians tended to have spirometers, whereas they tended to be limited to hospital specialists in the UK. Thus, given fairly similar populations in each country, this suggested a greater number of spirometers per capita in West Germany. West German physicians were also more knowledgeable and demanding in their requirements for product features: for example, inhalatory and exhalatory evaluations were needed to satisfy private health insurance reimbursement systems, which was not the case in the UK.

The main spirometry users in West Germany were specialist internists and a small group of hospital lung specialists who were dedicated 'heavy users'. These required more sophisticated spirometers. However, most hospital doctors had access to lung/body box machines which had superseded standard spirometers.

Family doctors, etc., unlike in the UK, did not generally use spirometers but possibly represented a valuable target market.

West Germans' demands were generally more technically sophisticated than those of U.K. users. They were less keen on hand-held machines, demand being limited to the patient in-home care market as an upmarket peak flow meter. The price break here was about £425, similar to the UK figure.

Competitive positions

A summary of market positions in the UK and West Germany is shown in Exhibit 6. Company image ratings, based on user surveys carried out in these two countries, are detailed for Vitalograph and other major rivals in the appendix, which also provides 'pen pictures' of all these companies.

Vitalograph was synonymous with spirometry in the UK. There was a universal existence of Vitalograph machines by establishment (92 per cent) and a 79 per cent market share by machine. The main competitors were P. K. Morgan and Micro Medical, each with a 10 per cent market share.

In West Germany, Jaeger and Vitalograph had leadership at 29 and 26 per

Exhibit 6 Market positions in the UK and West Germany

Company	Brands in use*		Market shares (by no. of machines)	
	UK (%)	WG (%)	UK (%)	WG (%)
Vitalograph	92	35	72	26
P. K. Morgan	10	–	7	–
Micro Medical	8	–	5	–
Gould	3	1	–	0.7
Jaeger	2	38	1	29
Chest Corp	0.5	7	1	5
Ohio	1	1	–	–
Hellige	–	14	–	10
Custo	–	5	–	4
Schiller	–	4	–	3
Siemens	–	4	–	3
Draeger	–	3	–	2
MIJN/FW/Polymed	–	2	–	5
Other	4	8	6	8
No idea/don't know	19	5	8	4

* 'Brands in use' refers to the percentage of organisations having *any* machines in use by respective suppliers. Market shares are based on the percentage of the number of spirometer machines in use.
Source: Milpro.

cent respectively, but Hellige's market share at 10 per cent, had also to be seen as a successful and serious threat. Additionally, Custo had achieved reasonable success (4 per cent) within a relatively short time. Market leaders had less dominating leadership than was the case in the UK, and the market was distinguished by more aggressive and successful competitive marketing.

Brand awareness was even less developed in West Germany than in the UK. On average, the West Germans considered their machines to be twice the price of UK machines. Vitalograph machines averaged £1,235 in the UK and DM 4,200 in West Germany. Typically, Jaeger machines were perceived to be the most expensive (emphasising the Rolls-Royce image) and Vitalograph the cheapest (emphasising a very functional but 'nothing special' product with no brand image).

Generally, spirometers currently available were considered satisfactory in West Germany. Dissatisfaction typically related to out-of-date machines which were slow or cumbersome to use and which produced inaccurate or unreliable results. Accuracy had even more important financial implications in the context of West German private medicine. Many such old machines were Vitalographs, which made it important for the company to ensure that its image was identified with newer, more elaborate line extensions. Jaeger's marketing created an image that was more highly rated on innovation, product durability, good product range and speed of response to enquiry; though qualitative research suggested perceptions of 'arrogance' with Jaeger.

Strategic options

To avoid the trap of strategic planning becoming divorced from action, 1991 was 'getting on with it year'. Norman Burden considered that there was still more to do to reinforce Vitalograph core business. An immediate priority was to exploit the 'huge shift' in the balance of the market (already discussed) by improving the existing product range even further. One product was being upgraded in terms of size and brightness to meet the needs of pharmaceutical companies' research laboratories – features which were also expected to appeal to other segments of the market. The flagship product was being further updated and provided with a better printer and a better screen, and further updating.

The company's new mission effectively precluded the option it had been 'drifting into', of going for big box lung-testing machines. No market research or costings had been carried out, but the strategy had been 'implicit in corporate thinking' up to the point where Norman Burden had joined the company. The view had simply developed that this was the natural progression once the market became saturated. Yet strategic reviews highlighted many distinctive features of this new type of market: it would involve major capital investment in production, and selling less user-friendly products in a different price range, to a different, somewhat limited market characterised by long drawn-out purchasing decisions. Norman Burden was against any plans for diversification, laid 'on sands'.

Market changes provided scope for more closely related diversification. One new, simpler product developed to meet general practitioners' needs was now being sold through pharmaceutical wholesalers (with whom previously the company had no contacts), who sold on to retail chemists, who were in turn responding to prescriptions issued by GPs. 'That really is a move across the [Ansoff diversification] grid. We've had to learn a whole new set of skills for that, that we didn't have before. So the pattern of our customer basis is very different than even three years ago.' Changes in the market were also opening up opportunities to sell existing products to new customers, and the company was engaged in a search to identify these.

Other possible related forms of diversification included software-driven products such as instruments for testing hearing or hearts, sold essentially to the same markets. Further analysis of market research could pin down exactly which new products and market segments the company should be targeting.

Norman Burden shared his predecessor's reservations about joint ventures, considering them as something of 'a mixed bag'. Acquisition was another route to growth, but involved sensitive stakeholder issues as 'it changes the essential nature of the company'.

Now that the restructuring was well under way, Norman Burden was reconsidering Vitalograph's strategic options in the light of a detailed strengths, weaknesses, opportunities and threats appraisal he had had carried out. Having been taken up with so many immediate matters, it was 'interesting to look at this, because I haven't looked at it for months'. There was no shortage of opportunities. For example, the 'EEC as a gateway for foreign licensing' had been recognised as an opportunity back in 1987, but perhaps it was time to take this seriously? Eastern Europe also represented an opportunity, having already contributed to the West German subsidiary's recent sales boom. France might also offer business opportunities? A lot of strategic thinking had been done, but the many options now needed evaluating to establish priorities for action over the next year or so.

Appendix Company image ratings

Vitalograph and Jaeger were assessed in both the UK and West Germany. Additionally, P. K. Morgan, Cardiokinetics and Mercury were assessed in the UK, and Dego, Hellige, Custo and Polymed in West Germany. Respondent users were asked to rate each company against each feature on a linear scale of 1–6, 1 being excellent. A summary of company image ratings by attribute is given below, after which brief 'pen pictures' are outlined for Vitalograph and each of its major competitors in these two major markets. Scores range from 1 to 6, a low score of 1 being excellent.

Vitalograph

> It's the Ford Escort or Fiesta – they do a good job without much mess . . . simple and reliable! (hospital specialist, Birmingham)

Overall, Vitalograph was ranked for each attribute as 'quite good' to 'good'. Vitalograph was also seen as offering the most complete after-sales service at a fair price. Product range was, however, not perceived as extensive or as sophisticated as Jaeger, and the company's representatives were less highly ranked. In Germany, Vitalograph was also perceived as market leader in terms of number of machines in use, but it was perceived as behind Jaeger and Hellige on quality.

Jaeger

In the UK Jaeger was largely associated with body box machines. It was per-

	Vitalograph	*P. K. Morgan*	*Jaeger*
UK			
Durability of equipment	4.5	3.5	3.8
New product development	3.6	3.3	3.8
Speed of enquiry response	4	3.8	3.7
Good product range	3.9	3	3.3

	Vitalograph	*Hellige*	*Jaeger*
West Germany			
Durability of equipment	4.4	4.2	4.3
New product innovation	3.3	4	4.3
Speed of enquiry response	4	3.4	4
Good product range	3.5	3.6	4.1

Source: Milpro.

ceived as above average on almost every front except on purchasing deals. Jaeger scored particularly highly on new innovations (1.8), product range (1.8), and durability of equipment (1.7). In West Germany it was perceived as number one on quality, range and commitment to the lung-testing market. On the other hand, Jaeger was associated with expensive products and its major interest was seen as limited mainly to body box units for hospital lung/chest specialists. It was not perceived as good on after-sales service, which all respondents felt to be a primary consideration when selecting new equipment.

P. K. Morgan

Overall, P. K. Morgan scored only mediocre to quite good. It was relatively stronger in the south of Britain, on its after-sales service and on its range of functions offered; but it was overpriced.

Mercury, Cardiokinetics and Micro Medical

Few respondents had heard of these, so scores were less reliable. Mercury scored an average rating of 3.0 (quite good), but was poorer on discounts, extent of product range and experience in lung function testing. Cardiokinetics scored above average at 2.0 in some areas such as discounting, and adequacy of response to enquiries, but was inconsistent and was particularly poor on after-sales service. Micro Medical had the worst company image overall, but did better on its level of innovation, the knowledgeability of its sales representatives, supply and delivery service and approachability. It was not rated as a prime competitor.

Hellige

Hellige had a reputation for high-quality, if expensive, products and was considered to have fairly good experience in the spirometry field; but users found products overcomplex, and difficult to use. Hellige was better known for ECG machines. It rather sells on its company name and its products were insufficiently user friendly.

Polymed

Polymed's products were known to a limited extent in Hamburg and Munich, but not Frankfurt. They were perceived as easy to use and they offered the routine range of evaluations required, and also the facility to assess the more specialist non-routine functions. Polymed's printers were considered poor. It performed relatively better on discounting and after-sales reputation, but in general it was well behind Hellige.

Custo

Custo was a new entrant. Its overall rating was 'quite good' (3.0); but it was considered poor in West Germany on after-sales service, on the quality of its representatives and on its 'willingness to negotiate prices'.

Dego

Dego was hardly known. It scored particularly poorly on its experience in lung function testing.

Of other competitors, *Draeger* was only mentioned in Hamburg and its products were considered cumbersome and expensive. *Siemens* was also involved, but the sole respondent comment referred to its poor after-sales service – a reputation likely to prohibit use of the company's products.

The News Corporation
Julie E. Norton and Leslie P. Willcocks

During the 1980s the group of companies constituting The News Corporation grew into one of the largest multinational communications businesses in the world. Based in Australia, the United Kingdom and the United States and with interests in newspapers, magazines, printing, publishing, paper making, film and television, turnover in the year to 30 June 1991 reached over £5 billion. Rupert Murdoch has been the chief executive since 1953.

Early years and growth to 1980

The company was established in Australia in 1923 by Rupert Murdoch's father, Sir Keith, and in its first year, with the founding of *The News* in Adelaide, made profits of A$8,000. Throughout the 1950s and 1960s growth was solely in Australia, with the company acquiring interests in regional newspaper and book publishing and television. By 1980 the company was publishing the only national newspaper, *The Australian*, two national magazines and over twenty provincial newspapers. Interests in book publishing and television continued along with the addition of film making, record production, farming and transport.

The profitability of this Australian base was the springboard to multinational status. It provided the financial backing for the 1968 purchase of the UK-based News of the World Organisation, publishers of the *News of the World* (*NOTW*) Sunday newspaper. Since then expansion in the UK has also been mainly in the areas of printing and publishing. By 1980 News International Ltd, the UK subsidiary, was publishing the *News of the World* and the *Sun*, newspapers with the largest circulation in the UK, and had interests in magazine and book publishing, printing, warehousing and transport. During the early 1980s this subsidiary was the major contributor to The News Corporation's profits.

From 1973 with the purchase of the Express Publishing Company of San Antonio, Texas, the company also operated in the United States. During the 1970s expansion in the USA occurred in the areas of local newspaper publishing (the *New York Post* was acquired in 1976) and in magazine publishing (the *Star*, a national magazine, was founded in 1974 and the *Village Voice* and *New York Magazine* were acquired in 1977).

However, it was not until 1980 that all the Australian, UK and US diverse interests were brought together under the full corporate control of the Australian parent company. Before then The News Corporation's investment in the UK had been achieved through a 49.9 per cent interest in News International Ltd. These two companies then each owned a 50 per cent interest in the US subsidiary, News America. In 1980 The News Corporation acquired the 50.1 per cent of News International that it did not already own.

This restructuring effectively transformed The News Corporation from a company with part-interests around the world into an integrated group with full control over the capital and resources if its subsidiaries. The full consolidation of these subsidiaries enabled reported turnover to increase from A$280m in June 1980 to more than A$1bn in June 1981. The structure and main operations of the multinational as at 30 June 1980 are shown in Appendix 1.

The Murdoch formula

The News Corporation's annual report for 1980 outlined the group's approach to its early growth and development:

> Over the years expansion has been both by original start-up and acquisition. Typically, acquisition has been followed by a mobilisation of energies and talents to transform both the professional quality and the market performance of old or failing publications . . . In virtually every market where [The News Corporation] operates it has achieved its position by first purchasing the weakest existing publication and slowly restoring its viability.

The management of the *Boston Herald-American* newspaper acquired in December 1982, saw this approach continuing into the 1980s. For a number of years the paper had been performing badly. It had only 18 per cent of the advertising market, compared with the 82 per cent of its competitor the *Boston Globe*, a circulation on weekdays of only 227,000 copies against the *Globe*'s 507,000 and 214,000 against 779,000 on Sundays. The paper had lost more than £6.5m in the twelve months before its acquisition.

As a precondition of ownership The News Corporation obtained an agreement with the unions on a reduction of staff from 826 to 542. Once in possession, its own management team was installed with a brief to brighten the paper's image and sharpen its editorial direction. The name was shortened to the *Boston Herald*. Graphics were redesigned. A switch was made from a four-column format to seven columns in order to print more news on the page. Sports, fashion and weather coverage were all expanded, and editorials were given a clearly defined point of view. In addition, an electronic editing system was installed, 2,000 new vending machines were put in place and, in April 1983, a Wingo competition was started.

In the first year of full ownership losses were halved. Weekday sales increased to 348,000 and Sunday sales to 287,000. Advertising revenues increased by 29 per cent, although the paper's market share remained at 18 per cent.

In September 1983 a Sunday sports pull-out was launched, and in 1984 a more comprehensive television book and new colour fashion section were added. In 1985 the paper was 'repositioned to appeal to a younger, more affluent readership'. As a result, in 1986 the *Boston Herald* reported its first profits in more than ten years.

Television and film making

The 1980s saw The News Corporation accelerate its real growth and development. During the early 1980s expansion continued to focus on traditional product areas. Major acquisitions included Times Newspapers Limited in the UK, and in the USA the *Boston Herald* and *Chicago Sun-Times* newspapers, *New Woman*, a general interest magazine and a group of technical and travel magazines. By 1984 turnover had nearly doubled to over £1.2bn (A$1.9bn). The financial results of The News Corporation during the 1980s are summarised in Appendix 2.

However, in 1984 a programme of expansion saw the beginnings of a major geographical and product shift. This expansion was USA based. It aimed to transform The News Corporation into an integrated global communications group, with a place in all parts of that industry from newspapers to television, from magazines to film.

In 1984 The News Corporation acquired the film company Twentieth Century Fox for £400m. This company was in a poor financial position. In 1984 it had lost £60m on revenues of £520m, it was heavily indebted and its net worth had fallen from £260m to just over £35m. A successful future would require large injections of cash, up to about £350m a year on making programmes, not to mention the £100m required to finance interest payments. On the plus side, the purchase created an integrated entertainments company, and provided access to studios for making films and TV programmes, and a film library valued at £700m. For one commentator.

> It was a brilliant thing that Murdoch did, coming into Hollywood when he did. It wasn't anything that required a mental giant to realise. It just took someone who understood media on a worldwide basis to realise that there would be a greater and greater need for software. So if you had a steady source of software, it would be very beneficial to you. (Lee Isgur, first vice-president, Paine Webber, New York)

To complete the picture, in 1985 six television stations in the USA were acquired from the Metromedia broadcasting group at a cost of £1.25bn. Though operationally very profitable, this company had suffered from high interest charges on debt incurred from an earlier leveraged buyout. Rupert Murdoch's purchase involved paying only £160m in cash but taking over £1bn in high-interest debt, most of it in the form of 'junk bonds'. These involved annual payments of £80m until 1988 when capital repayments fell due at a rate of an additional £130m per annum.

Refinancing packages were organised with the objective of replacing high-interest debt with sources of finance at lower rates of interest. In particular, in early 1986 News Corporation offered debt holders a swap of all the Metromedia 'junk bonds' for £1.2bn of preference shares in a newly established subsidiary. Fox Television. These shares at 13 per cent had a lower coupon initially than the Metromedia bonds but rose to 15 per cent after two years. Of particular advantage to The News Corporation was the fact that, under Australian accounting regulations, these preference shares could be classified as equity, thus having a beneficial effect on the group's reported gearing levels. To encourage acceptance, any of the shares not redeemed by 1989 could be converted into The News Corporation equity.

During 1985 and 1986 these US acquisitions were restructured into three principal operating groups:

- Twentieth Century Fox Film financed, produced and distributed television programmes and theatrical motion pictures throughout the world. The company had a film library of more than 2,000 titles, including such classics as *Star Wars* and *Butch Cassidy and the Sundance Kid*, plus syndicated TV series such as *M*A*S*H* and *Dynasty*.
- Fox Television Stations owned and operated seven independent television stations in New York, Los Angeles, Chicago, Washington DC, Dallas, Houston and Salt Lake City (acquired in 1989). These are all within the top ten US television markets (and include the first three).
- Fox Broadcasting Company (FBC) provided first-run original entertainment programming by satellite to independent television stations. By 1990 FBC had signed up over 120 independent stations as affiliates. Together with Fox Television stations they gave FBC the ability to deliver its programmes to 80 per cent of the total US network. The goal was to create, in effect, a fourth national television network for the USA.

For Rupert Murdoch this consolidation confirmed that:

> The News Corporation is now a multi-national, multi-media, company . . . at the forefront of global marketing, ready to encourage the cross fertilisation of ideas between continents, and the different media within them . . . The News Corporation is a citizen of the global village. (The News Corporation annual report, 1985)

However, these purchases had two further significant implications for The News Corporation. Revenues and operating profits increased, but so too did debt levels. Rupert Murdoch had to be careful that his acquisitions, and the debt associated with them, did not breach bank loan agreements which required that total borrowings should not exceed net worth by more than 10 per cent. Furthermore, as US law prevented foreign citizens from holding more than 25 per cent of any company with a broadcasting licence, in 1985 Rupert Murdoch became a US citizen.

The strategy of globalisation

In a speech to the International Institute of Communications in September 1988, Rupert Murdoch confessed that he did not have a very detailed strategic plan:

> If in 1980 we had attempted to chart on paper the destiny of our company, we would never have anticipated the 30 very diverse acquisitions we made on four continents, almost all of which arose from unique and unanticipated events. Business situations and business opportunities simply change too quickly for there to be much point in loading ourselves down with piles of strategic speculation.

He has, however, asked himself three questions about the globalisation of the media:

> Is a global communications network a reality? Yes. Are there really going to be world-wide media networks? Yes. Is it really going to be possible for an advertiser to achieve, in practice, a single order with the media of his choice across the world? Yes.

Other media groups had come to similar conclusions. For example, in its 1988 annual report, Time Inc. stated that 'by the mid-1990s, the media and entertainment industry will consist of a handful of vertically integrated, worldwide giants'. In this period the media could be perceived as tremendous growth industries, with long-term growth encouraged by rising real incomes and new technologies, which, for example, saw US communications spending growing half as fast again as GNP between 1960 and 1990.

The attraction of globalisation was based on the belief that tastes, income levels, technologies and even political philosophies around the world were converging on the American model, producing strong demand for American-style films and television programmes. In 1988, for the first time in history, foreign television stations spent more on American movies than stations in the USA itself.

Combining globalisation with integration was expected to increase profits through economies of scale. For example, a group's publishing house could gain preferential access to authors for potential movie subjects. Through its cable or satellite television network it would have a ready market for its film output and could pay more to attract best-selling authors or star directors by putting them to work on numerous related books, films or television projects under one roof.

Rupert Murdoch – The Wizard of Oz

> He's an expansion minded person, he's wanted to buy assets, he's wanted to take over, to move around the world, to build his media empire. But he also wants to retain control. (Australian financial analyst)

What was unique about The News Corporation was that it was not a faceless multinational, but an organisation keenly linked to its chief executive – as a 1990 UK television programme commented, it was Murdoch's 'Empire', built on his 'vision, ruthlessness and daring'.

Rupert Murdoch himself managed the various businesses through the 'formulae' that he had for their products. As a former newspaper editor explained: 'He talks in formulae terms. He has formulae for newspapers. There is the broadsheet formula, the popular formula. There is the downmarket tabloid formula, and so on.'

The implementation of these 'formulae' was achieved through the appointment of known and trusted lieutenants to run key products or business segments. However, the whole management structure was very informal with no defined responsibilities. One aide suggested that The News Corporation was 'an emotionally driven and bonded company, where executives don't spend time guarding territories because nobody has one nailed down'. Another suggested that Rupert Murdoch's idea of management was to put in a manager and put in someone beside him and not quite tell either of them what they were doing. A News International executive confirmed: 'I think he does do that. I don't think he does it to undermine the original person. I think he thinks that if the two can work off each other things will improve.'

Rupert Murdoch disliked committees, bureaucracy and red tape. The worldwide headquarters in midtown Manhattan, USA, employed barely 60 people, with hardly a memo in sight and communications kept to a bare necessity.

This management style was supplemented by an extremely efficient reporting system. This focused on a weekly document known as the 'Flash', for which each operating unit had to provide a summary of its operating results. These had to include the budgeted figures for every aspect of its affairs, set against the actual figures for the week, and then compared with the same week in the previous year. Each Thursday it was passed to headquarters with Rupert Murdoch studying it over the weekend. He might then casually ring to query a figure. The call might come only one week in a year, but it kept everyone on their toes for the other fifty-one. Control was also achieved by unannounced 'parachuting-in' trips to check in person on the details of a business's activities and management, or to take personal control at key moments. As a News International executive confirmed:

He really is the driving force and most major decisions are made by him . . . even relatively minor decisions – like whether we start our TV burst of advertising now or do we put it back three weeks. Those are the sort of things that would be discussed with him before the final timings are decided . . . He does like leading from the front and where there's likely to be a bit of excitement he'll wade in.

I think his biggest advantage is understanding the businesses that he's in . . . He can get down to the core of the business and has a lot of vision as to where that business ought to be going.

Maintaining control also required that Rupert Murdoch looked outside of the business to the regulatory environment that might constrain his activities. Most countries believed that the media was an industry whose importance required regulation, particularly regarding foreign ownership, concentration and cross-ownership. Controlling a business with a global reach, crossing several media products, Rupert Murdoch was likely to find himself affected by national regulatory systems. Many commentators have suggested that it is his political friendships that have bought him influence in this area.

The television programme *Empire* suggested that the support of Murdoch's newspapers for Margaret Thatcher in the 1979 general election helped to ensure that his acquisition of Times Newspapers in 1981 was not referred to the Monopolies and Mergers Commission, and certainly the government called a three-line whip to stop any referral.

In 1979 the Australian government amended the rules regarding the ownership of television stations from a requirement that an owner be resident in Australia to one requiring only that an owner be an Australian citizen. This enabled Rupert Murdoch to acquire Channel 10 in Melbourne even though he was no longer resident in Australia. These amendments were christened by the Australian press 'the Murdoch amendments'.

However, as one commentator has put it: 'his personal politics are right-wing . . . but he's opportunistic in his business dealings. He doesn't support only right-wing leaders – he supports winners. And he supports people who are going to promote his business interests.'

Often it was his own personal character, name and reputation that enabled him to affect perceptions and achieve his aims. As Mark Fowler, former US Federal Communications Commission Media regulator commented:

It became pretty evident, fairly quickly, that this man had big plans, had an enormous vision of what could be and had the courage and apparently the wallet to back it up. He saw things other people didn't see and was willing to take risks and was willing to pay some extraordinary high prices.

Progress in Fleet Street

I would rather buy a television station that is losing $1m for $20m than pay

$180 million for its competition . . . Our greatest assets are the ones we have created or bought for nothing: *The Times*, the *Sunday Times* and the *Sun*.

These comments from Rupert Murdoch in large part summarised his acquisition strategy. This is nowhere better exemplified than in his purchase of Times Newspapers Ltd (TNL) in 1981. In 1980 TNL lost in excess of £10m. The News Corporation, through its subsidiary News International, purchased the paper for £25m. The pattern of losses continued into 1981, even with investment of over £20m. The early 1980s also saw problems with the other newspapers in the Fleet Street stable.

The *News of the World*'s sales of 4 million copies, which made it the weekly newspaper with the widest circulation in the UK, disguised a basic weakness in the popular Sunday market of a contracting circulation base, 30 per cent smaller overall than a decade before. In September 1981 a free colour magazine, *Sunday*, was added to the paper. Its aim was to broaden the appeal of the *NOTW* to include more young people and the 50 per cent of the *Sun*'s readers who did not read the *NOTW*. As the only popular weekend magazine and with its large circulation, *Sunday* provided advertisers with an alternative to television and women's magazines. It was therefore able to command the highest page rate of any newspaper publication. Within a year the *NOTW* had reversed its trend of falling sales.

The *Sun* was being threatened by competition from a new paper, the *Daily Star*, whose circulation had grown to 1.5 million. The *Sun* made a move unprecedented in the industry and reduced its cover price from 12p to 10p to meet the *Daily Star*'s lower price, and in June 1980 began a promotion campaign, mailing 'Bingo' cards to every household in Britain. By 1981 the *Sun*'s circulation was established at 4 million copies – 1 million more than its nearest rival. However, the combined losses of *The Times* and the *Sunday Times*, together with the substantial investment in promoting the *Sun* and launching the *Sunday* magazine nearly eliminated the UK subsidiary's reported profits for 1982.

By 1985, however, *The Times*' circulation had risen to over 485,000, up 200,000 on the levels of four years previous. Advertising revenues in the year increased by 35 per cent (having increased by 31 per cent in the year before). This had been achieved on the basis of a traditionally loyal market, the appointment of new people in management and editorial, savings from economies of scale, some reduction in staffing and aggressive selling of the paper. However, the cost of maintaining a low cover price, coupled with costs of production, still kept it from making a profit. The paper's future profitability lay in cutting production costs, while its competitive strategy required uninterrupted production to make inroads into competitors' markets (particularly the *Daily Telegraph*) and to maintain advertising revenue.

The *Sun* in the same year increased circulation to 4.165 million and the *News of the World*, having been relaunched in 1984 in tabloid format, increased to 5.2 million. These two papers had become the dominant contributors from the UK to multinational profitability. The increasing profitability of the UK operations is detailed in Appendix 3.

The *Sun*'s production, however, was stuck at around 4 million due to limited printing press capacity at its Bouverie Street site. The *Sunday Times* was publishing larger and larger editions due to increases in advertising space, but was also held back from expanding and taking further advertising due to the lack of press capacity at the Grays Inn Road site. Negotiations to lengthen print runs did occur at both sites, but the wage increases expected by the print unions appeared prohibitive to management.

In terms of increasing revenues and profits from increased circulation and advertising, Rupert Murdoch's strategies at News International had been fairly successful. The major problem in 1985 seemed to be how to secure continued stable growth for all News International's Fleet Street titles.

Industrial conflict

It was in 1979 that Rupert Murdoch announced his intention to build a new printing plant at Wapping in Tower Hamlets, London. By 1982 plans had also been developed to build a new plant at Kinning Park, Glasgow, to enable the *Sun* to be faxed electronically and printed in Scotland, saving the £3m spent each year on airfreight. By summer 1984 News International had invested nearly £100m in these new plants.

That both plants remained idle was due to the nature of industrial relations within the newspaper industry. Changes in production and working required negotiation and agreement by the unions involved. As far as the Wapping plant was concerned, the design, layout and technology there, though offering better working conditions, did mean a reduction in the number of jobs on offer. The unions were not prepared to negotiate those jobs away quickly or cheaply. The managing director of News International, Bruce Matthews, indicated his frustration in this period by saying that the company could 'no longer tolerate being bled to death by unnecessary industrial action' by employees who 'have the advantage of industrial blackmail each night'.

Negotiations broke down in February 1985 and in March News International announced that it was to start a new London evening paper, *The Post*, to be printed at Wapping together with the *Sun* and the *News of the World*. The feasibility studies to determine the profitability of this new paper enabled News International management to install new technology and a new workforce at Wapping, and to establish a new distribution system for the papers, thus bypassing the involvement of all the old unions.

Much of this was kept secret from the unions, but in time they became concerned at developments and actively sought to negotiate terms and conditions for a transference to Wapping. In the negotiations that did take place up to January 1986 management put forward proposals that were so restrictive (as far as the unions were concerned) that acceptance was extremely unlikely and a resort to industrial action the only likely response. On 24 January 1986 the unions declared strikes across News International's four titles.

News International's immediate response was to issue dismissal notices to all those on strike on the grounds that their action constituted a breach of their contracts of employment. All production of News International's titles was transferred to Wapping, with the unions being able to bring little pressure to bear to disrupt production or distribution.

The report and accounts of News International to June 1986 included an exceptional item of £66m as the cost of moving to Wapping. However, operating profit before exceptional costs nearly doubled to £81m (and this included results for the six months prior to the move to Wapping), and increased again the following year by a further 65 per cent to £133m. In his review of 1986, Rupert Murdoch summed up the situation thus:

> Instead of being handicapped by the limitations of old technology and the restrictive practices of the print unions, we are now free to develop our British newspapers in a rational and business-like manner. No longer are we production-dominated and, in spite of extra costs incurred by the emergency move, the benefits are beginning to flow.

Towards the 1990s: the sky is the limit?

During the second half of the 1980s The News Corporation continued to expand and develop in its traditional product and market areas. Appendix 4 details the major acquisitions and disposals of this period, and Appendix 5 outlines the structure of the multinational by 1991.

The two major acquisitions of this period were the Australian *Herald and Weekly Times* (*HWT*) in 1987 and the American Triangle Publications in 1988. The first acquisition was made against the background of major changes to Australia's media ownership laws. In late 1986 the government proposed that the previous limit of two television stations per proprietor be replaced by a much larger limit: ownership of television stations broadcasting to 60 per cent of the national audience. At the same time no person was allowed to own a major national newspaper and a television station in the same city. This triggered a realignment of Australian media interests as companies saw the opportunity to create a national newspaper or television network. The News Corporation acquired the *Herald and Weekly Times* and divested itself of its television holdings.

This was the biggest newspaper takeover in the world at that time, adding more than 75 titles to The News Corporation, giving it nearly 70 per cent of Australia's print media and making it the largest publisher of English-language newspaper titles in the world. That Rupert Murdoch, a foreign national, could control so much of Australia's print media was due to the Australian government applying discretion, and refusing to implement its Foreign Takeover Act.

However, the increased debt involved with this acquisition and the acquisition of Triangle Publications was of such magnitude that Rupert Murdoch was obliged, in 1988, to commit The News Corporation to a debt reduction of £570m to £3.5bn by June 1989. This commitment did not restrain the company from its expansionist policies, exemplified by the launch in the UK on 5 February 1989 of Sky Television, a European television network broadcasting direct by satellite.

Satellite television was not a new venture for The News Corporation. In 1983 the company had acquired a controlling interest in Inter-American Satellite Network (renamed Skyband). Although soon withdrawing from this, The News Corporation went on to acquire a controlling interest in Satellite Television plc (SATV), which broadcasted English-language programming by satellite to cable systems across Europe. This venture, however, was never profitable, with advertising revenues far less than expected. It was this satellite operation that was relaunched in the UK and the Republic of Ireland in 1989 as Sky Television.

Sky offered four television channels, Sky Channel (renamed Sky One), a general entertainment channel targeted at a young (15–45) audience; Sky News, which offered a 24-hour news service; Sky Movies, a feature film channel, made available free of charge for a 'preview' period, but converted into a subscription channel early in 1990; and Eurosport, offering sports programmes.

The UK had regulations regarding the cross-ownership of media interests, including a requirement that no national newspaper proprietor might own more than 20 per cent of a television company. However, as Sky Television was beamed on channels rented from the Luxembourg-controlled Astra satellite, it fell outside the UK government's jurisdiction, even though its programmes were aimed almost exclusively at a UK audience. Rupert Murdoch was therefore able to own newspapers with 25 per cent of the national UK market as well as his four television channels.

There were fewer subscribers than expected. When Sky was launched advertisers were given guarantees that 2.5 million UK households would be receiving its programmes by the end of 1990. This was subsequently scaled down to a target of 1.5 million. By the middle of 1990 the company was able to claim that over 900,000 people had bought or rented satellite receiver dishes with 658,000 receiving Sky via cable and master antenna, and that about 770,000 homes had subscribed to the movie channel at £10 per month.

Although stringent cost reductions were implemented (one of Rupert Murdoch's maxims being that it was always easier to take a million off costs than add a million to revenues), the performance of Sky Television had marked financial consequences for The News Corporation. In the year to 30 June 1990, £134m had been invested in the venture; however, losses of nearly £10m per month were being incurred and it was estimated that £400m of investment would still be required through to the end of 1991. It was certainly true that, as Rupert Murdoch admitted at the 1989 Edinburgh Television Festival: 'were it not for the strength of our newspaper group and our human and capital resources, we surely could not have afforded to have doubled the number of television channels available in Britain'.

Rupert bears the debt burden

In March 1989 Rupert Murdoch announced plans to launch a new investment company – Media Partners International (MPI). The aim was to raise approximately £850m from shareholders which would then give the company access to £2.6bn when borrowings were included. This was to be spent on buying media and communications companies all over the world. The News Corporation was to hold only a minority (20 per cent) stake, but would have a ten-year management contract to run the company. The venture's first acquisition was to be Harper & Collins, the publishing interest of The News Corporation. This was to be sold for £560m with £170m remaining in MPI as The News Corporation's equity stake.

By June 1989, however, MPI was delayed, with firm commitments for equity stakes amounting to only £250m, and in January 1990 it was abandoned. There were reports of considerable resistance by potential investors to the idea of effectively making 'a blind bet' on Rupert Murdoch, and to the fact that the deal involved The News Corporation selling its publishing interests to reduce its debts. There was also concern at the disproportionately high return The News Corporation stood to earn – it planned a 20 per cent stake, but if MPI profits rose by 40 per cent or more in a year the management contract allowed for more than half the profits to accrue to The News Corporation.

Harper & Collins was, therefore, put into a joint venture company, established by The News Corporation, and its investment bankers, Credit Suisse First Boston. Effectively, the bank agreed to purchase, on a short-term basis, half of Harper & Collins. The News Corporation was then able to equity account for this investment and so move the debt associated with it off its balance sheet.

In November 1990 Rupert Murdoch announced the merger of Sky Television with its UK rival, British Satellite Broadcasting (BSB). BSB was the consortium (of Granada, Pearson, Reed International and Chargeurs) that in 1986 had obtained, from the UK's Independent Broadcasting Authority (IBA), a fifteen-year broadcasting franchise using the five high-powered satellite channels assigned to the UK for domestic use by the world's broadcasting authorities.

BSB had begun broadcasting in March 1990, after an investment of £1.5bn by its shareholders and bankers (this made it the largest single UK investment project after the Channel Tunnel). Start-up costs had been higher than expected due to heavier and lengthier advertising spend and competition with Sky dramatically increasing the cost of acquiring Hollywood film rights. There had been few problems launching the two satellites that the company owned and operated, but the newness of the technology it was using on the ground to receive programmes proved more difficult to develop, leading to a six-month launch delay. The purchase of satellite dishes by households was lower than expected. Six months after launch the venture was losing about £8m per week.

The News Corporation and the BSB consortium each owned 50 per cent of the equity of the newly created company, BSkyB (although, because BSB was a consortium, the next largest individual shareholder held only 11 per cent).

Besides merging all the assets and liabilities of the old companies, the BSB partners introduced a further £70m of equity and The News Corporation invested £30m as working capital. The venture also obtained £300m in debt financing. In April 1991 a further £200m was invested, with The News Corporation meeting its obligation mainly in kind by allowing the movie channel free access to almost £100m of future Twentieth Century Fox film broadcasts.

Under the terms of the merger the first £400m of distributable profits were paid out 80:20 in favour of The News Corporation. They were then divided 50:50 for twice the period it took to achieve the first £400m. Then it became 80:20 in favour of the old BSB shareholders for a final £400m, before returning to equal distribution. However, for accounting purposes, The News Corporation only had to account for 20 per cent of the venture's losses. Furthermore, as an equity-accounted investment, the merger allowed £470m of debt to be removed from The News Corporation's balance sheet.

The new company came to be dominated by Sky Television. The Astra satellite channels and the technology used by Sky Television were adopted, redundancies following the merger occurred mainly among the BSB staff (from employing 4,300 people at the time of the merger, the new company reduced staff to 980) and Sky executives came to dominate senior management, giving it operational and editorial control of the new company. Lord Thomson, former chairman of the IBA, called the merger 'a characteristically brutal Wapping in outer space carried out behind the backs of both the government and the IBA'.

The strains begin to tell

> I feel there is some deterioration setting in. It may be that this year (1990) will be the first year in some years when our earnings will not have their customary increase.

This was the warning issued by Rupert Murdoch at The News Corporation's annual general meeting in October 1989. Although profits before interest charges fell only slightly, 1990 profits before extraordinary items at £133m were 43 per cent lower than the previous year.

A protracted strike at the 50 per cent-owned Ansett Airlines reduced profits by about £45m. Fox Film Studios did not have a good year, and at this time the losses at Sky Television were reported in full. The News Corporation was also investing £500m in new printing presses in the UK. This was a heavy cash drain at a time when there was a slowing of the economies in each of The News Corporation's three main markets. The juxtaposition of the above problems resulted in a gap in working capital of £1.3bn that had to be financed by highly expensive short-term borrowing. By August 1990 interest payments on The News Corporation's debt were running at about £1.7m a day. For every £1 of profit earned, 80p was required to meet interest charges.

Furthermore, the group faced a tax audit by the Australian Taxation Office following complaints that The News Corporation paid an effective tax rate of only 1.76 per cent in 1989/90, compared with a nominal corporate tax rate of 39 per cent. The Australian parliament had legislated to block the use of subsidiary offshore tax havens – a strategy widely used by The News Corporation. The group expected its effective tax rate to increase to about 30 per cent in 1992 when the new legislation was fully operative. Had 1990 profits been taxed at 30 per cent, reported profit before extraordinary items would have been 45 per cent lower.

By January 1991, in response to these problems, The News Corporation shares had fallen to a low of 156p – way below their peak of 850p, touched ahead of the stock market crash of 1987. Even during 1990 the shares had traded as high as 680p (see Figure 1). The group's bonds were trading on yields of nearly 50 per cent and its debt had been downgraded by Moody's Investor Services, the US ratings agency, to near default levels. The News Corporation's market value of near £800m was a fraction of the £5bn net asset value of the 1990 accounts, and its borrowings of over £4.5bn were five times this stock market capitalisation. It was clear that without some form of restructing the company would default on loans due for repayment in 1991.

Operation Dolphin, the restructuring of The News Corporation's debt, took three months of negotiations with nearly 150 banks. Cynical commentators suggested that these banks could not afford to see The News Corporation bankrupted. As one European banker delicately put it: 'in a forced sale, asset values

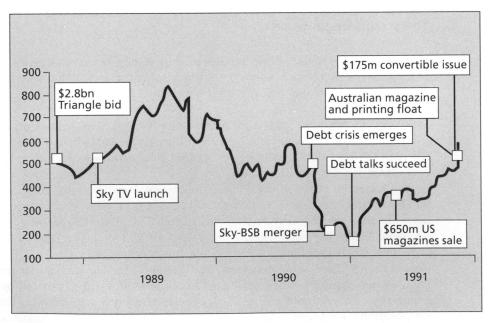

Figure 1 The News Corporation share price (pence per share)

would drop considerably to the detriment of the lenders. It is therefore impera-
tive that the Group's viability is maintained.'

The resultant deal, agreed in February 1991, involved a three-year, £3.8bn
debt restructuring agreement and a £300m bridging loan agreement. The debt
restructuring involved the following:

- Payment of interest at 1 per cent above the existing rate on each loan being
  rolled over (costing an extra £38m per annum).
- Payment of a front-end fee of 1 per cent to the banks involved (a one-off
  extra cost of £38m).
- The introduction of several strict financial covenants, including operating
  cash flow to interest coverage ratios, and operating earnings to debt ratios.
  Previous covenants relating to the size of the company's balance sheet and
  debt/equity ratios were abandoned.

The cost to Rupert Murdoch was not just financial. He agreed to quarterly
meetings with the banks to discuss the group's progress and to monitor the new
loan covenants. He also guaranteed to reduce debt levels by £1bn during the
course of the refinancing deal. This was difficult to achieve through increased
profitability alone. Most analysts believed significant asset disposals would also
be required.

In explaining The News Corporation's problems Rupert Murdoch admitted: 'I
had taken my eye off the financial side.' In retrospect he concluded that the decision to modernise printing plants in Australia and the UK should have been
delayed by three to four years, that the purchase of Triangle 'could have been a
deal of US$1bn too much' and that he 'wasted time' with the MPI initiative.

On the rebound

> We are the pin-up boys of the banks. Emotive words like bridge loans have
> gone.

These remarks by Rupert Murdoch reflect how much had changed in the eight
months following the company's refinancing. By October 1991 The News
Corporation had raised £900m through asset sales, and had announced plans for
the flotation of 45 per cent of its Australian printing and magazine interests to
raise a further £314m. These disposals reflected Rupert Murdoch's own priorities, where 'our publishing and newspaper assets come first, our television and
film assets are second, and then our books and magazines'.

The company had also placed £103m of convertible preference shares.
Unlike previous convertible issues (redeemed or converted into other equity
holdings), it was expected that these would be converted into The News
Corporation equity. This would reduce the Murdoch family interest to 41.4 per
cent. By the end of 1991 most of the £470m debt repayment due in February 1992

had been paid and it appeared that further obligations could be met from exist-ing cash flows without raising new money.

BSkyB was offering six television channels and claimed to be reaching 2.5 million homes through cable, dish and communal aerial. This was 11.6 per cent of television-owning households in the UK. More importantly for advertising rev-enues, ownership was concentrated among families with young children. Sixty per cent of the 1.7 million homes with dishes subscribed to the £11.99 per month film channel, and 60 per cent of these paid £16.99 per month for both film chan-nels offered. The losses of the combined companies had fallen to £1.8m per week (rising to £4.8m including financing charges). Continued growth on the same basis would enable operational break even to be reached in 1993. On this basis, in October 1991 Warburg Securities valued the new company at £2bn.

By 1991 Twentieth Century Fox had the largest share of the American film market, with its film *Home Alone* having been the third highest revenue earner in movie history. It was also a major source of programming for Fox Broadcasting and BSkyB.

This successful activity was reflected in the increase in the company's share price (see Figure 1) to 610p. Analysts were looking for further gains because of the 'double whammy' effect on The News Corporation's profits of a fall in debt and an upturn in profitability, as newspapers and television have high opera-tional gearing.

The future

The early 1990s had seen Rupert Murdoch and The News Corporation run into financial difficulties. By late 1991 it seemed to many commentators that the storm had been weathered. If The News Corporation was rumoured to be raising over £500m of both equity and long-term debt, surely this was a return to familiar themes: Murdoch's use of 'other people's money' and the confidence of a wide range of investing institutions in making the necessary loans.

The real questions seemed to lie with business directions. The perception of brokers Potter Warburg was that the company's super profits in the 1990s would come from BSkyB, Twentieth Century Fox and Fox Broadcasting. Other market analysts saw consumers turning increasingly to film and television, reflecting, perhaps, the fact that newspaper circulation was in long-term decline. According to the UK's *Sunday Telegraph* newspaper (October 1991), 'Murdoch watchers say that while his heart is always in newspapers his head is increasingly in televi-sion.' However, a review of the history of The News Corporation would suggest that Murdoch's financial acumen, his ability to stay 'one step ahead of the game' and his effectiveness in applying familiar recipes to new circumstances could never allow his intentions to be assessed so easily.

The possibility of his retirement, with all its implications for The News Corporation's future, seemed remote in late 1991. Moreover, whatever the vagaries of the economic and financial climate in the 1990s it would seem from the 1988–91 experience that the multinational had become too big to be allowed to founder and, especially if it learned from its recent history, too adroit to allow itself to do so. As so often before, however, the future of The News Corporation could not be separated from the motivations, personality and perceptions of Murdoch himself. The question remains whether patterns can be discerned in these through the history of the Corporation and, if so, whether such patterns will continue into the 1990s.

Appendix 1 The News Corporation Ltd structure at August 1980

THE MURDOCH FAMILY
controls
CRUDEN INVESTMENT PTY (VICTORIA)
which owns 43.5% of
THE NEWS CORPORATION LTD (ADELAIDE)
the principal activities of which are:

UNITED KINGDOM

Newspapers
National:
*Sun, News of
the World*
Regional:
Berrows Group

Printing
Eric Bembrose

Transport
Convoys Group

Paper making
Townsend Hook

AUSTRALIA

Newspapers
National:
The Australian
Regional:
Over a dozen papers
in Sydney, Adelaide
Perth, Queensland
and Darwin

Magazines
New Idea, TV Week

Printing
Progress Press

Television and film
Associated R&R Films
(joint venture)
TV stations in Sydney
Adelaide, Wollongong
and Melbourne

Other
Ansett Airlines (50%)
F. S. Falkiner
Festival Records

UNITED STATES

Newspapers
*San Antonio
Express, Houston,
New York Post*

Magazines
*Star, New York
Magazine, Village
Voice*

Source: The News Corporation annual report, 1981.

Appendix 2 The News Corporation Ltd: accounting policies

(a) Principles of consolidation

The consolidated accounts comprise all corporations in which The News Corporation Limited or its subsidiaries hold or control more than half the issued ordinary share capital or voting share capital or in which it controls the composition of the Board. They also incorporate the equity of the group in associated companies (companies in which it has a substantial interest and where there is capacity to significantly influence financial or operating policies).

(b) Publishing rights, titles and television licences

These assets are stated at cost or, from 30 June 1984, at valuation. Where at valuation assets are revalued triennially by Hambro's Securities Ltd (Australia and UK) and R. Gary Gomm & Assocs (USA), and are shown in the accounts at 70% of their latest revaluation (latest revaluation being 1990). Increments in the value of a class of assets are taken to the revaluation reserve.

No amortisation is provided on publishing rights and titles since, in the opinion of the Directors, they do not have a finite useful economic life. Although television licences in the United States are renewable every five years, the Directors have no reason to believe that they will not be renewed and, accordingly, no amortisation has been provided.

(c) Capitalisation of interest and new business start-up costs

Interest on funds invested in major projects with substantial development and construction phases are recorded as a capital cost until production or operations commence. Thereafter, the capitalised interest is amortised over the period that benefits are expected to be received. Capitalised interest for the year ended 30 June 1991 amounted to £72m.

Costs incurred in the development of major new activities are capitalised until the operations are commenced on a commercial basis. Thereafter, these costs are amortised over the period that benefits are expected to be received.

Up to 31 August 1989 the investment in the development of Sky Television plc was capitalised. This investment was to be amortised over the shorter of five years or the period the benefits are expected to be received. In June the directors determined it would be proper to charge the capitalised development cost of Sky to operating profit in the 1990 financial year. Accordingly, £134m of capitalised development cost was written off as an extraordinary item in the 1990 profit and loss statement.

Source: The News Corporation annual reports, 1982

Appendix 2 (*continued*)

Consolidated profit and loss accounts, 1982–91 (summarised)

	For year ending 30 June (£m)[1]									
	1982	1983	1984	1985	1986	1987	1988	1989	1990	1991
Turnover										
USA	136	198	319	525	909	1,233	1,050	1,780	2,321	3,105
UK	351	378	433	501	551	587	698	808	819	1,064
Australia	266	300	410	525	396	481	740	1,140	986	1,023
	753	876	1,162	1,551	1,856	2,301	2,488	3,728	4,126	5,192
Operating profit[2]										
USA	2	12	17	16	132	154	155	288	376	487
UK	7	39	39	48	83	145	153	191	62	93
Australia	30	25	40	40	33	49	100	208	200	157
	39	76	96	104	248	348	408	687	638	737
Interest payments	31	33	66	47	108	172	245	448	474	577
Profit after tax	22	51	60	61	118	159	192	235	133	152
Extraordinary items[3]	(2)	(25)	(38)	32	1	199	3	316	29	(338)
Profit after extraordinary items	20	26	22	93	119	358	195	551	162	(186)
Dividends paid:										
Ordinary shares	5	4.5	5.5	8	6.5	9	11	14	13.5	14
Preference shares	n/a	n/a	n/a	108	837	45	5.5	28	64	14
Dividend per share (pence)	n/a	1.5	2.0	3.0	2.5	3.0	3.7	4.7	4.7	n/a
Earnings per share (pence):										
After tax	n/a	18.0	22.0	23.0	43.0	55.0	62.0	75.0	48.0	52.5
After extraordinary items	n/a	9.0	8.0	35.0	44.0	122.0	63.0	167.0	57.0	(51.6)

Notes [1] Trading results have been converted at the average exchange rates for the year.

[2] Operating profit is shown before interest payments.

[3] Extraordinary items include the following:

1982–4 Foreign exchange losses totalling £100m

1986 Costs of relocating production facilities £66m

1987 Surplus on the disposal of non-current assets £255m

1988 Write-off of new business start-up and termination costs £57m

1989 Surplus on the disposal of non-current assets £400m

1990 Surplus on the disposal of non-current assets £209m
    Start-up and development costs of Sky Television £134m

1991 Losses on the disposal of non-current assets £82m
    Refinancing costs £91m.

Appendix 2 (*continued*)

Consolidated balance sheets, 1982–91 (summarised)

	For year ending 30 June (£m)[4]									
	1982	1983	1984	1985	1986	1987	1988	1989	1990	1991
Current assets										
Cash	3	11	12	74	29	95	60	78	72	96
Receivables, inventories and other items	206	248	332	394	746	887	876	1,188	1,478	1,454
Total current assets	209	259	354	468	775	982	936	1,266	1,550	1,550
Non-current assets										
Investments	110	136	255	300	213	1,156	1,600	1,616	1,556	1,419
Property, plant and equipment	164	196	266	305	459	550	744	932	1,561	1,538
Publishing rights, titles and TV licences	49	52	437	673	1,480	2,160	2,320	4,290	6,017	5,867
Goodwill					331	343	294	298	258	237
Other	12	21	37	44	447	434	609	840	848	1,149
Total non-current assets	335	405	995	1,322	2,930	4,643	5,567	7,976	10,240	10,210
Total assets	544	664	1,349	1,790	3,705	5,625	6,503	9,242	11,790	11,760
Current liabilities										
Borrowings	20	40	33	8	84	346	278	246	1,332	354
Creditors and accruals	143	202	359	382	637	800	874	1,059	1,395	1,499
Total current liabilities	163	242	392	390	721	1,146	1,152	1,305	2,727	1,853
Non-current liabilities										
Borrowings	162	154	266	607	1,068	1,626	2,296	3,568	3,419	4,698
Creditors and accruals	16	37	57	91	275	367	341	474	531	614
Total non-current liabilities	178	191	323	698	1,343	1,993	2,637	4,043	3,950	5,312
Total liabilities	341	433	715	1,088	2,064	3,139	3,789	5,348	6,677	7,165
Net assets	203	231	634	702	1,641	2,486	2,714	3,894	5,113	4,595
Shareholders' equity										
Share capital	20	20	20	28	28	628	661	683	635	667
Revaluation reserve			381	249	210	561	606	595	1,961	2,017
Other reserves	166	169	190	337	416	987	1,110	1,731	1,732	1,567
Minority interests	17	42	43	88	986	310	337	885	785	344
Total shareholders' equity	203	231	634	702	1,641	2,486	2,714	3,894	5,113	4,595

[4] The financial position has been converted at the exchange rate at balance sheet date.

Appendix 2 (*continued*)

Consolidated source and application of funds, 1982–91 (summarised)

	1982	1983	1984	1985	1986	1987	1988	1989	1990	1991
					($£m$)[1]					
Source of funds										
From operations	23	62	83	95	207	279	292	436	(35)	(968)
Issue of shares:										
Ordinary					3	167		8		
Redeemable preference		31	93				244	565	188	
Convertible notes						545				
Sales of assets	14	8	79	145	55	99	212	616	535	1,175
Gain on sale of businesses					39	240	5	318	89	
Increase in liabilities:										
Current	23	91	94	38	380	436	48	(37)	1,600	120
Non-current	17	(2)	120	443	801	693	661	1,130	253	(94)
Increase in minority interest					1,007					
Other	8	7	56	40	140	21	181	1	–	–
	85	197	432	854	2,632	2,480	1,643	3,037	2,630	233
Application of funds										
Increase in assets										
Current	28	60	77	175	385	225	(22)	257	388	(166)
Property, plant and equipment	23	53	81	97	281	171	250	314	779	44
Investments	1	25	95	156	41	868	603	426	72	(33)
Increase in publishing rights, titles and TV licences			37	321	992	404	210	1,758	667	(501)
Increase in goodwill					391			27	2	
Other non-current	1	4	12	16	400	50	257	116	144	272
Tax paid	18	8	4	31	20	20	28	24	17	20
Dividends paid	6	6	7	10	45	57	16	42	81	22
Redemption of preference shares			26			608	234	41	400	500
New business costs						26	57			
Other	8	37	119	22	77	51	10	32	80	75
	85	197	432	854	2,632	2,480	1,643	3,037	2,630	233

[1] See page 642.

Appendix 2 (*continued*)

Industry sector analysis, 1984–91

	1984	1985	1986	1987	1988	1989	1990	1991
					(£m)			
Revenues[1]								
Newspapers	781	1,014	953	875	1,062	1,374	1,420	1,461
Magazines	141	216	222	247	252	554	680	619
Television	84	122	170	297	233	352	552	630
Filmed entertainment			267	601	490	572	596	1,041
Commercial printing	70	77	72	77	107	224	243	234
Other	86	122	172	204	344	652	635	1,207
	1,162	1,551	1,856	2,301	2,488	3,728	4,126	5,192
Operating Income[1]								
Newspapers	47	50	74	150	198	325	306	247
Magazines	25	35	47	44	44	131	150	133
Television	5	6	26	50	34	47	3	58
Filmed entertainment			37	74	34	57	50	100
Commercial printing	4	4	8	8	9	23	27	26
Other	15	9	56	22	89	104	102	173
	96	104	248	348	408	687	639	737
Identifiable assets[4]								
Newspapers	619	686	647	1,367	1,754	2,345	3,596	3,612
Magazines	132	448	400	372	375	1,820	1,745	1,615
Television	169	133	1,332	1,324	1,249	1,696	2,222	2,003
Filmed entertainment			853	757	684	725	751	1,075
Commercial printing	28	36	35	56	141	171	164	145
Other	147	187	227	592	700	869	1,757	1,890
Corporate items	254	300	211	1,157	1,600	1,616	1,555	1,420
	1,349	1,790	3,705	5,625	6,503	9,242	11,790	11,760
USA	276	660	2,649	2,621	2,440	4,736	5,519	5,920
UK	348	442	463	911	989	1,420	2,804	2,448
Australia and Pacific Basin	471	388	382	936	1,474	1,470	191	1,972
Corporate items	254	300	211	1,157	1,600	1,616	1,555	1,426
	1,349	1,790	3,705	5,625	6,503	9,242	11,790	11,760
Capital expenditures:[4]								
Newspapers	20	70	63	50	115	179	536	248
Magazines	3	10	3	10	4	5	5	4
Television	1	4	6	9	8	81	206	48
Filmed entertainment			3	6	5	6	10	14
Commercial printing	4	6	3	7	6	12	21	9
Other	6	8	12	9	18	18	19	20
	34	98	90	91	156	301	797	343
USA	6	15	20	25	23	24	32	33
UK	9	58	44	33	90	220	634	207
Australia and Pacific Basin	19	25	26	33	43	57	131	103
	34	98	90	91	156	301	797	343

[1] See page 642.
[4] See page 643.

Appendix 3 News International plc accounts, 1980–91

Consolidated profit and loss account, 1980–91 (summarised)

For the year ending 30 June (£m)

	1980	1981	1982	1983	1984	1985	1986	1987	1988	1989	1990	1991
Turnover	114	293	380	412	458	493	546	581	686	785	796	755
Operating profit[1]	13	26	9	40	36	44	15	133	150	159	(61)	(55)
Investment income	n/a	n/a	3	3	11	33	89	86	95	167	191	177
Interest and other charges	n/a	n/a	8	7	7	31	92	107	157	306	396	457
Profit before tax	13	26	4	36	40	46	12	112	88	20	(266)	(336)
Tax (charge)/credit	(6)	–	–	(9)	(14)	(15)	9	(12)	(18)	(9)	21	(1)
Profit after tax	7	26	3	27	26	31	20	100	70	11	(245)	337
Minority interest	–				2	3	1	1	2	1	3	
Extraordinary items[2]		4	2	(3)	7	18	11	1	2	233	(35)	1
Dividends paid	3	13	2	3	50	3	48	6	7	9	7	8
Retained profit/(loss)	4	17	3	21	(15)	15	(16)	96	67	236	(284)	(344)

[1] 1986 operating profit is arrived at after deducting £66m in exceptional costs relating to the move to Wapping. 1990 operating profit is arrived at after deducting £134m in development costs for Sky Television plc.

[2] 1989 items relate to the surplus on disposal of non-current assets.

Consolidated balance sheets, 1980–91 (summarised)

	As at 30 June (£m)											
	1980	1981	1982	1983	1984	1985	1986	1987	1988	1989	1990	1991
Fixed assets												
Intangible	13	14	12	13	134	240	196	484	547	450	1,087	1,088
Tangible	47	90	96	112	106	146	171	177	274	361	769	798
Investments	29	30	22	23	136	542	918	1,674	1,698	3,169	2,842	4,094
	89	134	130	148	376	928	1,285	2,335	2,519	3,980	4,698	5,980
Current assets												
Stocks and debtors	59	92	97	93	157	206	234	278	247	673	1,141	1,292
Investments					1				410	15	10	185
Cash	18	7	7	25	33	86	16	115	22	47	6	1
	77	99	104	119	191	292	250	393	679	735	1,157	1,478
Creditors												
Due in one year	57	84	77	81	185	207	345	465	493	693	1,259	1,118
Net current assets	20	15	27	38	6	85	(95)	(72)	186	42	(102)	360

(Continued on p. 648)

Total assets less current liabilities	109	149	157	186	382	1,013	1,190	2,263	2,705	4,022	4,596	6,340
Creditors Due after one year	22	36	41	47	134	729	917	1,528	1,875	2,865	3,273	4,686
Net assets	87	113	116	139	248	284	273	735	830	1,157	1,323	1,654
Capital and reserves												
Share capital	12	22	22	22	22	22	22	23	99	99	99	99
Share premium								70				
Revaluation reserve		10	10	144	108	108	430	476	468	1,083	1,057	
Other reserves		2	3	3	59	65	41				566	
P & L account	75	79	81	103	77	95	77	171	254	586	141	(224)
Shareholders' funds	87	113	116	138	246	284	272	735	829	1,153	1,323	1,498
Minority interests				1	2		1		1	3		156
Capital employed	87	113	116	139	248	284	273	735	830	1,156	1,323	1,654

Appendix 4 Major acquisitions and disposals, 1984–91

Year	Acquisitions			Disposals		
1984	*Chicago Sun-Times*	(USA) ⎫	£16m	*Chicago Sun-Times*[1]	(USA) ⎫	£101m
	New Woman	(USA) ⎭		Houston Community Papers	(USA) ⎭	
	Ziff Davies Magazines	(USA)	£287m	Newspaper interests and	(Australia)	£535m
	Twentieth Century Fox	(USA)	£400m	Television stations[2]		
1985	Metromedia	(USA)	£160m	*New York Post*[1]	(USA) ⎫	£41m
1986	*South China Morning Post*	(Hong Kong)	£115m	Aviation Trade Publications	(USA) ⎭	
1987	*Herald & Weekly Times*	(Australia)	£1bn	*Elle Magazine*	(USA)	£110m
1988	Harper & Row	(USA)	£194m	Travel trade publications	(USA)	£480m
	Triangle Publications	(USA)	£1.7bn	*The Star*	(USA)	£243m
1989	William Collins[3]	(UK)	£400m	Medical journals	(USA)	£140m
1990				*South China Morning Post* (49%)	(Hong Kong)	£160m
1991				Magazine interests	(USA/UK)	£520m

[1] Disposed of in compliance with the USA Federal Communication Commission's general rule that joint ownership of a newspaper and television station in the same market is not permissible.

[2] Disposed of to comply with Australian Trade Practices Law.

[3] Acquisition of the outstanding 58% not already owned. Subsequently merged with Harper & Row to create HarperCollins.

Source: The News Corporation annual reports 1984–91.

Appendix 5 The News Corporation Ltd structure at June 1991

THE MURDOCH FAMILY
controls
CRUDEN INVESTMENT PTY (VICTORIA) and
KARAREM PTY (CANBERRA)
which owns 41% of
THE NEWS CORPORATION LTD (ADELAIDE)
the principal activities of which are:

UNITED KINGDOM	AUSTRALIA & PACIFIC BASIN	UNITED STATES
Newspapers *News of the World* *Sun* *The Times* *Sunday Times* *Today*	**Newspapers** National: *The Australian* Regional: Over 100 titles in Queensland, New South Wales, Victoria, Sth	**Newspapers** *Boston Herald* *San Antonio Express*
Television BSky B (48%) Sky Radio (75%)	Australia, Tasmania, Western Australia, Northern Territory Hong Kong: *S. China Morning Post* and *Sunday Post* (56%) Also papers in Fiji and Papua New Guinea	**Television and Film** 20th Century Fox Film Corp, Fox Broadcasting Co. Fox Television Stations Twentieth Television Corp.
Transport Convoys Ltd		
Magazines *Times Supplements*, *Sky* (50%), *TV* *Guide*	**Magazines** *New Idea, New Woman* *TV Week* (50%), *Home* *Beautiful, Family* *Circle, Australasian* *Post, Your Garden*	**Magazines** *TV Guide* *Mirabella*
Books HarperCollins	**Books** HarperCollins	**Books** HarperCollins
	Printing Interests in 13 companies	
	Paper manufacture Australian NewsPrint Mills (46%)	
Other News Gems Smart Card Int (50%) Circle K (UK) (50%) Times Network Systems	**Other** Ansett Airlines (50%) East West Airlines (50%) F. S. Falkiner Festival Records News Data Security Products (60%)	**Other** Quad Marketing, Product Movers, Etak Inc.

Electrolux: the acquisition and integration of Zanussi*
Sumantra Ghoshal and Philippe Haspeslagh

In recounting the story of Electrolux's acquisition of Zanussi, Leif Johansson, head of Electrolux's major appliance division, had reasons to feel pleased. Through a combination of financial restructuring and operating improvements Zanussi had, in only three years since the acquisition, gone from a massive loss of L120 billion in 1983 to a tidy profit of L60 billion in 1987[1] – a turnaround that had astounded outside analysts and was perhaps a shade more impressive than the expectations of even the extreme optimists within Electrolux. More important still was the progress made in integrating Zanussi strategically, operationally and organisationally within the Electrolux group, while protecting its distinct identity and reviving the fighting spirit that had once been the hallmark of the proud Italian company. Having been the first to suggest to president Anders Scharp that Electrolux should buy financially troubled Zanussi, Johansson had a major personal stake in the continued success of the operation.

By early 1988, however, the task was far from complete. Not everything was going well at Zanussi: the company had recently lost some market share within Italy to Merloni, its arch-rival, which had taken over domestic market leadership following its acquisition of Indesit, another large Italian producer of household appliances. There had been some delays in Zanussi's ambitious programme for plant automation. Moreover, a recent attitude survey had shown that, while the top 60 managers of Zanussi fully supported the actions taken since the acquisition, the next rung of 150 managers felt less motivated and less secure. It was not clear whether these problems were short term in nature and would soon be resolved, or whether they were the warning signals of more basic and fundamental maladies.

Though Leif Johansson felt that it would be useful to review the integration process, his own concerns were focused on what the next stage of the battle for

---

*A *Note on the Major Appliance Industry* by the same authors is available from the Case Clearing House of Great Britain and Ireland.

[1]$1 = L1,170 = Skr 5.85 (*International Financial Statistics*, December 1987).

This case was prepared by Dag Andersson, Nicola De Sanctis, Beniamino Finzi, and Jacopo Franzan under the supervision of Sumantra Ghoshal and Philippe Haspeslagh, Associate Professors at INSEAD. It is intended to be used as a basis for class discussion rather than to illustrate either effective or ineffective handling of an administrative situation. The co-operation of the Electrolux company and its executives is gratefully acknowledged. © 1989 INSEAD-CEDEP, Fontainebleau, France, revised 1990.

global leadership would be. The industry was changing rapidly with competitors like Whirlpool and Matsushita moving outside their home regions. At the same time some local European competitors like GEC-Hotpoint in the UK or Merloni (Ariston) in Italy were making aggressive moves to expand their shares in a relatively low-growth market. The Zanussi takeover, coupled with the subsequent acquisition of White Consolidated in the United States, had catapulted Electrolux to the top of the list of the world's largest producers of household appliances. The challenge for Johansson now was to mould all the acquired entities into an integrated strategy and organisation that would protect this leadership role and leverage it into a profitable world-wide operation.

In 1962 Electrolux was on a downward curve. Profits were falling and the company had not developed any significant in-house research and development capability. Compared with other appliance manufacturers such as Philips, Siemens, GEC and Matsushita, it had a limited range of products: the core business was made up of vacuum cleaners and absorption-type refrigerators. These refrigerators were increasingly unable to compete with the new compressor-type refrigerators developed by the competitors, and sales of the once highly successful lines of vacuum cleaners were rapidly declining.

That same year ASA, a company in the Wallenberg network (an informal grouping of major Swedish companies in which the Wallenbergs, the most influential business family in Sweden, had some equity shares) sold Electro-Helios to Electrolux for shares and thereby became a major shareholder. Electro-Helios was a technological leader in compressor-type refrigerators and a significant producer of freezers and cooking-ranges. This led to a major expansion of Electrolux's role in the Swedish household appliance market, but the company found itself in financial difficulty again due to rapid expansion of production capacity during a period of severe economic downturn.

In 1967 Hans Werthén was appointed CEO of Electrolux. In the next two decades he and the other two members of what was known as the 'Electrolux Troika', Anders Scharp and Gösta Bystedt, would manage to develop the company from a relatively small and marginal player in the business into the world's largest manufacturer of household appliances.

Growth through acquisitions

At the core of the dramatic transformation of Electrolux was an aggressive strategy of expansion through acquisition. At the beginning, Electrolux concentrated on acquiring firms in the Nordic countries, its traditional market, where the company already had a dominant market share. Subsequent acquisitions served not only to strengthen the company's position in its household appliance activities, but also to broaden its European presence and open the way to entirely new product areas. Exhibit 1 illustrates Electrolux's major acquisitions between 1964 and 1988.

With more than 200 acquisitions in 40 countries, and 280 manufacturing

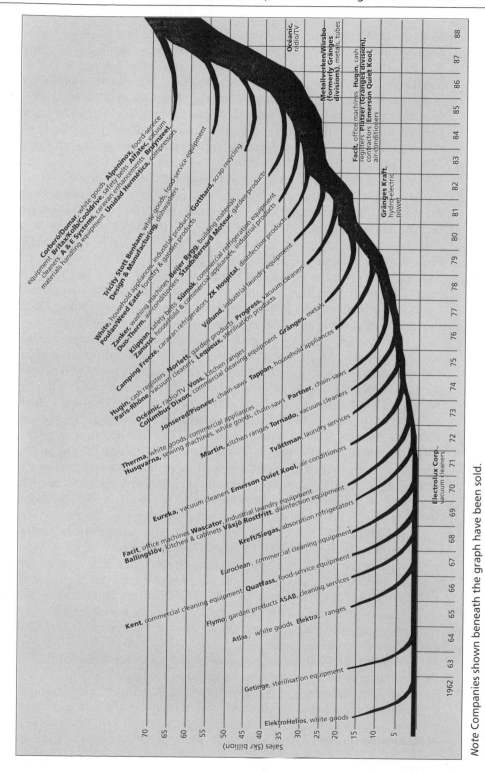

Note Companies shown beneath the graph have been sold.

Exhibit 1 Major company acquisitions and divestments since 1962.

facilities in 25 countries, the Electrolux Group had few equals in managing the acquisition and integration processes. The company generally bought competitors in its core businesses, disposing of operations which either failed to show long-term profit potential or appeared to have a better chance of prospering under the management of another company. In addition, Electrolux always tried to ensure that there were sufficient realisable assets available to help finance the necessary restructuring of the acquired company. Thus, from the beginning of the 1970s up to 1988, the group made capital gains from selling off idle assets of more than Skr 2.5 billion.

At the same time, flexibility had been maintained in order to pick up new product areas for further development. A typical example of this was the chain-saw product line that came with the acquisition of the Swedish appliance manufacturer Husqvarna in 1978. By developing this product line through acquisitions and in-house development, Electrolux emerged as one of the world's leading chain-saw manufacturers with about 30 per cent of the global market. Another example was provided by the new business area of outdoor products (consisting mainly of forestry and garden products), which had been grown from the small base of the Flugmo lawnmower business through the acquisition of firms like Poulan/Weed Eater in the USA and Staub/Bernard Moteur in France.

The two most notable departures from the strategy of buying familiar businesses had been the 1973 acquisition of Facit, a Swedish office equipment and electronics maker, and the 1980 purchase of Gränges, a metal and mining company. Both companies were in financial trouble. Electrolux had difficulty in fully mastering Facit. After having brought the profit up to a reasonable level, it was sold off to Ericsson in 1983. The borrowing necessary to buy Gränges, combined with the world-wide economic downturn and rising interest rates, pushed Electrolux into a sobering two-year decline (1981–3) in its profit margin. However, through the Gränges takeover Electrolux also acquired new businesses for future growth. An example was the manufacturing of seat belts, now concentrated in the subsidiary Electrolux Autoliv. Nevertheless, the acquisition of Gränges would be the last diversifying acquisition.

Even though Electrolux had dealt with a large number of acquisitions, specific companies were seldom targeted. In the words of Anders Scharp: 'You never choose an acquisition, opportunities just come.' The company made it a practice to simulate what the merger combination with other companies would result in should they come up for sale. The financial aspects of an acquisition were considered to be very important. The company usually ensured that it paid less for a company than the total asset value of the company, and not for what Electrolux would bring to the party.

Based on their experience, managers at Electrolux believed that there was no standard method for treating acquisitions: each case was unique and had to be dealt with differently. Typically, however, Electrolux moved quickly at the beginning of the integration process. It identified the key action areas and created task forces consisting of managers from both Electrolux and the acquired company in order to address each of the issues on a time-bound basis. Such joint task forces were believed to help foster management confidence and commitment and create avenues for reciprocal information flows. Objectives were clearly specified, milestones were identified, and the first phase of integration was generally completed with three to six months so as to create and maintain momentum. The top management of an acquired company was often replaced, but the middle management was kept intact. As explained by Anders Scharp: 'The risk of losing general management competence is small when it is a poorly performing company. Electrolux is prepared to take this risk. It is, however, important that we do not change the marketing and sales staff.'

Electrolux prior to the acquisition of Zanussi

The activities of the Electrolux Group in 1984, prior to the acquisition of Zanussi, covered 26 product lines within five business areas: namely household appliances, forestry and garden products, industrial products, commercial services and metal and mining (Gränges). Total sales revenue had increased from Skr 1.1 billion in 1967 to Skr 34.5 billion in 1984. The household appliance area (including white goods, special refrigerators, floorcare products and sewing machines) accounted for approximately 52 per cent of total group sales in 1984. Gränges was the second largest area with nearly 21.5 per cent of total sales. The third area, industrial products, provided heavy equipment for food services, semi-industrial laundries, and commercial cleaning.

By the 1980s Electrolux had become one of the world's largest manufacturers of white goods with production facilities in Europe and North America and a small presence in Latin America and the Far East. The group's reliance upon the Scandinavian markets was still considerable. More than 30 per cent of sales came from Sweden, Norway and Denmark. European sales, focusing mainly on Scandinavia and western Europe, constituted 65 per cent of total group sales. The United States had emerged as the single most important market with 28.9 per cent (1987) of total sales.

Electrolux's household appliances were manufactured in plants with specialised assembly lines. Regional manufacturing operations were focused on local brands and designs and established distribution networks. Sales forces for the various brands had been kept separate, though support functions such as physical distribution, stocking, order taking and invoicing might be integrated. With increasing plant automation and product differentiation, the number of models and the volume produced in any given plant had risen sharply. As described by Anders Scharp: 'We recognised that expansion means higher volumes, which create scope for rationalisation. Rationalisation means better margins, which are essential to boost our competitive strength.'

One important characteristic of Electrolux was the astonishingly small corporate headquarters at Lilla Essingen, 6 km outside the centre of Stockholm, and the relatively few people who worked in central staff departments. The size of headquarters was a direct outcome of the company's commitment to decentralisation. 'I believe that we have at least two hierarchical levels fewer than other companies of the same size,' said Scharp, 'and all operational matters are decentralised to the subsidiaries.' However, most strategic issues such as investment programmes and product range decisions were dealt with at headquarters. The subsidiaries were considered to be profit centres and were evaluated primarily on their returns on net assets as compared with the targets set by the corporate office. Presidents of the diversified subsidiaries reported directly to Scharp, while others reported to the heads of the different product lines. (Further information on Electrolux is provided in Exhibit 2.)

Exhibit 2 Electrolux Group key data

Group sales and employees world-wide

Nordic countries

	Sales (Skrm)	No. of employees
Sweden	11,128	29,456
Denmark	1,735	3,078
Norway	1,505	1,299
Finland	1,455	1,563
	15,813	35,396

North America

	Sales (Skrm)	No. of employees
USA	19,488	29,750
Canada	1,580	2,150
	21,068	31,900

Rest of Europe

	Sales (Skrm)	No. of employees
Great Britain	6,377	10,589
France	5,098	8,753
West Germany	4,445	3,317
Italy	3,684	15,282
Switzerland	1,818	1,814
Spain	1,445	2,851
Netherlands	1,238	1,016
Belgium and Luxembourg	913	1,040
Austria	392	958
Portugal	96	193
Others	604	41
	25,710	45,854

Latin America

	Sales (Skrm)	No. of employees
Brazil	302	6,215
Venezuela	208	1,032
Peru	181	750
Colombia	104	1,865
Mexico	66	1,735
Ecuador	34	232
Guatemala	24	31
Others	443	198
	1,362	12,058

Exhibit 2 *(continued)*

Asia	Sales (Skrm)	No. of employees
Japan	707	1,175
Saudi Arabia	215	738
Hong Kong	152	1,340
Philippines	150	525
Kuwait	147	2,220
Taiwan	119	2,178
Malaysia	72	1,833
Thailand	56	15
Singapore	50	556
Jordan	28	137
Lebanon	22	35
Others	720	1,729
	2,438	12,481

Africa	Sales (Skrm)	No. of employees
	414	

Oceania	Sales (Skrm)	No. of employees
Australia	497	2,216
New Zealand	114	557
Others	14	–
	625	2,773
Total	**67,430**	**140,462**

Sales by business area

	1987 (Skrm)	1986 (Skrm)	1985 (Skrm)	% of total sales of 1987
Household appliances	39,487	31,378	19,200	58.6
Commercial appliances	5,619	4,250	3,348	8.3
Commercial services	2,893	2,504	2,266	4.3
Outdoor products	4,475	2,909	2,990	6.6
Industrial products	11,784	9,087	9,232	17.5
Building components	3,712	2,962	2,652	4.7
Total	**67,430**	**53,090**	**39,688**	**100.0**

Operating income after depreciation by business area

	1987 (Skrm)	1986 (Skrm)	1985 (Skrm)	% of total sales of 1987
Household appliances	2,077	1,947	1,589	49.2
Commercial appliances	484	349	260	11.4
Commercial services	169	172	132	4.0
Outdoor products	421	241	373	10.0
Industrial products	910	474	657	21.5
Building components	164	138	126	3.9
Total	**4,225**	**3,321**	**3,137**	**100.0**

The acquisition of Zanussi

In June 1983 Leif Johansson, the 32-year-old head of Electrolux's major appliance division, received a proposal from Mr Candotti, head of Zanussi's major appliance division in France, from whom he had been 'sourcing' refrigerators for the French market. The proposal called for the investment of a small amount of money in Zanussi so as to secure future supplies from the financially troubled Italian producer. The next day Johansson called Anders Scharp to ask 'Why don't we buy all of it?', thereby triggering a process that led to the largest acquisition in the history of the household appliance industry and in the Swedish business world.

Zanussi

Having begun in 1916 as a small workshop in Pordenone, a little town in north east Italy, where Antonio Zanussi produced a few wood-burning cookers, Zanussi had grown by the early 1980s to be the second largest privately owned company in Italy with more than 30,000 employees, 50 factories and 13 foreign sales companies. Most of the growth came in the 1950s and 1960s under the leadership of Lino Zanussi, who understood the necessity of having not only a complete range of products but also a well-functioning distribution and sales network. Lino Zanussi established several new factories within Italy and added cookers, refrigerators and washing machines to the product range. In 1958 he launched a major drive to improve exports out of Italy and established the first foreign branch office in Paris in 1962. Similar branches were soon opened in other European countries and the first foreign manufacturing subsidiary, IBELSA, was set up in Madrid in 1965. Through a series of acquisitions of Italian producers of appliances and components, Zanussi became one of the most vertically integrated manufacturers in Europe, achieving full control over all activities ranging from component manufacturing to final sales and service. It is rumoured that, during this period of heady success, Zanussi had very seriously considered launching a takeover bid for Electrolux, then a struggling Swedish company less than half Zanussi's size.

The company's misfortunes started in 1968 when Lino Zanussi and several other company executives died in an aircrash. Over the next fifteen years the new management carved out a costly programme of unrelated diversification into fields such as colour televisions, prefabricated housing, real estate and community centres. The core business of domestic appliances languished for want of capital, while the new businesses incurred heavy losses. By 1982 the company had amassed debts of over L1,300 billion and was losing over L100 billion a year on operations (see Exhibit 3 for the consolidated financial statements during this period).

Between 1982 and 1984 Zanussi tried to rectify the situation by selling off many of the loss-making subsidiaries, reducing the rest of the workforce by over 4,400 people, and focusing on its core activities. However, given the large debt burden and the need for heavy investment in order to rebuild the domestic appliance business, a fresh injection of capital was essential and the company began its search for a partner.

Exhibit 3 Consolidated financial statements for the Zanussi Group

Consolidated income statement (Skr million)

	1980	1981	1982	1983
Sales	3,826	4,327	4,415	5,240
Operating cost	−3,301	−3,775	−3,957	−4,654
Operating income before depreciation	525	552	458	586
Depreciation	−161	−98	−104	−130
Operating income after depreciation	364	454	354	456
Financial income	192	330	284	279
Financial expenses	−407	−489	−647	−627
Income after financial items	149	295	−9	108
Extraordinary items	−53	−228	−223	81
Income before appropriations	96	67	−232	189
Appropriations	−53	−42	−409	−382
Income before taxes	43	25	−641	−193
Taxes	−7	−7	−10	−10
Net income	36	18	−651	−203

Consolidated balance sheet (Skr million)

	1980	1981	1982	1983
Current assets excl. inventory	1,559	1,987	1,811	2,108
Inventory	965	1,054	999	956
Fixed assets	1,622	1,539	2,366	2,902
Total assets	4,146	4,580	5,176	5,966
Current liabilities	1,590	1,832	1,875	2,072
Long-term liabilities	1,273	1,441	1,864	2,349
Reserves	259	301	472	627
Shareholders' equity	1,024	1,006	965	918
Total liabilities and shareholders' equity	4,146	4,580	5,176	5,966

The acquisition process

The process of Electrolux's acquisition of Zanussi formally commenced when Enrico Cuccia, the informal head of Mediobanca and the most powerful financier in Italy, approached Hans Werthén on 30 November 1983, about the possibility of Electrolux rescuing Zanussi from impending financial collapse. It was not by chance that the grand old man of Mediobanca arrived in Sweden. Mr Cuccia had close links to the Agnelli family – the owners of Fiat, the largest industrial group in Italy – and the proposal to approach Electrolux came from Mr Agnelli, who wanted to save the second largest private manufacturing company in his country. As a board member of SKF, the Swedish bearing manufacturer, Agnelli had developed a healthy respect for Swedish management and believed that Electrolux alone had the resources and management skills necessary to turn Zanussi around.

Meanwhile, Electrolux had been looking around for a good acquisition to expand its appliance business. Its efforts to take over AEG's appliance business in Germany had failed because the conditions stipulated for the takeover were found to be too tough. Later, Electrolux had to back away from acquiring the TI group in the UK because of too high a price-tag. Zanussi now represented the best chance for significant expansion in Europe. 'It was a very good fit', recalled Anders Scharp. 'There were not many overlaps: we were strong where Zanussi was weak, and vice-versa.' There were significant complementarities in products, markets and opportunities for vertical integration. For example, while Electrolux was well established in microwave ovens, cookers and fridge-freezers, Zanussi was Europe's largest producer of 'wet products' such as washing machines, traditionally a weak area for Electrolux. Similarly, while Electrolux had large market shares in Scandinavia and Switzerland where Zanussi was almost completely absent, Zanussi was the market leader in Italy and Spain, two markets that Electrolux had failed to crack. Zanussi was also strong in France, the only market where Electrolux was losing money, and had a significant presence in Germany where Electrolux had limited strength except in vacuum cleaners. Finally, while Electrolux had historically avoided vertical integration and sourced most of its components externally, Zanussi was a vertically integrated company with substantial spare capacity for component production that Electrolux could profitably use.

From 30 November 1983 until 14 December 1984, the date when the formal deal was finally signed, there ensued a twelve-month period of intense negotiation in which, alongside the top management of the two companies, Gianmario Rossignolo, the chairman of SKF's Italian subsidiary, took an increasingly active role. The most difficult parts of the negotiations focused on the following three issues:

1. *Union and work force reduction.* At the outset, the powerful unions at Zanussi were against selling the company to the 'Vikings from the North'. They would have preferred to keep Zanussi independent, with a government subsidy, or to merge with Thomson from France. They also believed that

under Electrolux management all important functions would be transferred to Sweden, thereby denuding the skills of the Italian company and also reducing local employment opportunities.

In response to these concerns, Electrolux guaranteed that all Zanussi's important functions would be retained within Italy. Twenty union leaders were sent from Sweden to Italy to reassure the Italians. The same number of Italian union leaders were invited to Sweden to observe Electrolux's production system and labour relations. Initially, Mr Rossignolo signed a letter of assurance to the unions on behalf of Electrolux confirming that the level of employment prevailing at that time would be maintained. Soon thereafter, however, it became obvious that Zanussi could not be made profitable without workforce reductions. This resulted in difficult renegotiations. It was finally agreed that within three months of the acquisition Electrolux would present the unions with a three-year plan for investments and reduction in personnel. Actual retrenchments would have to follow the plan, subject to its approval by the unions.

2. *Prior commitments of Zanussi.* A number of problems were posed by certain commitments on the part of Zanussi. One major issue was SELECO, an Italian producer of television sets. A majority of shares in SELECO were held by REL, a government holding company, and the rest were owned by Zanussi and Indesit. Zanussi had made a commitment to buy REL's majority holdings of SELECO within a period of five years ending in 1989. Electrolux had no interest in entering the television business but finally accepted this commitment despite considerable apprehension.

   Another major concern was the unprofitable Spanish appliance company IBELSA, owned by Zanussi. Zanussi had received large subsidies from the Spanish government against a commitment to help restructure the industry in Spain, and heavy fines would have to be paid if the company decided to pull out. Once again, Electrolux had to accept these terms despite concern about IBELSA's long-term competitiveness.

   Nevertheless, there was one potential liability that Electrolux refused to accept. In the later stages of the negotiations, an audit team from Electrolux discovered that a previous managing director of Zanussi had sold a large amount of equipment and machinery to a German company and had then leased them back. This could potentially lead to severe penalties and large fines, as the actions violated Italian foreign exchange and tax laws. Electrolux refused to proceed with the negotiations until the Italian government had promised not to take any punitive actions in this case.

3. *Financial structure and ownership.* Electrolux was not willing to take over majority ownership of Zanussi immediately, since it would then be required to consolidate Zanussi into group accounts and the large debts would have major adverse effects on the Electrolux balance sheet and share prices. Electrolux wanted to take minority holdings without relinquishing its claim

to majority holdings in the future. To resolve this issue, a consortium was organised that included prominent Italian financial institutions and industrial companies such as Mediobanca, IMI, Crediop and a subsidiary of Fiat. The consortium took on a large part of the shares (40.6 per cent), with another 10.4 per cent bought by the Friuli region. This allowed Electrolux to remain at 49 per cent. While the exact financial transactions were kept confidential, since some of the parties opposed any payment to the Zanussi family, it is believed that Electrolux injected slightly under $100 million into Zanussi. One third of that investment secured the 49 per cent shareholding, and the remainder went towards debentures that could be converted into shares at any time to give Electrolux a comfortable 75 per cent ownership. An agreement with over 100 banks which had some form of exposure to Zanussi assured a respite from creditors, freezing payments on the Italian debt until January 1987. At the same time the creditors made considerable concessions on interest payments.

One of the most important meetings in the long negotiation process took place in Rome on 15 November 1984, when, after stormy discussions between the top management of Electrolux and the leaders of the Zanussi union, a document confirming Electrolux's intention to acquire Zanussi was jointly signed by both parties. During the most crucial hour of the meeting, Hans Werthén stood up in front of the 50 union leaders and declared: 'We are not buying companies in order to close them down, but to turn them into profitable ventures ... and, we are not the Vikings, who were Norwegians anyway'.

The turnaround of Zanussi

It was standard Electrolux practice to have a broad but clear plan for immediate post-acquisition action well before the negotiation process for an acquisition was complete. Thus, by August 1984, well before the deal was signed in December, a specific plan for the turnaround and the eventual integration of Zanussi was drawn up in Stockholm. As stated by Leif Johansson: 'When we make an acquisition, we adopt a centralised approach from the outset. We have a definite plan worked out when we go in and there is virtually no need for extended discussions.' In the Zanussi case, the general approach had to be amended slightly, since a feasible reduction in the employment levels was not automatic. However, clear decisions were taken to move the loss-making production of front-loaded washing machines from France to Zanussi's factory in Pordenone. On the other hand, the production of all top-loading washing machines was to be moved from Italy to France. In total, the internal plan anticipated shifting production of between 600 and 800 thousand product units from Electrolux and subcontractors' plants to Zanussi, thereby increasing Zanussi's capacity utilisation. Detailed financial calculations led to an expected cost saving of Skr 400,000–500,000 through rationalisation. Specific plans were also drawn up to achieve a 2–3 per cent reduction in Zanussi's marketing and administrative costs by integrating the organisation of the two companies in different countries.

Immediate post-acquisition actions

On 14 December, a matter of hours after the signing of the final agreement, Electrolux announced a complete change in the top management of Zanussi. The old board, packed with nominees of the Zanussi family, was swept away and Mr Gianmario Rossignolo was appointed as chairman of the company. An Italian, long-experienced in working with Swedish colleagues because of his position as chairman of SKF's Italian subsidiary, Rossignolo was seen as an ideal bridge between the two companies with their vastly different cultures and management styles. Carlo Verri, who was managing director of SKF's Italian subsidiary, was brought in as the new managing director of Zanussi. Rossignolo and Verri had turned around SKF's Italian operations and had a long history of working together as a team. Similarly, Hans Werthén, Anders Scharp, Gösta Bystedt and Lennart Ribohn joined the reconstituted Zanussi board. The industrial relations manager of Zanussi was the only senior manager below the board level to be replaced. The purpose was to give a clear signal to the entire organisation of the need to change work practices.

Consistent with the Electrolux style, a number of task forces were formed immediately to address the scope of integration and rationalisation of activities in different functional areas. Each team was given a specific time period to come up with recommendations. Similarly, immediate actions were initiated in order to introduce Electrolux's financial reporting system within Zanussi, the clear target being to have the system fully in place and operative within six months from the date of the acquisition.

Direct steps were taken at the business level to enhance capacity utilisation, reduce costs of raw materials and components purchased, and revitalise local sales.

- *Capacity utilisation*. It was promised that Electrolux would source 500,000 units from Zanussi, including 280,000 units of household appliances, 200,000 units of components, and 7,500 units of commercial appliances. This sourcing decision was given wide publicity both inside and outside the company, and a drive was launched to achieve the chosen levels as soon as possible. By 1985, 70 per cent of the target had been reached.
- *Cost cutting in purchases*. Given that 70 per cent of production costs were represented by raw materials and purchased components, an immediate programme was launched to reduce vendor prices. The assumption was that vendors had adjusted their prices to compensate for the high risk of supplying to financially distressed Zanussi, and should lower their prices now that that risk was eliminated. A net saving of 2 per cent on purchases was achieved immediately. Over time about 17 per cent gains in real terms would be achieved, not only for Zanussi, but also for Electrolux.

- *Revitalising sales.* Local competitors in Italy reacted vigorously to the announcement of Electrolux's acquisition of Zanussi. Anticipating a period of inaction while the new management took charge, they launched an aggressive marketing programme and Zanussi's sales slumped almost immediately. After consulting with Electrolux, the new management of Zanussi responded with a dramatic move of initially extending trade credit from 60 to 360 days under specified conditions. Sales surged immediately and the market was assured once and for all that 'Zanussi was back'.

Agreement with the unions

In the next phase, starting from February 1985, the new management turned its attention to medium- and long-term needs. The most pressing of these was to fulfil a promise made to the unions before the acquisition: the presentation of a complete restructuring programme. This programme was finalised and discussed with the union leaders on 28 March 1985, at the Ministry of Industry in Rome. It consisted of a broad analysis of the industry and market trends, an evaluation of Zanussi's competitive position and future prospects, and a detailed plan for investments and workforce reduction. The meeting was characterised by a high level of openness on the part of management. Such openness, unusual in Italian industrial relations, took the unions by surprise. In the end, after difficult negotiations, the plan was signed by all the parties on 25 May.

The final plan provided for a total reduction of the workforce by 4,848 employees to be implemented over a three-year period (2,850 in 1985, 850 in 1986, and 1,100 in 1987) through early retirement and other incentives for voluntary exit. In 1985, as planned, the workforce was reduced by 2,800.

Paradoxically, from the beginning of 1986 a new problem arose. With business doing well and export demands for some of the products strong, a number of factories had to resort to overtime work and even hired new skilled workers, while at the same time the original reduction plans continued to be implemented. Management claimed that there was no inconsistency in these actions, since the people being laid off lacked the skills that would be needed in the future. With the prospect of factory automation clearly on the horizon, a more educated and skilled workforce was necessary and the new hires conformed to these future needs. Some of the workers resisted, and a series of strikes followed at the Porcia plant.

Management decided to force the issue and brought out advertisements in the local press to highlight the situation publicly. In the new industrial climate in Italy, the strategy proved effective and the strikes ended. In 1987 the company made further progress in its relationship with the unions. In a new agreement, wage increases were linked to productivity and no limits were placed on workforce reductions. Further, it was agreed that the company could hire almost 1,000 workers on a temporary basis, so as to take advantage of the subsidy provided by the government to stimulate worker training through temporary employment. It was clear that Zanussi management benefited significantly from the loss of union power that was a prominent feature of the recently changed industrial scene in Italy. However, its open and transparent approach also contributed to the success by gaining the respect of trade union leaders, at both the company and national levels.

Strategic transformation: building competitiveness

The new management recognised that, in order to build durable competitive advantage, more basic changes were necessary. The poor financial performance of the company before the acquisition was only partly due to low productivity, and sustainable profits could not be assured through workforce reduction alone. After careful analysis, three areas were chosen as the focal points for a strategic transformation of Zanussi: improving production technology, spurring innovations and new product development, and enhancing product quality.

1. *Improving production technology.* Recalling his first visit to Zanussi, Halvar Johansson, then head of Electrolux's technical R & D, commented: 'What we found on entering Zanussi's factories was, in many respects, 1960s technology! The level of automation was far too low, especially in assembly operation. We did not find a single industrial robot or even a computer either in the product development unit or in the plant. However, we also discovered that Zanussi's engineers and production personnel were of notably high standards.' As part of a broad programme to improve production technology, Electrolux initiated an investment programme of L340 billion to restructure Zanussi's two major plants at Susegana and Porcia.

   The Susegana restructuring proposal foresaw an investment of L100 billion to build up the facility into a highly automated, high-capacity unit able to produce 1.2 million refrigerators and freezers a year. The project was expected to come on stream by the end of 1988. The Porcia project anticipated a total investment of about L200 billion to build a highly automated, yet flexible plant capable of producing 1.5 million washing machines per year. This project, scheduled for completion in 1990, was the largest individual investment project in the history of the Electrolux group. When on stream it would be the largest washing machine factory in the world. Both projects involved large investments to build flexibility through the use of CAD-CAM systems and just-in-time production methodology. As explained by Carlo Verri: 'The automation was primarily to achieve flexibility and to improve quality, and not to save on labour costs.'

   Implementation of both the projects was somewhat delayed. While the initial schedules may have been over-optimistic, some of the delays were caused by friction among Zanussi and Electrolux engineers. The Electrolux approach of building joint teams for implementation of projects was seen by some Zanussi managers as excessive involvement of the acquiring company in tasks for which the acquired company had ample and perhaps superior capabilities. Consequently, information flows were often blocked, resulting in, for example, a more than one-year delay in deciding the final layout of the Susegana factory. The delays were a matter of considerable concern to the top management of Electrolux. On the one hand, they felt extensive involvement of Electrolux's internal consultants to be necessary for effective implementation of the projects, since Zanussi lacked the requisite expertise. On the other hand, they acknowledged Zanussi's well-established engineering skills and the need to provide the local engineers with the opportunity to learn and to prove themselves. They also worried about whether the skill levels of the local workforce could be upgraded in time for operating the new units, and looked for ways to expedite the training process.

2. *Innovation and new product development.* Zanussi had built its strong market presence on the reputation of being an innovator. This ability had, unfortunately, languished during the lean period. Both Rossignolo and Verri placed the greatest emphasis on reviving the innovative spirit of the company, and projects that had idled for years due to lack of funds were revitalised and assigned high priority.

   The results were quite dramatic and a virtual torrent of new product ideas emerged very quickly. The most striking example was a new washing machine design – the 'Jet System' – that cut detergent and water consumption by a third. The product was developed within only nine months and the new machine was presented at the Cologne fair in February 1986. Through a direct television link with Cologne, Carlo Verri himself presented the assembly line at Pordenone where the 'Jet System' was to be mass produced. By July 1986 demand for the new machine had reached the level of 250,000 per year and the company was facing delivery problems.

   While the 'Jet System' was the most visible outcome of the new emphasis on innovation, other equally important developments were in the pipeline. For example, the company developed a new rotary compressor to replace the reciprocating compressors that were being used in refrigerators. A major drive was also under way to improve product design and features through the introduction of IC chips. Interestingly, most of these proposals came not from the sophisticated and independent research centre of the company, but from development groups located within the line organisations which produced the products. How to maintain the momentum of innovation was a major concern for Verri, particularly as the company moved into the larger and more complex projects necessary for significant technological breakthroughs.

3. *Enhancing product quality.* Quality enhancement was viewed as the third leg of the strategy for long-term revitalisation of Zanussi. At Electrolux, high quality was viewed as an essential means of achieving the primary objectives of the company: satisfied customers, committed employees and sound

profitability. Zanussi had a good reputation for quality, but the standards had slackened during the turmoil faced by the company for almost a decade prior to the acquisition. Committed to the policy that quality levels must be the same within the group no matter where a product was produced, Electrolux initiated a major drive to enhance product quality at Zanussi and set extremely ambitious targets for failure rates and post-sales service requirements. The targets were such that incremental improvements did not suffice for their attainment and a new approach towards quality was necessary. The technical staff of Electrolux provided requisite guidance and assistance, and helped set up the parameters for a series of quality improvement programmes launched by Zanussi.

Carlo Verri was involved in these programmes on an almost day-to-day basis. First, he headed the working group that set up the basic policy on quality for the entire Zanussi organisation. In accordance with this policy, a total quality (TQ) project was started in May 1986 and a series of education and training programmes were introduced in order to diffuse the new philosophy and policy to all company employees. Supplier involvement was an integral part of the TQ project. As described by Verri: 'Supplier involvement was crucial. Zanussi's suppliers had to demonstrate their commitment to effective quality control. This meant that all the procedures for quality assurance, for tracking down failures, etc., had to be approved by us. In other words, suppliers had to have the capability to provide self-certification for the quality of their products. They had to provide service within days rather than weeks, given that our plants were becoming automated. Our gains in flexibility and quality through new production techniques could be lost if the suppliers did not become equally efficient.'

Organisational revitalisation: changing attitudes

One of the biggest challenges faced in the turnaround process lay in the area of revitalising the Zanussi organisation. During the troubled years the management process at Zanussi had suffered from many aberrations. Conflicts had become a way of life, and information flow within the organisation had become severely constrained. Most issues were escalated to the top for arbitration, and the middle management had practically no role in decision making. Front-line managers had become alienated because of direct dealings between the workers and senior managers via the union leaders. Overall, people had lost faith in the integrity of the system, in which seniority and loyalty to individuals were seen as more important than competence or commitment to the company.

In addition, the acquisition had also created a strong barrier of defensiveness within the Zanussi organisation. In its own acquisitions Zanussi typically eliminated most of the middle management in the acquired companies. As the acquired company it expected similar actions from Electrolux. Moreover, some Zanussi managers were not convinced of any need for change. They believed that Zanussi's financial problems were caused not by any strategic, operational or organisational shortcomings, but by the practices of the previous owners, including diversion of overseas profits through a foreign holding company in Luxembourg.

Finally, most of the managers were also concerned that both Rossignolo and Verri, with their backgrounds in the Italian subsidiary of a Swedish company, 'were closer to Stockholm than to Pordenone'.

In an attempt to overcome these barriers, Verri and the entire executive management group at Zanussi participated in a number of team-building sessions that were facilitated by an external consultant. These meetings gave rise to a number of developments that constituted the core of the organisational revitalisation of Zanussi.

1. *Statement of mission, values and guiding principles.* One of the direct outcomes of the team-building meetings was a statement of mission, values, and guiding principles, developed to serve as the charter for change (see Exhibit 4). The statement identified the four main values of the company: to be close to the clients and satisfy them through innovation and service; to accept challenges and develop a leader mentality; to pursue total quality not only in production but in all areas of activity; and to become a global competitor by developing an international outlook. Apart from these specific points, the statement also confirmed the new management's commitment to creating a context that would foster transparent and coherent behaviour at both the individual and company levels under all circumstances. As described by Rossignolo: 'We adopted the Swedish work ethic – everybody keeps his word and all information is correct. We committed ourselves to being honest with the local authorities, the trade unions and our customers. It took some time for the message to get across, but I think everybody has got it now.'

2. *Management development workshops.* In order to improve the flow of information among senior managers and to co-opt them into the new management approach, a set of management development workshops was organised. The 60 most senior managers of Zanussi, including Verri, participated in each of three two-day workshops that were held between November 1985 and July 1986. The next tier of 150 middle managers of the company were subsequently exposed to the same programme.

3. *Middle management problems.* An organisational climate survey in 1987 revealed an interesting problem. The top 60 managers of the company confirmed strong support for the mission statement and the new management style. Conversely, the 150 middle managers, who seemed to feel threatened by the changes, appeared considerably less enthused. Their subordinates – about a thousand front-line managers and professional employees – like the top management, fully approved the change and demanded greater involvement. In response to this problem, it was decided that the 60 top managers should establish direct communication with the 1,000 front-line managers, bypassing the middle management when

Exhibit 4 Mission, values and guiding principles of Zanussi

Mission

To become the market leader in Europe, with a significant position in other world areas, in supplying homes, institutions and industry with systems, appliances, components and after-sales services. To be successful in this mission, the company and management legitimisation must be based on the capability to be near the customer and satisfy his needs; to demonstrate strength, entrepreneurship and creativity in accepting and winning external challenges; to offer total quality on all dimensions, more than the competition; and to be oriented to an internal vision and engagement.

Values

Our basic values, ranked, are:
> to be near the customer; to accept challenges; to deliver total quality; with an international perspective.

Our central value, underlying all of the above, is transparence, which means that Zanussi will reward behaviour which is based on constantly transparent information and attitudes, safeguarding the interests of the company.

Guiding principles
1. A management group is legitimised by knowing what we want, pursuing it coherently, and communicating our intent in order to be believable.
2. Shared communication means shared responsibility, not power and status index.
3. The manager's task is managing through information and motivation, not by building 'power islands'.
4. Time is short: the world will not wait for our 'perfect solutions'.
5. Strategic management implies:
    *   Professional skills;
    *   Risk-taking attitudes and the skill to spot opportunity;
    *   Integration with the environment and the organisation, flexibility and attention to change;
    *   Identification with the mission of the firm, and helping in the evolution of a culture that supports it;
    *   Team work ability;
    *   Skill in identifying strengths and weaknesses.

Policies to be developed
Specific policies were being developed in the following areas to support the implementation of the above mission, values and guiding principles: personnel, image and public relations, administration, purchasing, asset control, legal representation, R & D and innovation, and information systems. Members of senior management were assigned responsibility for developing policies in each of these areas, with completion expected by the end of 1986.

necessary. The decision was made known within the organisation and a clear signal was sent to the middle managers that they should get on board or else they would risk missing the boat. At the same time, a special training programme was launched for the front-line managers and professional employees in order to broaden their management skills and outlook.

4. *Structural reorganisation.* Before the acquisition, Zanussi was organised in five 'sectors', with the heads of each sector reporting to the managing director. The sectors, in turn, controlled the operating companies in their business areas. In practice, the sector managers were closely involved with the day-to-day operations of the companies under their charge. Both the managing director at the corporate level and the different sector managers had strong staff organisations to support their activities.

Verri abandoned the sector concept, even though the operating companies continued to report to the former sector managers who were now called managing directors. However, staff at the sector level were virtually eliminated and the operating companies were given full responsibility and authority for taking all operating-level decisions. Similarly, staff at the corporate level were also reduced very substantially, and the heads of planning, finance and control, organisation and human resources, general administration, and legal and public affairs all reported directly to Verri. The four managing directors, the five heads of major corporate staff departments and Verri constituted the executive management group of Zanussi. As chairman, Rossignolo concentrated primarily on external relations.

Integration of the two companies

As described by Leif Johansson: 'With the acquisition of Zanussi, the Electrolux group entered a new era. In several respects we were able to adopt a completely new way of thinking.' Much of the new thinking emerged from the discussions and recommendations of the task forces that had been appointed, involving managers from both companies, to look at specific opportunities for integrating the activities of the two organisations. In total, eight such task forces were formed: two each for components, product development, and commercial appliances, and one each for the marketing function and management development. Each of these task forces had met three or four times, typically for half a day each time. Their recommendations formed the basis for the actions that were taken to integrate the production and sales operations of the two companies, rationalise component production and develop specialisation in product and brand development within the entire Electrolux group. At the level of individuals, a bridge had been built between the top management of Electrolux and the senior management team of Zanussi, and further actions were under way for creating similar understanding and mutual respect among managers lower down in the two organisations.

Electrolux Components Group (ECG)

Following Electrolux's acquisition of White Consolidated in the United States in March 1986, an international task force consisting of managers from Electrolux, White and Zanussi was created to explore the overall synergies that could be exploited within the activities of the three companies. The task force concluded that integration opportunities were relatively limited at the level of finished products because of factors such as differences in customer preferences and technical standards, and the high transportation costs.

However, at the component level there were many similarities in the needs of the three companies, implying greater scope for standardisation and production rationalisation. As a result of this analysis, the Electrolux Component Group was formed at the beginning of 1987 as part of the newly created industrial products division at Electrolux. The group was made responsible for the co-ordination and development of all strategic components used by Electrolux worldwide. Since over 50 per cent of the group's component production came from Zanussi, Verri was appointed head of this group in addition to his responsibilities as managing director of Zanussi, and the group headquarters were located in Turin, Italy. In order to preserve and enhance the competitiveness of the component sector, it was decided that 50 per cent of the component group's sales must be made to outside parties and at least 20 per cent of the internal requirement for components must be sourced from outside the newly formed group.

Integration of production

At Electrolux, production, sales and marketing had traditionally been integrated market by market. After the acquisition of Zanussi, all these activities would be reorganised into international product divisions and national marketing/sales companies.

The larger volumes from the combined operations made it feasible to switch to a system in which large-scale specialised plants, equipped with flexible manufacturing technology, would each produce a single product for the entire European market. This new 'one product–one factory' strategy was exemplified by the new plants in Susegana and Porcia. Each of the product divisions carried full responsibility not only for manufacturing, but also for development and internal marketing of their products. In order to co-ordinate long-term development among these 43 divisions, three co-ordinators were appointed for 'wet', 'hot' and 'cold' products respectively. Based in Stockholm without staff, each of these co ordinators would be on the road most of the time.

Integration of sales/marketing

Similarly, it was decided to create single umbrella companies over the separate sales/marketing organisations in all countries. Given the long-standing history of competition between the Electrolux and Zanussi organisations, this would turn out to be a difficult and complex process. It was planned that in each country the stronger organisation would absorb the weaker one. This did not mean, however, that the head of the larger organisation in each country would automatically receive the top slot in the combined organisation. A number of complaints arose on both sides over this issue, which became a source of much irritation. For example, it was because of this that Candotti, who had been the first to approach Electrolux for investment in Zanussi, resigned. In what remained a source of considerable frustration, Zanussi continued to operate through directly controlled sales companies in Germany, France, Denmark and Norway.

Co-ordination among the marketing companies was achieved through an equally lean co-ordinating structure reporting to Leif Johansson, with an Italian manager co-ordinating all European countries and a Swedish manager looking after the rest of the world.

To facilitate operational co-ordination between sales and production, a number of new systems were developed. One, the Electrolux Forecasting and Supply System (EFS), involved the automatic co-ordination of sales forecasts and delivery orders. By 1988 computer links with EFS would be established in all European sales subsidiaries and factories. The Zanussi evaluation system was changed to that of Electrolux, in which both sales and factories were assessed on the basis of return on net assets (RONA) rather than on a profit and cost basis. An overall RONA target of 20 per cent was set for the group as a whole.

Brand positioning and product development

One of the consequences of Electrolux's history of international expansion through acquisitions was a proliferation of brands, not only in Europe but also in the USA, where the acquisition of White had brought a number of brands. The task of co-ordinating these brands, some of which were local, others regional and a few international, would fall to the two marketing co-ordinators, working closely with Leif Johansson and a task force involving product styling and marketing managers. The challenge was complicated by the fact that even the international brands did not always have the same position from market to market. Zanussi, for example, was not a brand name in Italy itself, where its products sold as 'Rex'. And its image in Sweden was not nearly as upscale and innovative as in other countries like the United Kingdom.

The approach chosen in Europe was to group the brands in four brand-name families, each targeted at a particular customer profile and destined to become a separate design family (see Exhibit 5). Two of these families would be interna-

Exhibit 5 **Customer profiles**

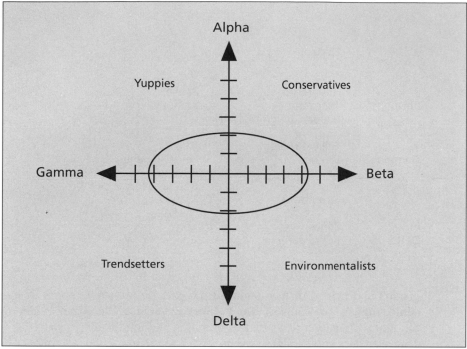

tional brands, based respectively on Electrolux and Zanussi, and the other two would regroup a number of local brands (see Exhibit 6). The goal was to develop an integrated pan-European strategy for each brand-name family. For the international brands, the strategy would involve high-scale production of standardised products in focused factories, and co-ordinated positioning and marketing across different countries. For the families representing a collection of national brands, the products would again be standardised as far as possible so as to allow manufacturing on a regional scale; but each brand would be 'localised' in its country through positioning, distribution, promotion and service.

Mutual respect and understanding among people

Since the acquisition Anders Scharp, Lennart Ribohn and Leif Johansson had ensured that they jointly visited Pordenone at least once every two months for a two-day review of Zanussi's activities and progress. Hans Werthén and Gösta Bystedt also visited Zanussi, though much less frequently. The visitors would typically spend some time touring one or another of Zanussi's facilities and then move on to pre-planned meetings with Zanussi's top management. Over time these meetings had built a strong bridge of mutual respect between the two

Exhibit 6 The brand-name families

α Alpha	Electrolux	
β Beta	Husqvarna Therma Boppas (Belgium, Italy)	Zakker Arthur Martin
γ Gamma	Elektro Helios Elektra Castor Voss Strömberg	Atlas Faure (Quelle) Privileg Boppas (Norway, France) Marykek
δ Delta	Zanussi Rex	

groups and helped diffuse some of the early apprehensions. As described by a senior manager of Zanussi: 'The top management of Electrolux really understand numbers. They look at a few key numbers and immediately grasp the essentials. That was very good training for us – we had the habit of analysing and analysing, without coming to any conclusions ... Besides, the top two or three people in Electrolux have the ability of immersing themselves in a particular problem and coming up with a solution and an implementation plan. They are also so obviously excited by what they do, their enthusiasm is very contagious.' For most senior managers at Zanussi these meetings provided stronger evidence than could any words that the top management of Electrolux did not consider the acquisition as a conquest but rather as a partnership. 'We have had a lot of exchanges, and have learnt a lot from them, but we have not had a single Swedish manager imposed on top of us here.'

At the next level of management the joint task forces had helped build some relationships among individuals, but the links were still weak and apprehensions remained. 'We don't know them, but our concern is that the next level of Electrolux managers may be more bureaucratic and less open. To them we might be a conquest', said a senior manager of Zanussi. 'In the next phase of integration, we must develop bridges at the middle and I frankly do not know how easy or difficult that might be.'

Future requirements

Whereas the acquisition of Zanussi and White Consolidated had catapulted Electrolux into a clear lead in the industry, the race was far from over. After initially failing to reach agreement with Philips in 1987, Whirlpool had come back in early 1988, agreeing to buy out 53 per cent of Philips's appliance operations as a first step to taking full control. Upon full completion Whirlpool would have paid or assumed debt totalling $1.2 billion for activities which in 1987 were generating $70 million pre-tax pre-interest income on sales of $2 billion. The Japanese had started moving outside south-east Asia. In the meantime, local European competitors such as GEC and Merloni were ensuring good returns and, more importantly, were gaining back market share.

All of this was taking place in a mature industry highly dependent on replacement demand. Industry analysts expected that, even in a moderately growing economy, appliance shipments would be on a downward trend for the next couple of years. Given the concentration of buyers and the shift towards specialised retailers, raw materials price increases were more and more difficult to pass on.

A strategy for change at KPMG
Gerry Johnson

Background to KPMG

KPMG is a large international firm of accountants and consultants. By 1992 the fee income of KPMG International was over $6 billion – number one world-wide – and about half of that was accounted for by Europe. Within that European total, the UK accounted for around $900 million – about 15 per cent of the world-wide total. The south-east region accounted for about 65 per cent of the UK fee income (see Figures 1 and 2). (The accountancy firms were all partnerships and did not publish their profits, so the main rankings were typically published in terms of fee income.) Table 1 shows the relative size of the main competitors, world-wide and in the UK, in terms of market share. KPMG was in the lead in several of its market sectors, and where not in the lead was generally placed second or third by external surveys. Overall, KPMG's competitive position was very close to that of its two main rivals: Coopers and Lybrand, and Price Waterhouse.

Within the UK, KPMG employed around 10,300 staff and partners. Over half of that total was in the south-east region – and the rest spread out over five other regions, each of which was significantly smaller than the south-east region. The south-east region was thus the major part of the UK practice (see Figure 2).

Colin Sharman, senior partner in the south-east, described the situation in the early 1990s:

> In the UK a little over half of the income is derived from audit and financial advice [see Figure 3 and Table 2 for comparable data for other firms]. That proportion has been coming down over the years. Around ten years ago it accounted for about two-thirds of the income: however, growth in the other main service areas of tax, management consulting and corporate recovery have gradually been taking a larger share of our total business. Although I have described the fee income in terms of the type of services that KPMG offers, we do not like to see ourselves defined as auditors or consultants. Rather, we describe ourselves as a firm that sells high quality professional services of a very wide variety. These services fall into two main categories: attest work and business solutions.

This case is based on a speech by Colin Sharman of KPMG in February 1992. It is intended for classroom discussion only rather than as an illustration of good or bad management practice. © KPMG Peat Marwick, 1992.

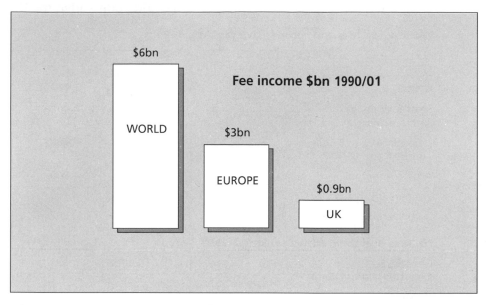

Figure 1 KPMG: an international perspective

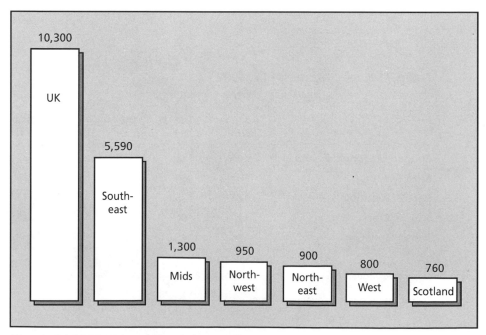

Figure 2 KPMG UK: staff numbers, 1991

Table 1 Relative size of KPMG competitors world-wide and in the UK

World-wide fees and competitive ranking, 1990

	Rank	$m
KPMG	**1**	**5,400**
Ernst & Whinney Arthur Young	2	5,006
Deloitte Haskins & Sells Touche Ross	3=	4,200
Arthur Andersen	3=	4,200
Coopers & Lybrand	5	4,100
Price Waterhouse	6	2,881

UK fees and competitive rankings, 1990

	Rank	$m
Coopers & Lybrand Deloitte Haskins & Sells	1	531
KPMG	**2**	**395**
Ernst Young	3	338
Price Waterhouse	4	300
Touche Ross	5	262
Arthur Andersen	6	194

Source: *International Accounting Bulletin.*

Table 2 UK fees: business mix, 1990

	Audit (£m)	Tax (£m)	MAS[1] (£m)	Corp. recovery insolvency (£m)	Total (£m)
Coopers & Lybrand Deloitte	244	122	128	37	531
Ernst & Young	162	84	68	24	338
Price Waterhouse	126	75	84	15	300
Touche Ross[2]	123	60	58	21	262
Arthur Andersen	56	45	85	8	194

[1] MAS = management advisory services.
[2] Estimated. Includes figures from merger with Spicer & Oppenheim.

Source: *International Accounting Bulletin.*

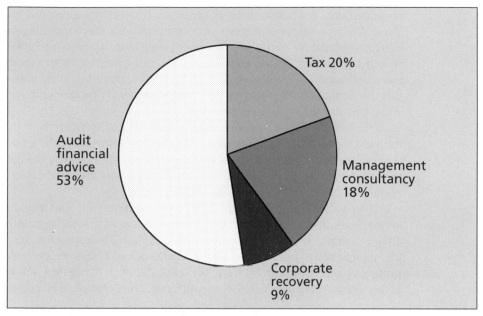

Figure 3 KPMG UK: fee income

Simply defined, attest work means we give opinions. The best known is, of course, audits but there are also a number of other circumstances where chartered accountants are required to sign their names to documents. The second category is business solutions. We help businesses to solve their business problems not just by management consulting advice, but also by our tax practice work, our corporate recovery work and to an increasing extent our accounting practice work helps clients find solutions and implement them.

It is also important to understand that KPMG is a *partnership*, which makes its structure, and the way it operates, quite different in many respects from that of a company. For example, in the south-east region of KPMG there are around 300 partners, each of whom is an owner/manager. As a matter of law all partners have to agree to certain things: for example, the taking of leases on new premises. This reinforces the feeling that partners are involved in major decision making. In practice, of course, we have moved a long way from the Victorian notion of partnership and we run ourselves increasingly on corporate lines. I am the senior partner, the managing director, and I have a management team who make many of the operational decisions of an executive board. But those 300 partners have to be consulted and have to agree – or at least not disagree – with any change. And that is not just an issue of communicating well through the organisation but also of winning the hearts and minds of my partners.

We have a matrix structure like many other professional service organisations. We have a delivery structure for services along discipline lines. We have different practice units for audit, for tax, for management consultants and for corporate recovery [see Figure 4]. Separately we focus on our market sectors through firm-wide multi-disciplinary groups that are industry based, focusing on banking, insurance, manufacturing and so on. But the dominant axis remains the discipline-based practice units, and that is the primary interface to the market.

Our mission involves providing the highest quality of services to our individual clients but our practice units are discipline based. The only way that we focus across disciplines is through our market sector groups, but they merely co-ordinate and do not run the business. Hence there is a conflict between our stated goals and our structure.

If we look at our marketplace, the 1980s were terrific. The demand for our services seemed to be infinite. Our top line fee growth was frequently 30 or 40 per cent p.a. In 1992 the market is far tougher. The recession has hit our clients and hence our market. Either clients are not buying – deferring some kinds of work is the easiest thing for some clients – or we find ourselves in highly competitive situations where differentiating ourselves is a major issue.

In addition to the recession, KPMG faced changed market circumstances in the 1990s. The client market was becoming increasingly concentrated. More especially, the expectations of clients were changing: they expected their advisors to

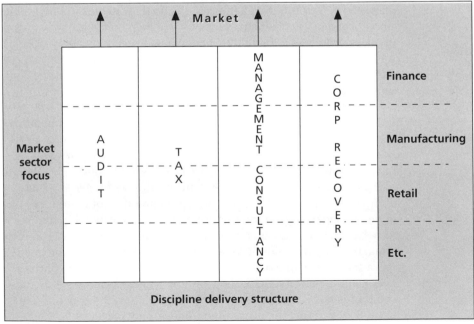

Figure 4 Delivery structure for services

understand the problems they faced, and to be able to provide a range of services to meet their needs. The issue for KPMG was, therefore, to ensure that partners were seen as, and performed the role of, business advisers.

Managing change at KPMG

In February 1992 Colin Sharman spoke at a Strategic Planning Society meeting in London about strategic change in KPMG:

> KPMG needs to change to survive in the tougher competitive environment of the 1990s. The right starting place was how we faced the market. We were facing the market not through our market sector focus but through our discipline structure. The key was to get client focus into our organisation.
>
> Having recognised the need to change we needed to work out how to get the organisation to change. Initially I thought that I could operate successfully by changing only the behaviour and skill sets of our people, in particular our partners. But I rapidly came to the conclusion that was not going to work. If I changed the behaviour of partners and staff to become more client focused, more market sector focused, more knowledgeable about the market place, that would rapidly fall apart. We would need to reinforce it by measurement systems to ensure that our people were measured by these new ways of doing things; and by a structure which aligned with what people were being asked to do. If people were accountable in one direction but were told to focus their efforts in another, it is likely that one or other would lose out, probably the new focus. And if our measurement systems and reward systems measure something other than the new behaviour we are asking for, it is fairly clear what will happen. So I concluded that we needed what I call a virtuous circle of change consisting of three interlinking elements – structure, measurement and behaviour, all needing to operate on each other. But of course changing all three elements is a much bigger task and takes much more time. So there is an issue of how much time can be afforded to achieve real change. Or looked at another way, what is the minimum time that we can take to achieve real change without damaging the business?

Blockages to change

Colin Sharman continued:

> KPMG can be characterised as professional, highly conservative and sometimes complacent. There is also an attitude that our partners can – and will – 'do anything', different from a 'do well' culture. And also a belief from right across the firm that being a generalist, rather than a specialist, is the

most desirable state. Partners believe they should have a say in decision making. It is not always seen like that from within the organisation and there is a belief that the senior partners in the organisation actually operate on the principle of management by edict. So we have partners who are struggling to keep the power to themselves and senior partners trying to manage but sounding like dictating. Either way, it does not help effective management.

In managing change, the way we run the business can sometimes be a problem. There is, for example, a widespread network of committees – the answer for most things in the organisation is to set up a committee, a retreat into collectivism at the drop of a hat. Alongside that the responsibilities of individuals within the organisation are so ill-defined that it makes achieving change very difficult. Our control systems are full of paradoxes. At lower levels our staff see controls as bureaucratic, taking time away from the real business of being a professional services firm. That may be true, but at the higher levels there is a belief that we have poor controls and poor management information to run the business. Both of those are probably right – we spend a lot of time collecting and controlling the things that don't help us to run the business. Alongside that we have too much poor discipline – a lack of rigour and not caring about doing it right the first time. That is not surprising if we are asking people to spend a lot of their time on data that are never used to manage the business. But poor discipline endemic through an organisation is a major barrier to new ways of working. For example there is too little value placed on managing carefully to timescales. It is regarded as much better to whirl around in frenzied activity at the last minute. That applies whether we are serving clients or whether we are trying to do something that contributes towards managing the business. You will hear people bragging about the extremely long hours that they work, doubtless to reinforce the air of crisis that they are managing (though never creating!).

The 'mystique of partnership' doesn't always help. Promotion to partner is seen as the summit of a KPMG person's career with virtually no second prizes for those who do not make it – we have a culture of 'up or out'. Partners, once created, are quite distinct and elevated people within the organisation. There are also problems with the discipline structure of audit, tax, consultancy and so on being dominant: problems illustrated, for example, by the tales people tell about how awful one of the other disciplines is. Nor is the 'cult of the individual' always helpful. The kind of people who are lionised are mavericks – people out of the mould; people who have broken the mould; people who don't conform, who are entirely individuals – there are lots of stories about individuals. You can imagine the way some of this expresses itself; especially when it comes to 'them and us' – partners and the rest or, at lower levels, senior managers and the rest. For example, in our London office we have three levels of dining room.

You might think from all of that, that KPMG is an organisation barely worth bothering with. But KPMG is a very successful organisation, which of course reinforces the aversion to change. Change is always all right provided someone else has to change. And if we are successful – winning new clients, making a reasonable amount of money – why on earth should partners change? But change is necessary. So let me tell you a bit about what we have been doing to achieve change.

The change process at KPMG

We organised a series of strategy workshops for the region's partners; and around one-third have now been through them. What those workshops did was to work through the strategic position of the firm, what the competitive strategy should be, what the blockages to change were, what the critical success factors were and crucially what actions needed to be put in place.

The messages that came out of the workshops and the key elements of change that were needed were remarkably consistent. These confirmed the need for increased client focus. Major issues of specialism and integrating our service delivery also emerged. Importantly, partners on the workshops recognised the need for major strategic change.

At the end of the series of workshops I arranged for some more detailed feedback sessions for all of the partners. I held ten evening sessions with all but a small handful of partners coming to one of the sessions. There we took the main messages from the workshops, discussed the main directions of the firm and tried to surface any real concerns. Those proved a very useful way of building the consensus that we need and also reinforcing the fact that change is definitely coming.

But I have not just worked with partners. The next group down, similar in size, are also critical to the success of the organisation. I used the senior management conference, which was an annual ritual for our senior managers to complain about the firm, as a way of getting them into strategic issues. The managers worked through much the same process as the partners had done on the workshops. At the end of that, the senior managers produced a serious analysis of the issues facing the firm and the kind of actions that were needed.

I tried to capture that enthusiasm, that commitment, that sense of change by holding a series of briefing sessions for partners and senior managers together to spread some of the messages. The messages I wanted to get across were that we were serious about change; that we needed to become a much more open organisation; that we needed to involve people at all levels in the development in the organisation and that we needed to communicate very much better than we had done in the past. All of those are fairly abstract messages but to make them have a real impact I had the sessions designed to reinforce the underlying message, which was that we are going to do things very differently in future.

We had to do things differently. So here is an example of the visuals that we used to accompany the presentations [see Figure 5]. Now you might think that this is pretty ordinary but my KPMG audience is accustomed to nothing more exciting than slides with a KPMG-blue background and logo. So if nothing else my pop art images made an impact. All of this contributed to a real atmosphere of change and a real desire for change in the organisation. People started talking openly about wanting to change, wanting to try new things and wanting to succeed.

But I also have to say that we have identified considerable fear of change in some people. We expected resistance to change in those most affected. That fear, which was predictable, is something that needs to be handled carefully so as not to destabilise the organisation.

We have now got to the stage where we have identified the main elements of our strategy. The major feature is that we need to be a client-focused organisation. That means that we need to work on the three elements of the virtuous circle that I described earlier to achieve client focus. We need to change the *structure* of the firm to put clients first and discipline second. We need to change the *behaviour* and *skills* of our partners so that they are client-focused professionals specialised and dedicated to client service. And we need to have *measurement systems* that line up with our new structure and reinforce the new behaviours and skills that our people must have.

The most important change to achieve is in the behaviour and skills of our people. This needs to be reinforced by ensuring that symbols of the old way of doing things, including committees, go. We have to have a proper identification of accountabilities and responsibilities for individuals. Stories of excellent client service across disciplines must replace ones about how part of the firm has failed.

I am also clear that our communication systems – which are primitive – have to be very much better. I will be using communications in a positive way to ensure that partners and staff understand and are committed to the direction we are going in.

I cannot yet report success in changing KPMG because we are still fairly near the beginning of the process. We have identified the main elements of change, the main blockages in the system and the main actions that we need to take to change the organisation. Now I and my partners need to manage that change. And if we are successful, we believe that we will have established competitive advantage in the marketplace. And that, after all, is why we are going through the process.

Figure 5 Visuals for the presentations

The Burton Group (A) 1969–1975

Gerry Johnson

Burton was the largest of the menswear retailers in the UK; yet in the mid-1970s it appeared near to collapse and led to the intervention of the City on matters concerning the internal management of the company – a step which remains unusual and emphasises the extent to which the company's demise was regarded as a matter of extraordinary concern.

At the beginning of the 1970s Burton had a turnover in excess of £80 million and over 1,000 properties (valued in excess of £70 million) in the UK and France, including 15 factories manufacturing mainly made-to-measure suits and over 600 menswear shops trading as Burton and, in the north, Jacksons. 27,000 people worked for the company, 10,000 of whom were employed at the Leeds Hudson Mills manufacturing base. Burton also owned Brown's of Chester, the quality departmental store, and Peter Robinson, a small chain of department stores concentrating on ladies' fashions.

From 1967 to 1969 the company had attempted to recruit a new senior management team; by 1970 this was in place under the direction of Ladislas Rice, an appointee of high reputation who had previously been chief executive of the Minerals Separation Company and a consultant with a leading management consultancy. Joining in June 1969, he was the first chief executive of any of the major UK clothing multiples to come from outside the industry.

Burtons before 1970

Montague Burton opened his first shop in Chesterfield in 1901. By 1929 the company had 300 shops and went public. In the intervening years the reputation and fortunes of Burton were built on the provision of good-quality, value-for-money, made-to-measure suits. However, by the end of the 1960s, despite increasing profitability (see Table 1), family control and paternalistic and centralised management had resulted in a lack of top management succession. The family themselves sought to remedy this in 1969 by the appointment of Ladislas Rice. Nevertheless the company was to remain in family control until the mid-1970s,

This case is intended for class discussion and not to illustrate either correct or incorrect handling of an administrative situation. © Gerry Johnson, 1986, revised 1988, 1992. The author wishes to acknowledge with thanks the assistance of Bridget Garnish in revising this case study.

Table 1 Burton's financial performance, 1965–69

Year	Turnover (£m)	Percentage change	Net profit before tax (£m)	Percentage change
1965	52.4	+ 8	4.2	+ 17
1966	57.2	+ 9	4.4	+ 5
1967	61.0	+ 6	4.9	+ 12
1968	65.6	+ 7.5	6.5	+ 32
1969	68.3	+ 4	7.2	+ 11

protected by a shareholding structured so as to retain voting within the family and the directors of the business.

Burton was a highly conservative company. Stories are told of the hierarchy existing in the shops, where the manager sat in his office, appearing occasionally to meet important 'clients' or inspect the staff, and where the young trainees or 'boys' recruited from school were not allowed to associate with customers until they were skilled in made-to-measure tailoring. Customers were predominantly married men; made-to-measure was the service provided, with ready-to-wear merchandise considered to be somewhat inferior and normally unavailable or low in stock, since the company lacked the stock control mechanism to handle it. Burton was essentially a manufacturer of made-to-measure garments with retail outlets as order points.

Yet the company was by the late 1960s operating in a retail environment undergoing rapid change. The 1960s was the era of the Beatles and the fashion-conscious young male who wore imported ready-to-wear Italian suits and colourful clothes. Market growth came from men under 25 who were increasingly purchasing ready-to-wear clothes, which they could buy at similar or better quality for less money at the increasing number of boutiques competing with Burton.

1969–72: Reorganisation

The new corporate management team appointed by Rice consisted of Peter Gorb as commercial director, who had been with Rice at Harvard in 1951 and had latterly been an executive with a textile manufacturer; Richard Stokes as personnel director; and Jim Power as finance director, the only internal Burton appointment at the most senior level. Rice immediately established a London head office away from the traditional base at Leeds for this team, and set about reconceiving the future strategy of the company.

At a corporate level Rice and his team sought a radical reorganisation. The company name was changed to the Burton Group Limited (from Montague Burton Limited) at the end of 1970; and Rice's team aimed to develop it as a group of separate retail businesses set up as profit-responsible divisions. Figure 1 shows the resulting structure of the group.

However, Rice and his colleagues believed that the central problem was the menswear business. Their aim was to achieve a switch from a manufacturing focus to a retailing focus: their solutions hinged on 'building a team of managers capable of buying and selling ready made men's suits and outerwear, and in controlling the purchasing, sales and stocks of ready to wear garments'.

It was Peter Gorb's brief to achieve this switch from a manufacturing focus to a retailing focus. At the menswear core of the business this entailed splitting off manufacturing from retailing with the dual purpose of releasing the menswear buyers from internal buying obligations, and also requiring the manufacturing division to produce to the needs of retailing – be it Burton retailing or any other customers it might deal with. It was known within the group that it was not an easy task to move towards ready-to-wear; two previous attempts had failed, in 1952 and in the 1960's. The major problem was stock management – since made-to-measure entailed low stock commitment compared with the higher stock levels necessary for a ready-to-wear business – and the need for accurate stock control.

Ivan Richardson was recruited from Marks and Spencer as retail menswear buying director and given the job of widening the product range to include competitively priced and profitable ranges of ready-to-wear suits. Martin Frankel, from Daks Simpson, was appointed managing director of the manufacturing divi-

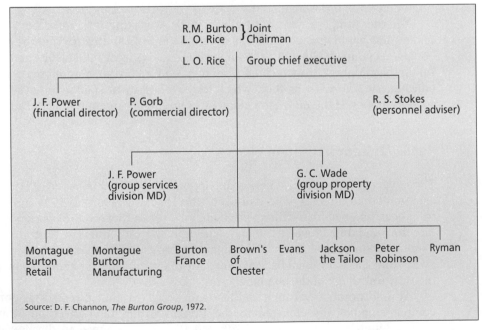

Figure 1 The Burton Group: management structure (in the early 1970s)

sion. His main task was to make the manufacturing operation profitable in its own right. He began by switching the emphasis from made-to-measure to ready-to-wear. Other major steps were the tightening of controls on costs and the increased mechanisation of manufacturing. Richard Stokes as personnel director was tasked with improving the company's management. By the end of 1970, 50 new senior executives had been recruited, new remuneration schemes including profit share were in place and a training centre had been established.

In addition, the planning mechanisms of the company received attention. The group executive set annual goals to divisions, which were required to demonstrate how they could contribute to these goals. The result was divisional plans, revised every six months and reported against monthly. Such plans also provided the basis for a system of management by objectives, so that all managers to middle management level knew how they were expected to contribute to the company's performance.

. . . and diversification

Burton also widened its portfolio of interests. Already involved in departmental stores, mail order and the French menswear operation, the years 1969 to 1973 saw a flurry of acquisitions for the company. Rice summarised his policy of diversification as 'To seek well-managed retail businesses, in any field, capable of expansion but needing, for real growth, the kind of property and financial strength which we can offer'. It was an attempt to utilise the asset base of the company and to move away from overreliance on the retail clothing sector.

The first move was, in fact, divestment. The mail-order operation, never a significant profit earner and currently unprofitable, was sold. In the six months from autumn 1970 to spring 1971 four acquisitions were made. The first was St Remy, a French operation which retailed men's and women's clothing through 35 shops throughout France. A major reason behind this acquisition was the need to provide additional volume to the Burton factory, which was running at 50 per cent capacity; in France the made-to-measure market was also holding up better than elsewhere.

This was followed by the acquisition of Trumps, an employment agency and package holiday operation which already traded in or adjacent to the Peter Robinson stores. However, this was not successful and by the beginning of 1972 Trumps had been sold to the Alfred Marks agency.

The third acquisition was Evans Outsize. It was bought for £4 million, and Burton acquired not only its 76 shops but also the computerised stock control systems operated by the company and the retail skills of Cyril Spencer, its chief executive. Evans was a profitable business which had been growing and could be seen as a potential beneficiary of the properties available through Burton.

The final acquisition in this spate of activity was Ryman Conran, the office supply company, which was purchased for £9 million. Ryman had 75 retail outlets selling office stationery, furniture and machines, and had four manufacturing units.

1971 also saw the internal development of a new retail venture, Orange Hand, which was aimed at the 5–15-year-old boy, and designed to exploit the growing fashion awareness of the young. The first shop opened in August 1971.

... and consequences

The financial consequences of these early decisions are shown in Table 2. Even by the end of 1971 there were some features of the performance of Burton which concerned outside observers. In 1970 turnover rose by just 3 per cent to £70 million and profit before tax fell by 13 per cent. The 14 per cent rise in turnover in 1971 to £80 million for the group, together with a profit increase of 19 per cent, hid a decline in menswear profits and a less than convincing trading performance – almost one-third of the group profits came from the property division. By mid-1972 it was clear that Burton faced considerable problems. The capital spent on its acquisitions was leading to increased borrowings and the swing away from made-to-measure suits was giving rise to under-utilised factory capacity.

Efforts were being made to improve performance, including the refurbishment of some 100 shops and the rationalisation of production capacity, involving redundancy programmes in three factories. But change was simply taking too long. Managers with the buying expertise required by Gorb or the computer and control skills required by Power took time to recruit; and the shops needed converting to present a more up-to-date image. One executive recalled:

> I remember there were window models that looked like something out of Joe Stalin's secret service. We needed to replace them but there wasn't the

Table 2 The Burton Group: financial performance, 1970–73 (£ million)

	1970	*1971*	*1972*	*1973*
Group turnover	70.2	80.2	100.2	113.8
Sales by activity:				
UK menswear retailing	55.9	n/a	n/a	71.0
UK menswear manufacturing	n/a	n/a	n/a	0.4
Other retailing	13.7	n/a	n/a	42.5
Profits				
Trading profit by activity:				
UK menswear retailing	7.6	n/a	n/a	6.6
UK menswear manufacturing	n/a	n/a	n/a	0.5
Other retailing	(0.1)	n/a	n/a	0.2
Property income	n/a	2.9	n/a	3.8
Group trading profit (before interest and taxation)	7.5	9.1	8.9	11.1
Group profit (before taxation)	6.3	7.4	6.6	8.7

manufacturing capacity to do it in less than five years. We had to change the heads in one year and so on down the body!

The strategy continues

The strategies agreed in 1970 were nevertheless maintained. The production focus was switching to ready-to-wear; the problem was that the capacity levels far outstripped the demand, despite the voluntary redundancies programme and some manufacturing cutbacks. Efforts were made to sell outside the group, but with little success. There was less resistance from the shop managers to the changes. They could see they were losing sales to ready-to-wear. Shops were being refitted and restocked with a wider selection of merchandise. The problems here were the time it took to refit, the failure of new ideas in merchandise to appeal to customers in shops that were out of date, and the 'learning curve' of the new merchandisers, which was 'much longer than expected'. Nonetheless the total number of shops owned by the group, discounting acquisitions, rose from 835 in 1972 to 920 in 1973.

In most other divisions there were strategies of both rationalisation and growth. Peter Robinson expanded its successful Top Shop venture, which was aimed at the fashion-conscious young woman, while cutting back on loss-making stores. Jackson launched 'Break Out', a more fashionable line of merchandise for younger men in 1973, while also pursuing a rationalisation of its manufacturing capacity. Ryman expanded its shop network, but in 1983 disposed of its manufacturing facilities. In Europe, Burton expanded the French operation in 1972 with the addition of fifteen new shops; and it launched a similar operation with two shops in Belgium. Also in May 1973 the group acquired Green's Leisure Centres, retailers of consumer electrical and photographic goods.

Rice and Power's financial strategy was to utilise Burton's assets to the full. This meant using the property base both as a means of raising capital and also as a yardstick against which to measure the viability of the store's operation. If properties could not be used by group retail businesses, they were to be let to other retail companies to gain income. Where properties could not generate adequate income or find outside users, they were to be disposed of. In 1972 a separate property company, Montague Burton Property Investment Limited, was established. The valuation of fixed assets, mainly properties, doubled from 1971 to 1972; and the Burton Group capital employed rose from £74.8 million to £144.4 million in 1972.

Within the corporate activities, divisions were encouraged to plan for profitable development through the annual divisional plan, which was to be compatible with the Group corporate plan. Divisional plans were revised every six months and divisional managers reported on a 'top-down, bottom-up' basis, with Rice and his team making clear to the divisions their general expectations, and the divisions responding with proposed plans in detail.

The 1973 results, particularly sales levels, were however disappointing, given a relatively buoyant market for the year in menswear. Group sales rose over the four years, but this was largely because of the acquisition of new businesses; menswear sales rose by only 27 per cent over the period compared with almost 63 per cent for the group. While menswear profits in 1973 were lower than in 1970, they had actually increased on 1972; the other retailing interests barely showed a profit at all. This depressed trading performance was bolstered by the income generated from the property company, which again accounted for about a third of group profits. The French operation was also giving rise to concern as the operation had proved to be unprofitable for the full year: management admitted that they were trying to 'buck the trend' on made-to-measure, even in France.

There were also concerns on two other fronts. First, the changed financial structure of the group (see Table 3) was worrying. Return on capital employed dropped from 10 per cent in 1971 to 5 per cent and 6 per cent in 1972 and 1973. The increased level of borrowing also meant that such profits as were earned were cut by high interest payments. The second concern was that the overcapacity in manufacturing was getting worse, and stocks remained stubbornly high at around 25 per cent of sales.

1974 and 1975: Attempted readjustment

In the 1974 annual report Ladislas Rice said:

> During this year and in view of the increasingly difficult national economic situation, the company undertook a reappraisal of its forward plans. Having achieved a better balance of retailing businesses we decided that the right course of action was to concentrate on their improvement rather than to continue to broaden our retailing base.

The action which was taken in line with this change in strategy included the disposal of the Boulogne factory and further cutbacks in UK manufacturing capacity, as well as the contraction of the Peter Robinson operation. Burton's menswear entered a period in 1974 when they had what amounted to a continual sale, in an effort to move stock. Throughout the company a major drive on cost reduction was implemented.

The success of this drive had to be seen in the light of the reluctance of the Burton family to implement closures. Burton had remained under the control of the Burton and Jacobsen families. The publicly quoted 'B' shares were non-voting shares, whereas voting rights were vested in the family controlled 'A' shares. The family had also long prided themselves on their responsibility to their employees and were reluctant to enforce redundancy by major factory closures.

The menswear retailing and manufacturing divisions were amalgamated and the emphasis continued to be on generating output through the mechanism of

Table 3 The Burton Group: summary balance sheets, 1970–75 (£000s)

	1970	1971	1972	1973	1974	1975
Properties and other fixed assets	61,134	63,237	131,761	137,190	140,672	138,919
Investments	138	127	219	497	456	476
Total fixed assets	61,272	63,364	131,980	137,687	141,128	139,395
Stocks	16,241	21,155	21,571	27,170	27,788	33,038
Debtors	12,507	15,724	17,732	22,837	27,007	32,356
Bank balances and cash	518	573	857	596	679	713
Short-term deposits				10,479	2,796	
Total current assets	29,266	37,452	40,160	61,082	58,270	66,107
Creditors	7,015	10,159	10,763	13,999	17,923	20,854
Bank overdraft and loans	7,430	8,082	11,235	25,665	22,595	28,604
Taxation	5,785	5,980	4,648	5,758	3,359	1,360
Dividends	1,594	1,823	1,021	1,613	1,618	1,570
Total current liabilities	21,824	26,044	27,667	47,035	45,495	52,388
Net current assets/liabilities	7,442	11,408	12,493	14,047	12,775	13,719
Less Medium-term bank loans	–	–	–	–	–	(7,856)
Total assets employed	68,714	74,772	144,473	151,734	153,903	145,258
Share capital	17,917	18,234	18,236	18,316	18,316	18,316
Reserves	39,196	31,335	100,310	99,981	101,128	100,736
Shareholders' funds	57,113	49,569	118,546	118,297	119,444	119,052
Loan capital, etc	11,601	25,203	25,927	33,437	31,692	26,206
Capital employed	68,714	74,772	144,473	151,734	151,136	145,258

price. In addition, new ranges were introduced. As one field retail manager of the time explained:

> They invited us up to Harrogate when Jim Power took over and gave us a presentation on what was going to happen. We were told it would be tough and we all had to pull together or we would go down. Most of the new merchandise we were shown was imported stuff, casual wear and cheaper ready-to-wear suits ... But when we got back out in the field not much changed. They put in some new merchandise, but it was added on to rather than instead of the bespoke tailoring ... we were still bespoke tailors ... We had a lot of cloth to sell.

Elsewhere in the groups Orange Hand, the fashion shop for boys, was closed down. The only area of investment in expansion was Top Shop, which was one of only two profitable businesses in 1974, the other being Evans with Cyril Spencer as chief executive.

In 1974 and 1975 profits declined further. It was clear by the end of 1974 that the costs of consolidation and rationalisation were high: the stock clearance policies depressed margins to 5 and 4 per cent respectively. The Boulogne closure incurred costs of £900,000 and the contraction of Peter Robinson £1.6 million. The 1974 results were called an 'unmitigated disaster' in the *Financial Times*.

External intervention

In April 1975 Scrimgeour's, the stockbroking firm with a special interest in retailing, took the unprecedented step of issuing a confidential report on Burton to the company's shareholders. The report was leaked to the *Sunday Telegraph*, which published extracts from it. Its comments were damning:

- The splitting of retailing and manufacturing had created 'competition between rather than coordination between the divisions'.
- 'We estimate that over the period [1969 to 1974] these [sales of made-to-measure] have fallen from approximately £1 million to approximately £550,000, a decline of 45 per cent. Nationally we believe the decline in made-to-measure suits over this period has been closer to 30 per cent.'
- The attempts by the company to move to more fashionable merchandise had not been successful because the 'trendy' clothes were not trendy enough to attract new customers, while being too trendy for the company's traditional customers.
- The attempted rationalisation of manufacturing was too slow, particularly at Leeds, and inadequately planned. This was made worse by inadequate stock control and distribution.
- It was a mistake to diversify. It would have been wiser to concentrate on the central problem of menswear. Many of the acquisitions placed strains on management resources because they had problems inherent within them, 'at a time when the major priority was the rejuvenating and restructuring of the "guts" of the business'.
- The setting up of the property company was done with the intention of attracting outside finance to support the property portfolio; instead the company was being financed in part by 'a bank overdraft of £3.3 million . . . Far from providing a method of long-term finance, this company has been obliged to return to its parent despite the Group's liquidity problems.'

The report concluded by saying that 'The present situation . . . rewards neither the shareholders nor the public and should not be allowed to continue.' The stockbrokers called on the institutions and the non-executive directors to put pressure on the company to replace Rice and his senior management team, and felt that Burton needed someone with more retail experience to head it.

The group results (see Tables 3 and 4) seemed to bear out the concern voiced in the report. Group turnover had increased by 16 per cent in 1974, but group trading profits, which had declined by 44 per cent in 1974, fell to just £5.6 million, or 4 per cent of sales. The overseas operation made losses in both 1974 and 1975. Both Ryman and Green were making losses, and the womenswear businesses were in profit only because Top Shop, with Ralph Halpern as managing director, was making £1 million profit. The manufacturing operation continued on a downward trend. In both 1974 and 1975, property revenue accounted for more than half the group profit before interest and taxation. Price reduction policy had little effect on stocks, which continued to run at more than 22 per cent of sales. By 1975 the return on capital employed had slumped to just 4 per cent – and it was only positive at all because of the property interests of the group.

The company did face some severe trading difficulties, including the three-day week in 1973, growing imports of cheaper and often good-quality garments, and the hot 1975 summer which depressed sales. There was also internal resistance to cutting back on manufacturing capacity too fast. There were other operational reasons for the failings of the strategy. The computerised stock control systems for both monitoring sales and reallocating stock were poor. So there

Table 4 The Burton Group: summary profit and loss account, 1974/75 (£ million)

	1974	*1975*
Group turnover	126.7	146.5
Sales by activity:		
UK menswear retailing	72.9	84.1
UK menswear manufacturing (external sales)	1.0	1.3
Womenswear retailing	19.5	23.7
Office and leisure retailing	22.1	23.0
Overseas retailing	11.3	14.3
Profits		
Trading profit by activity:		
UK menswear retailing	3.2	4.2
UK menswear manufacturing	(0.9)	(0.7)
Womenswear retailing	0.1	0.7
Office and leisure retailing	0.6	(0.9)
Overseas retailing	(0.6)	(0.8)
Property income	3.8	3.1
Group trading profit		
(before interest and taxation)	6.2	5.6
Income from/redemption of investment	0.7	1.6
Closure costs	(2.9)	(1.6)
Interest	(4.5)	(4.3)
Profit on sale of properties	3.9	1.2
Group profit (before taxation)	3.4	2.5

was inadequate knowledge about what was selling well and what stock was held, particularly in the branches. Similarly, cash control was lacking. Brian North, who took over as finance director when Jim Power took responsibility for menswear, recalled that although the group 'had the idea of profit centres, there was one key item missing – cash flow management'.

By the end of 1975, although Rice had not been replaced, management changes had occurred. Jim Power had taken over the running of menswear (retail and manufacturing) and Spencer, who was made responsible for the other retail operations, had joined Rice and Power in a triumvirate running the group. In fact, the public announcement of the greater involvement of Spencer disguised the fact that, at the very top of the company, a struggle for ascendancy was taking place between Power and Spencer.

The Burton Group (B) 1976–1984

Gerry Johnson

1976–80: Turnaround

In 1976 Cyril Spencer stated that his aim was 'to eliminate loss-making business which could not forecast return to profitability in the short term'. Brown's and Green's were sold off, as was Ryman's northern operation. The Paris factory of the French operation was closed, cutting out overseas manufacturing altogether. The provincial Peter Robinson shops were also closed. These disposals cut operating losses by £2.4 million, and the income from the sales went some way to reducing borrowings. There was also further expansion of womenswear with Top Shop in particular opening eleven more shops in 1976.

The central problem of menswear was, however, still not resolved. Power was pressing ahead with tighter controls, and nineteen loss-making Burton and Jackson shops were closed. But menswear retailing profits in 1976 decreased further to £1.4 million. To add to the problems facing the division, 1976 saw the repeat of a hot summer, which deflated the sales of traditional menswear garments and encouraged sales of leisurewear, of which the Burton shops had limited supplies. Since virtually all the other divisions – apart from Top Shop – were loss-makers, this meant that the group went into a trading loss situation for the first time in 1976, with group profits entirely dependent on the property income (see Table 1).

At the end of 1976 the boardroom struggle was resolved. Rice resigned as chief executive to become chairman, and Spencer was offered the position of chief executive. He accepted provided that Ralph Halpern was appointed to the board and North was given a full board post. The Halpern team, already running Peter Robinson and Top Shop, also assumed responsibility for Burton retailing. This team divided their week between London (and Top Shop) and Leeds (and Burton).

The emphasis of that year was recalled by North: 'We looked very hard at the sales we knew we could achieve. We knew what we wanted on the bottom line. Therefore, the middle is cost. We found we needed to take 30–35 per cent out of expenses – and no discussion.' In all, 90 unprofitable Burton and Jackson stores were closed and stocks reduced by £6 million (nearer £13 million in retail cash

This case is intended for class discussion and not to illustrate either correct or incorrect handling of an administrative situation. © Gerry Johnson, 1986, revised 1988, 1992. The author wishes to acknowledge with thanks the assistance of Bridget Garnish in revising this case study.

terms). The Jackson head office in Newcastle was closed down, which, with other staff reductions, produced a saving of 'several millions'; and the old staff incentive scheme, under which branch staff could earn more than their managers, was abolished

On the trading side, a major problem had to be faced. The branches were still ill-adapted to stock and display a wide range of clothing, from shirts to jeans and sweaters. Halpern recalled that one store had remained unmodernised since opening in 1923; in another, the manager had to stack the shirts on the floor, and eventually built some shelves for himself. Upwards of 300 branches had to be refitted, and speedily because the evidence was that sales responded immediately. According to North, the new merchandise produced an immediate 40 per cent

Table 1 The Burton Group: summary profit and loss account, 1976–79 (£ million)

	1976	*1977*	*1978*	*1979*
Group turnover	145.8	151.5	153.3	165.2
Sales by activity:				
UK menswear retailing/				
manufacturing	84.3	91.4	83.0	80.3
Women's retailing	22.6	27.1	36.6	49.0
Office and leisure retailing	22.4	17.2	18.8	22.0
Overseas retailing	16.5	15.8	14.8	13.8
Profits				
Trading profit by activity:				
UK menswear retailing	1.4	0.1	6.0	9.6
UK menswear manufacturing	(1.4)	(2.5)	(3.1)	
Womenswear retailing	0.8	1.7	4.2	5.3
Office and leisure retailing	(1.8)	(0.1)	0.6	0.8
Overseas retailing	(1.0)	(0.7)	(0.3)	0.1
Property income	3.1	3.0	2.5	3.9
Group trading profit				
(before interest and taxation)	1.2	1.6	9.9	19.8
Income from redemption of				
investments	1.0	0.4	–	–
Closure/reorganisation costs	(1.7)	(3.4)	–	–
Interest	(4.6)	(4.2)	(3.4)	(2.3)
Profit on sale of properties	2.8	0.5	1.0	–
Group profit (before taxation)	(1.4)	(5.1)	7.6	17.5
Taxation	–	1.0	(0.5)	(1.6)
Extraordinary items	(2.0)	(9.5)	(4.5)	2.9[1]
(mainly assets written off				
at closure and reducing costs)				
Total profit/(loss) to group	(3.4)	(13.6)	2.6	18.8

[1] The £2.9 million in 1979 represents disposal of investment properties less allocation to profit-sharing scheme.

boost in branch turnover, and that increase doubled as soon as the shop was properly fitted out. With the renewed emphasis on merchandising Halpern also moved the merchandising team back to London.

Despite the closures, menswear sales rose to £91 million. However, given the upheavals, menswear retail profits declined to just £100,000. On the manufacturing side, losses in 1977 rose to £2.5 million. However, the new team had closed four factories, one-third of capacity, immediately, with the Hudson Road Factory in Leeds reduced to cloth cutting and warehousing. The Hudson Mills closure in particular was seen by Ralph Halpern as a significant break with the past:

> People used to go to work in Hudson Road, Leeds and feel protected; it was a feudal castle. They had their lunch in the feudal canteen, the feudal barons called Burton turning up and administrating the rites and allowing employment to be granted; and there would be a medical man on the premises and a bit of billiards and a bowling green. So the whole of the village set-up was really to show that we could protect you there.

Losses were stemmed in Ryman, which was re-orientated towards consumer sales of stationery, rather than office equipment. But the European operations continued to lose money and decisions were taken to pull out of Belgium and cloth merchanting in France.

The reorganisation and closures mainly associated with menswear incurred costs in 1977 of £9.5 million – enough to send net losses to a total of £13.5 million after tax and interest. In financial terms, it was the low point in Burton's fortunes.

However, 1977 was, in many ways, also the turning point for the group. The strategy had become more focused on fashion retailing of both men's and women's clothing. Halpern's main success had been with Top Shop, a retailer of young women's clothes. He saw similar opportunities for menswear in the 15–24-year-old sector of the market, in which the spending power in men's fashions was to be found. He also believed that within Burton there was scope for several different types of men's retailer each appealing to different segments and backed up by product group merchandisers whose job it would be to ensure that the merchandise in each type of shop was compatible with its target market.

In addition, the image of Burton had to change, as Halpern explained: 'The future store will have the most beautiful shop fittings, the best deep-pile carpets, the best windows, but relatively good value, keenly priced merchandise.' The number of shops was further cut from 706 in 1972 to 585 in 1979, almost all of the reduction coming from the traditional menswear chain. Jackson was also incorporated into the Burton operation. However, within the total reduction there was growth in certain sectors. Some 44 of Halpern's 'trendsetter' shops for young men, called Top Man, were opened in just nine months; 55 new menswear shops were opened and 63 modernised totally, concentrating large sums of money to create 'flagship' shops. One executive who was a field manager at the time commented: 'This was not like the early 1970s: shops were completely refitted – gutted. There was real money spent on them. We were in retailing at last.'

The revitalisation of menswear retailing built up its own momentum given the increased sales from the changes:

> You could take decisions on the re-vamping of shops in the knowledge that you could fund it out of its own growth. And where market research showed that a town could not support a new Burton shop, then it was disposed of, so you were also able to fund the recovery out of disposals . . . You must remember Burton's had a tremendous asset base – a tremendous advantage.

By 1979 the company was able to spend £26 million on modernisation and still reduce borrowings and interest payments.

There were also continued attempts to come to terms with manufacturing. By the end of 1978 the number of factories was reduced to four and management were claiming that this was in line with retail needs, though it was still loss making. Halpern had also acted to improve stock control, switching over within two years to a centralised, computer-based monitoring and replenishment system. Providing little scope for the discretion of the shops in merchandise control, it was an approach which stressed information 'to tell people where they stand each month' and ensure that best-selling lines were made available and slow-sellers deleted early. The effects on stock were impressive with reductions in 1977 and 1978 to 14 and 12 per cent of sales respectively, a level hitherto unknown in the group.

Womenswear interests continued to be expanded with a concentration on the younger market. In 1979 the group made its first acquisition for six years, taking over Dorothy Perkins with its 240 women's fashion shops, and building its second major High Street presence in the UK in women's fashions. Halpern found similar problems with overstocking in the new acquisition and imposed the same centralised stock control and distribution system, after the removal of the Dorothy Perkins board.

By the end of 1979 the group's turnaround looked impressive. From the heavy losses of 1976 and 1977, the group returned to profitability in 1978, and in 1979 was able to show all retailing divisions as profitable and a group profit before tax of £17.5 million. Interest payments had been brought down by half in the four years, helped by the decision to fund credit sales externally and so reduce debtors from £21 million in 1978 to £12.5 million in 1979. Moreover, the high costs of closure and redundancy appeared to be behind them.

In 1980 the emphasis was on investment in the men's and women's retail chains and the pruning of loss-making peripheral ventures. A total of £36 million was spent on the shops, £12 million on new sites and £20 million on modernisation. One result was a hefty increase in borrowings from £12 million to £44 million. Other activities were cut: the Evans mail-order operation was disposed of and the number of Evans shops reduced; and two of the remaining four factories were also closed. By the end of 1980 it was also known that Burton was looking for buyers for its French operation and for Ryman; and both were sold the following year.

Changes in management

The period 1979 to 1981 saw activity at board level which changed the ownership structure and senior management of the company significantly. First, in 1979 the decision was taken to enfranchise the non-voting shareholders, a decision long called for by the City but resisted while the profit position, and share price, were so low. Burton ceased to be essentially a family controlled business.

The second move was the reorganisation of the board. At the end of 1979 Rice stepped down as chairman to become non-executive deputy chairman; Spencer was appointed chairman and joint managing director, with Halpern as the other joint managing director, and Brian North as deputy managing director. But dramatic changes were to occur in 1981. Prior to Burton's annual general meeting in 1981, it was revealed that Spencer had held secret discussions with Gerald Ronson of the Heron Corporation for the sale of Burton shares. Ralph Halpern was invited by Spencer to attend the meeting with Ronson:

> Spencer and Ronson were old friends. The deal which Ronson is reliably understood to have discussed involved a buy-out by Heron of the Burton family's interests accounting for some 15 per cent of the equity . . . At the time the Burton Group was valued on the stock market at a little under £240 million or 300p a share . . . Ronson's plan was clearly to buy Burton's at a discount to assets . . . Unknown to Ronson and Spencer, a recording system was hidden in his [Halpern's] bespoke Burton suit . . . Halpern's view of the . . . whispering was that it was improper for the deals to be discussed without the rest of the board's knowledge. (*Observer*, 24 January 1982)

At the board meeting on 2 July 1981, Spencer was asked to stand down. Ralph Halpern was appointed chairman and chief executive of Burton.

. . . and in management style

'You have to understand, he has immeasurable ego and immeasurable confidence – perhaps they are the same thing. The guy just exudes confidence.' This was a typical description of Ralph Halpern by one of his management team of the early 1980s. Halpern joined Peter Robinson in 1961 and progressed through the management hierarchy, increasingly being regarded as the man whose retail formula appeared to work. As chief executive of Top Shop and Peter Robinson in the mid-1970s he built a reputation for success when others in Burton gained a reputation for failure. By 1980 he was joint managing director of the group, and within another year he was its chairman and chief executive.

He operated by centralising what he considered to be the major policy decisions – final approval of merchandise ranges and shop design, shop acquisitions, senior appointments and financial structure – and then delegating their implementation to other teams in each of the operating divisions. The result was clear, explicit policy guidelines throughout the business, centred on fashion retailing of men's and women's clothes. All other activities were considered peripheral and unnecessary. Manufacturing was seen purely as a service to retailing, and as Halpern explained: 'If we can break even on that side I shall be happy. If there is no market in made-to-measure suits we will pull out.'

At the operational level, success in retailing was seen as linked to the total shopping environment – merchandise and shop appearance – and since the shops were fashion shops they had to change as fashion changed. By 1980 Top Shop was already going through its third refitting programme. Indeed, Halpern talked about 'institutionalising change':

> Change is always on the agenda: we don't just expect our executives to run the show, we expect them to change the show as well . . . We are positioned as the lifestyle clothing experts of the High Street and it's a tough position to maintain. Hence our management philosophy is that people are trained and motivated to plan for change. We believe this is crucial to our continued profitable growth . . . No store is allowed to go more than 4–5 years without complete modernisation . . . only the most visionary retailers recognise the need to change a successful formula while it is still working.

His view was that a positive attitude to risk taking should be encouraged, but within a tight framework. This was maintained by clear controls of expenditure, close attention to business planning and constant feedback of results. Planning was done on a two-tier basis: a fail-safe profit plan that managers could attain, but also a really challenging target with commensurate rewards for achievement. 'We believe in high pay and incentives and we stress promotion from within for those who succeed . . . For all our management and staff, substantial bonuses are linked to target plan . . . A senior executive member of a divisional board can double his salary for outstanding performance.' Given these demands on the managers of a business, 'Everything in that business has to change all the time to cope.' This was reinforced, for example, in rates of depreciation: 'Rates of depreciation are now adjusted to faster replacement of fixtures and fittings [from seven to three years] so that it can be expected frequently. The system is geared to change.'

It was this management approach that took over the running of Burton within a unique organisation structure. Each division had functional senior executives reporting directly to the main board of six functional managing directors: these functional areas were shop operations, merchandising, concessions, finance, personnel and systems. There were no divisional managing directors. As Ralph Halpern explained: 'If you have a series of managing directors in the divisions and you sit on top of that you are more likely to get out of touch. If you filter all knowledge through an individual it's very much filtered . . . It's really an explanation of his good performance or poor performance . . . What we wanted to happen was that central management should keep in touch with every facet of the business.' One executive commented: 'It's a very open system, it has to be:

you can't hide anything.' It was also an approach to management that bred mutual challenge within management teams: indeed, outsiders to the Burton system of management commented on how aggressive Burton's managers were.

The system also included quite explicit attempts to involve outsiders in the business. Ralph Halpern saw this as a means of ensuring that executives did not become overreliant on the way the company had always done things:

> You can't do it by getting the same people to think about visions of the future. You have to have other people who have not been infiltrated by this whole process . . . These are outside brains who are experts in their own particular field. We employ consultants in almost every single field in this company. Every top director has access to outside consultants, so he can make no excuse for becoming isolated.

1982–85: A success story

Ralph Halpern stated in the 1982 annual report:

> During the last two years the Group has pursued three specific objectives. The first was to improve the profitability of our successful retailing activities as a firm base for growth in the future. The second was to rationalise or dispose of those activities which were unlikely to contribute significantly to future profitability. The third was to reduce substantially our dependence on a high level of bank borrowing.

In 1981 and 1982 the policies of retail investment and divestment of all else were pursued, with both men's and women's fashion divisions growing as a result in terms of both sales and profits. By 1982 the losses from manufacturing had been reduced to £100,000 compared to £5.2 million in 1980; and group trading profits were in excess of £24 million. The third aim of reduced borrowings had also been achieved, with interest payments reduced to £100,000; profits after interest and tax were £19.4 million. More details of performance are shown in Tables 2, 3 and 4.

In 1983 Halpern turned his attention to future growth and repositioning. He attempted to acquire both Richard Shops and John Collier from the troubled UDS for between £75 and £90 million. The aim was to both build up the High Street representation in womenswear and also use the John Collier shops to appeal to a distinct men's market segment, the 30-plus age group. Burton regarded the need for moving away from an overreliance on the 15–25 age group as important because, as a population segment, its size was beginning to decline and would continue to do so through the 1980s. However, in 1983 it failed in the acquisition of the UDS chains and additional acquisition was postponed to January 1984, when the 93 Harry Fenton shops were purchased for £3.5 million and integrated into the retail operations.

Table 2 The Burton Group: summary profit and loss account, 1980–84
(£ million)

	1980	1981	1982	1983	1984
Group turnover	225.7	218.5	233.9	299.2	415.9
Sales by activity:					
Menswear	88.4	101.8	121.6	155.2	222.1
Womenswear	87.3	94.0	107.7	139.2	188.0
Others	22.2	–	–	–	
Overseas	13.5	17.8	–	–	
Mail order	4.9	–	–	–	
Manufacturing	6.3	1.7	0.4	0.6	5.8
Other activities	3.1	3.2	4.1	4.2	
Profits					
Trading profit by activity					
Menswear	12.7	13.0	15.6	23.3	34.6
Womenswear	7.6	7.6	8.7	14.2	20.5
Others	0.1	–	–	–	
Overseas	(1.2)	(0.2)	–	–	
Mail order	(1.3)		–	–	
Manufacturing	(2.7)	(1.1)	(0.1)	0.1	0.4
Other activities	0.1	(0.5)	0.1	0.2	
Other (mainly property)					
income	3.1	*	*	*	
Group trading profit					
(before interest and tax)	18.4	18.7	24.3	37.7	55.4
Interest	(5.2)	(4.1)	(0.1)	1.2	1.0
Taxation	(1.9)	(2.3)	(4.9)	(11.1)	(19.7)
Extraordinary items	(10.8)	3.8	0.1	0.2	–
(balance of the disposal of properties less closure and redundancy costs and allocation of profit sharing)					
Total profit/(loss) to group	0.3	16.1	19.4	28.0	36.7

* Income from property and credit operations distributed to divisions.

Within the existing shops, there was evidence of repositioning of the product range, particularly with womenswear. Top Shop, previously targeted almost exclusively at the 15–25 age group, introduced fashion for the 9–14-year-old, and, with Top Notch, fashion garments for the 25-plus, better-off woman. The aim was now growth of market share. For the first time in over ten years, the number of shops opened through internal development rather than acquisition increased from 748 in 1982 to 791. In addition, the new store development policy saw the opening of much larger 'superstores'. In April 1983 one such store, occupying three floors with men's, women's and children's clothes, was opened in Edinburgh with a second scheduled for Liverpool.

Table 3 The Burton Group: summary balance sheet, 1976–82 (£000s)

	1976	1977	1978	1979	1980	1981	1982
Fixed assets							
Properties and other assets fixed	128,962	142,179	137,314	150,114	161,954	150,307	217,145
Investments	4,583	8,402	12,797	8,781	10,133	11,375	9,043
Total	133,545	150,581	150,111	158,895	172,087	161,682	226,188
Current assets							
Stocks	27,214	21,421	18,967	28,224	29,691	26,553	27,630
Debtors	24,238	20,078	21,187	12,521	30,078	12,061	12,545
Bank balances and cash	473	442	3,127	20,467	599	318	10,851
Total current assets	51,925	41,941	43,281	61,212	60,368	38,932	51,026
Current liabilities							
Creditors	20,605	26,068	28,853	29,172	47,919	47,785	46,144
Bank overdraft and loans	21,778	17,464	14,975	25,287	21,877	448	–
Taxation	1,081	889	917	1,605	1,885	2,293	4,896
Dividends	785	558	1,658	2,627	2,712	3,594	4,370
Total current assets (liabilities)	44,249	44,979	46,403	58,691	74,393	54,120	55,410
Net current assets (liabilities)	7,676	(3,038)	(3,122)	(2,521)	(14,025)	(15,188)	(4,384)
Less medium-term bank loans	(8,088)	(6,720)	(5,246)	(1,948)	(22,588)	–	–
Total assets employed	133,133	140,823	141,743	154,426	135,474	146,494	221,804
Share capital	18,316	18,589	18,589	18,601	38,742	39,933	41,544
Reserves	97,459	107,250	108,186	123,235	86,950	99,104	174,648
Shareholders' funds	115,775	125,839	126,775	141,836	125,692	139,037	216,192
Loan capital, etc.	17,358	14,984	14,968	12,590	9,782	7,457	5,612
Capital employed	133,133	140,823	141,743	154,426	135,474	146,494	221,804

This expansion was to be only the beginning of what was Halpern's ambition to compete with the largest of the fashion retailers. He no longer regarded Burton as competing as a men's and womenswear multiple with other such multiples. The aim was to take shares from those dominating the market and that meant competing with market leaders such as Marks and Spencer. Such expansion would require growth backed by larger financial resources than even the new cash-rich Burton could draw upon. Consequently, in the 1983 annual report, Halpern announced the intention to increase share capital from the current £55 million to £125 million: the shareholdings of the family and directors were thus reduced to just 8 per cent.

Table 4 The Burton Group: summary balance sheet, 1983–84 (£000s)[1]

	1983	1984
Fixed assets		
Tangible assets	235,621	288,775
Investments	11,780	12,056
Total	247,401	300,831
Current assets		
Stocks	38,373	64,006
Debtors	12,350	15,546
Properties held for sale	–	–
Investments	2,064	2,934
Bank balances and cash	18,933	3,475
Total	71,720	85,961
Creditors (due within one year)	66,479	103,281
Net current liabilities/assets	5,241	(17,320)
Total assets less current liabilities	252,642	283,511
Creditors (due after one year)	7,733	11,610
Provisions for liabilities and changes	5,853	11,143
Minority interests	–	–
	239,056	260,758
Capital and reserves		
Called-up share capital	43,079	88,003
Share premium account	5,203	928
Revaluation reserve	110,193	71,978
Other reserves	150	150
Retained earnings	80,431	99,699
	239,056	260,758

[1] Separately stated due to changes in accounting policy.

The 1983 results showed sales of about £300 million, pre-tax profits up to £39 million and a return on capital employment of 16 per cent. These figures were achieved after a total of £29 million had been spent on the store openings and 79 shop modernisations, all of which expenditure had come from internal cash flow. The company had shown not only this ability to increase sales and profits, but also an ability through tightened retail controls, higher value merchandise and fewer markdowns, to increase margins from 10.3 per cent in 1982 to 12.6 per cent in 1983. By 1983 manufacturing was also profitable. The division had launched a high-quality, high-technology garment manufacturing service called Farndale, based on its Gainsborough factory, and this, together with increased manufacturing efficiency, produced a trading profit of just under £100,000 on sales of £600,000.

The success continued into 1984, when the company was able to claim record profits of £36.7 million from its wide range of fashion businesses:

- Top Shop, 'specialising in exciting fashion clothes, marketed in the right environments to young women of 15–25'.
- Top Man, 'presenting exciting high fashion merchandise to 15–30-year-old men . . . confident enough to express their personalities in the dramatic ways they dress'.
- Dorothy Perkins, 'providing up to date colourful, and good value fashion for women of 20–30. The aim here was to translate the fashion of the cities to the more versatile requirements of smaller towns.
- Evans, which had been a specialist store concentrating on clothes for 'larger' women, was during the year restyled as 'Evans Collection' with the aim of improving the fashionable image of the business.
- Principles, launched in 1984 'to fill a gap in the market', catered for the lifestyle needs of the 25–45-year-old sophisticated woman, 'seeking fashionable clothes and accessories produced to high standards but at sensible prices'.
- Finally, Burton itself concentrated on men's clothing. But, as the 1984 annual report emphasised: 'Burton's success in recent years has been achieved by identifying the change in men's clothing habits away from formal suits, towards more casual wear.'

'The rebirth of Burton': the underlying philosophy

Ralph Halpern's view of the reasons for success in fashion retailing were well publicised:

> Good management is making complicated things simple. The first thing you have to decide is what business you're in . . . Marketing is crucial. You have to decide which market you're trying to serve and find a way of serving it adequately. Retailing used to be a very slow business. You used to be able to

put up a formula that would last 30 or 40 years. Now you put a formula up, put it on the High Street and it could well be out of date in four or five years' time.

In addition, the retailer needed to be very clear about his or her proposition to the customer: 'The age of the generalist is over. The retailers to survive in the future will be those who offer a clear cut definition of what they're trying to do, to a clearly targeted audience.'

In 1983 Halpern addressed a retail conference on 'The Rebirth of Burton's' and explained the Burton's approach as follows:

> Underpinning our corporate success is the implementation of what has been referred to as multi-strategy market positioning, which simply means that Burton Group operates several companies with clear identities which are positioned to appeal to specific segments of the market . . . All planning systems, merchandise, financial policies for investment, personnel recruitment and trading must be in harmony and positioned to appeal to these specific segments.
>
> In an industry like ours which is not well known for up to date statistics we have to obtain the best available data on the state of the economy, demographics of population and income, distribution, intelligence about our competition, advance knowledge from the fashion designers, and most importantly, stock and sales financial information from within our own business. We are sitting on the fastest possible, and most accurate and instant form of market research, our own shops. Information from them must be accurate and instant, for the successful retailer to take advantage.
>
> Within each mainstream business we are able to experiment with new opportunities, for example in 75 Top Shops we added 'Top Girl' for 9 to 14-year-olds. And there is nothing to say that they have to be orientated towards young people, more recently we have seen a new economic force – women of over 25. The concentration of effort by retailers has been designing shops to cater for them, as personified and pioneered by Next, for example . . . by 1990, in six years time, there will be 1,000,000 more women between 25 and 44 years old than there were at the start of the decade. There will be many retailers, including ourselves, going into this expanding market. But only those who can develop a totally integrated business dedicated to serving it throughout everything they do will win the battle.

Later commentators, looking back at this period, also accounted for much of the success by reference to Ralph Halpern himself:

> Halpern provided Burton with outstanding leadership throughout the 1980s. He brought style and panache. He cared about the ambience in which people bought clothes and improved it out of all recognition. He catered brilliantly in clothes design and range for the career girl aged between 18 and 30 . . . At the top, Halpern lived out the fantasies of sales assistants the country over

with a £1 million a year salary, the gold Rolex and cufflinks, sessions in the gym and playing on his organ (a Yamaha synthesiser in the basement). Staff did not despise the style, they envied it. (*Sunday Telegraph*, 18 November 1990)

The Burton Group (C) 1985–1990

Gerry Johnson and Bridget Garnish

In 1985 the Burton Group was a major retailing force in the British clothing sector. Ralph Halpern was regarded as the epitome of the '80s entrepreneurial chief executive and could claim personal friendship with the Prime Minister. He was acknowledged as one of the prime movers in the revolution towards specialised retail chains that were now dominating the High Street. By 1991 the group announced profits less than half the 1986 level of £146 million and Sir Ralph Halpern stepped down from the posts of chairman and chief executive in November 1990.

The acquisition of the Debenhams Group

In 1985 the Burton Group made its largest acquisition: the Debenham Group. From its origins over 200 years ago, Debenhams had grown into one of the largest retail groups in the UK, with 68 department stores throughout the country. Floor space varied from 160,000 square feet down to 9,200 square feet, and the number of sales floors from six to one. Debenhams was also involved in retail distribution of toys through Hamleys, footwear manufacturing (and footwear retailing in the USA), financial services, property and investments. Debenhams had grown through the acquisition of individual department stores and small groups. Chairman in 1984, Bob Thornton, recalled that 'Each store was virtually a law unto itself and head office seemed to be virtually ignored.'

Traditionally, department stores offered a wide range of products on a single site. However, the appeal of a wide range under one roof suffered with the growth of specialist retailers such as Burtons, Top Shop, Next and others, particularly in the fashion goods sector. This trend accelerated with the increased popularity of shopping precincts and covered shopping areas, which in themselves offer the variety of choice that the department stores once claimed as unique to themselves. Meanwhile, other retailers – notably large supermarkets and 'out-of-town' operators – widened their product ranges and thus impinged on the traditional department store market. Such changes, coupled with the department stores' relatively high cost structure, placed them at a disadvantage to lower-cost retailers. Table 1 shows the financial position of Debenhams from 1983 to 1985.

The takeover of Debenhams in 1985 developed into a battle. On the one side was the Burton Group together with Sir Terence Conran's Mothercare/Habitat group. The basis of the alliance was that Terence Conran would bring his design skills to complement the marketing and merchandise skills of Burton. Deployed against them was an alliance of Debenhams and the Fayed brothers, who owned the House of Fraser, to resist the takeover. However, during the build-up to the bid the partnership between Burton and Conran dissolved when Sir Terence

Table 1 Debenhams plc: group three-year financial record (£000s)

	1983	1984	1985
Turnover (including VAT)	676,436	746,788	780,594
Trading profit before interest	26,408	41,270	48,348
Less interest	(5,045)	(5,768)	(6,074)
Trading profit after interest	20,910	35,502	42,274
Other items			
Profit before taxation	19,575	32,657	40.704
Taxation	4,308	7,729	10,619
Profit after taxation	15,267	24,928	30,085
Minority interests	601	1,670	1,585
Preference dividends	86	86	86
Profit before extraordinary items	14,580	23,172	28,414
Extraordinary items	–	–	8,635
Profit attributable to ordinary shareholders	14,580	23,172	19,779
Ordinary dividends	9,116	10,224	11,916
	5,464	12,948	7,863
Earnings per share (pence)	10.9	17.2	20.6
Assets employed:			
Fixed and other assets	350,623	364,498	392,661[1]
Net current assets			
(excluding bank borrowings)	51,808	59,089	53,142
	402,431	423,587	445,803
Financed by:			
Shareholders' interests (including minorities)	315,391	326,890	335,670
Deferred taxation	10,000	10,000	10,000
Lease obligations	10,648	7,778	6,074
Debenture, loan capital and other borrowings	66,392	78,919	94,059
	402,431	423,587	445,803

[1] Including: freehold property: £171,294
long leasehold property: £102,438
short leasehold property: £10,872   } £000 as valued at 29.1.84.
plant and machinery: £9,754
fixtures, fittings, etc.: £69,455

formed the Storehouse Group after acquiring British Home Stores – a competitor to Debenhams.

In a specially prepared video cassette, Ralph Halpern laid out his case for the takeover of Debenhams. The video argued that what customers were increasingly looking for from retailers was 'an environment which is spacious, comfortable, exciting, glamorous or just plain fun'. Using a theatre metaphor, he suggested that the management of stores such as Seibu in Tokyo regard 'each floor as a stage, where customers play the leading roles, the assistants the supporting cast: include in the scenario lighting, sound and set design and the show can begin'. The video went on to show examples of Trumptower in New York and the Watertower in Chicago as the sort of concept that Burton would build on for Debenhams.

> Every floor is as good as the ground floor. This is what is known as the galleria concept. Specialist shops on several levels under one roof. Easy access, wide entrances, attractive escalators that positively invite the customer to say let's go higher … The customer is surrounded by quality and service, by atmosphere, by sensation.

In the week before the closing date of the bid in August 1985, Burton's senior executives were busy visiting all the major institutional investors in an effort to get them to accept the Burton offer. They were aware that the House of Fraser had been buying Debenham shares, to the value of perhaps 25 per cent, a situation which made it a close contest. The eventual outcome was, however, success for Burton and Debenhams was acquired at a cost of around £570 million.

In a report to employees early in 1986 on the activities of 1985, Ralph Halpern was able to report further record profits of over £80 million before tax for the group (see the Appendix for financial information). He justified the Debenhams purchase as follows:

> We are retailers. We are here to serve our shareholders, and to provide them with opportunities for growth in profits. We saw in Debenhams a most marvellous opportunity in the high street – five million square feet that wasn't turning over sufficiently, wasn't making enough profit. We thought with our expertise we could turn the business round, and bring Debenhams more turnover and profits, as well as benefiting the Burton business.

There was, however, concern both inside and outside Debenhams that the Burton style would not fit with their kind of department store. It was not a concern that Halpern shared:

> I don't think anyone should be afraid of me, my team, or our techniques. I'm a human being who understands retailing, and people's hopes and fears. There's no reason to be afraid of me because I'm faster than most chief executives. The Burton people had the same problem in 1977. Burton was

almost dying on its feet. Now look at them. They're all rushing around and doing things and achieving profits. By comparison, the Debenhams people are quite fast.

As for the diverse nature of the Debenhams Group, he commented:

> We wouldn't have bought the Debenhams Group had we not wanted to run it. But there may be certain parts of it that cannot fit into the profit growth requirements that we will have in the future – because they are too small, or they are unsuitable, or because we don't want to invest the capital in them – and maybe somebody else could do it better than we could. I don't know which parts, if any, those are going to be. We haven't taken any decisions yet.

Ralph Halpern believed that this diversity caused a problem of image – about what Debenhams stood for. 'Think of Marks and Spencer. It stands for something. Burton stands for something. Now think of Debenhams. If you've got a blank in your mind, it's because the retailers have not successfully stamped a position and an image on the store.'

Burton's executives believed that their expertise in identifying a particular market opportunity, and going after it single-mindedly and with energy and panache, would be the solution. The transformation of Debenhams would be the reaffirmation of Halpern's commitment to the philosophy of retailing upon which Burton had been built since 1977:

> Consumers' aspirations are being fed with the possibility of new experiences, new ways of living their lives … The future belongs to the specialist. The age of the generalist is over. The retailers to survive in the future will be those who offer a clear cut definition of what they are trying to do, to a clearly targeted audience.

This was reinforced by a corporate advertisement issued during the takeover (see Figure 1), illustrating the lifestyle marketing concept adopted by Burton, and seen as just as relevant to Debenhams.

Early actions

By February 1986 the department store board was, according to personnel director Ian Murphy, 'looking at how best we can increase sales, control costs and improve margins'. This involved a redundancy programme affecting 330 staff in the stores, 46 at the London head office and 27 in management services. There were also plans to tighten up merchandising, stock control and distribution systems, and cut down on paperwork. The amount of space devoted to shop-in-shop operations was reduced, with merchandise from Burtons operations introduced.

The size of Debenhams meant that there had to be a restructuring of the Burton Group itself (see Figure 2). The structure was effectively based on the

The Young Market:
Dorothy Perkins

The Style Market:
Principles

The Teenage Market:
Top Shop/Top Man

The Larger Market:
Evans

The secret of successful retailing is giving the market what it wants

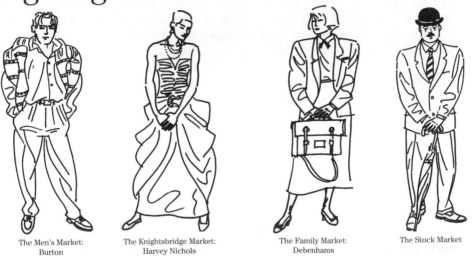

The Men's Market:
Burton

The Knightsbridge Market:
Harvey Nichols

The Family Market:
Debenhams

The Stock Market

Figure 1 Burton Corporate advertisement

three divisions: retailing; consumer financial services; and property, design and construction. Each had a managing director and operating board. The companies within each division also had an MD and board, except Debenhams which still supported a chairman. Ralph Halpern stated the purpose of the restructuring as to 'maintain strong central control whilst creating businesses with a more tightly focused view of their individual markets'. By 1986 there were 345 senior executives in the organisation.

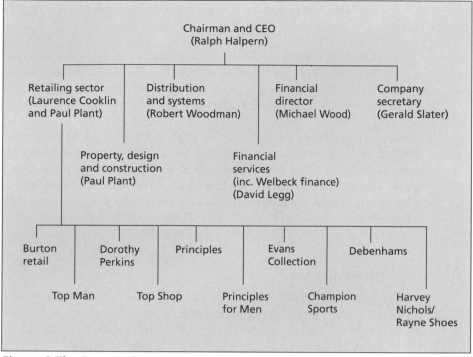

Figure 2 The Burton Group structure in 1986

Opinion in the trade and in the press was divided on the potential for Debenhams. Some argued that Burton really knew too little about department store retailing to follow through what amounted to grandiose plans for the business. Others believed that the Burton retail team would benefit from the challenge of taking department stores into the 21st century – a challenge which might take some years, but which past performance suggested they would achieve.

The success years

In November 1986 Burton could announce an increase in profit before tax of over 85 per cent to £146 million. All core businesses were reported as trading profitably. Those businesses were Burton, Harvey Nichols, Top Shop, Top Man, Dorothy Perkins, Principles, Evans, Colliers and Champion Sport. The group employed over 33,000 staff and in January 1987 was valued in excess of £1.56 billion. Personally Ralph Halpern was at the pinnacle of his reputation. Cited as an example of British business acumen and talent by Mrs Thatcher, he was rewarded with a knighthood. His personal standing seemed unassailable: even when the newspapers reported his dalliance with a young model, Fiona Wright, the shareholders and the City acknowledged few tremors of doubt.

In April 1987 the *Financial Weekly* quoted the future plans announced by Sir Ralph:

> The five year strategy included ambitious plans to increase market share in clothing. Menswear is targeted to grow from 9.5% to 13% – second only to Marks and Spencer – as 500 stores are added to the existing 700 … In five years time if all goes well, Burton will have doubled its selling space.

Womenswear market share was also expected to rise to 16 per cent, with the number of Principles outlets doubling. At the same time the group announced three new lines: Alias (leisure wear for men), Radius (for the individualistic 25–30-year-old man) and Secrets (underwear for women). In addition, ten sites were being sought for Harvey Nichols to move into the provinces. Debenhams refurbishment, expected to cost £200 million, was continuing with two additional stores (Hounslow and Colchester) opening in 1987.

Property and finance

To fuel this expansion and provide sites for new outlets Burton embarked on three years of property development and major financial deals. In 1986 the first move combined the two. Burton became the first retailer to negotiate a property-backed deal with the banks incorporating a holding company. The acquisition of Debenhams had provided 63 new properties for its portfolio but had left the group with a £300 million debt and 70 per cent gearing. Burton set up a new holding company, jointly owned (50 per cent) with the banks. It then sold £100 million of property to the holding company, using £30 million of Burton Group cash with the £70 million difference being met by the banks. This £70 million was then used to pay off some of the Debenhams acquisition debt. With some sales-and-leaseback deals, this left gearing at 30 per cent and debt at £130 million by the end of 1986.

The group was still short of new sites. In March 1987 the group brought Pengap Estates, a private property company. So aggressive was Burton for new sites, it offered incentives (of foreign holidays) to estate agents who found them suitable premises. The main thrust was to invest in the new shopping centres that were being developed throughout the country. Involvement varied from buying the initial site through to investing in existing schemes. In 1987 Dartford, Scarborough, Plymouth and Stockton were announced and the Fishergate centre in Preston was opened.

To help provide the finance, Burton announced a Eurobond[1], again a first in the retail sector. Michael Wood, group financial director, explained:

---

[1] A Eurobond is sold simultaneously in a number of foreign countries by an international syndicate of underwriters. Introduced from America in the 1970s, it was a popular form of cheap, long-term finance.

International capital markets have become one of the largest and most attractive sources of finance for British companies ... This equity linked transaction (*the Eurobond*) is specifically designed to attract new international investors to Burton, thereby developing an international market for our equity.

In addition, Burton went twice to the banks: firstly to Credit Suisse in April 1987 for a £400 million multi-option loan to replace all previous lines of credit, and secondly to Rothschild and County NatWest for a further £500 million in July 1987.

In November 1987 Burton announced profits up 23.3 per cent to £183.4 million (see the Appendix). The core retailing businesses contributed £124.7 million, with Debenhams providing a further £74.4 million. The group now had over 1,500 outlets and employed 33,428 staff.

For Sir Ralph this success was reflected in his annual income, up 35 per cent to £1,359 million. This was, at least in part, the result of the controversial share option scheme introduced at the beginning of the year. The design of the scheme was such as to give 80 senior executives bonuses after five years of up to eight times their salary and could have meant an £8 million bonus for Sir Ralph himself. It was, however, always a controversial scheme. In January 1987 Sir Ralph had written to shareholders explaining how the scheme would work:

All the options to be granted under our scheme will be subject to performance conditions which will ensure that employees will only benefit if the rise in Burton's share price is supported by a better financial performance to which they had personally contributed. Thus half of such options will only be exercisable if the target for real earnings per share growth is exceeded, and the other half if Burton's relative earnings per share performance is in the top quarter of the leading 100 UK companies.

Shareholders approved the scheme, though protests from City investors later in the year saw the package cut significantly.

Business expansion

There was expansion in types of business and within existing sectors of clothes retailing. The consumer financial services division concentrated mainly on the development of the in-house credit card. The Burton formula of differentiation by lifestyle was used here. Cards were produced for each shop. Though they were interchangeable, the customer was able to have a card that reflected his or her 'status' and style: for example, a Harvey Nichols card for the well-heeled executive, or a Top Shop card for the younger, fashion-conscious buyer. The commitment to the credit services sector was reflected in the creation of the BGFS Group by the merger of Burton's credit card group with the Welbeck credit card operation of Debenhams. Expert management was imported – David Legg was brought in from the financial services sector – to run the division.

Burton believed that its retailing expertise plus the lifestyle concept could be applied across a wider variety of products. It acquired Abroad Travel to develop this idea – holidays tailored to certain lifestyles, eventually to be retailed through the respective clothing outlets. Burton management needed to look no further than Champion Sports for evidence of the success of their ethos. By 1987 the chain was the second largest specialist sportswear retailer after Olympus. In addition, the group was pushing to move upmarket and up the age range: Principles for Men was heavily invested in, and Principles was given a more exclusive image including its own designer range. The jewel in the crown was to be Harvey Nichols: Sir Ralph transformed the store, once the epitome of the Sloane lifestyle, into a designer label emporium. Future plans including using the Harvey Nichols label in Principles store to exploit its upmarket image further.

Decline and fall

In 1988 pre-tax profits reached £211.7 million, 15 per cent up on the previous year. Sales were up 28 per cent in Debenhams, contradicting the sceptics who forecast disaster on the takeover. However, City analysts became unhappy as the Debenhams figures were kept consolidated into retailing profits with only portions declared. They complained that there was a lack of clarity as to the performance of the different parts of Burton. They were also concerned that the gearing of debt to equity at 47 per cent, while not particularly high for the level of profits, showed a continuing upward trend.

The Department of Trade and Industry investigation

A Department of Trade and Industry (DTI) investigation into the bitterly contested takeover of Debenhams was initiated in 1987. Inquiries centred around the business relationships entered into by the Burton Group with those who helped it gain control of Debenhams. Burton won control after a last-minute switch of allegiance by Gerald Ronson's Heron International, Sir Philip Harris and others. Sir Ralph Halpern insisted that the group's tactics and behaviour throughout the process were correct in all respects.

Inevitably, the inquiry took up the time of management for over a year, from January 1988 to May 1989 when it was finally concluded and it became clear that no action was to be taken. However, during that time it provided a focus of media attention, particularly as the investigation was poorly handled by the DTI. The existence of the investigation was leaked to the press, each side accusing the other of the lapse. The DTI continued to refuse to confirm or deny the investigation, so Sir Ralph announced it at the AGM in January 1988 – an unusual practice.

Investigations under Section 447 are usually confidential. However, the existence of an investigation into Burton had been rumoured in the stock market throughout 1987, and was confirmed by Sir Ralph at the AGM in

January 1988. The uncertainty created was one element in a poor share price performance for the company. (*Financial Times*, 23 May 1989)

Into recession

The move by Burton into property development had been typical of the mid-1980s when many businesses expanded via property-based deals. However, by 1989 the property slump had reached the balance sheet. Profits were up again (for the ninth successive year), but by only 5.7 per cent to £223 million, reflecting provisions of £100 million (as estimated by the financial media) against the decline in property value. By March 1990 the impact of the recession was leading to a reduction in property development. For example, shopping centres backed by the Burton property division were being placed on hold in Exeter and Plymouth. In this month there was also a sharp rise in debt to over 125 per cent of shareholders' funds. This was chiefly because of the cost of shopping centres that had been opened, and was aggravated by the low rental income that was not covering running costs. Provisions were made of £100 million against write-offs in property. By the end of the year these provisions had increased to £150 million.

As well as the problems in the property division, the credit and financial services were also being squeezed. Sir Ralph Halpern had been one of the first major retail chief executives to highlight the descent into retail recession. In company reports from 1987, despite the ever-growing profits, he was warning that each subsequent year would be harder, and margins tighter. After the credit boom of the mid-1980s consumer confidence was low as high interest rates and high unemployment discouraged both spending and borrowing. Inevitably, Burton's core business was affected; by mid-1990 the recession had surpassed even the gloomiest forecasts in the retailing sector. Keith Wills of Goldman Sachs was quoted as saying: 'It is as if the sales pattern has fallen off a cliff. The market for young women's clothing is usually very resilient, even when other sectors are suffering. But over the last few weeks demand has disappeared' (*Guardian*, 28 June 1990).

The reservations over Burton's ability to recover spread wider than the immediate recession:

> The question remains, however, whether the group can ever recapture its former glory days. Top Shop suited the early 1980s market of high-spending young people. In the 1990s the demographic bulge will have moved on. But Burton will have to prove that it can develop the retail formats to attract the over-30 age group which will be spending again when their mortgages fall. Most of its formats are old and tired, and the group's stack-it-high approach seems out of sympathy with the new times. (*Guardian*, 11 September 1990)

Meanwhile, the financial press continued to talk Burton down. Sir Ralph Halpern's share option scheme, which in 1989 brought him an income of £1.53

million, became increasingly unpopular. The City establishment were beginning to find fault, a symptom of the increasing pessimism and sobriety that was to characterise 1990. Attacks ranged from questioning the validity of combining the role of chairman and chief executive to articles on his private life. Headlines such as 'Burton in Bimbo Limbo' appeared even in serious newspapers such as the *Telegraph*, harking back to 1986 and the Fiona Wright affair. In the face of the market downturn and the criticisms from the financial press, executives were also accused of being defensive, in contrast to the openness, even razzmatazz, that had accompanied Burton announcements in the mid-1980s: 'If Burton is misunderstood it has only itself, or to be more specific its chairman, to blame. Communication with the major shareholders has become uncomfortable, spasmodic and hostile' (*The Times*, 19 July 1990).

Divestment and departure

Through June and July 1990 analysts were revising Burton profit forecasts for 1990 downwards to £150 million, as compared to the £223 million of 1989. Faced with the declining profit performance and mounting debt, in July 1990 the Burton Group announced its sale of the Burton Group financial services division to the financial services business of General Electric of the USA for £182.7 million. The main business of BGFS was the provision of consumer credit finance and it was the largest retail credit card operator in the UK with over 3 million cards in issue. The Burton Group press release stated that:

> During the past months, in response to these trading conditions, the Board
> has conducted a strategic review of operations with its financial advisers,
> S. G. Warburg and Co. Ltd. The result of the review has been the Board's
> decision to withdraw from financial services and property development and
> to concentrate the Group's financial and management resources on retailing
> ... Burton's retail businesses hold a leading position in the UK clothing
> market which we will continue to exploit for profitable growth in the 1990s.
> The challenges and opportunities created by the current retailing
> environment are being positively addressed by focusing on our strengths and
> reinforcing our balance sheet.

This was regarded as a sensible action by the City as it substantially reduced Burton's debt, but it was clouded by the simultaneous announcement that the property division was to be sold. Though this had been mooted by analysts, it provoked gloomy forecasts that it could take two years to sell, and in the meantime would drag down profits into the 'black hole of property'.

By September 1990 Burton's share price was sliding, from a 1990 high of 226p to 55p before recovering to 71p. Explanations varied for this. One analyst, John Richards of County NatWest, complained: 'It is a credibility problem. The reason people are worried is that the company is not telling us what is happening, so people are running around and worrying'. And given the importance of the declining value of property assets at that time, he was also concerned that 'We simply can't quantify the value of the company's assets'. Others pointed to the poor trading conditions and faltering profits, or to the financial structure of the group. Some analysts were forecasting profits for 1990 as low as £65 million with group debts of £400 million: in fact, profits before tax were declared at £133 million, certainly a dramatic reversal in Burton's fortunes. Moreover, the withdrawal from property development cost the group some £169 million and resulted in a loss after tax and dividends for the first time in over a decade (see Table 2).

The trend in the previous decade was to link closely the success of a corporation to the figure of its chairman, and there was increasing pressure from the City to remove Sir Ralph from the role of chief executive, leaving him as chairman. In fact, on 15 November 1990 Sir Ralph stepped down from both his roles as chairman and chief executive under a golden parachute of £2 million plus a £456,000 per year pension. There followed a flurry of press discussions on Sir Ralph's years at Burton and their success or failure:

> Halpern provided Burton with outstanding leadership throughout the 1980s. He brought style and panache. He cared about the ambience in which people bought clothes and improved it out of all recognition. He catered brilliantly

Table 2 The Burton Group: summary of sales and profit, 1990 (£ million)

Turnover	1,788.7
Trading	194.8
Other income	2.3
Interest (and similar charges)	(51.0)
Profit before exceptional costs	146.1
Exceptional costs[1]	(13.0)
Profit before taxation	133.1
Taxation	(36.8)
Profit after taxation	96.3
Extraordinary items[2]	(83.9)
Profit	12.4
Dividends	(33.6)
Deficit	(21.2)

[1]Including costs of reorganisation and rationalisation.
[2]Including costs of £169 million from withdrawal from property development.

in clothes design and range for the career girl aged between 18 and 30. Above all, he took Burton to a size and prestige not imaginable in its days as the 40 shilling tailor. His skill was to focus on an idea and squeeze it for all it was worth. Recalls designer Rodney Fitch: 'It was the right thing for the company and he was the right man for the time…' But the fantasy was flawed. For all the retail razzle, Halpern's skills as a group builder were thin. The diversification into financial services was scrapped and the plunge into property came dramatically unstuck. The big plans never made it on the scale envisaged … Halpern failed to create a retail group as solid as Kingfisher and Argos. And these examples cracked the myth that surrounded Halpern: you don't need flamboyance to be great in retailing. …

Others worry about Burton's perceived failure to adapt to the customer change: the demographic pig in the python. The 1980s thirtysomethings will be the 1990s fortysomethings. But Burton, overconcentrated in the younger market, needs to match today's more elegant, sober look. Perhaps most serious of all, Burton not only entered the recession with weak looking cost controls but the downturn caught it midway through a huge capital spending and store opening programme. The result, say critics, is that the brakes are being slammed on too late in the day (*Sunday Telegraph*, 18 November 1990). Halpern's attitude to those who accused him of personal greed was simple and even dignified, and lies at the core of his business strategy and philosophy. 'My wealth is minute to what I have created,' he said. 'Look at what the company has earned and what it is worth, and then look at my salary and my perks. And also look at the incentive bonuses that are paid right down the line, to every employee in the company, all 35,000 of them.'

His belief was that large and successful companies were not just created to provide an income for shareholders, and that everybody, from the chief executive down to the teenage shop assistants, deserved a spoonful of the gravy as a reward for hard selling … At one east London branch yesterday the assistant manager of a Burton store was right on cue: 'We all did well from Sir Ralph. He may have got millions, but we got the regular 50 to 100 quid extra in our pay-packets, right down to the trainee on the floor. He was good news in this industry …'

There are many in the City, including his enemies, who grudgingly admit that his sexual indiscretion and its accompanying lifestyle have been the ruination of what could have been an extraordinary business career. They can see the tragic element in the tale. His boast that he alone had been responsible, helped by a small group of hand-picked executives, for the astonishing success of the Burton empire is not disputed by many. And despite recent fumbles, his track-record and the figures prove it.

A merchant banker suggested that Halpern was a much more complicated character than many of the comments made about him would suggest. 'There is no doubt that he is an absolute megalomaniac,' he said, 'but he is a listener and was able to put together a strong team around him and right down through the organisation. A lot of the credit for that can be given to the remuneration package and generous option scheme. Two years ago he had the strongest and best retailing scheme in the whole industry.' (*Sunday Times*, 18 November 1990)

APPENDIX Summary of financial performance, 1985–89

	1985	1986	1987	1988	1989
	(£m)	(£m)	(£m)	(£m)	(£m)
Group turnover	551.0	1,217.2	1,338.6	1,590.2	1,818.5
Trading profit	81.6	179.9	200.1	229.2	244.8
Interest	(2.4)	(31.7)	(17.7)	(19.1)	(24.2)
Other income	1.0	0.5	1.0	1.6	3.2
Profit on ordinary activities before taxation	80.2	148.7	183.4	211.7	223.8
Taxation	(28.7)	(51.8)	(64.1)	(72.3)	(74.1)
Profit on ordinary activities after taxation	51.5	96.9	119.3	139.4	149.7
Extraordinary credit	–	3.7	6.9	0.4	–
Profit for the financial year	51.5	100.6	126.2	139.8	149.7
Dividends	(21.5)	(31.4)	(39.7)	(46.6)	(51.2)
Retained earnings	30.0	69.2	86.5	93.2	98.5
Tangible assets and investments	744.1	713.9	822.5	882.4	1,005.7
Current assets less liabilities, provisions and minority interests	(374.8)	(273.4)	(299.3)	(263.0)	(267.8)
Total assets employed	369.3	440.5	523.2	619.4	737.9
Share capital	135.1	274.4	276.0	276.8	278.3
Reserves	234.2	166.1	247.2	342.6	459.6
Capital employed	369.3	440.5	523.2	619.4	737.9
Earnings per share (undiluted)	14.6p	17.8p	21.7p	25.2p	27.0p
Dividend per share	4.4p	5.7p	7.2p	8.4p	9.2p
Dividend cover	2.4p	3.2p	3.2p	3.0p	2.9p

Index of companies and organisations

ABN (bank), 257
Air France, 324–5
Albani, 98
American Airlines, 325
AMRO (bank), 257
Amstrad, 128, 129
Antenne 2, 197
ANZ Bank, 404
Arthur D. Little, 250, 252
Asaki Breweries, 405
Association of British Travel Agents, 160
ATT, 299

Bass, 96, 98, 233
BBC, 122
Benetton, 128
Black and Decker, 124
BNP (bank), 214
BOC, 358
Boston Consulting Group, 130–1, 144, 145, 249
Braxton Associates, 25
British Aerospace, 271
British Airways, 14–15, 116, 119, 122, 325
British Insurance Brokers Association, 160, 162
British Petroleum, 290–1
British Rail, 25, 92, 247
British Telecom, 216, 271, 298, 299
Brother, 124
BSN, 233
BTR, 348, 361
Bundesbahn, 247

Cadbury Schweppes, 216, 358
Carnaud, 161,
CBS, 197
Cheshire County Council, 335
Chrysler, 67
Churchill Livingstone, 419
Churchill Pottery, 276–7
Clydesdale Bank, 81
CMB Packaging, 161
Coca-Cola, 238
Cokoladovny, 233
Companiex, 126–7
Conseil Superieur de Audiovisuel, 196–7

Courtaulds, 362

Degussa, 80
Deutsche Babcock and Metallgesellschaft, 81
Deutsche Eisenbahn AG, 247
Digital Equipment Corporation, 66
Dunsmore Chemical Company, 294–5

Elsevier–NDU, 224
Europa, 357

Ford, 27, 37

GEC, 98
General Motors, 27
Gossnab, 394
Guinness, 98, 117, 119

Hanson Trust, 229, 257, 361
HMSO, 271
Holiday Inns, 233
Honda, 89

IBM France, 196
ICI, 122, 188, 357, 362
ICL, 375
IKEA, 3–11, 17, 19–21, 23–4, 32, 213
Institute of Management, 197
Internationale Nederlanden Group, 237
ITT, 66–7

Kelloggs, 89, 207
Kia, 37
Kindercare, 388, 390–1
KLM, 325
Kronenbourg, 98

La Compagnie Bancaire, 214
Land Rover, 340–1
Lex, 358
Linfield, 255
London Transport, 271
Longman Publishing, 418–21
Lonrho, 233, 348, 361
Lufthansa, 325

McDonald's, 238, 359
Marks and Spencer, 89, 98, 208–9, 218
Mars, 101, 207, 232
Mazda, 37
Medic Aid, 24
Metal Box, 161
Michelin, 196
Midland Bank, 81, 122
Mitsubishi, 340
Monopolies and Mergers Commission, 89
Motorola, 80

National Australia Bank, 81
National Health Service, 81, 140–1, 217–19, 262
National House Builders Registration Council, 160
Nationale Nederland, 236–7
Nestlé, 101, 196, 233
NFC, 106, 108–9
NMB Postbank, 236–7

OFTEL, 299
OPEC, 87, 162
Opportunity 2000, 122

Pan Am, 325
Philips, 80, 399
Polytechnic and College Funding Council, 318–19
Post Office, 271
Project Medias 92, 197
Publishers' Association, 419

Reed International, 122
Rolls-Royce, 67, 80, 271, 284, 291

Royal Dutch Airlines, 325

Sabena World Airlines, 15
Sainsbury, 91, 122, 207–8, 209
SAS, 325
Savoy Hotel, 170
Sheffield City Council, 366–7
Sheffield Development Corporation, 179
Shell, 86–7, 352
SOGAT, 419
South Yorkshire Police, 189
STC, 358
Strategic Planning Institute, 263, 296

Tarmac, 361
Tesco, 208–9
TF1, 197
Training and Enterprise Council, 179
Trusthouse Forte, 170
TWA, 325

Unilever, 101, 227
United Stationers, 330
University Funding Council, 318

Vickers, 80
Virgin Records/Airlines, 222
VNU (publisher), 224
Volkswagen, 37

Wolters-Kluwer, 224

YMCA, 25

General index

acceptability, 246–8, 281–300
accountability, 379
acquisitions, 233–4, 238–9, 250, 256, 268, 270, 285, 356
action tasks, 12, 13, 15
adaptive model, 44, 159
adhocracy, 378, 380
amalgamation (of related areas), 317
analysers, 169, 171
annual revenue budget, 334
appraisal system, 373
asset management, 235–9 *passim*
asset stripping, 234
assumptions, 46, 48–9, 162, 164, 198, 332–4, 340, 399
audit, environmental, 76, 79–87
audit, resource, 119
authorisation, 60

backward integration, 228, 229, 254
balance sheet value (assets), 285
banking, 48–9, 135–6, 214–15, 316, 382
bargaining, 314, 315, 316, 334, 362
barriers
    to entry, 88–90, 91, 99, 216, 223
    to exit, 266
    to strategic change, 393–4
base budget reviews, 141–2, 334, 335
bases for comparison, 272–3
beliefs, 46, 48, 162, 198, 367, 399, 407
benchmarking, 136, 140, 141–2
best practice analysis, 136, 140–2
bidding, 315, 316, 317, 319, 334
'Big Bang', 61, 380, 382
brand name, 119, 255, 264, 270, 284
break-even analysis, 290, 301–2, 303, 333
budgeting, 333–4, 335
bureaucratic structures, 344, 380
business, role in society, 192–4
business-unit perspective, 374–5
business ethics, 138, 158, 191–7, 198
business level resource planning, 320–6
business strength, 106–7, 110, 250
buyers, 88, 90–3, 99
buyouts, 223

capacity fill/utilisation, 294

capital, 89, 333, 361
    goods, 227
    investment, 266, 284, 300
    structure, 289
career planning, 336
cash cow, 105, 145, 249–50, 268, 294, 372
centralisation, 358–67, 378, 379, 380
centrally planned economies, 370, 371
centres of excellence, 152
change, 272
    agency, 387–8, 401–5, 408–11, 413–14
    incremental, 388–9, 390–1
    operational, 415, 419
    see also strategic change, managing
charity sector, 25, 29, 30
chief executive (role/tasks), 346
child care (systems view), 390–1
China (state/company relationship), 371
citizens' charter, 138, 140–1
closed objectives, 190, 191
co-ordination, 353, 365–6, 367–70, 378
coercion (management style), 397, 398
coherence (change process), 416, 420
collaboration, 128, 167, 225, 226
communication (management style), 395–8, 399
communication channels, 180
communication skills, 413
community, 137–8, 194, 195
comparative analysis, 117–18, 138–42, 142–3
competition, 81, 219, 316, 317
competitive advantage, 116–17, 123–8, 130, 146,
        205–7, 209–10, 212–13, 219–21
competitive environment, 87–95
competitive position, 95–107, 252
competitive rivalry, 88, 91, 93–4, 99
competitive strategy options, 211
competitive tendering, 135, 223, 270, 273
competitor analysis, 96–8
competitor profiles, 140
conflicts of expectations, 172–3
consensus, 180
consistency, 245
consolidation, 36, 223–5, 247, 253, 264, 266-7
consortia, 235–6, 238, 254
contingency plans, 276

contracting-out, 273
contributors (subsidiaries), 356
control, 12, 13
    financial, 359, 361–2
    management, 370–6
    of resources, 133–5, 181
    by reward, 373–6
control systems, 60–3, 163, 165, 168
core competences, 115, 151–2, 221, 249, 256
corporate interest, 374–5
corporate level resource planning, 314–20
corporate objectives, 187, 188–9
corporate social responsibility, 194–5
corporate strategy, 3
    nature of, 4–14
cost, 89, 205–6, 217, 253
    efficiency (analysis), 128–31
    social, 137–8
    supply, 129–30
    value chain and, 216–17
cost/benefit analysis, 281, 284, 285–8
cost-drivers, 125, 128, 130, 288–9
cost leadership, 205–7, 210, 216–17, 252
critical path analysis, 337–9
critical success factors, 124, 327, 328-9
cultural context (strategy), 156, 157, 158–71
cultural fit, 173, 177, 234, 259–63, 297
cultural view (strategy development), 46–51, 55–7
cultural web, 60–3, 68, 156, 162–70, 259, 379, 386, 393
culture
    change (rites), 401–2, 403
    dominant, 169–70, 261
    shareholder expectations and, 156–98
customers, 138, 140–1, 217, 328–9, 332, 337–8

decentralised bureaucratic organisations, 380
decision-making, 56-65, 169, 171, 378, 379
decision flow, 41
decision matrices, 292–6
decision trees, 271, 274–5
decline, 224-5, 254, 260–1, 263, 317
decoupling trajectory, 67
defenders, 169, 171, 316, 379
demographics, 80
deregulation, 48, 89, 271
development
    internal, 231–3, 285
    joint, 234–9
    see also strategy development
devolution, 358–67, 378, 379, 380
diagnosing strategic change needs, 390–4
differentiation, 89–90, 203, 206–9, 253
    focused, 205, 211, 213–16
    strategies, 212–13, 323
    value chain linkages and, 217–19
directional policy matrix, 106–7, 108–9, 250
discounted cash flow, 282–3
discretion, 182, 195, 198
distribution channels, 89, 253, 330
diversification, 222, 256, 268, 270

related, 227–8, 230, 233
    unrelated, 228, 229, 231, 233
divestment, 272, 273
divisionalisation, 379
do-nothing situation, 272
dogs, 105, 106, 146, 250
dominant culture, 169–70, 261
Dupont model, 137

ecology, 81
economic factors, 80, 82–4
economies of scale, 88–9, 129, 130, 206, 317
edict (management style), 397, 398
education (management style), 395–8, 399
effectiveness, 128, 132–3
efficiency, 128–31, 218–19
electronic point of sale systems, 131, 378
embryonic stage (culture), 259–60, 261
emergent strategy, 38–9
employees, 136, 195, 223
endowed authority, 411, 413
Enterprise Zones, 288
entrepreneurs, 222
entry barriers, 88–90, 91, 99, 216, 223
environment, 18, 221–2, 380–1
environment (analysis), 75–6
    control, 181
    identifying competitive position, 95–107
    influence (audit), 79–87
    nature of, 77–9
    structural analysis, 87–95
    summary, 107–11
environmental assessment, 414, 418
environmental forces, 49–50
escape, 231
ethics, business, 138, 158, 191–7, 198
ethos, organisational, 160
European businesses, 214–15
evaluation, 20–1, 246–8
    see also strategy evaluation *entries*
exit barriers, 266
expectations, 172–3, 261
    stakeholders, 19, 135, 137–8, 156–98
experience curve, 130–1, 206, 217, 223, 225, 234
experimentation, 389–90, 392
exports, 227
external influences (strategy), 158–62, 344
external linkages, 128
external stakeholders, 173–4, 180, 184–5

failure strategies, 216
feasibility, 245, 247–8, 300–4, 313
financial analyses, 135–8
financial control, 359, 361–2
financial planning, 333–4, 335
financial ratio, 136, 137, 289–91
financial resources, 119
financial targets, 361
five-forces approach, 88, 90–1, 94–5, 106
flexibility analysis, 145–7

focus, 190, 206, 252, 253–4, 284
focused differentiation, 205, 211, 213–16
focusing trajectory, 66
formula-driven allocation, 314, 315–16
forward integration, 228, 229
frames of reference, 46, 47, 159
franchising, 8, 124, 238–9
functional structure, 345–6
funds flow analysis, 300–1

game theory, 298
Gantt charts, 339
gap analysis, 272–3, 274
gearing ratio, 136
generic strategies, 203, 223
    discussion, 204–9
    management challenge, 219–20
    market-based, 209–16
    sustaining/operationalising, 216–20
global co-operation, 354–5
global scenarios, 86–7
globalisation, 227
goals, 12, 13, 14, 413
'goodwill', 119
government, 28, 81, 89, 173, 192
green issues, 195
group rewards, 374, 376
growth, 131, 223, 225, 260–1, 316
    share matrix, 103, 105–6, 144–5
Gulf War, 194, 196–7, 324

Hawthorn effect, 271
heuristic models, 297
hierarchy, 167, 178, 180, 183, 186, 198
higher education (funding), 316, 318–19
historical analysis, 138–9, 169, 170
HIV/AIDS (politics of change), 52–3
holding company structure, 347–9
horizontal integration, 228, 229
human resource management, 121, 322, 416–20
human resources, 119, 134, 146, 374
hybrid strategy, 213

Icarus Paradox, 66–7
ideology, 365, 368
image, 119, 284
imitation, 125, 253
implementation, 182, 305–6, 332
implementors (subsidiaries), 356
imports, 225, 227
imposed strategy, 38, 39
inbound logistics, 120, 121
incentives, 272
    see also reward systems
incremental change, 388–9, 390–1
incremental strategy development, 35–7, 68
incrementalism, 43–6, 55–7, 68
individual rewards, 374, 376
individual (role), 195–7
industry norms, 139, 140, 148–9

industry recipe, 47, 50, 159–60
influence, 180, 388
'informal' stakeholder groups, 173
information, 79, 220–1, 370–3, 378–90, 392
    technology, 116, 378
infrastructure, 121
intangibles (resource audit), 119, 134
integration, 228–9, 233, 254
integrity, 196
intended strategy, 38, 67
interest-bearing loans, 135–6
intermediaries (role), 124–5
intermediate structures, 353
internal development, 231–3, 285
internal influences (strategy), 162–71
internal links, 182–3
internal markets, 135, 270, 364
internal rate of return, 282–3, 288
internal stakeholders, 173–4, 184–5
international division, 354
internationalisation, 135, 181, 227
intervention approach, 396–7, 398, 401
inventing trajectory, 67
investment, 135, 212, 266, 284, 300
    banks, 316, 382
issue awareness, 58–9

job design, 195
joint development, 234–9
joint ventures, 167–8, 235–6, 238–9, 253, 254, 353, 356
judgement, 305
just-in-time production, 332, 339

key assumptions (resource plans), 332–4, 340
key issues (identification), 118, 148–52
key skills, 323
key tasks (resource plans), 327–9, 340
knowledge, 181, 182

labour market, 81
language, 167, 403, 404
leadership, 253
    change agency and, 387, 411, 412–13, 414, 418
    cost, 205–7, 210, 216–17, 252
legislation, 89
licensing, 238–9
life cycle analyses, 249–54, 259–60
linkages, value chain, 135, 217–21
liquidation, 223
liquidity, 136, 290–1
local government, 178, 179, 222
logic, strategic, 248–58, 261
logical incrementalism, 43–6, 55–7, 68
'loops', 388–9, 390
low-price strategy, 323, 377–8

machine bureaucracy, 378, 379
management, 219–20, 223, 362
    control, 370–6
    information systems, 138, 220

management (*continued*)
  systems, 320, 323, 370–6
  women in, 121, 122
  see also strategic management in practice
managers, 136, 191, 195–7, 218, 219
managing up (change agents), 412
manpower planning, 334, 336–7
market, 230, 285
  attractiveness, 106–7, 110, 250
  decline, 224-5, 254, 317
  development, 226–7, 232–3, 253, 254
  growth, 103–6, 206–7
  maturity, 223, 225
  penetration, 225–6, 268
  power, 101–3, 104, 131, 206, 214, 263
  segments, 101–4, 131, 210, 231–16, 227, 253–4
  share, 103–6, 131, 206, 212, 216–17, 225, 263–4, 265–8
  market-based generic strategies, 209–16
marketing, 120, 121, 173, 184, 192, 195, 212, 226, 267
mass production, 378
matrix decision, 292–6
matrix structure, 349–52
mature markets, 223, 225
maturity phase (culture), 260, 261, 262
mechanistic organisations, 344, 376–8, 379, 380
merchandising, 134
mergers, 48, 161, 169–70, 236–9, 256, 257
mission, 12–14, 157, 186–91, 198
models/modelling, 296–7
monopoly organisations, 28, 134, 216
multidivisional structure, 346–7
multinational corporation, 24, 26–7, 192, 227, 306–7
  structural types in, 353–6, 357

national culture, 159, 160
nationalised industries, 28, 379
natural selection view, 40, 55–7
negative monitoring, 372
negotiation, 184, 185, 217, 413
net present value, 282–3, 288, 289
network analysis, 337–9
networks, 236–8, 240, 355, 364, 368–70
newspapers (cultural web), 164, 166, 167
niche strategy, 252, 253
not-for-profit sector, 25, 29, 30

objectives, 12–15, 157–8, 187–91, 304–5
oil industry, 87, 90–1, 162, 401
open competition, 316, 317
open objectives, 190
operational change, 416, 419
operational decisions, 9
operational management, 15–16
operational processes/technology, 378
operational resource plan, 320, 321
operational strategies, 11–12
operations, 120, 121
opportunism, 38, 39, 237–8
opportunities, 111, 148–51, 244–5

organic organisations, 376–8, 379, 380
organisation structure (and design), 344
  centralisation *vs.* devolution, 358–64, 365–7
  design elements, 356, 358
  influences on design, 376–81, 382
  management systems and control, 370–6
  organisational configurations, 364–70
  structural types, 345–56, 357
  summary, 381, 383
organisational configurations, 364–70
organisational design, 356, 358, 376–81, 382
organisational purposes, 157, 186–91
organisational routines, 397, 399
organisational structure, 61–3, 163, 165, 167–8
organisational type, 379–80
organised groups, 156–60, 162
outbound logistics, 120, 121
outside agencies, 306
owner control, 379

paradigm, 47, 49–50, 60–3, 68, 162–5, 167–9, 198, 259, 379, 386, 389
paradigm change, 63–5, 259
partial implementation, 305–6
participation, 396, 397, 398, 400
patent protection, 239
Patient's Charter, 140–1
payback period, 282, 283
performance, 133, 136, 268, 270, 361
  indicators, 168, 370, 372
personal traits (change agents), 413
personalities (balance of), 145, 146–7
PERT, 339
PEST analysis, 82–4, 106
physical resources, 119, 134
PIMS databank, 263, 264, 267, 269, 296
planning, 68, 276
  corporate level, 314–20
  financial, 333–4, 335
  resource, *see* resource planning/allocation
  strategic, 358–60, 379
  view (strategy development), 40–3, 55–7
police forces, 150–1, 189, 372
political
  factors (PEST), 82–4
  processes, 156, 171–86, 405–9, 410–12
  view (strategy development), 51–3, 55–7
Porter's generic strategies, 203, 204–5
portfolio analysis, 106–7, 142–5, 249–50, 313
portfolio life cycle, 250–1
position/ positioning strategy, 271, 298
power, 299, 405, 408
  assessment, 183–6
  of buyers/suppliers, 90–3
  indicators, 183–4
  management of strategic change, 405–8
  sources, 157, 178, 180–3
  structures, 60–3, 163, 165, 168
power/dynamism matrix, 175–6
power/interest matrix, 176–8

price, 210, 216, 217, 294, 298
primary activities, 120–1, 125, 128, 322
priorities, 327–8, 331, 351
privatisation, 89, 223, 270, 271, 272–3
problem-solving, 58–9
problem child, 105, 144
procurement, 120, 121, 128, 322
product
    development, 226–7, 232, 254, 268
    differentiation, 213–15
    market, 220, 222, 225, 353
    process design, 130
    range, 8
    safety, 195
    standards, 128, 129
production costs, 294
production departments, 173, 184
productivity, 225, 266, 297
professional bodies, 160
professional partnerships, 24–5, 29–30
profit, 192–3, 263, 265, 281, 282–5, 300
progressive organisations, 192–4
prospectors, 169, 171, 316, 379–80
public sector, 25, 27–9, 134–5, 194, 217–23
    expenditure, 142, 335
    strategies, 270–1
publishers, 214, 215, 224, 418–20
purposes (of organisation), 157, 186–91

Quaker companies, 193–4
quality, 225, 264
question mark, 105, 145, 249–50

railways, 25, 92, 247–8
ranking, 271, 273–4, 276–7
realised strategy, 38, 67, 148
reconfiguration, 247, 326
recruitment and selection, 336
referrals (strategy selection), 305
refreezing processes, 389, 392
related diversification, 227–8, 230, 233, 268
representation, 183, 185
research and development, 117, 226–7, 234, 264
    expenditure, 139, 148–9, 268, 269
research evidence, 263–71
resource
    allocation, 314–20
    analysis, *see* strategic capability
    audit, 117, 118, 119
    balance of, 118, 143–7, 313, 314
    -based strategies, 115
    claim on, 183, 185
    competitive advantage through, 116–17
    control, 133–5, 181
    dependence, 182, 184, 185
    deployment analysis, 302, 304
    fit (with others), 325–6
    human, *see main entries*
    identification, 321–5
    physical, 119, 134

plans, 326–39
profile, 149
utilisation, 117, 123–8
resource planning and allocation, 313
    business level, 320–6
    corporate level, 314–20, 321
    preparing resource plans, 326–39
    summary, 339–41
responsibility centres, 372, 373
retaliation, expected (market entry), 89
retrenchment (strategy), 252
return, analysing, 281–9
return on capital employed, 282, 283, 290
return on investment, 263, 264, 266
revenue budgets, annual, 34
reward systems, 12, 15, 167, 168, 370, 373–6
risk, 289–97, 374
rites, 401–3
rituals, 60–3, 163, 165–6, 401–3
roles (change agent), 412
'rolling-out' strategies, 307
route planning, 339
routines, 60–3, 163, 165–6, 397, 399, 403

sales, 120, 121
scenarios, 85–7, 271, 275–7
scheduling, 331, 332, 339
screening, 60, 245, 246, 248, 271–7
selection interviews, 401
selection of strategies, 304–7
sensitivity analysis, 284, 288, 291–5, 333
sequencing, 331
service departments, 120, 121, 346
service industries, 27, 223, 227
shareholder, 191, 270, 361
    value analysis, 135, 282, 288–91
shared resources, 317–20
simple structure, 345, 379
simulation modelling, 296–7
single European market, 129, 357
skills, 146–7, 181, 182
small businesses, 24, 26
social cost, 137–8
social responsibility, 191, 192, 194–5
society, role of business in, 192–4
society, values, of, 158–9, 161
socio-cultural factors, 80, 82–4
solution development/selection, 58, 59–60
specialisation, 125, 228
specialist knowledge/skills, 181
speculation, 222
sponsorship, 192, 195, 223
spreadsheets, 282, 333
stakeholder
    analysis, 171–8, 179
    identifying, 173–5
    mapping, 175–8, 184, 186, 246, 297
    reactions (analysing), 297–300
stakeholder expectations, 19, 135, 137–8, 156–7

stakeholder expectations (*continued*)
  business ethics, 191–7
  cultural context of strategy, 158–71
  organisational purposes, 186–91
  power, 178, 180–6
  stakeholder analysis, 171–8, 179
  summary, 198
standardisation, 366–7, 378
stars, 105, 106, 144, 249–50, 372
static markets, 225
status, 182, 184–5
stereotypes, 159, 192–4
stories, 60–3, 163, 165–6
strategic alliances, 234–9
strategic analysis, 17–20, 73–4
  culture and stakeholder expectations, 156–98
  environment, 75–111
  resources and strategic capability, 115–53
strategic business unit, 13–14, 103, 105–7, 110, 144,
      249–50, 288
strategic capability, 115–18
  assessing balance of resources, 143–8
  comparative analysis, 138–42
  key issues, 148–52
  resource audit, 119
  summary, 152–3
  value chain analysis, 120–38
strategic change, managing, 386
  conclusions, 414–17, 421
  diagnosing needs, 390–4
  leadership and change agency, 411, 412–14
  managing process, 394–409, 410
  understanding processes, 387–90
strategic choice, 20–21, 201–2
  strategy evaluation (making choices), 281–307
  strategy evaluation (suitability), 244–78
  strategy options, 203–41
strategic control, 359, 362–4
strategic decisions, 5–10, 56–65, 169, 171
strategic drift, 63–5, 68, 115, 169, 388, 389, 391–3
strategic group analysis, 98–101
strategy implementation, 311–12
  managing change, 386–421
  organisation structure and design, 344–83
  planning and allocating resources, 313–41
strategic investment thrusts, 288
strategic leaders, 355–6
strategic logic, 248–58, 261
strategic management
  challenge of, 30–2
  different contexts, 23–30
  process, 14–23
strategic management in practice, 34
  explaining strategy development, 39–55
  patterns of strategy development, 35–9
  strategic decision-making, 56–65
  summary and implications, 65–9
strategic options, 20–1, 203
  alternative directions, 220–30
  alternative methods, 230–9

generic strategies, 204–9
generic strategies (sustaining and
      operationalising), 216–20
  market-based generic strategies, 209–16
  summary, 239
strategic planning, 358–60, 379
strategic position, 76–7
strategic resources (control), 181
strategies, 12, 13, 15
  selection of, 304–7
'strategy clock', 205, 209–10, 211, 216
strategy development
  alternative directions, 203, 220–30
  alternative methods, 203, 230–9, 240–1
  explaining (views of), 39–55
  patterns of, 35–9
strategy evaluation (choices)
  analysing feasibility, 300–4
  analysing return, 281–9
  analysing risk, 289–97
  analysing stakeholder reactions, 297–300
  selection of strategies, 304–7
  summary, 307
strategy evaluation (criteria)
  cultural fit, 259–63
  evaluation criteria, 244–6
  framework, 246–8
  research evidence, 263–71
  screening options, 271–7
  strategic logic, 248–58
  summary, 277–8
strategy implementation, 21–2
strategy levels, 10–12
strategy vocabulary, 12–14, 15
strategy workshops, 337
strengths, 111, 148–52, 244–5
structural analysis of competitive environment, 76,
      87–95
structural types, 345–56
styles, management, 395–7, 398, 399
  strategic management styles, Figures 10.9, 10.10, 10.11
subcontracting, 238, 253, 266
subcultures, 261
suboptimisation, 128, 172
subsidiaries, 222, 353–6
substitutes, threat of, 88, 91, 93, 99
subsystems, 407
suitability (evaluation criteria), 244–8
suppliers, 88–93, 99, 136, 195, 218–19
supplies (environmental influence), 81
supply costs, 129–30
support activities, 120–1, 125, 128, 322
support staff, 365, 368
surrogate measures, 372
sustainable work, 86, 87
switching costs, 218–19
SWOT analysis, 111, 147–51
symbolic activity, 401–5, 408
symbols, 60–3, 163, 165, 167
  of power, 183, 184, 185

synergy, 228–9, 234, 249, 254–8, 270
systems view (incremental change), 388–9, 390–1,
    401

tariff barriers, 227
taskforce, 353
technical standards, 128, 129
technology, 80, 82–4, 116, 190, 217, 225, 378
    development, 121, 322
    transfer, 226, 268, 354
technostructure, 364–5, 368
telecommunications industry, 129, 299
television news, 194, 196–7
textile industry (Denmark), 240
threats, 88–91, 93, 99, 111, 148–51, 244–5
time horizons (perspectives), 374
'top-slicing', 317
total quality management, 134
training, 166, 336–7
transformational change, 35, 36, 388
transnational corporations, 355–6
triggering point (problems), 59
turnaround, 252

uncertainty, 77, 78
unfreezing, 389–90, 392, 403
unit objectives, 187, 190

unrelated diversification, 228, 229, 231, 233, 268
Urban Development Corporations, 288

value
    activities, 120, 123–4, 131, 136, 302, 320
    added, 120, 211–13, 217, 218–19
    -drivers, 125, 133, 288–9
    system, 121, 123, 128, 133–4, 249
value chain, 153
    analysis, 116–18, 120–38, 254–8, 313, 320, 372
    cost and, 216–17
    linkages, 135, 217–21
values, 162, 187, 188
    of society, 158–9, 161
venturing trajectory, 67
vertical integration, 133, 228, 233
visionary view (strategy development), 52–7
voting power, 297
voucher schemes, 273

weaknesses, 111, 148–52, 244–5
withdrawal option, 222–3
women in management, 121, 122
working capital, 300, 301
working conditions, 195

zero-based budgeting, 334, 335